Programming the M68HC12 Family

Gordon Doughman

Annabooks
San Diego

Programming the M68HC12 Family
by
Gordon Doughman

PUBLISHED BY

Annabooks
12860 Danielson Court
Poway, CA 92064
USA

858-391-5600
http://www.annabooks.com

Copyright © Gordon Doughman 2000

All rights reserved. No part of the contents of this book may be reproduced or transmitted in any form or by any means without the prior written consent of the publisher, except for the inclusion of brief quotations in a review.

Printed in the United States of America

ISBN 0-929392-67-1

First Printing March 2000

Information provided in this publication is derived from various sources, standards, and analyses. Any errors or omissions shall not imply any liability for direct or indirect consequences arising from the use of this information. The publisher, authors, and reviewers make no warranty for the correctness or for the use of this information, and assume no liability for direct or indirect damages of any kind arising from technical interpretation or technical explanations in this book, for typographical or printing errors, or for any subsequent changes.

The publisher and authors reserve the right to make changes in this publication without notice and without incurring any liability.

All trademarks mentioned in this book are the property of their respective owners. Annabooks has attempted to properly capitalize and punctuate trademarks, but cannot guarantee that it has done so properly in every case.

The author and publisher thank Motorola, Inc. for their permission to reprint the CPU 12 Reference Guide as Appendix A. We also appreciate Cosmic Software, Inc. for providing evaluation versions of their compilers and assemblers for the companion CD-ROM.

About the Author

Gordon Doughman received his B.S. in Applied Science from Miami University, in Oxford, Ohio in 1977. Before joining Motorola as a Field Applications Engineer in 1984, Gordon designed high precision crystal oscillators and consumer electronics products. During his years with Motorola, Gordon has authored several application notes and written numerous programs for the M68HC11 and M68HC12 microcontroller families including BASIC11, a basic interpreter for the M68HC11 family. In addition, he is the author of D-Bug12, a command line oriented debugger that currently runs on the MC68HC912B32 and MC68HC812A4 EVBs. Other than basic test patterns, D-Bug12 was the first piece of software to run on the first M68HC12 device when it emerged from the IC processing line.

In his current assignment as a Senior Field Applications Engineer, Gordon has spent the majority of his time working with automotive and industrial systems customers on their M68HC12 designs. Most recently he has been involved with the design of the hardware and firmware for a high-speed production Flash programmer utilizing the M68HC12's BDM interface.

Acknowledgments

I wish to express my appreciation to the following people for helping to make this book possible:

To Jim Sibigtroth for encouraging me to write this book, for contributing the material for Chapter 15 on the M68HC12's BDM and for being so willing to answer my questions on the various M68HC12 devices when the published documentation was unclear or incomplete.

To the numerous Motorola customers who were early adopters of the M68HC12 family devices. Answers to many of the questions and problems that arose during the early stages of their designs were used as material for this book.

To my son Chris Doughman for designing a vectorized version of the icon used to alert readers to important information within the text.

To my wife, Lin, and my sons, Steve and Chris, for being patient with me during the 18 months it took to write this book. In response to my younger son's frequent question: "Hey dad, is the book done yet?" Yes Chris, the book is done!

Contents

CHAPTER 1: THE CPU12 OVERVIEW 21
   1.1   OPERAND SIZE AND DATA ORGANIZATION IN MEMORY 22
   1.2   WEIGHTED BINARY FRACTIONS 24
   1.3   OPERAND ALIGNMENT 25
   1.4   CPU12 PROGRAMMING MODEL 25
   1.5   ACCUMULATORS 26
   1.6   INDEX REGISTERS 26
   1.7   STACK POINTER 26
   1.8   PROGRAM COUNTER 31
   1.9   CONDITION CODE REGISTER 31
       1.9.1   *S Control Bit* *32*
       1.9.2   *XIRQ (X) Mask Bit* *32*
       1.9.3   *H Status Bit* *33*
       1.9.4   *I Mask Bit* *33*
       1.9.5   *N Status Bit* *34*
       1.9.6   *Z Status Bit* *34*
       1.9.7   *V Status Bit* *34*
       1.9.8   *C Status Bit* *34*

CHAPTER 2: THE CPU12 INSTRUCTION SET 37
   2.1   ASSEMBLER SYNTAX 37
   2.2   ADDRESSING MODES 39
       2.2.1   *Inherent Addressing* *40*
       2.2.2   *Immediate Addressing* *40*
       2.2.3   *Extended Addressing* *41*
       2.2.4   *Direct Addressing* *42*
       2.2.5   *Relative Addressing* *43*
       2.2.6   *Indexed Addressing* *45*
   2.3   INSTRUCTION SET OVERVIEW 57
   2.4   LOAD AND STORE INSTRUCTIONS 58
   2.5   MEMORY-TO-MEMORY MOVE INSTRUCTIONS 61
   2.6   BRANCH INSTRUCTIONS 63
       2.6.1   *Unconditional Branch Instructions* *63*
       2.6.2   *Simple Branch Instructions* *64*
       2.6.3   *Unsigned Branch Instructions* *67*
       2.6.4   *Signed Branch Instructions* *69*
   2.7   REGISTER TRANSFER AND EXCHANGE INSTRUCTIONS 70
   2.8   ADDITION AND SUBTRACTION INSTRUCTIONS 73
   2.9   ADDRESS ARITHMETIC INSTRUCTIONS 75
   2.10   MULTIPLY AND DIVIDE INSTRUCTIONS 78

2.11	READ/MODIFY/WRITE INSTRUCTIONS	81
2.12	SHIFT AND ROTATE INSTRUCTIONS	83
2.13	BOOLEAN LOGIC AND COMPARE INSTRUCTIONS	86
2.14	STACK RELATED INSTRUCTIONS	88
2.15	15 BIT MANIPULATION INSTRUCTIONS	90
2.16	JUMP AND SUBROUTINE INSTRUCTIONS	92
2.17	CONDITION CODE REGISTER INSTRUCTIONS	95
2.18	LOOP PRIMITIVE INSTRUCTIONS	96
2.19	INTERRUPT RELATED INSTRUCTIONS	99
2.20	MINIMUM AND MAXIMUM INSTRUCTIONS	103
2.21	TABLE LOOKUP AND INTERPOLATE INSTRUCTIONS	105
2.22	FUZZY LOGIC INSTRUCTIONS	108
2.23	MISCELLANEOUS INSTRUCTIONS	113

CHAPTER 3: PROGRAMMING EXAMPLES 121

3.1	USING THE CPU12'S STACK	121
3.2	PARAMETER PASSING STRATEGIES	122
3.3	LOCAL VARIABLE ALLOCATION	124
3.4	ACCESSING PARAMETERS AND LOCAL VARIABLES	125
3.5	REMOVING LOCAL VARIABLES AND PARAMETERS	129
3.6	PRECAUTIONS WHEN ACCESSING PARAMETERS AND LOCAL VARIABLES	131
3.7	WRITING POSITION INDEPENDENT CODE	132
3.8	CLEARING ON-CHIP MEMORY	134
3.9	FIND MIN/MAX VALUE IN AN ARRAY OF 16-BIT VALUES	135
3.10	USES OF PRE/POST INCREMENT/DECREMENT INDEXED ADDRESSING	138
3.11	BINARY TO ASCII DECIMAL CONVERSION	142
3.12	ASCII DECIMAL TO BINARY CONVERSION	146
3.13	CRC CALCULATION	149

CHAPTER 4: MCU INITIALIZATION 159

4.1	PROTECTED REGISTERS	159
4.2	RESOURCE MAPPING	160
4.3	OPERATING MODE	163
4.4	FLASH MEMORY AND EXTERNAL ACCESS CONTROL	165
4.5	CONFIGURATION OF BUS CONTROL SIGNALS	167
4.6	PORT A, B, AND E DRIVE LEVELS	167
4.7	WATCHDOG TIMER	168
4.8	CLOCK MONITOR TIMER	171
4.9	REAL TIME INTERRUPT	173
4.10	INITIALIZATION CODE	176
4.11	SPECIAL MODE INITIALIZATION CONSIDERATIONS	179

CHAPTER 5: INTERRUPTS AND RESETS 185

5.1	EXCEPTION TYPES	186
5.2	NON-MASKABLE EXCEPTIONS	186

5.3	MASKABLE EXCEPTIONS (INTERRUPTS)	188
5.4	MASKABLE INTERRUPT PRIORITY	190
5.5	INTERRUPT SERVICE ROUTINE REQUIREMENTS	191
5.6	INTERRUPT LATENCY	195
5.7	INTERRUPT RESPONSE TIME	197
5.8	IRQ INTERRUPT EXAMPLE	198

CHAPTER 6: GENERAL PURPOSE PARALLEL I/O PORTS 209

6.1	ACCESSING PERIPHERALS	209
6.2	DATA DIRECTION REGISTERS	210
6.3	DATA REGISTERS	211
6.4	I/O PORT INITIALIZATION	212
6.5	UNUSED I/O PINS	212
6.6	GENERAL PURPOSE I/O EXAMPLES	214
6.7	INPUT SWITCHES	215
6.8	MULTIPLE INPUT SWITCH ROUTINE	221
6.9	SCANNED SWITCH MATRIX	224
6.10	OUTPUT INDICATORS	226
6.11	LCD ALPHA–NUMERIC DISPLAY MODULE	230
6.11.1	*Display Module Initialization*	*232*
6.11.2	*Displaying Data on the LCD*	*234*

CHAPTER 7: ON-CHIP BYTE ERASABLE EEPROM 241

7.1	EEPROM STRUCTURE	241
7.2	EEPROM CHARGE PUMP	242
7.3	BLOCK PROTECT MECHANISM	243
7.4	EEPROM CHARACTERISTICS	245
7.5	EEPROM PROGRAMMING AND ERASING PROCEDURES	248

CHAPTER 8: ON-CHIP FLASH EEPROM 259

8.1	FLASH MODULE CONFIGURATION	260
8.2	FLASH MODULE CONTROL REGISTERS	260
8.3	PROGRAMMING AND ERASE OPERATIONS	263
8.4	ERASURE OF THE FLASH EEPROM ARRAY	264
8.5	PROGRAMMING OF THE FLASH EEPROM ARRAY	266
8.6	A FLASH SERIAL BOOT LOADER EXAMPLE	268
8.7	BOOT LOADER REQUIREMENTS	269
8.8	BOOT LOADER STARTUP CODE	273
8.9	FLASH PROGRAMMING CONTROL LOOP	278
8.10	RECEIVING AND DECODING AN S–RECORD	280
8.11	PROGRAMMING A BLOCK OF FLASH	283
8.12	BOOT LOADER ERASE COMMAND	288
8.13	SUPPORT ROUTINES AND GLOBAL VARIABLES	291

CHAPTER 9: SERIAL COMMUNICATIONS INTERFACE 295

9.1	Physical Interface	296
9.2	Data Format	297
9.3	Receiver	298
9.4	Transmitter	300
9.5	Accessing Transmitted and Received Data	301
9.6	Single Wire Operating Mode	302
9.7	Baud Rate Generator	303
9.8	SCI Interrupts	307
9.9	Polled SCI Example	309
9.10	Interrupt Driven SCI Example	310

CHAPTER 10: SERIAL PERIPHERAL INTERFACE ... 321

10.1	Physical Interface	322
10.2	Operating Modes	324
10.3	Data Transfer Format	325
10.4	Bit Rate Selection	328
10.5	Accessing Transmitted and Received Data	329
10.6	SPI Interrupts	331
10.7	SPI Software Driver Strategy	331
10.8	SPI Parallel Output Port Example	331
10.9	SPI Parallel Input Port Example	336
10.10	SPI Display Driver Example	340

CHAPTER 11: STANDARD TIMER MODULE ... 355

11.1	Input Capture Concepts	356
11.2	Output Compare Concepts	357
11.3	Timer Structure and Physical Interface	358
11.4	Timer Prescaler and Counter Clock Source	361
11.5	Timer Counter Reset	363
11.6	Timer Channel Flags and Interrupts	364
11.7	Timer System Control	366
11.8	Special Timer Features	367
11.9	Timer Initialization	368
11.10	Period Measurement	369
11.11	Pulse Width Measurement	373
11.12	Pulse Train Pulse Measurement	375
11.13	Measuring Very Short Pulses	378
11.14	Alternate Uses For Input Capture Channels	378
11.15	Waveform Generation Using Output Compare	378
11.16	Pulse Width Modulated Waveform Generation	382
11.17	General Purpose Waveform Generation	387
11.18	Pulse Accumulator	390
11.18.1	*Event Counting*	*393*
11.18.2	*Gated Time Accumulation*	*395*

CHAPTER 12: PULSE WIDTH MODULATION MODULE 403
- 12.1 Left Aligned Operation 404
- 12.2 Center Aligned Operation 405
- 12.3 PWM Clock Sources 407
- 12.4 Calculating Duty Cycle and Period 408
- 12.5 PWM 16-bit Operation 412
- 12.6 Changing Duty Cycle and Period 413
- 12.7 Eight Bit, Left Aligned PWM Example 413
- 12.8 Sequenced Output Switching 416

CHAPTER 13: ANALOG-TO-DIGITAL MODULE 423
- 13.1 The ADC 423
- 13.2 ADC Initialization 425
- 13.3 Conversion Clock Prescaler and Final Channel Sample Time 426
- 13.4 Operating Mode Selection 429
- 13.5 Result Registers 430
- 13.6 Simple ADC Example 431
- 13.7 Timed Conversion Example 432
- 13.8 ADC Port Input Register 435

CHAPTER 14: HARDWARE BREAKPOINT MODULE 437
- 14.1 Breakpoint Operating Modes 437
- 14.2 SWI Dual Address Mode 439
- 14.3 BDM Full Breakpoint Mode 440
- 14.4 BDM Dual Address Mode 442
- 14.5 BDM Breakpoint Cautions 442
- 14.6 Program Counter at Data Breakpoints 443
- 14.7 ROM Code Patching Example 444
- 14.8 Protecting the EEPROM Table and Code Patch 447

CHAPTER 15: BACKGROUND DEBUG - A SOFTWARE PERSPECTIVE 449
- 15.1 An Unusually Cozy Relationship Between Hardware and Software 450
- 15.2 Separation of BDM vs User Applications 452
- 15.3 Entering Active Background Mode 454
- 15.4 Exiting Active Background Mode 457
- 15.5 Timing Considerations Between Debugger Hardware and BDM Firmware ... 460
- 15.6 Implementing a BDM Debugger Interface 468
- 15.7 BDM Communication Primitives 469
- 15.8 Implementing BDM Commands 474

APPENDIX A: INSTRUCTION SET SUMMARY 481

APPENDIX B: CONFIGURATION CODE 515

APPENDIX C: BDM PRIMITIVES LISTINGS 535

Foreword

At the dawn of the microprocessor age, in 1974, Motorola developed the M6800 8-bit CPU. At that time, the most useful form of documentation for these new devices came from the I.C. manufacturer in the form of a data sheet. The only source of application examples was the diagnostic code written by the designers during product development and evaluation. At the time, it was still possible for an individual engineer to comprehend the entire circuit (about 4,000 transistors in the MC6800) and thus fully understand what was happening in any situation.

Soon after the introduction of the M6800, Motorola added a few 16-bit instructions for a custom automotive microprocessor, and then in about 1979 they created the first microcontroller (MCU) by integrating memory and peripherals with the CPU to form the M6801. Although this was still a simple design by today's standards, the need for more extensive documentation was already becoming apparent. This led Bill Bruce, one of the Motorola product/test engineers, to write an authoritative reference manual for the M6801. This manual provided more detailed information about the subtle interactions of systems than the Motorola data sheets and included numerous examples to help users understand the MCU system.

The next big step in the M68xx family came with the M68HC11 in 1984. The 'HC11 added a second index register, divide instructions, and grossly enhanced the on-chip memory and peripherals. By this time the transistor count had increased to more than 167,000 and the design team grew to dozens of engineers working on separate pieces of the design. Even with ten years of history with compatible predecessors, there was a need for more detailed information and application examples which could not be found in traditional data sheets. Using the example of Bill Bruce's M6801 Reference Manual, I wrote the M68HC11 Reference Manual (a.k.a. the Pink Book). Even that was not a total answer to user needs, so several others have written textbooks to augment other documentation sources.

The M68HC12 is the biggest step yet in the evolution of this well established family of microcontrollers. It is still upward compatible with the original M6800 and M68HC11; in fact it can still execute old 'HC11 and even 6800 programs. Although an experienced 'HC11 programmer will find the M68HC12 familiar, the enhanced indexed addressing modes alone require them to view the M68HC12 differently than the M68HC11. The on-chip peripheral systems are so much more complex than previous microcontrollers that individual teams of engineers in design centers around the world were used to develop each memory or peripheral module.

In this book, Gordon Doughman provides a complete explanation of the M68HC12 from a programmer's point-of-view. Rather than simply providing facts as in a data sheet,

Gordon has included programming examples to show exactly how to set up and use the 'HC12s on-chip peripheral systems.

Although the book is primarily based on assembly language, Gordon's strong background in high-level languages shows through in his enlightening explanation of stack usage in Chapter 3. This chapter offers insights into alternative ways of using the stack for parameter passing and issues related to local variables. Many of these techniques are not well known to assembly language programmers.

Even though a lot of MCU programming is now done in high-level languages such as C, it is still very important to understand the underlying assembly language and architecture of the target MCU. There are many cases where assembly language must still be used, such as for device drivers or time-critical hardware interface code. It is also important to study the instruction set and addressing modes to understand the object code generated for the target processor by a C compiler. Armed with this knowledge, the C programmer can utilize the various facilities of the C language to write programs that are more compact and execute more efficiently. Because of Gordon's strong C programming background, this book will make an excellent reference for C programmers who need information about the assembly language and architecture of the M68HC12. It will also be helpful for those C programmers who are required to write assembly language device drivers for the M68HC12.

Gordon also has experience writing assemblers, and this talent is evident in a section in Chapter 2 on program counter relative addressing. Gordon explains both the PC-relative indexed addressing mode and the ,PCR assembler convention particularly well.

Jim Sibigtroth

Motorola Semiconductor Products Sector
Principal Member of the Technical Staff
Motorola Microcontroller Division

Introduction

To say that the microprocessor revolution that began in the early 1970s has changed the world is an understatement. The modern cousin of the microprocessor, the microcontroller, can be found in nearly every electronic product sold today. It has been estimated that the average household contains more than several dozen microcontrollers in products such as microwave ovens, blenders, toasters, refrigerators, washing machines, televisions, stereo receivers, CD players, personal computer systems, remote control devices, razors, phones, and even greeting cards that play music when they are opened. While most of these products may contain one, or maybe two, microcontrollers, the average family car may contain as many as two dozen. Some high-end luxury cars contain sixty or more microcontrollers operating together over a local area network to control and monitor nearly every imaginable point in the automotive system.

Over the years, Motorola has played a large part in making the power of the microprocessor available for use in both industrial and consumer products. Motorola's first single chip microcontroller family, the M6801, was originally developed in cooperation with the automotive industry for use as an engine controller. The MC6801 contained an enhanced M6800 CPU, 2048 bytes of ROM (EPROM), 128 bytes of RAM, a three function timer, serial communications interface and a crystal oscillator. A complete computer system on a chip. The enhanced CPU contained additional instructions for 16-bit arithmetic and for the manipulation of the single index register. While the M6801 family was not the first single chip microcontroller available, it was one of the first to be successfully used in automobiles.

As a result of the United States government's increasing demands on the automobile manufacturers to reduce engine emissions, increase fuel economy, and improve occupant safety, Motorola, in partnership with the automotive industry, developed a successor to the M6801 – the M68HC11 microcontroller family. In addition to integrating many more peripheral functions and memory, the M68HC11 CPU improved on the M6801 CPU by adding a second 16-bit index register to the programming model. In addition, numerous instructions were added improving the processor's performance in automotive and industrial applications. Because most programs were written in assembly language, the M68HC11 CPU maintained object code compatibility with the M6801 to preserve the customer's investment in previously written software and training.

As embedded systems continued to increase in sophistication and complexity, the amount of the software required to provide additional control and features began to explode. The first member of the M68HC11 family, the MC68HC11A8, contained 8k bytes of program ROM, but it wasn't long before M68HC11 family members were available with 12k, 16k, and even 32k bytes of program ROM or EPROM. Fortunately, the enhancements made to the M68HC11 CPU improved the instruction set's suitability for high-level language compilers. Numerous C compilers became available for the M68HC11 family. Using the C programming language for writing embedded control software greatly enhanced the software developer's productivity; however, because the instruction set was not specifically designed to allow efficient code generation by high-level language compilers, programmers typically saw their program's size grow by 20 - 30%. For many applications, this tradeoff of code size for programmer productivity was acceptable. Yet, for other high-volume applications such as those in the automotive industry, this code expansion was unacceptable. Consequently, much of the software for these applications continued to be written in assembly language.

Motorola developed the M68HC12 microcontroller as a result of an ever increasing demand for microcontrollers whose instruction set was well matched to high-level languages. This book explores the M68HC12 microcontroller family from the programmer's perspective. It also devotes considerable space to the description of selected on-chip peripherals available on various family members. Practical programming examples are included with the peripheral descriptions to provide the reader an illustration of how the peripheral might be used in an actual application. While this text does not assume the reader is familiar with any of Motorola's 8-bit microcontrollers prior to the M68HC12 family, it does assume the reader is familiar with computers and has some programming experience. Specifically, the concepts of basic computer architecture, number systems, digital logic elements and Boolean logic are not covered.

Even though the M68HC12's instruction set is well suited to efficient code generation by compilers, it is still necessary for high-level language programmers to be familiar with the underlying CPU architecture and instruction set. Therefore, all programming examples are presented in M68HC12 assembly language. Because most examples are short and well commented, C programmers should have no trouble understanding and rewriting the examples in C.

Though the CPU12's instruction set is a proper super set of the M68HC11 family, significant space is devoted to the description of the entire instruction set. This ensures that readers unfamiliar with the M68HC11 family will gain sufficient knowledge to understand the programming examples without having to refer to another text. Instructions and addressing modes that are new to the M68HC12 family are clearly marked so that the M68HC11 programmer may easily pick out and study those sections containing the new or updated information.

The programming examples in this book were written and assembled using Cosmic Software's ca6812 macro cross assembler which is part of their M68HC12 C cross compiler package. However, the examples should easily assemble with any M68HC12 cross assembler with little or no modification. A demo version of the compiler package including the assembler and linker may be downloaded from the Cosmic web site at: http://www.cosmic-us.com. This demo version is adequate to assemble and test any of the examples presented in this book.

All examples were tested using Motorola's M68HC12B32EVB evaluation board. This board is a low-cost development tool providing firmware developers or students with surprisingly sophisticated capabilities. The board contains an MC68HC912B32 microcontroller, an RS-232C level translator, a low-voltage reset circuit and various passive components and jumpers. The MC68HC912B32's 32k of Flash memory contains D-Bug12, a command line debugger allowing the M68HC12B32EVB to be used as a simple EVB or as a non-intrusive debugging tool utilizing the M68HC12's single-wire Background Debug interface.

Because of the complexity of the devices in a new microcontroller family such as the M68HC12, it is rare that initial parts meet every one of the device's original specifications. Motorola often provides such parts to engineers allowing them the opportunity to begin developing products as the device errata is being fixed. All documented errata for a device's mask set may be found on the web at: http://www.mcu.motsps.com/lit/errata/12err/err12.shtml. The examples in this book were tested on the 4J54E mask set of the MC68HC912B32. At the time of publication, this mask set was the one most widely available to customers. If the M68HC12 family member does not seem to operate as described in this book or as described in Motorola's documentation, it is possible that errata items may be the cause.

Two type-faces are used throughout this book. While the main body of the text is printed using the proportional Garamond font, CPU12 instruction mnemonics, I/O register names, I/O register bit names and program labels are printed in monospaced Courier font. All assembly source listings are printed using the Courier font.

Chapter 1 THE CPU12 OVERVIEW

The M68HC12 family of microcontrollers is Motorola's latest offering in the continuing evolution of its M6800 microprocessor architecture introduced in the mid 1970s. The original M6800 architecture, loosely based on Digital Equipment's PDP-8 minicomputer, has evolved over the years from the original multi-chip microprocessor based system, to the current state-of-the-art, highly integrated, single chip microcontroller.

The M68HC12 family is based on a modular design methodology similar to Motorola's M68HC16 and M68300 families of microcontrollers. The CPU12 is the Central Processing Unit used in all M68HC12 family members. It contains the registers that constitute the user's programming model, the instruction decode logic, and an instruction queue or pipe. Other modules on the same chip, such as program memory, RAM, peripherals and I/O ports, are connected to the CPU12 by a silicon bus known as the Lite Module Bus (LMB). Connection of the CPU12's address and data bus to off-chip memory or peripherals is actually performed by another module connected to the LMB.

The CPU12 is a significantly enhanced 16-bit version of the CPU contained in the popular M68HC11 family. Its instructions are a proper super set of the M68HC11 instruction set. All M68HC11 instructions are present in the CPU12 instruction set. However, the CPU12 is NOT object code compatible with the M68HC11. To run existing M68HC11 assembly language code on the CPU12, it must be reassembled using an M68HC12 assembler. Not all M68HC11 instructions have a directly corresponding CPU12 opcode. However, for those M68HC11 instruction mnemonics, M68HC12 assemblers translate the mnemonic into a CPU12 instruction that performs an equivalent operation. To ensure that reassembled M68HC11 assembly code will run on the CPU12, all CPU12 instructions and translated M68HC11 instructions, produce identical condition code register results.

Section 1.1: Operand Size and Data Organization in Memory

The experienced M68HC11 programmer will feel very comfortable with the M68HC12 family. Nevertheless, there are numerous techniques used by M68HC11 programmers that can be performed more efficiently because many new instructions and addressing modes have been added. The CPU12 instruction set provides the capabilities to use advanced programming techniques such as position independent code, access of extended memory space, and fuzzy logic inference.

Because the CPU12 is a full 16-bit CPU core utilizing internal 16-bit data paths, its performance for all arithmetic and logic operations is greatly enhanced. In addition, many other improvements were made to increase the performance of the CPU12 core. Examining the instruction set reveals that most instructions execute in fewer clock cycles than the equivalent M68HC11 instructions. In fact, internal 16-bit register transfer or exchanges execute in a single clock cycle.

Unlike other 16-bit architectures which require instructions to be multiples of 16-bits, the CPU12 allows instructions with odd byte counts, including many single byte instructions. This allows efficient use of program memory space. To take better advantage of the internal and external 16-bit data paths, the CPU12 contains an instruction queue or pipe. The queue, which resides between the system data bus and the CPU12's instruction decode logic, acts as an elastic buffer for program information. Because data is always fetched into the pipe 16-bits at a time, it allows program memory instructions to be fetched on 16-bit aligned word boundaries. This means that program fetches never need to be split into two 8-bit accesses. Having an instruction queue reside between the system bus and CPU decode logic can pose some challenges when connecting a logic analyzer to a part's external address and data bus.

1.1 OPERAND SIZE AND DATA ORGANIZATION IN MEMORY

Even though the CPU12 is a 16-bit CPU, it operates on several different data sizes and types. A byte is equal to 8-bits, a word is equal to two consecutive bytes in memory, and a long word is equal to four consecutive bytes in memory. Words and long words are not required to be aligned to a word or long word boundary. However, in some circumstances, a system wide performance penalty may be incurred for operand misalignment.

Bytes are individually addressable with the high order byte having an even address, the same as the word address as shown in Figure 1.1. The low order byte has an odd address that is one higher than the word address. This byte ordering is known as a "big endian".

Chapter 1: The CPU12 Overview

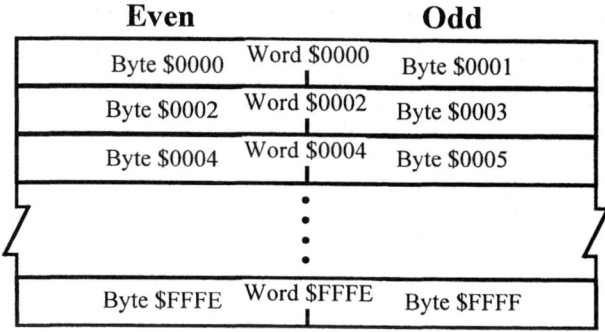

Figure 1.1: Word Organization in Memory

The data types supported by the CPU12 include bit data, integer data of 8, 16, and 32-bits, 16-bit addresses and binary coded decimal (BCD) data. All CPU arithmetic and logical operations are performed in binary arithmetic. The execution of branch instructions using the values in the CPU condition code register (CCR) determines whether programs interpret operation results as signed or unsigned numbers. Each of these data types is placed in memory as shown in Figure 2.

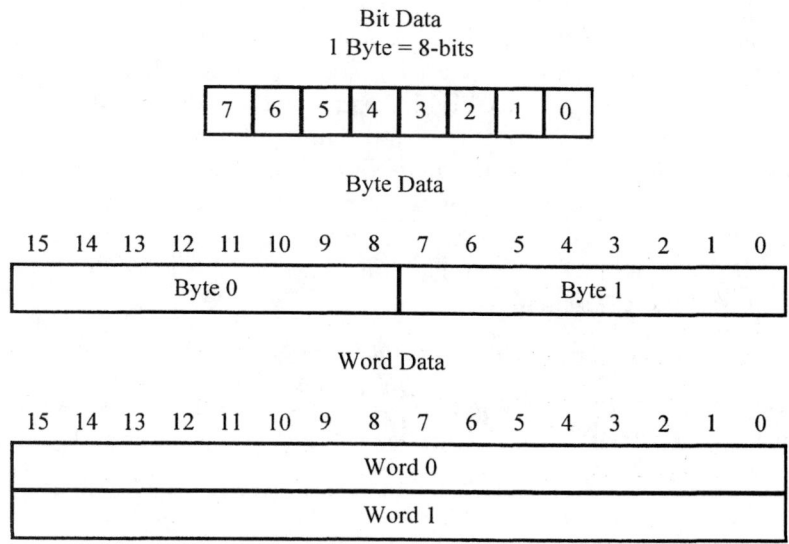

Section 1.2: Weighted Binary Fractions

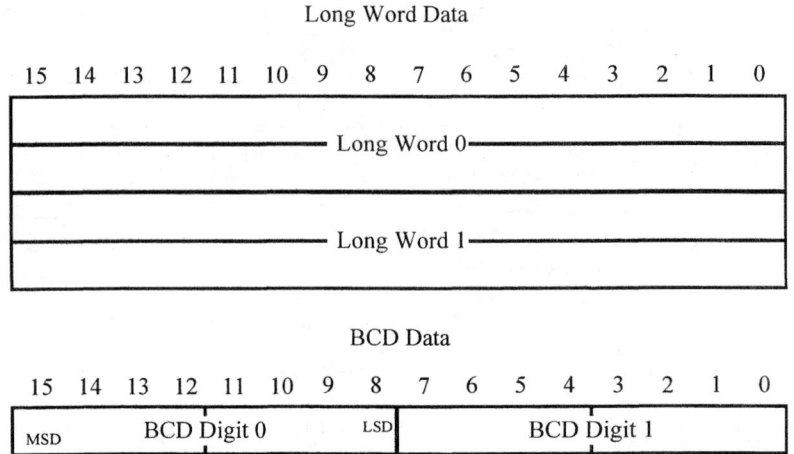

Figure 1.2: Data Organization in Memory

1.2 WEIGHTED BINARY FRACTIONS

In addition to the basic integer data types supported by the CPU12, two specialized data types are also supported. The fractional divide instruction, present in the M68HC11 CPU, produces an unsigned 16-bit weighted binary fraction as its result. The two table lookup and interpolate instructions present in the CPU12 both require an unsigned 8-bit weighted binary fraction to perform their function. Both the 8-bit and 16-bit weighted binary fraction data types have their radix or binary point to the *left* of the most significant bit. Placing the radix point to the left of the most significant bit rather than to the right of the least significant bit does not change the bit patterns stored in memory. It does, however, change the interpretation of the values of the bit patterns. Figure 1.3 shows the 8-bit and 16-bit weighted binary fraction representation.

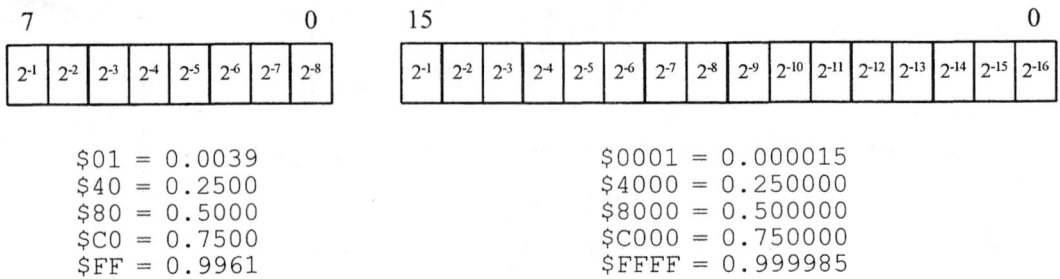

Figure 1.3: 8- and 16-bit Weighted Binary Fractions

Each bit, beginning with the most significant bit and moving towards the least significant bit, represents increasing negative powers of two rather than decreasing positive powers of two. As shown in the examples of Figure 1.3, the most significant bit represents the quantity of 2^{-1} or 0.5. The next least significant bit represents the quantity of 2^{-2} or 0.25 and so on. When more than one bit has a value of one, the quantities add together just as with integer numbers. As shown in the example, the hexadecimal number $C0 represents 0.75 which is 0.5 ($80) + 0.25 ($40).

1.3 OPERAND ALIGNMENT

The CPU12 does not require word or long word data to be aligned on a word boundary. However, not maintaining word alignment for these data types can result in a performance penalty each time the data is accessed. With the exception of data residing in the M68HC12's internal RAM module, access of a misaligned word requires two clock cycles instead of one, while a misaligned long word requires three clock cycles instead of two. The number of clock cycles required to access externally connected memory or peripheral devices may be greater if E-clock stretching is enabled.

1.4 CPU12 PROGRAMMING MODEL

The CPU12's basic architecture is known as an accumulator based architecture. This means that the result of most arithmetic and logical operations are placed in the CPU's accumulator. The CPU12 user programming model shown in Figure 1.4 is identical to the M68HC11 CPU. The CPU contains two general purpose 8-bit accumulators referred to as the A and B accumulators. For 16-bit arithmetic and logic operations, these two 8-bit accumulators are concatenated to form a single 16-bit D accumulator. As shown in the figure, the A accumulator contains the upper 8-bits of the 16-bit word and the B contains the lower 8-bits. The only other 8-bit register is Condition Code Register (CCR). The remaining registers, the X and Y index registers, the Stack Pointer (SP) and Program Counter (PC) are 16-bit registers.

Section 1.5: Stack Pointer

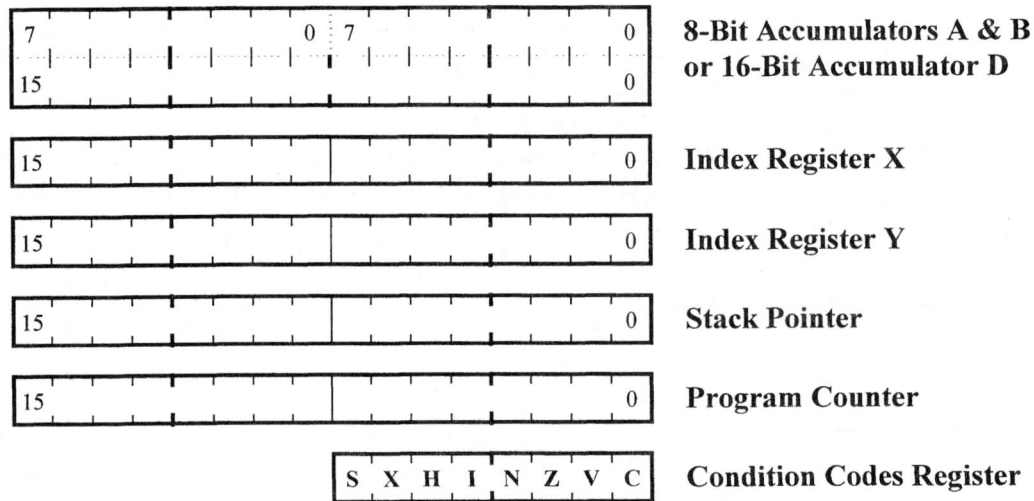

Figure 1.4: CPU12 User Programming Model

1.5 ACCUMULATORS

The two general purpose 8-bit accumulators, A and B, are used to hold operands and contain the results of operations. To improve the efficiency of handling 16-bit quantities, there are several arithmetic and logical operations that treat these as a single 16-bit accumulator. Most operations can use the A and B accumulator interchangeably. However, there are some exceptions which are discussed separately in Chapter 2.

1.6 INDEX REGISTERS

The two 16-bit index registers, X and Y, are primarily used with the indexed addressing mode. They generally contain a base address, to which a constant or the contents of one of the accumulators is added to form the effective address of an instruction's operand. Having two 16-bit indexable address registers is particularly useful when moving data around in memory or when performing calculations involving two separate data tables. In addition to their function as base address registers, the X and Y index registers are also used for some of the CPU12's extended arithmetic operations on 16-bit and 32-bit quantities.

1.7 STACK POINTER

The CPU12's stack pointer supports the automatic saving of the return address during subroutine calls and the CPU context when responding to interrupts. The memory area

Chapter 1: The CPU12 Overview

pointed to by the stack pointer can also be used for temporary data storage. This is memory area allocated at the beginning of a subroutine and released just before the subroutine returns. Because the stack pointer is 16-bits, the stack may be located anywhere within the 64k memory map occupied by RAM memory and may grow up to the size of the available memory. Each time data is placed on the stack, the stack pointer is automatically decremented. Conversely, when data is removed from the stack, the stack pointer is automatically incremented.

⚠ CPU12 Difference from the M68HC11

Unlike the M68HC11's stack which points to the *next available* byte on the stack, the CPU12 stack pointer points to the *last* byte placed on the stack. The "next available" style stack used on the M68HC11 is a carry over from the original M6800 design. For CPU's using an 8-bit data bus throughout the system and do not have direct access to data on the stack, it makes little difference which type of stack is used. However, for 16-bit designs, like the CPU12, using a "next available" stack can cause performance problems. The examples in Figure 1.5 show the inefficiency that would exist if the CPU12 used a "next available" style stack. When the M68HC11 places a 16-bit value on the stack, it first writes the low byte of the word to the location pointed to by the stack pointer, decrements the stack pointer, writes the high byte of the word and again decrements the stack pointer so that it points to the next available byte. Because the CPU12 has a 16-bit data bus and can write a word value to memory in a single operation, it only has to decrement the stack pointer once when using a "last used" style stack. If the CPU12 utilized a "next available" style stack it would still have to decrement the stack pointer twice even though it could write the entire 16-bit word to memory in a single operation. This would have resulted in additional instruction cycles for each stacking and unstacking operation.

In CPU12 (Last Used)
SP−2 ⇒ SP
(X_H:X_L) ⇒ M(SP) : M(SP+1)

If CPU12 had a Next Available stack
SP−1 ⇒ SP
(X_H:X_L) ⇒ M(SP) : M(SP+1)
SP−1 ⇒ SP

In M68HC11 (Next Available)
X_L ⇒ M(SP)
SP−1 ⇒ SP
X_H ⇒ M(SP)
SP−1 ⇒ SP

Figure 1.5: CPU12 and M68HC11 Stacking Operations

Section 1.7: Stack Pointer

Due to the fact the M68HC11 instruction set does not support stack pointer relative addressing, the only way to access data placed on the stack is to transfer the value of the stack pointer to the X or Y index register. Because the M68HC11 stack pointer points to the next available location on the stack, the transfer instructions, TSX and TSY, actually add one to the stack pointer value before placing it in the index register. Since the index register points to the last byte placed on the stack, the M68HC11 stack appears to be a "last used" stack from the programmers view point. Because the CPU12 supports stack pointer relative addressing (using the SP as an index register), a "last used" style stack was incorporated. This simplified the logic for the instructions providing general purpose register transfer and exchange.

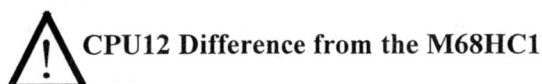
CPU12 Difference from the M68HC11

Although the CPU12's stack appears the same as the M68HC11's from the programmers viewpoint, there is one thing that changes. One of the first operations that must be performed in all programs is stack pointer initialization. With the M68HC11 the stack pointer is usually loaded with the last address of available system RAM. This address would be the "next available" memory location for stack storage. With the CPU12, however, the stack pointer should be loaded with the last address of available system RAM *plus one* since the CPU12 will decrement the stack pointer before it places data on the stack. For example, if a CPU12 and M68HC11 system both contained 1024 bytes of on-chip RAM located from $0800 to $0BFF, the CPU12's stack pointer should be loaded with $0C00 while the M68HC11's stack pointer should be loaded with $0BFF.

If M68HC11 source code is simply reassembled without making this simple change, it would function properly. The only consequence of not making the change is that one byte of memory would be wasted at the top of the stack. For most programs, this one byte of wasted stack space is not significant since the RAM allocated for the stack is generally larger than what is actually required.

As mentioned previously, the CPU12's stack is managed automatically for saving of the CPU context during subroutine calls and when responding to interrupts. When a subroutine is called, the address of the instruction following the calling instruction is automatically calculated and placed on the stack. When a return from subroutine instruction is executed, the saved address is pulled off the stack, placed in the program counter and execution continues from that address.

When an interrupt occurs, the currently executing instruction completes execution, and the entire CPU12 register set, with the exception of the stack pointer itself, is automatically placed on the stack as shown in Figure 1.6. The return address placed on the stack will be the address of the instruction following that which completed just prior to the recognition of the interrupt request. It is worth mentioning one additional item illustrated in Figure 1.6. All three 16-bit registers are placed on the stack with the high-byte of the 16-bit word at the lower address. Storing multi-byte quantities in this manner in the interrupt stack frame is consistent with the way store instructions place 16-bit quantities in memory. Notice, however, that the A and B accumulators are placed on the stack backwards compared to the order expected if the D accumulator was pushed onto the stack or stored in memory. This apparent inconsistency is a carry over from the original design of the M6800 microprocessor because the M6800 designers did not envision the A and B accumulators being used as a single 16-bit register. It may seem that this "problem" could have been fixed in the M6801 or M68HC11. However, in an effort to maintain complete compatibility with existing software that may have accessed these values from within an interrupt service routine, the stacking order of A and B was not changed.

While this may not be a problem for most interrupt service routines, it might be necessary in some situations to access the stacked value of the D accumulator. The simplest way to access the stacked values of A and B and have them in the proper order for a 16-bit value would be to load the D accumulator using stack pointer relative addressing and then exchange the values of the A and B accumulators.

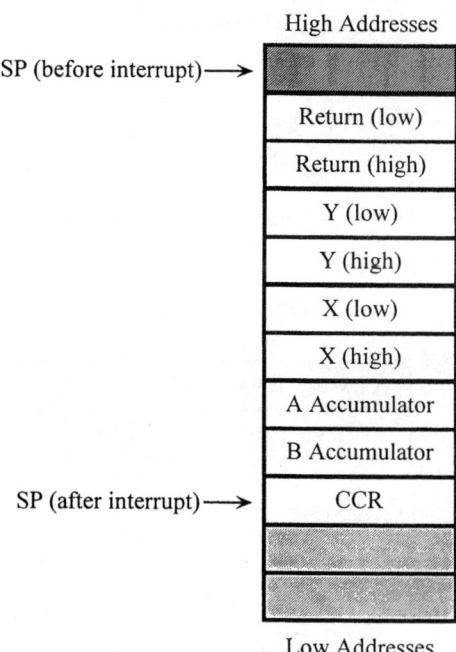

Figure 1.6: CPU12 Interrupt Stack Frame

Section 1.7: Stack Pointer

⚠ Important Information

There is one additional issue relating to the CPU12's stack pointer that was not a concern for the M68HC11 family. Unlike many other 16-bit microcontrollers, the CPU12 does not require the stack pointer to maintain alignment to a word boundary. However, not maintaining word alignment for 16-bit values can result in a system wide performance penalty if the stack is placed in external memory. Remember, because the CPU12 utilizes a 16-bit data bus, 16-bit data can be written to memory with a single write operation if the data is written to an even byte boundary. Therefore, if the stack pointer is pointing to an even byte address when a 16-bit value is pushed onto the stack, the stack pointer is decremented by two and a single 16-bit write operation is performed. If the stack pointer contains an odd byte address, two separate write operations and decrements must take place. First, the stack pointer will be decremented by one to point to the lower byte. Next, the lower byte of the 16-bit value is written to the even byte address (lower byte of a word address) contained in the stack pointer. The stack pointer is decremented again to point to the next lower byte in memory. Finally, the upper byte of the 16-bit value is written to the upper byte of the next lower word. Figure 1.7 shows the byte positions of a 16-bit word pushed on the stack when the stack pointer has an even byte address. Figure 1.8 shows the byte positions of a 16-bit word pushed on the stack when the stack pointer has an odd byte address.

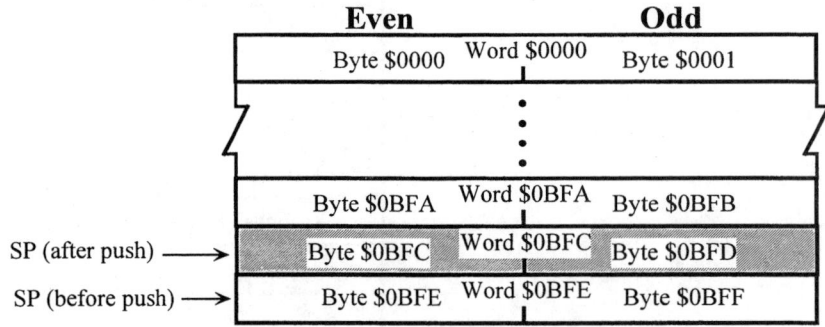

Figure 1.7: 16-bit data pushed on stack with even byte stack alignment

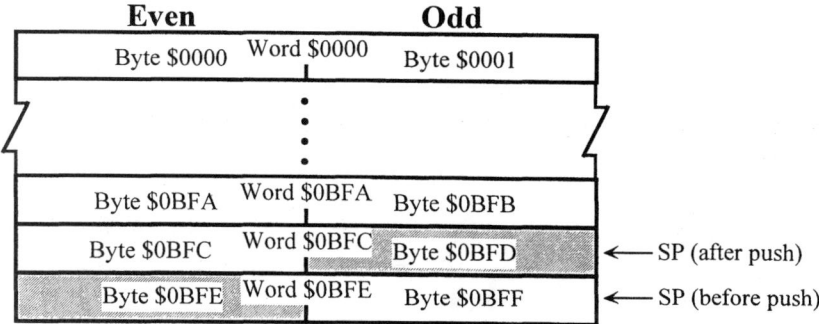

Figure 1.8: 16-bit data pushed on stack with odd byte stack alignment

As mentioned previously, the internal RAM module was specifically designed to allow misaligned word and long word accesses without imposing the extra bus cycle penalty. However, placing the stack in external memory will cause additional bus cycles to be inserted each time a subroutine is called, a return from subroutine is executed, or an interrupt is serviced if the stack pointer is not aligned to a word boundary. For many applications this performance penalty may not cause enough system performance degradation to be of concern. However, in an M68HC12 system that is heavily interrupt driven and is using the microcontroller near its computational capacity, this may be a concern. In such applications, the stack should be kept in internal RAM unless there is a very good reason for placing it elsewhere.

1.8 Program Counter

The Program Counter (PC) is a 16-bit register that holds the address of the next instruction to be executed. Each time an instruction is executed, the PC is automatically incremented. Because of the instruction queue contained within the CPU12, the program counter is not actually used to fetch the program instructions from memory. A separate register, the Instruction Pointer (IP), is used to fetch 16-bit aligned words from program memory to fill the instruction queue. The IP is not accessible to the programmer and is completely transparent to software execution.

1.9 Condition Code Register

The Condition Code Register (CCR) is an 8-bit register that contains five status bits, two interrupt masking bits and a STOP instruction control bit. The status bits reflect the results of CPU operations as it executes instructions. The five status bits are the half carry (H), negative (N), overflow (V), and the carry/borrow (C) bits. The half carry bit is only used for

Section 1.9: Condition Code Register

BCD arithmetic operations. The remaining status bits, N, Z, V, and C, allow program branching based on the results of previous operations.

The CPU12, unlike some other architectures, affects some or all of the five status bits based on more than just arithmetic and logical operations. It is rare that execution of separate instructions are required to modify these bits. In general, any data movement into or out of the CPU's registers will affect one or more of the flags. There are, however, a number of exceptions. Stack related push and pull instructions, the general purpose register transfer and exchange instructions and the memory-to-memory move instructions do not affect any of the condition code register status bits.

In general, instructions that move data into or out of the CPU's registers and logical bit operations will only affect the N, Z and V bits while arithmetic instructions generally affect all five bits. The detailed description of an instruction should be checked to determine the CCR bits affected by its execution. The following sections will discuss the function and meaning of each one of the condition code register bits.

1.9.1 S Control Bit

The S bit is used to control the operation of the CPU12 and its on-chip peripherals when the STOP instruction is executed. Execution of the STOP instruction causes the on-chip oscillator to cease operation placing the part in an very low power state. In some applications accidental execution of the STOP instruction may not be desirable. If the S-bit is set when the CPU12 executes a STOP instruction, it will be treated as a no-operation (NOP) instruction and simply continue execution with the next instruction. The S bit may be set or cleared at any time during a program's execution.

1.9.2 XIRQ (X) Mask Bit

The XIRQ bit is one of the two bits that allows program control of interrupt inputs to the CPU. The XIRQ input is an enhanced version of the Non-Maskable Interrupt (NMI) input used on previous generations of Motorola microprocessors and microcontrollers. Non-maskable interrupts are generally used to alert the CPU to an urgent request for peripheral service or a major system failure. However, if non-maskable interrupts are enabled before a system is fully initialized, it can lead to unexpected results. In fact, the execution of a non-maskable interrupt before the stack pointer is initialized could result in a total system failure. The X-bit allows software to control when the CPU12's one non-maskable interrupt is enabled.

During reset, the X-bit is automatically set, disabling the XIRQ input to the CPU12. As long as the X-bit remains set, any transitions on the XIRQ pin will be ignored by the CPU12. The application software must specifically clear the X-bit in order to recognize XIRQ interrupts. Once the X-bit is clear, software may not set it.

After XIRQ interrupts have been enabled and an XIRQ interrupt occurs, the CPU12's registers, with exception of the stack pointer, are pushed onto the stack. Then both the X-bit and I-bit are set to prevent further interrupts from being recognized during the execution of the service routine. The stacked value of the condition code register contains the state of the X-bit before the interrupt so that when a ReTurn from Interrupt (`RTI`) instruction is executed, the X bit will be restored to a value of zero, enabling the recognition of additional XIRQ interrupts.

Even though the XIRQ is considered to be a non-maskable interrupt, once enabled, there is a "back door" mechanism that may be used to disable XIRQ interrupts. Within the XIRQ interrupt service routine, it is possible to manipulate the stacked value of the condition code register to set the X-bit. When an `RTI` is executed at the end of the service routine, the modified value of the X-bit will be placed in the condition code register. This is the only way to disable XIRQ interrupts once they have been enabled. There is no direct way, through software, to set the X-bit once it has been cleared.

1.9.3 H Status Bit

Even though the CPU12 only performs binary arithmetic, programmers can operate on packed BCD data by performing a binary addition and then executing the Decimal Adjust accumulator A (`DAA`) instruction. The H-bit, or half carry, represents a carry out of bit three during a binary addition operation. This bit is used in conjunction with the `DAA` instruction to apply a correction factor to the A accumulator after the binary addition of two BCD numbers. The H-bit is only updated by the 8-bit add or add-with-carry instructions operating on the A or B accumulators or the add-B-to-A instruction. It should be noted, however, that the `DAA` instruction only operates on the A accumulator.

1.9.4 I Mask Bit

The IRQ bit is one of the two CCR bits that allows program control of the interrupt inputs to the CPU. The I-bit, set during reset, must be cleared by software before any maskable interrupts can be recognized. As long as the I-bit remains set, maskable interrupts from the external IRQ pin or one of an M68HC12's internal peripherals will become pending. As soon as the I-bit is cleared, any pending interrupts will be serviced in an order determined by a priority scheme set by the M68HC12's device integration module.

After IRQ interrupts have been enabled and an IRQ interrupt occurs, the CPU12's registers, with the exception of the stack pointer, are pushed onto the stack and the I-bit is set to prevent further interrupts from being recognized during the execution of the service routine. The stacked value of the condition code register will contain the state of the I-bit before the interrupt was recognized. When a ReTurn from Interrupt (RTI) instruction is

Section 1.9: Condition Code Register

executed, the I-bit will be restored with a value of zero, enabling the recognition of additional IRQ interrupts.

Unlike the X-bit, the I-bit can be set and cleared at any time under program control. This allows all IRQ interrupts to be disabled during critical portions of a program and then re-enabled. It also allows for nested interrupt service routines by clearing the I-bit within the interrupt service routine itself. This technique can allow for a faster response to a critical event, but should be used with great caution to avoid overflowing the stack.

1.9.5 N Status Bit

The N-bit reflects the state of the most significant bit of arithmetic, logic, or data movement operations involving the CPU12's registers or memory. It is most commonly used by software that treats numbers as signed two's compliment values. However it can be used simply to reflect the state of the most significant bit of any memory or I/O register.

1.9.6 Z Status Bit

The Z-bit is set to indicate that all of the bits from the result of an operation contain zeros. Most arithmetic, logic, and data movement operations involving the CPU registers affect the state of the Z-bit.

1.9.7 V Status Bit

The two's complement overflow bit, or V-bit, is set when the result of an operation produces a two's compliment arithmetic overflow. For example, if two positive 8-bit numbers (both numbers less than or equal to 127) are added together and produce a negative result (the most significant bit set), the V-bit is set to indicate that the result could not be properly represented in two's complement notation.

1.9.8 C Status Bit

When performing addition or subtraction operations, the C-bit is set to indicate either a carry or a borrow respectively. The shift and rotate also utilize the carry bit to allow multiple precision shifts and rotates. In addition, the carry bit has special meaning for several instructions. For example, if the carry bit is set after the execution of the divide instructions, it indicates division by zero.

Questions/Exercises

1.1 What feature of the CPU12 instruction set allows it to make effecient use of program memory when compared to other 16-bit microcontrollers?

Chapter 1: The CPU12 Overview

1.2 How many data types does the CPU12 support? Name them.

1.3 What are the memory operand alignment rules for 16-bit and 32-bit data? What happens if these rules are violated?

1.4 What is the "endian-ness" of the CPU12? What does this mean?

1.5 Is the most significant bit of a word stored at a higher or lower address than the least significant bit?

1.6 How many accumulators are available to a CPU12 programmer? What are their names?

1.7 What are the index registers used for? What are their names?

1.8 What is the difference in the implementation of the stack pointer on the CPU12 and the M68HC11? What implications does this have for the programmer?

1.9 How does the difference in the implementation of the stack pointer on the CPU12 affect M68HC11 code that is reassembled for execution on the CPU12?

1.10 What is different about the way the A and B accumulators are placed on the stack in response to an interrupt.

1.11 What restrictions are placed on stack pointer alignment? Is there any need to be concerned?

1.12 Briefly describe the function of each of the condition code register bits.

Chapter 2 THE CPU12 INSTRUCTION SET

While the CPU12 has a greatly enhanced instruction set compared to the M68HC11, the basic set of instruction mnemonics has been kept to a manageable size. Instructions have been added to perform extended precision math operations, fuzzy logic, memory-to-memory moves and table look-up, just to name a few. Perhaps the greatest enhancement though, is the expansion of the indexed addressing mode. In addition to eliminating the one byte, one cycle penalty present in the M68HC11 instruction set for using the Y index register, the indexing capability has been extended to include the use of the stack pointer and program counter as index registers.

The basic philosophy behind the CPU12 instruction set is to have a relatively manageable number of easy to remember instruction mnemonics, and then compliment them with flexible addressing modes. The instruction mnemonics determine the operation performed by the CPU12 while the addressing mode determines how data is accessed by the CPU12. In this chapter the various addressing modes supported by the CPU12 are examined and followed by a complete analysis of the instruction set.

2.1 ASSEMBLER SYNTAX

Before beginning a discussion of the CPU12's instruction set, it is necessary to define the basic assembly language syntax recognized by Motorola's and third party's assemblers. Each line of assembly language source consists of up to four fields, all of which are optional. Figure 2.1 shows the basic layout of a source line. Optional items are contained within square brackets. However, these are not to be confused with the square brackets used to specify the indexed indirect addressing mode. Items surrounded by less than (<) and greater than (>) symbols are meta symbols and are replaced with actual elements of the assembly

Section 2.1: Assembler Syntax

source. Any number of tabs or space characters may separate the fields. All lines are terminated with the system's end-of-line character(s). For DOS/Windows systems, the end-of-line characters consist of a carriage return/line feed sequence. For UNIX systems, the end of a line is marked only by a new line or line feed character. Macintosh systems use a single carriage return character to mark the end of a line.

```
[<Label>[:]]     [<Mnemonic>]    [<Operand>]]         [[;]<Comment>]
```

Figure 2.1: Assembly language source line

The first field, or label field, is used to mark an assembly language statement allowing a programmer to refer an instruction using a symbolic name rather than a hexadecimal address. The assembler assigns the value of the program or location counter to the name or symbol appearing in this field. In general, labels must begin with an alphabetic character, although some assemblers allow other non-numeric characters to be used as the first or succeeding characters. After the first character, most assemblers allow the use of any combination of alpha-numeric characters and/or special characters such as the period, question mark and underscore characters. Many assemblers require that the label be followed by the ASCII colon character. The colon is not considered part of the label but is simply used to terminate the label field. Many of Motorola's early M68HC11 assembler tools required only the label field be terminated with a space or tab character. Therefore, code written using these tools may require extensive modification before it can be reassembled using an M68HC12 assembler. If the source line does not contain the mnemonic, operand or comment field, the colon following the label should be followed by the system's end-of-line character sequence. In general, the alphabetic characters used in labels may be a mixture of upper and lower case characters. However, the documentation for each assembler must be examined to determine if the assembler recognizes labels in a case sensitive or case insensitive manner. Some assemblers include an option to select either choice. The maximum number of characters permitted in a label varies from assembler to assembler; however, some assemblers allow up to 255 significant characters.

The instruction mnemonic field consists of one of the CPU12 instructions as defined in Appendix A or an assembler directive as defined by the assembler being used. For most assemblers, the instruction mnemonics may consist of upper, lower or mixed case alphanumeric characters. The mnemonic field must be terminated by at least one space or tab character if it is followed by an operand field.

The operand field is used to supply additional address or data information that may be required by an instruction. However, not all instructions, specifically those utilizing inherent addressing and some utilizing special combinations of addressing modes, require the operand field. In general, the operand field consists of CPU register specifications and/or mathematical expressions. When multiple items are required by an instruction, the items must be separated by a comma. Register specifications consist of the eight CPU12 register names: A, B, D, X, Y, SP, PC, and CCR. Generally, register names may be supplied in either upper or lower case letters.

Address and/or data information is usually supplied as a general mathematical expression. Each assembler will have its own syntax regarding mathematical expressions, however, they will generally consist of symbols (labels) and/or numbers separated by mathematical operators. Numeric quantities may usually be represented in several number bases. Historically, Motorola's assemblers have used prefix characters to designate the various number bases. The dollar sign ($) precedes hexadecimal numbers, the "commercial at" character (@) precedes octal numbers, and the percent character (%) precedes binary numbers. Typically, the default numeric base of most assemblers is decimal, therefore any numeric quantities not preceded by one of the number base designators is interpreted as a decimal number. Some assemblers allow spaces to appear within a mathematical expression. While using spaces to separate operands and operators in a mathematical expression can make it more readable, it may prevent the source code from being used with other assemblers.

The last field of an assembly language source is the comment field. The comment field, ignored by the assembler, is used to contain information that documents the reason for the actions performed by the instruction mnemonic. Figure 2.1 shows that the comment field optionally begins with a semicolon (;), however, some assemblers use the semicolon as a comment field delimiter and require that it be present. Because all four fields of the assembly language source line are optional, a blank line is considered a comment line and is ignored by the assembler.

2.2 Addressing Modes

The CPU12 supports six basic addressing modes: inherent, immediate, extended, direct, relative and indexed. While some instructions use more than one addressing mode to access data, not all of the addressing modes are usable with every instruction,. All of the addressing modes, with the exception of inherent, calculate a 16-bit effective address that is used to access an instruction's data. The time required to perform the effective address calculation is included in each instruction's cycle count for a particular addressing mode. The use of various addressing modes does affect an instruction's execution time, however, the additional time is due to additional memory references that must be made by the CPU to obtain the data required by the instruction.

With the exception of inherent addressing, the addressing mode used by an instruction is specified in the operand field. Some addressing modes are specified by special characters, while other addressing modes are implied by the instruction mnemonic itself. In each of the following sections, a description of each addressing mode is given along with its assembler syntax and an example of instructions that use the addressing mode.

Section 2.2: Addressing Modes

2.2.1 Inherent Addressing

Inherent addressing is the simplest form of addressing since it does not require an operand specification other than the instruction mnemonic itself. The opcode specifies the location on which the data will be operated. Most of these instructions operate on one of the CPU12's internal registers. In general, inherent instructions residing on page 1 of the CPU12's opcode map require a single clock cycle to execute. Inherent instructions residing on page 2 of the opcode map require two clock cycles to execute.

```
Assembler Syntax:    none

Effective Address Calculation:   none

Examples:
         NOP        ; no operand required
         INCA       ; operation performed on a CPU register.
         ABX        ; add the B accumulator to the X index register.
```

Figure 2.2: Inherent Addressing Mode

In the example, the ABX instruction appears to be an instruction that uses inherent addressing. However, unlike the M68HC11, the CPU12 does not have an opcode for the ABX mnemonic. Instead, this mnemonic is translated by the assembler to the equivalent instruction, LEAX B,X. There are a number of M68HC11 instructions mnemonics in the CPU12 instruction set that are translated into equivalent operations for the CPU12. These instructions are discussed in other sections of this chapter.

2.2.2 Immediate Addressing

The effective address of the operand for immediate addressing is the byte address following the opcode of the instruction. Because the operand is included as part of the instruction stream, it will have already been fetched into the on-chip instruction queue. For this reason, most of the instructions utilizing immediate addressing only require one or two clock cycles to execute. The exceptions are those instructions utilizing more than one addressing mode. The size of the operand, or immediate data, depends on the size of the destination and is implied by the instruction mnemonic. When the destination is a register, the operand size will be 8-bits for the A and B accumulators and 16-bits for the D, X and Y index registers or the stack pointer. If an 8-bit value is supplied in the program source but the instruction mnemonic implies 16-bit immediate data, the assembler will generate a 16-bit value in the object code with the upper 8-bits containing zeros. When the destination is a memory location, the data can be either 8 or 16-bits.

Chapter 2: The CPU12 Instruction Set

The ASCII pound sign (#) is used to indicate immediate addressing and must be the first character in the operand field. One very common programming mistake is to inadvertently omit the pound sign when entering a program. Unfortunately this mistake can be very difficult to find because the assembler, in most cases, will interpret the number in the operand field as an address and generate the object code for either extended or direct addressing.

Assembler Syntax: #«data8 | data16»

Effective Address Calculation:

```
            ┌─────────────────────────┐
            │   Opcode Address + 1    │
            └───────────┬─────────────┘
                        │
                        ▼
            ┌─────────────────────────┐
            │        Operand          │
            └─────────────────────────┘
```

Examples:
```
    LDAA  #10           ; load A with the decimal value 10.
    LDD   #$1234        ; load D with the hex value 1234.
    MOVB  #5,$1234      ; place the decimal value 5 in address $1234.
```

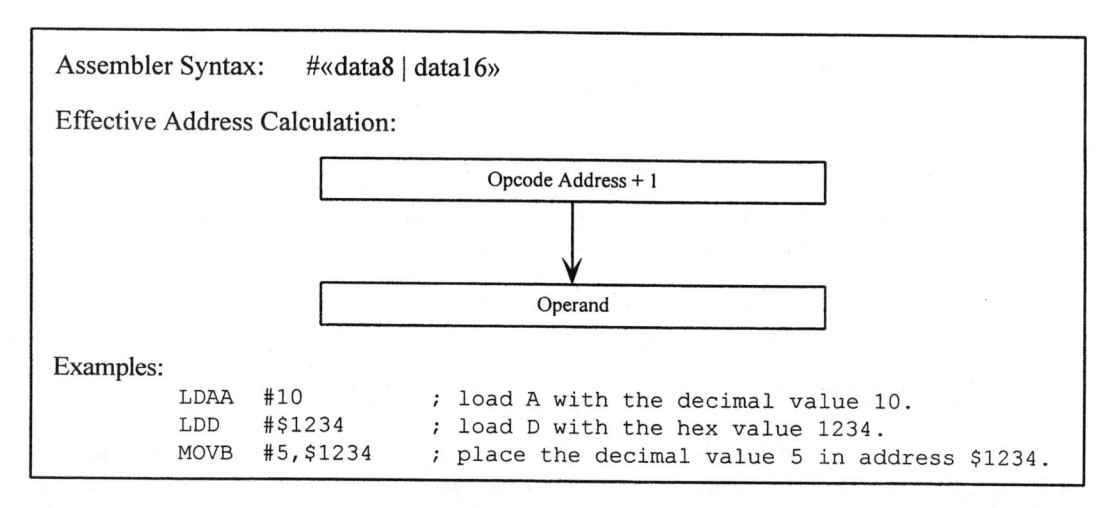

Figure 2.3: Immediate Addressing Mode

2.2.3 Extended Addressing

Extended addressing uses a full 16-bit address to specify the location of the operand. Using this addressing mode, any byte in the CPU12's 64k memory map may be accessed. The two bytes following the opcode form the address of the data to be operated on. Because the operand address is included as part of the instruction stream, it has already been fetched into the on-chip instruction queue several cycles before it is needed. However, because the CPU12 must use the supplied address to fetch the operand from memory, an additional bus cycle must be performed.

Section 2.2: Addressing Modes

Assembler Syntax: «address16»

Effective Address Calculation:

```
                    ┌─────────────────────────┐
                    │   Opcode Address + 1    │
                    └───────────┬─────────────┘
                                │
                                ▼
                    ┌─────────────────────────┐
                    │     Operand Address     │
                    └─────────────────────────┘
```

Examples:
```
    LDAA  $0010         ; load A with the byte at address $0010.
    LDD   $1234         ; load D with the bytes at $1234 & $1235.
    MOVB  $5678,$1234   ; move a byte from address $5678 to $1234.
```

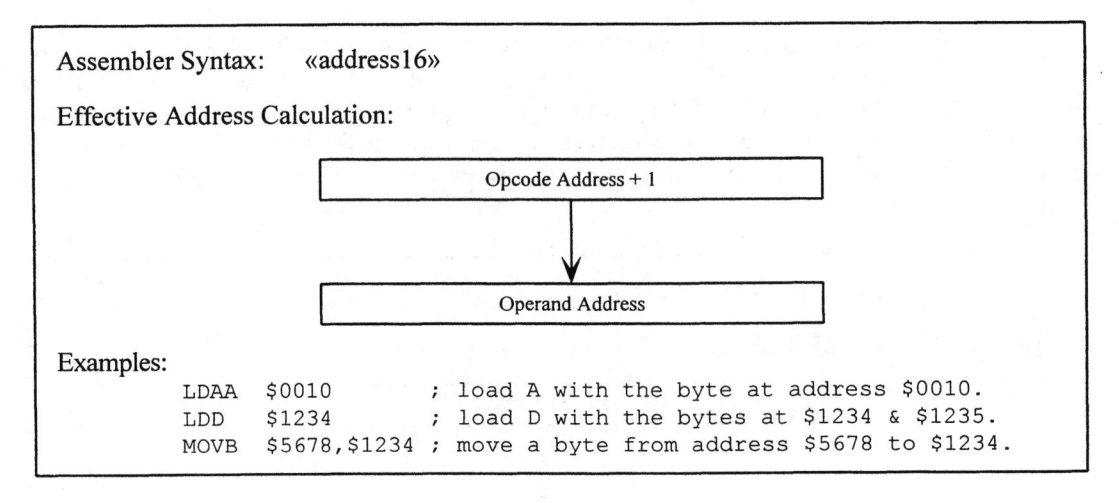

Figure 2.4: Extended Addressing Mode

2.2.4 Direct Addressing

The direct addressing mode, also known as zero-page addressing, is similar to extended addressing except that it can only access the lowest 256 bytes in the CPU12's 64k memory. Direct addressing only uses an 8-bit address to specify the location of the operand. The supplied 8-bit address, contained in the byte following the instruction opcode, is used as the lower 8-bits of the 16-bit address. The upper 8-bits of the address are set to zero when the address is used to fetch the operand. Because the direct addressing only supplies 8-bits of an operand address as part of the instruction, it uses one less byte of program memory. Placing often used program variables in page zero can significantly reduce the overall size of a program.

Chapter 2: The CPU12 Instruction Set

Assembler Syntax: «address8»

Effective Address Calculation:

```
        ┌─────────────────────────────┐
        │     Opcode Address + 1      │
        └─────────────┬───────────────┘
                      ▼
        ┌─────────────┬───────────────┐
        │    $00      │  8-bit Address │
        └─────────────┴───────┬───────┘
                              ▼
        ┌─────────────────────────────┐
        │       Operand Address       │
        └─────────────────────────────┘
```

Examples:

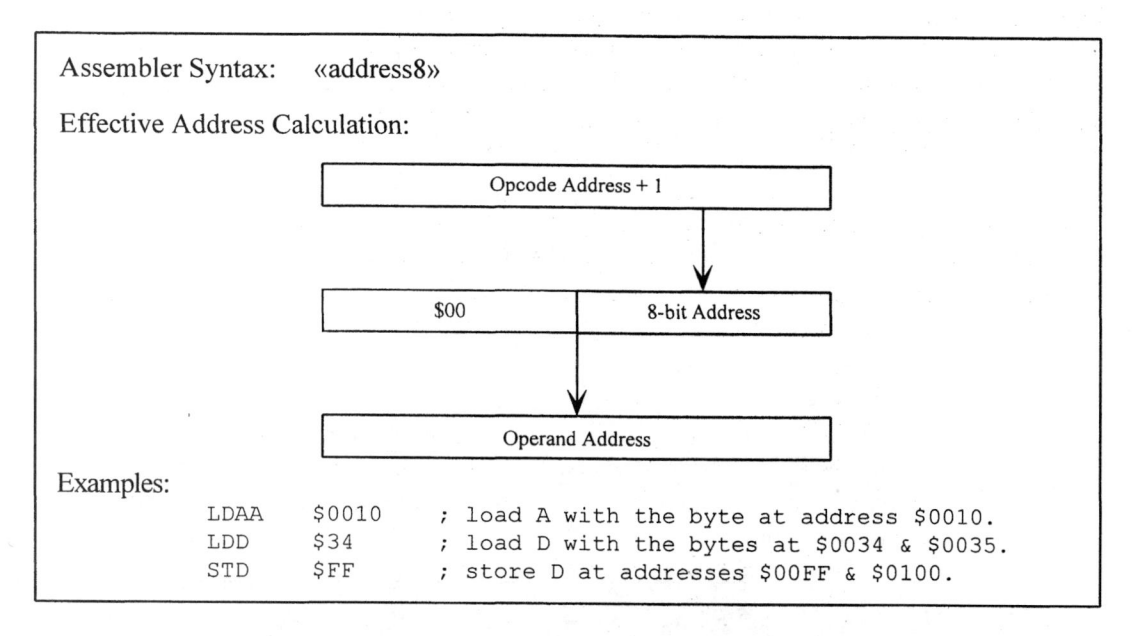

```
LDAA    $0010    ; load A with the byte at address $0010.
LDD     $34      ; load D with the bytes at $0034 & $0035.
STD     $FF      ; store D at addresses $00FF & $0100.
```

Figure 2.5: Direct Addressing Mode

The first example actually shows a four digit hexadecimal address supplied for the operand. However, because the upper 8-bits of the address are zero, the assembler will generate the object code for direct addressing rather than extended addressing, saving one byte of program code. The last line in the example is an interesting case. It shows the contents of the D accumulator, a 16-bit value, being stored at the last address on page zero. Although the high byte of the 16-bit value resides on page zero, the lower byte of the 16-bit value would have to be stored in the first byte address of page 1 ($0100). Even in this case, direct addressing will work properly. The CPU12 will automatically take care of generating the correct address to properly store the low byte of the 16-bit value.

2.2.5 Relative Addressing

Relative addressing, more accurately called *program relative addressing*, is used with both conditional and unconditional branching instructions. The term *program relative* refers to the fact that the effective address, or destination of the branch, is computed relative to the value of the program counter. While the branch instructions use relative addressing exclusively, the bit-test-and-branch and loop primitive instructions use it in combination with other addressing modes.

The CPU12's branch instructions use two types of relative addressing. Short branch instructions consist of a one byte opcode followed by an 8-bit *signed* offset. The long branch instructions consist of a two byte opcode followed by a 16-bit *signed* offset. Because the

Section 2.2: Addressing Modes

offsets are signed two's compliment numbers, it allows branching both forward and backward from the location of the program counter. The numeric range of the short branch instructions is -128 ($80) to +127 ($7F). The numeric range of the long branch instructions is -32768 ($8000) to +32767 ($7FFF). Because the destination address is calculated using the value of the program counter at the end of the instruction, the range of the short branch instructions is -126 to +129 from the first byte of the instruction. An offset of zero will cause the CPU12 to execute the instruction immediately following the branch instruction regardless of the test involved.

Calculation of the one or two byte two's compliment offset is performed by the assembler. In fact, some assemblers will optimize the generated object code by substituting short branch instructions when the programmer has specified a long branch and the destination address is within the range of a short branch. In some cases these types of optimizing assemblers will perform the reverse operation. Instead of generating an error when the destination of a short branch is out of range, the assembler generates the object code for a long branch instruction.

```
Assembler Syntax:     «address16»

Effective Address Calculation (short branch):

            15                                                    0
            ┌──────────────────────────────────────────────────────┐
            │                  Opcode + 2 (PC)                     │
            └──────────────────────────────────────────────────────┘

    15              8 7                    0
    ┌───────────────────────────────────────┐
    │   Sign extended 8-bit 2's Compliment Offset   │──▶( + )
    └───────────────────────────────────────┘

            15                                                    0
            ┌──────────────────────────────────────────────────────┐
            │                 Destination Address                  │
            └──────────────────────────────────────────────────────┘

Examples:
        BNE     Loop1       ; Branches to code marked by the label Loop1
        BRA     *           ; The '*' represents the value of the PC at
                            ; the first byte of the instruction. This
                            ; executes a loop forever!
        BHS     *+2         ; Produces an offset of zero. Executes the
                            ; next instruction regardless of the CCR bits.
```

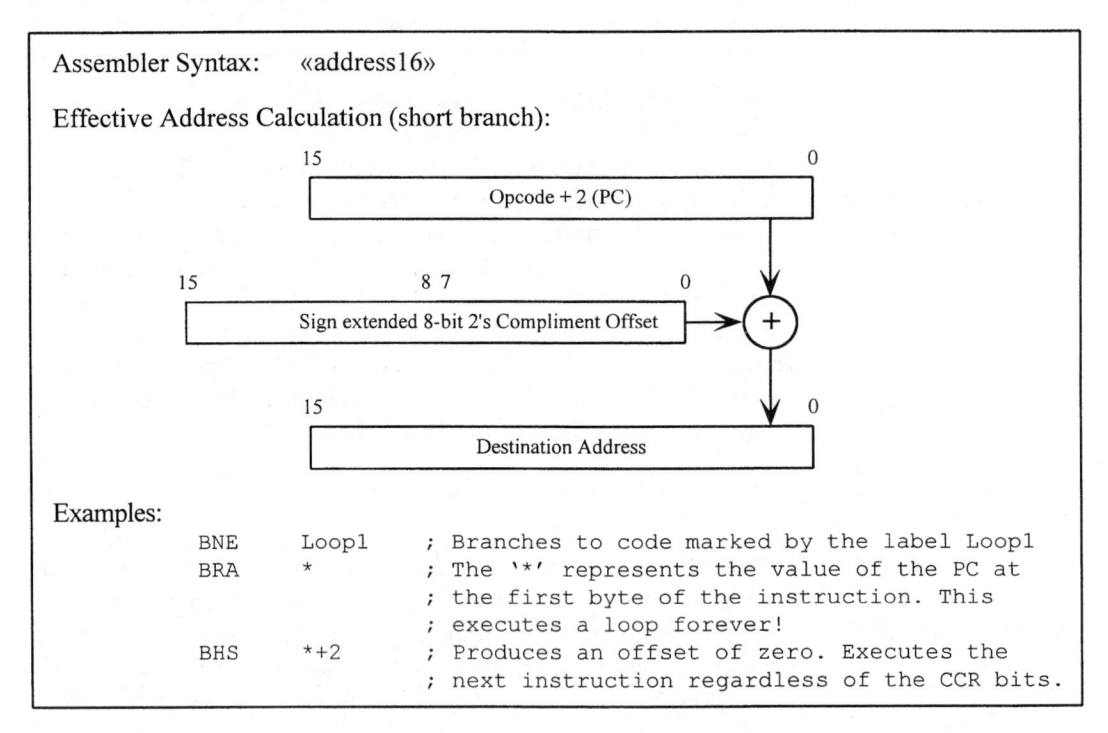

Figure 2.6: Short Program Relative Addressing

As mentioned previously, the bit-test-and-branch and loop primitive instructions also use relative addressing. In the case of the bit-test-and-branch instructions, the size of the instruction varies between four and six bytes. The effective address calculation is the same as the short branch except that the value of the program counter used for the calculation will be the instruction's opcode address plus four, five, or six.

The effective address calculation for the loop primitive instructions is similar to the short branch instructions except that a 9-bit two's compliment offset is used. Like the 8-bit offset, it is sign extended to a full 16-bits before the destination address is calculated. Because all loop primitive instructions are three bytes long, the value of the program counter used in the calculation will be the instruction's opcode address plus three.

```
Assembler Syntax:    «address16»

Effective Address Calculation (long branch):

                15                                    0
               [      Opcode Address + 4 (PC)         ]
                                                      |
         15                                    0      v
        [    16-bit 2's Compliment Offset     ]----->(+)
                                                      |
                15                                    v
               [        Destination Address           ]

Examples:
         LBNE    Loop1    ; Branches to code marked by the label Loop1
         LBRA    *        ; The '*' represents the value of the PC at
                          ; the first byte of the instruction. This
                          ; executes a loop forever!
         LBHS    *+4      ; Produces an offset of zero. Executes the
                          ; next instruction regardless of the CCR bits.
```

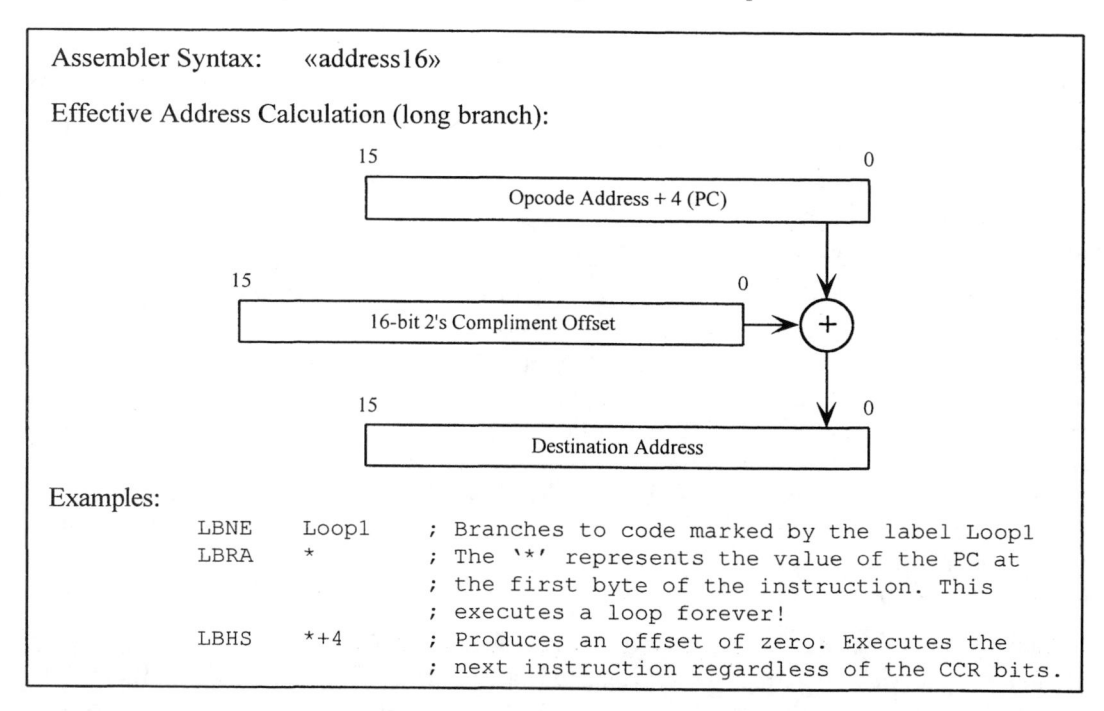

Figure 2.7: Long Program Relative Addressing

⚠ **CPU12 Difference from the M68HC11**

2.2.6 Indexed Addressing

The CPU12 uses a greatly enhanced variation of the indexed addressing modes available in the M68HC11 microcontroller family. The CPU12's indexed addressing mode capabilities offer reduced execution time in all cases and reduced code size for most operations. The one

Section 2.2: Addressing Modes

byte, one clock cycle penalty for using the Y index register has been eliminated. These reductions are the result of a fundamental difference in the way the indexed addressing information is encoded in the CPU12's object code.

Even with the addition of the Y index register, the M68HC11 had to remain object code compatible with the M6801 family of microcontrollers. Because there were relatively few spaces left in the M6801 family's opcode map, the M68HC11 designers faced a dilemma. Object code compatibility had to be maintained, yet it was required that all the instructions using the X index register also be able to use the Y index register. Their solution was to prefix each instruction that used X indexed addressing with one of the M6801's unused opcodes. This technique allowed the M68HC11's instruction decode logic to differentiate between the two index registers yet share much of the same logic for executing instructions using either the X or Y index registers. In addition, it allowed the M68HC11 to remain completely object code compatible with the M6801 family. Unfortunately, because of the extra byte associated with each instruction utilizing Y indexed addressing, many programmers avoided using the Y index register whenever possible. This made the additional index register less useful than it otherwise might have been.

Because the M68HC12 family only had to maintain *source code* compatibility with the M68HC11 family, and not object code compatibility, a more efficient method of encoding the indexed addressing modes was devised for the CPU12. Rather than use a prebyte for specifying the usage of a particular index register, the CPU12 utilizes a postbyte to fully specify both the index register and the particular type of indexed addressing used. At first glance, this method may not seem any more efficient than using a prebyte. However, because all 256 postbyte combinations are available for use by the instruction decode logic, the possibilities for indexed addressing mode enhancements are much greater. Remember, the prebyte method was restricted to using the few unused opcodes that were available in the M6801's opcode map.

The postbyte, plus zero, one, or two additional extension bytes, is used to fully specify the index register and one of seven types of indexed addressing. This method eliminates the execution time and code size differences between the X and Y index registers and dramatically enhances the indexed addressing capabilities of the CPU12 by allowing the use of other CPU registers as index registers. The extension byte(s) are used to specify a constant offset from the base address provided by the index register.

The major enhancements made to the CPU12's indexed addressing modes include: use of the stack pointer as an index register; use of the program counter as an index register, except with autoincrement and autodecrement modes; use of the contents of the A, B, or D accumulators for offsets; automatic pre- or post-increment or pre- or post-decrement by a count of 1 to 8; a choice of 5-, 9-, or 16-bit signed constant offsets; and two indexed indirect modes – one utilizing a 16-bit constant offset, the other using the contents of the D accumulator as an offset.

All indexed addressing modes use one of the CPU's four 16-bit registers, X, Y, SP, or PC, as the base address in calculating the effective address. In all cases, except for indexed-indirect, the effective address specifies the memory location(s) affected by the instruction operation. With the indexed-indirect variation, the address provided by the base register plus an offset points to a 16-bit address that points to the data affected by the instruction operation.

Because the M68HC11 family does not allow the stack pointer to be used as an indexable register, allocating, deallocating and manipulating stack data was a cumbersome process at best. Because the CPU12 allows the stack pointer to provide a base address for the indexed addressing modes, it provides a much more efficient method of accessing and manipulating data residing on the stack. This is especially important for the generation of efficient object code by high-level language compilers such as C. Furthermore, this important capability can also be utilized by assembly language programmers and can lead to more efficient programs that are easier to debug.

The use of the program counter as an index register may seem strange at first glance. However, referencing data with respect to the current value of the program counter allows programs to be written in a position independent manner. Position independent object code will execute properly at any address without reassembly or relinking. Because most embedded application code resides in nonvolatile memory, embedded applications generally do not warrant or benefit from position independent object code. However, there are certain situations, such as the Flash memory programming application discussed in Chapter 8, that can benefit from its use.

The following sections provide detailed descriptions of the various indexed addressing modes. Source syntax, effective address calculation and source examples are given.

Constant Offset Indexed Addressing

Constant offset indexed addressing is the only form of indexed addressing provided in the M68HC11 family. The CPU12 provides three basic variants that include 5-, 9-, and 16-bit constant offset values from the base index register value. Also unlike the M68HC11 family, the constant offset values are *signed* offsets. This offset is sign extended, if necessary, and added to the value of the base index register which may be X, Y, SP, or PC.

5-Bit Constant Offset Indexed Addressing

The 5-bit signed offset provides a range of -16 through +15 from the value in the base index register. While this range may not seem very large compared to the unsigned range, 0 to 255, provided by the M68HC11 indexed addressing, studies of many M68HC11 applications revealed that most offsets fell into the 5-bit positive offset range. Because the 5-bit offset value is actually stored in the index postbyte, no additional extension bytes are needed. This is a very important benefit for programmers that are converting existing M68HC11

Section 2.2: Addressing Modes

programs to the M68HC12 family. M68HC11 instructions using X as the base index register where the offset will fit into the 5-bit positive offset range, will produce the same size CPU12 object code. For M68HC11 instructions using Y as the base index register with an offset fitting into the 5-bit positive offset range, the CPU12 object code will actually be smaller than the original M68HC11 object code. M68HC11 programs that make intense use of the Y index register can become significantly smaller when translated to CPU12 object code.

Assembler Syntax: «offset5bit»,«X | Y | SP | PC»

Effective Address Calculation (5-bit Offset):

```
          15                                                    0
          ┌──────────────────────────────────────────────────────┐
          │         Index Register Value (X, Y, SP, PC)          │
          └──────────────────────────────────────────────────────┘
                                                         │
   15                     5 4                  0         ▼
   ┌──────────────────────────────────────────┐        ┌───┐
   │   Sign extended 5-bit 2's Compliment Offset │ ───▶│ + │
   └──────────────────────────────────────────┘        └───┘
                                                         │
          15                                             ▼  0
          ┌──────────────────────────────────────────────────────┐
          │                   Operand Address                    │
          └──────────────────────────────────────────────────────┘
```

Examples:
```
    LDAA    0,X      ; load A with contents of memory pointed to
                     ; by X plus zero.
    LDD     3,SP     ; load D with contents of memory pointed to
                     ; by SP plus three.
    LDX     -2,Y     ; load X with contents of memory pointed to
                     ; by Y minus two.
```

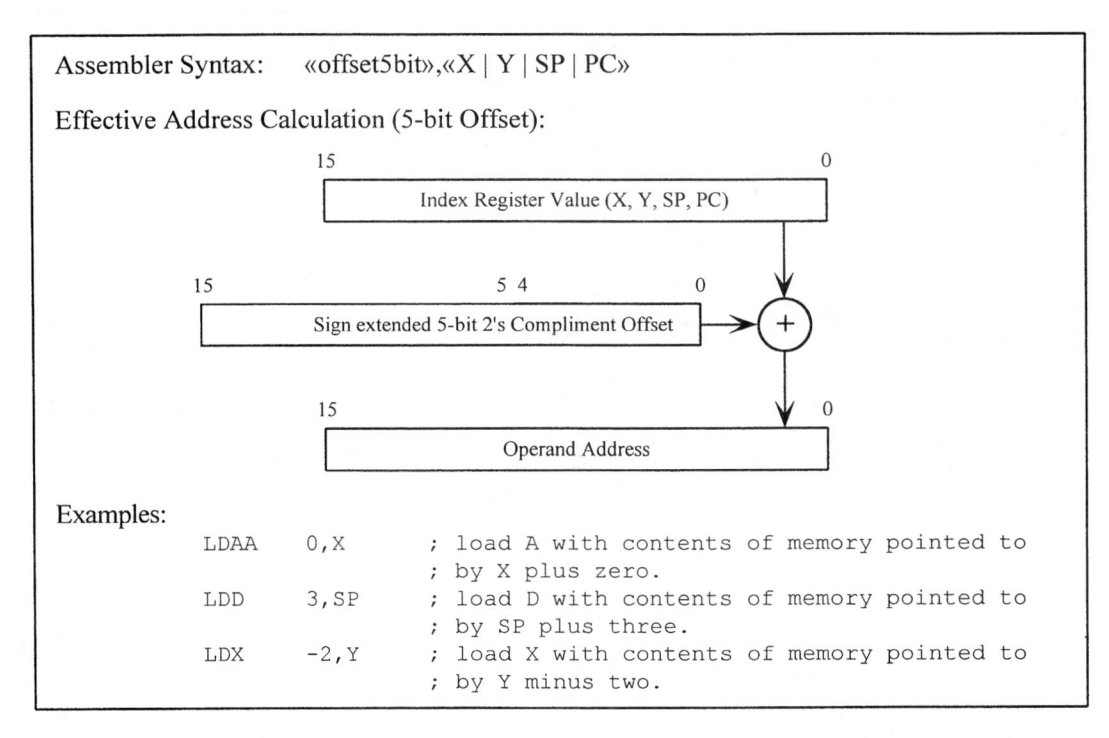

Figure 2.8: 5-bit constant Offset Indexed Addressing

9-Bit Constant Offset Indexed Addressing

The 9-bit offset indexed addressing mode provides an offset range of -256 through +255. This form requires a one byte extension beyond the postbyte. The most significant bit of the offset, the sign bit, is actually stored in the least significant bit of the postbyte. The remaining eight bits are stored in the extension byte. While this mode provides the same positive offset as M68HC11, the CPU12 object code will be one byte larger when it is used with the X index register. Translated M68HC11 assembly source code using the Y index register will be the same size.

48

Chapter 2: The CPU12 Instruction Set

```
Assembler Syntax:    «offset9bit»,«X | Y | SP | PC»
```

Effective Address Calculation (9-bit Offset):

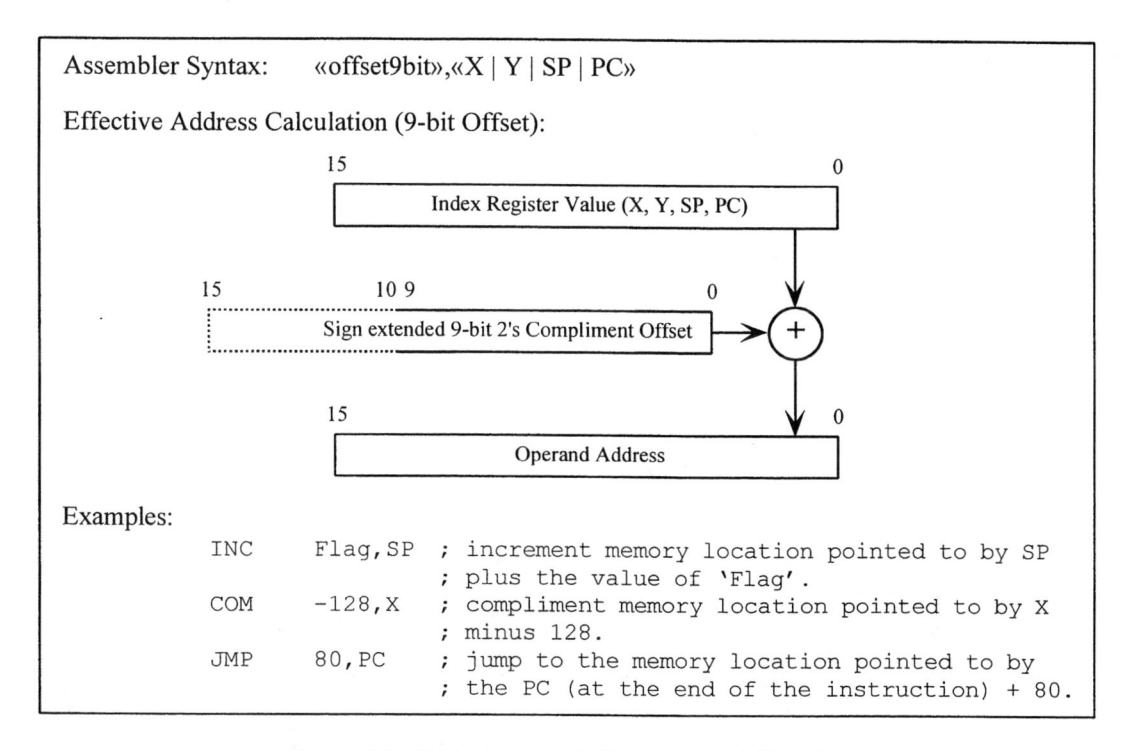

```
                 15                                            0
                 ┌──────────────────────────────────────────────┐
                 │      Index Register Value (X, Y, SP, PC)     │
                 └──────────────────────────────────────────────┘
                                                        │
         15       10 9                    0             ▼
         ┌─────────┬──────────────────────┐           ┌───┐
         │ Sign extended 9-bit 2's Compliment Offset │─▶│ + │
         └─────────┴──────────────────────┘           └───┘
                                                        │
                 15                                     ▼    0
                 ┌──────────────────────────────────────────┐
                 │              Operand Address             │
                 └──────────────────────────────────────────┘
```

Examples:
```
    INC    Flag,SP   ; increment memory location pointed to by SP
                     ; plus the value of 'Flag'.
    COM    -128,X    ; compliment memory location pointed to by X
                     ; minus 128.
    JMP    80,PC     ; jump to the memory location pointed to by
                     ; the PC (at the end of the instruction) + 80.
```

Figure 2.9: 9-bit constant Offset Indexed Addressing

16-Bit Constant Offset Indexed Addressing

The constant offset indexed addressing mode adds a 16-bit offset to the value of one of the base index registers. This varient forms the effective address of the memory location affected by the instruction. With a 16-bit offset, any byte or word in the entire 64k address space of the CPU12 can be accessed using indexed addressing. Because the 16-bit offset is the same size as the base index register, it can be thought of as either a signed or an unsigned value. For example, the value of $FFFF may be thought of as either +65535 or -1. The calculated effective address remains the same.

Section 2.2: Addressing Modes

Assembler Syntax: «offset16bit»,«X | Y | SP | PC»

Effective Address Calculation (16-bit Offset):

```
        15                                           0
        ┌─────────────────────────────────────────────┐
        │      Index Register Value (X, Y, SP, PC)    │
        └─────────────────────────────────────────────┘
                                                │
        15                              0       ▼
┌─────────────────────────────────────┐       ┌───┐
│          16-bit Offset              │──────▶│ + │
└─────────────────────────────────────┘       └───┘
                                                │
        15                                   0  ▼
        ┌─────────────────────────────────────────────┐
        │              Operand Address                │
        └─────────────────────────────────────────────┘
```

Examples:

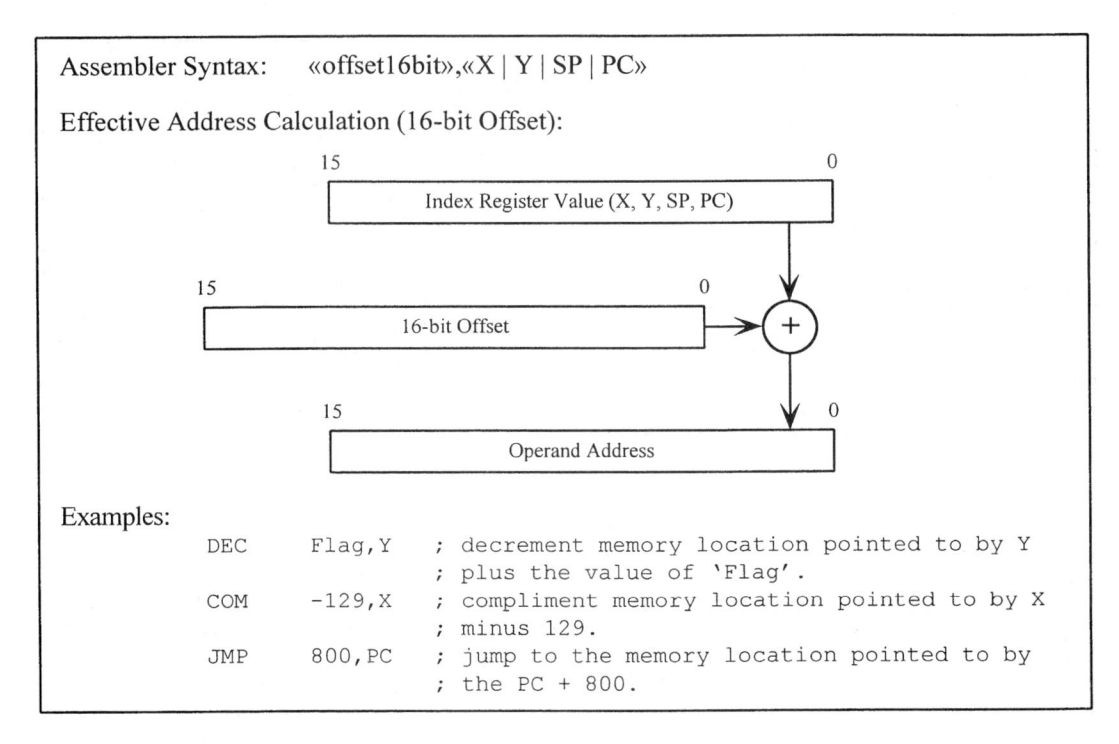

```
     DEC    Flag,Y    ; decrement memory location pointed to by Y
                      ; plus the value of 'Flag'.
     COM    -129,X    ; compliment memory location pointed to by X
                      ; minus 129.
     JMP    800,PC    ; jump to the memory location pointed to by
                      ; the PC + 800.
```

Figure 2.10: 16-bit constant Offset Indexed Addressing

Important Information

When using constant offset indexed addressing, it is not necessary for the programmer to specify the offset size. Under most circumstances, the assembler will choose the most efficient option. However, depending on the assembler, the generated object code might be something other than what the programmer expects. For example, because the 16-bit constant offset can be considered a signed or unsigned number, most assemblers will accept offset values from -32768 through +65535. A large positive number, such as +65535, would be converted to hexadecimal $FFFF. This is the same representation as the converted decimal value of -1. In this case, most assemblers would choose to use the 5-bit offset because it is the most efficient. From the CPU12's point of view, it does not matter whether the assembler encodes the value of $1F in the index postbyte using 5-bit offset or places the value $FFFF in two extension bytes following the index postbyte. The calculated effective address will be the same.

There are some cases where it seems that an assembler does not make an intelligent choice. For instance, if an offset is specified by a forward referenced symbol, the assembler may choose to use a 16-bit offset even though the value of the defined symbol is small enough to fit within a 5-bit offset. This is due to the the way the source code is scanned by the assembler and the assumptions it must make regarding the size of instructions when building its symbol table during the first pass of assembly. This most often occurs in simple absolute two-pass assemblers.

Accumulator Offset Indexed Addressing

Using this address mode, the effective address is the sum of the base index register and the contents of the A, B, or D accumulator. When the contents of either the A or B accumulator is used as the offset, the 8-bit value is *zero* extended, not *sign* extended. Because the D accumulator is the same size as the base index register, the 16-bit offset can be thought of as either a signed or an unsigned value. For example, the value of $FFFF may be thought of as either +65535 or -1. The calculated effective address is still the same.

Assembler Syntax: «A | B | D»,«X | Y | SP | PC»

Effective Address Calculation :

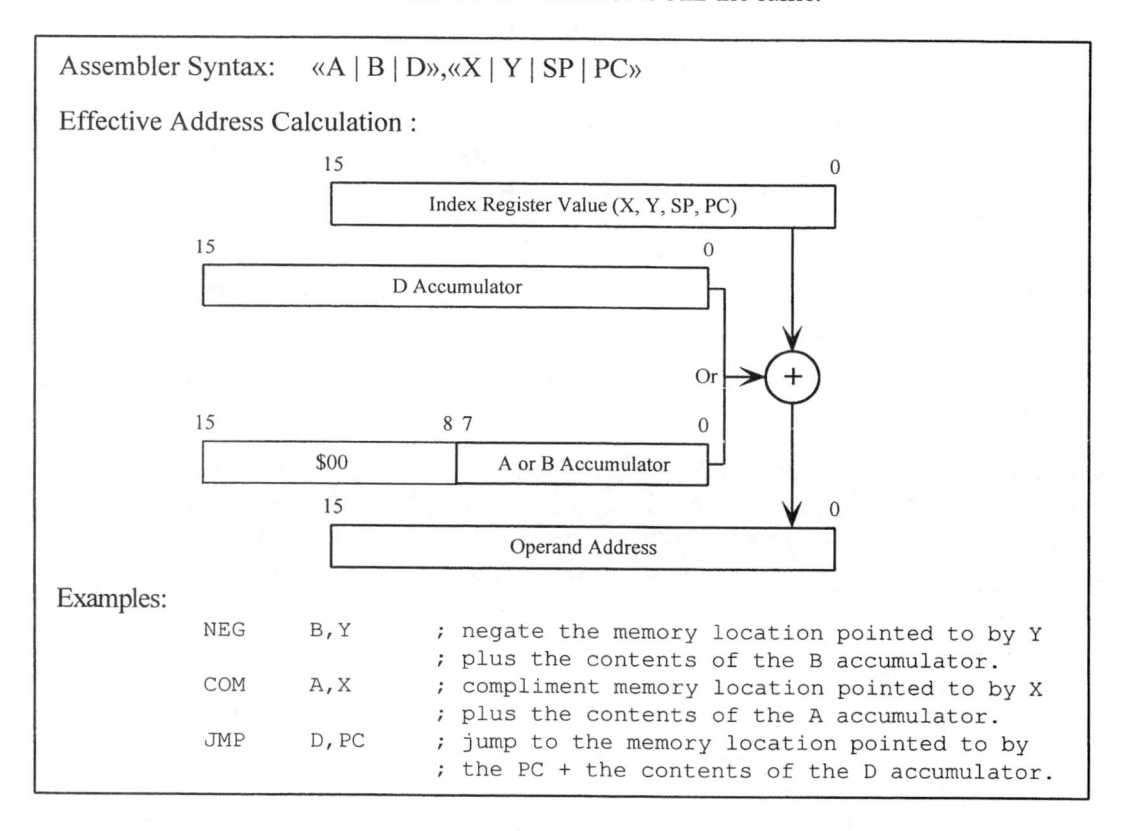

```
Examples:
          NEG    B,Y     ; negate the memory location pointed to by Y
                         ; plus the contents of the B accumulator.
          COM    A,X     ; compliment memory location pointed to by X
                         ; plus the contents of the A accumulator.
          JMP    D,PC    ; jump to the memory location pointed to by
                         ; the PC + the contents of the D accumulator.
```

Figure 2.11: Accumulator Offset Indexed Addressing

Section 2.2: Addressing Modes

The accumulator offset indexed addressing is quite useful when accessing elements of an array. The array could consist of simple elements that are 8- or 16-bit quantities, or the array elements could consist of a more complex data structure. Figure 2.12 shows how a C language statement might be translated to assembly language.

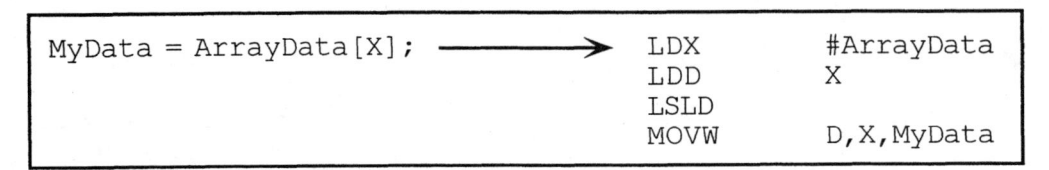

```
MyData = ArrayData[X];      ⟶      LDX         #ArrayData
                                    LDD         X
                                    LSLD
                                    MOVW        D,X,MyData
```

Figure 2.12: Using accumulator offset indexed addressing to move a 16-bit array element from the array into a variable.

Auto Pre/Post Increment/Decrement Indexed Addressing

This indexed addressing mode provides a great deal of flexibility in automatically adjusting the value of an indexable register. Adjustment of the base index register may be performed before or after its contents is used as the effective address of the operand. This mode can only utilize the X, Y, or SP as the base index register. Use of the program counter in this mode would not make any sense since it would disrupt normal program flow. The amount of adjustment is not related to the operand size manipulated by an instruction. In addition, instruction cycle times are not affected by the automatic increment or decrement operation.

Four bits in the postbyte allow the base index register to be adjusted by -8 through -1 or 1 through 8, either before or after the index register's contents is used as the effective address. Normally four bits would only allow a positive range of 0 through 7 to be represented. However, because a value of zero is not useful for auto increment indexed addressing, the CPU12 actually adds a value of one to positive postbyte values after it has been sign extended. Therefore, the postbyte values 0 through 7 actually represent increment amounts of 1 through 8 respectively. When a pre- or post- increment value is supplied in the assembly source, the assembler subtracting one from the value before placing it in the indexed postbyte.

Chapter 2: The CPU12 Instruction Set

Assembler Syntax: «1..8»,+«X | Y | SP»   (Pre-increment)
                    «1..8»,–«X | Y | SP»   (Pre-decrement)
                    «1..8»,«X | Y | SP»+   (Post-increment)
                    «1..8»,«X | Y | SP»–   (Post-decrement)

Effective Address Calculation :

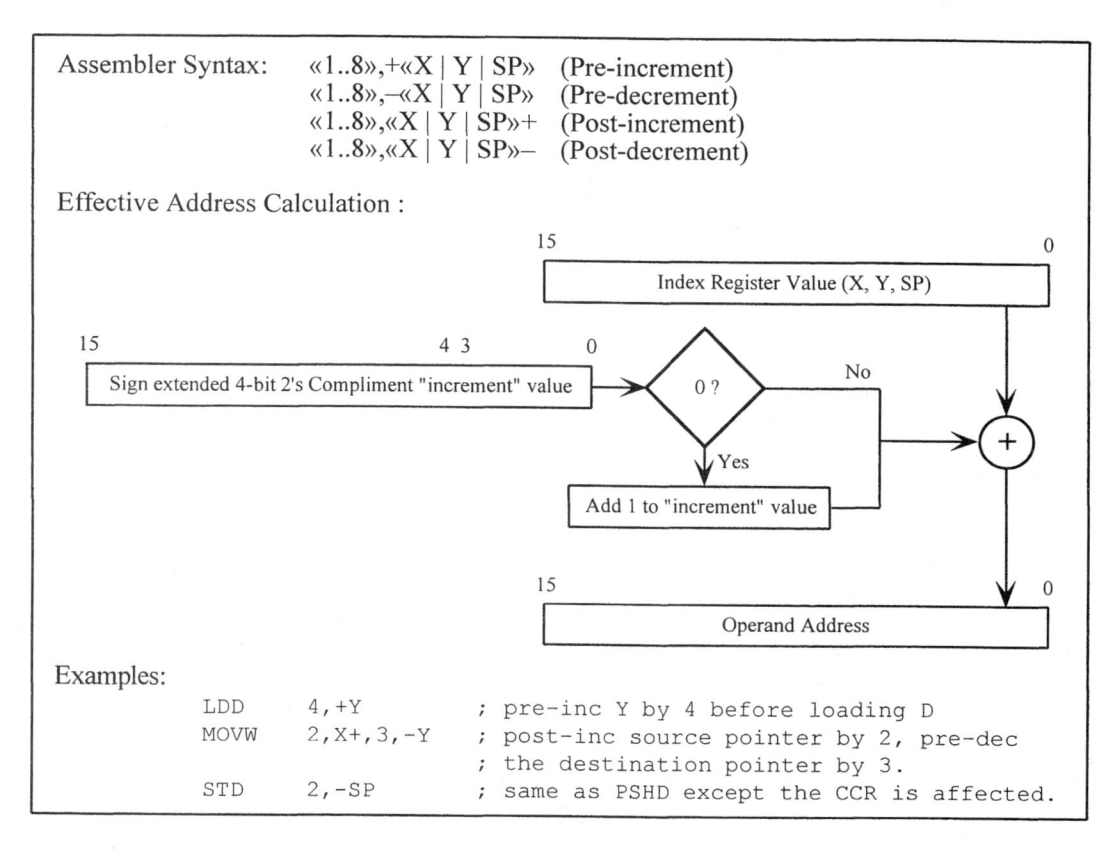

```
                                    15                                          0
                                   ┌────────────────────────────────────────────┐
                                   │       Index Register Value (X, Y, SP)      │
                                   └────────────────────────────────────────────┘
                                                                        │
 15              4 3          0                                         │
┌──────────────────────────────┐         ◇         No                   │
│ Sign extended 4-bit 2's      │───────▶ 0 ? ─────────────────────┐     │
│ Compliment "increment" value │         ◇                        │     │
└──────────────────────────────┘         │                        ▼     ▼
                                         │ Yes                     (+)
                                         ▼                          │
                              ┌────────────────────────┐            │
                              │ Add 1 to "increment"   │            │
                              │ value                  │            │
                              └────────────────────────┘            │
                                                                    │
                                    15                              ▼     0
                                   ┌────────────────────────────────────────────┐
                                   │              Operand Address               │
                                   └────────────────────────────────────────────┘
```

Examples:
```
        LDD     4,+Y         ; pre-inc Y by 4 before loading D
        MOVW    2,X+,3,-Y    ; post-inc source pointer by 2, pre-dec
                             ; the destination pointer by 3.
        STD     2,-SP        ; same as PSHD except the CCR is affected.
```

Figure 2.13: Pre/Post, Increment/Decrement Indexed Addressing

When used with the memory-to-memory move instructions, the auto increment/decrement addressing mode can be used to perform very efficient block move routines. In addition, is is easy to implement software stacks and queues using a combination of the auto increment/decrement indexed addressing mode. This addressing mode has a direct applicability to the increment and decrement operators in the C programming language when used with pointers. Figure 2.14 shows how a C source statement used to copy a null terminated string from one location in memory to another, could be directly implemented in CPU12 assembly language.

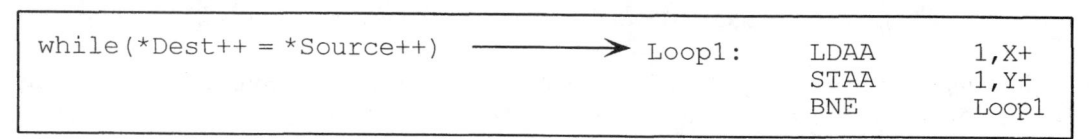

```
while(*Dest++ = *Source++)  ─────────▶  Loop1:   LDAA    1,X+
                                                 STAA    1,Y+
                                                 BNE     Loop1
```

Figure 2.14: Using the autoincrement/decrement addressing mode to move a null terminated string.

Section 2.2: Addressing Modes

Indexed Indirect Addressing

This form of indexed addressing is called indexed indirect because the effective address calculated by the CPU12 does not point directly to the data. Rather the calculated address points to a two byte area in memory containing a 16-bit value. This 16-bit value is an address that indirectly points to the data on which the operation will occur. Only two of the indexed addressing modes are supported with indirection by the CPU12: 16-bit constant offset and D accumulator offset. To distinguish the indirect forms of indexed addressing from the standard form, the index operand is surrounded by square brackets ([ ]).

```
Assembler Syntax:    [«offset16»,«X | Y | SP, PC»]  (16-bit constant offset)
                     [«D»,«X | Y | SP, PC»]         (D accumulator offset)
```

Effective Address Calculation :

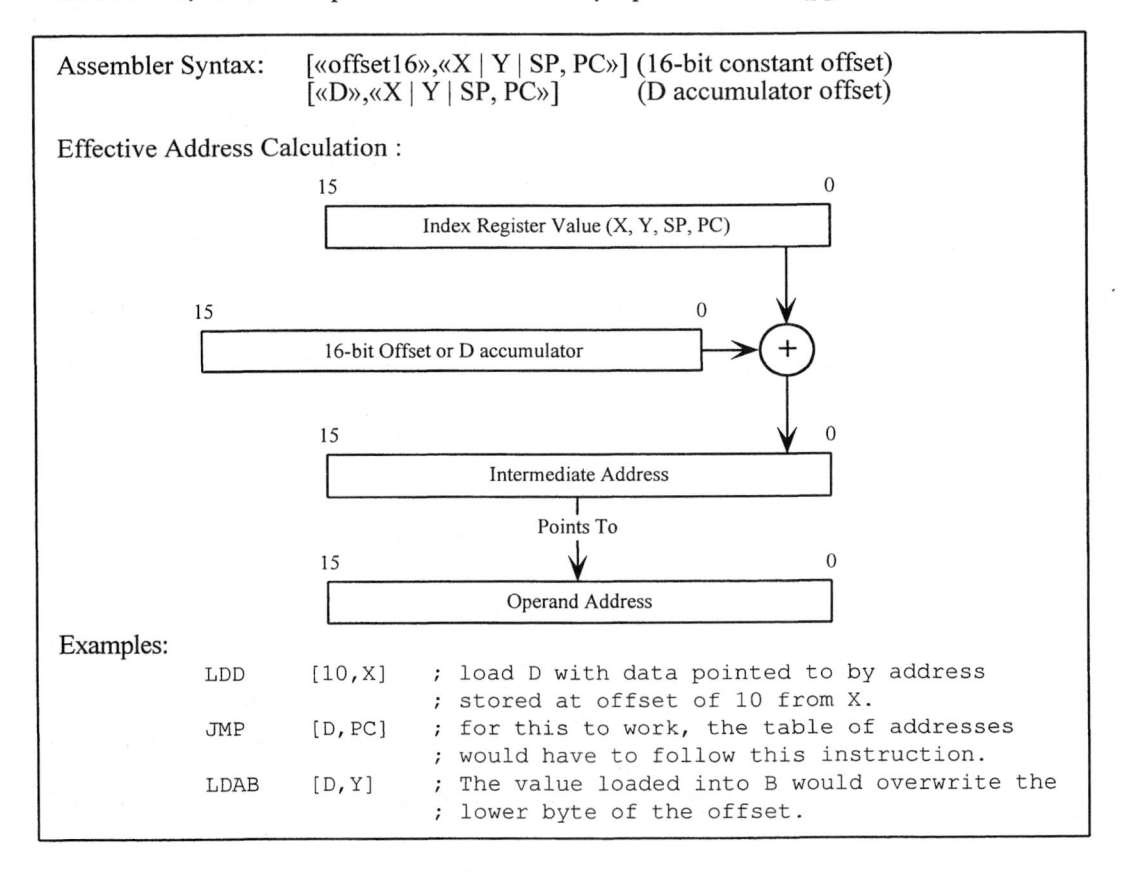

```
          15                                                0
          +--------------------------------------------------+
          |       Index Register Value (X, Y, SP, PC)        |
          +--------------------------------------------------+
                                                     |
     15                                      0       v
     +------------------------------------------+   +---+
     |       16-bit Offset or D accumulator     |-->| + |
     +------------------------------------------+   +---+
                                                     |
          15                                  0      v
          +--------------------------------------------------+
          |              Intermediate Address                |
          +--------------------------------------------------+
                              Points To
          15                                  0      v
          +--------------------------------------------------+
          |               Operand Address                    |
          +--------------------------------------------------+
```

Examples:
```
    LDD     [10,X]    ; load D with data pointed to by address
                      ; stored at offset of 10 from X.
    JMP     [D,PC]    ; for this to work, the table of addresses
                      ; would have to follow this instruction.
    LDAB    [D,Y]     ; The value loaded into B would overwrite the
                      ; lower byte of the offset.
```

Figure 2.15: Indexed Indirect Addressing

In a high level language such as C, functions may only return a single result. In many cases it is necessary to return more than one piece of information to a calling function. In C, this is usually done by passing the *address* of a variable as one of the parameters to a function. These parameters, usually passed on the stack, can easily be accessed using the indexed addressing with the stack pointer as the base index register. To place a return result in the variable without the benefit of indexed indirect addressing would require the use of one of the two index registers. With indexed indirect addressing, the returned data may be placed directly into the variable without having to disturb any of the CPU's registers. Figure 2.16 shows the benefits of using indexed indirect addressing for this purpose.

The astute reader, after gaining a thorough understanding of the CPU12's instruction set and addressing modes, may reexamine this example and realize that both instruction sequences could be the same length. Because indexed indirect does not allow constant offsets smaller than 16-bits, the STD indexed indirect instruction is four bytes long regardless of the offset value. If the offset defined by RtnData will fit into the postbyte, the two instruction sequences are equal in length. If the offset is any larger, the use of indexed indirect addressing will result in smaller code size. In any event, the use of indexed indirect addressing does not require the use of either the X or Y index register.

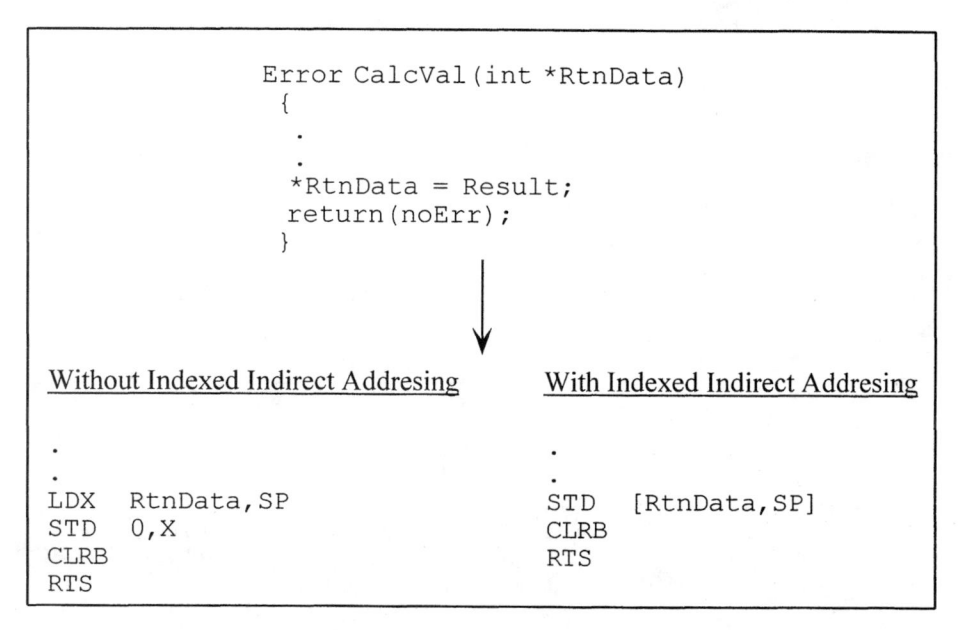

```
              Error CalcVal(int *RtnData)
              {
                 .
                 .
                 *RtnData = Result;
                 return(noErr);
              }
                            |
                            v

Without Indexed Indirect Addresing      With Indexed Indirect Addresing

 .                                       .
 .                                       .
LDX   RtnData,SP                        STD    [RtnData,SP]
STD   0,X                               CLRB
CLRB                                    RTS
RTS
```

Figure 2.16: Advantage of Using Indexed Indirect Addressing

Important Information

Program Counter Relative (PCR) Indexed Addressing

When using constant offset indexed addressing with the program counter as the index register, the calculation of the proper offset to the referenced data can be error prone and a

Section 2.2: Addressing Modes

nuisance to the programmer. Because the length of instructions can vary from as little as two bytes for page 1 instructions, to as many as five bytes for some page two instructions, the offset to the data will depend on the value of the program counter at the end of the instruction. Obviously it would be advantageous if the assembler calculated this offset just as it does for the program relative branch instructions.

To allow the assembler to calculate the offset based on the location of the data and the length of the instruction, the assembler mnemonic 'PCR' is substituted for the index register name. Obviously, this does not amount to a new indexed addressing mode, it simply instructs the assembler to calculate an offset to the address specified by the expression preceding the ',PCR' index specification. The offset is calculated by subtracting the value of the program counter at the address of the first object code byte of the *next* instruction from the value supplied in the index offset field. Generally the value supplied in the offset field will be a single label defining the address of the referenced data. However, the value may be a generalized expression. The 'PCR' notation may be used only when direct or indirect constant offset indexed addressing is employed. Attempting to use it with accumulator offset or with the pre/post increment/decrement indexed addressing modes will generate an assembler error.

Most programmers will prefer using the program counter relative notation because it eliminates the manual offset calculation. However, it *must* be used when writing a program in a position independent manner. Assembler syntax and source code examples are given below. No effective address calculation example is given because the 'PCR' notation is essentially a directive for the assembler to calculate the offset.

```
Assembler Syntax:    [«Label | expression»,PCR
                     [«Label | expression»,PCR]

Examples:
         LDD     Data1,PCR    ; load D in a position independent manner.
         LEAY    Msg2,PCR     ; load Y with pointer to Msg2 in a position
                              ; independent manner.
         JMP     Calc,PCR     ; same as LBRA (Long BRanch Always).
         JSR     Sub1,PCR     ; equivalent to LBSR.
```

Figure 2.17: Program Counter Relative Indexed Addressing

Invalid Indexed addressing Modes

While there are no invalid index postbyte values, some instructions cannot use every indexed addressing mode. Assemblers should make all the necessary checks to insure that only valid addressing modes are used with each instruction. If a program becomes lost and accidentally executes data representing one of these invalid combinations, the CPU12 will not perform the requested operation. However, the CPU12 will not lock up, refusing to execute any other instructions.

Indexed Addressing Mode Summary

Figure 2.18 is a summary of the CPU12's indexed addressing mode capabilities and a description of the postbyte encoding.

Postbyte Code	Source Code Syntax	Comments rr; 00 = X, 01 = Y, 10 = SP, 11 = PC	
rr0nnnnn	,r n,r -n,r	5-bit signed constant offset r can specify X, Y, SP, or PC	$-16 \leq n \leq +15$
111rr0zs	,r n,r -n,r	9- or 16-bit signed constant offset; z = 0; 9-bit with s = sign bit for extension byte z = 1; 16-bit, s = 0 r can specify X, Y, SP, or PC	$-256 \leq n \leq 255$ $-32768 \leq n \leq 65535$
111rr1aa	A,r B,r D,r	Accumulator Offset; (unsigned 8-bit or 16-bit) aa; 00 = A, 01 = B, 10 = D r can specify X, Y, SP, or PC	
rr1pnnnn	n,-r n,+r n,r- n,r+	Auto pre-decrement/increment or Auto post-decrement/increment p = 0, pre-decrement/increment p = 1, post-decrement/increment nnnn => 0000..0111 = +1.. +8; 1111..1000 = -1..-8 r can specify X, Y, or SP	
111rr011	[n,r]	16-bit offset indexed-indirect r can specify X, Y, SP, or PC	$-32768 \leq n \leq 65535$
111rr111	[D,r]	D accumulator offset indexed-indirect r can specify X, Y, SP, or PC	

Figure 2.18: Summary of Indexed Addressing Modes

2.3 INSTRUCTION SET OVERVIEW

The CPU12 instruction set is a proper super set of the M68HC11 family instruction set. Assembly language source code written for the M68HC11 can be assembled with an M68HC12 assembler and produce object code that is functionally identical. There are only two areas where modifications must be made to M68HC11 source code so that it will run properly on the CPU12. Any M68HC11 code involving software timing loops will most certainly need to be changed. First, the currently released M68HC12 family members run at a bus frequency of 8.0 MHz. This is four times the speed of the standard M68HC11 family members. If this were the only consideration, it might be a simple matter of scaling loop counters. However, most CPU12 instructions have reduced cycle counts. This means that

Section 2.4: Load and Store Instructions

each piece of M68HC11 code involving a software timing loop will have to be examined carefully and rewritten to account for these two factors.

The second area requiring some attention is M68HC11 code dealing with on-chip peripherals. While many of the M68HC12 family peripherals are similar to those on the M68HC11, there have been significant improvements to the peripherals that will require changes. It is important to carefully examine source code related to peripheral initialization, peripheral register interrogation and interrupt service routines. In a well written application, the software modules performing these functions should be isolated into small subroutines that can be easily located and changed.

As with the M68HC11, the M68HC12 architecture maps all memory and I/O registers into a single 64-Kbyte address space. Placing the I/O registers in the same address space as memory, known as memory-mapped I/O, allows the same set of instructions to access memory, I/O and control registers. In addition to the general purpose load and store instructions available on the M68HC11, the CPU12 has added memory-to-memory move instructions. These instructions allow data movement from one memory location to another without passing through one of the CPU's internal registers or affecting the CPU's condition code register. This is especially helpful in an accumulator-based architecture such as the CPU12 where the number of available registers is limited.

The CPU12 also supports a full set of arithmetic and logic instructions for manipulating both 8-bit and 16-bit signed and unsigned values. Both the execution speed and the precision of mathematical operations of the CPU12 have been greatly improved. In addition, more specialized instructions were added which perform multiply-accumulate operations, table look-up and interpolation, and fuzzy logic operations.

Detailed information about individual instructions, including cycle-by-cycle execution information, can be found in Motorola's *CPU12 Reference Manual* (P/N CPU12RM/AD). For convenience, Appendix A contains a complete instruction set summary including opcode maps, postbyte encoding for indexed addressing, register transfer/exchange and loop primitive instructions.

2.4 LOAD AND STORE INSTRUCTIONS

With some exceptions, the only way to perform an arithmetic or logical operation on a data value is to load a value into one of the CPU registers. To update or change a memory location, again with some exceptions, the value in one of the CPU registers must be stored to memory. Load and store instructions are provided for both 8-bit and 16-bit quantities. When values are loaded into CPU registers or stored into memory, the N-bit and Z-bit in the CPU12's condition code register are updated to reflect the state of the quantity being read from or written to memory. The V bit is always set to zero. Setting the condition code register in this manner can eliminate the need to execute a separate test instruction in certain code sequences.

Because the load and store instructions are so crucial to the efficient manipulation of a program's data, they are capable of using direct, extended and all indexed addressing modes. The load instructions are also capable of using the immediate addressing mode to load constant values into the CPU12's registers. Clearly, it would not make any sense to allow the store instructions to use immediate addressing. Such an action, if allowed, would cause the program to attempt modification of the one or two bytes immediately following the instruction. In most cases where a program resides in nonvolatile memory, this would not be possible. Figure 2.19 is a summary of the load and store instructions.

Load Instructions		
Mnemonic	Function	Operation
LDAA	Load Accumulator A	(M) → Acc. A
LDAB	Load Accumulator B	(M) → Acc. B
LDD	Load Accumulator D (A:B)	(M:M+1) → Acc. D
LDS	Load Stack Pointer (SP)	(M:M+1) → Stack Pointer
LDX	Load Index Register X	(M:M+1) → Index Register X
LDY	Load Index Register Y	(M:M+1) → Index Register Y
Store Instructions		
Mnemonic	Function	Operation
STAA	Store Accumulator A	Acc. A → (M)
STAB	Store Accumulator B	Acc. B → (M)
STD	Store Accumulator D (A:B)	Acc. D → (M:M+1)
STS	Store Stack Pointer (SP)	Stack Pointer → (M:M+1)
STX	Store Index Register X	Index Register X → (M:M+1)
STY	Store Index Register Y	Index Register Y → (M:M+1)

Figure 2.19: Load and Store Instructions

While examining Figure 2.19 it may seem that there are some missing instructions. As the table shows, there are no instructions to load or store the condition code register. It is rare that the entire value of the condition code register needs to be saved and/or loaded. As M68HC11 programmers may remember, two additional instructions are available which

Section 2.4: Load and Store Instructions

allow the condition code register to be transferred to the A accumulator (TPA) or the contents of the A accumulator to be transferred to the condition code register (TAP). These instructions are also available on the CPU12 as part of the general register transfer/exchange instructions. Because of the general nature of the transfer/exchange instructions, an additional option is available to the programmer. Even though separate mnemonics do not exist, the value of the B accumulator can be transferred to or exchanged with the condition code register and vice versa.

As shown in the table, values loaded into or stored from 16-bit registers occupy two consecutive bytes in memory. As mentioned in Chapter 1, 16-bit values do not need to be word aligned. However, loading or storing a misaligned 16-bit value to memory other than the on-chip RAM will cause the M68HC12 to perform an extra bus cycle to complete the read or write operation. This is true for constant values loaded from on-chip Flash or ROM memory. The only exception is constants loaded using the immediate addressing mode. If a program uses large or often accessed tables of 16-bit constant values, the programmer should ensure that the table is aligned to a word (even byte) boundary.

Figure 2.20 illustrates a very simple use of the load and store instructions. This type of sequence is often used when initializing on-chip peripheral registers or when assigning initial values to program variables. In this case the first and second lines load a 16-bit immediate value into the D accumulator and store it in the Serial Communications Interface's (SCI) baud rate register. The third and fourth lines load an 8-bit immediate value into the A accumulator and store it in one of the SCI's control registers, enabling the SCI's transmitter and receiver. If the SCI's control registers were located on page zero, the assembler would use direct addressing for the two store instructions. Otherwise the assembler would choose extended addressing.

```
InitSCI:   ldd     #52         ; Load D with value for 9600 baud
           std     SC0BDH      ; put in SCI baud rate register
           ldaa    #$0c        ; Load A with value to enable SCI
           staa    SC0CR2      ; Enable SCI Tx & Rx sections
```

Figure 2.20: Using Load and Store to Initialize the SCI

Figure 2.21 represents a slightly more involved example that copies a group of bytes from one area of memory to another. The group of bytes at the source are assumed to be ASCII characters that are terminated by an ASCII null ($00) byte. The first two lines of this program fragment load the source and destination address into the X and Y index registers respectively using immediate addressing. The third line retrieves a byte from the source memory area and *post increments* the source address by one so that the X register is pointing to the next source byte. The fourth line writes the byte in the A accumulator to the destination memory area and *post increments* the destination address by one so that the Y register is pointing to the next destination byte available. The last line consists of a branch instruction that continues execution at the label CopyLoop if the Z bit in the condition code register is not set. Because the store instruction automatically updates the N, Z and V bits in the condition code register, a separate test instruction is not needed. In this case, when the terminating null byte is stored at the destination, the Z bit is set, indicating an 'equal' or zero condition, the condition for the branch will be false, and the copy process will terminate.

```
            ldx       #Source     ; Load source address into X
            ldy       #Dest       ; Load dest address into Y
CopyLoop:   ldaa      1,x+        ; Get a byte & advance X
            staa      1,y+        ; Store a byte & advance Y
            bne       CopyLoop    ; continue if not done
```

Figure 2.21: Using Load and Store to copy a null terminated string

Remember that both the load and store instructions update the N, Z and V bits. By placing the branch instruction between the load and store and placing an unconditional branch after the store instruction, as shown in Figure 2.22, we create a copy routine that *does not* place the terminating null character from the source at the destination.

```
            ldx       #Source     ; Load source address into X
            ldy       #Dest       ; Load dest address into Y
CopyLoop:   ldaa      1,x+        ; Get a byte & advance X
            beq       Done        ; stop at the zero byte
            staa      1,y+        ; Store a byte & advance Y
            bra       CopyLoop    ; continue to copy
Done:
```

Figure 2.22: Copy a null terminated string not including the null byte

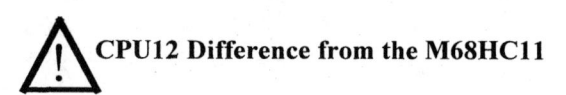

⚠️ **CPU12 Difference from the M68HC11**

2.5 MEMORY-TO-MEMORY MOVE INSTRUCTIONS

Closely related to the load and store instructions are the memory-to-memory move instructions. To enhance the data movement capabilities of the CPU12's accumulator based architecture, the CPU12 designers added two general purpose memory-to-memory move instructions. These instructions have the ability to move a byte or word from a source memory location to a destination location without using one of the CPU12's registers or

Section 2.5: Memory-to-Memory Move Instructions

affecting the condition code register. Separate addressing modes may be used for the source and destination addresses allowing for a great deal of flexibility. The move instruction mnemonics and the operand form are shown in Figure 2.23. The source address may use immediate, extended, or indexed addressing, while the destination address utilizes extended and indexed addressing exclusively. The source and destination address are separated from one another by a comma. Indexed addressing modes for both the source and destination are restricted to a subset that only includes 5-bit offsets, accumulator offsets and auto increment/decrement modes. Nine bit, 16-bit and indexed indirect modes are not allowed. However, any of the index registers, X, Y, SP, or PC may be used as the base index register.

\multicolumn{4}{c}{Memory-to-memory Move Instructions}
Mnemonic	Function	Operand Form	Operation
MOVB	Move Byte, source to destination	s,d	s $\rightarrow$ d
MOVW	Move Word, source to destination	s,d	s : s+1 $\rightarrow$ d : d+1

Figure 2.23: Memory-to-Memory move instructions

Important Information

When using the program counter as the base index register for either the source or destination address, there are special considerations. Because of the instruction pipe on the CPU12, there is a difference between actual value of the program counter and the programmers perception of the program counter's value. For instructions other than the memory-to-memory moves, dedicated queue management logic automatically compensates for this offset when using the program counter as an index register. However, because the program counter changes during the execution of the move instructions, the logic necessary to perform this function would be quite large. In fact, the logic was actually part of the original CPU12 design. However, because only short indexed offsets (-16...+15) are allowed, it was decided that programmers would make little use of the program counter as a base index register with the move instructions, so the logic was removed from the final design.

The program counter offsets vary for the different combinations of source and destination addressing modes, but are well documented in Motorola's CPU12 Reference Manual. However, assemblers should perform the necessary adjustments to the programmer supplied offset when using the program counter or PCR indexed addressing in conjunction with the move instructions. Be sure to check an assembler's documentation before using the program counter or PCR indexed addressing modes in conjunction with the memory-to-memory move instructions.

Chapter 2: The CPU12 Instruction Set

Figure 2.24 shows a simple example of using the MOVW instruction to move a block of 16-bit data from one area of memory to another. The MOVW instruction uses auto post increment indexed addressing in both the source and destination address to move the memory word and update the X and Y index registers. The size and execution speed of the MOVW instruction is no more efficient than if it were replaced with the LDD and STD instructions. However, the byte count would have to be placed in either a global variable or on the stack and would prevent the use of the DBNE loop primitive instruction.

```
           ldx      #Source    ; Load source address into X
           ldy      #Dest      ; Load dest address into Y
           ldab     #Count     ; get word count in B
CopyLoop:  movw     2,x+,2,y+  ; move a word, advance X & Y
           dbne     b,CopyLoop ; decrement count continue if not done
           .
           .
```

Figure 2.24: Block copy routine using MOVW

⚠ **CPU12 Difference from the M68HC11**

2.6 BRANCH INSTRUCTIONS

Both conditional and unconditional branch instructions are used to alter program flow based on external input and are what give computers their apparent intelligence. The CPU12 supports five types of branches: simple, unconditional, signed, unsigned and bit condition. All branch types, with the exception of the bit condition branches, support a short and long form. The M68HC11 family supports all of the same branch types but does not support the long branch form. The short branch form uses an 8-bit signed offset to allow a branch range of +127 through -128 from the program counter at the end of the branch instruction. The long branch form uses a two byte signed offset to allow relative branching throughout the entire 64-K byte address map. As shown in Figures 2.25, 2.26, 2.29 and 2.30, the instruction mnemonic for the short and long branches only differ by one letter. Preceding a short branch instruction mnemonic with the letter 'L' specifies the long branch form. The branch instructions are completely orthogonal. This means that for each branch instruction performing a conditional test, an instruction also exists that tests for the opposite condition.

2.6.1 Unconditional Branch Instructions

Of the two unconditional branch instructions shown in Figure 2.25, the BRA and LBRA instructions give the programmer the ability to alter program flow without checking for any

Section 2.6: Branch Instructions

conditions. This instruction is often used to jump to the top or bottom of a program loop to continue or initiate the loop execution. In such a situation, there will be one or more conditional tests within the loop to terminate its execution. This method is used in Figure 2.22 to branch back to the top of the loop to retrieve the next byte from the source memory area.

Unconditional Branches		
Mnemonic	**Function**	**Condition Code Test**
BRA, LBRA	Branch Always	*none*
BRN, LBRN	Branch Never	*none*

Figure 2.25: CPU12 Unconditional branch instructions

Because the BRN and LBRN instructions never branch, they are of little use. They were put into the instruction set simply to make the branch instructions completely orthogonal and to maintain M68HC11 code compatibility. In the M68HC11 family, the BRN instruction did provide a useful function to the programmer. Since execution of all branch instructions in the M68HC11 family require three clock cycles whether or not the branch was taken, the BRN instruction could be used as a two byte three cycle NOP instruction. Since the M68HC11 NOP instruction takes two clock cycles to execute, the BRN instruction was used to insert odd numbers of clock cycles within software timing loops to better control the accuracy of delays.

Because of the instruction queue, the CPU12 designers were able to optimize the execution of all branch instructions so that the execution time when the branch is not taken is shorter than when the branch is taken. When a branch is taken, the CPU12 must discard the contents of the instruction queue and refill the queue with instructions at the destination of the branch. If the branch is not taken, the next sequential instruction is already in the queue and the branch is treated as a NOP. This makes the BRN instruction a two byte, one cycle NOP. Obviously, it would not be code space efficient for software delay applications. Long branch instructions are four bytes long and require four cycles when taken and three cycles when not taken. This makes the LBRN instruction a four byte, three cycle NOP. Again, this would not be code space efficient for software delay applications.

2.6.2 Simple Branch Instructions

The simple branch instructions, shown in Figure 2.26, change program flow based on the state of a single status bit in the condition code register.

Chapter 2: The CPU12 Instruction Set

Simple Branches		
Mnemonic	**Function**	**Condition Code Test**
BCC, LBCC	Branch if Carry Clear	C == 0
BCS, LBCS	Branch if Carry Set	C == 1
BEQ, LBEQ	Branch if Equal	Z == 1
BNE, LBNE	Branch if Not Equal	Z == 0
BMI, LBMI	Branch if Minus	N == 1
BPL, LBPL	Branch if Plus	N == 0
BVC, LBVC	Branch if Overflow Clear	V == 0
BVS, LBVS	Branch if Overflow Set	V == 1

Figure 2.26: Simple branch instructions

The BCC and BCS instructions, as their mnemonics imply, check the state of the C bit and branch if the carry is cleared or set respectively. The carry, most often used during multi-precision addition, subtraction, shifts and rotates, can be tested using these two instructions to detect arithmetic overflow or underflow after operating on multi-precision, unsigned numbers.

The BEQ and BNE instructions test the state of the Z condition code register bit and branches if the Z bit is set or cleared respectively. Remember, when the Z bit is set, it means that all of the bits of the previous operation contained zeros. If the Z bit being set represents a result of zero, why do the mnemonics represent 'equal' and 'not equal' instead of 'zero' and 'not zero'? The original M6800 instruction set designers chose these mnemonics based on the fact that they would be executed after a compare operation. When a compare instruction is executed, a subtract operation is performed on the two quantities being compared. The actual result of the subtraction is discarded but the N, Z, V, and C condition code bits are updated based on the results of the subtraction. If the quantities being compared are equal, the result of the subtraction would be zero, resulting in the Z bit being set. While the mnemonics 'make sense' after compare operations, they don't seem as logical when testing for a zero or non-zero value. It would be quite easy using a macro assembler to write a simple macro that would allow the use of a mnemonic such as 'BZ' or 'BNZ' in place of the BEQ or BNE mnemonics.

The BMI and BPL instructions alter program flow based on the state of the N bit in the condition code register. The N bit reflects the state of the most significant bit of the result of an arithmetic, logic, and data movement operations involving the CPU registers or memory. These instructions are most commonly used by software treating numbers as signed two's

Section 2.6: Branch Instructions

compliment values; however, they can be used to alter program flow based on the state of the most significant bit of any memory location, I/O or CPU register.

The last pair of simple branch instructions, BVC and BVS, alter program flow based on the state of the V condition code bit. They are used to test for an overflow condition when performing arithmetic on two's complement numbers. Many control programs do not use signed two's complement numbers; therefore, these instructions may never be used by many programmers. Since the C programming language does not provide any method for detecting arithmetic overflow, even C compilers would not use this instruction when generating code for standard C statements.

Figure 2.27 shows a simple program fragment illustrating the use of two of the simple branch instructions and presents a technique that can be used to perform multiple precision arithmetic. The program code uses three instructions that have not been discussed, but their function will be detailed in the following explanation. The program fragment adds two 32-bit numbers overwriting one of the numbers with the result. When performing multi-precision arithmetic one byte at a time, the program must start with the least significant byte and work toward the most significant byte. As each pair of bytes are added, a possible carry from the previous addition must be added into the sum. As discussed previously, multi-byte numbers are stored in consecutive memory locations with the most significant byte at the lowest address and the least significant byte at the highest address.

```
Line 1              ldx      #Num1     ; Point to Num1
Line 2              ldy      #Num2     ; Point to Num2
Line 3              ldab     #3        ; Byte count to add.
Line 4              clc                ; clear the carry before 1st add
Line 5   AddLoop:   ldaa     b,x       ; Get a byte to add from Num1
Line 6              adca     b,y       ; Add it to the byte in Num2
Line 7              staa     b,x       ; overwrite byte in Num1.
Line 8              decb               ; subtract 1 from the byte count
Line 9              bpl      AddLoop   ; continue if not done
Line 10             bcc      OK        ; if carry clear, no error.
Line 11             lbra     AddError  ; if carry set, overflow
Line 12  OK:
```

Figure 2.27: Using Simple branch instructions

The first two lines begin by initializing the X and Y index registers to point to the most significant byte of each of the two numbers. The third line initializes the B accumulator with the value three. The reason this count is one less than the number of bytes being adding is so that the contents the B accumulator can be used as an indexed offset in the addition loop. On line four, the CLC instruction clears the C bit in the condition code register so that a carry is not added to the least significant byte the first time through the loop. The next line, beginning with the label `AddLoop`, loads a byte of `Num1` into the A accumulator using accumulator offset indexed addressing. The first time through the loop (when the B accumulator will contain three) the A accumulator is loaded with the byte at the address of `Num1 + 3`, the least significant byte of 'Num1.' Line six adds the contents of the A accumulator to the byte at `Num2 + 3` plus a possible carry. The seventh line stores the result at `Num1 + 3` overwriting the original byte. The `DECB` instruction subtracts one from the B accumulator and updates the N and Z condition code bits. The `BPL` instruction will branch back to the instruction at `AddLoop` until the fourth time through the loop when the `DECB` instruction will cause the B accumulator to go from a value of $00 to $FF, setting the N bit. At this point the `BPL` test will fail and the `BCC` instruction will be executed. If a carry was not generated as a result of adding the most significant byte of each number, the `BCC` instruction will branch to the label OK and continue execution. If not, an unconditional long branch is taken to an error routine.

Figure 2.28 (a) through (d) illustrates how the accumulator offset indexed addressing is used within the addition loop to access the four bytes of the 32-bit number.

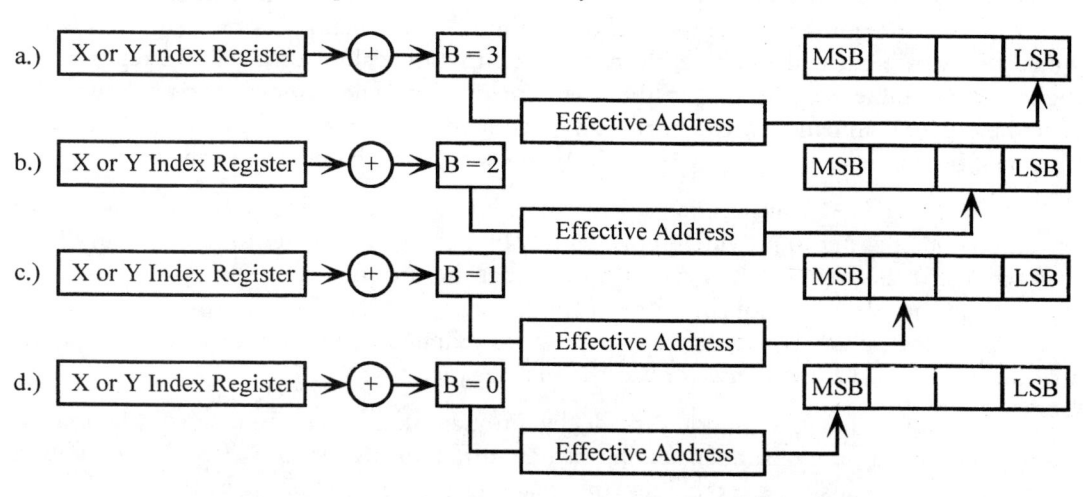

Figure 2.28: Use of accumulator offset indexed addressing

2.6.3 Unsigned Branch Instructions

The unsigned branch instructions shown in Figure 2.29 are used to change program flow when comparing unsigned data. Notice that the first two entries in the table, BHS and BLO, use the same condition code test as the BCC and BCS instructions and produce the same object code respectively. The BHS and BLO mnemonics are nothing more than a programming convenience provided by the assembler to help describe the condition being tested when CPU12 register and memory values are subtracted or compared.

Section 2.6: Branch Instructions

Unsigned Branches			
Mnemonic	**Function**	**Relation**	**Condition Code Test**
BHS, LBHS	Branch if Higher or Same	R ≥ M	C == 0
BLO, LBLO	Branch if Lower	R < M	C == 1
BHI, LBHI	Branch if Higher	R > M	C | Z == 0
BLS, LBLS	Branch if Lower or Same	R ≤ M	C | Z == 1

Figure 2.29: Unsigned Branch Instructions

The Relation column in Figure 2.29 uses a relational equation to describe the condition that exists when the branch is taken after a compare instruction is executed. For instance, if a memory location contains the value $44 and is compared with (subtracted from) the A accumulator, which contains a value of $47, ($47 - $44) the C bit will remain clear because a borrow was not required for the subtraction. If the BHS instruction is executed, the branch would be taken because the C bit is clear indicating that the value in the CPU12 register was higher or the same as the value in the memory location. The same reasoning is used to describe the BLO mnemonic. If a borrow was required as the result of a comparison, the C bit would be set indicating that the CPU12 register was lower than the value in memory.

The BHI and BLS instructions perform a logical OR of the C and Z bits in the condition code register to provide supplementary branching capabilities to the BCC and BCS instructions. If this logical OR is zero, it means that the previous compare did not require a borrow and the result was not zero. Therefore the register value was larger than the memory value. If the logical OR is one, either a borrow was required or the result was zero, meaning that the register had a lower value or was the same as memory.

One mistake that is commonly made by programmers is choosing incorrect branch instructions based on a misunderstanding of how different instructions affect the condition code register. For instance, examining the example in Figure 2.27 in light of the newly presented unsigned branch instructions, a programmer might be tempted to substitute the BHS instruction for the BPL in line nine. After all, the previous decrement instruction would subtract the value $01 from the accumulator value of $00 the last time through the loop; the register would be less than the subtracted value and the test should fail. Unfortunately, the decrement instruction *does not* affect the C bit. If it did, the decrement instruction could not be used in this manner because it would affect the state of the carry from the previous subtract operation.

2.6.4 Signed Branch Instructions

The signed branch instructions shown in Figure 2.30 are used to change program flow when comparing signed data. Because many programs do not used signed data, programmers must be careful not to use these instructions unless their programs manipulate signed two's compliment numbers.

Signed Branches			
Mnemonic	**Function**	**Relation**	**Condition Code Test**
BGE, LBGE	Branch if Greater Than or Equal	R ≥ M	(N ^V) == 0
BLT, LBLT	Branch if Less than	R < M	(N ^V) == 1
BGT, LBGT	Branch if Greater than	R > M	Z | (N ^V) == 0
BLE, LBLE	Branch if Less Than or Equal	R ≤ M	Z | (N ^V) == 1

Figure 2.30: Signed Branch Instructions

In reality, the CPU12 does not perform addition, subtraction or compare operations any differently for signed or unsigned numbers. All of its addition, subtraction and compare instructions perform simple binary arithmetic. Condition code register results are interpreted through the execution of branch instructions. This determines if a program interprets numbers as signed or unsigned quantities. Notice that for the signed branches, only the N, V and Z bits are involved in the condition code test, remember that the V bit is used to indicate a two's compliment overflow condition and the N bit is used to indicate a negative result.

A simple example may further help explain the difference between the signed and unsigned branched instructions. Suppose that a program reads an 8-bit unsigned value of $40 (64) from an A-to-D converter result register and compares it to the maximum conversion value, $FF, and branches if the A-to-D converter value is less than the maximum. Comparing the two values ($40 - $FF) will result in the Z, N, and V condition code bits being cleared and the C bit being set.

Understanding why the condition code bits are updated with these values should help in understanding how the signed and unsigned branches differ. Figure 2.31 shows that the value read from the A-to-D converter is positive whether the number is interpreted as a signed or unsigned value. However, the maximum A-to-D converter value of $FF has a positive value of 255 when interpreted as an unsigned number but has a value of -1 when interpreted as a signed number. For an unsigned subtraction, the C bit is set to indicate that a borrow was required for the subtraction operation. The result of the subtraction, $41, is

Section 2.7: Register Transfer and Exchange Instructions

based on the fact that a borrow was available for the operation. In other words, the answer is actually the result of subtracting the value of $FF from $140.

For a signed subtraction, a minus one is being subtracted from $40 (64 - (-1)). Just as in decimal arithmetic, subtracting a negative binary number is equivalent to adding the absolute value of the number. The Z bit is cleared indicating that the result is not zero, the N bit is cleared indicating that the result is not negative, and the V bit is cleared indicating that the subtraction did not result in a two's compliment overflow. The Z, N, and V bits, which are used to reflect the results of signed arithmetic, indicate that the A-to-D converter value, 64, is greater than the "maximum" value of -1.

Hex Value	Unsigned Decimal Value	Signed Decimal Value
$40	64	64
$FF	255	-1

```
C = 1      $40        Z = N = V = 0
         - $FF
         ──────
           $41
```

Figure 2.31: Comparing or subtracting signed and unsigned values

It should be pointed out that the BEQ and BNE instructions, grouped with the simple branch instructions, can be used with either signed or unsigned numbers. After a compare operation, the Z bit indicates that the compared quantities are equal, if set, or unequal if cleared.

⚠ **CPU12 Difference from the M68HC11**

2.7 REGISTER TRANSFER AND EXCHANGE INSTRUCTIONS

The CPU12 has replaced all of the individual M68HC11 transfer and exchange instructions with a single general purpose register transfer/exchange instruction. A single opcode is used along with a postbyte to specify the source and destination registers and the transfer or exchange operation. All of the original M68HC11 mnemonics are still recognized by M68HC12 assemblers. However, the assembler translates these mnemonics to the general purpose transfer and exchange instructions, with two exceptions. Because the M68HC11 TAB and TBA instructions update the N, Z, and V bits in the condition code register, separate instruction opcodes are used to perform these operations on the CPU12 to maintain complete M68HC11 compatibility. Other M68HC11 transfer and exchange instructions, like the general purpose transfer/exchange instructions, do not affect the condition code register. The only other obvious exceptions would be the TAP instruction for the M68HC11 and the TFR A,CCR or EXG A,CCR instructions for the CPU12.

Figure 2.32 through 2.34 show the register transfer and exchange instructions recognized by M68HC12 assemblers. Figure 2.35 shows the register transfer/exchange postbyte encoding.

\multicolumn{3}{c}{CPU12 Transfer/Exchange Instructions}
Mnemonic	Function	Operation
TFR	Register to Register Transfer	A, B, CCR, D, X, Y, SP → A, B, CCR, D, X, Y, SP
EXG	Register to Register Exchange	A, B, CCR, D, X, Y, SP ↔ A, B, CCR, D, X, Y, SP
TAB	Transfer Register A to B	A → B
TBA	Transfer Register B to A	B → A

Figure 2.32: CPU12 Transfer/Exchange Instructions

Four of the translated M68HC11 mnemonics, TSX, TXS, TSY, and TYS, execute differently when translated to the CPU12 instructions. From the programmers viewpoint, however, the results are identical. Remember that the M68HC11's stack pointer points to the next byte available. For this reason, the M68HC11's TSX and TSY instruction add one to the stack pointer's value during the transfer so that the value placed in the index register actually points to the last byte on the stack. This makes the stack appear as a "last used" stack from the programmers viewpoint. Conversely, the M68HC11's TXS and TYS instructions subtract one from the value of the index register during the transfer so that the value placed in the stack pointer points to the next available byte. Because the CPU12 incorporates a "last used" stack, the transfer and exchange instructions make no adjustments to register values involving the stack pointer.

\multicolumn{4}{c}{M68HC11 Transfer/Exchange Mnemonics}
Mnemonic	Function	CPU12 Instruction	Operation
TAP	Transfer Register A to CCR	TFR A,CCR	A → CCR
TPA	Transfer Register CCR to A	TFR CCR,A	CCR → A
TSX	Transfer Register S to X	TFR SP,X	SP → X
TXS	Transfer Register X to S	TFR X,SP	X → SP
TSY	Transfer Register S to Y	TFR SP,Y	SP → Y
TYS	Transfer Register Y to S	TFR Y,SP	Y → SP
XGDX	Exchange Register D and X	EXG D,X	D ↔ X
XGDY	Exchange Register D and Y	EXG D,Y	D ↔ Y

Figure 2.33: M68HC11 Transfer/Exchange Mnemonics

Section 2.7: Register Transfer and Exchange Instructions

Looking at the Operation column for the `TFR` and `EXG` instructions in Figure 2.33 it may not be completely obvious that the CPU12 allows register transfers and exchanges with registers of different sizes. This may seem illogical, however, the CPU12 designers used these special combinations for a useful function.

There are numerous times when a program's algorithm must perform arithmetic on a mixture of 8-bit and 16-bit values. For instance, when several readings from an 8-bit A-to-D converter have to be averaged, a 16-bit intermediate value is required to hold the sum of the readings. The operation performed when converting an 8-bit value to a 16-bit value depends on whether the 8-bit and 16-bit numbers are signed or unsigned values. Converting an 8-bit unsigned value to a 16-bit unsigned value is accomplished by zero extending the 8-bit value, making the the upper byte of the converted value zero. This operation is performed using the `TFR` instruction where the source is an 8-bit register and the destination is a 16-bit register. This is the most efficient way to zero extend the A or B accumulator into one of the 16-bit registers except if the 8-bit value is in the B accumulator and the destination is the D accumulator. In this case, because B is the lower byte of D, it is more efficient to execute the single byte `CLRA` instruction.

To convert a signed 8-bit value to a signed 16-bit value, the most significant bit of the 8-bit value must be propagated into the upper byte of the converted value. Using the `EXG` instruction with an 8-bit register as the source and a 16-bit register as the destination, properly sign extends the 8-bit value. Sign extending an 8-bit value is such a common operation, especially in the C programming language, that the mnemonic, `SEX`, is recognized by assemblers to help make a program more self documenting. Note that even though an `EXG` instruction is being executed, the source register *must* always be the 8-bit register.

CPU12 Sign Extension Instruction		
Mnemonic	**Function**	**Operation**
SEX	Sign Extend an 8-Bit Register	A, B, CCR → D, X, Y, SP

Figure 2.34: CPU12 Sign Extension Instruction

Figure 2.35 is a summary of the Transfer/Exchange postbyte encoding. In the Comments column the source and destination register bit patterns show two registers, `TMP2` and `TMP3`, that are not part of the CPU12 programmers model. These two 16-bit registers are internal temporary registers used by the CPU12 when executing various instructions and should not be used by normal programs. Many assemblers may not even recognize the `TMP2` and `TMP3` mnemonics. The `TMP2` and `TMP3` registers are used by the Background Debug firmware to save the state of the applications's Program Counter and D accumulator while the Background Debug Mode (BDM) firmware executes. This firmware was written by the CPU12 system architects, who took care not to use any instructions that disturb the contents of these temporary registers. Examples showing the use of these registers in the BDM firmware are presented in Chapter 15.

Postbyte Code	Source Code Syntax	Comments
esssxddd	r,r rs,rd r8,r16	e = 0, Transfer Register rs to rd e = 1, Exchange register r with register r x = don't care r8 = A, B, CCR r16 = D, X, Y, SP sss = <u>Source Register</u> ddd = <u>Destination Register</u> 000 - A 000 - A 001 - B 001 - B 010 - CCR 010 - CCR 011 - TMP3 011 - TMP2 100 - D 100 - D 101 - X 101 - X 110 - Y 110 - Y 111 - SP 111 - SP

Figure 2.35: Register Transfer/Exchange Postbyte Encoding

There is one final note regarding the Transfer/Exchange instruction. The actions performed by the CPU12 are clearly defined when an 8-bit source register is transferred or exchanged with a 16-bit destination register. However, what happens if a 16-bit source register is transferred or exchanged with an 8-bit destination register? Even though this type of operation is ambiguous and doesn't really make much sense, the CPU12 will perform a defined action. For all postbytes that transfer *or* exchange a 16-bit source register with an 8-bit destination register, the CPU12 transfers the lower byte of the 16-bit register into the 8-bit register.

2.8 ADDITION AND SUBTRACTION INSTRUCTIONS

The CPU12 provides addition and subtraction instructions for both 8-bit and 16-bit quantities. Both signed and unsigned operations can be performed between registers or the registers and memory. As expected with an accumulator based architecture, the results of the addition or subtraction operations end up in the A, B, or D accumulator. Addition and subtraction instructions that include the condition code register carry bit allow for multiple precision computation. However, as seen in Figure 2.36, this capability is supplied only for the A and B accumulators, there is no 'ADCD' instruction.

Section 2.8: Addition and Subtraction Instructions

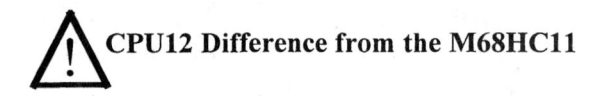

Arithmetic operations on BCD data are supported through the use of any of the binary 8-bit addition instructions that update the half-carry bit in the condition code register. After the binary addition, the DAA instruction must be executed to adjust the accumulator results and the carry bit for the binary addition of BCD data. Although binary additions involving the B accumulator properly update the half-carry bit, the DAA instruction only operates on the A accumulator. Because the subtract instructions do not properly update the half-carry bit, there is no way to directly perform BCD subtraction. To perform BCD subtraction, a method similar to performing two's compliment binary addition must be used.

Addition Instructions		
Mnemonic	**Function**	**Operation**
ABA	Add B to A	$B + A \rightarrow A$
ADDA	Add without carry to A	$A + (M) \rightarrow A$
ADCA	Add with carry to A	$A + (M) + CCR{:}C \rightarrow A$
ADDB	Add without carry to B	$B + (M) \rightarrow B$
ADCB	Add with carry to B	$B + (M) + CCR{:}C \rightarrow B$
ADDD	Add without carry to D	$D + (M : M{+}1) \rightarrow D$
DAA	Decimal Adjust A	$A + (\text{Correction Factor}) \rightarrow A$
Subtraction Instructions		
Mnemonic	**Function**	**Operation**
SBA	Subtract B from A	$A - B \rightarrow A$
SUBA	Subtract without borrow from A	$A - (M) \rightarrow A$
SBCA	Subtract with borrow from A	$A - (M) - CCR{:}C \rightarrow A$
SUBB	Subtract without borrow from B	$B - (M) \rightarrow B$
SBCB	Subtract with borrow from B	$B - (M) - CCR{:}C \rightarrow B$
SUBD	Subtract without borrow from D	$D - (M : M{+}1) \rightarrow D$

Figure 2.36: Addition and subtraction instructions

⚠ CPU12 Difference from the M68HC11

2.9 ADDRESS ARITHMETIC INSTRUCTIONS

The addition and subtraction instructions discussed in the previous section are only useful for manipulating values residing in the A, B, or D accumulators. There are many times that programs need to manipulate the values that reside in the X, Y, or SP registers. The M68HC11 has very limited address arithmetic capabilities only allowing one to be added to or subtracted from the X, Y, or SP registers. In addition, the M68HC11 allows the contents of the B accumulator to be added to the X or Y index register. If any complicated address arithmetic must be performed on the value in one of these registers, the register value must to be placed in the D accumulator, the calculations performed, and finally the calculated address placed into one of the address registers. This process is especially difficult when adjusting the stack pointer value because no M68HC11 instructions exist to transfer the value of the stack pointer directly to the D accumulator.

The CPU12 provides three more powerful, general purpose instructions for address calculations, but it also supports the M68HC11 instructions for compatibility. The first eight instructions shown in Figure 2.37 are the M68HC11 address arithmetic instructions. The last three entries in the table are unique to the CPU12. The Load Effective Address, or LEA instructions, use the address computation logic of the CPU12 associated with the indexed addressing modes to perform address calculations. The result of these calculations is placed in one of the address registers rather than being used to fetch data. The LEA instructions may use all indexed addressing modes, except the indexed indirect, for effective address calculations. The address register specified in the operand field can be X, Y, SP, or PC and is independent of the register in which the result is placed. The calculated effective address loaded into X, Y, or SP is the address that would have been placed on the address bus to fetch data from memory.

Section 2.9: Address Arithmetic Instructions

Address Arithmetic Instructions		
Mnemonic	**Function**	**Operation**
INX	Increment the X index Register	$X + 1 \rightarrow X$
INY	Increment the Y index Register	$Y + 1 \rightarrow Y$
INS	Increment the Stack Pointer	$SP + 1 \rightarrow SP$
DEX	Decrement the X index Register	$X - 1 \rightarrow X$
DEY	Decrement the Y index Register	$Y - 1 \rightarrow Y$
DES	Decrement the Stack Pointer	$SP - 1 \rightarrow SP$
ABX	Add B to the X index Register	$X + \$00{:}B \rightarrow X$
ABY	Add B to the Y index Register	$Y + \$00{:}B \rightarrow Y$
LEAX	Load effective address into X	$E.A. \rightarrow X$
LEAY	Load effective address into Y	$E.A. \rightarrow Y$
LEAS	Load effective address into SP	$E.A. \rightarrow SP$

Figure 2.37: Address Arithmetic Instructions

There are special considerations when using the LEA instructions with the auto increment/decrement addressing modes. For the following discussion, the source base index register (X, Y, SP, PC) is considered to be the register that appears as part of the index addressing mode specification in the operand field. The destination base index register (X, Y, SP) is the register specified by the LEA instruction mnemonic.

Both the pre-increment and pre-decrement addressing modes modify the value of the source base index register before being used to fetch data. As shown in Figure 2.38a, when the source and destination base index register is the same, the LEA instruction simply updates the value of the base index register by the increment or decrement amount. If, however, the the source and destination base index registers are different, the LEA instruction actually performs the equivalent of two instructions as shown in Figure 2.38b. It first updates the value of the source base index register and then copies that value to the destination base index register.

Using the LEA instruction with post-increment and post-decrement indexed addressing modes has no effect on the destination index register when the source and destination index register is the same. This result is shown in Figure 2.38c. Because the unmodified effective address that would have been placed on the address bus "overwrites" the post increment/decrement value, using the LEA instructions in this manner is of no use. The situation is quite different, however, when using different source and destination base index registers. In this case the pre-modified source register value is copied to the destination base index register, while the source base index register is post modified just as expected as shown in Figure 2.38d.

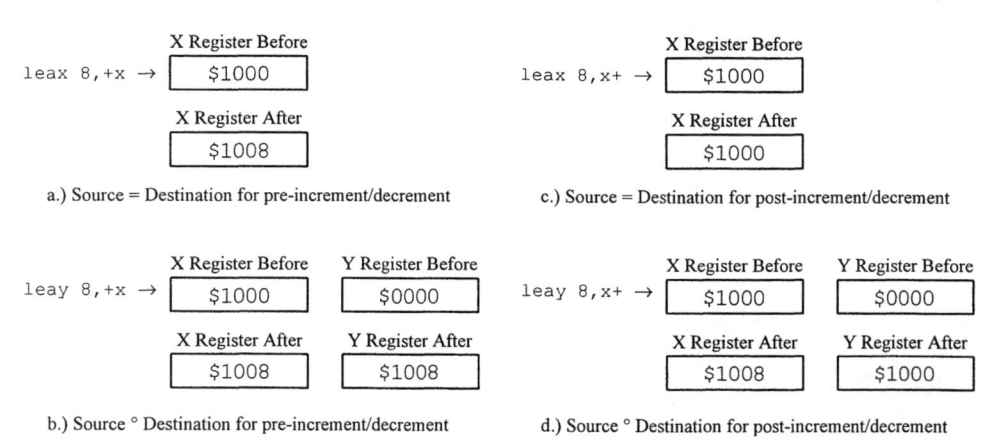

```
leax 8,+x  →   X Register Before
               $1000
               X Register After
               $1008
```
a.) Source = Destination for pre-increment/decrement

```
leax 8,x+  →   X Register Before
               $1000
               X Register After
               $1000
```
c.) Source = Destination for post-increment/decrement

```
leay 8,+x  →   X Register Before    Y Register Before
               $1000                 $0000
               X Register After     Y Register After
               $1008                 $1008
```
b.) Source ° Destination for pre-increment/decrement

```
leay 8,x+  →   X Register Before    Y Register Before
               $1000                 $0000
               X Register After     Y Register After
               $1008                 $1000
```
d.) Source ° Destination for post-increment/decrement

Figure 2.38: Using pre/post increment/decrement addressing with LEA

Examining at the opcode map in Appendix A, it is apparent that no entries exist for the INS, DES, ABX, and ABY instructions. Rather than add additional logic to the CPU12 and increase its size, the CPU12 designers choose to have these mnemonics translated into LEA instructions by the assembler. This, however, raises the question of why separate instruction opcodes exist for the INX, INY, DEX, and DEY instructions. The answer lies in the fact that the LEA instructions do not affect the condition code register. The M68HC11 INX, INY, DEX, and DEY instructions update the condition code register Z bit. Because one of the overriding design goals was to maintain complete execution compatibility with reassembled M68HC11 source code, these instructions had to have their own opcodes so that the Z bit could be properly updated.

The ability to calculate effective address values is a powerful feature that can enhance the efficiency of programs written in C or assembly language. The C language uses the stack for local or temporary variables within functions. Each time a function is entered, space for its local variables is allocated by subtracting the size of the local variables from the stack pointer. Just before a function returns, it must remove the local variable space from the stack. Having the ability to perform address arithmetic on the stack pointer using the LEAS instruction allows a compiler to generate efficient code for allocating and deallocating local variables. Figure 2.39 shows the code necessary to allocate 14 bytes of local variable space on the stack for both the M68HC11 family and the CPU12.

Section 2.10: Multiply and Divide Instructions

```
      M68HC11              CPU12
  ┌─────────────────┐  ┌─────────────────┐
  │ tsx             │  │ leas    -14,s   │
  │ xgdx            │  │                 │
  │ subd     #14    │  │                 │
  │ xgdx            │  │                 │
  │ txs             │  │                 │
  └─────────────────┘  └─────────────────┘
```

Figure 2.39: Local Variable Allocation

The M68HC11 requires five instructions producing seven bytes of object code. The CPU12 can allocate the 14 bytes of stack space with a single instruction producing only two bytes of object code. Deallocating the stack space would require an equivalent number of instructions and object code for each processor. The perceptive reader may realize that as the amount of required stack space grows, the M68HC11 code size will remain constant. However, the CPU12 code size will grow due to the need for additional index extension bytes to specify the amount to be subtracted from the stack pointer. In any event, the CPU12 code size will not exceed four bytes.

⚠ **CPU12 Difference from the M68HC11**

2.10 MULTIPLY AND DIVIDE INSTRUCTIONS

There was little emphasis on high speed mathematical operations in applications using the M68HC11 and earlier microcontrollers. However, as embedded applications were required to perform increasingly accurate closed loop feedback control, the need for high performance, high precision math operations became necessary. The M6801 family was Motorola's first MCU to offer an 8-bit multiply instruction. The M68HC11 family retained this instruction and added two 16-bit divide instructions. Including the hardware divide instructions provided a great performance improvement over implementing the divide routines in software. However, as applications for the M68HC11 family expanded, the need for higher performance arithmetic functions increased. In the M68HC11 family, this need was met by the addition of a math co-processor to some of the family members. While this extended the life of the M68HC11 family for numerically intensive applications, it was clear to the CPU12 designers that there would be an ever-increasing need for high speed, high precision numeric computations for increasingly sophisticated embedded applications.

Multiply and Divide Instructions

Mnemonic	Function	Operation
MUL	8 x 8 Unsigned Multiply	A x B → D
EMUL	16 x 16 Unsigned Multiply	D x Y → Y:D
EMULS	16 x 16 Signed Multiply	D x Y → Y:D
EMACS	16 x 16 Signed Multiply/Accumulate	$(M_x:M_{x+1})$ x $(M_y:M_{y+1})$ + M:M+3 → M:M+3
IDIV	16-bit ÷ 16-bit Unsigned Divide	D ÷ X → X; Remainder → D
FDIV	16-bit ÷ 16-bit Fractional Divide	D ÷ X → X; Remainder → D
IDIVS	16-bit ÷ 16-bit Signed Divide	D ÷ X → X; Remainder → D
EDIV	32-bit ÷ 16-bit Unsigned Divide	Y:D ÷ X → Y; Remainder → D
EDIVS	32-bit ÷ 16-bit Signed Divide	Y:D ÷ X → Y; Remainder → D

Figure 2.40: Multiply and Divide Instructions

As shown in Figure 2.40, the CPU12 supports extended precision multiply and divide instructions as well as multiply and divide operations for signed numbers. A signed multiply instruction is not provided for 8-bit values, however, it is quite easy to perform this operation using the 16-bit signed multiply. Figure 2.41 shows the necessary instruction sequence. Assuming that the two 8-bit signed numbers have been loaded into the A and B accumulators, the 8-bit value in A is sign extended into Y, then the value in B is sign extended into D overwriting the 8-bit value in A. Finally, the EMULS instruction is used to multiply the 16-bit signed values in Y and D. Even though a 32-bit result is contained in Y:D, the lower 16-bits in D will contain the desired result. The upper 16-bits contained in Y will simply be an extension of the most significant bit (the sign bit) of the result contained in D. If the value of the Y index register needs to be preserved, a PSHY instruction can precede the first SEX instruction and PULY could follow the EMULS instruction.

```
MULS:   sex     a,y     ; sign extend the a accumulator into y.
        sex     b,d     ; sign extend the b accumulator into d.
        emuls           ; perform a 16 x 16 signed multiply.
                        ; result is in d. value in y may be discarded.
```

Figure 2.41: Multiplying 8-bit signed values using EMULS

The fractional divide instruction (FDIV) was originally implemented on a custom automotive MCU just before the M68HC11 was designed. It can be used to resolve the

Section 2.10: Multiply and Divide Instructions

remainder of an integer division into a 16-bit binary fraction whose radix point is to the left of the most significant bit. Its primary use in automotive applications is to aid in linear interpolation between two points in table lookup operations. In the M68HC11, the use of the `FDIV` instruction is the only way to perform this type of function. However, performing the operation in this manner results in a fairly large routine that executes slowly. Because the CPU12 has two table lookup and interpolate instructions, the `FDIV` instruction was only kept for compatibility with existing M68HC11 code.

Requiring only 13 clock cycles, the `EMACS` instruction performs a 16-bit by 16-bit signed multiply and adds the 32-bit result to a 32-bit 'accumulator' residing in memory. This type of operation is used extensively in digital signal processing operations for implementing filters and other functions.Although the CPU12's `EMACS` instruction performs its function quickly, the `EMACS` instruction does not provide the necessary features found in dedicated multiply/accumulate units to allow it to perform digital signal processing operations on high frequency signals. Although additional software is required to perform saturation arithmetic when overflow occurs, the `EMACS` instruction can be quite capable of performing digital signal processing operations on signals up to frequencies of several hundred hertz.

By taking advantage of the CPU12's 16-bit Arithmetic and Logic Unit (ALU) and using some innovative logic design techniques, the execution speeds of the multiply and divide instructions have been dramatically increased over the equivalent M68HC11 instructions. Figure 2.42 compares execution speeds and required clock cycles for the various multiply and divide instructions. The instruction cycle times marked with an asterisk are only found on M68HC11 family members that contain a math co-processor.

Multiply and Divide Execution Times			
Mnemonic	Function	M68HC11 cycles/time 1 cycle = 250 nS	CPU12 cycles/time 1 cycle = 125 nS
MUL	8 x 8 Unsigned Multiply	10 / 2.5 μS	3 / 0.375 μS
EMUL	16 x 16 Unsigned Multiply	20 / 5 μS*	3 / 0.375 μS
EMULS	16 x 16 Signed Multiply	20 / 5 μS*	3 / 0.375 μS
EMACS	16 x 16 Signed Multiply/Accumulate	20 / 5 μS*	13 / 1.625 μS
IDIV	16-bit ÷ 16-bit Unsigned Divide	41 / 10.5 μS	12 / 1.5 μS
FDIV	16-bit ÷ 16-bit Fractional Divide	41 / 10.5 μS	12 / 1.5 μS
IDIVS	16-bit ÷ 16-bit Signed Divide	–	12 / 1.5 μS
EDIV	32-bit ÷ 16-bit Unsigned Divide	33 / 8.25 μS*	11 / 1.375 μS
EDIVS	32-bit ÷ 16-bit Signed Divide	37 / 9.25 μS*	12 / 1.5 μS

Figure 2.42: M68HC11 and CPU12 multiply and divide execution times

2.11 READ/MODIFY/WRITE INSTRUCTIONS

This group of instructions is discussed in relation to how they execute their function rather than the particular action performed. As the title of the section suggests, this group of instructions reads a value from a memory location or CPU register, modifies the value, and updates the original location. This group of instructions operates only on 8-bit register or memory values. Figure 2.43 contains a summary of the read/modify/write instructions.

Section 2.11: Read/Modify/Write Instructions

Read/Modify/Write Instructions		
Mnemonic	**Function**	**Operation**
INCA	Add 1 to A	$A + 1 \rightarrow A$
INCB	Add 1 to B	$B + 1 \rightarrow A$
INC	Add 1 to Memory Byte	$(M) + 1 \rightarrow (M)$
DECA	Subtract 1 from A	$A - 1 \rightarrow A$
DECB	Subtract 1 from B	$B - 1 \rightarrow B$
DEC	Subtract 1 from Memory Byte	$(M) - 1 \rightarrow (M)$
NEGA	Two's Complement A	$0 - A \rightarrow A$
NEGB	Two's Complement A	$0 - B \rightarrow B$
NEG	Two's Complement Memory Byte	$0 - (M) \rightarrow (M)$
COMA	One's Complement A	$\$FF - A \rightarrow A$
COMB	One's Complement B	$\$FF - B \rightarrow B$
COM	One's Complement Memory Byte	$\$FF - (M) \rightarrow (M)$
CLRA	Clear A	$0 \rightarrow A$
CLRB	Clear B	$0 \rightarrow B$
CLR	Clear Memory Byte	$0 \rightarrow (M)$
TSTA	Test A for negative or zero	$A - 0$
TSTB	Test B for negative or zero	$B - 0$
TST	Test memory for negative or zero	$(M) - 0$

Figure 2.43: Read/Modify/Write instructions

The read/modify/write instructions operating on memory values support extended and all indexed addressing modes. However, they do not support direct addressing. The alert reader may wonder why the CLR instruction is included in this group since its operation does not include reading memory before writing the value of zero. To save CPU logic in the M68HC11, M6801 and M6800 designs, the CLR instruction shared decode and execution logic with the other read/modify/write instructions. The sharing of execution logic actually caused a read cycle to execute before the memory location was written to zero in these CPUs. Because the CPU size is a relatively small portion of most M68HC12 family members, the CPU12 designers added the extra logic necessary to eliminate this spurious read cycle. This causes the CLR instruction to execute one cycle faster than all other read/modify/write instructions for each addressing mode.

Chapter 2: The CPU12 Instruction Set

It may also seem confusing that the `TST` instruction is included in this group because it does not perform modification of the data that is read. However, like the `CLR` instruction, `TST` shares the instruction decode and execution logic with the other read/modify/write instructions. Subtracting zero from the accumulator or memory value updates the N, Z, V, and C condition code register bits to reflect the results of the subtraction. The V and C bit will always be cleared. The N will be set if the most significant bit of the accumulator or memory value is set and the Z bit will be set only if the accumulator was zero before the subtraction.

2.12 Shift and Rotate Instructions

The shift and rotate instructions, shown in Figures 2.44 - 2.46, are actually part of the read/modify/write group. The logical shift left instructions shift every bit to the left by one bit position, putting the most significant bit into the carry and replacing the least significant bit with a zero. Each shift to the left effectively multiplies the accumulator or memory location by two. If the carry bit is set after a logical shift left, it indicates that an overflow occurred. The logical shift right instructions shift every bit to the right by one bit position, placing the least significant bit into the carry and replacing the most significant bit with a zero. This effectively divides the accumulator or memory location by two. However, if the least significant bit shifted out is a one, a loss of precision will occur. Unlike the other read/modify/write instructions, the CPU12 does have logical shift instructions that operate on 16-bit data in the D accumulator.

Logical Shift Instructions		
Mnemonic	**Function**	**Operation**
LSLA	Logical Shift Left A	
LSLB	Logical Shift Left B	
LSL	Logical Shift Left Memory Byte	
LSLD	Logical Shift Left D	
LSRA	Logical Shift Right A	
LSRB	Logical Shift Right B	
LSR	Logical Shift Right Memory Byte	
LSRD	Logical Shift Right D	

Figure 2.44: Logical Shift Instructions

Section 2.12: Shift and Rotate Instructions

Figure 2.45 contains the CPU12's arithmetic shift instructions. When comparing the actions in the Operation column of Figure 2.44 and 2.45 it can be seen that the operation performed by the logical shift left and the arithmetic shift left instructions is identical. In fact, the opcodes for these instructions are the same. The operation that is different, however, is the arithmetic shift right. This instruction's operation may seem strange, but it is meant for dividing two's compliment signed numbers by two for each shift to the right. Remember that negative numbers represented in two's compliment form use the most significant bit to indicate the sign of the number. By propagating the most significant bit back on itself, the sign of the number is preserved. For example, if accumulator A contains the signed two's compliment number $FE (%11111110) which represents the decimal value of -2 and an LSRA instruction is executed, the resulting value would be $7F (%01111111) which represents a value of +127 decimal. Clearly this would not produce the intended result. However, if the ASRA instruction is used on this same value, the result would be $FF (%11111111). This produces the intended result of -1. The CPU12 does not include an arithmetic shift right instruction for binary values larger than 8-bits. Performing this operation requires a combination of an 8-bit arithmetic shift right and an 8-bit rotate instruction.

Arithmetic Shift Instructions		
Mnemonic	**Function**	**Operation**
ASLA	Arithmetic Shift Left A	
ASLB	Arithmetic Shift Left B	
ASL	Arithmetic Shift Left Memory Byte	
ASLD	Arithmetic Shift Left D	
ASRA	Arithmetic Shift Right A	
ASRB	Arithmetic Shift Right B	
ASR	Arithmetic Shift Right Memory Byte	

Figure 2.45: Arithmetic Shift Instructions

The arithmetic and logical shift instructions discard the state of the carry, replacing it with either the most or least significant data bit of the accumulator or memory location; however, the rotate instructions preserve the state of the carry. Rotate left instructions place the value of the carry bit before the rotate into the least significant bit of the rotated data and places the most significant data bit into the carry. The rotate right instruction does just the opposite. These instructions effectively circulate data bits through the carry without loosing any data. Executing eight ROR or ROL instructions in a row leaves the carry and data in the same state it was in before the rotates.

Rotate Instructions		
Mnemonic	Function	Operation
ROLA	Rotate Left A Through Carry	
ROLB	Rotate Left B Through Carry	
ROL	Rotate Left Memory Byte Through Carry	
RORA	Rotate Right A Through Carry	
RORB	Rotate Right B Through Carry	
ROR	Rotate Right Memory Byte Through Carry	

Figure 2.46: Rotate Instructions

The rotate instructions can be used to examine each data bit within a byte without destroying the data. By placing each data bit in the carry, the BCC or BCS instructions can be used to perform some action based on the state of the carry. These instructions are critical to performing multi-precision arithmetic and logical shift operations. By combining a single shift instruction with multiple rotate instructions, a multi-byte value of any length may be shifted to the left or right one bit at a time. For instance, an arithmetic shift right on the high byte of a 16-bit value followed by a rotate on the low byte of the value will produce the equivalent of a 16-bit arithmetic shift right.

When shifting or rotating multi-precision values to the left, software should always begin with the least significant byte and work its way toward the most significant byte. The opposite is true when shifting or rotating multi-precision values to the right, i.e., software should begin with the most significant byte and work its way toward the least significant byte. When shifting multi-precision values, a shift operation must be performed on the first byte while succeeding bytes have rotate operations performed on them. Rotating multi-precision values, utilizes rotate instructions on all bytes.

Numerous techniques may be used when shifting or rotating multi-precision values. Figures 2.47 and 2.48 present simple pieces of code for performing a multi-bit shift on a 32-bit value. Both routines assume that the X index register points to the most significant byte of a 32-bit number and the B accumulator contains the number of bits to shift. It should be pointed out that neither of these small routines account for the condition where the B accumulator might contain a shift value of zero. Similar routines could be written to perform the arithmetic shift right, rotate left and rotate right functions on multi-precision values.

Section 2.13: Boolean Logic and Compare Instructions

```
LSL32:  lsl   3,x      ; perform lsl on the ls byte.
        rol   2,x      ; rotate carry into next ls byte, ms bit into carry.
        rol   1,x      ; rotate carry into next ls byte, ms bit into carry.
        rol   0,x      ; rotate carry into ms byte, ms bit into carry.
        decb           ; shifted the correct number of bits?
        bne   LSL32    ; no. shift until done.
```

Figure 2.47: Logical shift left of a 32-bit value

```
LSR32:  lsr   0,x      ; perform lsr on the ms byte.
        ror   1,x      ; rotate carry into next ls byte, ls bit into carry.
        ror   2,x      ; rotate carry into next ls byte, ls bit into carry.
        ror   3,x      ; rotate carry into ls byte, ls bit into carry.
        decb           ; shifted the correct number of bits?
        bne   LSR32    ; no. shift until done.
```

Figure 2.48: Logical shift right of a 32-bit value

2.13 BOOLEAN LOGIC AND COMPARE INSTRUCTIONS

The boolean logic instructions shown in Figure 2.49 perform a bitwise logical AND, OR, or exclusive OR between the contents of the A or B accumulator and a value in memory. With the exception of the BITA and BITB instructions, the results of each logical operation is placed in one of the 8-bit accumulators.

The BIT instructions perform a bitwise logical AND with the value in one of the 8-bit accumulators and a memory location, setting the condition code register accordingly. Neither the contents of the accumulator or the memory location is affected. The BIT instructions, which were part of the original M6800 instruction set, were used primarily to test the state of one or more bits within a memory byte and perform a branch based on the resulting state. However, these instructions have rarely been used since the introduction of the M68HC11 because of the bit test and branch instructions included in the M68HC11's instruction set. There may be times when it is desirable to use the BIT instructions because they record the results of the logical AND in the condition code register while the bit test and branch instructions have no effect on the condition code register. In addition, the BIT instructions support the indexed indirect addressing modes while the bit-test and branch instructions do not.

Chapter 2: The CPU12 Instruction Set

Boolean Logic Instructions		
Mnemonic	**Function**	**Operation**
ANDA	AND accumulator A with memory	A & (M) → A
ANDB	AND accumulator B with memory	B & (M) → B
ORAA	OR accumulator A with memory	A | (M) → A
ORAB	OR accumulator B with memory	B | (M) → B
EORA	EOR accumulator A with memory	A ^ (M) → A
EORB	EOR accumulator B with memory	B ^ (M) → B
BITA	AND accumulator A with memory	A & (M)
BITB	AND accumulator B with memory	B & (M)

Figure 2.49: Boolean Logic Instructions

The compare instructions are grouped with the boolean logic instructions because they share the same addressing modes. Both groups of instructions may be used with immediate, direct, extended, and indexed addressing modes. Unlike the boolean logic instructions, the compare instructions include mnemonics allowing comparison of 16-bit data. As shown in Figure 2.50 the compare instruction performs its operation by subtracting a value in memory from the contents of a CPU12 register. Neither the CPU12 register nor the contents of the memory location is affected, however, the N, Z, V and C bits in the condition code register are updated according to the results of the subtraction. All signed and unsigned branch instructions may be used immediately following a compare instruction to alter program flow.

Compare Instructions		
Mnemonic	**Function**	**Operation**
CMPA	Compare accumulator A with memory	A - (M)
CMPB	Compare accumulator B with memory	B - (M)
CBA	Compare accumulator A with B	A - B
CPD	Compare accumulator D with memory	D - (M : M + 1)
CPX	Compare X with memory	X - (M : M + 1)
CPY	Compare Y with memory	Y - (M : M + 1)
CPS	Compare SP with memory	SP - (M) : M + 1

Figure 2.50: Compare instructions

Section 2.14: Stack Related Instructions

> ⚠ **CPU12 Difference from the M68HC11**
>
> The CPS instruction was not part of the M68HC11 instruction set because the programmer did not have direct access to the value of the stack pointer. Although this instruction was added to the CPU12 instruction set, most programmers will have little use for the instruction. The stack is used for saving subroutine return addresses, temporary variables, and CPU register contents during interrupt processing and therefore the programmer rarely needs to compare its contents to another value. There are cases, however, where it could be used for debugging purposes. In particular, a real time kernel might use the CPS instruction to check the value of a task's stack pointer when a task switch occurs to ensure that the task's stack usage did not exceed its allocated amount of memory. Even this usage is of limited value. If a task has exceeded the amount of stack space allocated by the kernel, it is likely that the task may have already overwritten other data before the situation is detected by the real time kernel.
>
> ⚠ **CPU12 Difference from the M68HC11**

2.14 STACK RELATED INSTRUCTIONS

The M68HC11 instruction set allows the A, B, X, and Y registers to be pushed onto or pulled from the stack. As shown in Figure 2.51, the CPU12 adds the capability to push or pull the D accumulator and the condition code register on to or off of the stack. The single byte `PSHD` and `PULD` instructions replace the two instruction sequence required with the M68HC11 to save or restore the value of the D accumulator on the stack. Likewise, the `PSHC` and `PULC` instructions provide a way to save or restore the value of the condition code register without having to disturb the value in the A accumulator as required when using the M68HC11 instruction set. None of the pull instructions, with the exception of `PULC`, alter any of the condition code register bits. This feature allows the results of an intermediate computation to remain in the condition code register while restoring the original register contents. All of the push and pull instructions reside on page one of the opcode map and therefore require only a single byte of object code.

Chapter 2: The CPU12 Instruction Set

\multicolumn{3}{c}{**Stack Related Instructions**}
Mnemonic	**Function**	**Operation**
PSHA	Push accumulator A onto the stack	SP - 1 → SP; A → (SP)
PSHB	Push accumulator B onto the stack	SP - 1 → SP; B → (SP)
PSHC	Push CCR onto the stack	SP - 1 → SP; CCR → (SP)
PSHD	Push accumulator D onto the stack	SP - 2 → SP; D → (SP : SP + 1)
PSHX	Push X index register onto the stack	SP - 2 → SP; X → (SP : SP + 1)
PSHY	Push Y index register onto the stack	SP - 2 → SP; Y → (SP : SP + 1)
PULA	Pull accumulator A from the stack	(SP) → A; SP + 1 → SP
PULB	Pull accumulator B from the stack	(SP) → B; SP + 1 → SP
PULC	Pull CCR from the stack	(SP) → CCR; SP + 1 → SP
PULD	Pull accumulator D from the stack	(SP : SP + 1) → D; SP + 2 → SP
PULX	Pull X index register from the stack	(SP : SP + 1) → X; SP + 2 → SP
PULY	Pull Y index register from the stack	(SP : SP + 1) → Y; SP + 2 → SP

Figure 2.51: Stack Related Instructions

The ability to save and restore the contents of the condition code register may seem to have marginal utility, however, it is useful in certain situations. For instance, it may be necessary to execute a section of a program or a subroutine with interrupts disabled. A programmer's first thought may be to set the I-bit in the condition code register when entering the routine and then clear the I-bit when leaving the routine. Using this method would work fine if the I-bit were originally cleared; however, if the I-bit was set when the routine was entered, the original state of the I-bit would not have been preserved and may cause improper operation of other parts of the program. This type of situation may occur especially when a subroutine is shared by the main portion of a program and one of the program's interrupt handler routines. A simple way to prevent possible problems caused by this type of situation is to save the value of the condition code register with a PSHC instruction before setting the I-bit. At the end of the routine, a PULC instruction could be used to restore the original state of the I-bit.

This method will work if the routine does not need to return with any of the remaining condition code register bits in a particular state. If, however, the value of the other condition code register bits is important when the routine's processing terminates, a slightly different technique must be used to restore the original state of the I-bit. Figure 2.52 shows one way to perform this operation. In this case, just after executing the uninterruptable code, a

89

Section 2.15: 15 Bit Manipulation Instructions

BRSET instruction is used to test the state of the saved I-bit. If it was set, the CLI instruction is skipped and program execution continues. Notice that the BRSET instruction uses post auto-increment addressing to remove the old condition code register value from the stack after it tests the value of the saved I-bit.

```
          pshc                      ; save the current value of the I-bit by saving CCR.
          sei                       ; disable interrupts by setting the I-bit.
          .
          .                         ; execute the uninterruptable code.
          .
          brset 1,sp+,#$10,IbitSet  ; if the I-bit was set when we entered, leave it set.
          cli                       ; clear the I-bit if it was cleared when we entered.
IbitSet:  .
          .
```

Figure 2.52: Restoring the state if the I-bit in the CCR

Obviously, this same technique could be used to save and restore any of the bits in the condition code register with the exception of the X-bit. As discussed in Chapter 1, once the X-bit is cleared, it can only be set if the M68HC12 is reset or if the state of the X-bit in the stacked value of the condition code register is manipulated within the XIRQ interrupt handler.

⚠ **CPU12 Difference from the M68HC11**

2.15 15 Bit Manipulation Instructions

Before the introduction of the M68HC11, the only way to manipulate or test individual bits within a byte was to load the memory value into one of the 8-bit accumulators and perform a logical AND or OR using an 8-bit immediate value. While this method provided an adequate means to perform the desired function, modifying or testing and branching on bits within a memory byte required three instructions. In addition, the value of one of the accumulators and the value of the N, Z, V, and C bits in the condition code register were modified. The bit manipulation instructions give the programmer the capability to set, clear or test and branch one or more bits in a memory byte without modifying either of the accumulators or the condition code register. The four bit manipulation instructions contained in the CPU12 instruction set, shown in Figure 2.53, are the same ones contained in the M68HC11 instruction set.

Bit Manipulation Instructions		
Mnemonic	**Function**	**Operation**
BSET	Set bit(s) within a memory byte	(M) | mask → (M)
BCLR	Clear bit(s) within a memory byte	(M) & ~mask → (M)
BRSET	Branch if bit(s) within a memory byte are set	Branch iff ~(M) & mask == 0
BRCLR	Branch if bit(s) within a memory byte are clear	Branch iff (M) & mask == 0

Figure 2.53: Bit manipulation instructions

While the CPU12 does not add any additional bit manipulation instructions, it does allow the use of the extended addressing mode with each of the four instructions. This addition was an answer to a valid criticism of the M68HC11's bit manipulation instructions. Since the instructions only support the use of direct and indexed addressing modes, many M68HC11 programmers were forced to make difficult program design decisions.

To generate efficient object code, many M68HC11, programmers locate the on-chip RAM beginning at $0000 to allow a program to access its global variables using direct addressing. This choice not only allows efficient manipulation of 8-bit and 16-bit variables, but also allows efficient manipulation of bit or boolean variables using the bit manipulation instructions. However, placing the on-chip RAM on page zero precludes placing the I/O registers on page zero unless the programmer is willing to give up some of the precious on-chip RAM. In many cases, the I/O registers are left at their default address of $1000. To effectively utilize the bit manipulation instructions on the M68HC11's I/O registers, some programmers would dedicate the Y index register to point to the base of the I/O register block. In other cases, programmers load the M68HC11's X index register with the address of an I/O register just prior to executing a bit manipulation instruction. Obviously, neither of these techniques is very efficient and ties up the use of one of the CPU's index registers.

Important Information

The CPU12's ability to utilize the extended addressing mode for the bit manipulation instructions helps to increase the efficiency of programs that manipulate boolean variables and control bits in the I/O registers. In addition, the improvement to the indexed addressing modes has improved the flexibility and efficiency of these instructions. The use of the indexed addressing with the bit manipulation instructions, however, is restricted to the 5-bit, 9-bit, 16-bit, and accumulator offset modes. They may not use either of the indexed indirect addressing modes.

Section 2.16: Jump and Subroutine Instructions

To improve the efficiency of programs that manipulate and test boolean variables, it is a good idea to group related bits within the same byte when they are likely to be tested, set or cleared at the same time. This allows the programmer to use a single bit manipulation instruction to operate on multiple bits simultaneously.

Even though the `BSET` and `BCLR` instructions appear in this section, technically they can be grouped with the read/modify/write instructions. This is because they read an operand from memory, modify the selected bit(s) and write the result back to memory. Some care is required when using these instructions to manipulate control or status bits in one of the on-chip peripheral's registers. For example, each of the eight bits in the timer's `TFLG1` register is used to indicate an interrupt condition has occurred on one of the eight timer channels. To clear the interrupt, a one is written to the bit position corresponding to the timer channel causing the interrupt. A programmer's first thought might be to use the `BSET` instruction to write a one to the bit position corresponding to the interrupting timer channel. Unfortunately, this operation can have an unintended side effect if more than one of the interrupt flags is set. Because the `BSET` instruction performs a logical OR operation between the data read from the control register and the supplied bit mask, any bits that were set when the status register was read will be written back as ones, inadvertently clearing those flags as well as the intended interrupt flag. Specific techniques for clearing bits in the timer interrupt flag registers are discussed in Chapter 11.

⚠ **CPU12 Difference from the M68HC11**

2.16 JUMP AND SUBROUTINE INSTRUCTIONS

The `JMP` instruction causes an immediate change of program flow similar to the `BRA` and `LBRA` instructions. The destination of the `JMP` instruction can be specified using extended addressing or the various forms of indexed addressing. When using extended addressing the effective address is specified as an absolute 16-bit value following the single byte opcode. When using the indexed addressing modes, the destination of the jump follows the rules for effective address calculation determined by the various forms of indexed addressing. In either case, unlike the `BRA` and `LBRA` instructions, the destination of the jump is an absolute address with one exception. When the `JMP` instruction is combined with program counter relative, or `pcr`, indexed addressing it behaves in a manner identical to the `BRA` and `LBRA` instructions. In fact, combining the 9-bit constant offset, `pcr` indexed addressing with the JMP instruction gives the programmer a three byte relative branch always instruction with a range double that of the standard `BRA` instruction. Figure 2.54 shows the three combinations of `pcr` indexed addressing that can be combined with the JMP instruction to perform a relative branch operation and compares them with the closest equivalent of the relative branch instructions.

Chapter 2: The CPU12 Instruction Set

Jump Instructions			Branch Instructions		
Source	Bytes/Cycles	Range	Source	Bytes/Cycles	Range
JMP Label,pcr	2/3	-16..+15	BRA Label	2/3	-128..+127
JMP Label,pcr	3/3	-256..+255	———	———	———
JMP Label,pcr	4/4	-32768..+32767	LBRA Label	4/4	-32768..+32767

Figure 2.54: Comparing JMP using pcr indexed addressing with BRA

There is one caution that programmers should be aware of when substituting a JMP instruction utilizing pcr indexed addressing for a BRA instruction. When the label appearing in the operand field of the JMP instruction is forward referenced, many assemblers will choose the longest form of the JMP instruction because the assembler does not initially know how large an offset is required. This could result in a four byte, four cycle instruction being used where a two byte, three cycle BRA instruction would have worked. Some assemblers, however, have the ability to optimize the size of instructions containing forward references and will use the smallest instruction size possible.

Subroutines form the bulk of most computer programs. Having an efficient method for calling and returning from subroutines is essential for any CPU instruction set. The CPU12 supports all of the subroutine related instructions contained in the M68HC11 instruction set plus two new instructions that support an efficient method for calling subroutines located in expanded memory. As shown in Figure 2.55, the CPU12 contains the 8-bit offset BSR instruction, but does not contain a corresponding 16-bit offset LBSR instruction. This instruction was purposely omitted because the JSR instruction combined with pcr indexed addressing will accomplish the same function.

Section 2.16: Jump and Subroutine Instructions

Jump and Subroutine Instructions		
Mnemonic	**Function**	**Operation**
BSR	Branch to subroutine	SP - 2 → SP RTN_H → (SP); RTN_L → (SP+1) Subroutine Address → PC
JSR	Jump to subroutine	SP - 2 → SP RTN_H → (SP); RTN_L → (SP+1) Subroutine Address → PC
JMP	Jump to address	Address → PC
CALL	Jump to subroutine in expanded memory	SP - 2 → SP RTN_H → (SP); RTN_L → (SP+1) SP - 1 → SP PPAGE → (SP) Page# → PPAGE Subroutine Address → PC
RTS	Return from subroutine	(SP) → PC_H; (SP+1) → PC_L SP + 2 → SP
RTC	Return from subroutine in expanded memory	(SP) → PPAGE SP + 1 → SP (SP) → PC_H; (SP+1) → PC_L SP + 2 → SP

Figure 2.55: Jump and subroutine instructions

As embedded applications have become more complex over the years, their control programs have in many cases outstripped the 64k-byte address space available to 8-bit microcontrollers. Memory expansion in the M68HC12 family is supported through a simple bank switching scheme combining an 8-bit 'page' value with a 16-bit physical address to select one of 256 16k-byte memory pages. A special register, called the PPAGE register, located in the M68HC12's I/O register block, is used to hold the 8-bit page value.

Using this approach, each subroutine located in paged memory requires both a 16-bit physical address and an 8-bit page number to specify its full logical address. The CALL instruction supplies both a 16-bit physical address and an 8-bit 'page' value used to select one of 256 banked memory pages. When the CALL instruction is executed, it saves both the the 16-bit return address and the old value of the PPAGE register on the stack before writing the new page number to PPAGE. Stacking the value of the PPAGE register as part of the return address allows CALLs to be made from one bank to another while allowing the subroutine to return to the proper page number when an RTC is executed. All subroutines

Chapter 2: The CPU12 Instruction Set

executed using the `CALL` instruction must be terminated with an `RTC` instruction even if the subroutine is called from within the same bank. All subroutines called using the `JSR` or `BSR` instruction must be terminated with the `RTS` instruction and cannot be executed using the `CALL` instruction.

While the memory expansion supported by the `PPAGE` register and the `CALL/RTC` instructions is intended to support expanded program memory space, it does not preclude the use of the memory expansion pages for constant data or lookup tables. The most effective method to access large data tables residing in paged program memory is to place the table and a small data access subroutine on the same page. When the subroutine is called, the data table will be directly accessible to the subroutine. Performing a table lookup in this manner is adequate if the data can be returned in the CPU12's registers or copied from the lookup table into RAM.

If the combined size of a data table and the associated lookup and/or calculation routines will not fit into a single 16k-byte page, it will probably be necessary to access the data table by directly manipulating the value of the `PPAGE` register. Because the `PPAGE` register is located in the M68HC12's I/O register block, it can be written with a new value under program control. However, care must be taken when using the program expansion memory in this manner. The program code manipulating the value of the `PPAGE` register must reside in unpaged memory to prevent program run-away. In addition, the old value of the `PPAGE` register must be saved on the stack and restored after the data table is accessed. This allows the data access subroutine, located in unpaged memory, to be called from code residing in paged memory.

⚠️ **CPU12 Difference from the M68HC11**

2.17 CONDITION CODE REGISTER INSTRUCTIONS

The M68HC11 has six instructions to set or clear the C, I, or V bits in the condition code register. While these single byte instructions provided an efficient means for manipulating these three bits, setting or clearing other bits in the condition code register was an awkward process. To set or clear the S, X, H, or Z bit, the contents of the condition code register had to be transferred to the A accumulator. Next, the specified bits had to be set or cleared using a logical AND or OR instruction. Finally, the contents of the A accumulator would have to be transferred back into the condition code register. As shown in Figure 2.56 the CPU12 replaces these six instructions with two general purpose instructions allowing multiple bits in the condition code register to be set or cleared with a single instruction. The instructions perform a bitwise logical AND or OR with the value of the condition code register and an 8-bit immediate mask and write the result back to the condition code register. In addition to the obvious benefit of being able to manipulate the S, X, and N bits with a single instruction,

Section 2.18: Loop Primitive Instructions

implementing the condition code manipulation instructions only required two opcode positions. This allowed four new instructions to be placed on page one of the opcode map where instructions execute one clock cycle faster and use one less byte of memory than page two opcodes.

CPU12 Condition Code Register Instructions		
Mnemonic	**Function**	**Operation**
ANDCC	Logical AND CCR with mask	CCR & mask $\rightarrow$ CCR
ORCC	Logical OR CCR with mask	CCR | mask $\rightarrow$ CCR

Figure 2.56: CPU12 Condition Code Register Instructions

Certainly, these two new instructions require two bytes to manipulate the C, I, or V bits rather than the one byte instructions required by the M68HC11. However, because these instructions appear infrequently in most programs, the added object code byte is usually offset through the savings provided by the additional instructions residing on page one of the opcode map. As shown in Figure 2.57, the original M68HC11 instruction mnemonics are still accepted by M68HC12 assemblers and are simply translated into ANDCC or ORCC with the proper bit mask.

M68HC11 Condition Code Instruction Mnemonics			
Mnemonic	**Function**	**CPU12 Instruction**	**Operation**
CLC	Clear the carry (C) bit	ANDCC #$FE	CCR & $FE $\rightarrow$ CCR
CLI	Clear the interrupt mask (I) bit	ANDCC #$EF	CCR & $EF $\rightarrow$ CCR
CLV	Clear the overflow (V) bit	ANDCC #$FD	CCR & $FD $\rightarrow$ CCR
SEC	Set the carry (C) bit	ORCC #$01	CCR | $01 $\rightarrow$ CCR
SEI	Set the interrupt mask (I) bit	ORCC #$10	CCR | $10 $\rightarrow$ CCR
SEV	Set the overflow (V) bit	ORCC #$02	CCR | $02 $\rightarrow$ CCR

Figure 2.57: M68HC11 Condition Code Register Instructions

⚠ **CPU12 Difference from the M68HC11**

2.18 Loop Primitive Instructions

The loop primitive instructions combine a decrement, increment, or test operation followed by a branch on equal or not equal condition. Combining these two operations into a single

Chapter 2: The CPU12 Instruction Set

instruction, results in reduced execution time and in some cases results in smaller object code. A third advantage the loop primitive instructions have over a two instruction sequence is an extended branch range. The loop primitive instructions share the execution logic that is used to perform the signed 9-bit offset indexed addressing calculations to give them a branch range of +511 through -512 bytes from the first byte of the next instruction. Additionally, the decrement, increment, and test operations of the loop primitives do not affect the condition code register as an equivalent two instruction sequence would.

Unlike other instructions, all of the loop primitive instructions share the common opcode of $04. Each instruction's action is defined by a postbyte following the opcode. The anatomy of the postbyte is shown in Figure 2.58. The lower three bits of the postbyte define the CPU register used as the counter or test register. Note that two of the bit combinations do not produce valid postbyte encodings. Invalid postbyte encodings also occur if the two bits used to define the loop primitive operation are both ones. Normally, assemblers will not allow instructions to be generated using these bit patterns. However, because the possibility exists for loop primitive instructions with invalid postbytes to be executed during program run away, the CPU12 designers actually decode these combinations to perform innocuous operations.

Postbyte Code	Source Code Syntax	Comments
oobsxrrr	reg,Offset	b = 0, Branch if equal b = 1, Branch if not equal x = don't care s = 0, branch offset positive s = 1, branch offset negative rrr = <u>Count Register</u> oo = <u>Operation</u> 000 - A 00 - Decrement 001 - B 01 - Test 010 - invalid 10 - Increment 011 - invalid 11 - invalid 100 - D 101 - X 110 - Y 111 - SP

Figure 2.58: Loop Primitive Postbyte Encoding

The use of the stack pointer as a counter register has little value for most applications since it is used automatically by the CPU12 to stack subroutine return addresses and to save the CPU12's register contents during interrupt processing. Using the stack pointer in this manner with interrupts enabled is likely to cause complete system software failure. One

Section 2.18: Loop Primitive Instructions

limitation of the loop primitive instructions is their inability to utilize a memory location as a counter. While this may pose a limitation in some instances, it does not negate their usefulness in many applications. When the loop primitives are combined with other CPU12 instructions and addressing modes, such as the the memory-to-memory moves, they contribute to the efficient implementation of many program constructs. Figure 2.59, shows the six loop primitives.

\multicolumn{3}{c}{Loop Primative Instructions}		
Mnemonic	**Function**	**Operation**
DBEQ	counter = counter - 1 Branch if counter == 0	counter - 1 → counter if counter == 0 then branch else execute the next instruction
DBNE	counter = counter - 1 Branch if counter != 0	counter - 1 → counter if counter != 0 then branch else execute the next instruction
IBEQ	counter = counter + 1 Branch if counter == 0	counter + 1 → counter if counter == 0 then branch else execute the next instruction
IBNE	counter = counter + 1 Branch if counter != 0	counter + 1 → counter if counter != 0 then branch else execute the next instruction
TBEQ	Branch if counter == 0	if counter == 0 then branch else execute the next instruction
TBNE	Branch if counter != 0	if counter != 0 then branch else execute the next instruction

Figure 2.59: Loop Primitive Instructions

Figure 2.60 shows the use of the DBNE instruction in a short subroutine that receives 8-bit characters from the on-chip Serial Communications Interface (SCI) and places them in a buffer. When the subroutine is entered, the byte count is in the D accumulator and the X index register contains the address of the first byte of the buffer.

```
RcvLoop:    brclr   SC0SR1,#RDRF,*  ; Wait here till char available.
            movb    SC0DRL,1,x+     ; move character into buffer.
            dbne    D,RcvLoop       ; dec byte count, rvc till done.
            rts                     ; return
```

Figure 2.60: Loop Primitive Example

The BRCLR instruction is used to continually test the Receive Data Register Full (RDRF) bit in the SCI's SC0SR1 status register. The asterisk at the end of the BRCLR operand field is an indication to the assembler to use the address of the first byte of the instruction as the branch destination. As long as the RDRF bit is clear, the BRCLR instruction will continue to execute. When the RDRF bit becomes set, indicating that the SCI has received a data byte, execution continues with the MOVB instruction. Using extended addressing for the source and post increment indexed addressing for the destination addressing mode, the MOVB instruction moves the received data byte directly from the SCI data register into the buffer and advances the buffer pointer. Next DBNE decrements the byte counter in D and loops back to the BRCLR instruction if the counter is not zero.

In this particular example with the 16-bit byte count in D, the MOVB instruction combined with DBNE provides an efficient method of receiving a fixed number of bytes and placing them in a memory buffer. Of course, if the Y index register were available for use as the 16-bit counter register, the MOVB instruction could easily be replaced by load and store instructions using the A or B accumulator.

2.19 INTERRUPT RELATED INSTRUCTIONS

Interrupt inputs to the CPU12 allow it to respond quickly to external asynchronous events. They provide a way to temporarily suspend normal program execution so the CPU12 can execute a special routine called an interrupt service routine. Interrupt service routines are very similar to subroutines except that they are called through the CPU12's automatic hardware interrupt mechanism rather than through the use of the JSR or BSR instruction. Because the hardware interrupt mechanism saves the entire CPU register set on the stack, including a return address, interrupt service routines must be terminated with the return from interrupt or RTI instruction. The RTI instruction restores the contents of each CPU12 register and resumes normal program execution at the point where program execution was interrupted.

In addition to the CPU12's hardware interrupt mechanism, there are two instructions that produce a CPU response identical to a hardware interrupt. Execution of the software interrupt (SWI) instruction causes an interrupt without a hardware interrupt service request. Execution of SWI is not inhibited regardless of the state of the I or X bits in the condition code register. Once the SWI instruction is fetched and begins to execute, I-bit maskable interrupts are inhibited until the I-bit in the condition code register is cleared. This may occur when the RTI instruction is executed at the end of the software interrupt service routine, but only if the I-bit was cleared before the SWI instruction was executed. After an SWI interrupt service routine begins execution, it may be interrupted by an XIRQ interrupt if the condition code register X-bit is cleared.

While not used by most programmers, the SWI instruction is commonly used by ROM resident debug programs, such as D-Bug12 for the M68HC12 microcontroller family. D-Bug12 uses the SWI instruction to implement software breakpoints and for executing a single instruction of an application program. When a breakpoint is set using D-Bug12's breakpoint command, the entered address is placed in a breakpoint table. Just before

Section 2.19: Interrupt Related Instructions

execution is transferred from D-Bug12 to the application code by entering the 'go' command, the opcodes at the breakpoint addresses are replaced with the SWI opcode ($3F). When the application code executes the SWI instruction, the entire CPU state is saved on the stack and control is transferred back to D-Bug12. Before returning to the command line prompt, D-Bug12 removes the stacked registers and restores the original opcodes at the breakpoint addresses.

⚠ CPU12 Difference from the M68HC11

The CPU in the M68HC11 family detects the execution of unimplemented or illegal opcodes and produces an interrupt service request similar to when an SWI instruction is executed. In a related manner, the CPU12 detects the execution of unimplemented opcodes and produces a similar response. While the M68HC11 has unimplemented opcodes scattered across all four of its opcode pages, all 202 of the CPU12's unimplemented opcodes are contained on the second opcode page. In addition, the CPU12 defines an instruction mnemonic, TRAP, to represent these unimplemented opcodes. The TRAP instructions consist of the page two opcode prebyte, $18, followed by one of the unused opcodes, $30 through $39 and $40 through $FF, on page two. All 202 unimplemented opcodes share a single interrupt vector at $FFF8 and $FFF9.

As with other interrupts, the CPU's register contents, including a return address, are saved on the stack before beginning the TRAP interrupt service routine. However, because the M68HC11's unimplemented opcodes could consist of either one or two bytes, the stacked return address points to the first byte of the unimplemented opcode. This is the only way that software can determine if the M68HC11 unimplemented opcode is one or two bytes in length. Because all the CPU12's unimplemented opcodes are two bytes in length, the stacked return address is the address of the byte following the unimplemented opcode. This means that an interrupt handler would have to subtract one from the value of the stacked return address to determine the unimplemented opcode causing the interrupt exception.

The unimplemented opcode mechanism may be seen by some programmers simply as a means by which a system can recover from run away software conditions. However, it can be used as a way to request services from an operating system or to implement 'custom' instructions while saving the current CPU state on the stack. Figure 2.61 shows how a simple unimplemented opcode dispatch routine might be accomplished. First the return address is retrieved from the stack and is used to obtain the second byte of the TRAP instruction. A range check is then performed on the value to ensure that a valid trap service has been requested. The value is then used to develop an index into the trap dispatch table. Because a JMP instruction is used at the end of the dispatch routine, each TRAP service routine must end with an RTI instruction so that it will properly return to the calling task.

As mentioned, the other use of the unimplemented opcode mechanism is to provide a possible method of recovery from a software run away condition. At the very least, the unimplemented opcode vector should contain the same address as the reset vector. This will allow the system to be completely reinitialized if one of the unimplemented opcodes is executed. For many applications this method of recovery will be adequate. Some systems may require a more extensive strategy when recovering from such a situation. However, it must be remembered that the unimplemented opcode interrupt, like all interrupts, places nine bytes of data on the stack. Any error recovery strategy must remove this data from the stack before continuing normal program execution. Failure to eliminate these nine bytes may result in eventual stack overflow and may result in total system failure.

```
TrapDispatch: ldx     7,sp            ; get the return address off the stack.
              ldab    -1,x            ; get the 2nd byte of trap instruction.
              cmpb    #LoTrap         ; valid os trap?
              blo     BadTrap         ; no. go to bad trap handler.
              cmpb    #HiTrap         ; valid os trap?
              bhi     BadTrap         ; no. go to bad trap handler.
              andb    #TrapMask       ; yes. mask off unused bits.
              clra                    ; clear upper byte of d.
              lsld                    ; multiply by 2 for each table entry.
              ldx     #SrvcTable      ; point to the service jump table.
              jmp     [d,x]           ; go perform the requested service.
;
SrvcTable:    dw      DispatchTask
              dw      SendMsg
              .
              .
```

Figure 2.61: Simple TRAP Dispatch Routine

The last interrupt related instruction is the wait for interrupt (WAI) instruction. The WAI instruction is used to place the M68HC12 microcontroller into a low power state that disables clocks to the CPU12 module. All other M68HC12 modules continue to receive the system clock signals as normal. When the WAI instruction is executed, it pre-stacks the entire CPU12 register set including a return address. The CPU12 remains in the low power wait mode until it receives an unmasked interrupt or a reset. Upon receiving an unmasked interrupt, the CPU12 will set the X-bit and/or I-bit in the CPU condition code register, fetch the proper interrupt vector and continue execution with the appropriate interrupt service routine. If both the X-bit and I-bit in the condition code register are set when the WAI instruction is executed, a system reset is the only way the CPU12 can exit the wait mode.

The WAI instruction is generally used to reduce power consumption in an M68HC12 based system when there are no tasks to perform; however, it can also be used to provide a fast response to an interrupt event. Because the WAI instruction pre-stacks the CPU

Section 2.19: Interrupt Related Instructions

registers before entering the wait mode, it can respond quickly when an interrupt does occur. The CPU12 only needs to fetch the associated interrupt vector, fill the instruction prefetch queue, and begin executing the interrupt service routine. These actions require only five CPU clock cycles versus a minimum of 10 clock cycles if the CPU were executing program code when the interrupt occurred.

Figure 2.62 summarizes the CPU12's interrupt related instructions. Notice that the `SWI`, `TRAP` and `WAI` instructions place the X and Y index registers and the return address on the stack with the high-byte of the 16-bit word at the lower address. Placing multi-byte quantities on the interrupt stack frame in this manner is consistent with the way store instructions place 16-bit quantities in memory. However, the A and B accumulators are placed on the stack in reverse order than expected if the D accumulator were pushed onto the stack or stored in memory. This apparent inconsistency is a carry over from the original design of the M6800 microprocessor because the original M6800 designers did not envision the A and B accumulators being used as a single 16-bit register. It may seem that this "problem" could have been fixed in the M6801 or M68HC11. However, in a desire to maintain complete compatibility with existing software that may have accessed these values from an interrupt service routine, the stacking order of A and B has not been changed.

If the stacked value of the D accumulator needs to be accessed within an interrupt service routine, the programmer must remember that the high and low bytes are in reverse order from what would normally be expected. The easiest way to correct the byte reversal is to load the D accumulator and then exchange the A and B accumulators.

\multicolumn{3}{c}{Interrupt Related Instructions}		
Mnemonic	Function	Operation
RTI	Return from Interrupt	(SP) → CCR; SP + 1 → SP (SP) : (SP+1) → B:A; SP + 2 → SP (SP) : (SP+1) → X; SP + 2 → SP (SP) : (SP+1) → Y; SP + 2 → SP (SP) : (SP+1) → PC; SP + 2 → SP
SWI	Software Interrupt	SP - 2 → SP; RTN_H:RTN_L → (SP) : (SP+1) SP - 2 → SP; Y → (SP) : (SP+1) SP - 2 → SP; X → (SP) : (SP+1) SP - 2 → SP; B:A → (SP) : (SP+1) SP - 1 → SP; CCR → (SP)
TRAP	Unimplemented Opcode Trap	SP - 2 → SP; RTN_H:RTN_L → (SP) : (SP+1) SP - 2 → SP; Y → (SP) : (SP+1) SP - 2 → SP; X → (SP) : (SP+1) SP - 2 → SP; B:A → (SP) : (SP+1) SP - 1 → SP; CCR → (SP)
WAI	Wait For Interrupt	SP - 2 → SP; RTN_H:RTN_L → (SP) : (SP+1) SP - 2 → SP; Y → (SP) : (SP+1) SP - 2 → SP; X → (SP) : (SP+1) SP - 2 → SP; B:A → (SP) : (SP+1) SP - 1 → SP; CCR → (SP)

Figure 2.62: CPU12 Interrupt Related Instructions

> ⚠ **CPU12 Difference from the M68HC11**

2.20 MINIMUM AND MAXIMUM INSTRUCTIONS

The minimum and maximum instructions compare two 8-bit or 16-bit unsigned values and place the larger or smaller in the A or D accumulator or memory. Immediate, extended and direct addressing may not be used with these instructions. However, all of the indexed addressing modes may be used to specify the value in memory that is to be compared to the accumulator. While these are special purpose instructions, they can be used for the fuzzy logic fuzzification process and limit checking of values.

Figure 2.63 and 2.64 shows the CPU12 and M68HC11 code required to perform an upper and lower limit check on an 8-bit value. If the supplied 8-bit value exceeds the upper or lower limit set points, the upper or lower limit value is placed in the A accumulator. In both cases, the X index register points to two one byte constants residing in memory. The first byte contains the value of the lower limit and the second byte contains the upper limit. The CPU12 implementation requires just 11 bytes and executes in just 13 clock cycles. The M68HC11 implementation requires 19 bytes and takes a maximum of 24 clock cycles to execute when the input value exceeds the maximum limit. Even if the M68HC11 code were reassembled and executed on the CPU12 the code would require 18 clocks. In applications that must perform numerous limit checks on input or calculated values, the minimum and maximum instructions can save considerable code space and processing time.

```
LimitChk:   ldx     #LoHiLimit  ; Point to the low and high limit values.
            ldaa    InVal       ; get the input value to check.
            mina    0,x         ; place minimum value in a.
            maxa    1,x         ; place maximum value in a.
                    .
                    .
;
LoHiLimit:  db      LoLimit     ; low limit value.
            db      HiLimit     ; high limit value.
;
```

Figure 2.63: CPU12 Limit Check Routine

Section 2.20: Minimum and Maximum Instructions

```
LimitChk:    ldx     #LoHiLimit   ; Point to the low and high limit values.
             ldaa    InVal        ; get the input value to check.
             cmpa    0,x          ; compare value in a to minimum value.
             bhs     CheckHi      ; if larger or same, check against max.
             ldaa    0,x          ; replace value with the lower limit.
             bra     Done         ; branch around maximum check.
CheckHi:     cmpa    1,x          ; compare value in a to maximum value.
             bls     Done         ; value within range.
             ldaa    1,x          ; replace value with upper limit.
Done:        .
             .
;
LoHiLimit:   db      LoLimit      ; low limit value.
             db      HiLimit      ; high limit value.
;
```

Figure 2.64: M68HC11 Limit Check Routine

Figure 2.65 shows all eight of the minimum and maximum instructions. The mnemonics that begin with an 'E' perform the comparison and update between the D accumulator and memory. The last letter of the instruction mnemonic, 'A', 'D', or 'M', specifies the destination of the update. The N, Z, V, and C bits in the condition code register are updated as a result of the comparison rather than the optional store operation. This allows other possible program actions based on the results of the comparison. When the carry bit is clear after the execution of the MINA and EMIND instructions, it indicates that the value in the A or D accumulator has been replaced by the value in memory. If the carry bit is set after the execution of the MINM and EMINM instructions, it indicates that the value in memory has been replaced by the value in the A or D accumulator. Just the opposite is true for the maximum instructions. When the carry bit is set after the execution of the MAXA and EMAXD instructions, it indicates that the value in the A or D accumulator has been replaced by the value in memory. If the carry bit is clear after the execution of the MAXM and EMAXM instructions, it indicates that the value in memory has been replaced by the value in the A or D accumulator.

Chapter 2: The CPU12 Instruction Set

Minimum and Maximum Instructions		
Mnemonic	**Function**	**Operation**
MINA	Min of two unsigned 8-bit values Result to A accumulator	min(A, (M)) → A
MINM	Min of two unsigned 8-bit values Result to Memory	min(A, (M)) → (M)
EMIND	Min of two unsigned 16-bit values Result to D accumulator	min(D, (M:M+1)) → D
EMINM	Min of two unsigned 16-bit values Result to Memory	min(D, (M:M+1)) → (M:M+1)
MAXA	Max of two unsigned 8-bit values Result to A accumulator	max(A, (M)) → A
MAXM	Max of two unsigned 8-bit values Result to Memory	max(A, (M)) → (M)
EMAXD	Max of two unsigned 16-bit values Result to D accumulator	max(D, (M:M+1)) → D
EMAXM	Max of two unsigned 16-bit values Result to Memory	max(D, (M:M+1)) → (M:M+1)

Figure 2.65: Minimum and Maximum Instructions

⚠ **CPU12 Difference from the M68HC11**

2.21 TABLE LOOKUP AND INTERPOLATE INSTRUCTIONS

Many embedded control applications use complex control algorithms that cannot be represented by simple linear equations. Because most microcontrollers do not have sophisticated floating point hardware units capable of calculating non-linear functions, many applications use lookup tables to approximate these complex transfer functions. When using lookup tables, the software designer must make a trade off between the number of entries in the table and its accuracy. Generally, the greater the required accuracy, the larger table will be. To reduce the size of lookup tables representing complex functions, the curve representing the transfer function can be broken up into linear segments that are spaced equidistant along the x-axis with the table holding only the y-values corresponding to each x point. With this type of table and a software routine, it is possible to perform linear interpolation between two adjacent table entries to obtain results with an accuracy that would otherwise require a much larger lookup table.

The CPU12 designers added two instructions to perform this function since a routine to perform the linear interpolation is fairly large and executes slowly. The TBL and ETBL

Section 2.21: Table Lookup and Interpolate Instructions

instructions require only three bytes each and perform the table lookup and linear interpolation in eight and 10 clock cycles respectively. Both the table entries and the interpolated results for the TBL instruction are 8-bits, while the table entries and the interpolated results for the ETBL instruction are 16-bits. Because both instructions interpolate one of 256 result values falling between each pair of table entries, an effective table compression ratio of 256:1 is achieved.

Before executing the TBL or ETBL instruction, one of the index registers must be loaded with a value that points to the entry in a table that represents the starting point of one of the line segments represented in the table. This point is the table entry closest to, but less than or equal to the desired lookup value. In addition, the B accumulator must be loaded with an 8-bit binary fraction representing the distance between the two table entries over which the interpolation is to be performed. Both table lookup instructions use indexed addressing to identify the starting point of interest and thus provids a great deal of flexibility when construction tables. The most common method of constructing tables is to break the table into a maximum of 256 equally spaced segments and store the y values for each of the resulting endpoints. The D accumulator can then be used as input to the table. The A accumulator would hold the offset into the table containing the starting point of the line segment of interest. The B accumulator would contain the binary fraction that represented the interpolation distance between the starting point in the table and the next table entry.

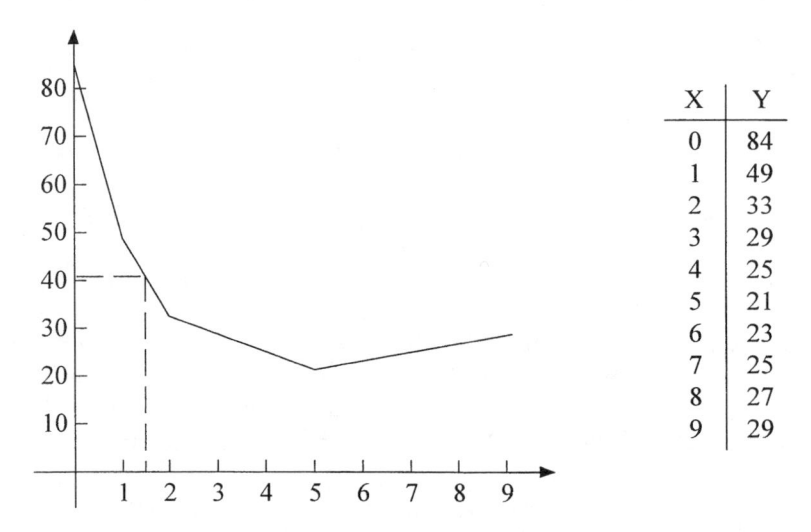

X	Y
0	84
1	49
2	33
3	29
4	25
5	21
6	23
7	25
8	27
9	29

Figure 2.66: TBL Example

Figure 2.66 shows a graph of a transfer function along with a table containing the x and y coordinate pairs describing the function. Using this data, suppose that a program needs to find the corresponding y value for an x value that is midway between the second (x = 1) and third (x = 2) table entries. In this case the X index register points to the start of the table, the

A accumulator would contain the the value of $01, and the B accumulator would contain $80, a binary fraction representing the value of 0.5 (Binary fractions are discussed in Chapter 1). Executing the TBL instruction using A accumulator offset indexed addressing with these register values would cause the CPU12 to compute a y value of 41 ($29) which corresponds to an x value of 1.5. Examining the graph in Figure 2.66 it can be seen that an x value of 1.5 does indeed correspond to a y value of 41. Figure 2.67 shows the CPU12 instruction sequence necessary to execute this simple example.

```
            ldd     #$0180          ; a = table entry, b = binary fraction.
            ldx     #Table          ; Point to the transfer function table.
            tbl     a,x             ; lookup & interpolate y value for x = 1.5.
              .
              .
;
Table:      db      84,49,33,29,25; Table entries 1 - 5.
            db      21,23,25,27,29; Table entries 6 - 10.
;
```

Figure 2.67: TBL Code Example

After executing the TBL instruction, the interpolated y value replaces the table offset contained in the A accumulator. In an actual application it is likely the value in the A and B accumulators would have been calculated by another part of the program. In this particular example, the y values for the transfer function were small enough to fit within a single byte. However, if any of the y values fell outside the range of 0..255, all the lookup table entries would have to be 16-bits and require the use of the ETBL instruction. The input parameters for the ETBL instruction are the same as for the TBL instruction, but the output is 16-bits and is placed in the D accumulator. One of the index registers must point to the table entry closest to, but less than or equal to the desired lookup value and the B accumulator must be loaded with the 8-bit binary fraction. Remember, however, that because each table entry is 16-bits, the index register must point to the high byte of the 16-bit table entry. This means that if a program calculates a *table entry* number, that value must be multiplied by two before being added to the table's base address. Utilizing the A accumulator offset indexed addressing as shown in the example would not work unless the table had fewer than 127 entries. Both the TBL and ETBL instructions are restricted to using indexed addressing modes that will fit within a single postbyte. This includes 5-bit offset, pre/post auto increment and decrement and accumulator offset modes but *does not* include the D accumulator offset indirect mode.

As shown in the example, when constructing line segment approximations of complex transfer functions it is not necessary for the slope of the line segment to change at each table

Section 2.22: Fuzzy Logic Instructions

entry. However, to maintain the best accuracy when performing the lookup and interpolation, line segment slope changes should occur only at table entry points.

Figure 2.68 contains a summary of the table lookup and interpolate instructions.

Table Lookup and Interpolate Instructions		
Mnemonic	Function	Operation
TBL	8-bit Table Lookup and Interpolate (no indexed indirect addressing)	$(M) + (B \times ((M+1) - (M))) \rightarrow A$ initialize B and index register before TBL indexed <ea> points to first 8-bit table entry B contains fractional table input value
ETBL	16-bit Table Lookup and Interpolate (no indexed indirect addressing)	$(M:M+1) + (B \times ((M+2:M+3) - (M:M+1))) \rightarrow D$ initialize B and index register before TBL indexed <ea> points to first 16-bit table entry B contains fractional table input value

Figure 2.68: TBL and ETBL Instruction Summary

⚠ **CPU12 Difference from the M68HC11**

2.22 FUZZY LOGIC INSTRUCTIONS

The CPU12 contains four instructions that specifically address the tasks required to efficiently implement a fuzzy logic inference kernel. Three of the four instructions are specific to the field of fuzzy logic, however, one of the instructions has other uses. Using these instructions allows a fuzzy logic inference kernel to be implemented in one-fifth the code space and execute fifteen times faster than a comparable kernel implemented on a midrange microcontroller such as the M68HC11. The additional logic required to implement the fuzzy logic instructions on the CPU12 is quite small compared to its total size, so there is no appreciable cost penalty for those not intending to use this feature.

This section is designed only to provide a basic description of the CPU12's fuzzy logic instructions. It is not meant to provide a tutorial on the theory and application of fuzzy logic using the M68HC12 family. Motorola's CPU12 Reference Manual (CPU12RM/AD) contains a chapter that explains the basic concepts of fuzzy logic along with a detailed explanation of the CPU12's fuzzy logic instructions. In addition there are numerous text books dedicated to the explanation of fuzzy set theory and the use of fuzzy logic in embedded applications.

Chapter 2: The CPU12 Instruction Set

A control system based on fuzzy logic uses three basic steps to perform its function. These steps are known as fuzzification, rule evaluation, and defuzzification, and are supported by the MEM, REV/REVW and WAV instructions respectively. The program code implementing these steps makes up the fuzzy inference kernel. To perform its control operation, the kernel processes a list of linguistic rules from a knowledge base provided by a human expert. Membership functions, also included in the knowledge base, define the meaning of labels used in the rules, in such a way as to provide a gradual transition from one state to another. This allows for different degrees of truth or membership based on system inputs.

The MEM instruction is used for the fuzzification step where the system inputs such as light, speed, or temperature, are compared against the rule base's membership functions to determine the degree of truth for each input. The MEM instruction performs this action by determining the y value that corresponds to the input value on a trapezoidal membership function. Figure 2.69 shows an example of a single trapezoidal membership function. The x axis represents the value of the current input and the y axis represents the degree of truth and varies from completely false ($00 or 0%) to completely true ($FF or 100%). The y value where each input (x value) intersects the trapezoidal membership function is the degree to which an input is true for a membership function.

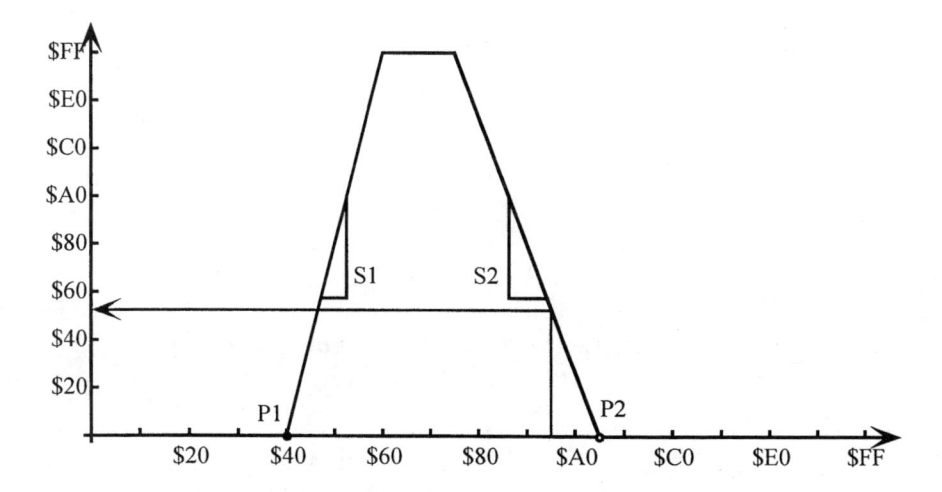

Figure 2.69: Single Trapezoidal Membership Function

The trapezoidal membership function is described by a four byte data structure that normally resides in nonvolatile memory. The first two bytes of the data structure contain the values for point P1 and point P2 respectively. The third and fourth bytes contain values that describe the slope of the leading (S1) and trailing (S2) edge of the membership trapezoid respectively. Normally, line slopes of less than one are not used, however, the MEM instruction reserves the slope value of $00 to indicate a membership function that begins or

Section 2.22: Fuzzy Logic Instructions

ends with a grade of $FF, signifying an infinite slope. A slope of $00 is used most often for the leading edge of the first membership function who's P1 value is $00 or the trailing edge of the last membership function who's P2 value is $FF. While Figure 2.69 only shows a single membership function, most systems contain from three to seven membership functions, however, there is no restriction on this number.

Before the MEM instruction is executed, the A accumulator must contain the value of a system input variable. The X index register must point to the four byte data structure describing the membership trapezoid, and the Y index register must point to a RAM memory location where the resulting grade of membership will be stored. After the execution of the MEM instruction, the A accumulator will remain unchanged, the value of the X index register will have been incremented by four and the Y index register will have been incremented by one. As long as the membership function data structures appear in sequential memory locations, the registers are properly setup for the execution of the next MEM instruction. Basically, the MEM instruction takes care of all the housekeeping chores required for the fuzzification process except for keeping a count of the number of MEM instructions to be executed. The end result of the fuzzification process is a table of fuzzy inputs that represents the current state of the system.

Once the fuzzification process is complete, the next step is to evaluate the fuzzy inputs using the system's expert rule base. This step, central to the fuzzy logic inference program, processes a list of rules using the fuzzy inputs generated in the fuzzification process. The CPU12 provides two instructions for rule evaluation. The REV instruction evaluates each set of fuzzy rules giving equal importance to each rule. The REVW is similar except that it allows each rule to have a separate weighting factor which determines how much each rule contributes to the fuzzy outputs. The rule base, which is usually constructed by a special fuzzy logic software tool running on a host computer, is stored in memory as a list of addresses to the fuzzy inputs and fuzzy outputs. For the REV instruction, the addresses are actually specified as 8-bit offsets from the Y index register. Because the REVW instruction requires the Y index register to point to the table of rule weights, the table contains complete 16-bit addresses for the fuzzy inputs and outputs. In addition to the address offsets, special reserved values appear in the table that are used to separate fuzzy input from fuzzy outputs and mark the end of the rule list.

The execution time of the REV or REVW instructions is dependent upon the size of the rule base. Because the execution time can be quite long compared to other system activity, both of these instructions are interruptible. Within each instruction, there exists a three clock cycle sequence that is executed for each rule processed. If an interrupt becomes pending, instruction execution will be suspended between the first and second clock cycle of this loop. All of the intermediate values are held within the CPU registers which are stacked in response to the interrupt. Normally, the stacked value of the program counter when responding to an interrupt would be the address of the next instruction. This, however, would not allow the REV or REVW instruction to resume execution when an RTI was executed. Instead, the program counter is decremented by two so that it points to the first byte of the instruction.

Before executing the REV or REVW instructions, the X index register must contain the address of the first byte of the rule list. The Y index register must be loaded with the base address of a table containing the fuzzy inputs and will contain the fuzzy outputs. The A accumulator must contain the value $FF and the V bit in the condition code register must be cleared. In addition, when using the REVW instruction, the C bit in the condition code register must be set to perform the weighted rule evaluation. Finally, all of the fuzzy outputs must be set to $00. When execution is complete, the X index register will point to the address after the address of the $FF byte used to mark the end of the rule table. The Y index register remains unchanged and the A accumulator will hold the truth value for the last rule evaluated.

The final step in the fuzzy inference process is defuzzification. The defuzzification process involves combining the fuzzy outputs generated in the rule evaluation process, into a single system output. The WAV instruction can be used to perform the sum-of-products and sum-of-weights calculations necessary for the weighted average calculation used in the defuzzification process. The values used in the calculation consist of the singleton membership functions from the knowledge base and the fuzzy outputs (weights) assigned to each fuzzy output during the rule evaluation step.

The WAV instruction uses the X index register to point to one source operand list and the Y index register to point to the second source operand list. The B accumulator contains a count of the number of elements in each list used in the calculations. For each pair of data points, a 24-bit sum-of-products and 16-bit sum-of-weights is accumulated in three 16-bit CPU temporary registers TMP1, TMP2, and TMP3. When the count in the B accumulator reaches zero, the 24-bit sum-of-products is transferred to Y:D (concatenation of the Y index register and the D accumulator) and the 16-bit sum-of-weights is transferred to the X index register. Because WAV only calculates the sum-of-products and sum-of-weights for the list elements, an EDIV must be executed immediately after WAV to obtain the weighted average.

Like the REV and REVW instructions, the weighted average's execution time is dependent upon the size of the source operand lists. To provide improved system response time, the WAV instruction is also interruptible. When an interrupt occurs during the execution of the WAV instruction, the three 16-bit CPU temporary registers are pushed onto the stack before interrupt processing begins. Once interrupt processing begins, the remaining CPU12 registers are placed on the stack. Unlike the rule evaluation instructions, however, the program counter is only decremented by one. This causes the return address to point to the second byte of the WAV instruction ($3C). Execution of this page one 'pseudo' opcode causes the CPU12 to restore the three temporary registers from the stack before resuming the execution of the WAV instruction.

Figure 2.70 summarizes the CPU12's fuzzy logic primitive instructions.

Section 2.22: Fuzzy Logic Instructions

<table>
<tr><th colspan="3">Fuzzy Logic Instructions</th></tr>
<tr><th>Mnemonic</th><th>Function</th><th>Operation</th></tr>
<tr>
<td>MEM</td>
<td>Membership Function</td>
<td>

μ (grade) $\rightarrow$ (Y)
$X + 4 \rightarrow X$; $Y + 1 \rightarrow Y$; A unchanged
if $A < P1$ or $A > P2$ then $\mu = 0$
else $\mu = \min((A - P1) \times S1, (P2 - A) \times S2, \$FF)$
where:
A = current crisp input value
X points to P1, P2, S1, S2; a 4 byte data structure describing the trapezoidal membership function
Y points to byte that will contain fuzzified input
</td>
</tr>
<tr>
<td>REV</td>
<td>MIN - MAX Rule Evaluation</td>
<td>

Find smallest rule input (min)
Store to rule outputs unless current fuzzy output is larger (max)
Rules are unweighted

Each rule input is an 8-bit offset from a base address contained in Y
Each rule output is an 8-bit offset from a base address contained in Y
$FE separates rule inputs from rule outputs
$FF terminates the rule list
REV is interruptable
</td>
</tr>
<tr>
<td>REVW</td>
<td>Weighted MIN - MAX Rule Evaluation</td>
<td>

Find smallest rule input (min)
Multiply by an 8-bit rule weighting factor (optional)
Store to rule outputs unless current fuzzy output is larger (max)

Each rule input is an 16-bit address of a fuzzy input value
Each rule output is an 16-bit address of a fuzzy output value
$FFFE separates rule inputs from rule outputs
$FFFF terminates the rule list
REVW is interruptable
</td>
</tr>
<tr>
<td>WAV</td>
<td>Calculates Sum-of-Products and Sum-of Weights for Weighted Average Calculation</td>
<td>

$$\sum_{i=1}^{B} S_i \cdot F_i \rightarrow Y{:}D$$

$$\sum_{i=1}^{B} F_i \rightarrow X$$

WAV is interruptable
</td>
</tr>
</table>

Figure 2.70: Fuzzy Logic Instruction Summary

> ⚠ **CPU12 Difference from the M68HC11**

2.23 MISCELLANEOUS INSTRUCTIONS

The last three instructions remaining to be discussed, NOP, STOP, and BGND, do not fit into any specific category. While the M68HC11 CPU contains both the NOP and STOP instructions, the BGND instruction is unique to the CPU12.

The NOP instruction does nothing other than increment the program counter by one. None of the other CPU registers or condition code register bits are affected. Very often, the NOP instruction is used within a small program loop to produce a programmed delay time. While this is a valid use of the instruction, this technique is sometimes discouraged because of the delay's dependence upon both the instruction execution time and the CPU's clock frequency. Obviously, because of the increased operating frequency of the M68HC12 family and the single clock instruction execution time of the CPU12's NOP instruction, any M68HC11 code using this technique would have to be rewritten before it was usable on the CPU12. The NOP instruction is sometimes used by programmers to effectively disable other instructions while debugging their code. Replacing each byte of an instruction with a NOP, effectively removes the instruction from the program. Caution must be exercised when using this technique, as the NOP's may have a different execution timing than the original instruction. This difference could lead to either the elimination of the problem that existed, or it could actually introduce additional problems.

The actions performed by the STOP instruction are dependent upon the state of the S-bit in the CPU12 condition code register. If the S-bit is set, the STOP instruction is treated as a one byte two cycle NOP. If the S bit is clear, execution of the STOP instruction will place an M68HC12 microcontroller in an extremely low power standby state by disabling the on-chip crystal oscillator. Before entering the stop mode, unlike the M68HC11, the STOP instruction pre-stacks the CPU registers. This allows quick recovery when an unmasked IRQ or XIRQ interrupt is used to recover from stop mode since the only actions required are fetching the interrupt vector and filling the CPU12's instruction pipe.

In addition to using unmasked interrupts to exit the stop mode, a masked XIRQ interrupt or an external reset may be employed. When the X bit in the condition code register is set, XIRQ interrupts are inhibited. However, if the CPU12 is in stop mode, a masked XIRQ interrupt will trigger the stop recovery process. Instead of a normal XIRQ interrupt response, the CPU12 executes a stop recovery process by adjusting the value of the stack pointer to remove the stacked registers and continues execution with the instruction following the STOP instruction. When using an external oscillator, this method allows recovery from stop mode in just two clock cycles.

When exiting the stop mode using one of the interrupt pins, an optional delay of 4096 E-clock cycles is inserted between the time the interrupt pin is asserted and the interrupt vector is fetched. This optional delay, controlled by the `DLY` bit in the `INTCR` register, is used to allow the on-chip oscillator to stabilize before the CPU12 begins to execute the stop mode recovery code. If an application uses an external oscillator that is not turned off when the microcontroller is placed in stop mode, this delay can be disabled by clearing the `DLY` bit. When using an external reset to recover from stop mode, the `DLY` bit is set automatically, enabling the 4096 E-clock delay.

Because the MC68H9C12B32 microcontroller is a completely static design, the contents of all CPU12 registers, peripheral registers and I/O lines remain unchanged while in the STOP mode. If the MC68H9C12B32 is being used in expanded mode, the multilpexed address bus will remain driven with the data of the last data byte pushed onto the stack. The R/W, DBE and LSTRB signals will be driven to a logic one and the E-clock will be driven to a logic zero.

The `BGND` instruction is generally used by debugger programs that work in conjunction with the M68HC12's single wire, non-intrusive background debug module. Background mode debuggers generally use the `BGND` instruction to implement software breakpoints in much the same way that ROM resident debuggers use the SWI instruction. The `BGND` instruction essentially follows the same instruction flow as a software interrupt, except that the CPU registers are not placed on the stack. Instead, the current program counter value is saved in the CPU12's TMP2 register and the BDM ROM and background registers are made active, overlaying any resources in the memory map from $FF00 through $FFFF. A substitute SWI vector contained in the BDM ROM is fetched and execution continues with the routines in the BDM ROM that control the background operation.

Once the CPU12 has entered the active background mode, the remaining CPU registers required by the BDM ROM code are saved either in CPU temporary registers or in the BDM background registers. The saved value of the program counter is incremented to point past the `BGND` instruction so that the instruction following the `BGND` opcode is executed when normal program execution resumes.

While the CPU12 is in active background mode, it receives debugging commands by way of a single wire serial interface. The commands include the ability to examine/change the CPU register values or system memory, execute a single instruction of a users program and resume normal program execution. Returning to normal program execution requires the reception of specific commands via the single wire serial interface. When exiting the active background mode, the CPU12 registers are restored, the BDM ROM and register block are disabled and the instruction queue is refilled beginning at the address contained in the CPU TMP2 register.

Before the active background mode can be entered, a command must be sent to the BDM module via the single wire serial interface to enable this mode. Executing a `BGND` instruction without the background debug mode enabled causes the BDM firmware to increment the program counter value in TMP2 and perform an immediate return to normal processing. Effectively the BGND instruction acts as a NOP requiring 48 clock cycles to complete in the current implementation of the BDM firmware.

Figure 2.71 summarizes the function and operation of the NOP, STOP and BGND instructions.

Miscellaneous Instructions		
Mnemonic	**Function**	**Operation**
NOP	Null Operation	PC + 1 → PC
BGND	Enter Active Background Mode	if BDM enabled, enter active background mode
STOP	Stop microcontroller clocks	SP - 2 → SP; RTN_H:RTN_L → (SP) : (SP+1) SP - 2 → SP; Y → (SP) : (SP+1) SP - 2 → SP; X → (SP) : (SP+1) SP - 2 → SP; B:A → (SP) : (SP+1) SP - 1 → SP; CCR → (SP)

Figure 2.71: Miscellaneous CPU12 Instructions

Questions/Exercises

2.1 How many addressing modes does the CPU12 utilize? Name them.

2.2 How are the addressing modes specified in the CPU12 source syntax.

2.3 How many CPU clock cycles are required for the execution of page 1 instructions utilizing the inherent addressing mode?

2.4 What is the size of the operand (in bytes) utilized by instructions employing the immediate addressing mode?

2.5 What ASCII character is used to indicate the immediate addressing mode? Where is the character placed?

2.6 Generally, what will an assembler do if the ASCII character used to indicate the immediate addressing mode is accidentally omitted in a program statement?

2.7 How much of the CPU12's memory map can be accessed using the extended addressing mode?

2.8 How much of the CPU12's memory map can be accessed using the direct addressing mode?

Section 2.23: Miscellaneous Instructions

2.9 Is the use of extended or direct addressing more desirable? Why?

2.10 What happens if a 16-bit value is stored at the last address accessible with direct addressing?

2.11 Which CPU register is used when computing the effective address for instructions that utilize the relative addressing mode?

2.12 What instruction groups utilize relative addressing?

2.13 What is the allowable range for short and long branch instructions?

2.14 What was one of the major M68HC11 indexed addressing mode problems solved with the CPU12 indexed addressing? How was this problem solved?

2.15 How many variations of the indexed addressing mode does the CPU12 support? Name them.

2.16 Which of the CPU12 registers can be used as index registers?

2.17 Which indexed addressing mode, specifically, allows C compilers to generate more efficient object code?

2.18 Which indexed addressing mode allows programs to be written in a position independent manner.

2.19 What is the major difference between the constant offset indexed addressing used by the CPU12 and the M68HC11's indexed addressing mode?

2.20 How many variations of constant offset indexed addressing does the CPU12 support?

2.21 How many extension bytes are required by instructions that utilize 5-bit constant offset indexed addressing?

2.22 How is each variation of constant offset indexed addressing specified in the assembly language source?

2.23 What is the numeric range that may be used to specify the constant offsets used with indexed addressing?

Chapter 2: The CPU12 Instruction Set

2.24 Which one of the CPU12's accumulators may be used to provide an offset for indexed addressing? Is the supplied value interpreted as a signed or unsigned quantity?

2.25 Which CPU12 indexable registers can be used with the auto increment/decrement indexed addressing modes?

2.26 How many different combinations of the auto increment/decrement indexed addressing modes does the CPU12 support?

2.27 What is the range of adjustment allowed utilizing the auto increment/decrement indexed addressing modes?

2.28 How many variations of indirect indexed addressing are supported by the CPU12? Name them.

2.29 What ASCII character(s) are utilized to distinguish indirect indexed addressing from other forms of indexed addressing.

2.30 What programming problems occur when using the program counter as an index register? How are these problems overcome?

2.31 What actions does the CPU12 take when it encounters an 'invalid' indexed postbyte?

2.32 What group of CPU12 instructions can be used to access an M68HC12's peripherals?

2.33 Which addressing modes can be used by the load and store instructions?

2.34 Which, if any, of the condition code register bits are affected by the load and store instructions?

2.35 Which, if any, of the condition code register bits are affected by the memory-to-memory move instructions?

2.36 Which addressing modes may be used for the source and destination of the memory-to-memory move instructions? Do any restrictions exist on the use of these addressing modes?

2.37 What are some of the possible uses of the BRN instruction?

Section 2.23: Miscellaneous Instructions

2.38   Explain the difference between unsigned and signed branches.

2.39   Which simple branch instruction(s) can be used on both signed and unsigned numbers? Why?

2.40   How do the TSX, TXS, TSY, and TYS instructions behave differently on the CPU12 than on the M68HC11? Does this difference affect M68HC11 code that is ported to the CPU12? Why?

2.41   What does the CPU12 do when the source and destination registers used with the transfer and exchange instruction are of different size.

2.42   What special CPU register are accessible via the transfer and exchange instructions?

2.43   Where are the results of addition and subtraction instructions placed?

2.44   What addressing modes may be used with the LEA instructions?

2.45   What special considerations must be observed when using the auto increment and auto decrement addressing modes with the LEA instructions?

2.46   Why do separate opcodes exist for the INX, INY, DEX and DEY rather than having them translated into LEA instructions by the assembler?

2.47   What is one of the most compelling uses of the LEA instruction?

2.48   The CPU12 does not contain an 8-bit signed multiply. How would this operation be performed using the CPU12?

2.49   What types of applications can the EMACS instruction be used for? What limitations does the EMACS instruction have for these types of applications?

2.50   Why is the FDIV instruction of less value to a CPU12 programmer than it was for an M68HC11 programmer.

2.51   What size data do the Read/Modify/Write instructions operate on?

2.52   What is unique about the execution of the CLR and TST instructions?

2.53   What is the difference between the shift and rotate instructions?

2.54   What is the difference between an arithmetic shift right and a logical shift right?

Chapter 2: The CPU12 Instruction Set

2.55   What is the difference between a logical shift left and an arithmetic shift left instruction?

2.56   What are the required actions necessary to perform a logical shift left or right on a multi-precision value?

2.57   Why would a programmer choose to use the BIT instructions instead of the bit-test-and-branch instructions?

2.58   What compare instruction is present in the CPU12 instruction set that is not part of the M68HC11 instruction set? Is the instruction useful? Why?

2.59   Why are the compare instructions grouped with the boolean logic instructions?

2.60   What additional push and pull instructions were added to the CPU12 instruction set? How useful are they?

2.61   What advantage do the bit manipulation instructions have over using the CPU12 logic instructions for setting, clearing, or testing individual bits?

2.62   What new addressing modes may be used with the bit manipulation instructions?

2.63   What restrictions are placed on the use of the indexed addressing modes with the bit manipulation instructions?

2.64   Why was the LBSR instruction omitted from the CPU12 instruction set?

2.65   What instructions were added to the CPU12's instruction set to allow easy access to program memory beyond 64k bytes?

2.66   What condition code register manipulation instructions are part of the CPU12's instruction set?

2.67   What are the advantages and disadvantages of the loop primitive instructions on the CPU12?

2.68   What do most programmers use the software interrupt (SWI) instruction for?

2.69   How is the illegal opcode trap different on the CPU12 from the M68HC11?

2.70   How can the illegal opcode trap be used by programmers?

Section 2.23: Miscellaneous Instructions

2.71   What can the WAI instruction be used for?

2.72   What is different about the way the D accumulator is placed on the stack in response to an interrupt versus executing a PSHD instruction?

2.73   What is the typical use of the MIN and MAX instructions?

2.74   What table compression ratio is achieved through the use of the TBL and ETBL instruction versus a 'straight' table encoding?

2.75   What addressing modes do the TBL and ETBL instructions use?

2.76   What are the three basic operations used for a control system based on fuzzy logic? What CPU12 instructions correspond to each step in the control process?

2.77   What happens if the CPU12 executes a BGND instruction and the background mode has not been enabled?

Chapter 3   PROGRAMMING EXAMPLES

This chapter presents programming examples and techniques using some of the new instructions and addressing modes discussed in the first two chapters. The examples include some basic utility routines that are useful in many applications. However, before presenting the programming examples, the topics of stack usage and position independent code are discussed.

3.1   USING THE CPU12'S STACK

The additions made to the indexed addressing modes of the CPU12 have made a tremendous improvement in its ability to access data and parameters stored on the stack. These features have not only made it possible for C compilers to generate more efficient code than the M68HC11, it also allows assembly language programmers to easily utilize the advantages of local data storage. Storing local or temporary data on the stack provides several advantages for programmers. First, because the storage space is allocated on entry to a subroutine and released before exiting the subroutine, the same temporary storage can be reused by subroutines that run in succession. This reuse has the potential to provide a substantial savings in the amount of RAM required by applications if subroutines utilize temporary stack storage rather than allocating global memory for this purpose.

Second, utilizing stack storage for local variables and parameters makes a subroutine both reentrant and recursive. A reentrant routine is one that may be interrupted during execution and used within an interrupt service routine without disturbing the original set of local variables. The properties that make a subroutine reentrant also make it recursive. Recursive subroutines are subroutines that call themselves. While the solution to certain problems lend themselves to an elegant implementation using recursion, recursive subroutines can require large amounts of stack space. Caution should be exercised when utilizing recursion in microcontroller applications where on-chip RAM is usually limited. However, both of these programming techniques can make debugging much easier in an interrupt driven, real time environment because a subroutine's local variables cannot easily be modified by another routine.

Third, placing local variables and parameters on the stack helps to promote modular programming. When the temporary memory required by a subroutine is allocated on the stack rather than as global storage, the subroutine can be easily detached from the main program for reuse or replacement.

Finally, because a subroutine's variables and parameters only exist while the subroutine is executing, it is less likely that one subroutine will accidentally modify the variables and parameters of another. Once a routine has been written and debugged, a programmer's time can be spent debugging logical errors and subroutine interaction among the routines within a program.

3.2 Parameter Passing Strategies

Historically, because of a lack of architectural support for efficient access to data residing on the stack, assembly language programmers have used CPU registers and/or global variables to pass information to subroutines. Note that there is nothing wrong with using either of these techniques and in many situations using one or both of these methods results in smaller, more efficient code. However, each of these methods has various pitfalls that can be avoided if subroutine parameters are passed on the stack.

Passing parameters directly in the CPU registers has the advantage of allowing a calling routine to place data required by a subroutine where it can be accessed directly. Obviously, this can lead to an efficient implementation of a subroutine, especially if no additional storage is required for the subroutine to perform its task. However, if a subroutine must call other subroutines requiring parameters to be passed in the CPU's registers, the original parameters must be saved on the stack and restored when a called subroutine returns. Another disadvantage of using only the CPU12's registers for passing parameters is the limited amount of data that can be passed to a subroutine. Essentially, parameters are limited to passing two 16-bit pieces of data in the X and Y index registers and either two 8-bit pieces of data in the A and B accumulators or a third 16-bit quantity in the D accumulator. Even with these disadvantages, for small, simple subroutines that do not call other subroutines, passing parameters in registers can produce efficient subroutine implementations.

Using the contents of global variables to pass data to subroutines has the advantage of not requiring any code to set up CPU registers or place data on the stack before calling a subroutine. While this method is attractive from a code efficiency standpoint, it can have some serious drawbacks unless the programmer is very careful with the overall software design and storage management. In a large, complex program, especially one utilizing numerous interrupt service routines, it can become quite difficult to manage the sharing of data among routines using global variables. Great care must be taken to ensure that the values of global variables used to share data among subroutines does not inadvertently get modified while a subroutine is using the data.

Placing subroutine parameters on the stack provides the greatest flexibility and modularity; however, these advantages do not come without a cost. Passing parameters on the stack requires additional code and processing time before calling a subroutine and again when a subroutine returns. Obviously, the more parameters passed to a subroutine, the greater the code space and time penalty incurred when placing the data on and removing the data from the stack. When implementing the software for an embedded system, a balance must be achieved that makes the best use of the stack, the CPU registers and global variables.

Placing parameters on the stack is usually accomplished by loading one of the CPU12's registers with the required value and pushing the register value onto the stack. After a subroutine's parameters are placed on the stack, a BSR, JSR or CALL instruction is used to execute the subroutine. After entering the subroutine, the parameters may be accessed using a fixed offset from the stack pointer. As shown in figure 3.1, the offset used to access the parameters must include the size of the return address plus any local variables allocated by the subroutine. If the subroutine is called using the BSR or JSR instruction, the return address will add two additional bytes to the parameter offsets. If the subroutine is located in the M68HC12's extended memory and is accessed using the CALL instruction, the return address will add three bytes to the offset – two bytes for the stacked return address and one byte for the stacked value of the PPAGE register. The memory area occupied by the parameters, return address, and local variables is known as a stack frame.

Section 3.3: Local Variable Allocation

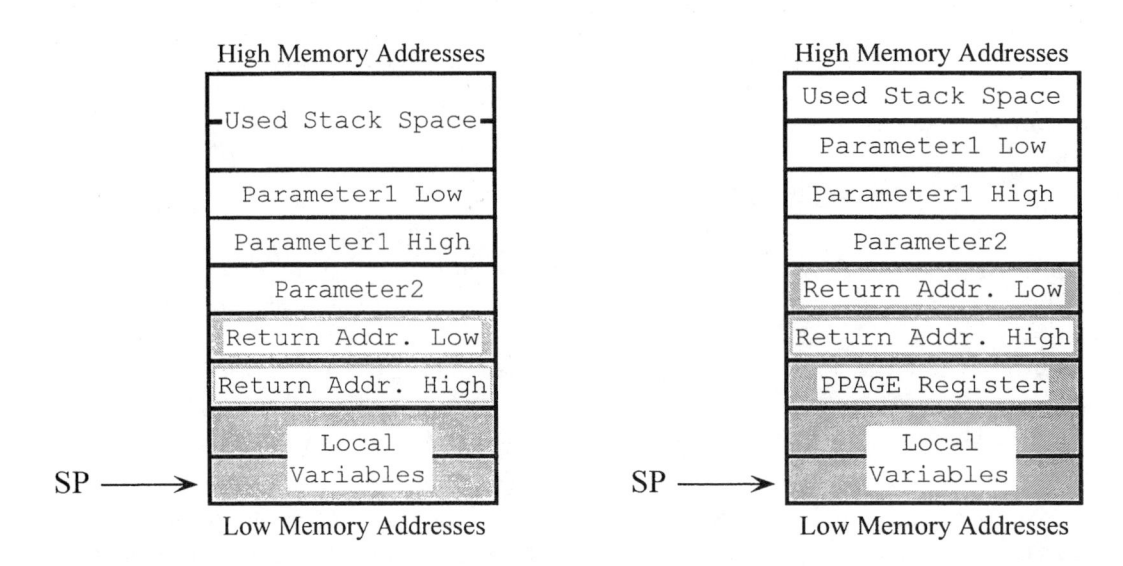

Figure 3.1: Parameter Location on the Stack for `BSR`, `JSR` and `CALL` Instructions

If parameters are passed in the CPU12's registers rather than on the stack, it nonetheless may be necessary to save some of the parameter values on the stack after entering the subroutine. In this case, stack space can be allocated for the parameter values along with other local variables saving the register contents in the appropriate locations. Obviously, in this case no offset adjustment needs to be made for the return address when accessing the parameters. Using this technique for passing parameters has the advantage of not requiring any code in the calling routine to remove the passed parameters from the stack. A single instruction at the end of a subroutine can remove both the local variables and parameters.

3.3 LOCAL VARIABLE ALLOCATION

The instruction set enhancements made to the CPU12's indexed addressing mode and the addition of the `LEAS` instruction make the allocation of stack space for local variables quick and efficient. Because the CPU12's stack grows from high memory to low memory, local variable storage space is allocated by subtracting the required number of bytes from the value of the stack pointer. Depending upon the amount of local storage necessary and the initial values of the variables required by the subroutine, different methods may be used to allocate local variable storage.

If the required amount of local variable storage space is only one or two bytes, one of the CPU12's 8-bit or 16-bit registers can be pushed onto the stack, decrementing the stack pointer by one or two counts. Because all of the push instructions are one byte in length, this is the most efficient way to allocate one or two bytes of storage space on the stack. It may be that the initial value of the variable is unimportant, however, if a variable requires a specific initial value, a CPU register can be loaded with the proper value before executing the push instruction. Another way to allocate a one or two byte local variable while initialing its value involves the use of the MOVB or MOVW instruction employing stack pointer predecrement indexed addressing as the destination addressing mode. An experienced CPU12 programmer will realize that using the memory-to-memory move instructions in this manner will not be as efficient as loading a CPU register with a value and pushing it on the stack. However, if subroutine parameters occupy all the CPU12's registers and there is no need to save the parameters during subroutine execution, the MOVB and MOVW instructions are an efficient method of allocating and initializing small amounts of local storage without disturbing the CPU registers.

The most common way to allocate local storage is to utilize the LEAS instruction with constant offset indexed addressing, subtracting the required number of bytes from the value of the stack pointer. Because the CPU12 supports 5-bit, 9-bit and 16-bit constant offset indexed addressing, stack space from one byte to 32,768 bytes can be allocated using a single instruction.

3.4 Accessing Parameters and Local Variables

As mentioned previously, subroutine parameters and local variables can be accessed within a subroutine using a fixed offset from the stack pointer. Being able to use the stack pointer as a base index register eliminates the need to dedicate either the X or Y index register as a stack frame pointer. However, there is one situation where the lack of a dedicated stack frame pointer can cause problems if the programmer is not careful. This will be discussed later in this section.

Instead of using numeric constants as offsets to data stored on the stack, it is more desirable to use symbolic variable names just as when declaring global variables. Utilizing an assembler directive to assign an offset value to a symbolic name, as shown in Figure 3.2, is one method that can be employed.

While this method will work with virtually any assembler, it creates a number of potential problems. First, it places the burden of calculating the variable offsets and the required amount of stack space on the programmer. While this may not seem to be an overwhelming task, it is a potential source of error. Performing these calculations when the subroutine is initially written is a fairly straightforward task. However, the largest chance for error is introduced if the subroutine must be modified during the debugging process or if modifying it at some point in the future. If a local variable is removed, not only will the local variable size have to be recalculated, but the programmer may have to recalculate the offsets for all the remaining variables. If a local variable is added, it will most likely be placed after the last variable in the list. In this case, the programmer must know the size of the previous variable to calculate the proper offset to the new variable. If the size of each variable is not

Section 3.4: Accessing Parameters and Local Variables

well documented in the comment field, the subroutine source code will have to be searched to determine the variable's size. This process can be particularly error prone especially if the last variable in the list is a multi-byte value manipulated as single bytes within the subroutine.

```
;
Var1:       equ     0               ; 16-bit variable.
Var2:       equ     2               ; 8-bit variable.
Var3:       equ     3               ; 16-bit variable.
;
LocSize:    equ     5               ; Number of bytes required by locals.
;
MySub:      leas    -LocSize,sp     ; allocate stack space for locals.
            clr     Var2,sp         ; initialize to 0.
                .
                .
                .
            leas    LocSize,sp      ; deallocate local storage.
            rts
;
```

Figure 3.2: Programmer Calculated Local Variable Offsets

An alternate method, illustrated in Figure 3.3, is much less prone to error. It uses the assembler's location counter together with assembler directives to automatically calculate the offset of each variable. In addition, it utilizes the assembler to calculate the amount of stack space required by the local variables. This method works particularly well with absolute assemblers supporting the required directives. Unfortunately, it may not work at all with relocatable assemblers.

```
PCSave      set     *               ; save the current value of the PC.
;
            org     0               ; set PC (location counter) to 0.
;
Var1:       ds      2               ; 16-bit variable.
Var2:       ds      1               ; 8-bit variable.
Var3:       ds      2               ; 16-bit variable.
;
LocSize:    set     *               ; Number of bytes required by locals.
;
            org     PCSave          ; reset PC to saved value.
;
```

Figure 3.3: Assembler Calculated Local Variable Offsets

Chapter 3: Programming Examples

Because local variables begin at an offset of zero, the assembler's location counter must be set to zero for this technique to work. However, the location counter cannot be arbitrarily set to zero in the middle of a source code file. Before assigning a value of zero to the location counter, its current value must be saved. The SET directive, used in the first line of the example, assigns a value to the symbol in the label field. The SET directive, unlike the EQU directive, may be used to assign or *reassign* a value to a symbol. Using the SET directive allows the reuse of the symbol PCSave to save the value of the assembler's location counter each time symbols representing local variables are declared in this manner. After saving the current value of the location counter, the assembler's ORG directive is used to set the location counter to zero.

The DS, or Define Storage directive is used to reserve an area of uninitialized. No code is generated by the directive; it simply advances the value of the assembler's location counter by the amount in the operand field. The symbol appearing in the label field is assigned the value of the location counter before the location counter is advanced. In the example, variable Var1 is assigned a value of zero, Var2 is assigned a value of two and Var3 is assigned a value of three. The DS directive is common to most assemblers; however, several variations exist. Some assemblers follow the letters 'DS' with an optional period and a single letter size designator 'B', 'W', or 'L' to indicate the size of the variable. The '.B' suffix indicates a byte size variable and increments the location counter by the amount of the expression in the operand field. The '.W' suffix indicates a word variable and increments the location counter by the amount of the expression in the operand field times two. Finally, the '.L' suffix indicates a long word variable and increments the location counter by the amount of the expression in the operand field times four.

When the assembler has finished processing the DS statements, the value of the location counter will be equal to the number of bytes occupied by the local variables, in this case five. The SET directive is then used to assign the value of the location counter to the symbol LocSize. LocSize can then be used by the LEAS instruction to allocate and deallocate the stack space for the local variables. Finally, the ORG directive is used to restore the assembler's location counter to the value that was saved in the symbol PCSave.

To allow access to parameters passed on the stack, additional DS directive statements can be placed between the second set of SET and ORG directives as shown in Figure 3.4. As discussed in Section 3.2 "Parameter Passing Strategies", the return address must be accounted for when calculating offsets to parameters. The line containing a DS statement with no symbol in the label field is used to reserve the space occupied by the return address when a subroutine is called using the JSR or BSR instruction. If the subroutine is located in the M68HC12's extended memory and is accessed using the CALL instruction, the amount of space reserved for the return address would be three bytes which includes the stacked value of the PPAGE register. Parameters should be listed in the reverse order that they are pushed onto the stack. In this case, Param3 would be pushed first, Param2 second and Param1 last.

Section 3.4: Accessing Parameters and Local Variables

```
PCSave      set     *               ; save the current value of the PC.
;
            org     0               ; set PC (location counter) to 0.
;
Var1:       ds      2               ; 16-bit variable.
Var2:       ds      1               ; 8-bit variable.
Var3:       ds      2               ; 16-bit variable.
;
LocSize:    set     *               ; Number of bytes required by locals.
;
            ds      2               ; Return Address.
Param1:     ds      2               ; Parameter 1.
Param2:     ds      2               ; Parameter 2.
Param3:     ds      2               ; Parameter 3.
;
            org     PCSave          ; reset PC to saved value.
;
```

Figure 3.4: Assembler Calculated Offsets to Parameters

As mentioned previously, the combination of assembler directives presented in Figure 3.3 and 3.4 utilizing the assembler to calculate the offset to local variables and parameters may not work with all relocatable assemblers. The key to using this method with relocatable assemblers is the assembler's ability to support both relocatable and absolute sections.

Sections are a feature of assemblers that allow it to maintain more than one location counter for different memory areas. Each section represents a contiguous area of memory that is generally associated with a specific portion of the target microcontroller's memory map. The physical address of program code and/or data placed in relocatable sections is not known at assembly time. Rather, the starting address of relocatable sections at assembly time is always zero. Another program called a linker is generally used to combine separately assembled relocatable modules and assign physical addresses to code and data. Code and data residing in an absolute section have their physical address determined at assembly time and operate in much the same manner as a simple absolute assembler.

The location counter within absolute sections can be used in much the same manner as an absolute assembler to automatically calculate the offset of each local variable and determine the required amount of stack space. Unfortunately, a common set of assembler directives does not exist for defining and switching among relocatable and absolute segments. The documentation for an assembler will need to be examined to determine what combinations of directives are required to implement the method presented here.

The examples in the remainder of the book will use the assembler syntax for Cosmic Software's ca6812 assembler. The Cosmic assembler supports a special absolute section called an offset section. The offset directive, as illustrated in Figure 3.5, starts an absolute section that is only used to assign offset values to symbols; no code or data can be placed in the offset section. The section starts at an address specified in the operand field, however, for the purposes of assigning offsets to stack based parameters and variables this address would always be zero. The offset section stays active until an assembler directive producing data or a CPU12 instruction is encountered.

```
;
            offset  0               ; switch to the absolute offset section.
;
Var1:       ds      2               ; 16-bit variable.
Var2:       ds      1               ; 8-bit variable.
Var3:       ds      2               ; 16-bit variable.
;
LocSize:    set     *               ; Number of bytes required by locals.
;
            ds      2               ; Return Address.
Param1:     ds      2               ; Parameter 1.
Param2:     ds      2               ; Parameter 2.
Param3:     ds      2               ; Parameter 3.
;
MySub:      leas    -LocSize,sp     ; allocate stack space for locals.
            clr     Var2,sp         ; initialize to 0.
              .
              .
            leas    LocSize,sp      ; deallocate local storage.
            rts
;
```

Figure 3.5: Using the offset Section in Cosmic's Assembler

3.5 REMOVING LOCAL VARIABLES AND PARAMETERS

Removing local variables and parameters from the stack is a relatively simple task; however, there are some considerations worth discussing. As shown in Figure 3.5, local variable space may be removed from the stack by executing an LEAS instruction with a positive offset just before the RTS instruction is executed. While this removes the local variables from the stack, any parameters passed on the stack will remain on the stack. In this case it is the *calling* routine's responsibility to remove the parameters from the stack.

Figure 3.6 shows an alternate method for removing parameters from the stack. This technique places the responsibility on the *called* routine to remove the entire stack frame including the parameters. Notice that just below the declaration of the parameters the symbol SFSize is set to the combined size of the local variables, return address and parameters. This symbol is used by the LEAS instruction at the end of the subroutine to remove the entire stack frame. Because the stack frame includes the return address, it must

Section 3.5: Removing Local Variables and Parameters

be loaded into one of the CPU registers before the stack frame is removed; in this case the X index register. Finally, a `JMP` instruction, using indexed addressing with an offset of zero, is used to return to the calling routine instead of an `RTS` instruction.

```
            offset  0              ; switch to the absolute offset section.
;
Var1:       ds      2              ; 16-bit variable.
Var2:       ds      1              ; 8-bit variable.
;
LocSize:    set     *              ; Number of bytes required by locals.
;
            ds      2              ; Return Address.
Param1:     ds      2              ; Parameter 1.
Param2:     ds      2              ; Parameter 2.
;
SFSize:     set     *              ; Total bytes for entire stack frame.
;
MySub:      leas    -LocSize,sp    ; allocate stack space for locals.
            ldd     Param2,sp      ; get Param2.
              .
              .
            ldx     LocSize,sp     ; get return address off stack.
            leas    SFSize,sp      ; remove locals & parameters.
            jmp     0,x            ; return.
;
```

Figure 3.6: Alternate Method For Removing Parameters From The Stack.

Having the called routine remove both the local variables and parameters from the stack has some distinct advantages. Because the size of the entire stack frame is automatically calculated by the assembler, it is less likely that a mistake will be made if part of the stack frame is removed by the called subroutine and part of it is removed by the calling routine. The greater advantage, however, is a potential savings in program size. The savings comes from the fact that each time a subroutine is called where parameters are passed on the stack, the `JSR` or `BSR` instruction does not have to be followed by an `LEAS` instruction to remove the parameters. The maximum savings would be obtained for programs that contain a relatively small number of subroutines that are frequently called.

Because of the program memory savings, it seems that this would always be the preferred method to use for removing parameters and variables from the stack. Unfortunately, this method does have one drawback. When a subroutine resides in M68HC12 extended memory and is accessed utilizing the CPU12's `CALL` instruction, the value of the `PPAGE` register is placed on the stack in addition to the 16-bit return address. Even though the `PPAGE` register resides in an M68HC12's I/O register block and can be directly read or written by a program, the only way to properly return from a subroutine accessed utilizing the `CALL` instruction is by executing an `RTC` instruction. In this case, the storage space utilized by stack based parameters must be removed by the calling routine.

No matter what strategy a programmer chooses for removing storage space allocated to parameters passed on the stack, care must be taken to ensure that the same amount of stack space allocated is removed. While this may seem like an obvious statement, the danger is very real, especially during the development cycle when changes are being made to the implementation of a program's design.

3.6 Precautions When Accessing Parameters and Local Variables

Utilizing the stack pointer as a base index register to access parameters and local variables is a valuable feature of the CPU12's instruction set. Not only does it allow efficient code to be written but it also eliminates the need to dedicate one of the two index registers as a stack frame pointer. However, there are some necessary precautions to avoid accessing incorrect data. First, programmers should be very careful when using the CPU12's push instructions to temporarily place items on the stack. Placing additional data on the stack will cause the offsets to all declared parameters and variables to change. While an additional constant can be added to succeeding accesses of stack based data, the danger exists that an incorrect value will be used. More likely, however, if changes are made to a program that remove the push and pull instructions, there is the risk that the the additional offset used to access parameters and variables will not be removed from the program code.

A second problem exists when a subroutine utilizing local variables and parameters must pass one or more of these values on the stack to another subroutine. Once again, as each new parameter is pushed onto the stack, the offset from the stack pointer to the current subroutine's parameters and variables change. In this situation a fairly simple solution to the problem exists. Before beginning the process of placing the new parameters on the stack, the value of the stack pointer can be transferred to one of the index registers. Then, instead of using the stack pointer as the base index register to access the variables and/or parameters, the X or Y index register can be utilized with the same offsets calculated by the assembler. Figure 3.7 illustrates this technique.

Section 3.7: Writing Position Independent Code

```
           offset   0              ; switch to the absolute offset section.
;
Var1:      ds       2              ; 16-bit variable.
Var2:      ds       1              ; 8-bit variable.
;
LocSize:   set      *              ; Number of bytes required by locals.
;
           ds       2              ; Return Address.
Param1:    ds       2              ; Parameter 1.
Param2:    ds       2              ; Parameter 2.
;
SFSize:    set      *              ; Total bytes for entire stack frame.
;
MySub:     leas     -LocSize,sp    ; allocate stack space for locals.
           tfr      sp,x           ; place sp in x to access vars & params
           ldd      Param2,x       ; get Param2.
           pshd                    ; place it on the stack.
           leay     Var2,x         ; get the address of local Var2
           pshy                    ; place it on the stack.
           jsr      CalcSpeed      ; go calc motor speed.
            .
            .
```

Figure 3.7: Using an alternate stack frame pointer

3.7 WRITING POSITION INDEPENDENT CODE

A program written in a position independent manner will run correctly when the same machine code is arbitrarily positioned in memory. Position independent code, which is sometimes referred to as relocatable code, should not be confused with relocatable object code that is produced by an assembler. Generally, entire programs written in a position independent manner do not provide any advantage in embedded systems where programs execute out of nonvolatile memory at a fixed address. In fact, programs written in a position independent manner are usually slightly larger and may execute somewhat slower than position dependent code. However, there are situations where position independence is valuable in embedded systems. One particular instance involves applications where a small program or subroutine must be copied from nonvolatile memory into RAM and then run from RAM. The Flash memory bootloader application discussed in Chapter 8 uses this technique to execute the Flash memory programming and erase bootloader out of RAM while the Flash array is being programmed or erased.

There are several characteristics that distinguish position independent code from position dependent code. Position independent code never makes use of absolute addressing when referring to other parts of a program, constant data, or even variables within a program. Instead, all references are made relative to the current value of the program counter or stack pointer. Address values loaded into index registers should always be calculated relative to the program counter or stack pointer. In particular, the JMP and JSR instructions should not be used with absolute (extended or direct) addressing.

The CPU12's instruction set provides instructions and addressing modes to allow a program, or even just a subroutine, to be written in a position independent manner. The inclusion of the short and long program relative branch instructions allow program control to be transferred to any location in the 64K byte memory map in a position independent manner. In addition, the capability of using the program counter as a base index register allows instructions to refer to data relative to the value of the program counter. Finally, the LEA instructions, combined with program counter relative addressing, allow position independent address calculation of constant data at run time. Figure 3.8 provides some examples of instructions that can be used for writing position dependent and position independent code. Note that two of the instructions, JMP and JSR, can be used when writing a program in either a position dependent or position independent manner depending on the addressing mode used with the instruction. Note the absence of an 'LBSR' instruction in the position independent column. This instruction was purposely omitted from the CPU12's instruction set because the JSR instruction, when combined with program counter relative indexed addressing, will accomplish the same purpose.

Position Dependent	Position Independent
JMP <address>	JMP <address>,pcr
	BRA <address>
	LBRA <address>
JSR <address>	JSR <address>,pcr
	BSR <address>
LDX #<address>	LEAX <address>,pcr
LDY #<address>	LEAY <address>,pcr

Figure 3.8: Position Dependent/Independent Instruction Comparison

The last two instructions in the position dependent column, LDX and LDY, are generally used with immediate addressing to obtain the address of a data table that is subsequently accessed using indexed addressing. To obtain the address of data tables in a position independent manner, an LEA instruction combined with program counter relative addressing must be used.

Even when programs are written in a completely position independent manner they are likely to require access to some global data storage and/or I/O registers. Because the location of the I/O registers and on chip RAM are generally known when a program is assembled, it is probably not necessary to access them in a position independent manner.

Section 3.8: Clearing On-chip Memory

However, there may be times where this is not the case. In such situations, the base address of the I/O registers could be placed in a global variable by a setup routine before the position independent code is called. The address can be loaded into one of the CPU12's index registers and the I/O registers can be accessed as an offset from the base address.

If a program's global data storage must be accessed in a position independent manner, there are a couple of techniques that may be employed. The easiest technique simply uses storage that preceeds or follows the program or subroutine and is accessed using program counter relative addressing. Obviously, this technique may only be used when a program is running out of RAM. The second technique can be used even if a program is running out of nonvolatile memory. The most effective way to obtain global data storage in a position independent manner is to acquire it from the stack, dedicating one of the index registers to access the global data. While this may seem to be an ineffective use of an index register, it does not mean that the index register cannot be used for other purposes during execution of a program. However, the programmer must ensure the index register value is properly saved and restored before accessing global data.

3.8 CLEARING ON-CHIP MEMORY

Like the CPU12's registers, the contents of the on-chip volatile memory used for global variable storage is undefined at powerup. Because a value of zero is used by many programmers to indicate an uninitialized state of a variable, it is generally desirable to clear global variable storage before the main portion of a program executes. Those familiar with the C programming language know that the language definition guarantees all volatile global variable storage is guaranteed to contain zero when a C program begins running. Programs written to run on desktop computers, have this this function performed by the operating system or startup code that is invisible to the user. For embedded systems this function must be performed by the programmer. Figure 3.9 shows the CPU12 code necessary to clear the on chip memory.

```
ClearMem:   ldx    #RAMBase    ; Point to the start of the on-chip RAM.
            ldd    #RAMSize    ; load D with the on-chip RAM size.
ClrMore:    clr    1,x+        ; clear a byte, point to the next byte.
            dbne   d,ClrMore   ; dec byte count, continue if not done.
            .
            .
```

Figure 3.9: Clearing on-chip memory

While this is a simple example, it does illustrate the power of the CPU12's post auto-increment indexed addressing and the loop primitive instruction. Clearing only a byte at a time may not seem to be the most efficient way to clear the memory on a 16-bit microcontroller; however it is the most simple and general way to implement the function. Because most on-chip memories contain an even number of bytes, it is possible to write an efficient routine to clear two bytes at a time.

```
ClearMem:   ldx    #RAMBase    ; Point to the start of the on-chip RAM.
            ldy    #RAMSize/2  ; load Y with the on-chip RAM size /2.
            clra               ; clear D
            clrb
ClrMore:    std    2,x+        ; clear a word, point to the next word.
            dbne   y,ClrMore   ; dec word count, continue if not done.
            .
            .
            .
```

Figure 3.10: Clearing on-chip memory 16-bits at a time

Figure 3.10 illustrates one way to implement such a routine. Because the CPU12 does not include an instruction that clears a word of memory, the D accumulator is initialized with a value of zero that is subsequently written to memory. Due to the fact that the value in the D accumulator is used to initialize memory, the Y index register is used as a loop counter. Notice that the value loaded into Y is the number of bytes of on-chip RAM divided by two. Because the STD instruction executes in the same number of clock cycles as the CLR instruction used in Figure 3.1, this routine will execute twice as fast on the same size memory block, ignoring the two clock cycles required for the CLRA and CLRB instructions.

3.9 FIND MIN/MAX VALUE IN AN ARRAY OF 16-BIT VALUES

The following example makes use of the CPU12's minimum and maximum instructions to find the smallest and largest unsigned values contained in an array of 16-bit numbers. In the example presented in Figure 3.11, the subroutine is entered with the B accumulator containing the number of 16-bit elements in the array and the X index register containing a pointer to the start of the array. The minimum value is returned in the Y index register and the maximum value is returned in the D accumulator.

Section 3.9: Find Min/Max Value In An Array of 16-bit Values

```
MinMax:  pshb              ; put array size on the stack.
         ldd     0,x       ; initialize d (max) with 1st entry in array.
         ldy     2,x+      ; initialize y (min) with 1st entry in array.
Loop:    dec     0,sp      ; decrement the array size. Done?
         beq     Done      ; yes. return.
         emaxd   0,x       ; place max of d or array element into d.
         exg     d,y       ; save the max in y, place min in d.
         emind   2,x+      ; place min of d or array element into d.
         exg     d,y       ; restore max in d, min in y.
         bra     Loop      ; go check next array value.
;
Done:    leas    1,sp      ; remove count byte from stack.
         rts               ; return with min in y, max in d.
;
;
```

Figure 3.11: Find Min/Max 16-bit Value

The `MinMax` routine begins by saving the array size on the stack so that the D accumulator can be used with the `EMIND` and `EMAXD` instructions for finding the minimum and maximum values in the array. The `LDD` and `LDY` instructions are used to initialize the return values with the first element of the array. The `LDY` instruction utilizes the post increment indexed addressing to advance the X index register to the next array element.

Placing the `DEC` instruction at the top of the program loop allows the subroutine to process array sizes of one element. While this may seem absurd, it improves the flexibility of the subroutine and allows its use in a program where the array may start with a single element and grow as the application runs. However, it does not cover the case where an array size of zero is passed in the B accumulator.

Because the `EMAXD` and `EMIND` instructions only compare the value in the D accumulator to values in memory, the `EXG` instruction is used to swap the minimum and maximum values in the Y index register and the D accumulator respectively. The `EMIND` instruction utilizes the post increment indexed addressing to advance the X index register to the next array element after the compare and potential load has been executed.

When the array size has been decremented to zero, the program branches to label `Done`. The `LEAS` instruction adds one to the value of the stack pointer, removing the counter from the stack. The reader may wonder why the two byte `LEAS` instruction is used rather than the `INS` instruction. Remember, the CPU12 does not have a separate opcode for the `INS` mnemonic. The `INS` instruction mnemonic is simply translated by the assembler into an `LEAS` instruction. Finally, the routine returns with the minimum value in the Y index register and the maximum value in the D accumulator.

Chapter 3: Programming Examples

While the minimum and maximum instructions are quite useful for finding minimum and maximum values or for limit check operations, they only operate on unsigned values. This may be adequate for many applications, however, there may be instances when these functions are required for signed numbers. Figure 3.12 contains a subroutine listing that substitutes compare, signed branch and load instructions for the EMIND and EMAXD instructions.

```
SMinMax: pshb              ; put array size on the stack.
         ldd    0,x        ; initialize d (max) with 1st entry in array.
         ldy    0,x        ; initialize y (min) with 1st entry in array.
Loop:    leax   2,x        ; point to the next entry.
         dec    0,sp       ; decrement the array size. Done?
         beq    Done       ; yes. return.
         cpd    0,x        ; compare max to mem value. memory < D?
         bgt    ChkMin     ; yes. D contains greater of two values.
         ldd    0,x        ; no. replace D with mem value.
         bra    Loop       ; Back to top of loop.
;
ChkMin:  exg    d,y        ; save the max in y, place min in d.
         cpd    0,x        ; compare min to mem value. D < memory?
         blt    GotMin     ; yes. go restore max in D, min in Y.
         ldd    0,x        ; no. D > memory. Load memory value in D.
GotMin:  exg    d,y        ; restore max in d, min in y.
         bra    Loop       ; go check next array value.
;
Done:    leas   1,sp       ; remove count byte from stack.
         rts               ; return with min in y, max in d.
;
```

Figure 3.12: Find Min/Max of Signed 16-bit Value

In addition to the elimination of the EMIND and EMAXD instructions, one other subtle change had to be made. Because of the arrangement of the load and branch instructions which were substituted for the EMIND and EMAXD instructions, the LEAX instruction had to be added to the top of the subroutine loop to increment the pointer to the array of numbers. The value of the minimum and maximum instructions are quite clear when comparing the code in Figure 3.11 and Figure 3.12. The code in Figure 3.11 requires only 24 bytes of code and finds the minimum and maximum values in a 10 element array in 170 clock cycles or 21.25 µS at 8.0 MHz. Figure 3.12 on the other hand requires 34 bytes of code and requires a maximum of 231 clock cycles or 28.875 µS at 8.0 MHz.

137

3.10 Uses of Pre/Post Increment/Decrement Indexed Addressing

The auto increment/decrement indexed addressing modes of the CPU12 are a powerful addition to the instruction set. The most obvious use for this addressing mode is in applications that move or compare blocks of memory. While it greatly improves the efficiency of these types of operations, other applications for these indexed addressing modes exist. This section will present several examples that make use of the auto increment and decrement indexed addressing modes.

Figure 3.13 shows a simple block move subroutine. In this example the Y index register contains the source address, the X index register contains the destination address and the D accumulator contains the byte count. While this subroutine is very small and efficient, it does have a limitation. This routine will only work if the source and destination blocks do not overlap. While this may be the case for most applications, there may be times when a more general routine is called for.

```
BlockMov:  movb    1,y+,1,x+   ; Move a byte & advance X & Y
           dbne    d,BlockMov  ; dec byte count, continue if not done.
           rts                 ; return.
```

Figure 3.13: Simple Block Move Subroutine

Writing a block copy routine that allows the source and destination blocks to overlap requires the use of two different copying techniques. If the destination address is less than the source address, the same technique used in the simple block move subroutine in Figure 3.13 may be employed. However, if the destination address is greater than the source address, the data must be copied from the source to the destination beginning at the end of both memory blocks. The data must be copied in this manner to prevent the data at the end of the source block from being destroyed as the copy progresses. In addition, a general purpose, robust block copy routine should check for a block size of zero and check for equal source and destination addresses. The subroutine shown in Figure 3.14 is a general purpose block move subroutine that allows the source and destination blocks to overlap.

Chapter 3: Programming Examples

```
BlockMov:   tbeq    d,Done          ; if byte count 0, just return.
            pshx                    ; put dest address on stack.
            cpy     2,sp+           ; start and end address the same?
            beq     Done            ; yes. just return.
            blo     MoveEnd         ; if the source addr is < dest addr,
                                    ; move data begining at end of block.
Move1:      movb    1,y+,1,x+       ; move a byte from source to dest.
            dbne    d,Move1         ; dec byte count, continue if not done.
Done:       rts                     ; return.
;
MoveEnd:    leax    d,x             ; calc ptr to the end of the dest + 1.
            leay    d,y             ; calc ptr to the end of the src + 1.
Move2:      movb    1,-y,1,-x       ; pre dec ptrs & move 1 byte
            dbne    d,Move2         ; dec byte count. continue if not done.
            rts                     ; return
;
```

Figure 3.14: General Purpose Block Move Subroutine

The subroutine begins by using one of the loop primitive instructions to test for a block size of zero. Next, the source and destination addresses must be compared. Because the CPU12 instruction set does not provide instructions to directly compare the contents of the X and Y index registers, the destination address is pushed onto the stack. Using the stack pointer as an index register, the source and destination addresses can be compared. Notice that the CPY instruction uses post increment indexed addressing to automatically remove the destination address from the stack after the comparison is performed. A BEQ instruction branches to an RTS instruction at label Done if the two addresses are equal. If the source address is greater than the destination address, the test performed for the BLO instruction fails and execution continues at label Move1 where the data is copied one byte at a time beginning at the start of the source and destination blocks.

If the source address is less than the destination address, execution continues at label MoveEnd. To begin the move at the end of the source and destination blocks, the block length, contained in the D accumulator, is added to both the source and destination address using the LEA instruction. However, simply adding the block length to the X and Y index register results in addresses that point one byte beyond the end of the source and destination blocks. For instance, a ten byte block of memory beginning at $0900 has an ending address of $0909 and not $090A which would result if the block length ($000A) were added to the starting address. To compensate for this, the MOVB instruction utilizes the predecrement indexed addressing mode to decrement the source and destination pointers before the first and succeeding bytes are moved.

The examples shown in Figure 3.15 and 3.16 illustrate the use of the MOVB instruction where only the source or destination utilizes post increment indexed addressing. The BRCLR

Section 3.10: Uses of Pre/Post Increment/Decrement Indexed Addressing

instruction that begins the `SendData` subroutine executes until the Transmit Data Register Empty (TDRE) bit in the Serial Communications Interface (SCI) status register is set indicating that a byte can be loaded into the data register. When the SCI is ready, the MOVB instruction moves a byte from a buffer, pointed to by the X index register, into the SCI data register and increments the pointer. The byte count is decremented and if not zero, branches to the `BRCLR` instruction to wait until the SCI is ready to accept or transmit the next character.

```
SendData:   brclr   SR1,TDRE,*    ; Wait till SCI is ready for next byte.
            movb    1,x+,DRL      ; move 1 byte from buf to SCI data reg.
            dbne    d,SendData    ; dec count, go wait till SCI ready.
            rts                   ; return.
```

Figure 3.15: Send Data From Buffer Out SCI

The `RcvData` subroutine in Figure 3.16 is almost identical to the `SendData` subroutine with the exception of the SCI status bit tested by the BRCLR instruction and the direction of data movement by the MOVB instruction. The `BRCLR` instruction executes until the Receive Data Register Full (RDRF) bit in the SCI status register becomes set, indicating that a byte is available in the SCI data register. The `MOVB` moves the data from the SCI data register into the receive data buffer and increments the buffer pointer.

```
RcvData:    brclr   SR1,RDRF,*    ; Wait till byte is available from SCI.
            movb    DRL,1,x+      ; move byte from SCI data reg to buff.
            dbne    d,RcvData     ; dec count, go wait till byte avail.
            rts                   ; return.
```

Figure 3.16: Receive Data From SCI, Store In Buffer

Because both of these subroutines utilize a 16-bit byte count contained in the D accumulator, it necessitates the use of the `MOVB` instruction to transfer data between the SCI data register and the data buffers. If an 8-bit byte count were utilized, held in one of the 8-bit accumulators, the other 8-bit accumulator could be used to transfer the data between the SCI data register and the send or receive buffer. Because the `MOVB` instruction does not support direct addressing for the source or destination address, implementing the subroutine utilizing load and store instructions would require one less byte if the SCI data registers were located on page zero. While this is not a large savings, these types of instruction set features should be kept in mind when writing programs.

Figure 3.17 shows an additional example utilizing the post increment indexed addressing to move data from the M68HC12 analog-to-digital converter's eight result registers into a data buffer. Even though the analog-to-digital converter's result registers are only 8-bits wide, the registers actually appear in the memory map at two byte intervals. This means that the source address pointer must be post incremented by two each time a byte is moved into the result buffer while the destination pointer must only be incremented by one. Fortunately, the amount of index register adjustment used with the auto increment/decrement indexed addressing modes does not depend on the size of the operand involved. As the MOVB instruction shows, the source index register is post incremented by two while the destination index register is only incremented by one.

```
GetA2DData: ldx     #ADR0H       ; Get address of A-to-D result reg #0.
            ldy     #A2DBuffer   ; point to result buffer.
            ldab    #8           ; number of A-to-D channels.
MoveMore:   movb    2,x+,1,y+    ; move byte A-to-D result reg to buff.
            dbne    b,MoveMore   ; dec count, go move next byte.
            rts                  ; return.
```

Figure 3.17: Move A-to-D Result Registers To Data Buffer

The last example presented in this section deals with the concept of a data element called a structure. In the C programming language, a structure is one or more related variables that are grouped together for practical handling. Because the pre/post auto increment/decrement indexed addressing has a range of -8 to +8 it can be used to step through or index into an array of small structures. The purpose of the subroutine shown in Figure 3.18 is to compare the first variable of each data structure in the array to the value in the D accumulator. If a value matches, the address returned in the X index register should point to the first element of the structure and a "true" or not equal condition should be returned in the condition code register.

The listing begins by defining a structure containing three data elements. Data1 and Data3 are 16-bit variables while Data2 is an 8-bit variable making the structure size a total of five bytes. The order in which the data elements are declared within the Offset section places Data1 at an offset of zero, Data2 at an offset of two and Data3 at an offset of three from the start of the structure. Note that within the Offset section, no data storage is allocated for the data structure, the ds directives simply assign an offset to each variable within the data structure. Fifty bytes of storage (10 array elements of the 5 byte structure) is allocated for the array of structures at the line beginning with the label MyStruct.

The subroutine begins at label Find by loading the X index register with an address that is SSize bytes less than the start of the array of structures. This allows the CPD instruction at label CmpMore to use preincrement indexed addressing to add SSize bytes to the X index register before the comparison is performed. This leaves the index register pointing to the proper array element if the comparison is successful. If the X index register had been loaded with the address of the first element of the array, the CPD instruction would have to use post-increment indexed addressing to advance the X index register. This would require an additional instruction at the end of the subroutine to adjust the X index register so the proper address was returned.

Two instructions, MOVB and TST, are used in unique but effective ways in this subroutine. The MOVB instruction combines immediate addressing for the source operand with predecrement indexed addressing for the destination operand to place a loop counter on the stack. While the subroutine could have used the Y index register for the loop counter, it was placed on the stack specifically to illustrate this use of the MOVB instruction. The TST instruction is used at the end of the subroutine for two purposes. First, it is used to check the value of the loop counter. If the loop counter contains a value other than zero, it indicates that the value in the D accumulator matched the first element of one of the structures in the array. This causes the Z-bit in the condition code register to be cleared indicating a not equal or "true" condition. Additionally, by utilizing post-increment indexed addressing, the loop count value is automatically removed from the stack.

```
             Offset  0
;
Data1:       ds.b    2              ; 1st element at offset of 0.
Data2:       ds.b    1              ; 2nd element at offset of 2.
Data3:       ds.b    2              ; 3rd element at offset of 3.
;
SSize:       equ     *              ;
;
             switch  .bss           ; switch to unitialized data section.
;
MyStruct:    ds.b    10*SSize       ; allocate storage for 10 element struct.
;
             switch  .text
;
Find:        ldx     #MyStruct-SSize ; point to SSize bytes before the array.
             movb    #10,1,-sp      ; put number of array elements on stack.
CmpMore:     cpd     SSize,+x       ; compare D to Data1. entry found?
             beq     Return         ; yes. rtn w/ x pointing to struct.
             dec     0,sp           ; no. dec array element count. done?
             bne     CmpMore        ; no. go compare the next one.
Return:      tst     1,sp+          ; yes. test element count & remove
                                    ; and remove it from the stack.
             rts                    ; return.
```

Figure 3.18: Accessing an Array of Structures

3.11 BINARY TO ASCII DECIMAL CONVERSION

There are numerous occasions in embedded applications when numeric quantities must be displayed on an output device. Often times the output device requires the information be supplied in ASCII character format. Because control system calculations are typically done using binary arithmetic, the binary quantities must be converted to a string of ASCII characters before they can be displayed. Converting a binary number to an ASCII string involves a process of breaking the number into individual decade digits through repeated division.

The division process is begun by choosing a divisor representing the largest decimal decade that can be represented by a binary number. For a 16-bit binary number, whose unsigned range is 0 through 65,535, the initial divisor is 10^5 or 10,000. The quotient of an initial division by 10,000 will be a single BCD digit, zero through nine, representing the number of ten thousands in the binary number. The remainder of the division represents the number of thousands, hundreds, tens and ones present in the original 16-bit number. The remainder is used as the dividend for the next division. The divisor for the next division will be the next lower decade, 10^4 or 1,000. The quotient of this second division will be a single BCD digit, zero through nine, representing the number of thousands in the binary number.

This process continues until the divisor reaches a value of 10^0 or 1. At this point the remainder from the previous division represents the number of ones in the original number. Figure 3.19 illustrates the process.

$$
\begin{array}{rcrcll}
65{,}535 & \div & 10{,}000 & = & 6 & \text{Remainder} \\
5{,}535 & \div & 1{,}000 & = & 5 & \text{Remainder} \\
535 & \div & 100 & = & 5 & \text{Remainder} \\
35 & \div & 10 & = & 3 & \text{Remainder} \\
5 & \div & 1 & = & 5 &
\end{array}
$$

Figure 3.19: Repeated Divisions by Powers of 10^x

As each division is performed, the resulting BCD digit must be converted to ASCII before being sent to an output device or placed in a buffer. Because of the arrangement of the ASCII numeric codes, a single unpacked BCD digit can be converted to ASCII simply by adding $30 to the BCD digit. In addition to the actual process of converting the binary number to ASCII, there are several other features that a general purpose conversion routine should have. First the routine should have the ability to convert both signed and unsigned numbers. Even though the CPU12 does have a signed integer divide instruction, its use is not practical for the conversion process. Instead, when converting a signed number, the conversion routine must first check the number being converted. If the number is negative, an ASCII minus sign ($2D) is placed in the output buffer and the two's compliment of the original number is converted. This simplifies the conversion routine by requiring it to operate only on positive values.

Section 3.11: Binary to ASCII Decimal Conversion

Another desirable feature for the conversion routine is the ability to suppress leading zeros. Without this feature, small one or two digit numbers would be displayed with three or four zeros in front of the significant digits making them much harder to read. For example, without leading zero suppression the number two would be displayed as "00002" instead of simply "2". A negative two would appear as "-00002" instead of "-2".

Figure 3.20 presents the code necessary for converting a 16-bit signed or unsigned binary number to a null (zero) terminated ASCII string with leading zeros suppressed. Three parameters are passed to the subroutine in the CPU12 registers. The Y index register should contain a pointer to a seven byte memory area used to contain the ASCII output of the routine. Seven bytes allows for a minus sign, five ASCII decimal digits and the terminating null byte. The X index register should contain the number to be converted. The B accumulator should contain a non-zero value if the number in the X index register should be converted as a signed value.

The subroutine begins by allocating space on the stack for three variables, initializes the decade divisor and the leading zero suppression flag. Next, to accommodate the leading zero suppression algorithm, a check must be made to determine if the number being converted is zero. If the value is zero, the ASCII character '0' and the terminating null byte are simply placed in the buffer and the subroutine returns. If this check were not made nothing would be placed in the buffer except the terminating null byte.

The instruction sequence between the labels `NotZero` and `Unsigned` check for the conversion of a signed number. The three instructions beginning at the label `NotZero` must be examined carefully to understand how they perform their function. The `STX` instruction saves the number to be converted in a local variable and at the same time updates the values of the N-bit and Z-bit in the condition code register. The `TBEQ` instruction checks the flag in the B accumulator to determine whether the number should be converted as a signed or unsigned number. If the B accumulator is zero, the number is converted as an unsigned value. Because the `TBEQ` instruction does not affect the condition code register, the `BPL` instruction immediately following it is actually using the condition code register results generated as a result of the `STX` instruction.

Chapter 3: Programming Examples

```
;          offset  0
;
zs:        ds      1              ; flag to supress leading 0's
Divisor:   ds      2              ; power of 10 divisor
Num:       ds      2              ; number/remainder being converted.
;
LocSize:   set     *              ; local variable size.
;
           switch  .text          ; restore original PC
;
Int2Asc:   leas    -LocSize,sp    ; allocate space for locals.
           movw    #10000,Divisor,sp ; initialize power of 10 divisor.
           clr     zs,sp          ; supress leading zeros.
           tbne    x,NotZero      ; number to convert == 0?
           movb    #$30,1,y+      ; yes. move ascii '0' into output buffer.
           bra     Return         ; return.
;
NotZero:   stx     Num,sp         ; save number to convert.
           tbeq    b,UnSigned     ; signed number? no. convert as unsigned.
           bpl     UnSigned       ; number positive? yes. convert as is.
           clra                   ; no. form twos compliment.
           clrb
           subd    Num,sp         ; by 0 - Num.
           std     Num,sp         ; save positive result.
           movb    #'-',1,y+      ; place minus sign in buffer.
UnSigned:  ldd     Num,sp         ; get number/remainder to convert.
           ldx     Divisor,sp     ; get power of 10 divisor.
           idiv
           std     Num,sp         ; save remainder of division.
           tfr     x,d            ; put quotient in d.
           tstb                   ; result != 0?
           bne     RNotZero       ; yes. go convert to ascii.
           tst     zs,sp          ; no. supressing leading 0's?
           beq     NextDig        ; yes. go convert next digit.
RNotZero:  addb    #'0'           ; convert result to ascii.
           stab    1,y+           ; place digit in buffer.
           inc     zs,sp          ; don't supress leading 0's.
NextDig:   ldd     Divisor,sp     ; get power of 10 divisor.
           ldx     #10            ; divide it by 10.
           idiv
           stx     Divisor,sp     ; save next lower pwr of 10.
           bne     UnSigned       ; convert next digit.
Return:    clr     0,y            ; null term converted string
           leas    LocSize,sp     ; deallocate locals
           rts                    ; return.
;
```

Figure 3.20: Binary to ASCII Decimal Conversion Routine

Section 3.12: ASCII Decimal to Binary Conversion

If the number is negative, the test performed by the BPL instruction fails and execution continues by negating the value to be converted and placing an ASCII minus sign in the output buffer.

The conversion of each decimal digit is performed by the code between the labels Unsigned and Return. The code within this loop is executed once for each of the five possible decimal digits. The conversion of each digit begins by dividing the initial number or the remainder of the previous division by the power of ten divisor. After the division, the remainder is saved in the local variable Num where it can be retrieved for the next division. The quotient is transferred from the X index register to the D accumulator where the converted digit can be easily examined and converted to ASCII. Before its conversion to ASCII however, it is checked to determine if the digit has a value of zero. If a non-zero value has been previously converted and placed in the output buffer, the leading zero suppression flag, zs, will contain a non-zero value causing the zero digit to be converted to ASCII and placed in the output buffer. If the leading zero suppression flag contains zero, nothing is placed in the output buffer and execution continues at the label NextDig.

Beginning at the label NextDig, the power of ten divisor is divided by ten to obtain the next lower power of ten enabling the next digit to be extracted from the binary number. When the quotient of this division reaches zero, the conversion process is complete. In reality, the last time the conversion loop is executed is unnecessary in terms of extracting the one's decimal digit from the remainder of the previous division. As shown in Figure 3.19, the divisor used for the last division is one. However, performing this last "unnecessary" division keeps the implementation of the subroutine simpler at the cost of a small increase in execution time.

Finally, there may be embedded applications that do not require ASCII coded data but instead require just BCD data for driving simple L.E.D. displays. In this case, removing the single line of the subroutine that adds the ASCII "0" character to the extracted BCD digit will place the converted number in the buffer in unpacked BCD format.

3.12 ASCII Decimal to Binary Conversion

Just as there is a need to display decimal numeric quantities on various output devices, there is often a need in embedded systems to allow operators to enter decimal numerals from a small keyboard or keypad. In addition to keyboard scanning, covered in Chapter 6, there is a need to convert the entered decimal digits to a binary number. This programming example converts an arbitrary number of ASCII decimal digits into an unsigned 16-bit binary number.

The process of converting a string of ASCII decimal digits into a binary number involves a process that is almost the opposite of the binary to ASCII conversion process. Rather than using a division process to break a binary number into decimal decades, a multiplication and addition process is used to build a binary number from individual decimal digits. As each decimal digit is processed, it is first converted from ASCII to BCD format. Next, the value of all previously processed digits is multiplied by ten and finally, the value of the most recently encountered digit is added to the total. While the basic process is quite simple, there are two additional considerations when converting data entered by a system operator. First, the possibility exists, depending on the keyboard input routines, that non-decimal characters may appear in the input buffer. A robust conversion routine should include checks for non-decimal characters in the input buffer. Second, the possibility exists that a decimal number larger than the maximum positive value that can be represented by a 16-bit number will be presented to the routine for conversion. Therefore, the routine must contain code that checks for overflow as each digit is processed.

Figure 3.21 contains the listing for an ASCII decimal to binary conversion routine. The only parameter required by the subroutine is a pointer to a null terminated string passed in the X index register. The converted result is returned in the D accumulator. If the conversion process completes normally, the subroutine will return with the condition code register Z-bit set. If a non-decimal ASCII character or an overflow condition occurs, the Z-bit will be cleared.

Section 3.12: ASCII Decimal to Binary Conversion

```
                offset  0
;
Num:      ds      2               ; number being converted.
BCD:      ds      1               ; temp storage for converted ascii char.
Error:    ds      1               ; error flag. 0 == no error.
;
LocSize:  set     *               ; local variable size.
;
          switch  .text           ; restore original PC
;
Asc2Int:  leas    -LocSize,sp     ; allocate locals
          clra
          clrb
          std     Num,sp          ; initialize converted result to 0.
          stab    Error,sp        ; initialize for no error.
Convert:  ldab    1,x+            ; get character from buffer.
          beq     Return          ; if it's $00, we're done.
          cmpb    #'0'            ; character < ascii 0 ($30)?
          blo     ErrRtn          ; yes. return error indication.
          cmpb    #'9'            ; no. character > ascii 9 ($39)?
          bhi     ErrRtn          ; yes. return error indication.
          andb    #$0f            ; no. convert to BCD.
          stab    BCD,sp          ; save it.
          ldd     Num,sp          ; get previous total.
          ldy     #10             ; multiply by 10 before the new
          emul                    ; BCD digit is added in.
          tbne    y,ErrRtn        ; if upper 16-bits != 0, overflow.
          addb    BCD,sp          ; add BCD digit to lower 8-bits.
          adca    #0              ; add carry into upper 8-bits.
          std     Num,sp          ; save result.
          bcc     Convert         ; if carry clear, no overflow. continue
ErrRtn:   inc     Error,sp        ; carry was set (or other error occurred).
Return:   ldd     Num,sp          ; retrieve result.
          tst     Error,sp        ; check error flag (sets ccr).
          leas    LocSize,sp      ; remove locals.
          rts                     ; return.
;
```

Figure 3.21: ASCII Decimal to Binary Conversion Subroutine

The Asc2Int subroutine begins by allocating stack space for its local variables and initializing the local variables Error and Num with zero. Beginning at label Convert, a character is retrieved from the input buffer and checked to ensure that it is a valid ASCII decimal digit. If the character is outside the valid range, the subroutine branches to label ErrRtn where the variable Error is assigned a non-zero value. Assuming a valid ASCII decimal digit, the character is converted to a BCD digit by masking off the upper four bits. Before the new BCD digit can be added to the value in Num, Num must first be multiplied by ten, therefore, the BCD digit is saved in the variable BCD. The value in Num is multiplied by ten using the EMUL instruction which produces a 32-bit result. The upper 16-bits are contained in the Y index register and the lower 16-bits are contained in the D accumulator. Following the multiplication, the TBNE instruction checks the upper 16-bits in the Y index register for an overflow condition. If the Y index register does not contain zero, the number being converted is larger than 16-bits.

After the multiplication and error check, the BCD digit is added to the contents of the D accumulator using a two step process. First the contents of the variable BCD is added to the B accumulator, this is followed by an ADCA instruction that adds an immediate value of zero plus the carry to the upper byte of the D accumulator. After saving the result in Num, the state of the C-bit is checked for an overflow condition. If the carry is clear, the conversion process continues by branching back to label Convert and fetching the next character from the buffer. The process continues until a null character is fetched from the buffer or an error condition occurs.

The Asc2Int subroutine finishes by loading the converted value into the D accumulator and testing the value of the variable Error. If an error occurred during the conversion process, Error will contain a non-zero value which leads to the Z-bit being cleared as a result of the TST instruction. Finally, the LEAS instruction, which does not affect the value of the condition code register, is used to remove the local variables from the stack.

3.13 CRC Calculation

Most communication protocols use some form of error checking to ensure the integrity of data for data transmission. Typically the sender computes a special signature value that is appended to the end of a data packet. As the receiver acquires data, it computes its own signature value which it compares to the received signature value. If an error occurred in transmitting the data, the two signature values should disagree. The two most popular error detecting signatures are the checksum and cyclic redundancy checks or CRCs. While the checksum is the easiest to understand and compute, it does not provide a robust error detection mechanism that is often required when data is sent through a wide variety of transmission mediums.

CRC calculations are based on a string of bits known as a "generating polynomial." Various generating polynomials are used, with each one generating a different CRC value for the same data. One of the most commonly used CRC calculations is that employed by the X/Y/ZModem protocol and is based on the generator polynomial of $x^{16} + x^{12} + x^5 + 1$ where the power of x represents which bits are set in the generating polynomial. Without explaining the theory behind CRC calculations, the method for calculating the 16-bit X/Y/ZModem CRC is shown in Figure 3.22.

Section 3.13: CRC Calculation

---

1. Set the initial CRC value to zero.
2. Get a byte of data, exclusive or it with the upper 8 bits of the CRC.
3. Examine the upper 8-bits of the CRC value 1 bit at a time.
4. Shift the CRC value to the left 1 bit.
5. If the most significant bit was set, exclusive or the generating polynomial ($1021) into the CRC.

Figure 3.22: 16-bit X/Y/ZModem CRC Calculation

While the basic operations performed by this algorithm are simple, it effectively involves examining each bit within the data block on which the CRC calculation is performed and results in a computationally intensive implementation. Figure 3.23 shows the CPU12 code necessary to perform the CRC calculation on an arbitrary block size. Two parameters are required by the subroutine. A pointer to the start of the data block is passed in the X index register and the size of the block is passed in the Y index register. The 16-bit CRC is returned in the D accumulator.

There are several features of the CPU12 architecture that lead to the efficient implementation of the CRC calculation. First, because the upper and lower bytes of the D accumulator can be individually accessed, it is easy to implement the second step of the CRC calculation. In addition, the MOVB instruction is essential to the space efficient implementation presented here. Without the memory-to-memory move instructions, one of the 8-bit accumulators would have to be saved and restored each time the `BitCnt` variable was initialized.

```
            offset  0
;
BitCnt:     ds      1                       ; bit counter.
;
LocSize:    set     *                       ; local variable size.
;
            switch  .text                   ; restore original PC
;
CRC16:      clra                            ; initialize CRC value to 0.
            clrb
            psha                            ; efficient way to allocate 1 byte.
;
CRCLoop:    eora    1,x+                    ; eor data byte w/ upper 8-bits of crc.
            movb    #8,BitCnt,sp            ; init loop counter for examining bits.
BitLoop:    lsld                            ; shift crc left 1 bit. ms bit goes to carry
            bcc     MSBClr                  ; c-bit clear, just examine next bit.
            eora    #$10                    ; c-bit set, eor crc w/ polynomial.
            eorb    #$21
MSBClr:     dec     BitCnt,sp               ; examined all 8 of upper crc bits?
            bne     Bitloop                 ; no. go shift crc left again.
            dbne    y,CRCLoop               ; yes. done with entire data block?
            leas    LocSize,sp              ; yes. remove local from stack.
            rts                             ; return.
;
```

Figure 3.23: 16-bit X/Y/ZModem CRC Subroutine

While this subroutine is code space efficient, it is not particularly time efficient. A CRC calculation for a 1024 byte data block requires approximately 11.3 mS. While this might be acceptable for applications handling small blocks of data or when communicating at low data rates, there may be applications where monopolizing the CPU for this amount of time is unacceptable. However, a slightly alternate technique may be employed to utilize this basic method of calculating the CRC. Rather than performing the calculation on an entire block of received data, the CRC can be calculated as each byte is received. This spreads the time required for the calculation over a longer period at the expense of a slight increase in total calculation time. The increase is due to the overhead required to repeatedly call the the subroutine and to load and save the intermediate CRC value. Figure 3.23 shows the subroutine modified to calculate the CRC of a single byte of data pointed to by the X index register. The initial or intermediate CRC value is passed in the D accumulator. Because the Y index register is used for the bit loop counter no local variables are needed. The first time the subroutine is called the initial CRC value passed in the D accumulator should be zero.

There is an interesting point to note for the subroutines in Figure 3.23 and 3.24. Because of the BCC branch statement between the BitLoop and MSBClr labels, it might be expected that the execution time for the subroutine would vary depending upon the contents

Section 3.13: CRC Calculation

of the data block. However, because branch instructions only require one cycle when not taken, and because the EORA and EORB instructions each require one cycle, the time required to calculate the 16-bit CRC is independent of the data.

```
CRC16.2:  ldy    #8            ; load bit count into y.
          eora   0,x           ; eor data byte w/ upper 8-bits of crc.
BitLoop:  lsld                 ; shift crc left 1 bit. ms bit goes to carry
          bcc    MSBClr        ; c-bit clear, just examine next bit.
          eora   #$10          ; c-bit set, eor crc w/ polynomial.
          eorb   #$21
MSBClr:   dbne   y,Bitloop     ; examined all 8 of upper crc bits?
          rts                  ; yes. return.
;
```

Figure 3.24: Single Byte 16-bit X/Y/ZModem CRC Subroutine

While one of these two approaches to a 16-bit CRC calculation will provide an acceptable solution in many applications, there may be some applications that require a higher performance approach. As is the case with many solutions to computing problems, a small compact implementation of an algorithm utilizing a repeating loop usually results in less than optimum performance. However, implementing an algorithm for maximum performance generally results in a solution with a larger code size. If the CRC operation involving the eight shifts and the exclusive OR of the generating polynomial is examined, it can be seen that the operation does not depend on the value of the bits being shifted into the low byte of the CRC. The operation depends only on what was in the high order byte before the shift and exclusive OR operation took place. Thus, for each of the 256 values in the upper byte of the CRC there exists a unique 16-bit value computed by the shift and exclusive OR operation. By precomputing these values and placing them in a table, a very time efficient table lookup implementation of the CRC calculation can be realized. However, the time efficiency comes at the expense of the space required for the lookup table. Because each table entry is 16-bits, the table requires 512 bytes.

Figure 3.25 shows a small C language program that can be used to generate the values in the lookup table presented in Figure 3.27.

Chapter 3: Programming Examples

```
static short CRC16Table[256];
main()
{
  short i;                          // outer loop counter
  short j;                          // inner loop counter
  short crc;                        // holds calculated 'CRC' value

  for (i = 0; i < 256; i++)         // loop through all 256 upper byte values
  {
    crc = i << 8;                   // put loop cntr in upper byte of CRC
    for (j = 0; j < 8; j++)         // look at each bit in the upper byte
      if (crc & 0x8000)             // if upper bit is set shift left 1 bit
        crc = (crc << 1) ^ 0x1021;  // and eor with the generating polynomial
      else
        crc = (crc << 1);           // otherwise, just shift to left 1 bit

    CRC16Table[i] = crc;            // place the result in the table
  }
}
```

Figure 3.25: CRC Table Value Generator

Figure 3.26 contains the assembly code necessary to utilize the data contained in the lookup table presented in Figure 3.27. Like the CRC16 subroutine in Figure 3.23, two parameters are required by the CRC16Tbl subroutine. A pointer to the start of the data block is passed in the X index register and the size of the block is passed in the Y index register. The 16-bit CRC is returned in the D accumulator. The subroutine begins by initializing the CRC value to zero and allocating the space for the DataP temporary variable on the stack. Allocation of the temporary is performed by using a PSHD instruction rather than an LEAS instruction because it requires one less byte of code. However, there is a danger in using this technique. If in the future this subroutine, or one like it, were to change by adding additional local variables, the programmer would have to remember to change the PSHD instruction to an LEAS. While using the PSHD instruction saved a byte of object code in this instance, it is possible that this programming "trick" could cause problems if the subroutine is modified at some point in the future.

Section 3.13: CRC Calculation

```
                offset  0
;
DataP:          ds      2               ; place to save pointer to data block.
;
LocSize:        set     *               ; local variable size.
;
                switch  .text           ; restore original PC
;
CRC16Tbl:       clra                    ; initialize CRC value to 0.
                clrb
                pshd                    ; allocate 2 byte local on stack.
;
CRCLoop:        eora    1,x+            ; eor data byte w/ upper 8-bits of crc.
                stx     DataP,sp        ; save updated pointer to the data block.
                pshb                    ; save the lower byte of the crc.
                exg     a,d             ; 0 extend a into d to use as table index.
                lsld                    ; x2, each table entry is 2 bytes.
                ldx     #CRCTable       ; point to start of table entry.
                ldd     d,x             ; get crc reduction from table.
                eora    1,sp+           ; eor old crc lower byte into upper byte.
                ldx     DataP,sp        ; restore pointer to data block.
                dbne    y,CRCLoop       ; dec byte count. Done?
                leas    LocSize,sp      ; yes. deallocate local.
                rts                     ; return.
;
```

Figure 3.26: Table Driven CRC16 Calculation

After performing an exclusive or of a data byte and the high byte of the CRC, the pointer to the next data byte is saved in the local variable DataP so that the X index register can be used to access the precomputed reduction value in the lookup table. Notice that after saving the value of the X index register, the low byte of the CRC is pushed onto the stack so that it can be used later in the calculation. Pushing data onto the stack in this manner to save a temporary value can be risky when local variables are referenced as offsets from the stack pointer. Unless the programmer is very careful to add a constant to the predefined offsets for the local variables, there is a high risk of accessing incorrect data. In a small subroutine such as this one, the problem is easily managed, however, in larger subroutines, the probability becomes much higher that erroneous data will be accessed. The use of this technique should be well documented in the subroutine header.

The EXG instruction is used in a manner to zero extend the value in the A accumulator to the D accumulator. This is required because the A accumulator value must be multiplied by two before being used as an index into the CRC constant table. After retrieving the new CRC value from the lookup table, the lower byte of the old CRC value is exclusive OR'ed with the upper byte of the new value and at the same time it is removed from the stack. The

Chapter 3: Programming Examples

X index register is then restored from the local variable DataP, the byte count decremented and the calculation continues if the byte count was not zero.

```
CRCTable   equ   *
:          dw    $0000,$1021,$2042,$3063,$4084,$50A5,$60C6,$70E7
           dw    $8108,$9129,$A14A,$B16B,$C18C,$D1AD,$E1CE,$F1EF
           dw    $1231,$0210,$3273,$2252,$52B5,$4294,$72F7,$62D6
           dw    $9339,$8318,$B37B,$A35A,$D3BD,$C39C,$F3FF,$E3DE
           dw    $2462,$3443,$0420,$1401,$64E6,$74C7,$44A4,$5485
           dw    $A56A,$B54B,$8528,$9509,$E5EE,$F5CF,$C5AC,$D58D
           dw    $3653,$2672,$1611,$0630,$76D7,$66F6,$5695,$46B4
           dw    $B75B,$A77A,$9719,$8738,$F7DF,$E7FE,$D79D,$C7BC
           dw    $48C4,$58E5,$6886,$78A7,$0840,$1861,$2802,$3823
           dw    $C9CC,$D9ED,$E98E,$F9AF,$8948,$9969,$A90A,$B92B
           dw    $5AF5,$4AD4,$7AB7,$6A96,$1A71,$0A50,$3A33,$2A12
           dw    $DBFD,$CBDC,$FBBF,$EB9E,$9B79,$8B58,$BB3B,$AB1A
           dw    $6CA6,$7C87,$4CE4,$5CC5,$2C22,$3C03,$0C60,$1C41
           dw    $EDAE,$FD8F,$CDEC,$DDCD,$AD2A,$BD0B,$8D68,$9D49
           dw    $7E97,$6EB6,$5ED5,$4EF4,$3E13,$2E32,$1E51,$0E70
           dw    $FF9F,$EFBE,$DFDD,$CFFC,$BF1B,$AF3A,$9F59,$8F78
           dw    $9188,$81A9,$B1CA,$A1EB,$D10C,$C12D,$F14E,$E16F
           dw    $1080,$00A1,$30C2,$20E3,$5004,$4025,$7046,$6067
           dw    $83B9,$9398,$A3FB,$B3DA,$C33D,$D31C,$E37F,$F35E
           dw    $02B1,$1290,$22F3,$32D2,$4235,$5214,$6277,$7256
           dw    $B5EA,$A5CB,$95A8,$8589,$F56E,$E54F,$D52C,$C50D
           dw    $34E2,$24C3,$14A0,$0481,$7466,$6447,$5424,$4405
           dw    $A7DB,$B7FA,$8799,$97B8,$E75F,$F77E,$C71D,$D73C
           dw    $26D3,$36F2,$0691,$16B0,$6657,$7676,$4615,$5634
           dw    $D94C,$C96D,$F90E,$E92F,$99C8,$89E9,$B98A,$A9AB
           dw    $5844,$4865,$7806,$6827,$18C0,$08E1,$3882,$28A3
           dw    $CB7D,$DB5C,$EB3F,$FB1E,$8BF9,$9BD8,$ABBB,$BB9A
           dw    $4A75,$5A54,$6A37,$7A16,$0AF1,$1AD0,$2AB3,$3A92
           dw    $FD2E,$ED0F,$DD6C,$CD4D,$BDAA,$AD8B,$9DE8,$8DC9
           dw    $7C26,$6C07,$5C64,$4C45,$3CA2,$2C83,$1CE0,$0CC1
           dw    $EF1F,$FF3E,$CF5D,$DF7C,$AF9B,$BFBA,$8FD9,$9FF8
           dw    $6E17,$7E36,$4E55,$5E74,$2E93,$3EB2,$0ED1,$1EF0
;
```

Figure 3.27: CRC16 Lookup Table

While the actual subroutine code only requires 26 bytes, the lookup table requires 512 bytes. This brings the total program memory requirements for this implementation to 538 bytes. However, at the expense of code space, the subroutine executes almost four times as fast as the CRC16 subroutine in Figure 3.23. For a 1024 byte block of data, the CRC16Tbl subroutine executes in slightly over 2.9 mS.

Section 3.13: CRC Calculation

Questions/Exercises

3.1 What advantages are provided by utilizing the stack for local variables and subroutine parameters?

3.2 What are the advantages of passing subroutine parameters in the CPU12's registers? What are the disadvantages?

3.3 What are the advantages and disadvantages of passing subroutine parameters in global variables?

3.4 What are the advantages and disadvantages of passing subroutine parameters on the stack?

3.5 What must be taken into account when accessing a subroutine's parameters?

3.6 What is the term used to describe the combination of a subroutine's parameters, return address and local variables?

3.7 What methods may be used to allocate local variable storage space? What are the advantages of each method?

3.8 What are the advantages and disadvantages of using the technique in Figure 3.2 to assign offsets to local variable names?

3.9 What are the advantages and disadvantages of using the assembler to calculate the offsets to local variables and parameters?

3.10 What must be taken into account when using the assembler to calculate the offsets to parameters?

3.11 What feature must a relocatable assemblers posess to allow it to calculate the offsets to local variables and parameters?

3.12 What two methods may be used to remove local variables and parameters from the stack? What are the advantages and disadvantages of each method?

3.13 What potential problems exist when using the stack pointer to access local variables and parameters placed on the stack? How can these problems be overcome?

3.14 What is the definition of position independent code?

Chapter 3: Programming Examples

3.15   What are the advantages of writting programs in a position independent manner for embedded applications?

3.16   What characteristics distinguish position independent code from position dependent code?

3.17   What features of the M68HC12 instruction set support the implementation of programs in a position independent manner?

3.18   Figures 3.9 and 3.10 contain subroutines that clear a block of memory. Write a subroutine that fills a block of memory with an 8-bit pattern. Write a subroutine that fills a block of memory with a 16-bit pattern.

3.19   Figures 3.11 and 3.12 contain subroutines that find the minimum and maximum values in an array of unsigned and signed 16-bit numbers. The maximum array size for both subroutines is 256 16-bit entries. Rewrite both subroutines to allow array sizes larger than 256 16-bit entries.

3.20   Rewrite the general purpose block move subroutine in Figure 3.14 to move data 16-bits at a time making sure the routine executes in the most efficient manner.

3.21   Figure 3.20 contains a 16-bit binary to ASCII decimal conversion subroutine. Write a subroutine to convert a 16-bit binary number to ASCII hexidecimal.

3.22   Write a subroutine to convert an 8-bit, 16-bit or 32-bit binary number to ASCII decimal.

3.23   Figure 3.21 contains an ASCII decimal to binary conversion subroutine. Write a general purpose subroutine to convert a numeric ASCII string containing binary, decimal, octal or hexidecimal number to a 16-bit binary number. Assume that binary numbers are preceded by an ASCII %, octal numbers are preceded by an ASCII @ and hexidecimal numbers are preceded by an ASCII $. Allow for negative decimal numbers.

Chapter 4 MCU Initialization

One of the most important pieces of code written for any application is the code executed immediately after a microcontroller comes out of reset. At best, if the initialization sequence is incorrect or incomplete it can cause problems with proper execution of the main application program that may be vary difficult to track down. At worst, if some of the basic microcontroller systems are not properly initialized, the MCU may never begin execution of the main application program. Because each microcontroller in the M68HC12 family contains differing numbers and types of peripherals, the exact initialization sequence will vary from part to part. In addition, because various applications will not utilize each of the peripherals contained on a microcontroller, initialization code is not required for every peripheral. Most peripherals or microcontroller subsystems are disabled when the MCU exits the reset state. To utilize a peripheral, one or more of its control registers must be written with specific values. The initialization software required for the various peripherals are covered in the chapter devoted to each particular subsystem. This chapter covers the initialization of some of the very basic hardware systems required for an M68HC912B32 based system to begin functioning properly. While most of the initialization process described here can be used on other M68HC12 family members, each part may require a slightly different initialization sequence.

⚠ **CPU12 Difference from the M68HC11**

4.1 Protected Registers

Those familiar with the M68HC11 family may remember that several control registers governing the basic configuration of the microcontroller are protected from accidental

Section 4.2: Resource Mapping

modification. The protection mechanism involves a timeout mechanism requiring the programmer to configure the protected registers within the first 64 E-clock cycles after the microcontroller exits the reset state. After the first 64 E-clocks, writes to these protected register are ignored. One of the advantages of using such a timeout mechanism means that if the default configuration is suitable for a particular application, the programmer does not have to write a value to the register for it to be protected. Additionally, the timeout mechanism will protect all of the sensitive configuration registers even if the programmer forgets to properly initialize them all.

Unfortunately, the timeout mechanism becomes less effective as more flexibility is added to microcontrollers through the addition of many highly configurable peripherals. While the timeout period could be extended, the microcontroller designers would have to guess what the longest timeout requirements would be for future derivatives. Also, as the timeout period is lengthened, the the probability becomes greater that software in the target system may cause an erroneous write to one of the protected registers.

To avoid these pitfalls, the M68HC12 system designers choose to protect the sensitive configuration registers through a "write once" mechanism. In Normal operating modes, each protected configuration register may be written exactly once after the microcontroller exits the reset state; additional writes are simply ignored. While this protection mechanism certainty avoids the main problem with the timeout mechanism, it does require that each each protected configuration register is written with a value even if its default value is the correct for the application. Not writing to one of the MCU's protected registers leaves a system vulnerable to accidental reconfiguration.

To allow for additionally flexibility during factory testing, and during the development and testing of M68HC12 based systems, the write once protection mechanisms are overridden in the Special operating modes. With one exception, protected bits within control and configuration registers may be repeatedly changed without going through a reset sequence. The exception is the SMODN bit in the MODE register controlling Special or Normal mode operation of the M68HC12. The SMODN bit, which has a value of zero when operating in Special mode, may only be changed from zero to one once without going through a reset sequence. If a system requires the M68HC12 to exit the reset state in Special mode and later switch to Normal mode, the application program should write or rewrite all of the protected registers since the write once protection mechanism is enabled when switching from Special to Normal mode.

4.2 RESOURCE MAPPING

To provide for flexible system configuration, the internal I/O register block and on-chip memory systems may be remapped from their default locations in the 64k-byte memory map. The bits within the resource mapping registers associated with setting the base address of the associated resource are write once protected in Normal modes. As explained in the previous section, even if the default base address is acceptable for a particular application, the registers should still be written with the default values to prevent accidental modification later. Writes to the mapping registers go into effect between the cycle following the write and the cycle after that. To ensure that invalid accesses do not occur to resources that are being remapped, writes to each of the remapping registers should be followed by a single NOP instruction.

Because the internal resource remapping scheme allows for the various resources to be mapped to the same starting address, the remapping logic contains fixed priority rules allowing only the resource with the highest priority to be accessed. When resources overlap, the resource with a lower priority will be inaccessible in the overlapping address range. The BDM ROM, unlike the bootstrap ROM in the M68HC11 family, is never visible to a running program. The BDM ROM is only switched into the memory map when the CPU12 enters the active Background mode or for a single memory access cycle of the serial BDM commands READ_BD_BYTE, READ_BD_WORD, WRITE_BD_BYTE or WRITE_BD_BYTE. The BDM serial commands are discussed in Chapter 14. Figure 4.1 shows the resource mapping priorities.

Priority	Resource
1	BDM ROM (if active)
2	I/O Register Space
3	RAM
4	EEPROM
5	Flash EEPROM
6	External Memory

Figure 4.1: Internal Resource Mapping Priority

The INITRG register controls the mapping of the internal I/O register block. The upper five bits of the register define the base address of the block, allowing it to be remapped to any 2K byte boundary. The register block occupies a 512 byte portion of the address space beginning at address $0000 after reset. All 512 bytes of the register space are not implemented in every M68HC12 family member, however, all 512 bytes are reserved for I/O registers. When the register block overlaps a lower priority resource, access to the entire 512 bytes of the lower priority resource is lost. For instance, if the on-chip RAM and the I/O register block of an MC68HC912B32 were both configured with a base address of $0000, only the 512 bytes of on-chip RAM from $200 - $3FF would be accessible.

Because the value written to the INITRG controls the location of all other control registers, including the other mapping registers, it should be written immediately out of reset.

Section 4.2: Resource Mapping

When writing to the `INITRG` register, either a numeric value or a symbol representing the default address should be used. All other registers should be accessed using symbolic names whose values have been defined as an offset from the I/O register base address. The register definition files that appear in Appendix B are defined in this manner.

Some M68HC12 family members implement an extra control bit in the least significant bit of the `INITRG` as shown in Figure 4.2. When the `MMSWAI` bit is set, internal clocks to memory mapping logic are turned off when the CPU12 enters the wait mode. While this can result in some additional power saving, access to all of the on-chip resources including the I/O register block and internal program memory is disabled. The only manner to exit the wait mode when using this feature is through a system reset.

Bit 7	6	5	4	3	2	1	Bit 0
REG15	REG14	REG13	REG12	REG11	0	0	MMSWAI

Figure 4.2: INITRG Register

Because the RAM mapping register, `INITRM`, determines the base address of the on-chip RAM, it must be initialized before any accesses are made to the on-chip RAM. This not only includes accesses using direct or extended addressing, but also the usage employed by the automatic stacking of return addresses when calling subroutines. The default base address and the number of bits used to define the base address of the on-chip RAM will vary depending on the size of the RAM and the size of other on-chip resources such as the on-chip EEPROM.

The upper four bits of the `INITEE` register control the base address of the on-chip EEPROM allowing it to be mapped to any 4K-byte boundary within the 64K-byte address space. The actual starting address of the EEPROM within the 4K-byte block will depend on the size of the EEPROM memory. For instance, the 768 bytes of EEPROM in the MC68HC912B32 begins at $D00 while the 1K-byte of EEPROM on the MC68HC912D60 begins at $xC00. In addition, the default base address of the EEPROM block will vary not only by device but also by the MCU operating mode. For example, the 4K-byte block of EEPROM on the MC68HC812A4 has a default base address of $1000 in Expanded and Peripheral modes and $F000 in Single-chip modes. Placing the 4K-byte EEPROM block at the top of the memory map in Single-chip mode allows programs to executed from EEPROM when the part comes out of reset.

The least significant bit of the `INITEE` register, as shown in Figure 4.3, controls the presence of the EEPROM block in the memory map. While the upper four bits of the `INITEE` register are write-once protected in Normal modes, the `EEON` bit may be read or written at any time. This feature allows the EEPROM block to be switched into and out of the memory map under program control. Note that even when the EEPROM block is

Chapter 4: MCU Initialization

switched out of the memory map, the EEPROM control registers may still be accessed and EEPROM locations may be programmed or erased.

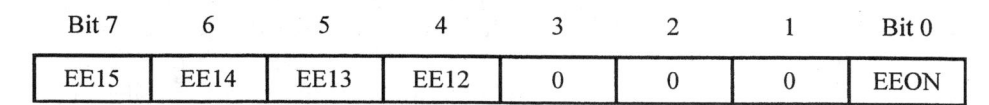

Bit 7	6	5	4	3	2	1	Bit 0
EE15	EE14	EE13	EE12	0	0	0	EEON

Figure 4.3: INITEE Register

4.3 OPERATING MODE

The initial operating mode of an M68HC12 microcontroller is determined by the voltage level applied to three of the MCU's pins when the reset pin transitions from a logic zero to a logic one level. The state of each of the three pins, BKGD, MODB and MODA, is reflected in the upper three bits of the MODE register bits, SMODN, MODB and MODA, as shown in Figure 4.4.

Bit 7	6	5	4	3	2	1	Bit 0
SMODN	MODB	MODA	ESTR	IVIS	EBSWAI*	0	EME*

Figure 4.4: Mode Register

While the initial operating mode of the microcontroller is determined by hardware, the MODE register allows the mode to be changed by the initialization software. Figure 4.5 shows the various operating modes associated with the eight combinations of the three mode selection pins.

BKGD	MODB	MODA	MODE
0	0	0	Special Single Chip
0	0	1	Special Expanded Narrow
0	1	0	Special Peripheral
0	1	1	Special Exapnded Wide
1	0	0	Normal Single Chip
1	0	1	Normal Expanded Narrow
1	1	0	Reserved (Forced to peripheral)
1	1	1	Normal Exapnded Wide

Figure 4.5: M68HC12 Operating Modes

Section 4.3: Operating Mode

The state of the BKGD pin, reflected in the SMODN bit, chooses one of two major operating modes, either special mode, when BKGD is zero, or normal mode, when the BKGD pin is one. Because Special mode allows unrestricted access to a peripheral's protected control and test registers it is generally unwise to allow an application to run in Special mode. Because the MODE register is one of the microcontroller's protected registers, it is possible and sometimes even desirable to reset the microcontroller in Special mode and later change to one of the normal modes by writing a new value to the mode register. In fact, many development tools utilizing the M68HC12's Single Wire Background Debug interface place the target microcontroller in Special Single-Chip mode when the developer requests that the target system be reset. Special Single-Chip mode forces the target microcontroller into active background mode, allowing the development system to gain control of the target microcontroller even if the target's memory does not contain program code.

The SMODN bit may be written from a zero to a one allowing the mode to be changed from Special to Normal; however, the SMODN bit must be written twice. This seemingly strange requirement, also shared by the IVIS bit, was designed into the write mechanism of the MODE register to allow development tools more control over a target microcontroller. Development tools typically place the target microcontroller in Special mode so the operating mode may be reconfigured by the development tool. If only a single write were required to change the SMODN bit, an application could inadvertently change to Normal mode when writing to the MODE register to lock the state of the write-once protected bits.

The MODB and MODA bits may be written anytime while in Special mode except that Special Peripheral and Reserved modes may not be selected. In Normal mode, MODB and MODA may be written only once. The value of being able to switch operating modes under program control allows an application to come out of reset in Single-chip mode and begin executing code out of internal Flash EEPROM or ROM. The application can then switch to one of the Expanded modes, allowing access to additional program memory, RAM or peripherals. When exiting reset in Expanded mode, any internal program memory is disabled allowing the reset vector to be fetched from an external memory device.

The ESTR bit controls how the E-clock behaves during both internal and external instruction and data accesses. When the ESTR bit is zero, the E-clock behaves as a free running clock signal that has a 50% duty cycle and a frequency of one half of the crystal for M68HC12 family members without a phase-locked loop clock system. When the ESTR bit is one, its default value in all operating modes, the E-clock stretches high during external accesses and stretches low during non-visible internal accesses. Unless an external peripheral device requires a free running clock signal, it helps to reduce electromagnetic radiation and power consumption if the E-clock is allowed to remain in a static state when not required for external access cycles. The ESTR bit is write-once in Normal modes and may be read or written anytime in special modes.

The `IVIS` bit allows internal bus activity to be reflected on the microcontroller's external bus. This capability allows development tools such as emulators and logic analyzers to monitor a program's activity involving on-chip resources. In Special modes the default value of the IVIS bit is one and must be written twice to change it to a zero. In Normal modes the default value is zero and it may only be written once.

Bits zero, one, and two of the `MODE` register contain control bits that vary among M68HC12 family members. Bit two of the `MODE` register in the MC68HC912B32 and MC68HC912D60, `EBSWAI`, has a function similar to the `MMSWAI` bit in the `INITRG` register. When the `EBSWAI` bit is set, internal clocks to external bus logic are turned off when the CPU12 enters the wait mode resulting in additional power savings. However, because this bit is not automatically cleared when exiting the wait mode, it should not be used if the program is being executed out of external memory. Failure to observe this restriction will cause the CPU12 to fetch random values from the floating internal data bus and will result in CPU run away. The default value of the `EBSWAI` is zero in all operating modes which results in the external bus remaining active in the CPU wait mode.

The `EME` and `EMD` bits are used to remove the control registers for I/O ports E and D respectively when operating in expanded mode. This allows an emulator to replace the ports with external logic so an emulator can emulate a single-chip system while operating in Expanded mode. In single chip modes the associated port registers remain in the memory map regardless of the state of these bits.

4.4 Flash Memory and External Access Control

When operating the MC68HC912B32 in either Single-chip or Expanded modes, at least two other registers must be initialized. The MISC register, shown in Figure 4.6, contains configuration bits that control bus timing to external memory and peripherals and the state of the internal Flash memory. All of the bits in this register are write-once protected in Normal modes and may be read or written any time in Special modes.

Bit 7	6	5	4	3	2	1	Bit 0
0	NDRF	RFSTR1	RFSTR0	EXSTR1	EXSTR0	MAPROM	ROMON

Figure 4.6: MISC (Miscellaneous Mapping Control) Register

When operating in Single-chip mode the ROMON and MAPROM bits both have default values of one which enables the on-chip Flash and places it in the memory map from $8000 - $FFFF. This is the configuration normally desired for Single-chip operation. The remaining bits in the register may be written to either zeros or ones as they have no meaning or effect for Single-chip operation. In Expanded modes, the remaining bits control bus timing to external memory and peripherals. The four combinations of the EXSTR0 and EXSTR1 bits

Section 4.4: Flash Memory and External Access Control

allow the external E-clock to be stretched zero, one, two or three integral E-clock cycles. This effectively inserts wait states for all external accesses enabling the M68HC912B32 to interface to devices that cannot meet the full speed bus timing. When operating the M68HC912B32 with an 8.0 MHz E-clock, current device specifications require that external memory or peripheral devices must have an access time under 25 nS for operation without the E-clock stretching. While it is quite easy to obtain relatively inexpensive RAM devices with access times in this range, Flash or EPROM devices, if they can be acquired, can be quite expensive. Obviously, as M68HC12 family speeds increase, the external bus timing specifications will become increasingly difficult to meet. Executing programs from external memory accessed with even a single E-clock stretch can impose severe performance penalties on the entire system. If all program execution and data accesses take place in clock stretched memory, overall system performance will be approximately half of what it would be if a program and its data were contained in non-stretched memory.

If a system design includes a mixture of external memory and peripherals, it would seem the bus timing would have to be set to the speed of the slowest connected device. Fortunately, the M68HC12 system designers put some extra logic in the expansion address mapping logic to accommodate a mixture of fast external memory and slow peripheral devices. The `RFSTR0` and `RFSTR1` bits provide the ability to separately control E-clock stretching for external accesses to the 512 byte area just above the memory space reserved for internal I/O registers. As shown in Figure 4.7, the Register Follow Stretch bits provide the same range of E-clock stretching as Expanded Stretch bits.

EXSTR1	EXSTR0	E-Clocks Stretched
0	0	0
0	1	1
1	0	2
1	1	3

RFSTR1	RFSTR0	E-Clocks Stretched
0	0	0
0	1	1
1	0	2
1	1	3

Figure 4.7: E-clock Stretch Bits

Some additional logic built into the expansion address mapping logic accommodates a mixture of 16-bit external memory with 8-bit peripherals. This logic, enabled by writing a one to the `NDRF` bit, configures the 512 byte area just above the memory space reserved for internal I/O registers to respond in the same manner as if the external data bus were configured for Narrow mode. This allows 8-bit peripherals to be connected to the upper byte of the 16-bit external bus while having the peripheral's 8-bit registers appear at sequential byte addresses. Without this feature, connecting an 8-bit peripheral to either the upper or lower byte of the data bus would cause the peripheral's data registers to appear in the memory map at every other byte address.

4.5 CONFIGURATION OF BUS CONTROL SIGNALS

When operating the M68HC912B32 in the expanded mode, the two 8-bit general purpose I/O ports A and B become the multiplexed 16-bit address and data buses while six of the general purpose Port E pins are used for bus control signals. In normal expanded modes the only bus control signal enabled by default is the E-clock because it is often used as an enable signal for external address decoding logic. The remaining pins associated with the bus control signals remain configured as general purpose I/O lines and must be configured via software. However, because Port E's internal pullup resistors are automatically enabled out of reset in all operating modes, the bus control signals, including the R/W signal, are pulled to a logic one. The exact combination of bus control signals required for an application will depend upon the types of memory and/or peripherals connected to the external bus. At any rate, because the Port E Pin Assignment Register, or PEAR, contains write-once protected bits, the register should be written with a configuration value even when operating in Single-chip mode.

4.6 PORT A, B AND E DRIVE LEVELS

When Ports A, B and E are used for the multiplexed address, data, and bus control signals, they are required to drive the signals to specific voltage levels within the timing constraints specified in the M68HC912B32's electrical characteristics. The memory and/or peripheral devices connected to the bus and control signals essentially represent a capacitive load to the microcontroller. The timing specifications of the MC68HC912B32 are guaranteed with a capacitive load of 90 pf on each of the pins. This number includes not only the capacitance of the connected devices but also the stray capacitance of the circuit board and/or associated socket. Including the stray capacitance this would still allow for the connection of more than a half a dozen devices to the bus. To help provide for the more likely situation where only one or two devices might be attached to the external bus, the M68HC12 designers provided the capability to reduce the amount of drive current supplied to the Port A, B and E pins. Three bits in the `RDRIV` register, shown in Figure 4.8, allow each port to be programmed for reduced drive capability.

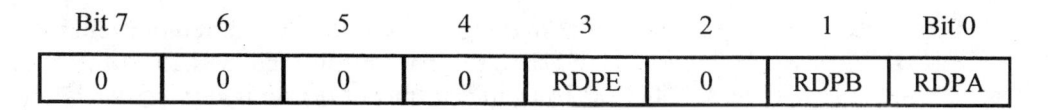

Bit 7	6	5	4	3	2	1	Bit 0
0	0	0	0	RDPE	0	RDPB	RDPA

Figure 4.8: Reduced Port Drive Configuration Register

Reducing the amount of drive current available to each pin on a port helps to reduce the total power consumption of the microcontroller. But perhaps even more important, it can help to reduce possible Radio Frequency Interference (RFI) problems associated with high

Section 4.7: Watchdog Timer

speed digital signal transitions. Each of the three bits defaults to a value of zero enabling the full drive capability on each port pin. When reduced drive is enabled, the drive capability is reduced to approximately one third the normal level. The capability for reduced drive is available for each port regardless of the function assigned to the port. The RDPA, RDPB and RDPE bits are all protected by the write-once protection mechanism.

⚠ **CPU12 Difference from the M68HC11**

4.7 WATCHDOG TIMER

Even in the most robust systems having the most carefully designed and implemented software, it is still possible for software to become stuck in an endless loop waiting for a condition that may never occur. While the COP (Computer Operating Properly) watchdog timer system cannot prevent such situations from occurring, it can initiate a system reset allowing a software recovery from such a situation. When the COP watchdog timer is enabled, the application software is responsible for keeping the timer from expiring and generating a reset.

Unlike the M68HC11 family, the COP watchdog system is **always** enabled when an M68HC12 exits the reset state in Normal modes but is disabled in Special modes. This fact can cause a great deal of difficulty and confusion for developers who forget to disable the watchdog if it is not going to be used. The problem stems from the fact that most development tools place a target device in Special mode thus disabling the COP watchdog timer. Firmware not disabling the watchdog timer will run just fine in a development environment, however, when the firmware is placed in an MCU in the final target system, the system appears totally dead. Because the default timeout period for the MC68HC912B32 is usually shorter than the time necessary to perform a system's initialization tasks, the M68HC12 is reset before it begins to execute its normal system tasks. This situation can be very easily detected by monitoring the M68HC12 reset pin with an oscilloscope. If the watchdog timer is timing out during the firmware initialization process, the reset pin will be driven low for approximately 16 E-clock cycles at a periodic rate.

The initial timeout period for the COP watchdog varies among the different M68HC12 family members. For instance, the M68HC912B32's initial timeout period is 1.024 mS with an 8.0 MHz E-clock, while the MC68HC812A4's initial timeout period is approximately one second with an 8.0 MHz E-clock. The time out period can be selected from one of seven rates as shown in Figure 4.9.

CR2	CR1	CR0	Divide E By:	At E = 4.0 MHz Timeout -0/+2.048 mS	At E = 8.0 MHz Timeout -0/+1.024 mS
0	0	0	OFF	OFF	OFF
0	0	1	2^{13}	2.048 mS	1.024 mS
0	1	0	2^{15}	8.1920 mS	4.096 mS
0	1	1	2^{17}	32.768 mS	16.384 mS
1	0	0	2^{19}	131.072 mS	65.536 mS
1	0	1	2^{21}	524.288 mS	262.144 mS
1	1	0	2^{22}	1.048 S	524.288 mS
1	1	1	2^{23}	2.097 S	1.048 S

Figure 4.9: COP Watchdog Timeout Rates

As shown in the column headings for the timeout rates, the implementation of the watchdog prescaler stages causes a positive tolerance in the timeout period equal to the period of the prescaler. The prescaler is made up of a free-running counter chain that is asynchronous to the watchdog service software. Because the prescaler chain is not reset when the service routine resets the watchdog timer, the possibility exists that the prescaler count will have rolled over to zero just prior to the watchdog timer being reset. While tolerance varies with the frequency of the E-clock, it is always equal to the shortest selectable timeout rate. For the longer timeout rates this tolerance is insignificant, however when utilizing the shortest rate, a careful analysis of software execution times and watchdog service routine placement must be performed to ensure that the watchdog is always reset within the minimum timeout period.

The MC68HC912D60 and MC68HC912DA128 has an additional selectable feature associated with its COP timer called the Window COP Mode. When enabled, the watchdog timer must be reset within the final 25% of the timeout period. Attempting to to reset the COP outside this window will cause a reset the same as if the watchdog had timed out. This feature is quite useful for systems containing firmware executing a regular interval under all operating conditions. However, its use would not be recommended for systems where control program execution time varies widely depending on external events.

The watchdog timer is reset by writing two values in the proper sequence to the COP Reset register (COPRST). First, a value of $55 must be written to the COPRST register to arm the COP timer clearing mechanism. This must be followed by a write of the one's complement of $55 or $AA. The second write does not have to immediately follow the first. The only requirement is that both writes occur within the selected timeout period. When

Section 4.7: Watchdog Timer

used with the Window COP Mode on the MC68HC912D60 or MC68HC912DA128, both writes must occur within the final 25% of the timeout period. As an additional protection against errant software execution, writing any values other than $55 or $AA to the COPRST register will cause an immediate watchdog reset to occur.

Placement of the COP clearing sequence within the control system's firmware will require careful analysis of the overall control program design. There is certainly nothing wrong with clearing the COP timeout mechanism more often than necessary, however, the firmware designer should avoid the temptation to randomly scatter the COP reset sequence throughout the program. Having too many reset sequences scattered throughout the program will increase the likelihood that an errant system condition will go undetected.

If a program is organized as a series of subroutines that are called from a main loop, two simple strategies may be used to determine the selection of the timeout rate and the placement of the clearing sequence. If the total execution time for all of the subroutines is relatively short and each one executes in approximately the same amount of time, a timeout period can be selected based on the total time required for the subroutines to execute in succession. In this case, a single clearing sequence can be placed any where within the main loop. While this method is simple and straightforward, the timeout rate may have to be lengthened as more and more subroutine calls are added to the main loop. This can result in a poor response to an erroneous condition that exists in the control system. An alternate strategy for a similarly structured control program, especially one where subroutine execution times varied widely, would be to select a timeout period based on the execution time of the longest subroutine and place a COP clearing sequence before each subroutine is called. While this would improve the overall system response time to a software problem, it may allow possible problems within short subroutines to go undetected for longer than is acceptable.

There are many other strategies that can be used to determine the watchdog timeout period and the clearing sequence placement. However, the basic principle that guides the selection of a strategy should be governed by the acceptable amount of time that a system may be inoperative without causing permanently destructive side effects. In this regard, a COP clearing sequence should **never** be placed in an interrupt service routine. It is quite possible for an interrupt routine to continue to execute properly and to occur often enough to keep the watchdog from generating a reset even though the main portion of the program is no longer functioning. In addition, because the COP watchdog timer system is part of the M68HC12 device, it, like any other block of logic on the chip, is susceptible to improper operation caused by electrical noise and/or electromagnetic radiation form a source outside the chip. Such problems usually occur in a poorly designed system or in systems placed in an environment for which they were not designed. The fact is, the COP timer system should not be viewed as a complete fail-safe mechanism for systems designed with the M68HC12.

The COP Control register (`COPCTL`), shown in Figure 4.10, contains the COP rate select bits `CR0`, `CR1` and `CR2`. In addition, the `FCOP` and `DISR` bits are also associated

Chapter 4: MCU Initialization

with the watchdog timer system, however, neither may be written in Normal operating modes. The `FCOP` bit, used to force a watchdog reset, is mainly used to test the M68HC12's interrupt logic during factory testing. The `DISR` bit is used to disable system resets from either the COP watchdog or the Clock monitor system. This bit is automatically set when the M68HC12 is reset in Special modes effectively disabling the watchdog timer system.

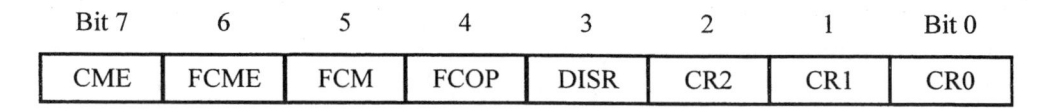

Bit 7	6	5	4	3	2	1	Bit 0
CME	FCME	FCM	FCOP	DISR	CR2	CR1	CR0

Figure 4.10: COP Control Register

The `DISR` bit may only be written in Special operating modes. All writes to this bit are ignored in Normal operating modes. If a target system is designed to come out of reset in one of the Special modes and then later switch to Normal mode, the `DISR` bit must be cleared before changing modes if the COP watchdog timer or Clock Monitor timer is used in the application. If it is not cleared, the `DISR` bit will remain set in Normal mode keeping the COP timer and Clock Monitor reset functions disabled no matter what value is written to the `COPCTL` register.

4.8 Clock Monitor Timer

Because the watchdog timer is based on the M68HC12's clock, the COP timer cannot detect difficulties that may result from problems with the M68HC12 clock source. The Clock Monitor timer system provides an additional level of system protection if a problem occurs with the microcontroller's clock source. The Clock Monitor consists of a simple resetable monostable timer controlled by an internal resistor-capacitor (RC) network. If the system E-clock edges do not keep the timer reset within the delay set by the RC time constant, a system reset is generated. Because this mechanism operates on a simple RC delay, the Clock Monitor can operate even without a clock present.

Standard CMOS semiconductor processing allows for the production of very accurate capacitor elements. However, the absolute value of resistive elements varies widely from wafer to wafer. Because of this variation, the timeout period may vary greatly from device to device. The timeout periods presented in Figure 4.11 show that when operating with a V_{DD} level of 5 volts ± 10%, the Clock Monitor will generate a system reset when the operating frequency falls between 500 KHz (2 µS period) and 50 KHz (20 µS period). When operating with a V_{DD} level of 3 volts ± 10%, the Clock Monitor will generate a system reset when the operating frequency falls between 200 KHz (5 µS period) and 10 KHz (100 µS period). Obviously this prevents the use of the Clock Monitor timer on systems operating below 500 KHz when powered by a 5 volt supply, and 200 KHz when powered by a 3 volt supply.

Section 4.8: Clock Monitor Timer

V_{DD}	Clock Frequency Range
5 V ± 10%	500 KHz - 50 KHz
3 V ± 10%	200 KHz - 10 KHz

Figure 4.11: Clock Monitor Minimum Frequency Range

Three bits in the COPCTL register, Force Clock Monitor reset (FCM), Clock Monitor Enable (CME) and Force Clock Monitor Enable (FCME), are used to control the operation of the Clock Monitor timer. The FCM bit has a similar function to the FCOP bit. It is used to force a Clock Monitor reset during factory testing. Like the FCOP bit, it can only be written in Special modes. The use of the Clock Monitor function is controlled by the CME bit. Unlike all the other bits in the COPCTL register that are write-once protected or may not be written in Normal modes, the CME bit may be read or written at any time in all operating modes. This feature allows system designers to make use of the Clock Monitor function even if the application must place the M68HC12 in the low power stop mode. In this case the CME bit would have to be cleared just prior to executing the STOP instruction and then set after exiting the stop mode.

Allowing the Clock Monitor function to be enabled and disabled in this manner provides a great deal of flexibility for applications that must utilize the low power stop mode or must switch to lower operating frequencies to reduce power consumption. However, this flexibility does present an opportunity for possible problems by allowing accidental writes to the CME bit to disable the Clock Monitor function. For those applications requiring it, the FCME bit provides a mechanism to permanently enable the Clock Monitor, preventing it from being accidentally disabled. The FCME bit is write-once protected in normal modes and may be read or written at any time in Special modes.

While most systems utilize a reliable clock source and do not require the Clock Monitor function, it can be used as a backup to protect against the accidental execution of the STOP instruction. When the M68HC12 executes the STOP instruction, all on-chip clocks are stopped thus halting program execution and the functioning of the on-chip peripherals. The critical nature of many applications will not tolerate the microcontroller entering this state. A stop disable bit (S) in the condition code register, when set, causes the STOP instruction to be treated like a NOP instruction continuing execution with the next sequential instruction. For added protection against accidentally entering the stop mode, the Clock Monitor can be enabled. If the S bit accidentally gets cleared and a STOP opcode is executed, the Clock Monitor will generate a system reset, restarting the clock and beginning program execution from the Clock Monitor interrupt service routine.

The operation of the Clock Monitor timer with a complete loss of the MCU clock source actually introduces a paradoxical situation for the M68HC12. Because the completion of the reset operation requires the MCU clocks, the reset pin will be driven to a low level and will remain asserted until a clock source is reapplied. Fortunately, however, a complete loss of the clock source is not the usual case. In many cases the system wide assertion of reset will correct the cause of the stopped clock and recovery can proceed much as if a COP watchdog timeout had occurred.

4.9 REAL TIME INTERRUPT

While the initialization of the Real Time Interrupt (RTI) is not critical to the basic operation of the microcontroller, it very often plays an essential part in the operation of a system's control program. The Real Time Interrupt can be used to generate a hardware interrupt at a fixed periodic rate without using one of the main timer channels. One of the uses of a periodic interrupt is for generating the basic system 'tick' for a Real Time Operating System (RTOS). The tick or heartbeat of a real time operating system is the basic rate used by the operating system to allocate time to the various system tasks. Each time the basic tick interrupt occurs the RTOS suspends the currently executing task and uses its internal task scheduling algorithm to determine if other tasks require some of the CPU's time. Each scheduled task is given a 'time slice' equal to the period of the Real Time Interrupt based on the tasks priority and the urgency of other events occurring in the system.

Applications not using a conventional real time operating system often organize the software into a series of subroutines called from a main program loop. Generally the entire set of subroutines is called once each time through this main loop. However, the amount of time required to execute each subroutine varies because of changing conditions in the system even though the maximum execution time for all the subroutines is well defined. In many cases it is desirable for the entire group of subroutines to execute only once during a fixed time interval. The Real Time Interrupt can be used as the execution pacing signal in a design of this type. When the end of the main loop is reached, the software could wait for a signal from the Real Time Interrupt service routine before returning to the top of the main loop.

One of the applications for which the RTI timer is not well suited is keeping the time of day. There are two reasons for this limitation. First, because the RTI rates are based on a simple binary divider chain, interrupts cannot be generated at a rate consistent with keeping track of seconds, minutes, and hours unless a clock source representing an even power of two is used. For instance to generate an interrupt of exactly 1, 2, 4, 8 or 16 mS which could then be divided further in software to produce seconds, minutes and hours counters, would require a crystal frequency of exactly 16.384 MHz; not a commonly available crystal.

The second reason has to do with the initial accuracy and the relatively poor long term frequency stability of common microprocessor quartz crystals. The initial accuracy of all quartz crystals is specified with a specific drive level, load capacitance, and oscillator circuit. Duplicating these three factors in large volume production situation may be difficult. To trim the frequency of the oscillator, a variable capacitor would have to be added to the circuit and a calibration operation would have to added to the production operation. While the short

Section 4.9: Real Time Interrupt

term stability of even inexpensive quartz crystals is very good, their frequencies tend to shift over time and temperature, many times by hundreds of parts per million. If an application must keep an accurate time of day clock, the 50 Hz or 60 Hz power line should be used as a frequency reference. While the power line does not provide good short term frequency stability, its long term frequency stability is excellent.

The operation of the Real Time Interrupt is controlled by the Real Time Interrupt Control register (`RTICTL`) and the Real Time Interrupt Flag register (`RTIFLG`). In addition, the `RTICTL` register contains additional control bits governing the operation of both the Real Time Interrupt and COP watchdog timer in the CPU12 during wait and background operating modes. As shown in Figure 4.12, the `RTICTL` contains three bits, `RTR0`, `RTR1` and `RTR2` allowing the selection of one of seven Real Time Interrupt rates. Because the initial state of these three bits after reset is zero, the Real Time Interrupt system is disabled by default. The RTI rates are based on the M68HC12's E-clock divided by 2^{13} and provide rates of increasing time period based on successive powers of two. Figure 4.13, shows the RTI periods based on both 4.0 MHz and 8.0 MHz E-Clocks. Unlike the rate select bits for the COP watchdog timer, the Real Time Interrupt rate select bits may be read or written at any time in any of the operating modes.

Bit 7	6	5	4	3	2	1	Bit 0
RTIE	RSWAI	RSBCK	0	RTBYP	RTR2	RTR1	RTR0

Figure 4.12: Real Time Interrupt Control Register (`RTICTL`)

At the expiration of the selected RTI period, the Real Time Interrupt Flag (`RTIF`) bit in the `RTIFLG` register is set. However, an interrupt will only be generated if the Real Time Interrupt Enable (`RTIE`) bit in the `RTICTL` register is set. Having a separate control bit to enable RTI interrupts allows the RTI timer to be used in applications that require polled operation of the RTI timer. In either case, software must clear the `RTIF` bit by writing a one to it when it is set. Because the clock source for the RTI timer is a free running counter that cannot be stopped or interrupted, the RTI timeout periods will remain constant regardless of any software latencies associated with clearing the `RTIF` bit. A new RTI period begins from the completion of the previous RTI period and not from the clearing of the `RTIF` bit. Note that both the RTI rate select bits and the `RTIE` bit may be read or written any time in both Normal and Special operating modes.

RTR2	RTR1	RTR0	Divide E By:	E = 4.0 MHz Timeout Period	E = 8.0 MHz Timeout Period
0	0	0	OFF	OFF	OFF
0	0	1	2^{13}	2.048 mS	1.024 mS
0	1	0	2^{14}	4.096 mS	2.048 mS
0	1	1	2^{15}	8.196 mS	4.096 mS
1	0	0	2^{16}	16.384 mS	8.196 mS
1	0	1	2^{17}	32.768 mS	16.384 mS
1	1	0	2^{18}	65.536 mS	32.768 mS
1	1	1	2^{19}	131.72 mS	65.536 mS

Figure 4.13: Real Time Interrupt Rates

The RTI and COP Stop in Wait (RSWAI) and RTI and COP Stop in Background (RSBCK) bits can be used to exercise additional control over the Real Time Interrupt and COP watchdog timers in the CPU12 Wait and Background Debug modes. Both the RSWAI and the RSBCK bits may only be written once in Normal Modes and may be written any time in Special modes. Setting the RSWAI bit in the RTICTL register cause both the RTI and COP timers to be disabled when the CPU12 executes the WAI instruction and enters the wait mode. This control bit does more than just inhibit interrupts from the RTI timer or a reset from the COP watchdog, it actually turns off the clock source to these modules leaving them in a suspended state until the CPU12 exits the wait mode. This feature is quite useful for applications that must enter the Wait mode for long periods of time to conserve system power, yet require the services of the RTI or COP watchdog timer when running. There is one precaution that must be taken when using this feature in conjunction with the COP watchdog timer. Because the COP watchdog timer runs asynchronously to the executing software, it is possible that the COP may be ready to expire just before the Wait mode is entered. Because of the latency involved in exiting the CPU12 Wait mode, it's possible that the COP could timeout during the recovery period. To prevent this potential problem, the watchdog should be reset just before entering the Wait mode.

The RSBCK bit performs a function similar in nature to the RSWAI bit. When the RSBCK is set both the RTI and COP timers are disabled when the CPU12 enters the active Background Debug mode. Because the Background Debug firmware does not service the COP timer, it would initiate a system reset when the active Background Mode was entered during the development process. If the Real Time Interrupt were not disabled while in active Background Mode, it would most likely time out and cause an RTI interrupt to be pending when returning to normal program execution. These features, while extremely valuable

Section 4.10: Initialization Code

during the debugging process, should not be enabled in the production release of the target application code. In general it is not possible to enable the Background Debug mode without the use of a debug tool attached to the M68HC12 BDM interface. However, it has been observed in systems with inadequate power-down reset circuits and in systems designed with insufficient attention to system electrical noise. In these cases, a BGND instruction was inadvertently executed, placing the M68HC12 in active Background Mode. If the COP watchdog is disabled because the RSBCK bit is set, the M68HC12 will remain in active Background Mode waiting for a command from the debug tool. For such cases, if the RSBCK bit is not set, the watchdog timer would time out generating a reset of the target system.

Finally, the Real Time Interrupt Divider Chain Bypass (RTBYP) bit is used specifically for factory testing and is only writeable in Special modes. Setting this bit substitutes a divide by four counter for the normal divide by 2^{13} counter.

4.10 INITIALIZATION CODE

The assembly listing shown in Figure 4.14 is typical of the code sequence necessary to initialize the basic functions of an MC68HC912B32 microcontroller as discussed in this chapter. The first file included at the top of the listing, Config.Asm shown in Figure 4.15, contains basic configuration information required to perform the initialization of an MC68HC912B32 running in Normal Single Chip mode. The LimRegs.Asm file, also included in the startup code, contains symbolic register name definitions for the Lite Integration Module (LIM). The contents of this file can be found in Appendix B. Because the addresses of the register names in the LimRegs.Asm and other files in Appendix B are based on the value of the symbol RegBase, the Config.Asm file should always be included before any of the register name definition files.

Chapter 4: MCU Initialization

```
;
        include "Config.Asm"     ; Config info for single chip mode.
        include "LimRegs.Asm"    ; register & bit definitions for the LIM.
;
StartUp: lds    #RAMBase+RAMSize ; init the SP to top of RAM + 1.
         ldaa   #Regbase>>8      ; get upper 8-bits of the reg base addr.
         staa   _INITRG          ; move base address of the I/O registers.
         nop                     ; rqt of moving the I/O base address.
         ldaa   #RAMBase>>8      ; get upper 8-bits of the RAM base addr.
         staa   INITRM           ; move the base address of the RAM.
         nop                     ; rqt of moving the RAM base address.
         ldaa   #((EEBase>>8)&$f0)+EEON ; get upper 4-bits of EE base addr.
         staa   INITEE           ; move the base address of the EEPROM.
         nop                     ; rqt of moving the EEPROM base address.
         ldaa   #COPOff          ; disable the COP & clock monitor timers.
         staa   COPCTL
         ldaa   #NSCMode         ; Normal Single Chip operating mode.
         staa   MODE             ; lock the operating mode.
;
         ldaa   #ROMON+MAPROM    ; make sure that the Flash remains on
         staa   MISC             ; in the upper half of the memory map.
         ldaa   #NDBE+NECLK      ; config Port E pin functions for general
         staa   PEAR             ; purpose I/O (default for Single chip).
         ldaa   #0               ; config Port A, B & E for normal
         staa   RDRIV            ; pin drive levels.
         bclr   RTICTL,RSWAI+RSBCK ; enable RTI & COP in wait & Bkgd.
         .
         .
         .
```

Figure 4.14: MC68HC912B32 Startup code for Normal Single Chip Mode

The initialization process begins at the label Startup by initializing the stack pointer and fixing the base address of the I/O registers. Notice that the symbol used to initialize the base address of the I/O registers, _INITRG, begins with an underline. This alternate symbol, defined in the Config.Asm, is used because the value of the symbol INITRG, defined in LimRegs.Asm, is based on the value assigned to the symbol RegBase. In this particular case, where the base address of the internal I/O registers are not moved from their default position, this extra symbol would be redundant. However, this allows the registers to be moved by simply changing the value of the RegBase symbol rather rather than having to change the startup code. After relocating the internal I/O registers, the remaining on-chip resources are move to their desired locations.

Next the COP watchdog timer and Clock Monitor is disabled by writing the value COPOff to the COP Control Register. This symbol is defined to have a value of zero in the file LimRegs.Asm. Because COP timeout rates are dependent on the target clock

Section 4.10: Initialization Code

frequency, the symbol definitions for COP timeout rates are contained in the `Config.Asm` rather than in the `LimRegs.Asm` file. Even though the Clock Monitor function is disabled here, remember that it can be enabled and disabled at anytime by writing to the `CME` bit in the `COPCTL` register. However, if an application requires the Clock Monitor function be permanently enabled, the defined value of `FCME` can be added to the value `COPOff` before writing to the COP control register. Next, the `MODE` register is written to lock the operating mode of the MC68HC912B32, in this case Normal Single-chip mode. Remember, even if the operating mode is not changed from the mode set by the levels on the BKGD, MODB and MODA pins, this register must be written to prevent the it from accidentally being changed.

The next three protected registers, `MISC`, `PEAR` and `RDRIV`, are initialized to keep the on-chip Flash turned on in the upper half of the memory map, configure the `PORTE` pins for general purpose I/O and set ports A, B and E for normal drive levels. The final instruction in the initialization sequence, BCLR, is used to clear the `RSWAI` and `RSBCK` bits to enable the COP watchdog and Real Time Interrupt timer when the the CPU12 is in the Wait and Background Debug modes. Using bit manipulation instructions is not normally recommended for initializing individual write-once bits. However, because these two bits are the only protected bits in the register and because both of the bits are being set to the same value, using the bit manipulation instruction is safe. If these two bits were being written with different values or if the register contained other write-once protected bits programmed with different values, the bit manipulation instructions could not be used. In that case, the load/store sequence used to initialize the other protected registers should be used.

```
;
NSCMode:    equ     $90             ; Normal Single-Chip Mode.
NEWMode:    equ     $f0             ; Normal Expanded Wide Mode
;
_INITRG:    equ     $0011           ; default addr of INITRG register.
;
RegBase:    equ     $0000           ; base address of I/O register block.
SysClock:   equ     8000000         ; system clock frequency.
RAMBase:    equ     $0800           ; base address of on chip RAM.
RAMSize:    equ     1024            ; number of bytes of on-chip RAM
EEBase:     equ     $0d00           ; base address of on-chip EEPROM.
EESize:     equ     768             ; number of bytes of on-chip EEPROM.
FEEBase:    equ     $8000           ; base address of on-chip Flash EEPROM.
FEESize:    equ     32768           ; number of bytes of on-chip Flash EEPROM.
;
COP1mS:     equ     1               ; 1 mS timeout based on 8.0 Mhz clock.
COP4mS:     equ     2               ; 4 mS timeout based on 8.0 Mhz clock.
COP16mS:    equ     3               ; 16 mS timeout based on 8.0 Mhz clock.
COP65mS:    equ     4               ; 65 mS timeout based on 8.0 Mhz clock.
COP262mS:   equ     5               ; 262 mS timeout based on 8.0 Mhz clock.
COP524mS:   equ     6               ; 524 mS timeout based on 8.0 Mhz clock.
COP1S:      equ     7               ; 1 Sec. timeout based on 8.0 Mhz clock.
;
```

Figure 4.15: Basic Configuration Equate File

4.11 SPECIAL MODE INITIALIZATION CONSIDERATIONS

Most applications will utilize the M68HC12 in one of the Normal operating modes from the moment the microcontroller comes out of reset. However, there may be some specialized applications that require the special privileges or access to some of the M68HC12's test registers when the M68HC12 is operated in Special mode. Resetting an M68HC12 in Special single-chip mode always places the microcontroller in active background mode. Consequently, this operating mode is only valuable during target system development and software debugging when a development tool is connected to the M68HC12's Single-Wire Background Debug interface. The only two Special operating modes available for normal program execution are Special Expanded Wide or Special Expanded Narrow. As mentioned previously, it is not a good idea to allow an application to run in Special Mode any longer than necessary because the write-once register protection mechanism is disabled. Switching from a Special to a Normal operating mode requires additional considerations for the initialization code.

When switching from Special to a Normal operating mode, the write-once register protection mechanism is re-enabled. This requires the initialization software to rewrite any of the protected registers initialized while running in Special mode. Failure to follow this

Section 4.11: Special Mode Initialization Considerations

recommendation may lead to total program failure if the registers are left unprotected and are accidentally written with an improper value.

In addition to reinitializing any of the protected registers written while running in Special mode, specific consideration must be given to the initialization of the `COPCTL` register before switching operating modes. Remember that the `DISR` bit in the `COPCTL` register is automatically set in Special modes. This effectively disables the COP and Clock Monitor functions by *inhibiting* either of these modules from generating system resets. Although the Clock Monitor function is disabled when the M68HC12 exits reset, the COP watchdog function is actually enabled, though a reset from a timeout is inhibited. Because the `DISR` control bit in the `COPCTL` register may only be changed while running in Special mode, it must be written from a one to a zero before switching operating modes. However, if the COP Timer Rate Select Bits `CR2:CR0` are written to a value other than zero at the same time the `DISR` control bit is written to zero **and** enough time has elapsed that a COP timeout occurred, a watchdog reset will take place immediately. This will restart the microcontroller initialization sequence which will eventually result in another COP watchdog reset when the `DISR` control bit is cleared. This sequence of events will continue to occur in an endless loop never allowing the CPU12 to complete its initialization sequence and begin running the target application code.

If the COP watchdog timer or the Clock Monitor are used in the application, one of two different methods must be used to prevent this condition from occurring when switching from Special to Normal mode. Writing a value of $00 to the `COPCTL` register will not only clear the `DISR` bit and the COP Timer Rate Select Bits, but it also has the effect of resetting the COP timer. Using this method has the advantage of keeping the COP timer disabled indefinitely until the MODE register is written and a new value is written to the `COPCTL` register in Normal operating mode. The assembly listing shown in Figure 4.16 illustrates the use of this method.

The second method involves using the standard COP reset sequence to reset the COP timer before clearing the `DISR` control bit and writing a non-zero value to the COP Timer Rate Select Bits. In this case, the watchdog timer is enable during the remainder of the initialization process and must be serviced accordingly. Figure 4.17 shows the use of this method.

The code in Figures 4.16 and 4.17 illustrate two other subtle points regarding the re-initialization of the Internal I/O Register Position register and other resource mapping registers. Notice that when the `INITRG` register is written the second time, the register name used is not preceded by an underline character. Instead the symbol name defined in the `LimRegs.Asm` file must be used because the I/O register block has already been relocated. In addition, notice that the second time the resource mapping registers are written, `NOP` instructions do not follow the store instructions. This requirement is not necessary the second time these registers are written because the registers are not being moved to a new location.

Chapter 4: MCU Initialization

```
;
        include "Config.Asm"      ; Config info for single chip mode.
        include "LimRegs.Asm"     ; register & bit definitions for the LIM.
;
StartUp: lds    #RAMBase+RAMSize  ; init the SP to top of RAM + 1.
        ldaa    #Regbase>>8       ; get upper 8-bits of the reg base addr.
        staa    _INITRG           ; move base address of the I/O registers.
        nop                       ; rqt of moving the I/O base address.
        ldaa    #RAMBase>>8       ; get upper 8-bits of the RAM base addr.
        staa    INITRM            ; move the base address of the RAM.
        nop                       ; rqt of moving the RAM base address.
        .
        .
        .
        ldaa    #COPOff           ; disable the COP & clock monitor timers.
        staa    COPCTL
        ldaa    LSTRE+RDWE        ; enable all bus control signals for
        staa    PEAR              ; external memory access.
        ldaa    #NEWMode          ; Normal Expanded Wide operating mode.
        staa    MODE              ; store twice to switch from Special
        staa    MODE              ; to Normal mode.
;
        ldaa    #Regbase>>8       ; re-initialize the INITRG register
        staa    INITRG            ; to lock its value.
        ldaa    #RAMBase>>8       ; re-initialize the INITRM register
        staa    INITRM            ; to lock its value.
        .
        .
        .
        ldaa    #COP65mS          ; set the COP for 65 mS timeout.
        staa    COPCTL
        .
        .
        .
```

Figure 4.16: Resetting and Disabling the COP Timer Before Switching Modes

Important Information

An additional point illustrated in Figures 4.16 and 4.17 involves the initialization of the NECLK bit in the PEAR register when switching from single chip to expanded mode. When operating an M68HC12 family device in expanded mode the E-clock signal is normally required for de-multiplexing the external address and data bus. When a device is reset in Normal Single Chip mode the NECLK bit has a value of zero configuring pin PE4 as general purpose I/O. As stated in the M68HC912B32 documentation, the NECLK bit may be written once in Normal Single Chip mode but writes to NECLK are ignored in Expanded

181

Section 4.11: Special Mode Initialization Considerations

modes. When changing from Normal Single Chip to either Expanded operating mode, the PEAR register *must* be written with NECLK equal to zero *before* the MODE register is written to enable the E-clock on pin PE4. Failure to perform these writes in the proper order will result in PE4 remaining configured as a general purpose I/O pin.

```
;
          include "Config.Asm"      ; Config info for single chip mode.
          include "LimRegs.Asm"     ; register & bit definitions for the LIM.
;
StartUp:  lds     #RAMBase+RAMSize  ; init the SP to top of RAM + 1.
          ldaa    #Regbase>>8       ; get upper 8-bits of the reg base addr.
          staa    _INITRG           ; move base address of the I/O registers.
          nop                       ; rqt of moving the I/O base address.
          ldaa    #RAMBase>>8       ; get upper 8-bits of the RAM base addr.
          staa    INITRM            ; move the base address of the RAM.
          nop                       ; rqt of moving the RAM base address.
          .
          .
          .
          ldaa    #$55              ; value to arm the COP reset mechanism.
          staa    COPRST
          coma                      ; value to complete the reset sequence.
          staa    COPRST
          ldaa    #COP1S+FCME       ; clear the DISR bit and enable
          staa    COPCTL            ; the COP & clock monitor timers.
          ldaa    LSTRE+RDWE        ; enable all bus control signals for
          staa    PEAR              ; external memory access.
          ldab    #NEWMode          ; Normal Expanded Wide operating mode.
          stab    MODE              ; store twice to switch from Special
          stab    MODE              ; to Normal mode.
;
          staa    COPCTL            ; lock the COPCTL register.
          ldaa    #Regbase>>8       ; re-initialize the INITRG register
          staa    INITRG            ; to lock its value.
          ldaa    #RAMBase>>8       ; re-initialize the INITRM register
          staa    INITRM            ; to lock its value.
          .
          .
          .
```

Figure 4.17: Resetting and Enabling the COP Timer Before Switching Modes

Questions/Exercises

4.1   How are sensitive configuration registers protected from accidental alteration in the M68HC12 family? Why is this method more desirable than the method used in the M68HC11 family?

Chapter 4: MCU Initialization

4.2   What restriction does this method place on the initialization of protected registers?

4.3   How is access to these registers affected by operating mode?

4.4   What programming restriction must be followed when remapping internal resources?

4.5   What happens when two internal resources are mapped to the same address space?

4.6   What are the advantages and disadvantages of setting the MMSWAI bit before wntering the CPU wait mode?

4.7   What precautions should be used when moving the on-chip I/O register block by writing to the INITRG?

4.8   What precautions should be used when moving the on-chip EEPROM by writing to the INITEE?

4.9   How is the initial operating mode of an M68HC12 microcontroller determined?

4.10 What is the purpose of the IVIS bit in the MODE register?

4.11 When operating the M68HC12 in expanded mode, what is the benefit of having the external E-clock signal stretch during internal accesses? What controls the stretching of the E-clock?

4.12 What considerations must be made when executing programs from external memory?

4.13 What special feature of the M68HC12 family allows easy connection of 8-bit peripherals to a 16-bit external bus?

4.14 What important difference exists between the M68HC12 and M68HC11 COP watchdog timers?

4.15 What difference exists in the operation of the COP watchdog timer when the M68HC12 operates in Special mode?

4.16 What clearing sequence must be used to keep the COP timer from generating a system reset?

Section 4.11: Special Mode Initialization Considerations

4.17   What things should be considered in the placement of the COP clearing sequence within the control system's program.

4.18   What system level restrictions are placed on the use of the Clock Monitor timer? What feature of the Clock Monitor allows this restriction to be overcome.

4.19   The Real Time Interrupt timer is best suited for what types of applications?

4.20   What feature is shared by both the COP and Real Time Interrupt timer that aids the debugging process?

4.21   What special precaution(s) must be observed when switching from Special to Normal operating modes?

Chapter 5   INTERRUPTS AND RESETS

The CPU12 responds to a general class of processing exceptions that include resets and interrupts. Each exception or group of exceptions has one or more associated 16-bit exception vectors containing the address of an exception handler. In the case of reset exceptions, the 16-bit address should point to software that initializes or reinitializes the entire microcontroller and target system. Interrupt exception vectors point to code known as an interrupt service routine. An interrupt service routine is much the same as a subroutine. It is generally written to perform a specific task, usually involving an event occuring asynchronous to the execution of the main program. The primary difference between a subroutine and an interrupt service routine is the final instruction used to return to the previously executing code. Subroutines are terminated by executing either the RTS or RTC instruction. The RTS instruction terminates subroutines called with a JSR or BSR instruction while the RTC instruction terminates subroutines located in expanded memory invoked with a CALL instruction. Because the entire internal state of the CPU12 is placed on the stack in response to an interrupt exception, an RTI instruction must be used to terminate an interrupt service routine.

The exception vector table is located in the upper 128 bytes of the CPU12's standard 64K-byte address space. Because each exception vector is comprised of two bytes, this allows for 64 separate interrupt sources. Because the exception vectors are only two bytes in length, the initial instructions comprising the exception handler may not be located in expanded memory. This does not mean that the majority of the interrupt handler could not reside in expanded memory or that the interrupt handler cannot call subroutines located in expanded memory.

This chapter contains a general discussion of exception processing as it relates to the CPU12. It does not contain specific information on the interrupt capabilities of the

Section 5.1: Non-maskable Exceptions

peripherals contained on various M68HC12 family members. Chapters in this book describing the functionality of various M68HC12 family peripherals discuss each one's interrupt capabilities.

5.1 EXCEPTION TYPES

There are basically two classes of exceptions recognized by the CPU12. Non-maskable exceptions include three reset sources, a software interrupt, an unimplemented opcode trap, and a pseudo non-maskable interrupt. The resets, unimplemented opcode trap, and `SWI` instruction exceptions are unaffected by the state of the I-bit or X-bit in the condition code register. The XIRQ interrupt is actually a pseudo non-maskable interrupt. Service requests from the XIRQ input pin are ignored when the X-bit in the CPU12's condition code register is set. All other interrupt sources are masked when the I-bit in the condition code register is set.

5.2 NON-MASKABLE EXCEPTIONS

Vectors for the six non-maskable exceptions occupy the highest vector addresses in the 64K-byte memory map. The remaining 58 interrupt vectors, as shown in Figure 5.1, are used for all of the maskable interrupt sources. A hardware priority encoder determines the exception source serviced first when multiple exception requests are pending. In general, the higher the interrupt vector address' value, the higher its priority. While the non-maskable exception sources always have priority over the maskable sources, independent service priorities exist within the two groups.

Within the group of non-maskable exception sources, the reset exceptions have priority over the remaining three sources. When a reset exception occurs, the current CPU activity is immediately terminated. Reset exception processing begins by setting the X-bit and I-bit in the condition code register and filling the CPU12's instruction queue starting at the address contained in the associated reset vector. The M68HC12 distinguishes between an externally applied reset and an internally generated reset by sensing the state of the reset pin after the initial reset condition is recognized. As soon as a reset condition is detected, the M68HC12 drives the reset pin low for a period of 16 E-clock cycles and then releases it. After an additional period of eight E-clock cycles, the reset pin is sampled by the M68HC12. If the reset pin remains low, the POR/External reset vector is fetched. However, if the pin returns to a high level, either the Clock monitor or COP watchdog vector is fetched. To prevent an incorrect reset vector from being fetched, externally applied resets must hold the reset pin low for at least 32 E-clock cycles.

Vector Address	Priority	Exception Source
$FFFE - $FFFF	1	POR or External Reset
$FFFC - $FFFD	2	Clock Monitor Reset
$FFFA - $FFFB	3	COP watchdog Reset
$FFF8 - $FFF9	4	Unimplemented Instruction Trap
$FFF6 - $FFF7	5	Software Interrupt Instruction (SWI)
$FFF4 - $FFF5	6	XIRQ Signal
$FFF2 - $FFF3	1	IRQ Signal
$FF80 - $FFF1	*	Device Specific Interrupt Sources

Figure 5.1: CPU12 Exception Vector Map

Even though the SWI and unimplemented opcode trap instructions are grouped with the non-maskable exceptions, these sources actually have a low priority if an enabled interrupt source is pending before either of these instructions begins to execute. However, once the CPU12 begins execution of either the SWI or one of the TRAP instructions, no maskable interrupts will be recognized until the I-bit in the condition code register is cleared.

The XIRQ interrupt is an improved implementation of a non-maskable interrupt input. A non-maskable interrupt input is generally used in systems to notify a microcontroller of an extremely urgent service request or catastrophic system failure. One of the problems associated with a truly non-maskable interrupt is the possibility of the input being asserted before a system has been adequately initialized to a state where the system can properly respond to the request. To prevent such a situation from occurring in an M68HC12 system, XIRQ interrupts are inhibited by automatically setting the X-bit in the condition code register when the microcontroller exits the reset state. Once an adequate amount of system initialization has been performed, the X-bit may be cleared, enabling XIRQ interrupts. Once the X-bit is cleared, it may not directly be set by software. However, within the XIRQ interrupt service routine, the stacked value of the condition code register may be manipulated. Setting the *stacked* value of the X-bit within the XIRQ service routine causes the X-bit to remain a one when an RTI instruction is executed. This is the only way to change the value of the X-bit from a zero to a one without going through an MCU reset sequence. Figure 5.2 shows an XIRQ interrupt service routine fragment that manipulates the stacked value of the condition code register.

A second problem associated with true non-maskable interrupts allows a non-maskable interrupt service routine may be interrupted by another non-maskable interrupt request. Obviously, if a problem developed in a system causing multiple non-maskable interrupt requests, the system's stack would quickly overflow resulting in system run away. To prevent such a situation form occurring in an M68HC12 system, both the X-bit and the I-bit in the condition code register are set in response to an XIRQ interrupt request.

Section 5.3: Maskable Exceptions (Interrupts)

```
;
XIRQSrvc:   equ     *               ; beginning of xirq service.
            bset    0,sp,#$40       ; set the x-bit in stacked ccr.
              .
              .
              .
            rti                     ; restore all regs leaving the x-bit set.
;
```

Figure 5.2: Setting Stacked value of the X-bit

5.3 Maskable Exceptions (Interrupts)

Much like the M68HC11 family, the maskable interrupt sources include the external IRQ interrupt pin and the various on-chip peripheral systems. All of the maskable interrupt sources are controlled by the I-bit in the condition code register. When the I-bit is set, its default state out of reset, all maskable interrupts are inhibited. Unlike the X-bit, the I-bit may be set or cleared by software at any time. On-chip interrupt sources typically have interrupt mask bits allowing individual interrupt sources to be enabled or disabled without inhibiting all maskable interrupts. In addition, the M68HC12 family provides the ability to disable the external IRQ interrupt input without setting the the I-bit and thereby disabling all maskable interrupts. The Interrupt Control Register (INTCR), shown in Figure 5.3, contains the IRQ Enable (IRQEN) control bit allowing software control of the external IRQ interrupt input. When the IRQEN bit is set, its default state out of reset, the IRQ pin is connected to the interrupt control logic. When cleared, interrupts from the IRQ pin are inhibited regardless of the state of the I-bit in the condition code register.

Bit 7	6	5	4	3	2	1	Bit 0
IRQE	IRQEN	DLY	0	0	0	0	0

Figure 5.3: Interrupt Control Register

In addition to the IRQEN bit, the INTCR register contains the IRQ edge select (IRQE) bit and the oscillator startup delay (DLY) bit. The IRQE bit is used to select the manner in which the internal interrupt control logic responds to a signal applied to the IRQ pin. When the IRQE bit is cleared, the IRQ pin is configured as a level sensitive input, generating IRQ interrupts as long as the IRQ pin is held low. This operating mode is useful when several external peripheral devices are connected to the IRQ line as shown in Figure 5.4, and is similar to the way the internal peripherals are connected to the IRQ logic inside the M68HC12. In both instances, this simple wired-OR arrangement allows a peripheral to maintain a valid interrupt request to the CPU until the interrupt is recognized by the software. It is the software's responsibility to manipulate a peripheral's control registers to remove the interrupt request.

The exact manner in which peripherals are connected to an M68HC12 system will obviously depend on the hardware interface contained in the peripherals. However, the use of the IRQ interrupt input by peripherals is not restricted by the type of physical connection used to communicate with the peripheral. Peripherals may be connected to the address and data bus when operating in expanded mode, the Serial Peripheral Interface (SPI) or to the parallel ports and still utilize the IRQ interrupt to request service. Because the M68HC12 does not contain any interrupt priority logic or automatic interrupt vector generation for externally connected peripherals, the software for the IRQ interrupt service routine must perform these functions. Since all externally connected peripherals share a single interrupt vector, the IRQ interrupt service routine must check each peripheral to determine the one generating the interrupt. The order in which the peripherals are checked determines each peripheral's relative priority within the IRQ interrupt level. Deciding the priority to assign to each peripheral is a system design issue that depends on both the speed and frequency with which each peripheral is capable of generating service requests. Because software is required to determine the source of the interrupt, the average interrupt response time becomes progressively longer as more external peripherals are added to a system.

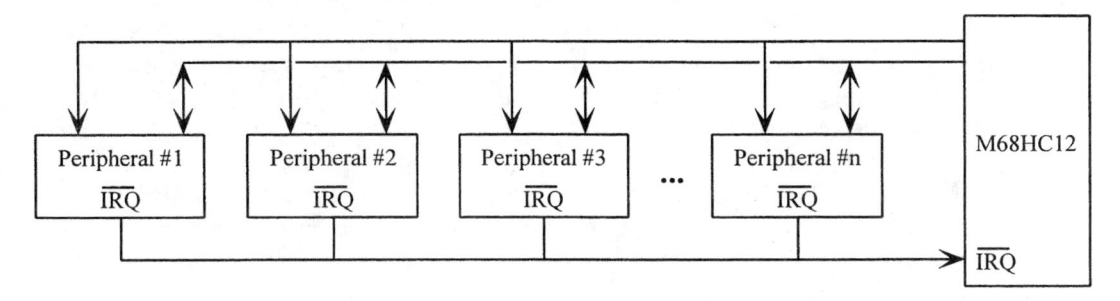

Figure 5.4: Level Sensitive IRQ Connection

Setting the `IRQE` bit configures the IRQ input to recognize only falling edges. This arrangement is only useful if a single peripheral is connected to the IRQ pin or if the IRQ pin is being driven by a periodic signal. Because the edge detect circuitry consists of a simple single bit latch, the interrupt must be serviced before the next falling edge occurs or the second interrupt request will be lost. When configured to recognize falling edges, no software is required to clear the latched interrupt request. It is cleared automatically by hardware when the IRQ vector is fetched. Note that the `IRQE` bit may be read at any time but is protected by the write-once mechanism in Normal operating modes.

The `DLY` bit in the `INTCR` register is not related to the control of the IRQ pin. This control bit is used to impose a 4096 E-clock cycle delay when exiting the CPU12's STOP mode. This delay allows for crystal oscillator stabilization before enabling clocks to the rest

Section 5.4: Maskable Interrupt Priority

of the M68HC12 device. This feature is enabled out of reset and should be used if the M68HC12's on-chip oscillator is utilized. While this delay does prevent an immediate recovery from the STOP mode, it helps to ensure that accurate clock timing is present before resuming microcontroller operation. If an external oscillator is used as a clock source for the M68HC12, a stabilization period is not required allowing immediate recovery from STOP mode. Like the `IRQE` bit, the `DLY` bit is protected by the write once mechanism in Normal operating modes and should be initialized even if its value is not changed from its default state.

5.4 Maskable Interrupt Priority

All maskable interrupt sources are prioritized in a fixed order as determined by the M68HC12's interrupt control block with the external IRQ interrupt having the highest priority. Like the M68HC11 family, the M68HC12 family provides the ability to elevate the priority of one maskable interrupt source above all other maskable interrupts. The highest priority maskable interrupt source is determined by the value contained in the `HPRIO` control register, shown in Figure 5.5. The implementation of bit six in the `HPRIO` register will vary to accommodate the total number of interrupt sources contained on a particular M68HC12 family member. For instance, on the MC68HC912B32 bit six is a read-only bit with a fixed value of one. On the other hand, the MC68HC912DA128 implements bit six as a read/write bit to accommodate its expanded number of interrupt sources. Note that bit zero is a read-only bit containing a fixed value of zero allowing only even values to be written to the HPRIO register.

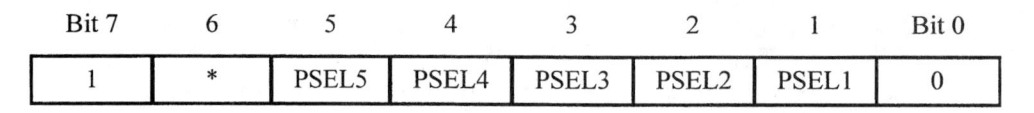

Bit 7	6	5	4	3	2	1	Bit 0
1	*	PSEL5	PSEL4	PSEL3	PSEL2	PSEL1	0

Figure 5.5: Highest Priority Maskable Interrupt (HPRIO) Register

At reset, the value of the `HPRIO` register is $F2 placing the external IRQ interrupt at the highest priority. The value of the `HPRIO` register can be read at any time; however, it may only be updated when the I-bit in the condition code register is set. This restriction is required to prevent race conditions from occurring in the CPU12 if an interrupt occurred when the `HPRIO` was written. Figure 5.6 contains a detailed interrupt vector map for the MC68HC912B32. As shown, the value written to the `HPRIO` register consists of the low byte of the even interrupt vector address. If, for instance, it were desired to elevate the Real Time Interrupt above other maskable interrupt sources, a value of $F0 would be written to the `HPRIO` register. Writing a value greater than $F2 or a value assigned to a reserved vector location will cause the IRQ interrupt to assume the highest priority.

Chapter 5: Interrupts and Resets

Vector Address	HPRIO Value	Exception Source
$FFFE - $FFFF	–	POR or External Reset
$FFFC - $FFFD	–	Clock Monitor Reset
$FFFA - $FFFB	–	COP watchdog Reset
$FFF8 - $FFF9	–	Unimplemented Instruction Trap
$FFF6 - $FFF7	–	Software Interrupt Instruction (SWI)
$FFF4 - $FFF5	–	XIRQ Signal
$FFF2 - $FFF3	$F2	IRQ Signal
$FFF0 - $FFF1	$F0	Real time Interrupt
$FFEE - $FFEF	$EE	Timer Channel 0
$FFEC - $FFED	$EC	Timer Channel 1
$FFEA - $FFEB	$EA	Timer Channel 2
$FFE8 - $FFE9	$E8	Timer Channel 3
$FFE6 - $FFE7	$E6	Timer Channel 4
$FFE4 - $FFE5	$E4	Timer Channel 5
$FFE2 - $FFE3	$E2	Timer Channel 6
$FFE0 - $FFE1	$E0	Timer Channel 7
$FFDE - $FFDF	$DE	Timer Overflow
$FFDC - $FFDD	$DC	Pulse Accumulator Overflow
$FFDA - $FFDB	$DA	Pulse Accumulator Edge
$FFD8 - $FFD9	$D8	Serial Peripheral Interface
$FFD6 - $FFD7	$D6	Serial Communications Interface 0
$FFD4 - $FFD5	–	Reserved
$FFD2 - $FFD3	$D2	Analog-to-Digital Converter
$FFD0 - $FFD1	$D0	Byte Data Link Controller
$FF80 - $FFCF	–	Reserved

Figure 5.6: Interrupt Vector Map for the MC68HC912B32

5.5 INTERRUPT SERVICE ROUTINE REQUIREMENTS

As mentioned at the beginning of this chapter, interrupt service routines are similar to subroutines with the exception of the final instruction. In addition, other issues that must be addressed when writing an interrupt service routine. The first and most important issue to address in the interrupt service routine is clearing the interrupt status flag causing the interrupt. Each on-chip peripheral capable of generating interrupts contains status flag bits in one of its control registers indicating the peripheral requires service. If a peripheral's local

Section 5.5: Interrupt Service Routine Requirements

interrupt enable bit has been set, the status bit will generate an interrupt when a particular peripheral occurs. It is the interrupt service routine's responsibility to clear the status flag before the service routine returns. Failing to clear the interrupt status bit will cause the peripheral to generate an endless string of interrupt requests. In most cases this will cause the M68HC12 to become stuck in an endless loop, continually executing the same interrupt service routine.

The method for clearing interrupt status flags varies from peripheral to peripheral, but in general it involves writing a value to the status bit's associated control register. In some instances, however, interrupt status bits are automatically cleared by software's normal response to the interrupt. For example, the Receive Data Register Full (RDRF) bit in the SCI system is automatically cleared when the SCI status register is read followed by a read of the SCI data register when the RDRF bit set. Caution must be exercised when reading or writing a peripheral's status and control registers to ensure that multiple status bits are not accidentally modified. When a peripheral is being initialized for interrupt driven operation, care should be utilized if it is necessary to read or write status registers outside of the interrupt service routine.

Important Information

All internal and external interrupt requests are latched when they occur and, with the exception of some of the fuzzy logic instructions, are only recognized and processed between instructions. However, because of a design fault in some M68HC12 peripheral modules, if an interrupt occurs during the execution of an instruction clearing a peripheral's local interrupt enable bit, the interrupt will remain latched in the interrupt controller even though the interrupt source has been removed. Under these conditions, the interrupt controller will fetch the Software Interrupt vector (SWI) and execute the SWI's interrupt service routine. To avoid this unintentional spurious interrupt recognition, it is **strongly** recommended that a peripheral's interrupt enable bit(s) only be cleared when the I-bit in the condition code register is set.

Because many applications only disable a peripheral's interrupt enable bit(s) from within an interrupt service routine, the I-bit will already be masked. For those applications disabling a peripheral's interrupts outside the interrupt service routine, it is **strongly** recommended that the instruction used to disable the peripheral's interrupts be preceded by an SEI instruction and followed by a CLI instruction. For instances where the state of the I-bit is unknown when disabling a peripheral's interrupts, the condition code register should be saved and restored as shown in Figure 5.7

```
;
        .
        .
        pshc                    ; save current state of the I-bit.
        sei                     ; disable all I-bit interrupts.
        bclr    TMSK1,#$01      ; disable timer Ch. 0 interrupts.
        pulc                    ; restore ccr.
        .
        .
;
```

Figure 5.7: Disabling I-bit maskable interrupts before disabling a peripheral's interrupts

Another important consideration when writing an interrupt service routine is the length of time spent in the service routine itself. Remember that after all of the CPU12's registers are stacked, the X-bit and/or I-bit in the condition code register is set. This prevents the CPU12 from recognizing additional pending interrupt requests while executing the interrupt service routine. This automatic mechanism, which prevents the nesting of interrupts, can result in a slow overall interrupt response time, especially if interrupt service routines require a large amount of CPU time. Keeping the length of the interrupt service routines to an absolute minimum is the best way to ensure that a system's interrupt response time is adequate. The interrupt service routine should contain the smallest amount of code necessary to clear the interrupt source and prepare the peripheral for the next interrupt event. Any data gathered or generated by the interrupt event can be passed to the main program through global variables for further processing and notifying the main program of the data's availability through a software semaphore flag. While this may be an adequate solution in systems that are heavily interrupt driven, it may not be effective for many systems.

Systems requiring faster interrupt response times or systems required to perform lengthy calculations in the interrupt service routine do have another option. Although the CPU12's hardware mechanism prevents nested interrupts, the system software designer may elect to allow interrupt nesting by clearing the condition code register interrupt mask bit(s) within an interrupt service routine. Great care must be exercised when using this technique to prevent a situation where multiple nested interrupts could cause the CPU12's stack to overflow. Before clearing the condition code register interrupt mask bit(s), software must ensure the status flag causing the interrupt has been cleared. If this operation is not performed, the stack will very quickly overflow resulting in CPU run away.

In observing the general rule of keeping interrupt service routines as short as possible, subroutine calls from within an interrupt service routine should be avoided or kept to an absolute minimum. In the event that subroutine calls are necessary, there are several precautions to observe. All subroutines called from within an interrupt service routine

Section 5.5: Interrupt Service Routine Requirements

should be reentrant. This is especially important if the subroutine is shared with main program code or is called after interrupts have been re-enabled from within the interrupt service routine. Failure to follow this recommendation will likely result in random failure of a system when a shared subroutine is interrupted. When programming in a high-level language such as C, care must be exercised when utilizing library functions provided by the compiler vendor to ensure that they are reentrant.

Important Information

Like the M68HC11, there is a subtle difference in the way the I-bit is set and cleared. When the I-bit is set by an instruction, interrupts are immediately inhibited. If an interrupt occurs during the execution of an instruction that sets the I-bit, the interrupt remains pending until the I-bit is later cleared. However, when an instruction is executed that clears the I-bit, the actual clear operation is delayed for one E-clock cycle. This means that the instruction following the I-bit clearing instruction is always executed. This one cycle delay is required for proper use of the Wait for Interrupt (WAI) instruction as shown in Figure 5.8. If the one E-clock cycle delay was not imposed when clearing the I-bit, it is possible that an interrupt could be recognized between the CLI and WAI instructions. If the interrupt was recognized and serviced between these two instructions, the WAI instruction would cause the CPU to incorrectly wait for the interrupt source that had just been serviced.

```
    ;
            .
            .
            .
            cli    ; enable I-bit maskable interrupts.
            wai    ; wait here for the next interrupt.
            .
            .
    ;
```

Figure 5.8: CLI/WAI Instruction Sequence

A common error for programmers that are new to Motorola microcontroller architectures is to place an SEI (ORCC #$10) instruction at the beginning of the interrupt service routine and a CLI (ANDCC #$EF) instruction just before the RTI instruction at the end of the interrupt service routine. The SEI instruction at the beginning of the routine is simply redundant because the I-bit is automatically set by the CPU12 hardware before the service routine is entered. The CLI instruction is also redundant because the I-bit will automatically be cleared when the condition code register is restored from the stack. Because

Chapter 5: Interrupts and Resets

of the one E-clock cycle delay in the clearing of the I-bit, the `RTI` instruction would not allow an interrupt to be recognized and serviced between the CLI and RTI instructions.

5.6 Interrupt Latency

One of the concerns of many real-time system designers is a microcontroller's response speed to an unmasked interrupt. This time period, known as the interrupt latency period, is defined as the maximum time required by a microcontroller to begin execution of an interrupt service routine in response to an unmasked interrupt request. In addition to the operating frequency of the M68HC12 there are three additional factors that contribute to interrupt latency: the execution time of the longest CPU12 instruction in a program, the time required to save the CPU context and the time required to fetch the interrupt vector and begin execution at a new memory location.

Just before the execution of each instruction, the CPU12 interrupt control logic checks for an unmasked pending interrupt. If no interrupt is pending, the CPU begins executing the instruction and, with one exception, will not recognize an interrupt until the instruction execution is complete. The longest uninterruptable CPU12 instruction is the EMACS requiring 13 E-clock cycles instruction to perform a 16-bit by 16-bit multiply and 32-bit addition. Even if a program does not make specific use of the EMACS instruction, it is probably a good idea to use 13 clock cycles when calculating interrupt latency times. Even though the `WAV`, `REV` and `REVW` fuzzy logic instructions can require hundreds of cycles to complete execution, each of these instructions is interruptible.

The second factor to consider in interrupt latency calculations is the amount of time required to save the CPU12's context at the time the interrupt is recognized. Like the M68HC11 and all other M6800 derivatives, the CPU12 automatically saves the contents of the entire register set as part of the interrupt processing sequence. The automatic register stacking sequence does add four clock cycles to the interrupt latency, however, it relieves the programmer from having to push each of the registers onto the stack individually. It can be argued that only the program counter and condition code register should be automatically saved on the stack by the CPU's hardware interrupt response mechanism. This, in fact, would allow the programmer to improve interrupt response time by only stacking those registers required by the interrupt service routine. While this is a valid argument, it would only improve the interrupt response time by three clock cycles if none of the CPU12's registers were used in the interrupt service routine. At 8.0 MHz this only amounts to an improved response time of 375 nS. It must be remembered that the five clock cycles required to save the internal CPU state on the stack is only valid if the stack is located in on-chip RAM. If the stack is located external RAM and the stack pointer contains an odd byte address when an interrupt occurs, the register stacking sequence would require a minimum of nine clock cycles to complete. This results from the fact that the word write cycles for the program counter, X and Y index registers and the D accumulator or would require two bus

Section 5.6: Interrupt Latency

cycles for the misaligned accesses. The stacking of the 8-bit condition code register would still only require a single bus cycle. The nine clock cycles assumes that the external RAM can be accessed without using E-clock stretching. If the external memory cannot be accesses in a single E-clock cycle, interrupt latency times would increase proportional to the number of cycles the E-clock is stretched.

The third consideration when figuring maximum interrupt latency times is the amount of time required to fetch the associated interrupt vector and begin execution of the interrupt service routine. The time required to fetch the interrupt vector address is only affected by the number of bus cycles required to access an aligned word of program memory. When the interrupt vector is located in on-chip memory, only a single bus cycle is required. However, if the interrupt vector is located in external memory, any E-clock stretching required to access the external memory device would have to be taken into consideration. Because all of the interrupt vectors are word aligned, misaligned reads cannot occur during the vector fetch portion of the interrupt service response. If, however, the external memory is connected in narrow mode, the vector fetch will require two bus cycles. An additional factor that contributes to the CPU12's interrupt latency is caused by the instruction queue. Before execution of the interrupt service routine can begin, the three word instruction queue must be filled. The three word aligned accesses require a minimum of three bus cycles when executing from on-chip memory or wide-mode connected external memory.

This whole discussion may sound like the CPU12 requires a complex set of calculations to determine maximum interrupt latency. In reality, for most applications executing their programs entirely out of internal memory and utilizing on-chip RAM for the stack, the calculations are very simple and straightforward. Maximum interrupt latency is simply the cycle count of the longest instruction used in a program plus nine. For programs utilizing the EMACS instruction, this translates to a total of 22 E-clocks, requiring only 2.75 µS at 8.0 MHz. For systems utilizing off-chip program and/or RAM memory, Figure 5.9 presents two formulas to use when calculating maximum interrupt latency times.

$$I_{LW} = IC_{MAX} + 4(PE_{STRETCH} + 1) + 9(DE_{STRETCH} + 1)$$

$$I_{LN} = IC_{MAX} + 8(PE_{STRETCH} + 1) + 9(DE_{STRETCH} + 1)$$

Where:
- I_{LW} = Interrupt Latency for Expanded Wide-Mode
- I_{LN} = Interrupt Latency for Expanded Narrow-Mode
- IC_{MAX} = Cycle Count of Longest Instruction
- $PE_{STRETCH}$ = Program Memory E-clock Stretch Cycles
- $DE_{STRETCH}$ = Data Memory E-clock Stretch Cycles

Figure 5.9: Interrupt Latency Calculation Formulas Using External Memory

Chapter 5: Interrupts and Resets

There are several important things to take into consideration when using these formulas. The initial term of both equations, ICMAX, can vary greatly for Wide and Narrow operating modes for the same instruction. Examining the cycle-by-cycle execution information for the EMACS instruction as as presented in Appendix A reveals that there are eight cycles within the instruction that are affected by both the speed and width of external memory connected to the M68HC12 microcontroller. Six of the cycles are word access to data memory while two of the eight cycles are word accesses to program memory. When executing code out of external program memory at a bus speed of 8.0 MHz, it is very likely that the E-clock will have to be stretched at least one E-clock cycle. This will double the number of E-clock cycles required for those bus cycles when operating in wide mode and quadruple the E-clock cycle count when operating in narrow mode.

The six cycles accessing data contained in external memory can most likely be performed without any E-clock stretching. However, even when operating the M68HC12 in wide mode, care must be taken to ensure that the accessed operands reside on an even byte boundary. If these operands reside on odd byte boundaries, each word access will require two bus cycles, thus imposing the same performance penalty on the instruction as if the part were operating in Narrow mode. In both cases the six bus cycles would require 12 E-clocks. With these cycle counts, 12 E-clocks for data access and 8 E-clocks for program memory access, total execution time for the EMACS instruction would require 25 E-clocks when operating in Narrow mode. This is more than double the 13 E-clock cycles required when executing the instruction utilizing on-chip memory.

In the last term of both equations, notice that the multiplier used for calculating the data accesses during interrupt processing are the same for both Wide and Narrow modes. Because the equations are used to calculate worse case interrupt latency times, the word writes to data memory even in Wide mode cannot assume that the stack pointer is aligned to a word boundary. Therefore, accounting for worse case conditions the equation for wide mode assumes that each word write will require two bus cycles.

5.7 INTERRUPT RESPONSE TIME

The basic interrupt latency of a microcontroller such as the M68HC12 can easily be defined as discussed in the preceding paragraphs. However, there are additional considerations in applications where multiple interrupts can be pending at the same time or where interrupts can be masked for an extended period of time. In such cases, the interrupt response time, can become an extremely complex issue and more of a concern than the basic interrupt latency of the M68HC12. The interrupt response time for any particular interrupt is the maximum time required for the interrupt to be serviced after the interrupt becomes pending. While there are numerous software techniques that can be used to minimize interrupt response time, the M68HC12 microcontroller provides two hardware mechanisms to help reduce total interrupt response time.

Section 5.8: IRQ Interrupt Example

⚠ M68HC12 Difference from the M68HC11

Normally, at the end of an interrupt service routine, the execution of an `RTI` instruction will restore the CPU12's internal state from the stack, fill the instruction prefetch queue, and resume program execution at the point where it was interrupted. However, if another interrupt is pending after the registers have been restored, the CPU12 will simply adjust the stack pointer to preserve the stack contents rather than actually re-stack the register contents. Adjusting the stack pointer is functionally identical to re-stacking the registers but is much faster. After the adjustment of the stack pointer, the CPU12 performs a vector fetch operation, fills the instruction prefetch queue beginning at the address contained in the interrupt vector, and begins execution of the new interrupt service routine. Note that the `RTI` instruction requires two additional clock cycles for execution with an interrupt pending - one cycle for the stack adjustment and one for the vector fetch.

The second hardware mechanism that can be used to improve overall interrupt response time is the Interrupt Priority Control Register or `HPRIO`. As discussed earlier in the chapter, the `HPRIO` register allows the priority of one maskable interrupt source to be elevated above all others. Because the contents of the `HPRIO` register can be changed any time the I-bit is set, maskable interrupt priorities may be dynamically changed as an application executes. This can be extremely useful when utilizing peripherals in a manner where they have time critical, interrupt driven tasks to perform occasionally. For instance, suppose that an application utilizes the Serial Communications Interface (SCI) to receive short, high-speed messages from a master controller. The first byte of each message would contain the address of the node for which the message was intended. After receiving the first byte of a message, the receiving node would compare its address to the received address and continue to acquire the message if the address matched. After confirming the validity of the address, the `HPRIO` register could be written with a value of $D6 to ensure that the SCI receiver had the highest priority of the maskable interrupt sources. When message reception was complete, the `HPRIO` could be restored with its previous value.

5.8 IRQ INTERRUPT EXAMPLE

One common use of the external interrupt input is for a timing reference based on the 50 Hz or 60 Hz power line. This timing reference can be used to keep track of elapsed time or the actual time of day and date. Keeping track of the time of day is a fairly easy process because the time of day repeats every 24-hour period. It simply requires maintaining a set of counters for the seconds, minutes, and hours. Because of the different number of days in each month, maintaining the month, day of the month, and year is a little more complicated; and then of course there's leap year. Figure 5.10 presents the definitions for the counters required to maintain the time of day and date. In addition to defining variables for the seconds, minutes, hours, month, day of the month and year, several other variables are necessary. The `Ticks` variable is used as a counter to divide the line frequency time base into one second periods that can be used for time keeping functions. Each time the input to the IRQ pin generates an interrupt, this variable is decremented. When the counter reaches zero, the seconds counter is incremented and the `Ticks` variable is reinitialized with the value contained in the `TicksPSec` variable. The `LeapYear` variable is used as a boolean flag to indicate whether or not the value contained in the variable `Year` is a leap year. Keeping track of the day of the week may not be important for many applications, however, there are applications such as HVAC control or security access control where knowing the day of the week is important. The `DayOfWeek` variable is maintained as a modulo 6 counter that keeps track of the day of the week. This counter is incremented when the `Hours` variable rolls over from 23 to 0.

```
;
Hz55:         equ   SysClock/8/55 ; Loop count (uS) for 55 Hz.
;
TicksPSec:    ds    1        ; number of ticks per second.
Ticks:        ds    1        ; tick counter (60 - 0).
CVarStart:    equ   *        ; start address of clock variables
DayOfWeek:    ds    1        ; day of the week (Sun = 0, Sat = 6).
Hours:        ds    1        ; hour counter (0 - 23).
Minutes:      ds    1        ; minutes counter (0 - 59).
Seconds:      ds    1        ; seconds counter (0 - 59).
Month:        ds    1        ; month (1 - 12).
DayOfMonth:   ds    1        ; day of month (1 - 31)
Year:         ds    2        ; year (0 - 32767).
CVarEnd:      equ   *        ; end address of clock variables
LeapYear:     ds    1        ; Leap year flag (1 = leap yr., 0 = non-leap yr).
;
```

Figure 5.10: Time-of-Day Clock Variables

Figure 5.11 contains the code necessary to perform the initialization required by the remainder of the time keeping software. The first action performed by this subroutine configures the IRQ interrupt input for negative edge sensitive operation by programming the `IRQE` bit in the `INTCR` register to a one. This causes one interrupt to be generated for each cycle of the AC power line. In addition the `IRQEN` bit is cleared to ensure that IRQ interrupts are not automatically enabled when the I-bit in the condition code register is cleared. Other software must specifically set the `IRQEN` bit to begin the time of day function. In addition to providing initial values for the time and date counters, the initialization software calls a subroutine, `LineFreq`, to measure the line frequency. Having the initialization software perform this function allows the clock to be used in either a 50 Hz or 60 Hz power line environment without having to make changes to the firmware. The value returned by this subroutine, either 50 or 60, is used to initialize both the `TicksPSec` and the `Ticks` variables.

Section 5.8: IRQ Interrupt Example

Note that the values maintained in all of the counters are binary rather than BCD. This allows simple increment and decrement operations to be performed in the IRQ interrupt service routine where the counters for the time of day clock are maintained. This helps to keep the interrupt service routine as small and fast as possible, placing the burden of format conversion outside the interrupt service routine. The time and date counters are initialized to 12:00 P.M., January 1, 1900. While there is no real significance to these particular values, care should be exercised if initializing the counters with another date to ensure that the variables LeapYear and DayOfWeek are properly set.

```
;
TODInit:    equ     *
            ldaa    #$a0        ; set irq for edge sensitive,
            staa    INTCR       ; disable ext. irq, enable osc dly from stop.
            bsr     LineFreq    ; go measure the AC line frequency.
            stab    TicksPSec   ; save the number of Ticks/sec.
            stab    Ticks       ; init the Tick count.
            clr     Seconds     ; set seconds & minutes to 0.
            clr     Minutes
            clr     LeapYear    ; the initial year, 1900, is not a leap year.
            ldab    #12         ; set hour for 12 noon.
            stab    Hours
            ldab    #1          ; day of month & month to 1.
            stab    Month
            stab    DayOfMonth
            stab    DayOfWeek   ; set DOW to Monday (1).
            ldd     #1900       ; make the year 1900
            std     Year
            rts                 ; return.
;
```

Figure 5.11: Time-of-Day Clock Initialization

The LineFreq subroutine, shown in Figure 5.12, utilizes a simple software method of determining the line frequency. While this method does not result in a precise measurement of the actual line frequency, it is accurate enough to determine whether the power source is operating at a frequency of 50 Hz or 60 Hz. While the use of software timing loops is generally discouraged, in this case it leads to a simple implementation that depends on nothing other than the operating frequency of the M68HC12. Using the on-chip timer system for this measurement would result in a more accurate measurement. However, it would require initialization of the timer system in a configuration that may not be compatible with its use by the remaining system software. Because the state of the IRQ pin is available in bit one of the Port E data register, the line frequency reference signal does not have to be connected to another I/O pin to perform the measurement. The period measurement is performed by measuring the low and high time of the signal separately and adding the results.

```
;
LineFreq:   clra                          ; clear the count accumulator.
            clrb
            brclr   PORTE,#$02,*          ; wait here till irq goes high.
            brset   PORTE,#$02,*          ; wait here for falling edge.
LoTime:     addd    #1                    ; [2] add 1 to the half period count.
            nop                           ; [1] cycle delay.
            nop                           ; [1] cycle delay.
            brclr   PORTE,#$02,LoTime     ; [4] (dir) count till irq goes high.
HiTime:     addd    #1                    ; [2] add 1 to the half period count.
            nop                           ; [1] cycle delay.
            nop                           ; [1] cycle delay.
            brset   PORTE,#$02,HiTime     ; [4] (dir) count till irq goes low
            cpd     #Hz55                 ; count > 55 Hz count?
            bhi     Fifty                 ; yes. longer period, 50 Hz line.
            ldab    #60                   ; no. assume a 60 Hz line.
            rts                           ; return.
Fifty:      ldab    #50                   ; 50 Hz line frequency.
            rts                           ; return.
;
```

Figure 5.12: Line Frequency Measurement Subroutine

At the beginning of the LineFreq subroutine a pair of BRCLR/BRSET instructions is used to wait for the IRQ pin to transition from a one to a zero before beginning to measure the low time of the applied signal. When the transition from high to low is detected, the loop beginning at label LoTime is executed, adding one to the D accumulator for each loop iteration. As indicated by the bracketed numbers in the comment field, each loop iteration requires eight E-clock cycles. For an MC68HC912B32 running at 8.0 MHz, this equates to a time period of 1.0 µS for each loop. When the IRQ pin transitions from a low to a high state and exits the low time measurement loop, the D accumulator should contain a count of approximately 8333 ($208D) for a 60 Hz or 10000 ($2710) for a 50 Hz signal. Because each loop requires 1 µS, this directly represents the low period of the waveform in microseconds. Next the subroutine enters a similar loop at the label HiTime that measures the high time of the waveform in a similar manner. Because it is not necessary to retain separate values for the high and low periods of the waveform, the high time loop simply continues to add one to the low period measurement in the D accumulator. When the high time measurement is complete, the D accumulator will contain a value of approximately 16667 ($411B) for 60 Hz or 20000 ($4E20) for 50 Hz signal.

Rather than return the measured period, the nominal line frequency is returned in the B accumulator. To determine the nominal line frequency, the measured period is compared to

Section 5.8: IRQ Interrupt Example

the value `Hz55` as defined in Figure 5.10. This value represents the period of a 55 Hz signal in relation to the number of loop iterations executed for the high and low period measurement. Comparing the value of the measured period to the value of the calculated period for a signal half way between the two expected frequencies provides the greatest immunity against instantaneous variations in the power line frequency. Even though the AC power line provides a stabile long term timing reference, instantaneous frequency variations are not only possible, but probable. Because of the possibility of short term power line frequency shifts or noise that may affect the period measurement, it may be a good idea to call the `LineFreq` subroutine at least twice and compare the returned results. If the two values do not match the subroutine should be called a third time, comparing the three results and using the value that is returned two of the three times.

It is important to emphasize that the two loops performing the period measurement are dependent upon the execution time of the instructions within the loop. While this may seem to be an obvious fact, the execution time of the `BRCLR` and `BRSET` instructions will vary depending on the addressing mode used to access the tested byte. In this case, the Port E data register is accessed using direct addressing, thus requiring four E-clock cycles for the execution of each instruction. If an application relocates the I/O registers to an address requiring these instructions to use extended addressing, their execution times would increase to five E-clock cycles. This would require either one of the `NOP` instructions to be removed from each of the period measurement loops or the calculation of the `Hz55` constant to be changed by replacing the divide by eight with a divide by nine.

The actual time and date keeping functions are performed in the IRQ interrupt service routine shown in Figure 5.13. While the interrupt service routine appears to be lengthy, the average execution time is quite small. The `Ticks` variable, decremented at the start of the service routine, is used to divide the incoming line frequency by 50 or 60. When the `Ticks` variable reaches zero, it is reloaded with the contents of `TicksPSec` and the `Seconds` variable is incremented. Both the `Seconds` and `Minutes` variables are incremented modulo 60. That is, when the variables reach a value of 60, they are reset to zero and the next higher time period is incremented. The `Hours` counter is maintained as a modulo 24 counter. Keeping time in 24 hour format avoids the necessity of maintaining a separate variable to indicate A.M. or P.M. If an application requires the time to be displayed in 12 hour format, the display formatting software can easily perform the necessary conversion. When the `Hours` variable rolls over from 23 to zero, the `DayOfWeek` variable is incremented modulo 7. As shown in Figure 5.10, a value of zero represents Sunday, a value of one represents Monday and so on with a value of six representing Saturday. While the assignment of the days of the week to these values is arbitrary, any other assignment must make sure that the value contained in `DayOfWeek` has the proper relationship to the value in the `DayOfMonth` variable.

```
;
IRQISR:     equ     *
            dec     Ticks           ; Ticks = Ticks - 1. Has 1 sec. elapsed?
            lbne    Return          ; not yet. Just return.
            ldab    TicksPSec       ; yes. reinitialize the tick counter.
            stab    Ticks
            ldab    #60             ; compare count for seconds & minutes.
            inc     Seconds         ; Seconds = Seconds + 1.
            cmpb    Seconds         ; 60 seconds elapsed?
            blo     Return          ; not yet. Just return.
            clr     Seconds         ; yes. set seconds counter to 0.
            inc     Minutes         ; add 1 to the minutes counter.
            cmpb    Minutes         ; 60 minutes elapsed?
            blo     Return          ; not yet. Just return.
            clr     Minutes         ; yes. set minutes counter to 0.
            inc     Hours           ; add 1 to the hours counter.
            ldab    Hours           ; get the hours counter.
            cmpb    #24             ; did it roll over to the next day?
            blo     Return          ; no. return.
            clr     Hours           ; yes. 00:00 = 12:00 A.M.
            inc     DayOfWeek       ; go to the next day of the week.
            ldab    DayOfWeek       ; get the DOW counter.
            cmpb    #7              ; did it go from Sat (6) to Sun?
            blo     ChkDay          ; no. go adjust the Day of the Month.
            clr     DayOfWeek       ; yes. Sun = 0.
```

Figure 5.12: IRQ Interrupt Service Routine

The remaining portion of the interrupt service routine, beginning at label ChkDay, is devoted to maintaining the calendar portion of the time keeping function. If the calendar is not required for an application, all of the code from ChkDay up to the line just before the label Return may be removed. Of course, the program line blo ChkDay would have to be changed to blo Return.

After adjusting the day of the week, one is added to the DayOfMonth variable. Because the number of days in each month varies, the maximum value of this counter will vary depending on the current month of the year. Two lookup tables, one for 'normal' years and one for leap years, are used to determine the maximum number of days in a particular month. These tables are presented in Figure 5.13. The value contained in Month, minus one, is used as an index when comparing the value in DayOfMonth to the maximum number of days for that month. Note that if the value contained in LeapYear is non-zero, the lookup table at label DaysPMonL is used rather than the lookup table for a non-leap year. If the new value in DayOfMonth exceeds the value found in the table it is reset to the first day of the next month. If the DayOfMonth variable is set to the first day of the next month, the of Month is incremented and compared to the value 12. If its value exceeds 12, it is reset to the first month of the next year. Finally, if the calendar transitions into a new

Section 5.8: IRQ Interrupt Example

year, one is added to the `Year` variable. At this point the software must determine if the new year is a leap year so that the `LeapYear` variable can be properly initialized.

```
ChkDay:   ldx    #DaysPMon      ; point to the days per month table.
          tst    LeapYear       ; are we in a leap year?
          beq    NoLeap1        ; no.
          ldx    #DaysPMonL     ; yes. point to days/month tbl for leap yr.
NoLeap1:  ldaa   Month          ; get the current month.
          deca                  ; subtract 1 from month for index.
          inc    DayOfMonth     ; go to the next day.
          ldab   DayOfMonth     ; get the last day of the current month.
          cmpb   a,x            ; did we go into the next month?
          bls    Return         ; no. return.
          ldab   #1             ; yes. Start at the first day of next month.
          stab   DayOfMonth
          inc    Month          ; go to the next month.
          ldab   Month          ; get the month count.
          cmpb   #12            ; did we go into the next year?
          bls    Return         ; no. return
          ldab   #1             ; yes. initialize to January.
          stab   Month
          ldd    Year           ; get the year count.
          addd   #1             ; go to the next year.
          std    Year           ; save the year count.
          bitb   #$03           ; year evenly /4 (first check for leap year).
          beq    Century        ; yes. Next check the century.
NoLeap2:  clr    LeapYear       ; no. new year is not a leap year.
          rti                   ; return.
Century:  ldx    #400           ; only centuries evenly divisible by
          idiv                  ; 400 are leap years.
          tbne   d,NoLeap2      ; remainder != 0, not a leap Century.
          ldaa   #1             ; we are in a leap year/century.
          staa   LeapYear       ; set the leap year flag.
Return:   rti                   ; return.
;
```

Figure 5.12: IRQ Interrupt Service Routine (cont.)

Determining the type of year is actually a two step process. As most people know, each year is composed of approximately 365.25 days, so every fourth year an extra day is added to February to make up for the quarter day 'lost' in the previous three years and the additional quarter day in the current year. However, the additional quarter day is not quite six hours long, in fact it is much closer to 5 hours, 48 minutes, an 46 seconds. This fact requires an additional adjustment be made. This adjustment, which was originally defined in the year 1582 when the Gregorian calendar was adopted, states that every fourth year is a leap year except for century years that are not evenly divisible by 400. Thus the years 1700, 1800 and 1900 were not leap years, but the year 2000 is a leap year since 2000 is evenly divisible by

400. This second rule eliminates three leap years every four centuries and ensures the long term accuracy of the Gregorian calendar. Even this correction is not perfect since it results in a three day error in 10,000 years. Obviously, a correction will have to be done at some point in the future, however, any software written today need not take this slight inaccuracy into account.

After adjusting the value in Year and saving its new value, the value is checked to see if it is evenly divisible by four. This test is performed by checking the lower two bits of the 16-bit value. If these two bits are zero, it indicates the number is evenly divisible by four. If this condition is true, the year is divided by 400. If the remainder of the division, the result of which is placed in the D accumulator, is not zero, it indicates that the new year is not a leap century and the LeapYear variable is cleared. If the remainder is zero, a value of one is written to the variable indicating a leap year.

```
;
DaysPMon:   fcb     31              ; Days in January.
            fcb     28              ; Days in February.
            fcb     31              ; Days in March.
            fcb     30              ; Days in April.
            fcb     31              ; Days in May.
            fcb     30              ; Days in June.
            fcb     31              ; Days in July.
            fcb     31              ; Days in August.
            fcb     30              ; Days in September.
            fcb     31              ; Days in October.
            fcb     30              ; Days in November.
            fcb     31              ; Days in December.
;
DaysPMonL:  fcb     31              ; Days in January.
            fcb     29              ; Days in February (leap year).
            fcb     31              ; Days in March.
            fcb     30              ; Days in April.
            fcb     31              ; Days in May.
            fcb     30              ; Days in June.
            fcb     31              ; Days in July.
            fcb     31              ; Days in August.
            fcb     30              ; Days in September.
            fcb     31              ; Days in October.
            fcb     30              ; Days in November.
            fcb     31              ; Days in December.
;
```

Figure 5.13: Days per Month Lookup Tables

Section 5.8: IRQ Interrupt Example

Accessing The Time and Date

The need for keeping track of the time and date in an application might be to time stamp events, to limit access to specific system functions depending upon the time of day or day of the month, or even to perform specific operations that must be synchronized to the time of day. At first thought it may seem as though retrieving the time and date is simply a matter of reading the variables associated with the time keeping software. However, utilizing this procedure can result in reading a time and date that are off by as much as a year. Because the IRQ interrupts driving the time keeping software occur asynchronously in relation to the software reading the time-of-day clock variables, it is quite possible that an IRQ interrupt will occur while the variables are being read.

For instance, if the time and date counters contained 23:59:59, 12/31/1998 when software began to read the variables and an IRQ interrupt occurred just prior to reading the value in Year, the date read by the software would be 12/31/1999. Obviously, the chance of this occurring is unacceptable for any application.

The solution to this problem is to simply mask IRQ interrupts when reading the time and/or date variables. However, instead of requiring the programmer to remember this detail, it is better to create a small subroutine to retrieve the time and date values while interrupts are masked. Figure 5.14 presents the simple subroutine to perform this task. Notice that the external IRQ interrupt is masked by clearing the IRQEN bit in the INTCR register rather than setting the I-bit in the condition code register. This allows other maskable interrupts to be serviced while the time and date variables are being retrieved. Before calling the GetTimeDate subroutine, the X index register must be loaded with an address that points to an eight byte memory area that will receive the time and date data.

```
;
GetTimeDate: bclr    INTCR,#IRQEN            ; inhibit IRQ interrupts.
             ldab    #CVarEnd-CVarStart      ; number of bytes to move.
             ldy     #CVarStart              ; start of time/date data block.
TDMove:      movb    1,y+,1,x+               ; move a byte at a time.
             dbne    b,TDMove                ; done? if b != 0, cont. move.
             bset    INTCR,#IRQEN            ; re-enable IRQ interrupts.
             rts                             ; return.
;
```

Figure 5.14: GetTimeDate Subroutine

The problem involved when reading the clock variables also exists when setting the time and date variables. The subroutine in Figure 5.15, SetTimeDate, is used to copy an eight byte memory area into the clock's variables. This subroutine is identical to the GetTimeDate subroutine except that the source and destination index registers for the MOVB instruction have been reversed.

Chapter 5: Interrupts and Resets

```
;
SetTimeDate:    bclr    INTCR,#IRQEN           ; inhibit IRQ interrupts.
                ldab    #CVarEnd-CVarStart     ; number of bytes to move.
                ldy     #CVarStart             ; start of time/date data block.
TDMove2:        movb    1,x+,1,y+              ; move a byte at a time.
                dbne    b,TDMove2              ; done? if b != 0, cont. move.
                bset    INTCR,#IRQEN           ; re-enable IRQ interrupts.
                rts                            ; return.
;
```

Figure 5.15: SetTimeDate Subroutine

Questions/Exercises

5.1   Explain the difference between a subroutine and an interrupt exception handler.

5.2   How many exception vectors are supported in the M68HC12 architecture?

5.3   Where are the exception vectors located? What restrictions does this place on interrupt exception handlers?

5.4   How many exception classes are recognized by the M68HC12 family? Name them.

5.5   List the non-maskable exception sources recognized by the M68HC12 family?

5.6   What is the difference between the IRQ and XIRQ interrupt inputs?

5.7   Can XIRQ interrupts be inhibited after they have been enabled? Explain.

5.8   Is it possible to inhibit interrupts from the IRQ pin while allowing maskable interrupts from other sources to be recognized? Explain.

5.9   How many different ways can the IRQ pin be configured? What is the default configuration? Under what conditions would each configuration be used?

5.10 What control bit appears in the Interrupt Control Register (INTCR) that is not specifically related to interrupts? What is its use?

5.11 Can on-chip maskable interrupt sources have their priority changed? How is this accomplished?

5.12 What determines the default priority of the on-chip maskable interrupt sources?

Section 5.8: IRQ Interrupt Example

5.13 What one critical operation must be performed by an interrupt service routine? How is this critical operation performed?

5.14 What other important considerations must be observed when writing interrupt service routines.

5.15 Does the M68HC12 interrupt mechanism allow nested interrupts? Explain.

5.16 What is unique about the way the CLI (ANDCC #$EF) instruction is executed?

5.17 What factors must be considered when calculating interrupt latency times?

5.18 What is the difference between interrupt latency and basic interrupt response times?

5.19 What hardware feature of the M68HC12 helps in reducing the interrupt response time when multiple interrupts are pending.

5.20 Add an alarm function to the time keeping software. The alarm function should call a subroutine when when the clock time matches the alarm time and should repeat every 24 hours.

5.21 Modify the time keeping software to automatically compensate for daylight savings time.

Chapter 6   GENERAL PURPOSE PARALLEL I/O PORTS

The general purpose I/O ports on the M68HC12 family provide the most basic facilities for controlling the environment outside the microcontroller. The number and type of general purpose parallel I/O pins vary with each M68HC12 family member. Each I/O port is ordinarily associated with one of the on-chip peripheral systems and is used to gain access to, or control its functions. However, when a peripheral's associated I/O pins are not being used for their specific purpose, the pins can usually be configured for general purpose I/O. At a minimum, each peripheral port has two registers associated with it. The data register, which can be read or written at any time, is used to read data from input pins and write data to output pins. The data direction register, which also can be read or written at any time, allows each pin to be individually configured as an input or an output. In addition to these two registers, some peripherals contain a register, known as the pin assignment register. This register provides additional control over the function of each I/O pin when it is associated with a peripheral. This register allows a pin's function to be assigned to its peripheral function or utilized as general purpose I/O. In general, pin assignment register settings override data direction register settings when determining a pin's use as an input or an output. During and immediately after reset, all I/O pins are automatically configured as inputs.

6.1   ACCESSING PERIPHERALS

The control and status information for all on-chip peripherals and general purpose I/O ports appear to the CPU12 as data bits in memory locations. Using this type of arrangement for accessing peripherals is known as memory mapped I/O. There is a great advantage to accessing peripherals in this manner. Instead of requiring special purpose instructions to

Section 6.2: Data Direction Registers

manipulate peripherals, any CPU12 instruction operating on a memory location can be used to control or check the status of a peripheral. This type of I/O architecture is especially advantageous to the M68HC12 family because of the CPU12's bit manipulation instructions. Combined with the the extended addressing mode of the bit manipulation instructions, it provides the ability to set, clear, or test the state of any bit in the peripheral registers regardless of where they are located in the memory map.

Both the data and data direction register ports are addressable as 8-bit bytes. Depending on the number of physical pins associated with a peripheral, not every bit in each register may be implemented. In general, reads of unimplemented bits return a value of zero, and writes to these bits have no effect. Even though the port control and data registers are byte addressable, some general purpose I/O ports, such as Port A and Port B on the MC68HC912B32, are arranged in such a manner as to allow both 8-bit data and data direction registers to be read or written with a single 16-bit access. At first, this may not seem any different from similar arrangements on the M68HC11 family of microcontrollers. However, because the M68HC11 family is only an 8-bit microcontroller, two bus cycles are required to read or write 16-bits of data appearing at two successive memory locations. Because the M68HC12 family is capable of 16-bit reads or writes in a single bus cycle, both the upper and lower bytes of the 16-bit word can be read or written at the same time. While this minor timing difference will not affect most applications, it is something that should be kept in mind.

6.2 DATA DIRECTION REGISTERS

As mentioned previously, the role of the data direction registers is to provide programmable control of each general purpose I/O pin. Writing a value of one to a pin's associated data direction register configures an I/O pin as an output. Writing a zero to a data direction register bit configures its associated I/O pin as an input. During reset, all data direction register bits are cleared, configuring all I/O pins as inputs. While the programmability of each I/O pin provides a great deal of flexibility in the assignment of pins to particular functions in a system, it also allows for the possibility of accidental reprogramming of an I/O pin's function. In most cases, the accidental reprogramming of data direction register bits is not a result of program failure, but is usually a result of electrical noise. Obviously, a properly designed hardware system should not allow electrical noise of such magnitudes to reach the microcontroller. However, because the operating environment of many embedded systems cannot be completely controlled, there are occasions when externally radiated or conducted electrical noise can cause corruption of data direction register contents, even in a well designed system. To help reduce the possibility of system failure caused by the corruption of data direction registers, many programmers periodically 'refresh' the contents of the data direction registers. While this technique is used successfully in many systems existing in harsh environments, it should not be used as a substitute for an adequate hardware design.

6.3 Data Registers

Using the data registers for I/O operations is a reasonably straightforward operation. When pins are configured as outputs, writing a one to the associated data register bit causes a logic one to be driven onto the external pin. When pins are configured as inputs, reading the data register returns the logic level applied to the external pin. There are, however, additional subtleties regarding their use that merit discussion.

As mentioned previously, a peripheral's data registers may be read or written at any time. This implies that data register bits may be written to when they are configured as an inputs and read when they are configured as an outputs. This is, in fact, the case. However, the results of these operations may not be what is expected. Reading data register bits configured as outputs will return the value last written to the data register rather than the actual logic level present on the output pin. Writing to the data register of I/O pins configured as inputs causes the value of each written bit to be latched into an output flip-flop. If the input pin is later reconfigured as an output, the logic level driven onto the pin will be the last value written to the associated data register bit. This behavior must be carefully considered if an I/O pin is being used in a bidirectional manner, particularly if different parts of a program manipulate several bits within a single port data register.

Consider the situation illustrated in Figure 6.1. In this case, bit seven of Port A is used in a bidirectional manner. The code fragment shown on the left of the figure begins by clearing the associated data direction register bit making bit seven an input. Next, the BSET instruction writes a one to the bit seven output data latch so a logic one will be driven onto the pin when it is reconfigured as an output. If an interrupt service routine executes after the output data latch has been written to a one, any manipulation of the Port A data register by the interrupt service routine will result in a zero being written to the output data latch if the the input data register bit reads zero. Because interrupts usually occur asynchronously in relationship to main program code, these types of problems tend to appear randomly and can be extremely difficult to debug.

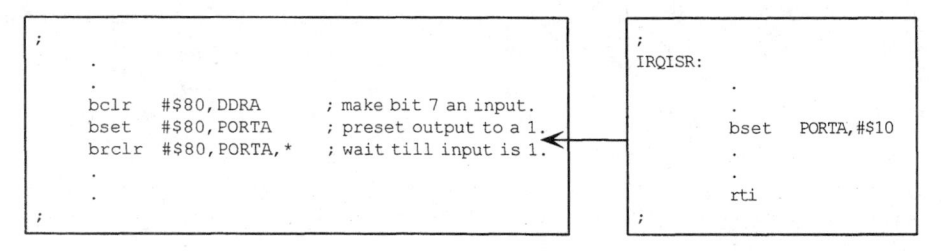

```
;
        .
        .
        .
    bclr    #$80,DDRA       ; make bit 7 an input.
    bset    #$80,PORTA      ; preset output to a 1.
    brclr   #$80,PORTA,*    ; wait till input is 1.
        .
        .
;
```

```
;
IRQISR:
        .
        .
        .
    bset    PORTA,#$10
        .
        .
    rti
;
```

Figure 6.1: Accidentally changing the output pin data latch

To prevent this type of problem from occurring, the output data register should not be preset with a value until it is going to be configured as an output. Even in this case,

Section 6.4: Unused I/O Pins

interrupts should be disabled during the two instruction sequence required to preset the output data register and configure the pin as an output. If interrupts are not disabled, the same situation can occur as illustrated in Figure 6.1.

6.4 I/O PORT INITIALIZATION

While the initialization of the general purpose I/O ports may seem to be a trivial matter, there are several precautions that should be observed to prevent the unintended operation of devices connected to the pins. As mentioned previously, all general purpose I/O pins are automatically configured as inputs during reset. This action ensures that external devices connected to input pins will not accidentally have their outputs driven by the I/O pin during the reset period. While this provides a benign condition for pins that remain configured as inputs, pins that are eventually configured as outputs are allowed to 'float' during this time period. In situations where output pins control the operation of mechanical devices and/or high power electrical equipment, this time period can present a potentially hazardous condition. To ensure safe operation of the system during this period, it is essential that either a pull-up or pull-down resistor be placed on the I/O pin to ensure that the controlled equipment remains off.

Even if an embedded system does not control equipment that could present a safety hazard prior to I/O port initialization, it is still a good idea to initialize the I/O ports soon after exiting reset, preferably before any lengthy system wide diagnostics are performed. When configuring pins as outputs, it is essential to initialize the data register *before* a pin is configured as an output. Because the state of the output data latches are not guaranteed when the M68HC12 exits reset, this sequence is necessary to ensure that the proper level appears on the output pin when the data direction register is written.

6.5 UNUSED I/O PINS

The diverse nature of systems utilizing general purpose microcontrollers invariably creates situations where there are either not enough or too many general purpose I/O pins for a particular application. Additional I/O ports can be added by operating the microcontroller in expanded mode and connecting general purpose I/O peripherals to the expansion bus. However, too frequently, the opposite situation is simply ignored by the hardware designer. Most often, unused I/O pins are simply left unconnected and remain as inputs – their default configuration. To avoid undesired operation of the microcontroller, all unused I/O pins must be connected and/or configured properly.

Allowing unused I/O pins to remain unconnected and configured as inputs can lead to undesirable operation. Each general purpose I/O pin is essentially connected to a high impedance input buffer and an N-channel and P-channel output driver as shown in Figure 6.2. When pins are configured as inputs, the N-channel and P-channel output devices are both turned off. As long as the input remains at a voltage level between VDD + 0.3 volts and VSS - 0.3 volts, this complimentary transistor pair remains in a high impedance tri-state mode. If the input pin exceeds VDD + 0.3 volts, the P-channel transistor effectively becomes a diode connected to VDD. Conversely, if the input pin becomes less than VSS - 0.3 volts, the N-channel transistor becomes a diode connected to VSS. These two situations, illustrated in Figure 6.3 a and b respectively, can cause permanent damage to the output devices if the maximum per pin current ratings of the device are exceeded. Leaving input pins unconnected to either VDD or VSS increases the likelihood of electrical noise entering the pin and exceeding these ratings.

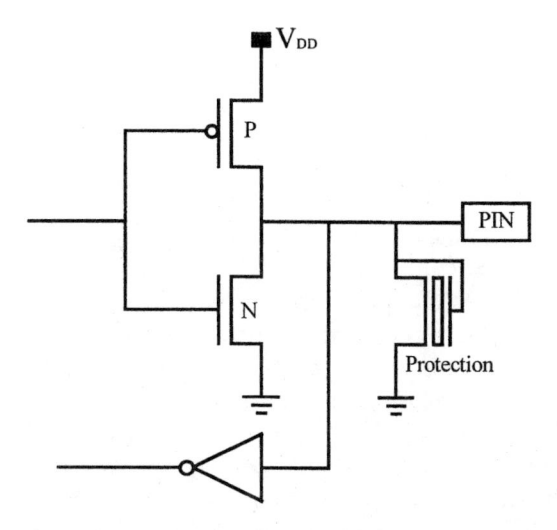

Figure 6.2: General Purpose I/O Pin

Even if electrical noise in a system were never to be of sufficient magnitude to harm the output devices, electrical noise entering the pin would still be applied to the input buffer. While this condition would not cause harm to the N-channel and P-channel devices comprising the input buffer, it would cause the devices to become active when the noise passes through the switching threshold of the buffer. The result of the inadvertent switching of unconnected input buffers can cause an increase in overall device current consumption. The amount of additional current consumption caused by the random switching depends upon the magnitude and frequency of the electrical noise and the level of accumulated charge on the input pin.

Section 6.6: General Purpose I/O Examples

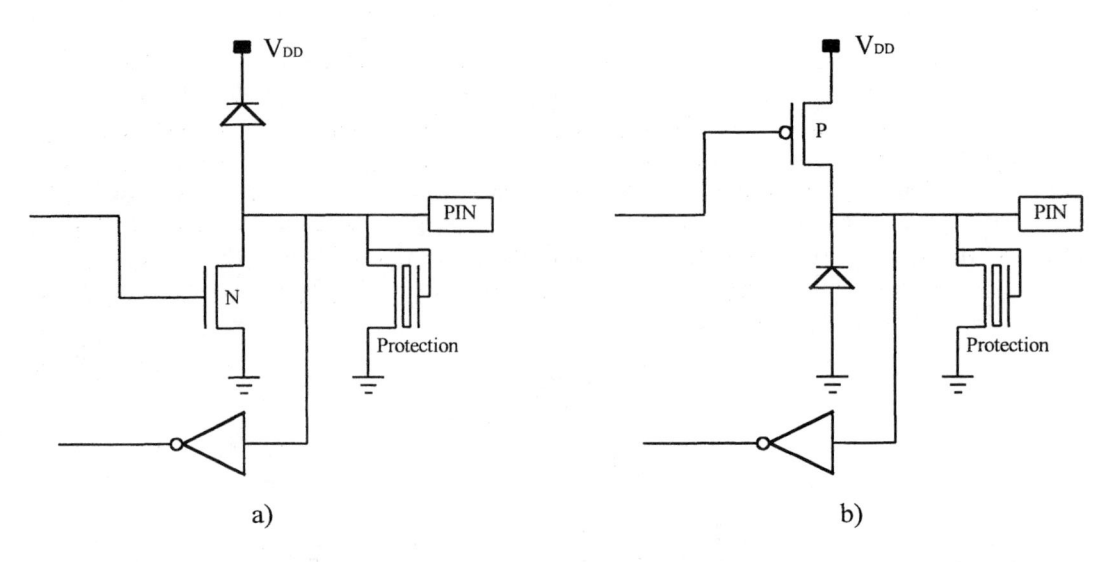

Figure 6.3: General Purpose I/O Pin exceeding VDD (a) or becoming less than VSS (b)

One way to solve this potential problem without adding external pull-up or pull-down resistors to the design, is to enable the built-in active pull-up devices on the port containing the unused I/O pins. While this provides the simplest and least costly solution to the problem, the capability to individually enable or disable the pull-up device for each port pin is not available. In general, each port's pull-up control bit enables or disables the active pull-up devices for *all* I/O pins on a port. This may or may not pose a problem in an application depending on how the remainder of the port pins are utilized. When I/O pins are configured as outputs, the active pull-ups are disabled regardless of the state of the pull-up enable bit and therefore are not a concern. If, however, some of the remaining port pins are configured as inputs, the effect of the active pull-up will depend upon the exact manner in which the input pin is utilized. If possible, unused I/O pins should be assigned to ports where the remainder of the pins are configured as outputs. If it is not possible to utilize the port's active pull-ups and the unused pins must be configured as inputs, external pull-up or pull-down resistors should be added to the design. To avoid having to use external pull-up or pull-down resistors when the active pull-ups cannot be used, the unused I/O pins can simply be configured as outputs.

6.6 General Purpose I/O Examples

There are many ways that applications can utilize general purpose I/O pins. However, many embedded applications require interaction with users through the use of simple input and output devices such as switches and display devices. The remainder of this chapter provides some practical examples demonstrating the use of the M68HC12's general purpose I/O ports.

6.7 INPUT SWITCHES

The most common method used to provide input data to a microcontroller application program is through a set of simple switches. The style of switches used in an application can be comprised of a variety of types and forms, however, there are common issues involved with them all. This example demonstrates techniques and issues involved detecting the closure and/or opening of mechanical switches connected to the M68HC12's general purpose I/O ports.

All mechanical contact switches exhibit a common characteristic known as 'bounce'. This phenomenon occurs whenever a switch is opened or closed and is a result of the mechanical process of bringing two conductors in contact with one another. The mechanical bounce of a switch causes multiple on-off transitions to occur for a short period of time. The length of time depends primarily the physical size and mass of the two contacts involved but can vary from a few milliseconds for small, low current switches, to hundreds of milliseconds for large switches controlling high current loads. Switches used as inputs to the M68HC12 device would generally be small, low current switches having bounce times in the order of one to tens of milliseconds.

Because of switch bounce and the speed at which the CPU12 operates, a switch closure cannot be detected simply by checking the state of an I/O pin. If a single `BRSET` or `BRCLR` instruction were used to test the state of an input switch, hundreds or even thousands of switch transitions might be detected by a running application. To ensure a single transition is reported to an application, a debounce period must be allowed to elapse after the initial detection of an I/O pin state change. After the debounce period expires, the I/O pin must be checked again to ensure that a valid switch transition occurred.

Once a switch transition is confirmed, a 'switch pressed' status can be reported to the main portion of the application, allowing it to perform an action based on the change in switch status. However, returning a 'switch pressed' status when the initial switch transition occurs may not produce the desired result in an application if the switch is held down by an operator. To avoid detecting and reporting multiple 'switch pressed' events, a switch scanning routine must be able to distinguish between the initial transition, the switch remaining pressed and the release of the switch. In fact, some applications may need to detect and react to all three conditions for a single switch.

Consider, for example, an application where the speed of a motor is controlled by two momentary contact push button switches, one of the buttons is used to increase motor speed, the other is used to decrease motor speed. A momentary closure of either button causes the speed of the motor to increase or decrease the motor speed by a fixed amount. If

Section 6.7: Input Switches

either button remains pressed longer than some predetermined period, the motor speed will be continuously increased or decreased.

When connecting individual switches to the M68HC12's general purpose I/O ports, almost any style switch can be used: normally open or closed, momentary, or latching contact. No matter what style is chosen, it is most efficient from a hardware perspective to connect one side of the switch to an I/O pin and the other side of the switch to ground. Such a connection can take advantage of the built-in pull up resistors available on most I/O port pins. When the pull up resistors are enabled and the switch is open the port pin will be read as a logical one and when closed it will be read as a logical zero.

Figure 6.4 presents a very elementary subroutine that will detect the closure and release of a single normally open, momentary contact switch connected to port pin PA0. The inefficiencies of this particular subroutine will be obvious to a programmer with experience writing code to detect switch closures. However, it provides a simple example for those with less experience and provides a framework that can be expanded to provide a more efficient implementation.

```
;
ChkSw:      brclr   PORTA,#$01,ChkSw1    ; if switch pressed, go debounce.
NoPress:    clrb                         ; if not return an == condition.
            rts                          ; return.
;
ChkSw1:     ldab    #10                  ; switch pressed was detected.
            bsr     mSDelay              ; delay for 10 mS debounce.
            brset   PORTA,#$01,NoPress   ; rtn if switch not pressed after db.
ChkSw2:     brclr   PORTA,#$01,*         ; wait here until released.
            ldab    #10                  ; debounce the release for 10 mS.
            bsr     mSDelay
            brclr   PORTA,#$01,ChkSw2    ; if false release, wait for release.
            ldab    #1                   ; switch released. return != condition.
            rts                          ; return.
;
mSDelay:    ldx     #2000                ; 1 mS delay constant @ 8 MHz E-clock.
Delay:      dex                          ; [1]
            bne     Delay                ; [3/1]
            dbne    b,mSDelay            ; times the number in b.
            rts                          ; return.
;
```

Figure 6.4: Simple Switch Closure Detection Subroutine

The subroutine begins by checking bit zero of Port A. If a switch closure is detected, the subroutine continues at label `ChkSw1` where the switch closure debounce delay begins, otherwise, the subroutine returns with a zero in accumulator B. The debounce delay is performed by executing a simple software delay routine for 10 mS. After returning, bit zero is checked again to determine if the switch is still pressed. If bit zero of Port A is a logic one the subroutine returns with the B accumulator clear indicating that the switch is no longer pressed. However, if PA0 remains clear, the `BRCLR` instruction at label `ChkSw2` will execute until the switch is released.

Once the switch is released, a second debounce delay period begins to ensure that multiple transitions associated with switch release are not accidentally reported to the main program. After the release debounce period, a final check of the switch state is made to ensure that port pin PA0 has returned to a logic one. If not, the `BRCLR` instruction will return execution to the label `ChkSw2`. When the final `BRCLR` instruction fails to branch, a one is returned in the B accumulator, indicating that the switch was pressed and released.

While this example shows the proper way to debounce a switch connected to a port pin, the implementation does have some major shortcomings. Due to the fact the debounce delay routine utilizes a simple software delay loop, and because the CPU12 remains within the subroutine during the entire time the switch is pressed, the CPU12 is unable to perform any other tasks. Adapting this subroutine to perform more efficiently requires changes allowing the subroutine to return to the main portion of the program before the completion of a switch press and release.

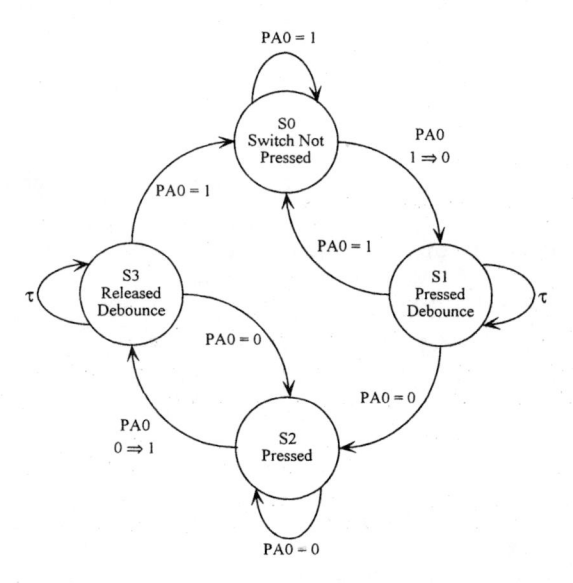

Figure 6.5: Switch State Transition Diagram

Section 6.7: Input Switches

Figure 6.5 contains a simple state diagram describing various states of the switch detection software in Figure 6.4 and will help in understanding the revised software. As shown, the detection of a switch press consists of four basic states and events that trigger the transition from one state to another. As long as a transition from a logic one to a logic zero is not detected on PA0, the state machine will remain in state S0. When a logic zero is detected on pin PA0, a transition is made from state S0 to S1 and begins the switch pressed debounce period. During the switch pressed debounce period, the state machine remains in state S1 until the expiration of the debounce time period represented by τ. Upon expiration of the debounce period, a transition is made to state S2 if port pin PA0 remained a logic zero or will transition back to state S0 if a logic one is detected on the pin. The state machine remains in state S2 as long as PA0 remains a zero. When a transition from a logic zero to a logic one is detected on PA0 the state machine moves to the release debounce period, state S3. Like state S1, the state machine remains in state S3 until the expiration of the debounce period. Finally, if pin PA0 remains a logic one at the end of the debounce period a transition is made back to state S0.

Remember that the software in Figure 6.4 returns a zero in the B accumulator if a switch press is not detected and returns a one only if the software makes a complete transition through the subroutine. To properly understand the revised subroutine, it is important to understand that the 'switch-not-pressed' status returned by the subroutine is distinctly different from the state machine being in state S0. In addition, returning a status of 'switch-pressed' is not the same as the state machine being in state S2. As shown in Figure 6.7, a 'switch-pressed' status is returned by the subroutine only when the state machine transitions from state S3 to S0.

Basic state machine control, presented in Figure 6.6, is implemented utilizing a jump table and a computed GOTO. Each time the `CheckSw` subroutine is called, the value contained in the variable `CurState` is used to index into the jump table at `StateTbl`, executing the portion of the subroutine applicable for the current state. Because each jump table entry consists of a two byte address, the value in `CurState` must be multiplied by two before being used as an offset. Notice that a check is performed on the variable `CurState` to ensure that it contains a valid state value. Even though during normal program execution `CurState` should always contain a valid state value, the small amount of additional code for the range check provides added protection against potential program failure. The most likely cause of an invalid state value would be the failure of software to initialize the value of `CurState` to `St0` before calling the subroutine for the first time.

```
;
CurState:   ds      1                   ; current state of the state machine.
DBDlyCnt:   ds      1                   ; debounce delay.
;
St0:        equ     0                   ; switch press not detected.
St1:        equ     1                   ; debounce after press.
St2:        equ     2                   ; pressed after DB down
St3:        equ     3                   ; debounce after release.
;
CheckSw:    ldx     #StateTbl           ; point to the state table.
            clra                        ; we'll use D for indexing
            ldab    CurState            ; get the current state machine state.
            cmpb    #St3                ; valid state?
            bls     StateOK             ; yes.
            clrb                        ; no. go back to state 0.
            stab    CurState            ; fix the bad value.
StateOK:    lsld                        ; mult. by the # of bytes/table entry.
            jmp     [d,x]               ; go check the current state.
;
StateTbl:   dc.w    State0              ; state #0, switch press not detected.
            dc.w    State1              ; state #1, debounce after press.
            dc.w    State2              ; state #2, pressed after DB down.
            dc.w    State3              ; state #3, debounce after release.
;
```

Figure 6.6: State Machine Control Implementation

The code in Figure 6.7 implements all four states of the switch check state machine. Remember that the whole goal of rewriting the CheckSw subroutine was to allow the CPU12 to perform other tasks during the detection of a switch press and release. Following the execution path through any of the four states reveals that the CPU12 never spends more than a few dozen cycles within the subroutine during the detection process. Even if the switch remains pressed for an extended period of time, the subroutine returns to the calling routine with a 'switch-not-pressed' status. Notice that with the exception of state S3, all states exit through the label NoPress returning a 'switch-not-pressed' status to the calling application.

Section 6.7: Input Switches

```
State0:     brclr   PORTA,#$01,PressDn  ; if sw pressed, go to debounce state.
NoPress:    clrb                        ; if not return an == condition.
            rts                         ; return.
;
PressDn:    ldab    #St1                ; set to state #1.
SetupDB     stab    CurState
            bsr     InitDB              ; setup RTI for debounce timer
            bra     NoPress             ; return a not pressed condition.
;
State1:     tst     DBDlyCnt            ; press debounce period expired?
            bne     NoPress             ; no. return a not pressed condition.
            brclr   PORTA,#$01,GotoS2   ; switch really pressed?
            clr     CurState            ; no. false press. Goto State 0
            bra     NoPress             ; and return a not pressed condition.
;
GotoS2:     ldab    #St2                ; yes. set to state #2.
            stab    CurState
            bra     NoPress             ; return a not pressed condition.
;
State2:     brclr   PORTA,#$01,NoPress  ; still pressed, return not pressed.
            ldab    #St3                ; if released, go to state 3 & setup
            bra     SetupDB             ; debounce after release.
;
State3:     tst     DBDlyCnt            ; release debounce period expired?
            bne     NoPress             ; no. return a not pressed condition.
            brclr   PORTA,#$01,GotoS2   ; yes. check switch once more.
            clr     CurState            ; switch was released, back to state 0
            ldab    #1                  ; return a switch pressed condition.
            rts                         ; return.
;
```

Figure 6.7: State S0 through S3 Implementation

In the original subroutine, one of the areas where the CPU12 spent a significant amount of time was the software delay loop implementing the debounce periods. To avoid this inefficiency, the Real Time Interrupt (RTI) timer is used in conjunction with a software counter to time these two periods. The subroutine `InitDB` is called during the transition from state S0 to S1 and from S2 to S3 to enable and initialize the RTI timer and the variable `DBDlyCnt`. As shown in Figure 6.8 the RTI timer is initialized to produce an interrupt every 1.024 mS which allows the debounce period to be adjusted in approximate 1 mS increments. The `DBDlyCnt` variable is decremented by the RTI interrupt service routine and tested by the code implementing states S1 and S3. Observe that each time the value of

`DBDlyCnt` is decremented in the RTI interrupt service routine, its value is checked for zero. When the variable reaches zero, the debounce period has expired and the RTI timer is disabled. Testing for the expiration of the debounce period is performed by the `TST` instructions at the beginning of States S1 and S3. If the debounce period has not expired, the code for both states returns immediately, allowing the CPU12 to perform other tasks. When the debounce period does expire, transition to the next state is allowed.

Two items should be pointed out regarding the use of the RTI timer for timing the debounce period. First, employing the RTI timer for this type of application is not a typical use of this timer. However, because the RTI timer was discussed in Chapter 4, it was thought that most readers would be familiar with its initialization and application. It would be more common to use one of the timer module's channels configured as an output compare to produce a delay equal to the total debounce delay period. The second item is revealed in the comment of first line of the `InitDB` subroutine where it explains that a delay of 10 to 11 mS will be produced by initializing the `DBDlyCnt` variable with a constant of 11. Because the input to the RTI timer block is fed by a 2^{12} divider circuit there will always an uncertainty of one RTI clock period when the timer is enabled and disabled as used in this application.

```
;
InitDB:   ldab    #11             ; 10 - 11 mS delay.
          stab    DBDlyCnt        ; each RTI is 1.024 mS
          bset    RTIFLG,#RTIF    ; clear RTI flag before we enable RTI Ints.
          ldab    #$81            ; set rate & enable RTI ints.
          stab    RTICTL
          rts                     ; return.
;
RTIISR:   bset    RTIFLG,#RTIF    ; clear RTI flag
          dec     DBDlyCnt        ; debounce count == 0?
          bne     RTIRtn          ; no. return.
          clr     RTICTL          ; yes. disable the RTI.
RTIRtn:   rti                     ; return.
;
```

Figure 6.8: Debounce Timer Initialization and RTI Interrupt Service Routine

6.8 MULTIPLE INPUT SWITCH ROUTINE

The switch input example presented in the previous section provides a basic framework for detecting the press and release of a single momentary contact push button switch in an efficient manner. Obviously, most applications requiring end user interaction are likely to

Section 6.8: Multiple Input Switch Routine

require more than a single input switch. Accommodating more than one switch can be accomplished in a variety of ways depending on the number of inputs required. In general, if five or fewer switch inputs are required, the best approach is to simply connect push button switches to adjacent port input pins.

Figure 6.9 shows a state machine implementation for four pushbutton switches connected to port pins PA0 through PA3. While changes had to be made to the code implementing all four states, the majority of the changes were made to state zero. Rather than using bit manipulation instructions to detect a switch press, a program loop is used to test each of the four port bits to determine if one of the switches is pressed. Using this method allows the generation of a bit mask containing a one in the bit position corresponding to the switch that is pressed. This value is saved in the byte variable `SwMask` and is used by the remaining states to check the status of the pressed switch. This is also the value returned in the B accumulator after the successful detection of a switch closure and release.

Inspecting the portion of state zero that examines the status of each switch reveals a limitation of the implementation. Observe that each time state zero is called, it begins by checking port pin PA0 and proceeds to check the next higher numbered port pin until a pressed switch is found or all four inputs have been checked. By halting the scanning process with the first input where a pressed switch is found, the program logic negates the possibility of detecting more than one switch being pressed at the same time. This feature, known as key rollover capability, may not pose a problem for most embedded applications; however, if required, it will necessitate a significant change in the state machine implementation.

```
;
State0:     ldab    #$01            ; init the bit mask.
            stab    SwMask
            ldaa    #4              ; number of switches to check.
            ldab    PORTA           ; get switch inputs on port A.
            andb    #$0f            ; mask off upper 4 bits.
ChkLoop:    bitb    SwMask          ; any switches pressed?
            beq     PressDn         ; yes. go save new mask & process.
            lsl     SwMask          ; move bit mask to next sw position.
            dbne    a,ChkLoop       ; loop until all switches are checked.
NoPress:    clrb                    ; no. return an == condition.
            rts                     ; return.
;
PressDn:    ldab    #St1            ; set to state #1.
SetupDB     stab    CurState
            bsr     InitDB          ; setup RTI for debounce timer
            bra     NoPress         ; return a not pressed condition.
;
State1:     tst     DBDlyCnt        ; press debounce period expired?
            bne     NoPress         ; no. return a not pressed condition.
            ldab    PORTA           ; retrieve switch inputs.
            bitb    SwMask          ; same switch pressed?
            beq     GotoS2          ; yes. move state #2
            clr     CurState        ; no. false press. back to state #0.
            bra     NoPress         ; return.
;
GotoS2:     ldab    #St2            ; yes. set switch to state #2.
            stab    CurState
            bra     NoPress         ; return a not pressed condition.
;
State2:     ldab    PORTA           ; get switch inputs on port A.
            bitb    SwMask          ; same switch pressed?
            beq     NoPress         ; yes. just wait until its released.
            ldab    #St3            ; no. go setup
            bra     SetupDB         ; debounce after release.
;
State3:     tst     DBDlyCnt        ; release debounce period expired?
            bne     NoPress         ; no. return a not pressed condition.
            ldab    SwMask          ; get the switch bit mask.
            bitb    PORTA           ; switch pressed after debounce?
            beq     GotoS2          ; yes. false release detected.
            clr     CurState        ; no. switch released, back to state 0.
            rts                     ; return w/ port switch bit in acc b.
;
```

Figure 6.9: Checking Four Switches Attached to PA0 through PA3

Section 6.9: Scanned Switch Matrix

6.9 SCANNED SWITCH MATRIX

When more than five individual push button switch inputs are required in an application, it is more efficient from an I/O port pin utilization to arrange the switches in an X-Y matrix as shown in Figure 6.10. With this arrangement, twice as many input switches (16) can be accommodated using the same number of I/O port pins as would be required applying the connection strategy used in the previous example. In the figure, each switch is connected at the point where a row and a column *cross*. When a switch is closed, a connection is made between a row and column I/O pin and the connection can be detected with software. As shown, the resistors connected to the row *inputs* may be connected to VDD or VSS. If connected to VDD, a logic zero placed on any one of the column output lines will result in a logic zero being read at a row input pin where a key switch is closed. If the resistors are connected to VSS, a logic one placed on any of the column output lines will result in a logic one being read at a row input pin where a key switch is closed. Because the M68HC12 family has built in, configurable pull up resistors on most of its I/O port pins, the external resistors would not be required.

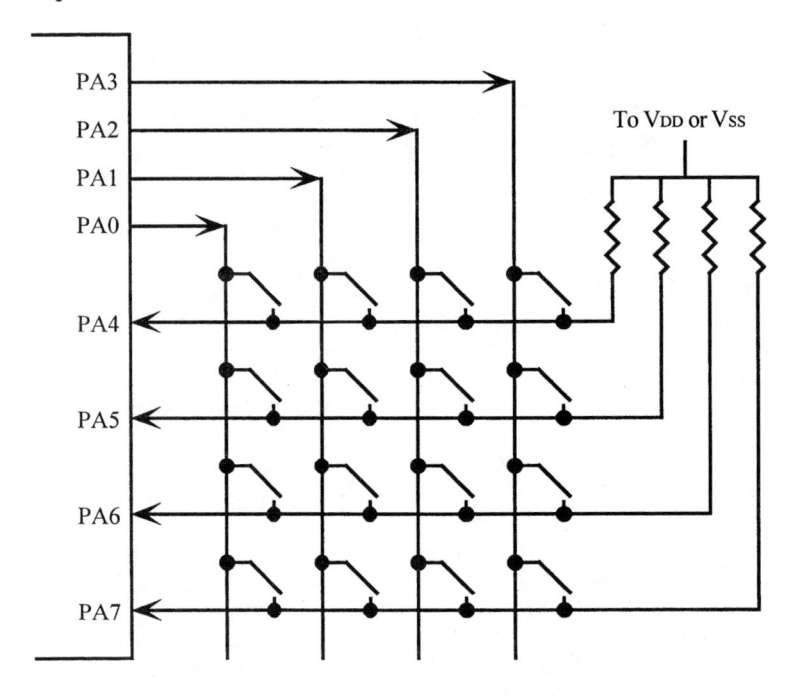

Figure 6.10: A 4 x 4 Key Matrix

The actual key scanning process is actually quite simple and begins by placing a logic zero on port pin PA0 while the remainder of column outputs remain at a logic one. The row inputs are then checked to see if any of the pins are at a logic zero. If PA4 through PA7 all

Chapter 6: General Purpose Parallel I/O Ports

contain logic ones, a logic zero is placed on PA1 while PA0, PA2, and PA3 stay at a logic one. Again, PA4 through PA7 are checked for a switch closure. The process of shifting a logic zero to the next higher column output and shifting a logic one into the least significant column output continues until one or more of the row inputs contain a logic zero or until all four column outputs have been strobed. It should be noted that even though the columns were used as the strobe outputs and the rows used as the inputs, nothing prevents the reverse strategy from being used.

```
;
State0:    ldaa   #4              ; number of columns to check.
           ldab   #$0e            ; init the columns strobe mask.
           stab   PORTA           ; strobe column 1.
ChkLoop:   ldab   PORTA           ; get row inputs in upper 4 bits
           andb   #$f0            ; mask off the column strobe pattern.
           cmpb   #$f0            ; any row inputs low (key pressed)?
           bne    PressDn         ; yes. go determine which row.
           sec                    ; no. set carry to rotate a 1 into
           rol    PORTA           ; the lsb & the 0 to the next column.
           dbne   a,ChkLoop       ; strobe all 4 columns.
NoPress:   clrb                   ; no rows contained 0. return 0 in b.
           rts                    ; return.
;
PressDn:   ldaa   #$10            ; find row with the pressed switch.
           staa   SwMask
           ldaa   #4              ; check each of 4 rows to determine
RowLoop:   bitb   SwMask          ; AND row info w/ row mask. found row?
           beq    FoundRow        ; yes. go create row/column mask.
           lsl    SwMask          ; no. shift row mask to next row.
           dbne   a,RowLoop       ; check all rows.
           bra    NoPress         ; should never get here. JIC.
;
FoundRow:  ldab   PORTA           ; get column strobe info.
           comb                   ; make strobed row a 1 for mask.
           andb   #$0f            ; get rid of Port A row info.
           addb   SwMask          ; add in generated row mask.
           stab   SwMask          ; save column/row mask pattern.
           ldab   #St1            ; set to state #1.
SetupDB    stab   CurState
           bsr    InitDB          ; setup RTI for debounce timer
           bra    NoPress         ; return a not pressed condition.
;
```

Figure 6.11: State 0 modified for a 4 x 4 key matrix

225

Section 6.10: Output Indicators

The changes required to the example in Figure 6.9 are isolated to State 0. The remainder of the state machine implementation may be used as-is. Figure 6.11 contains the source code necessary to scan and detect a switch press for the 4 x 4 key matrix shown in Figure 6.10. State 0 begins with a program loop that shifts a zero through each of the column outputs and checks for one or more zeros on the row inputs. When a zero is detected on the row inputs, the code branches to label `PressDn` where it is determined which row input contains a zero. If more than one row input contains a zero, the first zero found, scanning from PA4 to PA7, is used for the bit mask. After the detection of a zero on a row input, execution continues at the label `FoundRow` where a combined bit mask is generated. This bit mask contains a one in the row and column bit positions corresponding to the pressed switch. This bit mask is saved in the variable `SwMask` and is used by subsequent machine states to determine the status of the pressed switch.

Once the state machine has transitioned through all four states, the value returned to the calling program is the bit mask representing the row and column of the detected switch press. Depending on the application, this value may be used directly by a program or it may be converted to a key number using a simple table look up.

6.10 OUTPUT INDICATORS

The scanned key matrix example in the previous section provided an illustration of how general purpose I/O pins can be used in a combination of inputs and outputs for a specific function. When output pins are required to drive actuators or power devices requiring more than a few milliamps of drive current, an external buffer device must be connected between the I/O pin and the driven device to boost the current drive capability. There are many such devices whose function and drive capabilities will vary depending on the device's intended application.

For applications requiring interaction with an operator, some form of output indicator or display is generally required to provide feedback on a system's operation. Indicators can range from individual LEDs to multi-digit seven segment numeric displays to multi-character alpha-numeric Vacuum Fluorescent or Liquid Crystal displays. Even though the M68HC12 family's I/O pins are not specified for LED drive capability, each I/O pin is easily capable of sinking 5 - 10 mA of current. At these current levels, high efficiency, low current LEDs can be driven directly using I/O pins configured as outputs. The total number of outputs that can simultaneously illuminate LEDs depends on the ambient operating temperature and the internal power dissipation of the M68HC12. The currently published electrical characteristics of the individual M68HC12 family members provide the necessary information to calculate junction temperature rise due to internal and I/O power dissipation.

Figure 6.12 shows four LEDs connected to port pins PA0 through PA3. The cathode of each diode is connected directly to the I/O pin while the anode is connected to VDD through a current limiting resistor. The size of the current limiting resistor is chosen to limit

Chapter 6: General Purpose Parallel I/O Ports

the amount of current flowing into the I/O pin and will depend on the voltage drop across the LED and the voltage drop across the N-channel transistor making up the lower portion of the I/O driver. The forward voltage drop across an LED will typically be from 1.5 to 3.5 volts. The currently published electrical characteristics for the MC68HC912B32 specifies an I/O pin voltage of VSS + 0.4 volts at an IOL of 1.6 mA. While this specification is valid over the entire temperature range, which extends to +125•C, it is *extremely* conservative. Typical measurements are much lower. Measurements taken on a recent mask set show voltage drops across the internal N-channel transistor of 150 - 160 mV on Port A pins sinking approximately six milliamps and 260 - 270 mV when sinking 12 mA. When directly driving LEDs in this manner, initialization software should write ones to the port data register before configuring the pins as outputs. This will ensure that the LEDs remain off when the data direction register is written.

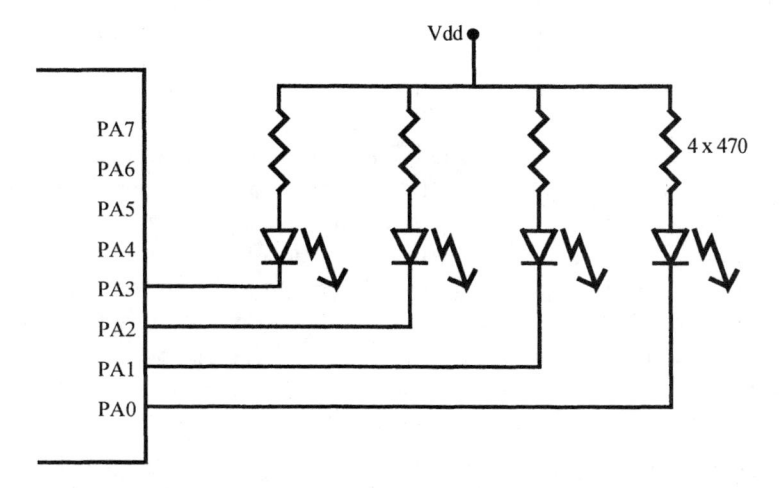

Figure 6.12: Driving LEDs directly with I/O port pins

For applications requiring a single digit numeric display, it is feasible to directly drive a seven segment display using a single 8-bit I/O port. A common anode display, one where all of the anodes of the LEDs are tied together, can be connected to an I/O port as shown in Figure 6.13. As the figure shows, because of the common cathode connection, the current limiting resistors must be moved to the cathode side of the LEDs. In this instance, because of the possibility of all eight segments being illuminated at the same time, it is a good idea to keep segment current to 10 mA or less. This current level is more than adequate to provide good luminous intensity for a high efficiency numeric display. As when driving individual LEDs connected to I/O port pins, writing a zero to a port pin's data register illuminates a segment of the display while writing a one will extinguish the segment.

Section 6.10: Output Indicators

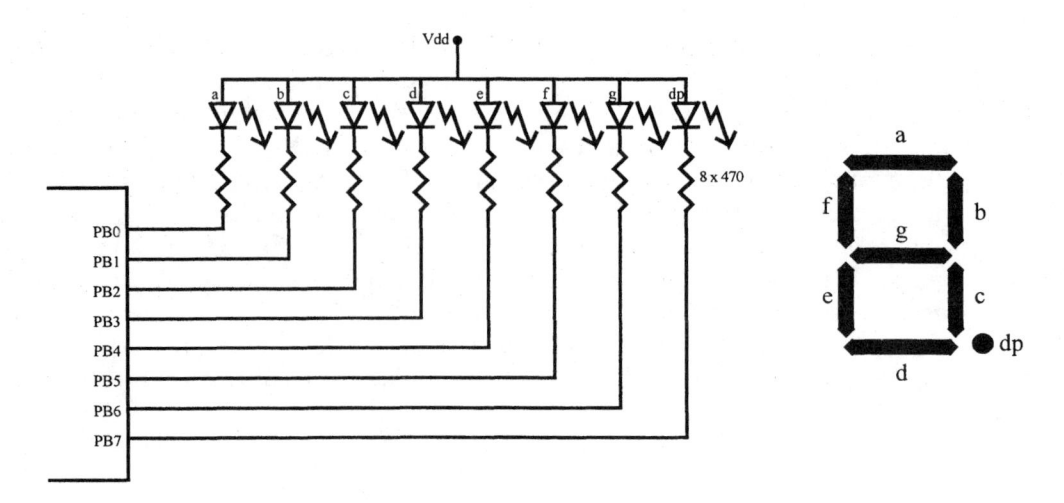

Figure 6.13: Driving a single digit 7-segment display with I/O port pins

The software necessary to drive a single digit numeric display connected as shown in Figure 6.13 is presented in Figure 6.14. The initialization subroutine, beginning at label `DigitInit`, configures all pins of Port B as outputs and writes ones to all eight bits, blanking the display. The order of the initialization writes to the Port B data register before configuring the port pins as outputs to prevent unknown data from appearing on the port momentarily. The subroutine beginning at `DispDigit` accepts a hexadecimal number in the B accumulator having a value of $00 through $0F that is shown on the 7-segment display. In addition, a value of $FF passed to the subroutine results in a blanked display. A value outside this range is ignored, resulting in the display remaining unchanged.

The translation from the hexadecimal parameter to the data pattern representing a 7-segment digit is performed by a simple table look up. The data pattern for each digit was built by examining Figure 6.13 and placing a zero at each bit location where a segment is to be illuminated. Notice that the most significant bit of all table entries is zero. This would seem to indicate that this bit, which controls the decimal point, is illuminated for all digits. However, examining the source code reveals that the table entry for each digit is OR'ed with the value contained in the most significant bit of the Port B data register. Formatting the table in this manner and performing the operation in this fashion allows the decimal point to be controlled independently from the displayed digit. Although no subroutine is provided for illuminating and extinguishing the decimal point, the operation can easily be performed using bit manipulation instructions.

Even though this example presents a subroutine and translation table that displays the hexadecimal digits $0 through $F, it is possible to display additional alphabetic characters and symbols. Extending the range checking of the subroutine and the translation table can provide additional capability for communicating a system's status to an operator.

```
;
DigitInit: ldab    #$ff            ; all outputs & ddr set to 1s.
           stab    PORTB           ; blank display.
           stab    DDRB            ; config port b as outputs.
           rts
;
DispDigit: cmpb    #$ff            ; blank the display?
           bne     NoBlank         ; no. check for valid hex digit.
           stab    PORTB           ; yes. store $ff to turn off all segments.
           rts
NoBlank:   cmpb    #$0f            ; b greater than max. hex digit?
           bhi     Error           ; yes. don't change display.
           ldx     #LEDTable       ; no. point to translation table.
           ldaa    PORTB           ; get value of port b
           anda    #$80            ; mask off all but decimal point.
           oraa    b,x             ; OR in info from seg. table.
           staa    PORTB           ; update display data.
Error:     rts                     ; return.
;
LEDTable:  fcb     %01000000       ; zero
           fcb     %01111001       ; one
           fcb     %00100100       ; two
           fcb     %00110000       ; three
           fcb     %00011001       ; four
           fcb     %00010010       ; five
           fcb     %00000010       ; six
           fcb     %01111000       ; seven
           fcb     %00000000       ; eight
           fcb     %00011000       ; nine
           fcb     %00001000       ; A
           fcb     %00000011       ; b
           fcb     %01000110       ; C
           fcb     %00100001       ; d
           fcb     %00000110       ; E
           fcb     %00001110       ; F
;
```

Figure 6.14: Single Digit 7-segment Display Driver Software

When a single 7-segment digit is not adequate for communicating a system's status, it is possible to add more digits on additional I/O ports; however, this method is not practical for most applications. Instead, multiple digits are usually connected in an arrangement where

Section 6.11: LCD Alpha–numeric Display Module

the cathodes of all digits are connected in parallel and the anodes of each digit are connected to a transistor switch. Software, usually interrupt driven, is used to display each digit for a brief period of time at a rapid rate giving the illusion that each digit is illuminated continuously. This technique, known as multiplexing, is commonly used for multi-digit displays because it reduces the number of I/O port and display connections required. The main disadvantage of this technique is an increase in the number of required components, the additional software, and the CPU time required to multiplex the display. In some cases, especially where component assembly costs are high, it may be advantageous to utilize a dedicated multiplex display driver I.C. such as the Motorola MC14489A. This part can be used to drive up to five digit displays, including decimal points, or up to 25 individual LEDs. Connection to the M68HC12 is made via three of the Serial Peripheral Interface's (SPI) four pins. A complete application example using the MC14489A to drive a four digit display plus four LED indicator lamps is presented in Chapter 10.

6.11 LCD Alpha–numeric Display Module

Applications requiring more sophisticated operator interaction than is possible with simple numeric digits and indicators can utilize alpha–numeric display modules to communicate the status of a system by employing text messages. Numerous types and sizes of display modules are available utilizing a variety of display technologies. Preassembled display modules usually contain their own microcontroller. These microcontrollers generally include specialized circuitry for driving the display and a serial or parallel interface for communication with a host microcontroller. In addition, it will generally contain firmware to manage various display functions and allow the host microcontroller to send it ASCII data to display.

A block diagram for the Optrex DMC-16249 16 character by 2 line LCD display is shown in Figure 6.15. Each of the 32 characters is formed in a 5 x 7 dot matrix, with the built in character generator ROM providing 192 standard characters, numbers and symbols. The host computer interface consists of a parallel 8-bit data bus and three control signals. These signals, with the proper decoding logic, may be connected directly to a microcontroller's data bus allowing the control registers and display memory to be accessed as memory locations. For applications where the microcontroller operates in single chip mode, these same signals can be connected to general purpose I/O pins and can be manipulated by software.

Chapter 6: General Purpose Parallel I/O Ports

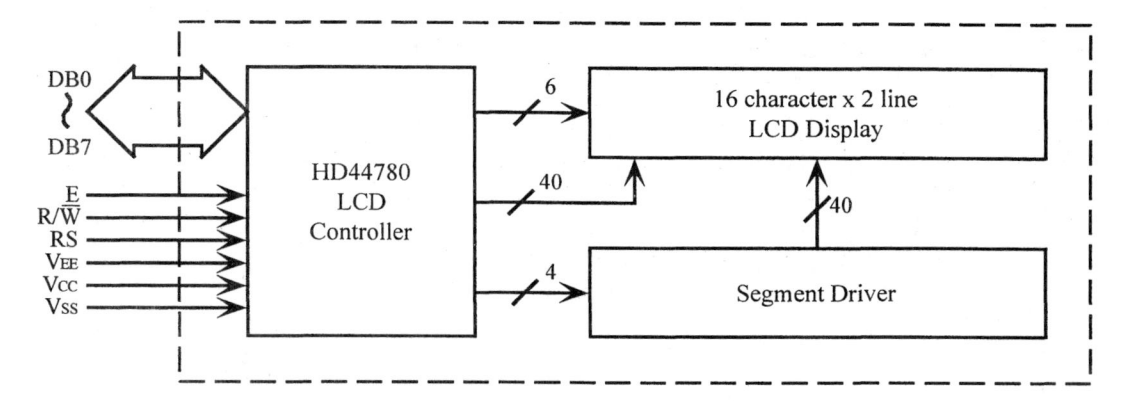

Figure 6.15: Optrex DMC-16249 Block Diagram

In addition to the firmware necessary to convert ASCII data to the 5 x 7 dot patterns forming the display characters, the module firmware provides 11 commands allowing manipulation of basic display characteristics. The commands, shown in the table of Figure 6.16, can be combined by the host microcontroller software to provide a higher level of display functionality. Examining the table, notice that each command has an execution time associated with it. After issuing a command, the host software must delay the specified time before issuing another command. As an alternative to utilizing a software delay loop, the controller's busy flag may be polled to determine when the module is idle and can accept a command.

Many of the commands utilize bits within the command word to configure and/or control characteristics of the display. The function of each bit is explained at the bottom of the table. Configuration bits marked with an asterisk (*) are don't care bits and may be written with a value of one or zero. The DL bit in the Function Set command will be of particular interest for designs where the number of I/O port lines are limited. This bit can be used during the module's initialization sequence to specify a 4-bit wide data bus interface rather than the standard 8-bit data bus. Utilizing the 4-bit data bus would complicate the host microcontroller software since two data transfers are required for each command; however, it would allow the module to be controlled utilizing only seven I/O pins. For the example presented here, the standard 8-bit data bus is utilized with the data bus connected to Port A and the three control lines, E, R/w and RS connected to port pins PB0, PB1 and PB2 respectively.

The clock signal, E, is used to initiate all transfers to and from the module. Because the module's signals are manipulated by software, timing for the data and control signals is not critical in most cases. However, for write operations, RS and R/w signals must be stable a minimum of 40 nS before the rising edge of the E-clock. This specification imposes a restriction on the software that will not allow the RS and R/w signals to change using the same instruction that transitions E from low to high.

Section 6.11: LCD Alpha–numeric Display Module

Instruction	RS	R/W	DB7	DB6	DB5	DB4	DB3	DB2	DB1	DB0	Execution Time (max)
Clear Display	0	0	0	0	0	0	0	0	0	1	1.64 mS
Home Cursor	0	0	0	0	0	0	0	0	1	*	1.64 mS
Set Entry Mode	0	0	0	0	0	0	0	1	I/D	S	40 μS
Display/Cursor On/Off	0	0	0	0	0	0	1	D	C	B	40 μS
Display/Cursor Shift	0	0	0	0	0	1	S/C	R/L	*	*	40 μS
Function Set	0	0	0	0	1	DL	N	F	*	*	40 μS
CGRAM Address Set	0	0	0	1	Character Generator Address						40 μS
DDRAM Address Set	0	0	1	Display Data Address							40 μS
Busy Flag/ Address Read	0	1	BF	CGRAM/DDRAM (Cursor) Address						0 μS
CGRAM/DDRAM Data Write	1	0	Character Generator/Display Data							40 μS
CGRAM/DDRAM Data Read	1	1	Character Generator/Display Data							40 μS

I/D = 1 : Increment	R/L = 1 : Shift Display/Cursor to Right	N = 0 : One Row
I/D = 0 : Decrement	R/L = 0 : Shift Display/Cursor to Left	F = 1 : 5 x 10 Dot Matrix
S = 1 : Display Shift	DL = 1 : Use 8-bit Data Interface	F = 0 : 5 x 7 Dot Matrix
S/C = 1 : Shift Display	DL = 0 : Use 4-bit Data Interface	BF = 1 : Module Busy
S/C = 0 : Shift Cursor	N = 1 : Two Rows	BF = 0 : Module Idle
D = 1 : Display On	C = 1 : Cursor On	B = 1 : Cursor Blink
D = 0 : Display Off	C = 0 : Cursor Off	B = 0 : Cursor Solid

Figure 6.16: Optrex DMC-16249 Display Module Commands

6.11.1 Display Module Initialization

Before data can be sent to the display module, a specific sequence of commands must be written to the display to initialize the module's firmware. Because the Busy Flag cannot be accessed during this initialization process, fixed delays, specified in the data sheet, must be inserted between sending each command. After the initialization process is complete, the Busy Flag may be used to check for command completion. Figure 6.17 contains the software necessary to properly initialize the display module. The eight commands used to initialize the display are stored in a data table beginning at label `InitCmdTbl`. Each entry in the table consists of two bytes. The first byte of the entry is the command byte sent to the display.

Chapter 6: General Purpose Parallel I/O Ports

The second byte is a constant representing the number of 100 µS delay periods that the software must wait before issuing the next command. The data sheet does not provide details on the actions performed by the display module during the first three commands, however, the fourth command is used to set the interface length, number of display lines and the font matrix size.

```
;
LCDInit:     clr    PORTB          ; RS, R/w & E = 0.
             ldab   #$07           ; make signals outputs.
             stab   DDRB
             ldaa   #$ff           ; make port a outputs.
             staa   DDRA
             ldaa   #8             ; 8 commands are used to init the module.
             psha                  ; put the count on the stack.
             ldy    #InitCmdTbl    ; point to the command table.
NextCmd:     ldaa   1,y+           ; get a command byte.
             staa   PORTA          ; put command on module's data bus.
             bset   PORTB,#EClk    ; clock it into the module.
             bclr   PORTB,#EClk
             ldab   1,y+           ; get the delay time between commands.
             bsr    uS100Delay     ; delay for 100 uS * count.
             dec    0,sp           ; done with the commands?
             bne    NextCmd        ; no. loop until done.
             pula                  ; yes. remove command count.
             rts                   ; return.
;
InitCmdTbl:  db     $30, 42        ; get the module's attention.
             db     $30, 1
             db     $30, 1
             db     $38, 1         ; specify interface width, lines & font.
             db     $08, 1         ; turn display off.
             db     $0c, 1         ; turn display on.
             db     $06, 1         ; increment cursor, no display scroll.
             db     $01, 1         ; clear display & home the cursor.
;
uS100Delay:  ldx    #200           ; 100 uS delay constant @ 8 MHz E-clock.
Delay:       dex
             bne    Delay
             dbne   b,uS100Delay   ; times the number in b.
             rts                   ; return.
;
```

Figure 6.17: Optrex DMC-16249 Initialization Code

Section 6.11: LCD Alpha–numeric Display Module

The sixth command, used to turn the display back on, can also be used to enable the cursor and cause it to blink, however, in this case the cursor remains disabled. The seventh command, Set Entry Mode, configures basic display behavior during the entry of ASCII text. The mode set by this command causes each character to be displayed at the current cursor position and causes the cursor to be incremented to the next display location. The last entry in the table is not a required initialization command; however it ensures that the module's display memory is cleared and returns the cursor to the home position (display address zero).

Finally, the data sheet specifies that VCC must remain at a level above 4.5 volts for a minimum of 15 mS before the display initialization sequence may begin. Depending on other initialization tasks required by a system and the amount of time required to perform those tasks, a 15 mS delay may need to be inserted at the beginning of the initialization subroutine. This can easily be accomplished by loading the B accumulator with a value of 150 and calling the `uS100Delay` subroutine.

6.11.2 Displaying Data on the LCD

The HD44780 LCD controller used in the Optrex DMC-16249 display is designed to support a variety of LCD display sizes. The display data memory consists of an 80 byte array that is logically split into two 40 byte areas. The lower 40 bytes, addressed from $00 through $27, are used for the first line of a display while the upper 40 bytes, addressed from $28 through $4F, are used for the second line. Because the DMC-16249 display only contains 16 characters for each of its two lines, the display data memory for the first line is accessed at addresses $00 through $0F and the second line is accessed at addresses $40 through $4F. For this reason, when the end of the first line is reached, the cursor will not automatically wrap to the beginning of the second line. Instead, the HD44780's firmware will continue to store data data at increasing display memory addresses where the data will not be visible. If automatic line wrapping of text is desired, the host software must perform the function.

```
;
SendCmd: bsr    IsBusy              ; is the module busy?
         bne    SendCmd             ; yes. keep checking until it's not.
         bclr   PORTB,RS+Rw         ; RS & R/w = 0.
         ldaa   #$ff                ; change port a to outputs.
         staa   DDRA
         stab   PORTA               ; put command on module data bus.
         bset   PORTB,#EClk         ; latch command into module.
         bclr   PORTB,#EClk
         clr    DDRA                ; return port a to inputs.
         rts
;
IsBusy:  clr    DDRA                ; setup port a for reads.
         bclr   PORTB,RS            ; RS = 0 for commands.
         bset   PORTB,Rw            ; set R/w for read.
         bset   PORTB,#EClk         ; data output 160 nS after rising
         nop                        ; edge of E.
         ldaa   PORTA               ; get status data from module.
         bclr   PORTB,#EClk         ; put E-clock back low.
         bita   #BUSY               ; busy bit set if module is busy.
         rts
;
```

Figure 6.18: Sending commands to the Optrex DMC-16249 display module

The ability to format text sent to the module and perform basic text display maintenance requires the capability to send control commands to the DMC-16249. Figure 6.18 presents two subroutines that provide this capability. The `SendCmd` subroutine transmits one of the nine commands, passed in the B accumulator, to the display module. Before latching the command into the module, the `IsBusy` subroutine is called to ensure that the module is able to accept the command. If `IsBusy` returns with the Z condition code register bit set, the module's busy bit was clear indicating that the module is idle and ready to accept the command. If the module was busy, `IsBusy` is repeatedly called until an idle condition is returned.

Examining the `IsBusy` subroutine reveals two subtle issues that must be observed when reading from the display module. First, notice that a `NOP` is placed between the `BSET` and `LDAA` instructions. Because the module's data access time is specified at 160 nS from the rising edge of E, the `NOP` is required to ensure that the data is available and stable before it is read by the CPU12. The need for the `NOP` instruction can be understood by examining the cycle-by-cycle instruction timing of the `BSET` and `LDAA` instructions in Appendix A. As Appendix A shows when both instructions utilize direct addressing, the `BSET` instruction

Section 6.11: LCD Alpha–numeric Display Module

performs its write on the *last* cycle of the instruction while the `LDAA` instruction performs its read on the *first* cycle of the instruction. With an 8.0 MHz operating frequency, this would only provide 125 nS between the time the module's E signal went high until the data was read. Clearly this does not meet the module's 160 nS timing specification. Inserting the `NOP` adds an additional 125 nS to the access time which easily meets the specification. The second issue involves the placement of the `LDAA` instruction between the `BSET` and `BCLR` instructions. This arrangement is required because the DMC-16249 data bus is only valid while E is high.

Figure 6.19 presents a very basic `putchar` subroutine that allows writing a single 8-bit ASCII character to the display. Like the `SendCmd` subroutine, it calls `IsBusy` before writing data to the display to ensure the module is ready to accept the character. The subroutine does not perform automatic line wrapping of text and does not process carriage return or line feed characters. Before writing text to the display, the cursor must be positioned to the desired location where the text is to appear. Note, however, because the display module is configured to increment the cursor location after each character is written, the cursor location only needs to be set prior to writing the first character of a string.

```
;
putchar: bsr     IsBusy           ; is the module busy?
         bne     putchar          ; yes. must wait until it's not.
         bclr    PORTB,Rw         ; set R/w for write.
         bset    PORTB,RS         ; set RS = 1 for data write.
         ldaa    #$ff             ; make port a outputs.
         staa    DDRA
         stab    PORTA            ; put character on module's data bus.
         bset    PORTB,#EClk      ; clock it into the module.
         bclr    PORTB,#EClk
         clr     DDRA             ; make port a inputs.
         rts                      ; return.
;
```

Figure 6.19: `putchar` Subroutine

The final set of subroutines presented in Figure 6.20 provides some basic display utilities. The first subroutine, `SetCursPos`, is used to place the cursor at a specific character location on the display. To simplify the task of displaying text messages, this subroutine accepts a number from $00 through $1F in the B accumulator as a cursor position. Line one contains character positions $00 through $0F while line two contains character positions $10 through $1F.

```
;
Line1:          equ     $80
Line2:          equ     $c0
;
SetCursPos:     cmpb    #$0f            ; first row ($00 - $0f)?
                bls     FirstLine       ; yes. go send command.
                cmpb    #$1f            ; no. second row ($10 - $1f)?
                bhi     BadCursPos      ; no. bad position.
                addb    #$30            ; yes. module cursor addr. is $40 - $4f.
FirstLine:      addb    #$80            ; msb is cursor command.
                bsr     SendCmd         ; move the cursor.
BadCursPos:     rts                     ; return.
;
DispLineE:      pshx                    ; save pointer to the message.
                pshb                    ; save 'line number'.
                bsr     SendCmd         ; place cursor at start of line.
                ldx     #ClrLine        ; point to spaces string.
                bsr     OutStr          ; clear the line.
                pulb                    ; restore line number.
                pulx                    ; restore the message pointer.
DispLine:       bsr     SendCmd         ; place cursor at start of line.
                bsr     OutStr          ; display the message.
                rts
;
ClrLine:        db      "                ", 0
;
OutStr:         ldab    1,x+            ; get next character. Done?
                beq     MsgDone         ; yes. return.
                bsr     putchar         ; no. send it to the display.
                bra     OutStr          ; send next character.
MsgDone:        rts                     ; return.
;
```

Figure 6.20: Optrex DMC-16249 Display Utilities

The second subroutine actually has two entry points depending on the desired action. Both entry points accept a pointer to a null (zero) terminated string in the X index register and one of the constants, Line1 or Line2, in the B accumulator. The entry point at label DispLineE will display a text string on the first or second line of the display after erasing any existing text on the selected line. Because the display module does not contain a command for erasing a single display line, a text string of 16 space characters is sent to the display effectively erasing the line. The entry point at label DispLine displays a text string

Section 6.11: LCD Alpha–numeric Display Module

on the first or second line without first erasing the line. The second entry point is useful if only the beginning of a display line needs to be updated. This may be the case in an application where the time of day is displayed using the first few characters of a line and the remainder of the display remains constant most of the time.

The last subroutine in the listing, `OutStr`, is used by the `DispLineE` subroutine to send null terminated strings to the display module. On entry the X index register should point to a null terminated string. This general purpose subroutine can be used with the `SetCursPos` subroutine to place text messages at any location on either of the display's two lines.

Questions/Exercises

6.1   At a minimum, how many control registers are associated with a general purpose I/O port? What are the purposes of these registers?

6.2   What is the purpose of a pin assignment register? What effect does it have on the function of other registers that control the characteristics of general purpose I/O pins?

6.3   What type of I/O architecture does the M68HC12 family support? What are the advantages and disadvantages of this type of I/O architecture?

6.4   What value is normally read from unimplemented I/O register bits?

6.5   What value is written to a Data Direction Register (DDR) to configure a pin as an output?

6.6   What is the default value of the bits in a Data Direction Register? What is significant about this?

6.7   When pins are configured as outputs, what value is read from the associated I/O port data register?

6.8   Can the output data latch associated with an I/O pin be written when the pin is configured as an input? What implications does this have when I/O pins are used in a bidirectional manner?

6.9   To ensure safe operation of a system after the M68HC12 exits the reset state, what precautions should be taken with regards to I/O port initialization? What special precautions should be taken for pins that are configured as outputs?

6.10 What should be done with unused I/O pins?

Chapter 6: General Purpose Parallel I/O Ports

6.11   Describe the problem common to all switch devices connected to inputs of a microcontroller. What complications can this cause programs that must detect switch transitions?

6.12   What three conditions of a switch press must a program be able to distinguish among?

6.13   For the M68HC12 family, what is the most efficient method of connecting input switches to I/O port pins?

6.14   What are the limitations of the switch input routine presented in Figure 6.4?

6.15   The multiple switch input routine presented in Figure 6.9 has what limitation?

6.16   When is it more advantageous to utilize an X - Y switch matrix for key input rather than attaching switches to individual I/O pins?

6.17   Briefly describe the scanning process for an X - Y switch matrix.

6.18   Write a subroutine that translates the row and column number returned by the scanned key matrix to key numbers 0 through 15. Key numbering should begin with 0 in the upper left corner of the array and proceed left to right, top to bottom, ending with key number 15 in the lower right corner of the array.

6.19   Modify the scanned key matrix software to return a "key pressed" status every 250 mS if any key is held down for more than one second.

6.20   What value must be written to a port's data register to illuminate LEDs connected as shown in Figure 6.12.

6.21   Expand the subroutine in Figure 6.14 to translate the hexadecimal values $10 through $17 to the alphabetic characters 'P', 'H', 'L', 'r', 'J', 'U', 'y', 't' respectively.

6.22   Write a subroutine that calls the key translation subroutine written for question 6.18 and then displays the keycode on the 7-segment display shown in Figure 6.13.

6.23   Design the hardware and software for a four digit, 7-segment multiplexed display.

6.24   Rewrite the `putchar` subroutine in Figure 6.19 to automatically wrap text to line two when the cursor is at Display Data RAM address $10 and putchar is called. Hint: the `IsBusy` subroutine returns the module's Display Data RAM address in the lower seven bits of the A accumulator.

Section 6.11: LCD Alpha–numeric Display Module

6.25 Rewrite the `putchar` subroutine in Figure 6.19 to recognize the carriage return and line feed characters. Have the carriage return character place the cursor at the start of the current line. The line feed character should place the cursor on line two if it is currently on line one and should scroll the display up one line if the cursor is already on line two.

Chapter 7 ON-CHIP BYTE ERASABLE EEPROM

The M68HC11 was the first microcontroller family to include CMOS byte erasable EEPROM on-chip. It was also the first microcontroller to combine CMOS UV erasable EPROM and byte erasable EEPROM on the same chip. The M68HC12 family continues the tradition of firsts by being the first commercially available microcontroller family to combine Flash EEPROM and byte erasable EEPROM on the same device. The merit of byte erasable EEPROM has proven valuable in many applications for items such as unique product serial numbers, calibration and set point information, and even masked ROM program patching. Any information that must be retained when VDD power is removed can be retained in EEPROM memory indefinitely. The amount of EEPROM available on each M68HC12 family member varies from part to part. However, the EEPROM on current M68HC12 devices varies from as little as 768 bytes to 4096 bytes. As with the M68HC11 family, the on-chip EEPROM can not only be used for data, but can also be used to contain executable programs. Because the on-chip EEPROM block contains a high-voltage charge pump for programming and erase operations, no external high-voltage supplies are required. The EEPROM block described in this chapter is the 768 byte EEPROM module contained on the MC68HC912B32. While some details of EEPROM operation may vary slightly for other M68HC12 family members, the basic concepts and software presented here can be applied to other family members.

7.1 EEPROM Structure

The 768 byte block of on-chip EEPROM is arranged as 384 byte addressable words. Word reads of the array do not require that the data be aligned to an even byte

Section 7.2: EEPROM Charge Pump

boundary; however, misaligned word reads require two bus cycles to complete. Unlike read accesses, program and erase operations of 16-bit data are restricted to aligned words. Misaligned program and erase operations must be performed a byte at a time, therefore doubling the time required to update EEPROM data and increasing the complexity of the programming software. For consistent, optimum performance all 16-bit data should be kept aligned to even byte boundaries.

⚠ **M68HC12 Difference from the M68HC11**

All M68HC12 family members allow remapping of the on-chip EEPROM through the `INITEE` register as described in Chapter 4. The default base address varies depending on the size of the EEPROM array and the location and size of other on-chip resources. The default base address of the 768 byte array on the MC68HC912B32 is $0D00 and may be remapped to any 4K-byte boundary. The 768 byte block is arranged as 24 rows of 32 bytes each. Note that the arrangement is different from the M68HC11 where the on-chip EEPROM was arranged in 16-byte rows. This difference results from the fact that the EEPROM array is arranged as 16-bit words rather than a byte wide array. This arrangement allows erasure of individual bytes, 16-bit aligned words or a complete row of 32 bytes. In addition, the entire EEPROM array may be erased in a single operation requiring no more time that a byte or word erase.

7.2 EEPROM Charge Pump

The on-chip charge pump that generates the high-voltage necessary for program and erase operations utilizes extremely small on-chip capacitors to boost VDD to the required voltage levels. The efficiency of the charge pump and its ability to program or erase the array are affected by VDD and the frequency of the clock driving the charge pump. The charge pump is guaranteed to operate properly over the entire VDD supply range specified in each family member's electrical characteristics document. However, because the clock driving the charge pump is derived directly form the system E-clock, a minimum microcontroller operating frequency of 1 MHz is required to maintain the guaranteed minimum program and erase times while maintaining a data retention life of 10 years.

To allow program and erase operations of systems operating with an E-clock below 1 MHz, a simple on-chip RC oscillator may be selected to drive the charge pump. The RC oscillator is enabled by setting the `EERC` bit in the EEPROM Module Configuration Register (`EEMCR`) as shown in Figure 7.1. The nominal frequency of the RC oscillator is approximately 10 MHz; however, the frequency varies with processing, voltage, and temperature, and can be as low as 8.8 MHz.

Chapter 7: On-chip Byte Erasable EEPROM

Bit 7	6	5	4	3	2	1	Bit 0
1	1	1	1	1	EESWAI	PROTLCK	EERC

Figure 7.1: EEPROM Module Configuration Register (EEMCR)

In addition to the `EERC` bit, the `EEMCR` register contains two additional bits effecting the operation of the EEPROM module. The `EESWAI` bit provides the option to reduce total chip power consumption by disabling clocks to the module during wait mode. When the bit is set, which is its default value, clocks to the module are inhibited after the `WAI` instruction is executed. Clearing the `EESWAI` bit leaves the EEPROM block unaffected during wait mode. If the EEPROM module has been relocated to the top of the memory map so that the interrupt vectors are fetched from EEPROM when exiting the wait mode, this bit must be cleared. In this situation, failure to clear the `EESWAI` bit will cause the EEPROM array to be inaccessible when the microcontroller exits the wait mode resulting in an incorrect address to be fetched from the interrupt vector.

The `PROTLCK` bit is part of the EEPROM's block protect mechanism discussed in the next section. Its purpose is to prevent accidental changes to the registers controlling the block protect mechanism. The default value of zero allows changes to the registers controlling the block protect mechanism. Writing a one to the `PROTLCK` bit prevents any further changes to the block protect and bulk erase protect bits. Because the `PROTLCK` bit itself is protected by the write once mechanism in Normal modes, it should be written with the desired value even if its default value is correct for the intended application.

⚠ **M68HC12 Difference from the M68HC11**

7.3 BLOCK PROTECT MECHANISM

Some of the early M68HC11 family members provided minimal protection to prevent the accidental programming or erasure of EEPROM memory locations. A block protect mechanism was added to later M68HC11 family members and has been retained in the M68HC12 EEPROM module. This feature allows a great deal of flexibility in preventing both accidental or *intentional* erasure of blocks of EEPROM data. The block protect mechanism utilizes control bits in three separate registers to perform its function. The `PROTLCK` bit contained in the EEPROM Module Configuration Register adds a second level of protection against accidental program and erasure of the EEPROM by protecting the block protect and bulk erase protect control bits.

Section 7.3: Block Protect Mechanism

For the purposes of write and erase protection, the on-chip EEPROM is divided into various size blocks that may be individually protected. The number and size of the blocks vary among M68HC12 family members depending on the size of the EEPROM module. However, each block has an associated control bit contained in the EEPROM Block Protect register (EEPROT) preventing any byte within the block from being programmed or erased. The EEPROT register for the MC68HC912B32, shown in Figure 7.2, contains five block protect bits BPROT0 through BPROT4.

Bit 7	6	5	4	3	2	1	Bit 0
*	1	1	BPROT4	BPROT3	BPROT2	BPROT1	BPROT0

Figure 7.2: MC68HC912B32 EEPROM Block Protect register (EEPROT)

After reset, each of the block protect bits has a value of one, preventing the EEPROM from being programmed or erased. To perform either operation in a memory range controlled by the block protect bits, the bit must be cleared. Those familiar with the M68HC11 family parts may remember that its block protect register must be written in the first 64 E-clock cycles to remove the EEPROM protection. The M68HC12 family's EEPROT register may be read or written at any time as long as the PROTLCK bit in the EEMCR register and the EEPGM bit in the EEPROM Programming Control register (EEPROG) are both zero. This feature allows much greater flexibility for applications requiring the bulk erasure and reprogramming of individual sections of the EEPROM memory array. The range of EEPROM memory controlled by each block protect bit is shown in Figure 7.3. The lower case 'x' appearing as part of the protected address range represents the upper four bits of the module address as defined by the upper four bits of the INITEE register.

Block Protect Bit Name	Address Range Protected	Block Size
BPROT4	$xD00 - $xDFF	256
BPROT3	$xE00 - $xEFF	256
BPROT2	$xF00 - $xF7F	128
BPROT1	$xF80 - $xFBF	64
BPROT0	$xFC0 - $xFFF	64

Figure 7.3: MC68HC912B32 Block Protect Address Range

The implementation of bit seven of the EEPROM Block Protect register varies among M68HC12 family members. Currently, all M68HC12 devices, with one exception, implement this bit as read-only, returning a value of one. The MC68HC912B32 implements bit seven for use as the Shadow and Test Row Protection control bit (STPROT). This bit is utilized to control the programming and erase operation of special EEPROM memory locations that are not normally visible to the programmer. These special EEPROM memory cells are used to retain information about various EEPROM tests that have been run during factory testing of the device. Under normal operating conditions this bit should be written with its default value of one.

In addition to the Block Protect control bits, the EEPROM Programming Control register (EEPROG) contains a Bulk Erase Protection (BULKP) control bit that can be used to protect the EEPROM array from a bulk or row erase operation. Like the Block Protect control bits, BULKP may be read or written at any time as long as the PROTLCK bit in the EEMCR register and the EEPGM bit in the EEPROG are both zero. The default value of BULKP is one which prevents the EEPROM array from being bulk erased. To perform a bulk or row erase operation on the EEPROM array, both the BULKP bit and the BPROT bit associated with the address range for the erase operation must be cleared.

7.4 EEPROM Characteristics

Each EEPROM byte in its erased state contains a value of $FF. Programming a value into a byte or aligned word involves programming zeros into specific bit locations. Those bit locations containing ones remain in the erased state. Bits may only be programmed from ones to zeros. It is possible to modify a programmed location by selectively programming additional zeros into the byte or word. However, if a bit within a byte or word must be changed from a zero to a one, the entire contents of the location must be erased and then reprogrammed with the new value. For most applications it is recommended that a strict erase-before-write method be used when updating the value of an EEPROM location.

EEPROM programming and erasure involves the movement of an electrical charge through a thin oxide insulation layer on to or off of a floating gate. The charge movement through the oxide layer requires a relatively large electrical field, supplied by the on-chip charge pump, be applied for a significant amount of time. After many program and erase cycles, charge may become trapped in the thin oxide layer surrounding the floating gate. The trapped charge causes the program and erase times to lengthen until a bit cannot be programmed to a zero in the specified time. At this point, the EEPROM bit is worn out. In many cases these bits can still be programmed by increasing the program and erase times, but the wear-out mechanism tends to reduce the transistor's ability to retain a value of zero over a long period of time. Motorola currently guarantees a minimum of 10,000 erase and write cycles for each

Section 7.4: EEPROM Characteristics

byte of the EEPROM array over the entire temperature and voltage range of each device. In addition, a typical write/erase endurance of 30,000 cycles is specified if the average maximum temperature is below 85° C. While these numbers of write/erase cycles are adequate for most applications, the potential for EEPROM failure does have implications when designing an application's software.

In most applications, EEPROM locations are only written and erased several times over the life of a product. There are applications, such as an automobile odometer, where a variable must be updated hundreds of thousands of times. In these cases, it is usually best to find an alternate solution that does not require the EEPROM location to be updated each time the variable value is updated. In the case of the automobile odometer, it might be possible to maintain the actual odometer value in RAM and only update the value contained in EEPROM every 10 miles and/or each time the ignition is switched off. This scheme does present some possible accuracy problems if power is inadvertently removed from the odometer module before the EEPROM location is updated. However, the occurrence of such an event would likely be rare in the actual application.

For applications requiring a higher degree of accuracy or more frequent updates of count values stored in EEPROM, a method can be used to encode an eight count counter in a single byte of EEPROM. This method would successively program each one of the eight bits to a value of zero until the byte reached a value of $00. This method of bit position encoding would only be needed for the low order bits of a counter since the upper bits would change much less frequently. Using this method, an EEPROM location would only experience a write/erase cycle once every eight counts, thus effectively extending the useful life of an EEPROM location by a factor of eight.

Utilizing this technique requires a programming method known as 'selective-write'. In this method, a value is calculated containing zeros in bit positions that need to change from ones to zeros and contains ones in all other bit positions. This pattern is programmed into the EEPROM location with the result that the bit positions containing zeros become programmed to zeros. All bit positions in the calculated value containing ones are not programmed but retain their former value. EEPROM bit locations containing ones remain unprogrammed while bit locations containing zeros remain programmed. The objective of the 'selective-write' method is to avoid programming some bits more than others. Figure 7.4 shows a program fragment implementing an eight count counter utilizing a single byte of EEPROM memory. If a count of eight does not fit an application well, a 16-bit word can be used to implement a count up to sixteen.

Chapter 7: On-chip Byte Erasable EEPROM

```
        .
        .
        .
        ldab    0,x             ; get eeprom counter byte.
        pshb                    ; save current value.
        com     0,sp            ; put 1's in programmed locations (0).
        lslb                    ; add a zero to the byte value.
        beq     EraseCnt        ; if new value 0, erase byte counter.
        tfr     b,a             ; save value for compare after program.
        orab    1,sp+           ; val to prog is OR of new value & ~old val.
        bsr     ProgEEByte      ; go program the new ee byte value.
        cmpa    0,x             ; program properly?
        bne     Error           ; no. handle the problem.
        .
        .
        .
```

Figure 7.4: 'Selective-write' Programming Example

In this example, the X index register contains a pointer to the counter byte. The fragment begins by retrieving the current value of the counter and saving it on the stack. Next, the saved value is complimented, producing a value containing ones in the bit positions that have been programmed to zero in the EEPROM byte. The current value is modified using a logical shift left left.This results in a zero being placed in the next most significant bit of the count value. If the result of this shift is zero, a branch is taken to code that erases the encoded 8-bit counter and presumably increment the next stage of the counter.

The alert reader might notice that erasing the encoded count byte before programming it with a value of $00 will result in the most significant bit never being programmed to zero. This may seem to be an error; however, an 8-bit byte can actually represent nine unique values using this encoding method, as shown in Figure 7.5. In this particular example an eight count encoded counter is implemented using the values $FF through $80 to represent the counts zero through seven.

After the check for zero, a copy of the shifted value is placed in the A accumulator allowing a verify operation to be performed after the byte has been programmed. Finally, the original complimented value on the stack is logically OR'd with the shifted value. The result is a byte value containing a zero in the next bit position to be programmed. For example, if the value of the encoded count byte currently contains %11111000 a value of %11110111 is required to program the next bit in the count sequence. Complimenting the value %11111000 produces a result of %00000111. Shifting the current value left one bit produces a value of %11110000. Performing a bitwise OR of this result with the complimented value produces a result of %11110111.

Section 7.5: EEPROM Programming and Erasing Procedures

EEPROM Byte Value	Count Value
$FF	0
$FE	1
$FC	2
$F8	3
$F0	4
$E0	5
$C0	6
$80	7

Figure 7.5: Encoded EEPROM Byte Count Values

Encoding a count value in this manner means that the value contained in the EEPROM byte cannot be directly manipulated by software. Instead the encoded count value must be converted to a binary value that can be easily manipulated. A subroutine to perform the conversion is presented in Figure 7.6. The subroutine is entered with the value to convert in the B accumulator and returns the converted result in B. The conversion is performed by repeatedly shifting the encoded byte count to the right until a one is shifted into the carry. Each time a shift operation is performed, one is added to the conversion result.

```
;
CvtEncCnt:clr   1,-sp       ; allocate & init binary result.
CvtLoop:  lsrb              ; place ls bit in carry. found first 1?
          bcs   CvtDone     ; yes. go get result from stack & return.
          inc   0,sp        ; no. add 1 to intermediate result.
          bra   CvtLoop     ; back for next shift.
CvtDone:  pulb              ; retrieve result from stack.
          rts               ; return
;
```

Figure 7.6: Encoded Count Conversion Subroutine

7.5 EEPROM Programming and Erasing Procedures

The programming and erasure of the on-chip EEPROM array is accomplished through software manipulation of bits contained in the EEPROM Programming Control

Chapter 7: On-chip Byte Erasable EEPROM

register (EEPROG). The contents of the EEPROG register, shown in Figure 7.7, may be read or written at any time. However, special hardware logic enforces a specific sequence of writes to program or erase the EEPROM. Having to follow a prescribed sequence of writes helps prevent accidental alteration of the EEPROM contents.

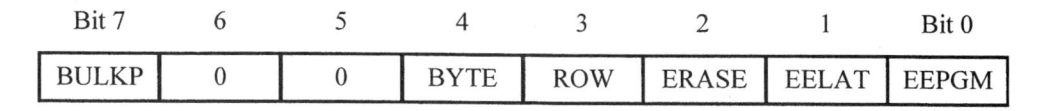

Bit 7	6	5	4	3	2	1	Bit 0
BULKP	0	0	BYTE	ROW	ERASE	EELAT	EEPGM

Figure 7.7: EEPROM Programming Control register (EEPROG)

⚠ M68HC12 Difference from the M68HC11

The programming and erase operations follow the six basic steps listed below:

1. Write the BYTE, ROW and ERASE bits to the desired value; write EELAT = 1.
2. Write a byte or aligned word to a valid EEPROM address.
3. Write EEPGM = 1.
4. Delay for the programming (t_{PROG}) or erase (t_{ERASE}) time.
5. Write EEPGM = 0.
6. Write EELAT = 0.

Executing any of the six steps out of order will cause the EEPROM memory location to remain unaltered. Unlike the M68HC11 family, the last two steps cannot be combined into a single operation. The EEPGM and EELAT bits must be cleared with two separate writes to the EEPROG register. When programming or erasing more than one byte or aligned word in the EEPROM array, it is only necessary to repeat steps two through five for each location programmed or erased. However, it should be noted that as long as the EELAT bit is set, the contents of the EEPROM array cannot be read by the CPU12. This restriction means that each program or erase operation cannot be verified until the operation at all locations are complete. This characteristic also implies additional considerations for software utilizing data stored in the EEPROM array. Care should be taken so that no references are made to the EEPROM array during program or erase operations. In particular, if interrupts remain enabled during the program or erase time period, interrupt service routines must not access EEPROM data.

While most applications utilize the on-chip EEPROM strictly for nonvolatile data storage, it is common for executable code or jump tables to be placed in the on-chip

Section 7.5: EEPROM Programming and Erasing Procedures

EEPROM memory. This might be especially true for applications utilizing the M68HC812A4 in single-chip mode, using the 4k bytes of on-chip EEPROM for both program and data storage. Because the EEPROM array cannot be read when the EELAT bit is set, the code used to program and erase the EEPROM data cannot be run from the EEPROM array. In such a case, it is necessary to copy the subroutine implementing the program and/or erase algorithm into RAM and jump to the subroutine in RAM during the program and/or erase operation.

Before presenting subroutines that can be used for programming and erasing EEPROM locations, the function of each of the bits in the EEPROG register will be discussed. The EELAT bit, which is used for both program and erase operations, is used to enable both the address and data latches associated with the EEPROM array. For erase operations, this bit can be written to a value of one at the same time as the BYTE, ROW and ERASE bits.

The EEPGM bit is used to begin the program or erase process by applying the charge-pump high voltage output to the EEPROM array. The EEPGM bit can only be set after the EELAT bit has been set. If an attempt is made to set the EEPGM and EELAT bits simultaneously, only the EELAT bit will be set; the EEPGM bit will remain clear. While the EEPGM bit is set, the BULKP, BYTE, ROW and ERASE bits cannot be changed. In addition, none of the block protect bits in the EEPROT register can be changed while EEPGM is set.

The ERASE control bit is used to configure the EEPROM array for either programming or erase operations. When the ERASE bit is zero, the array is configured for programming or read operations. When set the EEPROM is configured for erase operations.

The BYTE, ROW and BULKP bits are used in conjunction with the ERASE control bit to determine the type of erase operation to perform. Figure 7.8 presents the five meaningful combinations of these bits along with a concise description of the erase operation allowed. Notice that when the BYTE control bit is set, the ROW and BULKP bits are ignored. Also notice that if a row or bulk erase is attempted when the BULKP bit is set, the byte or aligned word location written will be erased while the remainder of the EEPROM array remains unchanged. The intent of the BULKP control bit is only to prevent an accidental bulk or row erasure from occurring while attempting a byte or aligned word erase operation.

Chapter 7: On-chip Byte Erasable EEPROM

BULKP	BYTE	ROW	Block Size
0	0	0	Bulk Erase Entire EEPROM Array
0	0	1	Row Erase 32 Bytes
X	1	X	Byte or Aligned Word Erase
1	0	0	Defaults to Byte or Aligned Word Erase
1	0	1	Defaults to Byte or Aligned Word Erase

Figure 7.8: Erase Operation Selection

Figures 7.9 and 7.10 present assembly listings for performing byte and word programming of EEPROM memory respectively. Before calling either subroutine, the X index register must be loaded with a valid EEPROM address. The data must be loaded into the B accumulator for the ProgEEByte subroutine or into the D accumulator for the ProgEEWord. As required by the EEPROM array, both subroutines attempt to erase the memory location before it is programmed. If the erase operation fails, a not equal (Z condition code register bit = 0) condition is returned.

```
ProgEEByte:  bsr    ErasEEByte         ; go erase the byte first.
             bne    PByteRtn           ; if erase wasn't successful, return.
             bset   EEPROG,#EELAT      ; arm the address & data latches.
             stab   0,x                ; place the data in the latches.
             bset   EEPROG,#EEPGM      ; apply programming voltage to byte.
             jsr    Dly10mS            ; delay 10 mS.
             bclr   EEPROG,#EEPGM      ; remove programming voltage.
             bclr   EEPROG,#EELAT      ; disarm the address and data latches.
             cmpb   0,x                ; byte program properly?
PByteRtn:    rts                       ; return == ok, != bad.
;
```

Figure 7.9: EEPROM Byte Program Subroutine

```
ProgEEWord:  bsr    ErasEEWord         ; go erase the word first.
             bne    PWordRtn           ; if erase wasn't successful, return.
             bset   EEPROG,#EELAT      ; arm the address & data latches.
             std    0,x                ; place the data in the latches.
             bset   EEPROG,#EEPGM      ; apply programming voltage to byte.
             jsr    Dly10mS            ; delay 10 mS.
             bclr   EEPROG,#EEPGM      ; remove programming voltage.
             bclr   EEPROG,#EELAT      ; disarm the address and data latches.
             cpd    0,x                ; word program properly?
PWordRtn:    rts                       ; return == ok, != bad.
;
```

Figure 7.10: EEPROM Word Program Subroutine

Section 7.5: EEPROM Programming and Erasing Procedures

After setting the `EELAT` bit, writing data to the the address and data latches and applying the programming voltage by setting the `EEPGM` bit, a subroutine is called producing a 10 mS delay before it returns. After returning from the delay subroutine, the `EEPGM` and `EELAT` bits are cleared to allow verification of the programmed data. If the `EEPROM` contents do not match the data in the B or D accumulator, a not equal condition is returned. Both subroutines are nearly identical, only differing in the size of data used in the erase, program, and compare operations. Note that the address passed to the `ProgEEWord` subroutine *must* be an aligned word (even byte) address. If the X index register contains an odd address, only the upper byte of the data will be programmed into EEPROM at the odd address. The next higher address will remain unaffected.

Figures 7.11 and 7.12 contain the byte and word erase subroutines respectively. Like both of the programming routines, the X index register must be loaded with a valid EEPROM address prior to calling either subroutine, however, no data is required for the erase operation. Both subroutines preserve the contents of all CPU12 registers.

```
EraseEEByte: pshb                          ; preserve b.
             ldab  0,x                     ; get contents of byte to erase.
             incb                          ; if EEByte + 1 == 0
             beq   ByteErased              ; if already erased just return.
             bset  EEPROG,#EELAT+ERASE+BYTE ; set latches & byte/word erase.
             stab  0,x                     ; place the address in the latches.
             bset  EEPROG,#EEPGM           ; apply erase voltage to byte.
             jsr   Dly10mS                 ; delay 10 mS.
             bclr  EEPROG,#EEPGM           ; remove programming voltage.
             bclr  EEPROG,#EELAT+ERASE+BYTE ; clr latches & byte/word erase.
             ldab  0,x                     ; get byte data (should be $ff)
             incb                          ; byte erased properly?
ByteErased:  pulb                          ; restore b.
             rts                           ; return == ok, != bad.
;
```

Figure 7.11: EEPROM Byte Erase Subroutine

Chapter 7: On-chip Byte Erasable EEPROM

```
ErasEEWord: pshd                            ; preserve d.
            ldd   0,x                       ; get contents of word to erase.
            addd  #1                        ; if EEWord + 1 == 0
            beq   WordErased                ; already erased, just return
            bset  EEPROG,#EELAT+ERASE+BYTE  ; set latches & byte/word erase.
            std   0,x                       ; place the address in the latches.
            bset  EEPROG,#EEPGM             ; apply erase voltage to byte.
            jsr   Dly10mS                   ; delay 10 mS.
            bclr  EEPROG,#EEPGM             ; remove programming voltage.
            bclr  EEPROG,#EELAT+ERASE+BYTE  ; set latches & byte/word erase.
            ldd   0,x                       ; get word data (should be $ffff)
            cpd   #$ffff                    ; word erased properly?
WordErased: puld                            ; restore d.
            rts                             ; return == ok, != bad.
;
```

Figure 7.12: EEPROM Word Erase Subroutine

To help extend the life of EEPROM memory locations and to reduce total programming time, both erase subroutines check the state of the location to be erased. If the location is already erased, each subroutine returns without performing the erase operation. With the exception of the erased state check and the setting and clearing of the ERASE control bit in the EEPROG register, these two subroutines are very similar to the ProgEEByte and ProgEEWord subroutines. It might seem that the two instruction sequence used at the beginning of the subroutines to check for an erased EEPROM location could have been more efficiently performed using the IBEQ instruction. However, because the IBEQ instruction does not modify the condition code register, the value returned in the condition code register would be the result of the accumulator load.

When having to erase large blocks of EEPROM memory it is much more efficient to utilize the row erase feature of the EEPROM array instead of erasing a byte or aligned word at a time. A row of EEPROM memory consists of 32 sequential bytes that begins on a 32 byte boundary. The row erase procedure follows the same basic steps as an aligned word erase except the ROW bit is set and the BYTE bit remains clear. As with the byte and word erase procedures, the data written to the EEPROM array after the address and data latches are enabled is unimportant. However, for the row erase function to work properly an aligned word write must be performed to any one of the 16 words in the row. If a byte or misaligned word write is performed, only a single byte will be erased. The subroutine presented in Figure 7.13 avoids this possible problem by masking off the lower five bits of the address passed in the X index register so that the address points to the first word in the row. After the row erase operation is performed, the 32 byte row is checked for an erased state. If any locations are not erased, the subroutine returns with the Z condition code register bit cleared, otherwise, the subroutine returns with the Z bit set. For the row erase operation to

Section 7.5: EEPROM Programming and Erasing Procedures

complete properly, the `BULKP` bit in the `EEPROG` register must be cleared prior to calling the `ErasEERow` subroutine. Attempting to perform a row erase with the `BULKP` bit set will cause the first word of the 32 byte block to be erased. The remainder of the block will remain unchanged.

```
ErasEERow: pshx                            ; save pointer to byte in row.
           exg  d,x                        ; mask pointer to point to 1st byte
           andb #$e0                       ; in the row.
           exg  d,x                        ; restore x.
           bset EEPROG,#EELAT+ERASE+ROW    ; set to row erase (32 bytes).
           std  0,x                        ; set addr latches (data dont care)
           bset EEPROG,#EEPGM              ; apply erase voltage to byte.
           jsr  Dly10mS                    ; delay 10 mS.
           bclr EEPROG,#EEPGM              ; remove programming voltage.
           bclr EEPROG,#EELAT+ERASE+ROW    ; reset addr, data latches & erase.
           movb #16,1,-sp                  ; put word count on stack.
EraseChk:  ldd  2,x+                       ; get word data, advance pointer.
           cpd  #$ffff                     ; word erased properly?
           bne  BadRtn                     ; no. return w/ != condition.
           dec  0,sp                       ; yes. dec word count. Done?
           bne  EraseChk                   ; no. check next word in the row.
BadRtn:    leas 1,sp                       ; yes. remove word count.
           pulx                            ; restore ptr.
           rts                             ; return == ok, != bad.
;
```

Figure 7.13: Row Erase Subroutine

Another method that may be used to selectively erase portions of the EEPROM array involves the use of the bulk erase operation in conjunction with the block protect bits. If most or all of the EEPROM array must be erased, this method is very efficient since the bulk erase operation requires no more time than a row, aligned word, or byte erase operation. To protect individual blocks of the EEPROM from being erased, one or more of the block protect bits in the `EEPROT` register must be set before the bulk erase operation. If it is desired to erase the entire array, all of the block protect bits must be cleared and the `BULKP` bit in the `EEPROG` register must be cleared.

A bulk erase subroutine appears in Figure 7.14. Before calling the subroutine, the X index register must be loaded with the address of the first byte in the EEPROM block to be erased. While any address in the EEPROM array may be written when performing the bulk erase operation, passing the address of the first byte in the block allows an erase verify to be performed after the bulk erase operation. In addition, the D accumulator must be loaded with the size of the block so the erase verification can be performed. If any locations in the specified block are not erased, the subroutine returns with the Z condition code register bit cleared; otherwise, the subroutine returns with the Z bit set.

Chapter 7: On-chip Byte Erasable EEPROM

```
EEBulk:     bset    EEPROG,#EELAT+ERASE     ; set latches set for bulk erase.
            stab    0,x                     ; place the address in the latches.
            bset    EEPROG,#EEPGM           ; apply erase voltage to array.
            jsr     Dly10mS                 ; delay 10 mS.
            bclr    EEPROG,#EEPGM           ; remove programming voltage.
            bclr    EEPROG,#EELAT+ERASE     ; clr latches & erase bit.
            lsrd                            ; we'll check a word at a time.
BulkChk:    ldy     2,x+                    ; get word data, advance pointer.
            iny                             ; word erased properly?
            bne     BadBulk                 ; no. return w/ != condition.
            subd    #1                      ; yes. dec word count. Done?
            bne     BulkChk                 ; no. check next word in the row.
BadBulk:    rts                             ; return == ok, != bad.
;
```

Figure 7.14: EEPROM Bulk Erase Subroutine

All of the EEPROM programming and erase subroutines presented call the `Dly10mS` subroutine to delay for a 10 mS period while the programming voltage is applied to the EEPROM array. This subroutine, presented in Figure 7.15, utilizes a simple software loop to delay for the 10 mS programming and erase period. The delay time is based on the two instruction 'do nothing' loop defined by the DEX and BNE instructions requiring four CPU clock cycles for each loop iteration. The 10 mS delay does not take into account the small amount of time required by other instructions in the subroutine or the time required to call the subroutine. Though, for most E-clock frequencies this additional time is negligible.

```
;
Dly10mS:    pshx                        ; save register we'll use for delay count.
            ldx     #SysClock/400       ; delay count, 4 clks/loop, 8 MHz SysClock.
DlyLoop:    dex                         ; dec delay count.
            bne     DlyLoop             ; loop till done.
            pulx                        ; retrieve result from stack.
            rts                         ; return
;
```

Figure 7.15: 10 mS Delay Subroutine

Utilizing 100% of the CPU12's time during programming and erase delays may not be acceptable for many systems. Because it is possible to perform other tasks during the 10 mS program or erase operation, it is feasible to begin the EEPROM operation and then return to the main program loop until the 10 mS has expired. Unfortunately, because the entire EEPROM array is inaccessible during program and erase operations, a danger exists that another program routine or even an interrupt service routine may attempt to read an EEPROM location resulting in invalid data being returned. Utilizing

Section 7.5: EEPROM Programming and Erasing Procedures

this technique would require that special software interlocks be designed into all parts of the system software performing read accesses of the EEPROM array.

For highly interrupt driven systems it is quite possible for an interrupt to occur during a program or erase operation. If a single interrupt service routine requires a lengthy execution period or if multiple interrupt service routines must be executed sequentially, it is possible that a programming or erase operation could extend beyond the specified maximum time of 10 mS. A small extension of the time the program or erase voltage is applied to the EEPROM array will not damage the EEPROM or compromise the operation. However, extended application of the programming and erase voltage may result in an accelerated wear-out of the affected EEPROM locations. In addition, the application of program and erase voltages to the EEPROM array for extended periods can result in the possibility of high-voltage breakdown of the array's row and column devices.

Because EEPROM memory modification does take a relatively long period of time and because its contents cannot be read during the process, careful consideration must be given to the points during program execution at which EEPROM modification is permitted. Even if a system's software is carefully designed to prevent accesses or interrupts during the modification process, the possibility still exists that a power failure or system reset may occur during the programming or erase process. This can result in an EEPROM location containing incorrect or unreliable data because the modification procedure was interrupted. One way of protecting against EEPROM data loss due to a power failure might be to generate an XIRQ interrupt at the initial stage of power loss allowing the programming operation to finish before a complete loss of system power occurs.

Recovering from an unintended system reset during the program or erase process is also possible. One method might involve saving information on the state of the program and/or erase operation in on-chip RAM at various states of the modification process. When a reset occurs, the status information could be checked by the initialization software and any operation that was in process could be redone. At a minimum, the required status information would need to include the EEPROM address and data, the size of the data (byte or word), and some indication of the operation that was interrupted. In addition, to protect against situations where repeated resets from an internal or external source might continuously interrupt the program or erase operation to the same memory location, a counter should be maintained as part of the status information. Each time an attempt is made to repeat the program or erase operation, the counter should be incremented. When the counter reaches some maximum value, additional modification operations should not be attempted. Using this final protection mechanism can prevent an EEPROM location from being 'worn out' if a system failure causes repeated resets.

Chapter 7: On-chip Byte Erasable EEPROM

Questions/Exercises

7.1 What restrictions, if any, are imposed for read and write operations involving the on-chip EEPROM?

7.2 What is the difference in the arrangement of the M68HC11 and M68HC12 EEPROM arrays?

7.3 What is the function of the on-chip charge pump?

7.4 What must be done for proper EEPROM programming and erase operation if the M68HC12 is operated with an E-clock below 1 MHz?

7.5 What registers are connected with the block protect mechanism of the M68HC12?

7.6 What is the function of the PROTLCK bit in the EEPROM Module Configuration Register?

7.7 What is the default state of the block protect bits in the EEPROT register?

7.8 After reset, how many times may the block protect bits be written?

7.9 What is the erased state of an EEPROM byte?

7.10 What effects of the erase/program cycle tend to wear out an EEPROM bit?

7.11 List the six basic steps required to program or erase an EEPROM location. Are all six steps required for each location?

7.12 What mus be done before an EEPROM location can be programmed?

7.13 What occurs if a bulk or row erase operation is attempted when the BULKP bit is set?

7.14 What is the main difference in byte and word erase and programming operations?

7.15 What operation can be performed by the EEPROM erase code to help extend the life of the EEPROM locations?

7.16 What data must be written to an EEPROM address for an erase operation?

Section 7.5: EEPROM Programming and Erasing Procedures

7.17 Which EEPROM address must be written to for a row erase operation? What precaution must be used when performing the write?

7.18 Does the bulk erase operation affect the entire EEPROM array?

7.19 Rewrite the ProgEEWord subroutine so that it will properly program either an aligned or misaligned word value.

Chapter 8 ON-CHIP FLASH EEPROM

The on-chip Flash EEPROM memory residing on many of the M68HC12 family members, serves primarily as reprogrammable nonvolatile program and constant data storage. While the Flash EEPROM is both byte and aligned word programmable like the EEPROM described in Chapter 7, it can only be bulk erased. Including Flash EEPROM, rather than EPROM or ROM, on a microcontroller has significant advantages for both the manufacturer and the end customer.

Placing system firmware in Flash EEPROM memory provides distinct benefits for the manufacturer. Because the on-chip Flash memory can be programmed at any time during the manufacturing process, firmware development can be extended late into the product development cycle by eliminating the lead times associated with masked ROM. In addition, when a manufacturer has several products based on the same microcontroller, Flash memory can eliminate inventory problems associated with ROM based microcontrollers. Finally, if a severe bug is found in the product's firmware during the manufacturing process, the in-circuit reprogramability of Flash EEPROM memory prevents the manufacturer from having to scrap any of the work-in-process.

Because the M68HC12's Flash memory has the capability to be electrically erased and reprogrammed in-circuit, a customer's products can be updated or enhanced with new features and capabilities without having to replace any components or return their product to the factory.

8.1 FLASH MODULE CONFIGURATION

The amount of Flash memory varies among M68HC12 family members to accommodate various applications. However, the maximum size of a single Flash module is 32,768 bytes. M68HC12 family members with greater than 32K bytes of Flash contain more than one module of Flash memory. For instance the MC68HC912D60 contains 61,440 bytes of Flash implemented as one 32,768 byte module, located from $8000 through $FFFF and one 28,672 byte module located from $1000 through $7FFF. The MC68HC912DA128 contains 128K bytes of on-chip Flash implemented as four 32K byte modules. Much of the 128K bytes is accessed using the expanded memory capabilities of the CPU12.

All Flash memory blocks are arranged in a 16-bit wide configuration allowing byte, aligned, and misaligned word access. Byte and aligned word accesses require only a single bus cycle while misaligned word accesses require two bus cycles. Fortunately, because the CPU12 always fills its prefetch queue by performing aligned word fetches, no access penalty is paid for instructions that are not aligned on even byte boundaries. On the other hand, each access to misaligned constant data stored in Flash will suffer the additional bus cycle penalty. For applications depending heavily on data tables containing a mixture of byte and word data, care should be taken to ensure that word data remains aligned on an even byte address when constructing the tables.

Each Flash memory module has independent hardware interlocks protecting the memory's contents from accidental erasure or corruption. In addition, each Flash module has an erase protected boot block residing in the upper portion of the memory array. This erase protected area generally contains customer developed code used to erase and reprogram the remainder of the microcontroller's on-chip Flash. In most cases, the boot block area will also contain communications routines that may utilize the Serial Communications Interface (SCI), Byte Data Link Controller (BDLC), or a Controller Area Network (CAN) communications interface to load the required data into the device. As discussed later in the chapter, there are several special considerations for this type of software that present some software design challenges.

The size of the boot block varies among family members. The 32K Flash module on the MC68HC912B32 has a 2K boot block that resides in the upper 2K of the block while the MC68HC912D60 contains an 8K boot block that resides in the upper 8K of *each* of its Flash memory modules. In most applications, the 8K boot block in the 28K Flash module would be erased and reprogrammed with the remainder of the module.

8.2 FLASH MODULE CONTROL REGISTERS

Each Flash module has an associated four byte register block controlling the operation of the module. Two of the four control registers, shown in Figure 8.1, are associated with the protection of the boot block. The LOCK bit in the Flash EEPROM Lock Control register

Chapter 8: On-chip Flash EEPROM

(FEELCK) register is a write once protected register used to write protect the BOOTP bit in the Flash EEPROM Module Configuration Register (FEEMCR). This double level of protection may seem unnecessary; however, it provides programming and erase software some extra flexibility in controlling the erasability of the boot block. The default state of the LOCK bit is zero allowing the BOOTP bit to be changed as often as required by an application. Writing a one to the LOCK bit causes the BOOTP bit to become read-only and remain in the last written state until the microcontroller is reset. The BOOTP bit has a value of one out of reset, thus protecting the boot block from either intentional or accidental erasure. If a module's boot block contains boot loader software used to reprogram the remainder of the Flash module, this bit should remain set. When a system's application software is running under normal operating conditions, the LOCK bit should simply be written to a one after reset to prevent any modification of the BOOTP bit.

Bit 7	6	5	4	3	2	1	Bit 0	
0	0	0	0	0	0	0	LOCK	FEELCK

Bit 7	6	5	4	3	2	1	Bit 0	
0	0	0	0	0	0	0	BOOTP	FEEMCR

Figure 8.1: FEELCK and FEEMCR Control Registers

With one exception, the control and status bits bits contained in the Flash EEPROM Control Register (FEECTL), shown in Figure 8.2, are associated with the erasure and programming of the Flash module. The exception is the FEESWAI bit which controls the application of the module or E-clock to the Flash module during the CPU12 wait mode. Setting FEESWAI can result in lower power consumption when the the microcontroller enters wait mode. However, because the FEESWAI effectively turns the Flash array off during wait mode, it cannot be asserted if the reset or interrupt vectors reside in the Flash array. Doing so would cause the CPU12 to read the levels present on the floating data bus when performing the vector fetch rather than the proper interrupt vector contents.

Bit 7	6	5	4	3	2	1	Bit 0
0	0	0	FEESWAI	SVFP	ERAS	LAT	ENPE

Figure 8.2: Flash EEPROM Control Register (FEECTL)

The SVFP is the only status bit in the register. It reflects the state of the voltage applied to the VFP pin of the microcontroller. When SVFP is set, it indicates that the voltage on the

Section 8.2: Flash Module Control Registers

VFP pin is above approximately 10.5 volts. While this is outside the specified range for proper programming of the Flash, it can be checked by the programming software as a basic diagnostic indicator before programming or erasure begins or if the operation fails.

The remaining three bits in the `FEECTL` register are used to control the programming operation of the Flash. The programming and erasure of the on-chip Flash array is accomplished through software manipulation of these three bits. The `FEECTL` register may be read or written at any time; however, special hardware logic enforces a specific sequence of writes to the `ERAS`, `LAT`, and `ENPE` bits to program or erase the Flash. Having to follow a prescribed sequence of writes helps prevent accidental alteration of the Flash contents.

The `ERAS`, `LAT`, and `ENPE` bits have functions very similar to the `ERASE`, `EELAT` and `EEPGM` bits that are used to control the programming of the byte erasable EEPROM. The `ERAS` bit is used to select either the programming or the bulk erase mode. The default state of the `ERAS` bit is zero configuring the Flash for programming operation. This bit can be read or written at any time but cannot be changed during an erase operation.

The `LAT` bit controls the transparent latches used during program and erase operations. When programming a byte or aligned word, the latches hold the address and data of the location being programmed. When an erase operation is performed, writing to any address in the Flash array simply serves to trigger the hardware sequencing logic allowing the erase voltage to be applied to the array. While the data written to the array is unimportant for an erase operation, an aligned word write must be performed. As part of the hardware protection mechanism, the high voltage detection circuit controlling the `SVFP` bit will prevent the `LAT` bit from being set if the programming voltage is not applied to the VFP pin.

Finally, once the `LAT` bit has been set and a write operation is performed, the `ENPE` control bit is used to apply VFP to the Flash array. If an attempt is made to set the `ENPE` bit before the `LAT` bit is set and before the latches have been written, the value of `ENPE` will remain zero and the Flash array will remain unchanged. When the `ENPE` is set the state of the `LAT`, `ERAS` and `BOOTP` bits may not be changed.

Even though the `ERAS`, `LAT`, and `ENPE` bits perform functions similar to the associated programming and erase control bits for the byte erasable EEPROM, there are some important differences in the accessibility of the Flash and byte erasable EEPROM memory arrays during program and erase operations. Any time the byte erasable EEPROM's `EELAT` and/or `EEPGM` bits are set, the contents of the array cannot be read. However, the Flash array is only inaccessible when the `ENEP` bit is set. As summarized in Figure 8.3, this difference allows the Flash module to be read whenever the `ERAS` and/or `LAT` bits are set. Notice the difference in the Flash accessibility for programming and erase operations. During a programming operation, when the `ERAS` bit is clear, only the location being programmed may be read. During an erase operation, all locations in the Flash module may be read. This feature can help to simplify the implementation of the program and erase algorithms.

ENPE	LAT	ERAS	Result of Read Access
0	0	—	Normal Read of Location Accessed
0	1	0	Read of Location Being Programmed
0	1	1	Normal Read of Location Accessed
1	—	—	Read Access Ignored

Figure 8.3: Flash Module Read Access During Program and Erase Operations

Because the Flash module cannot be read during a program or erase operation when the ENEP bit is set, the programming software that applies VFP to the array must not reside in the Flash array itself. Instead, as discussed in the Flash serial boot loader application later in the chapter, this portion of the programming software must reside in other memory that is accessible to the microcontroller during this time period. The memory may be other on chip memory or externally connected memory. Most often, however, this portion of the Flash programming algorithm is copied from the Flash into the on-chip RAM before the programming operation begins. For M68HC12 family members such as the MC68HC912D60 that contain more than one Flash module, it is possible to program or erase one module while executing the program or erase software from the other module.

The location of the control registers within the I/O block vary among family members; however, the four registers are always in the same order within the block. Because the MC68HC912B32 contains a single block of Flash, it has a single set of control registers located at $x0F4. Due to the fact that the MC68HC912D60 contains two blocks of Flash, it has a two sets of control registers located at $x0F4 and $x0F8. It would seem to follow reason that the MC68HC912DA/DG128 having four blocks of Flash would have four sets of control registers. This is, in fact, the case. However, all four sets of control registers appear at the same four memory addresses, $x0F4 through $x0F7. Each set of control registers is accessed by manipulation of the value in the PPAGE register. Additional information on the MC68HC912DA/DG128's Flash paging mechanism can be found in the MC68HC912DA/DG128 technical summary.

8.3 Programming and Erase Operations

Like the M68HC12's byte erasable EEPROM, the erased state of each bit in the Flash EEPROM is a logic one. Bits are changed from a logic one to a logic zero through a specific sequence of programming operations. Individual bits may only be changed from a logic zero to a logic one through a complete erasure of the Flash array. It is possible to reprogram a location in the Flash array without erasing the entire array if the new value does not involve changing the value of any bits from a zero to a one. Currently, Motorola specifies the program/erase life to be a maximum of 100 cycles. For embedded system developers used to

Section 8.4: Erasure of the Flash EEPROM Array

working with external Flash memory devices this may seem to be an extremely low number of program/erase cycles. However, this number guarantees a 10 year data retention at ambient temperatures of 125•C, which is typical of an under-the-hood automotive application. At lower temperatures, especially at room temperature during development, the number of program/erase cycles is in the thousands.

The Flash module requires an externally applied program/erase voltage (VFP) to program or erase the array. The programming/erase voltage is applied statically to the VFP pin, however, the VFP pin must always be kept greater than or equal to VDD - 0.5 volts to prevent damage to the Flash array. To prevent the accidental erasure or programming of the Flash array, VFP should only be applied during the erase or programming procedure.

As mentioned previously, programming is restricted to a single byte or aligned word. Instead of using a control bit in one of the Flash array's control registers, the size of the programming operation is determined by internal signals generated when data is written to the programming latches. Writing only to an odd or even byte will perform a byte programming operation. Writing to an aligned word selects a word programming operation. If a misaligned word write is performed after the LAT bit is set, only the odd byte of the word will be programmed.

8.4 ERASURE OF THE FLASH EEPROM ARRAY

To ensure that the erasure of the Flash EEPROM is reliable and to provide the maximum possible life expectancy for the Flash, an intelligent erase algorithm is used providing successive erase pulses to the array until all locations are erased. Once all locations in the Flash array are erased, or the maximum number of erase pulses are applied, the same number of erase pulses required to erase the array are applied again. This procedure provides a 100% erase margin to the Flash array ensuring that any bits that were programed to zeros remain in the erased state. Failure to apply the erase margin pulses could result in data retention problems. After the margin pulses are applied, the Flash array should again be checked to ensure that it was properly erased. The simplified flowchart in Figure 8.4 depicts these basic steps.

Chapter 8: On-chip Flash EEPROM

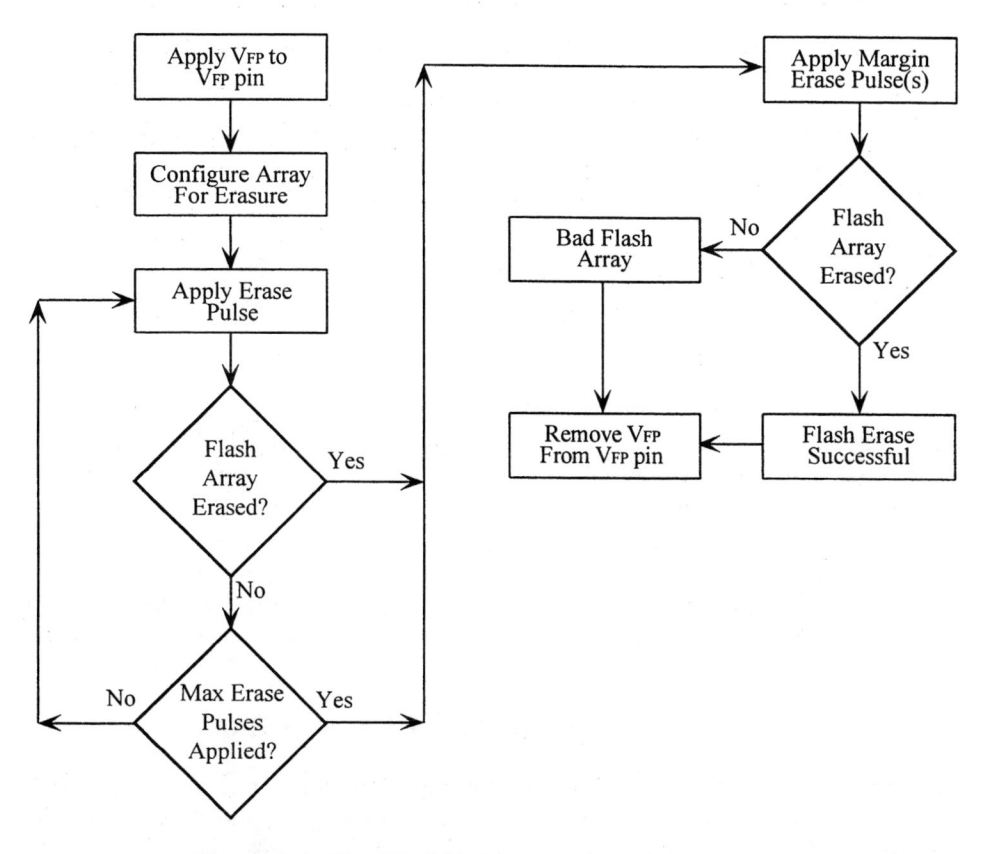

Figure 8.4: Simplified Flash Erase Algorithm Flowchart

The following sequence of steps presents, in detail, the recommended procedure for erasing the Flash EEPROM. Note that the erase voltage must be at the proper level prior to the first execution of step number 4.

1. Turn on VFP - apply the erase voltage to the VFP pin.

2. Set the LAT and ERAS bit to configure the Flash array for erasure.

3. Perform an aligned word write to any valid address in the Flash array.

4. Set the ENEP bit, applying the erase voltage to the array.

5. Delay for t_{EPULSE}, which is currently specified at 10 mS.

6. Remove the erase voltage from the array by clearing ENEP.

7. Delay for a period of t_{VERASE} while the erase voltage is being removed from the array. This time period is currently specified to be a minimum of 1 mS.

Section 8.5: Programming of the Flash EEPROM Array

8. Read the array checking to ensure that all locations are erased.
   - If any of the locations remain unerased, repeat steps 4 through 8, until the array is completely erased or n_{EP} (currently 5) erase pulses have been applied.
   - When all locations are erased, repeat steps 4 through 7 the same number of times that was required for erasure of the array.
9. Check the array again to ensure that all locations are erased.
10. Clear the LAT and ERAS bits.
11. Remove the erase voltage from the VFP pin.

Even though the maximum number of erase pulses is specified at five, the Flash array will typically be erased with the application of one or two pulses, plus the margin pulses. Because the erase process involves moving electrical charge through an oxide insulator, a higher potential VFP, within the limits of the device specification, may result in faster erase times. The currently specified program and erase voltage (VFP) is 12 volts ±5%. While the erase timing and VFP specifications are not likely to change, the most current data sheets or technical summaries should be consulted to ensure that the M68HC12 device is operated within the proper design limits.

8.5 PROGRAMMING OF THE FLASH EEPROM ARRAY

Programming of the Flash array follows a procedure very similar to the erase procedure. Each programmed location has successive programming pulses applied until the data read from the location is the same as the data written to the latches. Programming margin pulses are applied and the data is once again verified. The simplified flowchart in Figure 8.5 illustrate these basic steps.

Chapter 8: On-chip Flash EEPROM

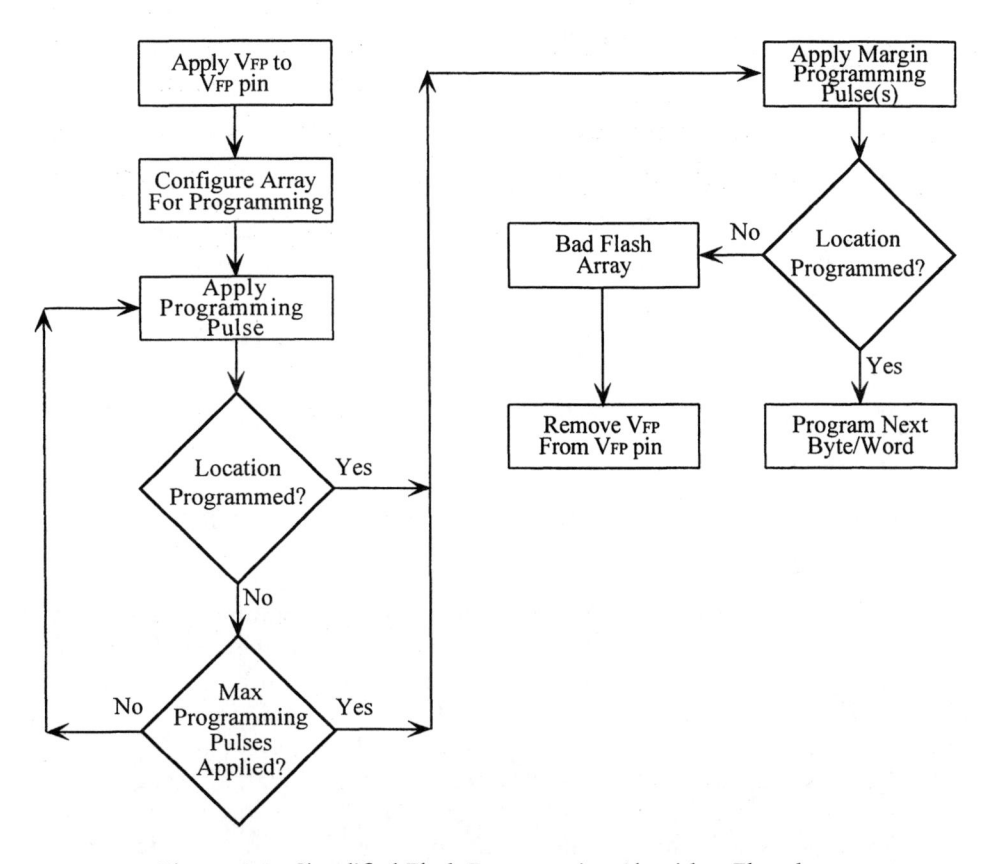

Figure 8.5: Simplified Flash Programming Algorithm Flowchart

The following sequence of steps presents, in detail, the recommended procedure for programming the Flash EEPROM. As with the erase procedure, the programming voltage must be at the proper level prior to the first execution of step number 4.

1. Turn on VFP - apply the erase voltage to the VFP pin.
2. Set the LAT bit to configure the Flash array for programming.
3. Perform a byte or aligned word write to a valid address in the Flash array, latching both the address and the data.
4. Set the ENEP bit, applying the erase voltage to the array.
5. Delay for t_{PPULSE}, which is currently specified to be between 20 µS and 25 µS.
6. Remove the programming voltage from the array by clearing ENEP.

Section 8.6: A Flash Serial Boot loader Example

7. Delay for a period of t_{VPROG} while the programming voltage is being removed from the array. This time period is currently specified to be a minimum of 10 µS.

8. Read the addressed location to ensure that it has been programmed.
   - If any of the location remains unprogrammed, repeat steps 4 through 8, until the location is programmed or n_{PP} (currently 50) programming pulses have been applied.
   - When the addressed location is programmed, repeat steps 4 through 7 the same number of times that was required program the addressed location.

9. Check the location again to ensure that it contains the proper data.
10. Clear the LAT bit.
11. Repeat steps 2 through 10 for each byte or word programming operation.
12. Remove VFP.

As with the erase process, the required number of programming pulses to properly program a byte or aligned word should rarely, if ever, approach the specified maximum of 50. Typically, a Flash location should retain the desired data with the application of one or two programming pulses. The total time required for each programming pulse is t_{PPULSE} plus t_{VPROG}. If the minimum times are used for t_{PPULSE} and t_{VPROG} and two pulses are required for initial programming, plus an additional two pulses for the 100% margin, programming each location would require a minimum of 120 µS not including any software overhead. If the M68HC12 operates at an E-clock of 8.0 MHz, the amount of time required for software overhead would be minimal compared to the programming pulse times. If the data were immediately available to the programming software and the Flash array were programmed a word at a time, the total time required to program a 32,768 byte array would be just under two seconds (120 µS x 16,384).

In many applications, the data to be programmed into the Flash memory will not be immediately available to the programming software. Instead it will be sent, a block at a time, through one of the on-chip communications interfaces. In this case, the speed at which the data can be obtained through the communications interface will generally be the limiting factor in the time required to program the Flash array.

8.6 A FLASH SERIAL BOOT LOADER EXAMPLE

Unlike the the M68HC11 family, the M68HC12 family of devices does not have a Bootstrap ROM containing firmware to allow initial programming of the Flash directly through the on-chip Serial Communications Interface (SCI) port. Initial programming of the on-chip Flash requires either special test and handling equipment to program the device before it is placed in the target system or a Background Debug Mode (BDM) programming tool capable of programming the Flash through the BDM interface after the device has been placed on the circuit board.

During the initial programming process, a boot loader can be placed in the erase protected boot block allowing subsequent programming of the remainder of the Flash through the on-chip SCI. In addition to implementing the Flash programming and erase algorithms described earlier, the boot loader firmware must implement a simple serial communications protocol that allows the on-chip SCI port to be used for obtaining the data to be programmed into the Flash. Even though this example is written for the MC68HC912B32, the techniques and even most of the code is usable for other members of the M68HC12 family.

Programming and erasing the on-chip Flash memory of the MC68HC912B32 presents some unique challenges. As mentioned earlier in the chapter, even though the the firmware implementing the programming and erase algorithms reside in the erase protected boot block, the code cannot be run from the boot block during the erase or programming procedure. Consequently, during the erase and programming process, the code must reside in other on-chip memory. In this example, the boot loader is small enough to allow the code comprising the program, erase and serial communications routines to fit into the on-chip RAM simultaneously. Therefore the entire boot loader is simply copied into RAM and executed from RAM during the entire program and erase process. Applications requiring a more sophisticated serial communications protocol using the BDLC or CAN peripherals may not be able to copy the entire boot loader into RAM. In this case, only the portion of the routines performing the actual program and erase operations need to reside in RAM as a subroutine. As each block of data is received or when the Flash is erased, the boot loader can jump to the subroutine, perform the necessary actions and return to the boot loader in Flash when finished. It is important to note that the `LAT` bit in the `FEECTL` register **MUST** be cleared before resuming execution from the Flash.

In addition, because the erase protected boot block resides in the top 2k of the memory map ($F800 - $FFFF), the reset and interrupt vectors cannot be changed without erasing the boot block. This necessitates that a secondary reset/interrupt vector table be located outside the 2k boot block.

8.7 BOOT LOADER REQUIREMENTS

The two most important requirements for a program such as the Flash serial boot loader are that it have minimal impact on the final product's software performance and add little or nothing to the product's hardware costs. The Flash serial boot loader described here meets both of these requirements.

Section 8.7: Boot loader Requirements

Because the MC68HC912B32 includes an on-chip SCI, no additional external hardware is required to communicate with a host computer. The possible exception might be the addition of an RS-232 level translator chip to the hardware design. In many systems, this may already be a part of the design because the SCI is often used as a diagnostic port. If an RS-232 level translator is not part of the system design, a small adapter board could be constructed containing the level translator and RS-232 connector. The adapter board would only be required when updating the system firmware and would not add the cost of the level translator and connector to each system. In addition to the SCI port, a single input pin is required to advise the serial boot loader startup code to execute the Flash serial boot loader instead of beginning execution of the system application program. In this example the PDLC6 pin is used for this purpose; however, any input pin may be used.

Because the boot loader code is copied from the Flash boot block into the on-chip RAM where it is executed, the code must be written in a position independent manner. That is, it may not refer to any absolute addresses. With the exception of references to the peripheral I/O registers, all references to program or data are made relative to the value of the program counter.

Because the MC68HC912B32's interrupt and reset vectors reside in the 2k byte boot block, they cannot be changed without erasing the boot block itself. Even though it is possible to erase and reprogram the boot block from within the boot loader program, it is inadvisable to do so. If anything were to go wrong during the process of reprogramming the boot block, it would be impossible to recover from the situation without the use of BDM programming hardware. For this reason, the serial boot loader includes a jump table that utilizes a secondary interrupt and reset vector table located just below the 2k boot block. Each entry in the secondary interrupt table consists of two byte addresses that mirror the primary interrupt and reset vector table located in the erase protected boot block. Figure 8.6 shows the correspondence between the primary and secondary interrupt vector tables.

Making use of the CPU12's indexed-indirect program counter relative addressing, each jump table entry consists of a single four byte `JMP` instruction. This form of the `JMP` instruction executes in only six CPU clock cycles, adding just 750 nS to the interrupt latency for a system operating with an E-clock of 8.0 MHz. In most applications this small amount of additional interrupt latency will not affect the overall performance of a system.

Chapter 8: On-chip Flash EEPROM

Interrupt Vector Address	Interrupt Source	Secondary Vector Address
$FFC0 - $FFCF	Reserved	$F7C0 - $F7CF
$FFD0 - $FFD1	BDLC (J1850)	$F7D0
$FFD2 - $FFD3	ATD	$F7D2
$FFD4 - $FFD5	Reserved	$F7D4
$FFD6 - $FFD7	SCI 0	$F7D6
$FFD8 - $FFD9	SPI	$F7D8
$FFDA - $FFDB	Pulse Acc. Input Edge	$F7DA
$FFDC - $FFDD	Pulse Acc. Overflow	$F7DC
$FFDE - $FFDF	Timer Overflow	$F7DE
$FFE0 - $FFE1	Timer Channel 7	$F7E0
$FFE2 - $FFE3	Timer Channel 6	$F7E2
$FFE4 - $FFE5	Timer Channel 5	$F7E4
$FFE6 - $FFE7	Timer Channel 4	$F7E6
$FFE8 - $FFE9	Timer Channel 3	$F7E8
$FFEA - $FFEB	Timer Channel 2	$F7EA
$FFEC - $FFED	Timer Channel 1	$F7EC
$FFEE - $FFEF	Timer Channel 0	$F7EE
$FFF0 - $FFF1	Real Time Interrupt	$F7F0
$FFF2 - $FFF3	IRQ	$F7F2
$FFF4 - $FFF5	XIRQ	$F7F4
$FFF6 - $FFF7	SWI	$F7F6
$FFF8 - $FFF9	Illegal Opcode Trap	$F7F8
$FFFA - $FFFB	COP Failure Reset	$F7FA
$FFFC - $FFFD	Clock Mon. Fail Reset	$F7FC
$FFFE - $FFFF	Reset	$F7FE

Figure 8.6: Correspondence Between Primary and Secondary Interrupt Vector Addresses

The instructions implementing the interrupt and reset jump table are shown in Figure 8.7. Noticeably absent from the jump table is an entry for the reset vector. This apparent omission is not an oversight. Rather, the boot loader startup code executes immediately after reset so that the state of the PDLC6 pin can be examined to determine if the serial boot loader should be executed. If the PDLC6 pin is at a logic one level, an indirect jump is made to the address contained in the secondary reset vector.

The symbols appearing in the label field of Figure 8.7 are used by the assembler to generate addresses for the hardware reset and interrupt vectors table as shown in Figure 8.8. Also notice the symbols appearing in the label field of Figure 8.8 are used in the operand field of the JMP instruction. This allows the assembler to calculate the proper offset to

Section 8.7: Boot loader Requirements

secondary interrupt and reset address table. By having the assembler subtract the value of the symbol `BootBlkSize` from the address of the hardware interrupt or reset vector, the source for this jump table can be used with a boot block of any size simply by redefining the value of the symbol `BootBlkSize`.

The only additional changes required to use these listings with other M68HC12 family members is the addition of JMP instructions and addresses to accommodate a larger number of interrupt vectors.

```
;
JBDLC:       jmp    [BDLC-BootBlkSize,pcr]      ; jump to BDLC ISR.
JATD:        jmp    [ATD-BootBlkSize,pcr]       ; jump to A2D ISR.
JSCI0:       jmp    [SCI0-BootBlkSize,pcr]      ; jump to SCI ISR.
JSPI:        jmp    [SPI-BootBlkSize,pcr]       ; jump to SPI ISR.
JPACCIE:     jmp    [PACCIE-BootBlkSize,pcr]    ; jump to Pulse Acc ISR.
JPACCOv:     jmp    [PACCOv-BootBlkSize,pcr]    ; jump to Pulse Ovfl ISR.
JTimerOv:    jmp    [TimerOv-BootBlkSize,pcr]   ; jump to Tmr Ovfl ISR.
JTimerCh7:   jmp    [TimerCh7-BootBlkSize,pcr]  ; jump to Timer Ch7 ISR.
JTimerCh6:   jmp    [TimerCh6-BootBlkSize,pcr]  ; jump to Timer Ch6 ISR.
JTimerCh5:   jmp    [TimerCh5-BootBlkSize,pcr]  ; jump to Timer Ch5 ISR.
JTimerCh4:   jmp    [TimerCh4-BootBlkSize,pcr]  ; jump to Timer Ch4 ISR.
JTimerCh3:   jmp    [TimerCh3-BootBlkSize,pcr]  ; jump to Timer Ch3 ISR.
JTimerCh2:   jmp    [TimerCh2-BootBlkSize,pcr]  ; jump to Timer Ch2 ISR.
JTimerCh1:   jmp    [TimerCh1-BootBlkSize,pcr]  ; jump to Timer Ch1 ISR.
JTimerCh0:   jmp    [TimerCh0-BootBlkSize,pcr]  ; jump to Timer Ch0 ISR.
JRTI:        jmp    [RTI-BootBlkSize,pcr]       ; jump to RTI ISR.
JIRQ:        jmp    [IRQ-BootBlkSize,pcr]       ; jump to IRQ ISR.
JXIRQ:       jmp    [XIRQ-BootBlkSize,pcr]      ; jump to XIRQ ISR.
JSWI:        jmp    [SWI-BootBlkSize,pcr]       ; jump to SWI ISR.
JIllop:      jmp    [Illop-BootBlkSize,pcr]     ; jump to Trap ISR.
JCOPFail:    jmp    [COPFail-BootBlkSize,pcr]   ; jump to COP Reset.
JClockFail:  jmp    [ClockFail-BootBlkSize,pcr] ; jump to Clk Fail Rst.
;
```

Figure 8.7: Interrupt/Reset Jump Table

Chapter 8: On-chip Flash EEPROM

```
;
BDLC:       dc.w    JBDLC       ; BDLC interrupt vector.
ATD:        dc.w    JATD        ; A2D interrupt vector.
            dc.w    $ffff       ; Reserved interrupt vector.
SCI0:       dc.w    JSCI0       ; SCI interrupt vector.
SPI:        dc.w    JSPI        ; SPI interrupt vector.
PACCIE:     dc.w    JPACCIE     ; Pulse Acc input edge interrupt vector.
PACCOv:     dc.w    JPACCOv     ; Pulse Acc overflow interrupt vector.
TimerOv:    dc.w    JTimerOv    ; Timer overflow interrupt vector.
TimerCh7:   dc.w    JTimerCh7   ; Timer channel 7 interrupt vector.
TimerCh6:   dc.w    JTimerCh6   ; Timer channel 6 interrupt vector.
TimerCh5:   dc.w    JTimerCh5   ; Timer channel 5 interrupt vector.
TimerCh4:   dc.w    JTimerCh4   ; Timer channel 4 interrupt vector.
TimerCh3:   dc.w    JTimerCh3   ; Timer channel 3 interrupt vector.
TimerCh2:   dc.w    JTimerCh2   ; Timer channel 2 interrupt vector.
TimerCh1:   dc.w    JTimerCh1   ; Timer channel 1 interrupt vector.
TimerCh0:   dc.w    JTimerCh0   ; Timer channel 0 interrupt vector.
RTI:        dc.w    JRTI        ; Real Time Interrupt interrupt vector.
IRQ:        dc.w    JIRQ        ; IRQ interrupt vector.
XIRQ:       dc.w    JXIRQ       ; XIRQ interrupt vector.
SWI:        dc.w    JSWI        ; SWI interrupt vector.
Illop:      dc.w    JIllop      ; TRAP instruction interrupt vector.
COPFail:    dc.w    JCOPFail    ; COP watchdog reset vector.
ClockFail:  dc.w    JClockFail  ; Clock fail reset vector.
Reset:      dc.w    BootStart   ; Powerup/Reset vector.
;
```

Figure 8.8: Hardware Interrupt and Reset Vector Table

8.8 BOOT LOADER STARTUP CODE

Figure 8.9 presents the serial boot loader's startup code along with constant definitions required by the boot loader. While most of the items in the constant definitions area are self explanatory, there are several items worth discussing. Even though the MC68HC912B32's timer module is not discussed until Chapter 11, the serial boot loader utilizes the timer's output compare function for the programming and erase time delays. Utilizing the timer instead of software delay loops in this example does not provide any particular advantages in terms of timing accuracy, but it shows one way the timer can be used to generate accurate time delays.

Because of the orders of magnitude difference in the erase and program pulse lengths, the timer must be used with two different timer prescale values to produce accurate time delays. For the short time delays required by the programming algorithm, the timer prescaler is set to a divide by one scale factor. For the MC68HC912B32 this uses the system E-Clock

Section 8.8: Boot loader Startup Code

to directly drive the timer counter register. To obtain the number of timer ticks equivalent to 1 µS, the system clock should be divided by 1,000,000. In this case, the result would be eight. This result is then multiplied by 22 to yield the total number of timer ticks equal required to produce a 22 µS delay. However, to avoid truncation errors, the system clock is first multiplied by the 22 µS delay time before being divided by 1,000,000 as shown in Figure 8.9. The timer tick value for the program verification delay, t_{VPROG}, is calculated to be half of the programming delay time and is assigned to the symbol `uS11`.

A 22 µS programming pulse was chosen because it represents approximately the midpoint of the allowed program pulse time. Examining the actual programming code in Figure 8.17, reveals that the instruction overhead added from testing the timer output compare flag and clearing the `ENEP` bit causes the actual programming time to be somewhat longer than 22 µS. When the M68HC12 is operating at a clock frequency of 8.0 MHz, this additional time is well within the specified programming pulse limit. When operating the microcontroller at frequencies below 2.0 MHz, the additional time that VFP is applied to the array due to the instruction overhead becomes significant. In these cases, the programming pulse should be reduced to 20 µS. In fact, if operating an M68HC12 at 1.0 MHz or below, the timing of the programming pulse would have to be performed with some very carefully written software delay loops.

```
;
                include   ConfigSC.Asm
                include   LIMRegs.Asm
                include   MSI.Asm
                include   FlashEE.Asm
                include   BDLC.Asm
                include   Timer.Asm
;
Baud9600:       equ  SysClock/16/9600      ; baud reg, based on clock freq.
mS10:           equ  SysClock/3200         ; 10 mS delay for /32 prescaler.
mS1:            equ  SysClock/32000        ; 1 mS delay for /32 prescaler.
uS22:           equ  (SysClock*22)/1000000 ; 22 uS delay for /1 prescale.
uS11:           equ  us22/2                ; 11 uS delay for /1 prescale.
;
BootBlkSize:    equ  2048                  ; Erase protected bootblock size.
MaxProgPls:     equ  50                    ; max number of programming pulses.
MaxErasePls:    equ  5                     ; max number of erase pulses.
;
StackTop:       equ  RAMBase+RAMSize       ; address to init the stack pointer.
;
S0RecType:      equ  '0'                   ; ASCII '0' used as S0 rec. indicator.
S1RecType:      equ  '1'                   ; ASCII '1' used as S1 rec. indicator.
S9RecType:      equ  '9'                   ; ASCII '9' used as S9 rec. indicator.
;
;
BootStart:      brclr PORTDLC,#$40,BootCopy ; PortDLC bit #6 == 0?
                jmp   [Reset-BootBlkSize,pcr] ; no. jump to users program
                                            ; pointed to by the the
                                            ; secondary 'reset' vector.
;
BootCopy:       lds   #StackTop            ; initialize the stack pointer
                clr   COPCTL               ; disable watchdog
                ldx   #BootLoad            ; point to start of bootloader.
                ldy   #RAMBase             ; point to the start of on-chip RAM.
                ldd   #BootLoadEnd         ; calc. size of the bootloader code.
                subd  #BootLoad
MoveMore:       movb  1,x+,1,y+            ; move a byte of bootloader into RAM.
                dbne  d,MoveMore           ; dec byte count, move till done.
                jmp   RAMBase              ; execute the bootloader code.
;
```

Figure 8.9: Boot loader Constant Definitions and Startup Code

The boot loader begins execution at label BootStart by checking the state of port pin six on PORTDLC. If the pin is at a logic zero, execution continues at label BootCopy where the boot loader code between the labels BootLoad and BootLoadEnd is copied, one byte at a time, into the on-chip RAM. When the copy is complete, execution of the boot loader continues by jumping to the instruction at the beginning of RAM. Note, before

Section 8.8: Boot loader Startup Code

the copy process is begun, the stack pointer is initialized and the COP watchdog timer is disabled.

```
;
BootLoad:    ldd    #Baud9600       ; set SCI to 9600 baud @ 8.0 MHz
             std    SC0BD
             ldab   #TE+RE          ; enable the transmitter & receiver.
             stab   SC0CR2
             ldab   #LOCK           ; protect the 2k bootblock.
             stab   FEELCK
             ldab   #TEN+TFFCA      ; enable timer system, fast flag clear.
             stab   TSCR
             ldab   #$01            ; config timer Ch. 0 as output compare.
             stab   TIOS
BLLoop:      leax   BLPrompt,pcr    ; point to the bootloader prompt.
             jsr    OutStr,pcr      ; display it.
             jsr    getchar,pcr     ; get the command from the user.
             jsr    putchar,pcr     ; echo it.
             pshb                   ; save it.
             leax   CrLfStr,pcr     ; go to the next line.
             jsr    OutStr,pcr
             pulb                   ; restore the entered character.
             andb   #$df            ; simple convert to upper case.
;
CheckFErase: cmpb   #'E'            ; erase command entered?
             bne    ChkProg         ; no. go check for the program command.
             jsr    CheckVfp,pcr    ; yes. check for Vfp present.
             bne    BLLoop          ; go print prompt if not present.
             jsr    FErase,pcr      ; yes. go erase the Flash.
             leax   ENot,pcr        ; point to the 'not erased' string.
             bne    BadErase        ; branch if it didn't erase properly.
             leax   Erased,pcr      ; if it did, point to the 'erased' string
BadErase:    jsr    OutStr,pcr
             bra    BLLoop          ; go back & print the prompt again.
;
ChkProg:     cmpb   #'P'            ; program command entered?
             bne    BLLoop          ; no. go redisplay the command prompt.
             jsr    CheckVfp,pcr    ; yes. check for Vfp present.
             bne    BLLoop          ; go print prompt if not present.
             jsr    FProg,pcr       ; yes. go program the Flash.
EEProgStat:  pshc                   ; save the success/fail condition.
             leax   CrLfStr,pcr     ; go to the next line.
             jsr    OutStr,pcr
             pulc                   ; restore the success/fail condition.
             leax   PNot,pcr        ; point to the 'not programmed' string.
             bne    BadErase        ; display string if programming failed.
             leax   Programmed,pcr  ; else, point to the 'programmed' string.
BadProg:     bra    BadErase        ; go display the prompt again.
;
```

Figure 8.10: Boot loader Initialization and Main Loop

Chapter 8: On-chip Flash EEPROM

The software in Figure 8.10 comprises the boot loader initialization and the main execution loop. The instructions between the labels `BootLoad` and `BLLoop` comprise the initialization portion of the code. It sets the SCI baud rate register for 9600 baud, enables the transmitter and receiver, sets the LOCK bit in the FEELCK register to protect the 2K boot block from program or erasure, enables the timer system and configures timer channel 0 for the output compare function.

The code at label `BLLoop` comprises the main control loop of the serial boot loader and begins by displaying the following prompt on the host terminal's screen:

```
(E)rase or (P)rogram:
```

After displaying the prompt, the `getchar` subroutine is called where the CPU12 waits for a single character to be entered from the keyboard. After a character is entered, it is echoed back to the terminal by calling the `putchar` subroutine. Finally, the character is converted to upper case ASCII by clearing bit six of the received character. This method of converting characters from lower to upper case only works if the received character is an alphabetic character. In an application that may need to receive and process the ASCII characters with a value greater than an ASCII 'z', a check must be performed to ensure the received character is a lower case alphabetic character before clearing bit six. The converted character is checked for a valid command entry by comparing it to an upper case 'E' and 'P'. If an invalid character was entered, the prompt is simply displayed on the next line.

Before executing either the erase or program command, the `CheckVfp` subroutine is called to verify the programming voltage is present on the VFP pin. If the programming voltage is not present, a message is displayed on the terminal and the subroutine returns with the condition code register Z-bit cleared, indicating a 'not equal' condition. If VFP is not present, the main control loop simply displays the prompt on the next line. If VFP is present, either the `FErase` or `FProg` subroutine is called to perform the requested action. The successful execution of both of these routines is indicated by returning with the condition code register Z-bit set. When returning from the `FErase` subroutine, notice that the X index register is loaded before executing the branch instruction that checks for the success or failure of the erase process. This arrangement is possible because the `LEAX` instruction does not alter the condition code register. At the conclusion of either command, execution of the boot loader resumes at label `BLLoop` where the prompt is displayed.

Figure 8.11 contains the source code for the `CheckVfp` subroutine and the string declarations for the prompt and success/failure messages.

Section 8.9: Flash Programming Control Loop

```
CheckVfp:       clra                            ; assume Vfp is present (Z == 1).
                brset   FEECTL,#SVFP,VfpOK      ; programming voltage present?
                leax    NoVfpError,pcr          ; no. inform the user.
                jsr     OutStr,pcr
                inca                            ; return Z == 0 (not zero condition)
VfpOK:          rts
;
CrLfStr:        dc      $0d,$0a,0
BLPrompt:       dc      $0d,$0a,"(E)rase or (P)rogram:",0
ENot:           dc      "Not "
Erased:         dc      "Erased",0
PNot:           dc      "Not "
Programmed:     dc      "Programmed",0
NoVfpError:     dc      $0d,$0a,"Vfp Not Present",0
;
```

Figure 8.11: `CheckVfp` Subroutine and Prompt/Message Strings

8.9 FLASH PROGRAMMING CONTROL LOOP

The `FProg` subroutine, called by the boot loader main loop, is itself a small subroutine utilizing other subroutines to perform its task. It controls the flow of data between the host computer and the MC68HC912B32 by sending an asterisk to the host computer when it is ready to receive the next S-Record. This handshaking arrangement is required because of the variable amount of time required to program each Flash memory location. To use this form of software handshaking, the host communication program must have the ability to wait for a single character or character string before it sends a line of data. This form of software handshaking was chosen over hardware handshaking or Xon/Xoff software handshaking for several reasons.

While hardware handshaking would provide a slight increase in the overall performance of the programming process, the complexity of the connection between the microcontroller and the host computer seems to outweigh the slight benefit in performance. Even though the cost of the cabling and connector may not be a factor, making sure that a cable supporting the proper handshaking signals is the main concern.

Because almost all communications programs support Xon/Xoff software handshaking, this might seem to have been the best choice. Unfortunately, Xon/Xoff handshaking presents some challenges that would dramatically increase the complexity of the SCI character receive routine. Most modern PC computers have UARTs containing a hardware First-In-First-Out (FIFO) buffer. This allows the host CPU to write several characters, many times up to 16, to the UART without waiting for each character to transmit. Once the FIFO has been loaded with data, it cannot be kept from sending them unless stopped by hardware handshaking. If the host computer has loaded the FIFO with characters just as the

MC68HC912B32 sends an Xoff character to the host, the SCI receive routine would have to be able to receive a variable number of characters and place them in a buffer until they were needed. This increase in software complexity does not meet one of the original goals of keeping the boot loader as small as possible.

```
;
FProg:       ldab    #$00            ; set the prescaler to /1.
             stab    TMSK2
             bra     FSkipFirst      ; don't send 'pace' character first time.
FSendPace:   ldab    #'*'            ; the asterisk as the pace character.
             jsr     putchar,pcr     ; tell host it's ok to send next S-Rec.
FSkipFirst:  jsr     GetSRecord,pcr  ; go get the S-Record.
             bne     ProgDone        ; non-zero condition means an error occ.
             ldab    RecType,pcr     ; check the record type.
             cmpb    #S9RecType      ; was it an S9 record?
             beq     ProgDone        ; yes. we're done.
             cmpb    #S0RecType      ; no. was it an S0 record?
             beq     FSendPace       ; yes. just ignore it.
             jsr     ProgFBlock,pcr  ; no. an S1 rec. go prog data into Flash.
             beq     FSendPace       ; zero condition means all went ok.
ProgDone:    rts                     ; if prog failed, non-zero condition ret.
;
```

Figure 8.12: `FProg` Subroutine

The `FProg` subroutine begins by clearing the timer prescaler bits and selecting a divide by one prescale value. Except for first time an S-Record is received, an asterisk is sent to the host informing it that the boot loader is ready to receive a complete S-Record. The `GetSRecord` subroutine is called to receive an entire S-Record, placing the decoded data in global variables. If the S-Record was not properly received the condition code register Z-bit is set upon return. Receipt of an S0 header record is simply ignored while an S9 record terminates the Flash programming process. Because the `GetSRecord` subroutine, shown in Figure 8.13, receives only S0, S1, and S9 S-Records it can be assumed that a valid S1 record was received if the received S-Record type was not an S0 or an S9. The reception of a valid S1 record causes the `ProgFBlock` subroutine to be called where the received S-Record data is programmed into the Flash.

Section 8.10: Receiving and Decoding an S–Record

```
;
              offset  0
SRecBytes:    ds      1               ; holds number of bytes in rcvd S-Rec.
CheckSum:     ds      1               ; used for calculated checksum.
LocSize:      set     *               ; number of bytes required for locals.
;
GetSRecord:   leas    -LocSize,sp     ; allocate stack space for variables.
LookForSOR:   jsr     getchar,pcr     ; get a character from the receiver.
              cmpb    #'S'            ; start-of-record character?
              bne     LookForSOR      ; no. go back & get another character.
              jsr     getchar,pcr     ; yes. found start-of-record character.
              cmpb    #'0'            ; found an S0 (header) record?
              beq     SaveRecType     ; yes. save S-Rec type & rcv S0 Rec.
CheckForS9:   cmpb    #'9'            ; no. found an S9 (end) record?
              beq     SaveRecType     ; yes. save S-Rec type & rcv S9 Rec.
ChkForS1:     cmpb    #'1'            ; found an S1 (code/data) record?
              bne     LookForSOR      ; no. false SOR rcvd. check for another.
SaveRecType:  stab    RecType,pcr     ; yes. set the record type to '1'
              jsr     GetHexByte,pcr  ; get the S-Record length byte.
              bne     BadSRec         ; return if there was an error.
              stab    SRecBytes,sp    ; save tot number of S-Rec bytes to rcv.
              stab    CheckSum,sp     ; init checksum with data byte count.
              subb    #3              ; rmv load addr & chksum field from cnt.
              stab    DataBytes,pcr   ; save the code/data field size.
              leax    LoadAddr,pcr    ; point to addr/code/data/chksum buffer.
RcvData:      jsr     GetHexByte,pcr  ; get an S-Record data byte.
              bne     BadSRec         ; return if there was an error.
              stab    1,x+            ; save the byte in the data buffer.
              addb    CheckSum,sp     ; add the byte into the checksum.
              stab    CheckSum,sp     ; save the result.
              dec     SRecBytes,sp    ; received all the S-Record bytes?
              bne     RcvData         ; no. go get some more.
              inc     CheckSum,sp     ; if chksum was ok, result will be zero.
BadSRec:      leas    LocSize,sp      ; remove locals.
              rts                     ; return.
;
```

Figure 8.13: `GetSRecord` subroutine

8.10 RECEIVING AND DECODING AN S-RECORD

An S-Record is comprised of six fields as shown in Figure 8.14. After allocating space on the stack for two local variables, the `GetSRecord` subroutine begins to look for the Start Of Record (SOR) character. It repeatedly calls the getchar subroutine ignoring all characters except an ASCII 'S'. The field following the Start Of Record character is the S-Record type and consists of a single ASCII numeral. Though there are eight defined S-Record types, the `GetSRecord` subroutine only recognizes the S0, S1, and S9 record types. If the character following the Start Of Record character is anything other than an ASCII '0', '1', or '9', the search for a Start Of Record character is begun again. When a valid record type is received, the ASCII value is stored in the global variable `RecType`. Saving the S-Record type is necessary so the `FLoad` subroutine can determine what action to take if an S-Record is successfully received. The length field is comprised of two ASCII hexadecimal characters representing the number of *character pairs* present in the Load Address, Code/Data and Checksum fields. The Length field is received and converted to a single hexadecimal byte by the `GetHexByte` subroutine.

| SOR | Type | Length | Load Address | Code/Data | Checksum |

Figure 8.14: S-Record Field Layout

If the Length field is successfully received, the value is saved in the local variable `SRecBytes` and is used to initialize the calculated checksum value. Because the Length field includes the three bytes in the Load Address and Checksum fields, three is subtracted from the received value before saving the value in the `DataBytes` global variable. After loading the address of the `LoadAddr` global variable into the X index register, a loop is entered that receives the Load Address, Code/Data, and Checksum fields by repeated calls to the `GetHexByte` subroutine. Each received byte is placed in successive memory locations until the count in the local variable `SRecBytes` is exhausted. Placing the three received fields in successive memory locations is possible because of the declaration order of the global variables.

Just before returning to the `FLoad` subroutine, an error check is performed by incrementing the calculated checksum. Because the received checksum is the ones compliment of the sum of the bytes in the Length, Load Address, and Code/Data fields, adding it to the calculated checksum should produce a result of $FF if all bytes were received correctly. Incrementing the calculated checksum, which includes the received checksum should result in a value of zero if no errors occurred. This results in the the Z-bit in the condition code register being set. The `FLoad` subroutine checks the condition of the Z-bit to determine if the S-Record was received properly.

The `GetHexByte` subroutine is presented in Figure 8.15 along with two additional subroutines it requires to perform its task. The `IsHex` subroutine is called each time `GetHexByte` receives a character from the `getchar` routine to verify that the received character is an ASCII hexadecimal character. If the received character is not an ASCII numeral, '0' through '9' or one of the letters 'A' through 'F', `IsHex` returns with the condition code register Z-bit cleared as an error indication. For valid ASCII hexadecimal characters, `IsHex` returns with the Z-bit is set.

After verifying the received character as a valid ASCII hexadecimal character, it must be converted to a binary hexadecimal value. The `CvtHex` subroutine performs this function by

Section 8.10: Receiving and Decoding an S–Record

first subtracting the ASCII value of the character '9' ($39) from the hexadecimal character in the B accumulator. If the the character was an ASCII numeral, the result will be less than or equal to nine. If not, it means that the character was one of the letters 'A' through 'F'. Because the ASCII letters 'A' through 'F' have values that are $08 greater than the ASCII '9', an additional seven is subtracted from the original result to produce the proper binary value. For example, if the character in the B accumulator were the ASCII letter 'D' ($44) subtracting ASCII '0' would produce $14. Subtracting seven produces the correct binary result, $0D.

After receiving and converting the first ASCII character comprising the upper four bits of a byte, the converted result must be shifted into the upper four bits of the B accumulator so that it can be combined with the next converted character. Notice that this is done using an 8 x 8 multiply instead of four successive logical shift left (LSL) instructions because it requires one less byte of object code yet requires the the same number of clock cycles to complete.

```
;
GetHexByte:   bsr   getchar      ; get the upper nybble from the SCI.
              bsr   IsHex        ; valid hex character?
              beq   OK1          ; yes. go convert it to binary.
              rts                ; no. return with a non-zero ccr indication.
OK1:          bsr   CvtHex       ; convert the ascii-hex character to binary.
              ldaa  #16          ; shift it to the upper 4-bits.
              mul
              pshb               ; save it on the stack.
              bsr   getchar      ; get the lower nybble from the SCI.
              bsr   IsHex        ; valid hex character?
              beq   OK2          ; yes. go convert it to binary.
              pulb               ; remove saved upper nybble from the stack.
              rts                ; no. return with a non-zero ccr indication.
OK2:          bsr   CvtHex       ; convert the ascii-hex character to binary.
              addb  1,sp+        ; add it to the upper nybble.
              clra               ; simple way to set the Z ccr bit.
              rts                ; return.
;
IsHex:        cmpb  #'0'         ; less than ascii hex zero?
              blo   NotHex       ; yes. character not hex. return ccr Z = 0.
              cmpb  #'9'         ; less than or equal to ascii hex nine?
              bls   IsHex1       ; yes. character is hex. return ccr Z = 1.
              cmpb  #'A'         ; less than ascii hex 'A'?
              blo   NotHex       ; yes. character not hex. return ccr Z = 0.
              cmpb  #'F'         ; less than or equal to ascii hex 'F'?
              bhi   NotHex       ; no. character not hex. return ccr Z = 0.
IsHex1:       orcc  #$04         ; yes. return a zero ccr indication.
NotHex:       rts
;
CvtHex:       subb  #'0'         ; subtract ascii '0' from the hex character.
              cmpb  #$09         ; was it a decimal digit?
              bls   CvtHexRtn    ; yes. ok as is.
              subb  #$07         ; no. ascii hex letter ('A' - 'F').
CvtHexRtn:    rts
;
```

Figure 8.15: `GetHexByte`, `IsHex` and `CvtHex` Subroutines

8.11 PROGRAMMING A BLOCK OF FLASH

After an S1 record has been successfully received, `FLoad` calls the `FProgBlock` subroutine to program the received data into the Flash. Because of the length of the `FProgBlock` subroutine and because of the number of branches within it, a complete flowchart is provided in Figure 8.16 as an aid to understanding the source code listing in Figure 8.17.

Section 8.11: Programming A Block of Flash

To simplify the implementation of the programming algorithm and to keep the boot loader code as small as possible, the `ProgFBlock` routine only programs a single byte of the Flash at a time. This may seem to impose a severe time penalty when programming 30k of Flash. However, the actual time saved would be extremely small in relation to the amount of time required to send an S-Record file containing 30k of object code. Consider, for example, that most Flash locations are able to be programmed with the application of, at most, three programming and three margin pulses. Therefore using a total time of 33 μS per byte, 22 μS programming time and 11 μS read recovery time, would require 33 μS x 6 x 30720 or approximately 6.1 seconds to program 30K bytes a byte at a time. If words were programmed instead, the time would be cut approximately in half.

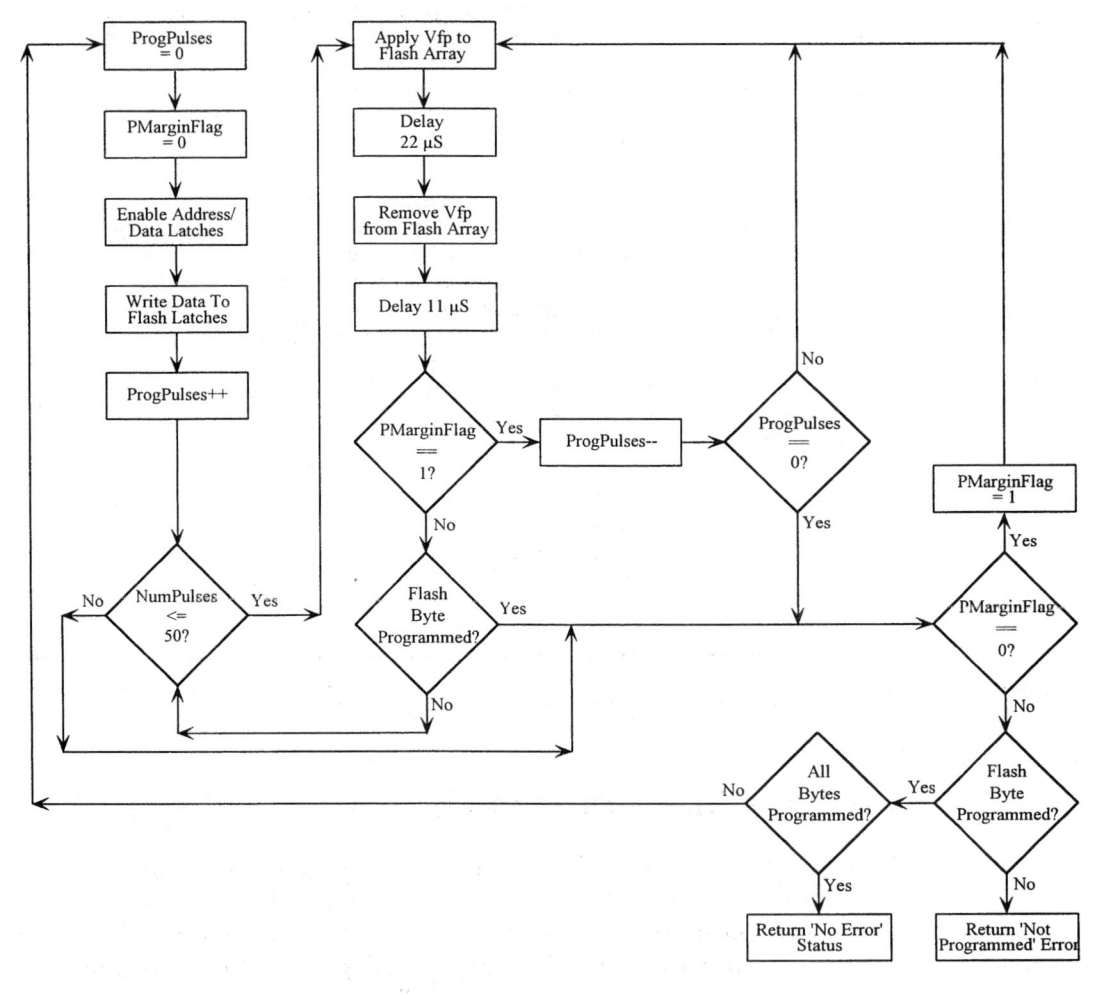

Figure 8.16: `ProgFBlock` subroutine flowchart

Chapter 8: On-chip Flash EEPROM

For the serial boot loader, the communication baud rate is the limiting factor in the length of time required to program the Flash. Consider an S-Record file containing 30k of object code. If each S-Record contains 32 bytes in the code/data field, each S-Record would be comprised of 74 ASCII characters not counting carriage return and/or line feeds. The file would contain 960 S-Records for a total file size of 71,040 bytes The time to transmit this much ASCII data at 9600 baud with no pauses between characters requires approximately 74 seconds. This is more than an order of magnitude greater than the three seconds that would be saved by programming a word at a time. Even at a baud rate of 38,400 it would require approximately 19 seconds to transmit 71,040 bytes.

The `FProgBlock` subroutine essentially consists of three nested loops. The outer loop beginning at label `ProgLoop` is executed for each byte. It begins by clearing the programming pulse counter, `ProgPulses`, and the the programming margin flag, `PMarginFlag`. During programming, the `ProgPulses` is used to maintain a count of the programming pulses applied to each byte up to a maximum of `MaxProgPls` pulses. When applying the programming margin pulses, this value is decremented until it reaches zero. `PMarginFlag` is a boolean variable used to indicate that programming margin pulses are being applied. When its value is non-zero, it modifies subroutine execution so that the contents of the Flash memory is not compared to the S-Record data after the application of each margin pulse. In addition the outer loop enables the Flash address and data latches and writes a byte of the S-Record data to the latches.

The next inner most loop, beginning at label `PPulseLoop`, is executed once for each programming pulse applied to the Flash array. At the beginning of each loop, the `ProgPulses` variable is incremented and checked to see if the maximum number of programming pulses have been applied. If the maximum count has been reached, a value of one is stored in the `PMarginFlag` so that the programming pulse loop will be terminated *after* the next programming pulse is applied.

Because of the requirement to produce short, accurate time delays, the timer is used in a slightly unusual manner. Before each program or read recovery cycle begins, the timer subsystem is disabled by clearing the Timer Enable (`TEN`) bit in the Timer Status and Control Register (`TSCR`). When the timer is disabled, the contents of all timer registers, including the value of the Timer Counter Register (`TCNT`), are maintained. This allows software to read the value of the `TCNT` register, add a value to it that will produce a delay of 22 μS and write the result to the `TC0` register. Using the timer in this manner allows a delay constant to be calculated without having to compensate for any intervening instruction execution time. Next, the programming voltage is applied to the array by setting the Enable Programming/Erase bit (`ENPE`) in the Flash EEPROM Control register (`FEECTL`) and the timer system is enabled. When the programming time period has expired, the programming voltage is removed from the Flash array. Because the programming read recovery time is specified as a minimum of 10 μS, the delay does not have to be as accurate as the programming pulse. Even though the output compare is setup to produce a delay of 11 μS,

Section 8.11: Programming A Block of Flash

the actual delay will be slightly longer due to the fact that the timer is not disabled when setting up the delay.

At the end of each programming cycle, if the `PMarginFlag` contains a value of zero, the byte of Flash data is compared to the byte of received S-Record data. If the two values do not match, the programming cycle is repeated until the data matches or the maximum number of programming pulses have been applied. When the data matches or the programming pulse limit has been reached, an equal number of program pulses are applied to the Flash memory location to provide 100% programming margin. Finally, the Flash data is again compared to the received S-Record data. If the two do not match, the `ProgFBlock` routine terminates returning with the condition code register Z-bit clear indicating that the programming operation failed. If the byte is successfully programmed, the received S-Record byte count is decremented and the programming operation continues until the value reaches zero. Successfully programming all received bytes of the S-Record is indicated by returning with the Z-bit set.

Chapter 8: On-chip Flash EEPROM

```
;
            offset   0                    ; offset section for defining locals.
;
ProgPulses: ds       1                    ; holds the number of prog pulses.
PMarginFlag:ds       1                    ; flag for applying margin pulses.
;
ProgFBlock: pshd                          ; easy way to allocate 2 bytes on stack.
            ldx      LoadAddr,pcr         ; get the S-Record (Flash) load address.
            leay     SRecData,pcr         ; point to the received S-Record data.
ProgLoop:   clr      ProgPulses,sp        ; init the ProgPulses local variable.
            clr      PMarginFlag,sp       ; init the PMarginFlag local variable.
            bset     FEECTL,#LAT          ; turn on Flash address/data latches.
            movb     0,y,0,x              ; put the addr/data into the latches.
PPulseLoop: inc      ProgPulses,sp        ; add 1 to prog pulses applied.
            ldab     ProgPulses,sp        ; get the new value.
            cmpb     #MaxProgPls          ; applied max programming pulses?
            bls      PMarginLoop          ; no. go apply a programming pulse.
            movb     #1,PMarginFlag,sp    ; yes. apply 'MaxProgPls' of margin.
PMarginLoop:bclr     TSCR,#TEN            ; stop timer for accurate delays.
            ldd      #us22                ; get the constant for a 22 uS delay.
            addd     TCNT                 ; add to value of timer counter reg.
            std      TC0                  ; init the OC register with delay val.
            bset     TSCR,#TEN            ; turn on the timer.
            bset     FEECTL,#ENPE         ; turn on Vfp
            brclr    TFLG1,#$01,*         ; wait until Vfp is applied for 22 uS.
            bclr     FEECTL,#ENPE         ; turn off Vfp.
            ldd      #uS11                ; get the constant for a 11 uS delay.
            addd     TCNT                 ; add it to the timer counter reg value.
            std      TC0                  ; init the OC reg. with the delay value.
            brclr    TFLG1,#$01,*         ; wait until Vfp is removed for 11 uS.
            tst      PMarginFlag,sp       ; applying the margin pulses?
            beq      CmpData              ; no. see if the data programmed ok.
            dec      ProgPulses,sp        ; yes.applied all margin pulses?
            bne      PMarginLoop          ; no. go apply more margin pulses.
            bra      PMarginDone          ; yes. go check the data again.
;
CmpData:    ldab     0,x                  ; get the data from the Flash memory.
            cmpb     0,y                  ; same as the S-Record data?
            bne      PPulseLoop           ; no. apply more programming pulses.
            movb     #1,PMarginFlag,sp    ; yes. set the prog margin flag.
            bra      PMarginLoop          ; apply the margin programming pulses.
;
PMarginDone:bclr     FEECTL,#LAT          ; turn off latches to prog next loc.
            ldab     1,x+                 ; get data from Flash for final compare.
            cmpb     1,y+                 ; same as the S-Record data?
            bne      PDone                ; no. bad Flash memory (or Vfp lost).
            dec      DataBytes,pcr        ; done with all the S-Record bytes?
            bne      ProgLoop             ; no. program the next location.
PDone:      puld                          ; remove the locals.
            rts                           ; return.
;
```

Figure 8.17: FProgBlock Subroutine

Section 8.12: Boot loader Erase Command

8.12 BOOT LOADER ERASE COMMAND

The code implementing the erase command is comprised of the `FErase` subroutine. The subroutine implements the Flash erase algorithm described earlier in the chapter. Because the erase algorithm is similar to the programming algorithm the flowchart in Figure 8.18 looks similar to the one for the `FProgBlock` in Figure 8.16.

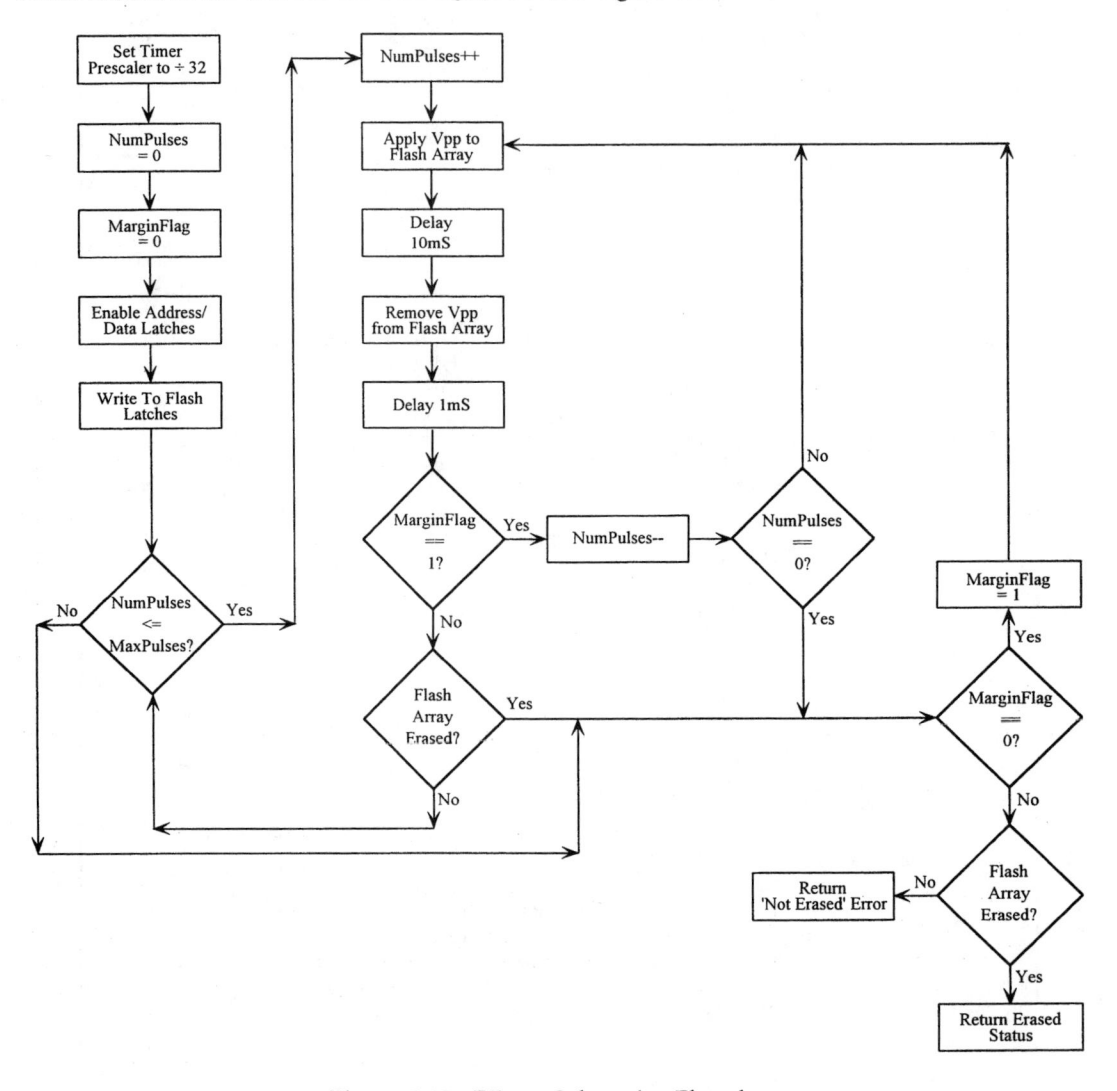

Figure 8.18: FErase Subroutine Flowchart

Because the length of the erase pulse timing is more than 2 orders of magnitude greater than the programming pulse, the timer prescaler is set to the highest available scale factor of ÷ 32. Because of the greater length of the erase pulse, the software overhead required to setup the output compare function does not contribute significantly to the total time the erase voltage is applied. Therefore, it is not necessary to disable the timer system prior to configuring the output compare register to produce an accurate delay. After initialization of the timer prescaler, two of the three local variables, `EMarginFlag` and `NumPulses`, are initialized with zero. Finally, prior to applying erase pulses, the Flash is configured for erasure by setting the `LAT` and `ERAS` bit in the `FEECTL` register and performing an aligned word write to a valid Flash address.

Section 8.12: Boot loader Erase Command

```
;
              offset  0                ; offset section for defining locals.
;
NumPulses:    ds      1                ; number of erase pulses applied.
EMarginFlag:  ds      1                ; flag for applying margin erase pulses.
NotErasedF:   ds      1                ; != 0 indicates Flash array not erased.
;
FErase:       leas    -3,sp            ; allocate stack space for locals.
              ldab    #$05             ; set the prescaler to /32.
              stab    TMSK2
              clr     EMarginFlag,sp   ; clear the margin pulse flag.
              clr     NumPulses,sp     ; clear the erase pulse count.
              bset    FEECTL,#LAT+ERAS ; turn on latches & erase bit.
              std     FEEBase          ; write to any Flash address.
;
EraseLoop:    ldab    NumPulses,sp     ; get the 'pulse' count
              cmpb    #MaxErasePls     ; applied the max num of erase pulses?
              beq     DoEMargin        ; yes. go apply the erase margin pulse.
              inc     NumPulses,sp     ; inc the 10 mS erase pulses count
PulseLoop:    bset    FEECTL,#ENPE     ; turn on Vfp.
              ldd     #mS10            ; timer constant for a 10 mS delay.
              addd    TCNT             ; add it to current value of the timer.
              std     TC0              ; init the output compare register.
              brclr   TFLG1,#$01,*     ; wait for output compare flag to set.
              bclr    FEECTL,#ENPE     ; turn off Vfp.
              ldd     #mS1             ; timer constant for a 1 mS delay.
              addd    TCNT             ; add it to current value of the timer.
              std     TC0              ; init the output compare register.
              brclr   TFLG1,#$01,*     ; wait for output compare flag to set.
              tst     EMarginFlag,sp   ; are we applying erase margin pulses?
              beq     CheckErase       ; no. did last pulse erase the array?
              dec     NumPulses,sp     ; yes. applied enough margin pulses?
              bne     PulseLoop        ; no. go apply some more.
;
CheckErase:   clr     NotErasedF,sp    ; clear the erased flag.
              ldx     #FEEBase         ; point to start of the flash block.
              ldy     #(FEESize-BootBlkSize)/2 ; count of num words to chk.
              ldd     #$FFFF           ; the value of an erased word.
EraseCkLoop:  cpd     2,x+             ; this word erased?
              bne     NotErased        ; no. set flag, apply another erase pls.
              dbne    y,EraseCkLoop    ; yes. dec count & go check next word.
;
DoEMargin:    tst     EMarginFlag,sp   ; already applied the margin pulse?
              bne     EraseDone        ; yes. we're done.
              inc     EMarginFlag,sp   ; no. set the 'margin pulse' flag.
              bra     PulseLoop        ; go apply the margin erase pulse.
;
NotErased:    inc     NotErasedF,sp    ; array not erased. flag the condition.
              tst     EMarginFlag,sp   ; have we applied the margin pulse?
              bne     EraseDone        ; yes. we're done. the Flash is bad.
              bra     EraseLoop        ; no. go apply another erase pulse.
;
EraseDone:    clr     FEECTL           ; clear the LAT & ERAS bit.
              ldab    NotErasedF,sp    ; get the erase result.
              leas    3,sp             ; get rid of the locals.
              rts                      ; return.
;
```

Figure 8.19: FErase Subroutine

After initialization, the erase process begins at the label `EraseLoop`. This loop begins by checking the value of the local variable `NumPulses` against the maximum allowable erase pulses. If less than the maximum number of erase pulses have been applied, execution continues by applying a single erase pulse and then checking the entire array for the erased state. If every location in the array is not erased, additional erase pulses are applied until the array becomes erased or the maximum number of erase pulses have been applied. When the Flash array is checked for the erased state, it is checked a word at a time to speed the erase verification process. As soon as a word is found that does not contain $FFFF, the verification process is stopped. Note that when checking the array for an erased state as the erase pulses are being applied, it is not necessary to recheck check the entire Flash array. It is only necessary to continue the verification process form the location where the verification failed from the application of the previous erase pulse. In this example, to keep the software as simple as possible, the entire array is checked after the application of each erase pulse.

Finally, after the application of the margin pulse(s), the array is once again checked for the erased state before returning. If during the final erase verification a location is found that did not erase, a non-zero value is placed in the the `NotErasedF` variable. This value is returned in the B accumulator, indicating the result of the `FErase` subroutine.

8.13 SUPPORT ROUTINES AND GLOBAL VARIABLES

In addition to the support routines in Figure 8.15 the serial boot loader also utilizes the three subroutines presented in Figure 8.20. The `getchar` and `putchar` subroutines receive and send characters through the on-chip SCI. These subroutines utilize a simple software polling technique to receive and send characters. When the `getchar` routine is called, it waits in a single instruction loop until the SCI's Receive Data Register Full (RDRF) status bit is set, indicating a character was received. The character is retrieved from the SCI data register and returned in the B accumulator. The `putchar` subroutine is called with an 8-bit character in the B accumulator and waits in a single instruction loop until the SCI's Transmit Data Register Empty (TDRE) status bit is set before writing the character to the SCI data register. The final subroutine, `OutStr`, repeatedly calls the `putchar` subroutine to send a null terminated string out the SCI.

The final declarations appearing in the listing of Figure 8.20 reserves space for the bootloader's global variables. These declarations simply advance the assembler's location counter, assigning addresses to each of the variable's labels. No space in the boot block is utilized by the global variable declarations. Notice that these declarations appear just following the end of the boot loader which is marked by the label `BootLoadEnd`. Because the variables are always referenced utilizing program counter relative indexed addressing, the variables will immediately follow the boot loader code in the on-chip RAM. Note that this particular technique of placing the global variables immediately following the code only works for relocatable code that is copied to and run from RAM.

Section 8.13: Support Routines and Global Variables

```
;
getchar:        brclr   SC0SR1,#RDRF,*  ; wait for the RDRF bit to be set.
                ldab    SC0DRL          ; retrieve the character.
                rts                     ; return.
;
putchar:        brclr   SC0SR1,#TDRE,*  ; wait for the TDRE bit to be set.
                stab    SC0DRL          ; send the character.
                rts                     ; return.
;
OutStr:         ldab    1,x+            ; get a char, advance pointer, null?
                beq     OutStrDone      ; yes. return.
                jsr     putchar,pcr     ; no. send it out the SCI.
                bra     OutStr          ; go get the next character.
OutStrDone:     rts
;
BootLoadEnd:    equ     *               ; end of S-Record Bootloader code.
;
;               Global Variables
;
RecType:        ds.b    1               ; received record type
DataBytes:      ds.b    1               ; number of data bytes in the S-Record.
LoadAddr:       ds.b    2               ; load address of the S-Record.
SRecData:       ds.b    65              ; S-Record data storage.
;
```

Figure 8.20: Serial Boot loader Support Routines and Global Variables

Questions/Exercises

8.1   What are some of the advantages of Flash EEPROM over ROM or OTP/EPROM.

8.2   Why is it important for word data accesses to be aligned to an even byte address? Is there the same concern for program instructions? Why?

8.3   Typically, what is the Flash boot block used for? Where is it located in the Flash array?

8.4   Explain the role of the LOCK and BOOTP control bits. How are the functions of these bits related?

8.5   What is the purpose of the FEESWAI control bit. What precautions must be observed regarding its use?

8.6   What is the purpose of the SVFP control bit?

8.7 What are the functions of the ERAS, LAT, and ENPE bits? What is the relationship between the LAT, and ENPE bits?

8.8 Explain the difference in the Flash array accessibility when performing programming and erase operations. What implications does this have on the Flash programming software?

8.9 What is the maximum number of guaranteed erase/program cycles of the Flash?

8.10 What precautions must be observed with regards to voltage applied to the VFP pin?

8.11 Which control bits are used to select between byte or word programming?

8.12 What is the maximum number of erase pulses that may be applied to the Flash? How many erase pulses are typically required to erase the Flash?

8.13 What is the maximum number of programming pulses that may be applied to the Flash? How many erase pulses are typically required to erase the Flash?

8.14 What special considerations must be made for the interrupt and reset vectors for applications utilizing the boot block for a Flash bootloader?

8.15 What programming technique was used in writing the Flash serial bootloader presented in this chapter? Why was this technique used?

8.16 Rewrite the bootloader startup code in **Figure 8.10** to allow the selection of an alternate communication baud rate.

8.17 Why was the software handshaking method used in the serial bootloader chosen?

8.18 What S-Record types are received and processed by the GetSRecord subroutine.

Chapter 9 SERIAL COMMUNICATIONS INTERFACE

The Serial Communications Interface or SCI, is probably the most commonly used peripheral on embedded microcontrollers. The SCI provides an asynchronous communications port used to communicate with other microcontrollers, host computers or as a diagnostic port utilized during software development and during actual product usage. The MC68HC912B32 contains a single SCI utilizing the standard Non-Return to Zero (NRZ) data format transmitting and receiving the least significant bit of data first. The transmitter and receiver sections are separate and can be independently enabled and disabled; however they do share a single baud rate generator. The baud rate generator is based on a 13-bit modulus counter providing a great deal of flexibility in choosing standard baud rates for various microcontroller operating frequencies. Hardware parity generation and checking have been incorporated into the M68HC12 SCI module to reduce the amount of software overhead necessary for applications requiring the additional error checking parity provides. A number of additional advanced features are included allowing the SCI to be utilized in robust networking applications. The SCI is actually part of the Serial Interface module on the M68HC912B32. As shown in Figure 9.1, the Serial Interface module contains a Serial Peripheral Interface and general purpose I/O in addition to the SCI. The Serial Interface module on the MC68HC812A4 contains a second SCI in place of the General purpose I/O. The SCI on the MC68HC912B32 and the MC68HC812A4 are nearly identical to the SCI modules on the M68HC11 K series and M68HC11 N series parts. In fact, assembly language or C software drivers written for either of these M68HC11 parts would operate properly on the MC68HC912B32 and the MC68HC812A4 when reassembled or recompiled.

Section 9.1: Physical Interface

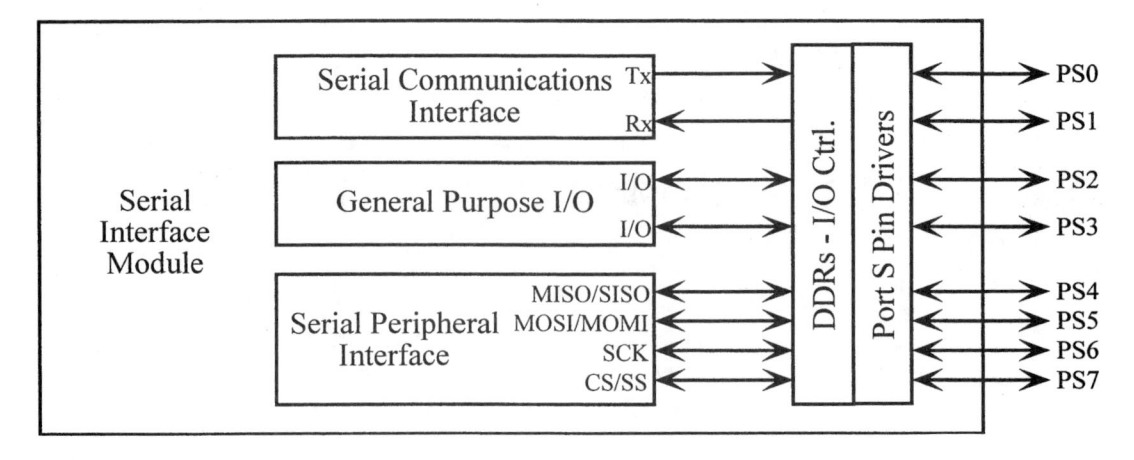

Figure 9.1: SCI Block Diagram

9.1 PHYSICAL INTERFACE

As shown in the block diagram, the SCI physical interface consists of two pins. One is associated with the SCI transmitter, the other with the receiver. There is no hardware support for handshaking signals that may be required for interfacing with a modem or host computer. However, these functions can be implemented in software utilizing the Port S or other general purpose I/O lines. The characteristics of the pins associated with the transmitter and receiver will vary depending on the SCI operating mode and the various options available for the Port S pins. However, when the SCI is configured for normal operation and the transmitter and receiver are both enabled, PS0 will be configured as an output and PS1 will be configured as an input regardless of the state of the data direction register bits associated with these pins. As with other I/O pins associated with on-chip peripherals, the Port S pins provide the option of active pull-ups and/or reduced drive capability. Unlike some of the other peripheral ports where the active pull-up and reduced drive options must be enabled or disabled for all pins on a port, the Port S pin control logic provides the capability to individually enabled and disabled these two options for the SCI, SPI, and General Purpose I/O pins. As shown in Figure 9.2 the Pull-up and Reduced Drive (PURDS) control register for Port S provides three control bits for each option. The PUPS0 and RDPS0 bits control the active pull-ups and reduced drive options respectively for the two pins associated with the SCI. PUPS1 and RDPS1 control these options for the two General Purpose I/O pins while PUPS2 and RDPS2 control pull-ups and reduced pin drive for the four pins associated with the SPI. By default, all bits in this register are cleared disabling all of the Port S pull-ups and selecting normal port drive capability. As with other I/O ports, if a pin is configured as an output, the active pull-ups, if enabled, are automatically disconnected from the I/O pin.

Chapter 9: Serial Communications Interface

Bit 7	6	5	4	3	2	1	Bit 0
0	RDPS2	RDPS1	RDPS0	0	PUPS2	PUPS1	PUPS0

Figure 9.2: Pull-up and Reduced Drive (PURDS) for Port S Control Register

In addition to the active pull-up and reduced drive options, the two SCI port pins may be configured for Wired-Or or open drain operation. When configured in this manner the gate signal of the P-channel output device, which is connected between the output pin and VDD, is disabled so that the drain of the N-channel is effectively the only output device connected to the pin. In reality, because the P-channel device is still physically connected to the pin, an inherent diode to VDD is still present. For this reason, the open drain configured outputs cannot be connected to a supply source higher than VDD. To allow open drain output pins to assume a logic level of one when a one is written to the associated data register, a current limiting pull-up resistor must be connected between the output pin and VDD. The size of the pull-up resistor should be kept above 3K • to insure that a valid logic zero can be attained when the pin is driven low. Note that the open drain configuration is available even when the pins are configured as general purpose outputs.

9.2 DATA FORMAT

As already mentioned, the SCI utilizes the standard Non-Return to Zero (NRZ) data format transmitting and receiving the least significant bit first. This data format is compatible with personal computers, modems, and stand alone computer terminals. Even though the start and stop bits are fixed at a single bit time, the data portion of the transmitted and received character is programmable to be eight or nine data bits. The hardware parity generation and detection can be programmed for even or odd parity. When enabled, the generated and received parity bit *replaces* the eight or ninth data bit in the transmitted character. An additional bit is not added to the data stream. Figure 9.3 illustrates a single transmitted character for eight and nine bit character formats.

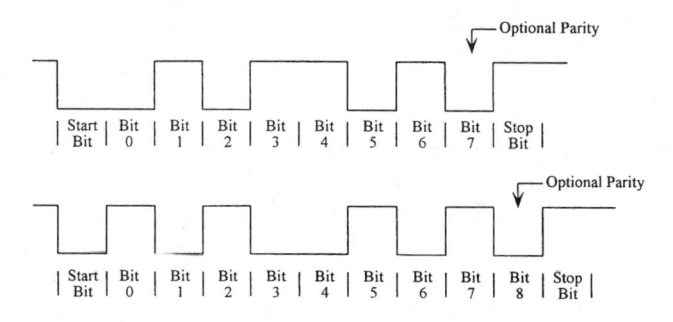

Figure 9.3: Eight and Nine Data Bit Formats

Section 9.3: Receiver

In addition to the eight and nine data bit formats, the SCI transmitter is capable of sending a special data stream known as a break. When a break is sent, the transmit data (TxD) pin is held at the space (zero) level level for a time period determined by software. The SCI break logic always ensures that the TxD pin is held low for an even multiple of the selected character time, but never shorter than 10 or 11 bit times. The break sequence is recognized as a special condition by some telecommunications and computer equipment and is useful in attempting to gain the attention of the connected device when it has not responded in some predetermined time period.

The data format, optional parity, and parity type is selected through control bits contained in the SCI Control Register 1 (SC0CR1) register shown in Figure 9.4. The M control bit selects the eight or nine bit data format. The PE bit is used to enable the parity option and the PT control bit selects even parity when it has a value of zero and odd parity when its value is one. The WOMS bit controls the Wired-Or or open drain SCI pin option described in the previous section. The default value of all bits in the SC0CR1 is zero which selects one start bit eight data bits, one stop bit, no parity and normal port pin operation with both high and low drive capability.

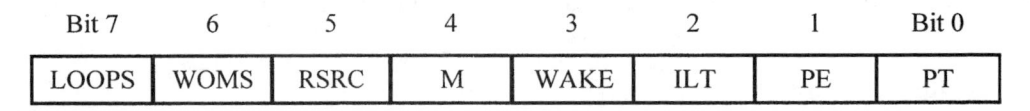

Bit 7	6	5	4	3	2	1	Bit 0
LOOPS	WOMS	RSRC	M	WAKE	ILT	PE	PT

Figure 9.4: SCI Control Register 1 (SC0CR1)

9.3 RECEIVER

The receiver is responsible for synchronizing the SCI to the incoming serial data stream and properly recovering the transmitted data bits. Because the NRZ data format contains no embedded clock information, the data recovery process depends on the transmitter and receiver operating at close to the same speed. Because of the advanced start bit synchronization, data sampling techniques, and stop bit detection used by the receiver section, the SCI can receive data containing a moderate amount of noise without error. Special status flags in the SCI Status Register 1 (SC0SR1) register indicate four separate error conditions when the SCI is unable to properly receive a character.

Essentially, the SCI receiver consists of a receive shift register, which performs the bit serial to bit parallel conversion, and a receive data register. When the serial conversion is complete, the contents of the receive shift register is transferred to the receive data register where the data is made available to software. This arrangement, known as double buffering, allows the receiving software a minimum of a complete character time, 10 or 11 bit times, to read a received character before the reception of the next character is complete. Without double buffering, the received character would have to be read before the next start bit was detected.

The SCI receiver, enabled by writing a one to the Receiver Enable (RE) bit in the SCI Control Register 2 (SC0CR2) register, utilizes a clock operating at 16 times the selected baud rate. Using a higher frequency clock in the receive logic allows multiple sampling points within each bit cell of the received data stream. For instance, for a valid start bit to be detected, the receiver logic must sense that the receive pin has been at a logic one level for three consecutive receive clock periods followed by one receive clock period at logic zero. When this condition is detected, the first condition for a valid start bit is met. To further validate the start bit, the receive pin is sampled again at the third, fifth and seventh receive clock periods. If at least two of the three samples are zero, a valid start bit is assumed and synchronization with the source is established. If at least two of the samples are logic ones, the initial start bit detection is considered to have been noise and search for a valid start bit is begun again.

During each bit time, including the start, stop, and each data bit, samples of the receive pin are taken during the eighth, ninth, and tenth receive clock times to determine the level of the receive pin at each clock time. The value of the received bit is considered to be the majority of the three samples. For data bits, this is the value shifted into the receive data shift register. If all three samples of each bit time within the character frame do not agree, the Noise Flag (NF) in the SC0SR1 register is set to indicate a possible corruption of the received data. The Noise Flag can be checked by the SCI receiver software and appropriate action taken. Note that the Noise Flag is not set if an overrun error occurs.

The three additional error conditions detected by the receiver are overrun errors, framing errors and parity errors. Overrun errors, indicated by the setting of the OR bit in the SC0SR1 register, indicates that a new character is ready to be transferred from the receive shift register into the receive data register before the previously received character has been read. In this condition, all received characters are lost until the receive data register is read. If overrun errors are a chronic problem when operating in a software polled mode, it indicates that the SCI receive software is not checking the Receive Data Register Full (RDRF) status bit often enough. This could be the result of poorly designed software or an indication that the baud rate is too high for the particular application. One way to avoid overrun errors, especially if data is received in short bursts at high speed, is to operate the SCI receive in an interrupt driven mode. This will allow short bursts of high speed data to be correctly received and placed in a buffer by the interrupt service routine. The data can then be retrieved by other system software when required.

Framing errors, indicated when the FE bit is set, indicate that a level of zero was detected on the receive data line when a stop bit was expected. Framing errors are generally the result of electrical noise corrupting the stop bit, a baud rate mismatch, or simultaneous character transmissions by more than one master when the SCI is used in a networking application. Recovery from a framing error due to baud rate mismatch may be nearly

Section 9.4: Transmitter

impossible depending on the cause of the mismatch. If the source baud rate is more than ± 4.5% of the receiver baud rate for 8-bit data or ± 4% for 9-bit data, characters will be received incorrectly. Both of these variations assume that one of the communicating devices is operating at the exact baud rate frequency. One SCI operating four percent too fast and one operating four percent too slow would not be able to communicate. A framing error is likely to occur when the baud rate of the transmitting SCI is slightly slower than these percentage tolerances.

Parity errors, indicated when the PE bit is set, indicate that the *calculated* parity of the received data did not match the value of the *received* parity bit. Parity errors can occur for the same reasons as framing errors. However, assuming that baud rates are matched, the most common reason for a parity error is the corruption of transmitted data by electrical noise. The Parity Error flag remains zero if the SCI's parity feature is disabled.

All four receiver error flags are cleared by reading the SC0SR1 followed by a read of the low byte of the SCI transmit/receive register. However, only those bits set when the SC0SR1 is read will be cleared when the low byte of transmit/receive register is read. If it is desired to detect and report any of the receiver error conditions, the receiver software must take care to preserve the contents of the SC0SR1 before reading the transmit/receive register low byte. Figure 9.5 shows one approach that might be used to return the contents of the SC0SR1 in accumulator A while utilizing a bit manipulation instruction to test the RDRF bit.

```
;
      .
      .
Here: brclr SC0SR1,#RDRF,Here; wait here till RDRF is set.
      ldaa   SC0SR1           ; get error flags while (if) they're set.
      ldab   SC0DRL           ; get character, clearing the error flags.
      .
      .
;
```

Figure 9.5: Retrieving SCI Receive Error Flags

9.4 Transmitter

The SCI transmitter section is much simpler than the receiver because it does not require the sophisticated data recovery circuitry contained in the receiver front end. The clock utilized by the transmitter has a frequency equal to the selected baud rate. Like the receiver, the transmitter is double buffered, containing a transmit data register and a transmit shift register. Transmission of a character begins when data is written to the low byte of the transmit data register. If the transmitter is idle, the data is immediately transferred from the transmit data register to the transmit shift register. As soon as the transfer occurs, another character can be written to the transmit data register. If new data is written to the transmit data register before the previous data is transferred to the transmit shift register, the data contained in the transmit data register is overwritten by the new data. SCI transmit software should always check the Transmit Data Register Empty (TDRE) bit in the SC0SR1 to ensure the transmit data register is empty before writing a new value to it.

The transmitter is enabled separately from the receiver by writing a one to the Transmitter Enable (TE) bit in the SC0CR2 register. When the TE bit is written to a one, a check is made to determine if the transmit shift register is empty. This condition is indicated when the Transmit Complete (TC) bit in the SC0SR1 register is set. If it is empty, a preamble word of ones with no start bit is transmitted before normal data transmission begins. If the transmit shift register is not empty when the TE bit is written to a zero and then to a one, the remaining bits in the shift register continue to be shifted out, including the stop bit. When the transmit shift register is empty, a preamble word consisting of 10 or 11 ones is transmitted before normal data transmission begins again. This behavior may seem strange and even unnecessary. Why would any application disable the SCI transmitter and re-enable it while data is still being sent out the transmit shift register? This particular feature was designed into the SCI transmitter to allow a forced idle period of minimum duration to be transmitted. This behavior is useful in a multi-drop network system where the receiving node's SCIs are configured for idle line wake-up. Momentarily disabling and re-enabling the transmitter forces an idle time of one data frame to be inserted into the message stream, thus forcing the receiving node's SCIs into an active mode when the idle line is detected.

9.5 Accessing Transmitted and Received Data

The SCI Data Register High byte (SC0DRH) and the SCI Data Register Low byte (SC0DRL) registers are utilized by both the transmitter and receiver. The SC0DRL register corresponds to the low seven or eight data bits in a transmitted or received data frame while the SC0DRH register contains the received and transmitted ninth data bits when the SCI is configured for nine bit operation. Reads of the SC0DRL return the contents of the lower 8-bits of the read-only receive data register. Writes to the SC0DRL access the lower 8-bits of the write-only transmit data register. The SC0DRH, unlike the SC0DRL, utilizes two separate bit positions for the received and transmitted ninth data bit. Bit number seven of the byte corresponds to the ninth data bit received by the SCI system. While bit number six corresponds to the ninth data bit transmitted by the SCI system. When using nine bit data transmission, the ninth data bit does not have to be rewritten for each frame transmitted. The same value is transmitted for each frame until the bit is changed. The SC0DRH and SC0DRL are shown in Figure 9.6.

Section 9.6: Single Wire Operating Mode

Bit 7	6	5	4	3	2	1	Bit 0	
R8	T8	0	0	0	0	0	0	SC0DRH

Bit 7	6	5	4	3	2	1	Bit 0	
R7/T7	R6/T6	R5/T5	R4/T4	R3/T3	R2/T2	R1/T1	R0/T0	SC0DRL

Figure 9.6: Transmit and Receive Data Register

When operating the SCI in eight bit mode only the SC0DRL needs be read or written; the contents of the SC0DRH can be ignored. However, when operating in nine bit mode, the T8 bit in the SC0DRH register may be written at the same time as the SC0DRL register using a 16-bit write instruction. If software dictates that these two registers be written separately, the SC0DRH should be written before the SC0DRL register. Reading the data registers when the RDRF bit is zero will return the last character received by the SCI. Writing to the SCI transmit data register with the transmitter disabled will latch the value into the data register and clear the TDRE and TC bits. When the transmitter is subsequently enabled, the contents of the transmit data register is transferred to the transmit shift register and sent after an idle frame is transmitted.

9.6 SINGLE WIRE OPERATING MODE

The M68HC12 SCI supports a half-duplex single wire operating mode allowing bidirectional communication utilizing a single wire. This mode of operation is supported on the M68HC11 family. However, the M68HC11 family requires Port D be operated in the Wire-Or mode, the transmit and receive pins must be electrically connected on the circuit board, and a pull-up resistor must be connected to the transmit and receive pins. In addition, if any of the other pins on Port D are utilized as outputs, they must also have pull-up resistors connected to them. The M68HC12 family provides the option to configure the SCI in this mode simply by using the LOOPS, WOMS, RSRC, and DDS1 control bits in the SC0CR1 register. When configured for this operating mode, PD0, the SCI receive pin, becomes available for use as general purpose I/O. Both the transmitter and receiver must be enabled to use the loop or single wire mode.

When the LOOPS bit is set to one, the SCI receiver is disconnected from the receive data pin and the receiver source is determined by the Receiver Source (RSRC) control bit. If the RSRC bit is zero, the receiver is *internally* connected to the transmitter output, placing the SCI in the loopback test mode. When the RSRC bit is one, the receiver input is actually connected to the TxD pin, placing the SCI in the single wire mode. In this mode, for any transmitted data to appear on the TxD pin, the data direction bit for Port S pin 1 (TxD) must be configured as an output when the RSRC bit is one. If the TxD pin is configured as an input when the `LOOPS` bit is set to one, the TxD pin will be driven to a logic one when the `RSRC` bit is zero and will be high impedance when `RSRC` bit is one.

In addition to being useful for operating the SCI in single wire mode, the `LOOPS` and `RSRC` can also be used when performing diagnostics on the SCI and its associated port pin. For example, if a system is having difficulty transmitting and receiving data, diagnostic software could configure the SCI enabling the transmitter and receiver, setting a baud rate and setting the `LOOPS` bit. In this configuration if the same character can be written to and read from the SCI data register with the proper status flags set or cleared, the SCI logic can be assumed to be operating properly. Next, the `RSRC` control bit can be set to one, connecting the receiver to the TxD pin. If transmitted characters are not received properly, it is likely that an external transceiver or other logic is faulty. As a final step the TxD pin can be configured as an output to allow transmitted characters to be monitored by an oscilloscope or communications protocol analyzer.

The most useful application for the SCI single wire mode (`LOOP` = 1 and `RSRC` = 1) is a simple local area network where multiple devices utilize a single single wire to transmit and receive messages. When the `RSRC` bit is set, the receiver is always connected to the TxD pin. However, before data can be transmitted, the TxD pin must first be configured as an output, connecting the transmit data shift register to the TxD pin. While the transmitter and receiver are both connected to the TxD pin, all characters transmitted by the SCI will also be received by the SCI. This allows the integrity of each transmitted character to be verified immediately after transmission. If more than one device on the single wire bus were to begin transmitting at the same time, the received character most likely would not match what was transmitted, indicating an error condition.

So, unlike the receiver, the transmitter cannot remain connected to the TxD pin while other devices on the network are transmitting unless the Wire-or mode is selected by setting the `WOMS` bit in the `SC0CR1` register. If utilizing CMOS drive mode the TxD pin must be reconfigured as an input to remove the CMOS driver from the network bus after the transmission of each message.

9.7 BAUD RATE GENERATOR

The SCI's baud rate generator is based on a 13-bit modulus counter rather than a simple binary counter chain as found on most of the M68HC11 family devices. Utilizing a modulus counter gives the baud rate generator a great deal of flexibility allowing the generation of both standard and non-standard baud rates that are relatively independent of the CPU12's operating frequency. On the MC68HC912B32, the clock source for the baud rate generator is the E-clock, so the available baud rates will depend on frequency of the CPU12. On other M68HC12 family members, such as the MC68HC812A4, the clock used to drive the baud rate generator, the timer counter, the Real-time Interrupt, the COP watchdog timer, and other modules is derived separately from the E-clock. This clock, known as the Module or

Section 9.7: Baud Rate Generator

M clock, allows the CPU12's speed to be increased or decreased during program execution without affecting the SCI's baud rate.

The 13-bit SCI Baud Rate Control Register (`SC0BDH` and `SC0BDL`) consists of two eight bit registers that are normally treated as a single 16-bit register. The lower 13 bits of this 16-bit register are utilized for the baud rate count while the upper three bits are reserved for controlling factory test functions. Writing to the upper three bits in Normal operating modes has no effect and reading them returns a value of zero. Care must be taken when operating in special mode to write only zeros to these bits to avoid placing the baud rate generator in test mode. The baud rate counter bits may assume any value from zero through 8191. However, when written with a value of zero, the baud rate generator is disabled, effectively disabling the SCI even if the transmitter and receiver are enabled.

The 13-bit value written to the Baud Rate Control Register is loaded into a down counter and is used to divide the input clock by the counter value. The output of this counter is then used to drive a simple divide by two counter to obtain a symmetrical square wave at the output. The square wave is then synchronized to the M68HC12's CPU clock before being used as the receiver clock which is 16 times the desired baud rate. The receiver clock is divided by a four bit counter ($\div$ 16) to produce the SCI transmitter clock. The formula for calculating the the Baud Rate Control Register value given the Module clock frequency and he desired baud rate is shown in Figure 9.7.

$$BR = \frac{\text{M-clock}}{16 \times \text{Desired Baud Rat}}$$

Figure 9.7: Baud Rate Control Register Formula

In this formula, remember that the M-clock is the timing clock supplied to the SCI module in Hz. On the MC68HC912B32, the M-clock is the same frequency as the E-Clock. On M68HC12 family members that contain on-chip Phase-locked Loop clock circuits, such as the MC68HC812A4 and the MC68HC912D60, the M-clock can be a different frequency than the CPU's clock.

Because the SCI baud rate is dependent on the frequency of the clock supplied to the module, some of the higher standard baud rates are not available with all module clock frequencies. Figure 9.8 summarizes the Baud Rate Control Register values for M-clock frequencies of 2.0 MHz, 4.0 MHz, and 8.0 MHz corresponding to most standard baud rates. While it is possible to calculate Baud Rate Control Register values for higher baud rates than those listed, the calculated results will generally not allow reliable communications at the higher baud rates.

Desired Baud Rate	BR Divisor for M-Clock of 2.0 MHz	BR Divisor for M-Clock of 4.0 MHz	BR Divisor for M-Clock of 8.0 MHz
110	1136	2273	4545
300	417	833	1667
600	208	417	833
1200	104	208	417
2400	52	104	208
4800	26	52	104
9600	13	26	52
14400	–	17	35
19200	–	13	26
38800	–	–	13

Figure 9.8: Baud Rate Control Register Values for Standard Baud Rates

For example, calculating a Baud Rate Control Register value for a baud rate of 57,600 baud utilizing an M-clock frequency of 8.0 MHz will produce a result of 8.68 which would be rounded up to 9. Rearranging the formula in Figure 9.7 will allow a calculation of the exact baud rate resulting from a specific Baud Rate Control Register value. The rearranged formula, shown in Figure 9.9, yields an actual baud rate of 55,556. This value, which is approximately 3.5% lower than the desired baud rate, would be within the 4% or so tolerance previously discussed; however, the receiving device would have to operate at *exactly* 57,600 baud for the communication to be reliable. If the receiving device were to be operating at more than 0.5% above 57,600 baud the devices would fail to communicate properly.

$$\text{Actual Baud Rate} = \frac{\text{M-clock}}{16 \times \text{BR Control Reg. Value}}$$

Figure 9.9: Actual Baud Rate Formula

In many embedded systems the SCI will operate at a single baud rate and not be changed. In those situations, the Baud Rate Control Register can be initialized with a precalculated constant. Some applications, such as a software debugging program or a piece of test or diagnostic equipment may require the flexibility to allow an operator to change the communications rate. A subroutine performing this calculation is presented in Figure 9.10.

Section 9.7: Baud Rate Generator

Before calling the subroutine the D accumulator must be loaded with the desired baud rate. If the subroutine is successful in calculating a new Baud Rate Control Register value for the requested baud rate, the Baud Rate Control Register is updated and a zero is returned in the B accumulator. If an error occurs in the calculation and range check, a non-zero value is returned.

```
;
BSysClock:   equ    SysClock>>4         ; pre-calc SysClock/16.
;
SetSCIBaud:  tfr    d,x                 ; put desired BR in x for ediv.
             ldy    #BSysClock>>16      ; upper 16-bits in y for ediv
             ldd    #BSysClock&$ffff    ; lower 16-bits in d for ediv
             ediv                       ; (SysClock/16)/Desired BR.
             bvc    NoOvf               ; v = 0, no error.
BadBaud:     ldab   #-1                 ; v != 0, quotient > $ffff, error.
             rts                        ; return non zero for error.
;
NoOvf:       fdiv                       ; resolve remainder into fraction
             stx    -2,sp               ; equ to tstx, MSB set? (fraction > 0.5)
             bpl    NoRound             ; no. don't round result up.
             iny                        ; yes. round result up.
NoRound:     cpy    #0                  ; was calc. BR reg value 0?
             beq    BadBaud             ; yes. can't set requested baud rate.
             cpy    #8191               ; greater than max BR reg value?
             bhi    BadBaud             ; yes. can't set requested baud rate.
             sty    SC0BD               ; BR reg value ok. set new baud rate.
             clrb                       ; return a no error indication.
             rts
;
```

Figure 9.10: Subroutine to Calculate Baud Rate Control Register value

In implementing the formula in Figure 9.7, the equ assembler directive is used to divide the SysClock value by 16 and assign it to the symbol BSysClock. Utilizing the assembler to precompute this value at assembly time avoids the additional code and time required to compute the value at run time. Utilizing this technique assumes, of course, that the module clock frequency is the same as the system clock frequency and that the clock frequency does not change. The first three instructions set up the registers properly to perform the 32-bit by 16-bit unsigned divide. The desired baud rate is transferred from D into X and the scaled system clock value is loaded into Y:D 16-bits at a time. After the divide is performed, the condition code register V-bit is checked for division overflow. If the V-bit is set, the quotient of the division was larger than $FFFF. If overflow occurred, the B accumulator is loaded with a non-zero value and the subroutine returns.

To calculate an accurate value for the Baud Rate Control Register, the remainder of the division cannot simply be ignored. Instead, the remainder is used to determine if the integer quotient needs to be rounded up. The fractional divide instruction, `FDIV`, is used to resolve the remainder into a weighted binary fraction (weighted binary fractions are discussed in Chapter 1). If the fractional result is greater than 0.5 ($8000), one is added to the quotient of the 32-bit by 16-bit unsigned divide. Notice that no registers must be set up before the execution of the `FDIV` instruction. The results of the `EDIV` instruction leave the divisor unchanged in the X index register while the remainder is placed in the D accumulator. This is right where the `FDIV` instruction requires the values. The `STX` instruction following the `FDIV` instruction is used in an unusual manner. Normally, a program would NEVER store a value at a negative offset from the stack pointer. Doing so would pose the risk of the value being overwritten if an interrupt occurred after the store operation. In this case, however, we are not really interested in saving the value. Instead we simply want to check the X index register for a value greater than $8000. The `STX` instruction will update the N-bit and Z-bit and clear the V-bit in the condition code register. If the value of X is $8000 or larger, the N-bit will be set indicating a remainder of 0.5 or greater. In this case, one is added to the original quotient in the Y index register rounding the result up.

After the rounding operation, a limit check is made of the resulting quotient to ensure that the calculated Baud Rate Control Register value is valid. The check at the label `NoRound` checks for a result of zero from either the rounding operation or the result of the initial divide. In either case, a result of zero is invalid. Finally, a check is made to ensure that the calculated Baud Rate Control Register value does not exceed the maximum allowable value of 8191.

9.8 SCI INTERRUPTS

Even though there are four conditions that can potentially generate an SCI interrupt, the SCI utilizes only one of the 64 interrupt vectors available on the M68HC12 family. Resolution of the condition causing the interrupt must be determined by an interrupt service dispatch routine. Determining the cause of the interrupt requires examining the interrupt control bits in SCI control Register 2 (`SC0CR2`) and the transmitter and receiver status bits in the SCI Status Register 1 (`SC0SR1`). The upper four bits of `SC0CR2`, shown in Figure 9.11, correspond one for one to the upper four status bits in the `SC0SR1`. Transmitter related interrupts are controlled by the upper two bits of `SC0CR2` while receiver interrupts are controlled by bits four and five. By default, all SCI interrupts are disabled. Individual interrupts are enabled by writing a one to the desired interrupt control bit. An SCI interrupt is generated whenever a bit in the `SC0CR2` is set and the corresponding bit in the `SC0SR1` is set.

Section 9.8: SCI Interrupts

Bit 7	6	5	4	3	2	1	Bit 0	
TIE	TCIE	RIE	ILIE	TE	RE	RWU	SBK	SC0CR2

Bit 7	6	5	4	3	2	1	Bit 0	
TDRE	TC	RDRF	IDLE	OR	NF	FE	PF	SC0SR1

Figure 9.11: SCI control Register 2 (SC0CR2) and SCI Status Register 1 (SC0SR1)

Figure 9.12 contains a generic SCI interrupt dispatch routine that examines the various status and control bits in SC0CR2 and SC0SR1 and calls the appropriate interrupt service routine. At first glance, checking the state of each interrupt control bit before checking the associated status flag may seem redundant. However, this check is necessary for situations where status flags are set but the associated interrupts are disabled. For example, when the transmitter is in the idle state, the TDRE and TC bits are both set. If there are no characters to transmit, the TIE and TCIE bits must remain clear to prevent spurious SCI interrupts from being generated. If only the TDRE and TC bits were checked in the interrupt dispatch routine, the associated interrupt service routines would be executed when there was no data to transmit. While the same situation does not exist with the receiver, there may be situations where a program needs to inhibit one or both receiver interrupts. In this case, the receiver interrupt control bits must each be checked before checking the associated status flag in SC0SR1. If, however, the SCI receiver interrupts are always enabled, a check of the interrupt control flags is unnecessary.

```
;
SCIISR:   brclr SC0CR2,#RIE,CkIdle   ; Chk idle line if Rx int not enabled.
          brset SC0SR1,#RDRF,RxIRQ   ; get data if RDRF set.
ChkIdle:  brclr SC0CR2,#ILIE,CkTxD   ; Chk TxD if idle line int not enabled.
          brset SC0SR1,#IDLE,IdleIRQ ; Svc idle line request if IDLE set.
CkTxD:    brclr SC0CR2,#TIE,CkTC     ; Chk Tx compl. if Tx int not enabled.
          brset SC0SR1,#TDRE,TxIRQ   ; send data if TDRE set.
CkTC:     brclr SC0CR2,#TCIE,NoISRQ  ; if TCIE not set we shouldn't be here.
          brset SC0SR1,#TC,TCIRQ     ; Svc Tx complete if TC is set.
NoSIRQ:   rti                        ; we should never get here.
;
```

Figure 9.12: Generic SCI Interrupt Dispatch Routine

Checking the receiver interrupt status and control bits before those associated with the transmitter was not an arbitrary choice. To avoid the loss of received data, an SCI interrupt dispatch routine should *always* check the receiver control and status flags before checking those associated with the transmitter. Failure to follow this convention will most likely result

Chapter 9: Serial Communications Interface

in receiver overruns when data is received during message transmissions longer than a couple of bytes.

9.9 POLLED SCI EXAMPLE

Operating the SCI in a polled mode is the most common way this peripheral is utilized. The initialization, transmit, and receive routines require only a minimal amount of code as shown in Figure 9.13.

```
;
Baud9600:   equ     SysClock/16/9600    ; have assembler calc BR val for 9600
;
SCIInit:    ldd     #Baud9600           ; get BR value for 9600 baud.
            std     SC0BD               ; initialize the baud rate register.
            ldab    #TE+RE              ; get bit mask for Tx & Rx enable.
            stab    SC0CR2              ; enable Tx & Rx.
            rts                         ; done.
;
getchar:    brclr   SC0SR1,#RDRF,*      ; loop on self until RDRF is set.
            ldab    SC0DRL              ; get received byte.
            rts                         ; return.
;
putchar:    brclr   SC0SR1,#TDRE,*      ; loop on self until TDRE is set.
            stab    SC0DRL              ; send byte.
            rts                         ; return.
;
charavail:  pshb                        ; save b.
            ldab    SC0SR1              ; get contents of SC0SR1
            bitb    #RDRF               ; RDRF bit set?
            pulb                        ; restore b.
            rts                         ; return
;
```

Figure 9.13: Polled Mode SCI Subroutines

The SCI initialization subroutine, SCIInit, configures the SCI for 9600 baud, eight data bits, and no parity. Because none of the SCI features controlled by the SC0CR1 are utilized in this example, the register need not be initialized. Its default value of $00 automatically selects eight data bits, no parity and 'normal' SCI operation. The getchar and putchar subroutines provide only very rudimentary capability to receive and transmit characters using the SCI. While both subroutines are small and very simple, neither one makes good use of the CPU's processing time. Examining the first instruction of each subroutine gives a clear indication why. If the TDRE bit is clear when the putchar subroutine is entered, indicating that both the transmit shift register and the transmit data

Section 9.10: Interrupt Driven SCI Example

register are full, the CPU12 simply executes the BRCLR instruction until the TDRE bit becomes set. During this time, which could be as long as one character time, the CPU12 cannot perform any useful work unless the execution of the BRCLR is suspended in response to an interrupt service request. The getchar subroutine poses a potentially worse situation if it is called before checking for the availability of a character in the receive data register. Once the getchar subroutine is called, it will execute the BRCLR instruction until the RDRF bit is set indicating a character has been received. If a problem were to develop with the transmitting source, a program could become trapped in the getchar subroutine forever. To prevent this from occurring, the charavail subroutine is provided to check the state of the RDRF before getchar is called. If charavail returns with a 'not equal' condition (Z-bit = 0), the RDRF bit is set and a character is available in the receive data register. Even with the drawbacks associated with the getchar and putchar routines presented here, they are adequate for many applications. To overcome these limitations, the SCI must be utilized in a buffered, interrupt driven mode as described in the next section.

9.10 INTERRUPT DRIVEN SCI EXAMPLE

To overcome the CPU utilization problems of operating the SCI in a polled mode, the SCI must be configured so that its interrupt capabilities are used. When configured in this manner, the SCI only requires attention from the CPU12 when the RDRF bit is set indicating a character has been received or when the TDRE bit is set indicating that the transmitter is ready to accept another byte of data. To utilize the interrupt driven method effectively, a circular queue or buffer must be associated with both the transmitter and receiver. Because of the relative difference in operating speeds of the SCI and the CPU12, the queue acts as an elastic buffer providing a software interface to help match this speed difference, while providing an overall improvement in system performance and response. For instance, if the CPU12 is busy performing time critical I/O tasks, an entire message can be received and placed in the buffer where the CPU12 can later retrieve the information when it is not as busy. The same is true for data transmission. An entire message can be placed in the transmit buffer very quickly by the CPU12 allowing it to resume with other tasks. Each time the TDRE bit is set, the transmit interrupt service routine removes a character from the transmit buffer and writes it to the transmit data register until the buffer is empty.

In addition to the transmit and receive queues themselves, several other pieces of information are needed for management of each queue. This information is required by the software to keep track of the next available storage location in the queue, the next piece of data to be removed from the queue, and a way to determine if the queue is full or empty. Rather than utilize 16-bit pointers to manage the queues, the example presented here employs four one byte variables. RxIn, RxOut, TxIn, and TxOut are used in conjunction with the 8-bit accumulator offset indexed addressing to access data in the transmit and receive queues. In addition, two one byte variables, RxBAvail and

Chapter 9: Serial Communications Interface

`TxBAvail`, are used to keep track of the number of bytes available in each queue. When the value in each of these variables is equal to the size of the queue, the buffer is empty. When the value is zero, the queue is full. Using a byte for the index does not allow this example to support queue sizes greater than 255 bytes. However, with a limited amount of on-chip RAM, this should not pose severe restrictions for most applications.

Figure 9.14 shows the declarations for the queue management variables and the queues themselves. As shown, both the transmit and receive queues are 32 bytes in length. This size was an arbitrary choice for this example. The proper queue size for a particular application will depend on the expected length of messages transmitted and received. If the selected queue size is too small, the routines essentially will behave the same as the polled SCI example. Once the transmit queue fills, the CPU12 will have to wait until a character is transmitted before the next character can be placed in the queue. If the receive queue is too small, there will be a risk that received characters will be lost if the queue becomes full and CPU12 does not remove some of the data before the next piece of data is received. Conversely, picking a queue size larger than necessary does not have a detrimental effect on program performance or loss of data. However, it will consume the valuable on-chip memory unnecessarily. If uncertain on the exact queue size for a particular application, it is best to make it larger than necessary. Note that the transmit and receive queues do not have to be the same size, nor is their size required to be an even power of two.

```
;
RxBufSize:  equ   32            ; receive queue size.
TxBufSize:  equ   32            ; transmit queue size.
;
RxBuff:     ds    RxBufSize     ; allocate receive queue storage.
TxBuff:     ds    TxBufSize     ; allocate transmit queue storage.
RxIn:       ds    1             ; next available location in the Rx queue.
RxOut:      ds    1             ; next char. to be removed from the Rx queue
TxIn:       ds    1             ; next available location in the Tx queue
TxOut:      ds    1             ; next char. to be sent from the Tx buffer.
RxBAvail:   ds    1             ; number of bytes left in the Rx queue.
TxBAvail:   ds    1             ; number of bytes left in the Tx queue.
;
```

Figure 9.14: Interrupt Driven SCI Data Declarations

The `SCIInit` subroutine in Figure 9.15 is similar to that of the polled example with some obvious additions. When called, the D accumulator should contain the value to be stored in the baud rate register. This value can be obtained by loading the D accumulator with a precalculated constant or it can be calculated by a subroutine similar to the `SetSCIBaud` subroutine presented earlier in this chapter.

Section 9.10: Interrupt Driven SCI Example

```
;
SCIInit: std     SC0BD           ; initialize the baud rate register.
         clr     RxIn            ; set Rx queue index values to 0.
         clr     RxOut
         clr     TxIn            ; set Tx queue index values to 0.
         clr     TxOut
         ldab    #RxBufSize      ; init number of available Rx
         stab    RxBAvail        ; queue bytes to RxBuffSize.
         ldab    #TxBufSize      ; init number of available Tx
         stab    TxBAvail        ; queue bytes to TxBuffSize.
         ldab    #TE+RE+RIE      ; get bit mask for Tx, Rx & Rx interrupt.
         stab    SC0CR2          ; enable Tx & Rx & Rx interrupts.
         rts                     ; done.
;
```

Figure 9.15: Interrupt Driven SCI Initialization

After initializing the baud rate register, the transmit and receive queue index values are set to zero placing the logical start of the queue at the physical start of the memory area allocated for the queue. In reality, these values could be initialized to any value between zero and the queue size minus one as long as RxIn is equal to RxOut and TxIn is equal to TxOut. The RxBAvail and TxBAvail variables are initialized to the size of the receive and transmit queues respectively, indicating empty queues. Finally a value is written to SC0CR2 that enables the transmitter, receiver, and receiver interrupts; however, transmitter interrupts are *not* enabled at this point. Unlike the receiver interrupts, which may be enabled at all times, the transmit interrupt may only be enabled when the transmit queue contains characters to be sent out the SCI. Enabling transmit interrupts at initialization would immediately cause a transmitter interrupt even though the transmit queue is empty. This is because the TDRE bit is set whenever the SCI transmitter is in an idle state.

The SCI interrupt dispatch routine, presented in Figure 9.16, is a pared down version of the SCI interrupt dispatch routine presented in Figure 9.12. It could be argued that the two BRCLR instructions that check the state of the RIE and TIE interrupt enable bits are not required in this example because only one receive and one transmit interrupt source are enabled. However, it is a good idea to leave these checks in the dispatch routine in case it is modified to include the idle line or transmit complete interrupt.

```
;
SCIIRQ:      brclr SC0CR2,#RIE,ChkRxInt ; Rx interrupts enabled?
             brset SC0SR1,#RDRF,RxIRQ   ; yes. RDRF = 1 service Rx ints.
ChkRxInts:   brclr SC0CR2,#TIE,NoSCIInt ; Tx interrupts enabled?
             brset SC0SR1,#TDRE,TxIRQ   ; yes. TDRE = 1, service Tx ints.
NoSCIInt:    rti                        ; return w/o any action.
;
```

Figure 9.16: Interrupt Driven SCI Interrupt Dispatch routine

The receive interrupt service routine, RxIRQ shown in Figure 9.17, basically performs two functions. It removes a character from the SCI receive data register and, if there is space available, places it in the receive queue. It also adjusts the RxIn index to point to the next available location in the queue. Notice that the test for available queue space is performed at the start of the RxIRQ service routine by checking the value of RxBAvail. If the queue is full, the received data is read from the receive data register so that the RDRF bit causing the interrupt is cleared, but nothing is done with the data. This condition, known as a *software* overrun error, will occur if the main program does not call the getchar routine often enough to remove characters from the queue. If this condition occurs often, it is a sign that the receive queue is not large enough or that there is a bottleneck elsewhere in the program. Utilizing the interrupt driven receive method presented here, a *hardware* overrun error, indicated by the OR bit in the SC0SR1 register being set, should not occur unless interrupts are disabled for more than one character time.

If space is available in the queue, the character is read from the receive data register, placed in the queue, and the queue index is incremented. If the increment operation causes the index to point past the physical end of the queue storage area, the value of the index is initialized to zero to 'wrap' the pointer around to the start of the storage area. Finally, an RTI instruction resumes program execution at the point it was interrupted.

Note that the receive interrupt routine does not report any errors that may have occurred as each piece of data is received. If desired, this capability could easily be added to the interrupt service routine. Each time a character is received, the value of the SC0SR1 register could be read and the upper four bits masked off. This value would be OR'd with the result from the previously received character and stored in a variable that could be examined by other parts of the program. When adding such a feature, remember that the read of the SC0SR1 register must occur *before* the data is read from the receive data register. Otherwise, any of the error flags that might have been set will be cleared.

Section 9.10: Interrupt Driven SCI Example

```
;
RxIRQ:      tst     RxBAvail    ; any room left in the Rx queue?
            beq     Buffull     ; no. just throw the character away.
            dec     RxBAvail    ; yes. there'll be one less now.
            ldx     #RxBuff     ; point to the physical start of the Rx queue.
            ldaa    RxIn        ; get index for the next avail queue location.
            ldab    SC0DRL      ; get the received character.
            stab    a,x         ; place it in the queue.
            inca                ; next available queue location.
            cmpa    #RxBufSize  ; wrap around to start of queue?
            blo     NoRxWrap    ; no. just update the index.
            clra                ; yes. start at begining of queue.
NoRxWrap:   staa    RxIn        ; update the next avail. queue location index.
            rti                 ; return from the SCI Rx interrupt.
;
Buffull:    ldab    SC0DRL      ; queue full. get character & throw it away.
            rti                 ; return.
;
```

Figure 9.17: SCI Receive Interrupt service Routine

The `getchar` subroutine provides the ability to retrieve data from the receive queue one byte at a time. Before attempting to retrieve data from the receive queue, a check is performed to see if the queue contains any data. If no data is available, the subroutine simply waits until a byte is received and placed in the queue. While this behavior may seem less than desirable, a separate subroutine, `SCIGetBuf`, presented in Figure 9.18, allows a program to check for the availability of data in the receive queue before calling the `getchar` subroutine. This allows a program to continue to perform other functions if the queue is empty. There may be times, however, when a program cannot continue execution until it receives some required data. In this case, the behavior of the `getchar` subroutine provides the required functionality.

```
;
SCIGetBuf:  ldab    #RxBufSize  ; are there any characters in the Rx queue?
            subb    RxBAvail
            rts                 ; return number available.
;
```

Figure 9.18: `SCIGetBuf` Subroutine

The remainder of the `getchar` subroutine behaves similar to the receive interrupt service routine except that it removes a character from the queue at an offset defined by the `RxOut` variable. After removing the data, `RxOut` is updated to point to the next available byte in the queue and one is added to `RxBAvail`. Notice that SCI receiver interrupts are not disabled during the execution of the `getchar` subroutine allowing an SCI receiver interrupt to be executed, placing new data in the receive queue. To allow this flexibility, both routines must be written in a manner as to minimize the interaction between any variables manipulated by both routines. Examining the listings of `RxIRQ` and `getchar` reveals that `RxBAvail` is the only variable manipulated by both routines. Observe in the `getchar` subroutine that the value of `RxBAvail` is not modified until the very end of the subroutine after the character has been removed from the queue and the queue index has been adjusted. Only one condition can occur resulting in data loss that could be prevented by disabling SCI receiver interrupts during the execution of the `getchar` subroutine. Suppose that the receive queue is full when the `getchar` subroutine is called. If `getchar` is interrupted by a receiver interrupt after a character has been removed from the receive queue but *before* the `RxBAvail` has been updated, a software overrun error would occur. If receiver interrupts were disabled until after `RxBAvail` had been updated, the pending interrupt would be serviced and the received character properly placed in the queue. If the receive queue is properly sized for an application this condition should not occur.

```
;
getchar:    pshx                        ; save the registers we'll use.
            psha
RxChk:      ldab    #RxBufSize          ; any characters available?
            subb    RxBAvail
            beq     RxChk               ; no. just wait until some are.
            ldx     #RxBuff             ; point to the physical start of Rx queue.
            ldaa    RxOut               ; get index to next avail char in Rx queue.
            ldab    a,x                 ; get the character.
            inca                        ; point to the next location in the queue.
            cmpa    #RxBufSize          ; reached the end of the queue?
            blo     NogcWrap            ; no.
            clra                        ; yes. wrap to the start.
NogcWrap:   staa    RxOut               ; update the queue index.
            inc     RxBAvail            ; removed a char from queue, 1 more's avail.
            pula                        ; restore what we saved.
            pulx
            rts                         ; return.
;
```

Figure 9.19: `getchar` Subroutine

The transmit interrupt service routine is very similar to the receive interrupt service routine except that data is removed from the transmit queue and written to the SCI transmit data register. In addition to managing the `TxOut` queue index and the `TxBAvail` variables, the transmit interrupt service routine has one additional responsibility not required by the receive interrupt service routine. At the end of the `TxIRQ` routine the transmit queue must be checked for an empty condition. If the queue is empty, SCI transmitter interrupts

Section 9.10: Interrupt Driven SCI Example

must be disabled to prevent an interrupt from occurring the next time TDRE is set. The method used to detect an empty transmit queue is slightly different that that used by the getchar subroutine to detect an empty receive queue. Rather than checking the value of TxBAvail to see if its value matches the size of the transmit queue, the value of the TxOut queue index is compared to the TxIn queue index value. The only time these two values will be equal *after* a character has been removed from the transmit queue by the TxIRQ routine is when the queue has become empty. This method was chosen simply because the value of TxOut is already in the A accumulator. Checking the value of TxBAvail would have required an additional instruction to load the value into one of the accumulators.

```
;
TxIRQ:     ldx     #TxBuff         ; point to physical start of the Tx queue.
           ldaa    TxOut           ; get index for the next character to send.
           ldab    a,x             ; get the data.
           stab    SC0DRL          ; send it.
           inca                    ; advance to next character to send.
           cmpa    #TxBufSize      ; reached the end of the queue?
           blo     NoTxWrap        ; no.
           clra                    ; yes. wrap to the start.
NoTxWrap:  staa    TxOut           ; update the queue index.
           inc     TxBAvail        ; one more byte available in the queue.
           cmpa    TxIn            ; TxIn = TxOut?
           bne     TxRTI           ; no. more characters to send.
           bclr    SC0CR2,#TIE     ; yes. queue is empty turn off TDRE ints.
TxRTI:     rti                     ; return.
;
```

Figure 9.20: Transmit Interrupt Service Routine

The final routine presented in this example is the putchar subroutine which is used to place data into the transmit queue. A test is performed at the start of the routine to see if any space is available in the queue. If not, putchar remains in a loop checking the value of TxBAvail until it becomes non-zero. After updating the values of TxIn and TxBAvail and just before restoring the registers used by the subroutine, the TIE bit is set to enable SCI transmitter interrupts. If the TDRE bit is set when the BSET instruction is executed, an SCI transmitter interrupt will be generated immediately causing the character placed in the queue to be transmitted even before the putchar subroutine returns. This situation occurs when a byte is placed in an empty queue.

```
;
putchar:    pshx                        ; save the registers we'll use.
            psha
TxChk:      tst     TxBAvail            ; Any room left in the Tx queue?
            beq     TxChk               ; no. just wait here till it is.
            ldx     #TxBuff             ; point to physical start of the Tx queue.
            ldaa    TxIn                ; get the index to the next available spot.
            stab    a,x                 ; put the character in.
            inca                        ; point to the next available spot.
            cmpa    #TxBufSize          ; go past the end of the queue?
            blo     NopcWrap            ; no.
            clra                        ; yes. wrap around to the start.
NopcWrap:   staa    TxIn                ; update the queue index
            dec     TxBAvail            ; one less byte available in the Tx queue.
            bset    SC0CR2,#TIE         ; enable transmitter interrupts.
            pula                        ; restore what we saved.
            pulx
            rts                         ; return
;
```

Figure 9.21: putchar Subroutine

Questions/Exercises

9.1 Which M68HC11 parts have an SCI nearly identical to the SCI on the M68HC12? How compatible are software drivers written for these M68HC11 family members.

9.2 What hardware handshaking signals are supported by the M68HC12 SCI?

9.3 How do the Port S data direction register bits effect the TxD and RxD pins when the SCI transmitter and receiver are enabled?

9.4 What is different about the reduced drive and pull-up control bits on Port S?

9.5 What other special configuration options are available for the TxD and RxD pins?

9.6 What data format is utilized by the SCI? What are its characteristics?

9.7 Where in the data stream is the parity bit placed?

9.8 What special data stream is the SCI capable of sending?

9.9 How long does a program have to read a received character after it has been transferred to the receive data register?

Section 9.10: Interrupt Driven SCI Example

9.10 At what speed does the SCI receive clock operate? What are the advantages or disadvantages of using this rate?

9.11 How many times is each bit sampled? Which sample is used as the received bit value?

9.12 How many error conditions are detected by the receiver? Name each one and give a brief description of the error condition.

9.13 What sequence of operations is required to clear the receiver error flags?

9.14 At what speed does the SCI transmit clock operate?

9.15 What status bit should be checked before writing to the transmit data register?

9.16 What occurs if the transmitter is disabled while the SCI is transmitting a character?

9.17 What occurs when data is written to the transmit data register with the transmitter disabled?

9.18 What is he most common application for the SCI single-wire operating mode?

9.19 On what is the baud rate generator based? What are its advantages?

9.20 What frequency clock is used as an input to the baud rate generator?

9.21 What limits the highest standard baud rate that can be generated using a given clock frequency as an input to the baud rate generator?

9.22 What is the maximum value that may be written to the baud rate register? What baud rate would this produce on an MC68HC912B32 with an E-clock frequency of 8.0 MHz?

9.23 What is the minimum value that may be written to the baud rate register? What baud rate would this produce on an MC68HC812A4 with an E-clock frequency of 2.0 MHz?

9.24 How many interrupt vectors are utilized by the SCI?

9.25 How many conditions can generate an interrupt? What are they?

Chapter 9: Serial Communications Interface

9.26 Why is an SCI interrupt dispatch routine necessary? Which interrupts should be check for first? Why?

9.27 What are the advantages of operating the SCI in a polled mode? What are the disadvantages?

9.28 What are the advantages of operating the SCI in an interrupt driven mode? What are the disadvantages?

9.29 What precaution is necessary when initializing the SCI for operation in the interrupt driven mode?

9.30 What condition occurs if the receive queue is full and another character is received before some of the data is removed from the queue?

9.31 What might cause a hardware overrun error to occur when operating the SCI in the interrupt driven mode?

9.32 What behavior is exhibited if the interrupt driven getchar subroutine is called with no characters in the receive queue.

9.33 What function must the transmit interrupt service routine perform when the transmit queue becomes empty? What might happen if this action is not taken?

9.34 What must be done when data is placed in the queue by the putchar subroutine?

Chapter 10 SERIAL PERIPHERAL INTERFACE

The Serial Peripheral Interface, or SPI, is a synchronous serial interface allowing high speed communication with peripherals or even other microcontrollers equipped with an SPI interface. Connected peripherals can range in complexity from simple CMOS shift registers to a multi-megabit Flash memory device. Due to the fact that the SPI system is a synchronous system, data transfers depend on a clock signal provided to the slave devices by the SPI master. Because data is transferred into or out of the SPI system on the edges of the supplied clock, reliable data transfers are dependent upon the electrical integrity of both the clock and data signals. This characteristic, for the most part, makes the SPI system unsuitable for communications with peripherals over long distances. In general, the SPI system is designed for communication with devices residing on the same printed circuit board, however, with careful system design and printed circuit board layout, it can be used to communicate with several boards within the same system.

The programmability of the clock and idle state of the data line make the SPI directly compatible with numerous standard SPI peripherals available from various manufacturers. Even if an SPI peripheral requires a non-standard clock and/or data format, the SPI pin driver logic is flexible enough to generate the required format through direct manipulation of the pins associated with the SPI clock and/or data lines. Data rates as high as the E-clock frequency divided by two are possible when the SPI is configured as a master or slave.

The SPI is actually part of the Serial Interface module on the M68HC912B32. As shown in Figure 10.1, the Serial Interface module also contains a Serial Communications Interface (SCI) and general purpose I/O in addition to the SPI.

Section 10.1: Physical Interface

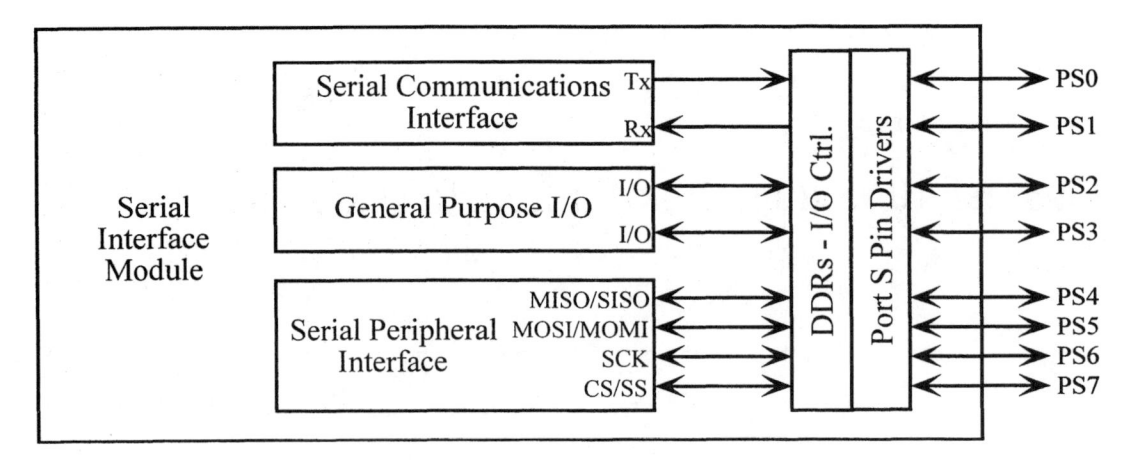

Figure 10.1: Serial Interface Module Block Diagram

10.1 PHYSICAL INTERFACE

As shown in the block diagram, the SPI physical interface consists of four pins. When the SPI is enabled, all pins defined as inputs by the selected configuration will be inputs regardless of the state of the Port S data direction register bits. However, all pins that are defined as outputs will be outputs only if the data direction register bits associated with that pin contain a one. Any pin whose SPI function is defined as an output but has its associated data direction register bit equal to zero may be used as a general purpose input.

Two of the pins, PS4 and PS5, are associated with the transmission and reception of SPI data. The function and characteristics of these pins vary depending on the SPI operating mode and the various options available for the Port S pins. When configured as a master, pin PS6 becomes the SPI clock output providing the synchronous transfer clock to all connected slave devices. When configured as a slave, pin PS6 becomes the SPI clock input requiring a clock signal from an SPI master to complete the serial data transfer. Remember that when the SPI is configured as a master, port pin PS6 *must* be configured as an output for the SPI system to operate.

⚠ **M68HC12 Difference from the M68HC11**

The fourth port pin, PS7, associated with the SPI is the Chip Select/Slave Select (CS/SS) function. In addition to its normal function as the Slave Select input, this pin has the option of being configured as a Chip Select *output* when the SPI is operated in master mode. The CS/SS output is enabled if the SSOE bit in the SP0CR1 is set and the associated Port S data direction register bit is set. Each time the master initiates an SPI transfer, the

CS/SS output pin is asserted low one half clock cycle before the first clock edge and is negated one half clock cycle after the last clock edge of the transfer. Because the CS/SS pin is negated between each 8-bit transfer, this feature will probably not be compatible with peripherals requiring data transfers of more than 8-bits. However, this feature is quite useful when two M68HC12's are interconnected in a master/slave arrangement where each device can be a master or a slave. If the master and slave M68HC12's have their Clock Phase (CPHA) control bit configured with a value of zero, the slave microcontroller *must* have its Slave Select line negated between each 8-bit transfer. In this case, the CS/SS output can be used to automatically perform this function.

As with other I/O pins associated with on-chip peripherals, the Port S pins provide the option of active pull-ups and/or reduced drive capability. However, unlike some of the other peripheral ports where the active pull-up and reduced drive options must be enabled or disabled for all pins on a port, the Port S pin control logic provides the ability to enable and disable these options for the SCI, SPI, and General Purpose I/O pins individually. As shown in Figure 10.2 the Pull-up and Reduced Drive (PURDS) Control Register for Port S provides three control bits for each option. The PUPS2 and RDPS2 bits control the active pull-ups and reduced drive options, respectively, for the four pins associated with the SPI. As with other I/O ports, if a pin is configured as an output, the active pull-ups, if enabled, are automatically disconnected from the I/O pin.

Bit 7	6	5	4	3	2	1	Bit 0
0	**RDPS2**	RDPS1	RDPS0	0	**PUPS2**	PUPS1	PUPS0

Figure 10.2: Pull-up and Reduced Drive (PURDS) for Port S Control Register

In addition to the active pull-up and reduced drive options, the four SPI port pins may be configured for Wired-Or or open drain operation. When configured in this manner the gate signal of the P-channel output device, which is connected between the output pin and VDD, is disabled so that the drain of the N-channel is effectively the only output device connected to the pin. In reality, because the P-channel device is still physically connected to the pin, an inherent diode to VDD is still present. For this reason, the open drain configured outputs cannot be connected to a supply source higher than VDD. To allow open drain output pins to assume a logic level of one when a one is written to the associated data register, a current limiting pull-up resistor must be connected between the output pin and VDD. The size of the pull-up resistor should be kept above 3K• to insure that a valid logic zero can be attained when the pin is driven low. Note that the open drain configuration is available even when the pins are configured as general purpose outputs.

⚠ **M68HC12 Difference from the M68HC11**

Section 10.2: Operating Modes

10.2 OPERATING MODES

The SPI supports two basic operating modes for data transfer. The 'Normal' mode, most familiar to M68HC11 developers, utilizes the Master Out/Slave In (MOSI) and the Master In/Slave Out (MISO) pins to perform full duplex synchronous data transfers. In this mode, a data bit is shifted out of the master and into the slave on one clock edge then out of the slave and into the master on the opposite clock edge.

The new mode added to the M68HC12's SPI is the bidirectional mode utilizing a single pin for transferring data to and from peripheral devices. When bidirectional mode is selected, the MOSI pin becomes the serial data I/O (MOMI) when configured as a master and the MISO pin becomes the serial data I/O (SOSI) when configured as a slave. The direction of the data transfer is determined by the corresponding data direction bit of the associated pin. If the pin is configured as an output, the serial data is driven out on the corresponding pin and is also used as the input to the SPI shift register. If the pin is configured as an input, the output of the shift register is discarded while the data applied to the external pin is clocked into the shift register. The master and slave pin connections for the two operating modes are shown in Figure 10.3 a - d.

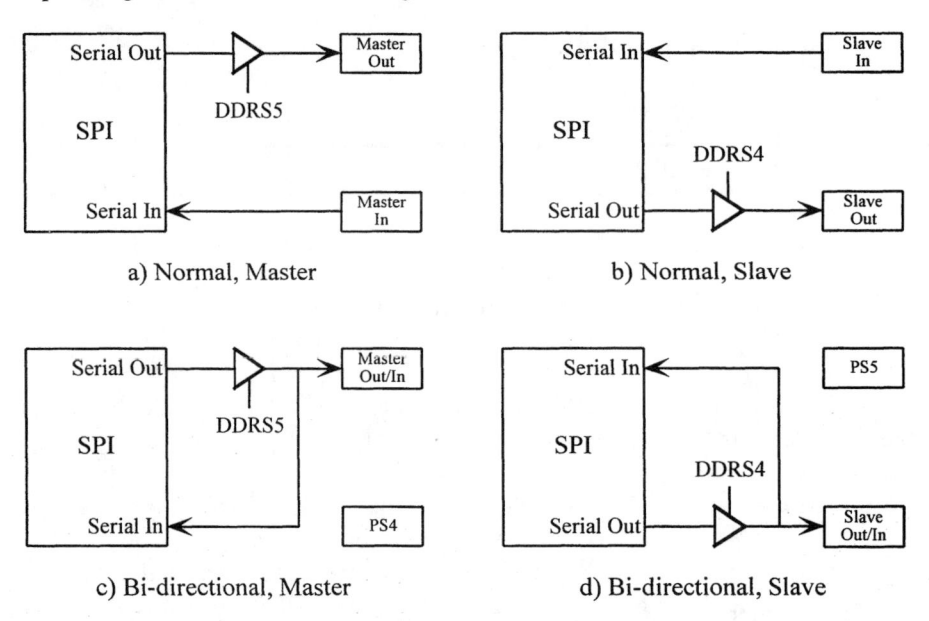

a) Normal, Master

b) Normal, Slave

c) Bi-directional, Master

d) Bi-directional, Slave

Figure 10.3: SPI Operating Modes

In bidirectional mode, the function of the CS/SS pin and the SCK pin are unchanged. When configured as a master, the SCK pin supplies the synchronizing clock signal if the associated data direction register is programmed as an output. When configured as a slave, the SCK pin is always an input which receives the synchronizing clock signal from the master. The CS/SS pin may be an input or an output when the SPI is configured as a master and is always an input when configured as a slave.

10.3 Data Transfer Format

The SPI has two fundamental data transfer formats controlled by the CPHA bit in the SP0CR1 control register, shown in Figure 10.4. In addition, when configured as a master, the state of the clock pin can be configured to assume either a logic one or a logic zero state when not transferring data. When the CPOL bit in the SP0CR1 control register has a value of zero, the SCK line will remain zero when idle. When CPOL has a value of one, the SCK line will be one when not transmitting data. A third option, controlled by the LSBF bit in the SP0CR1 register allows the selection of shifting out either the most significant or least significant bit first. The default value of the LSBF bit is zero causing the most significant bit to be shifted out first. This is the format used by most peripherals. When communicating with other microcontrollers the clock phase, polarity, and the bit shift direction should be configured identically for both the master and slave. When connecting to standard peripherals, the state of the CPHA, CPOL and LSBF bits will depend on the transfer format supported by the device manufacturer. However, the flexibility provided by these control bit settings will allow the M68HC12's SPI to work with most existing SPI type peripherals.

Bit 7	6	5	4	3	2	1	Bit 0
SPIE	SPE	SWOM	MSTR	CPOL	CPHA	SSOE	LSBF

Figure 10.4: SPI 0 Control Register 1 (SP0CR1)

Figure 10.5 and 10.6 are basic timing diagrams illustrating the two data transfer formats with the SPI configured as a master. The key to understanding the difference between the two data transfer formats lies in the examination of the beginning of each transfer. The first transfer format analyzed is presented in Figure 10.5. Notice that as soon as the slave's select line is asserted, the slave places the most significant bit of its shift register on the MISO pin. In this case, because the timing diagram depicts the master automatically asserting the slave's select line using CS/SS pin, this occurs coincident with the beginning of the first SCK clock cycle. If, however, the slave's chip select line is asserted earlier, the slave would drive the MISO line with the shift register's most significant bit from that point until the end of the first SCK clock cycle. The master, on the other hand, waits until the beginning of the first SCK clock cycle to place the most significant bit of its shift register on the MOSI pin. Notice that this is exactly one half SCK cycle before the first clock edge appears on the SCK line.

Section 10.3: Data Transfer Format

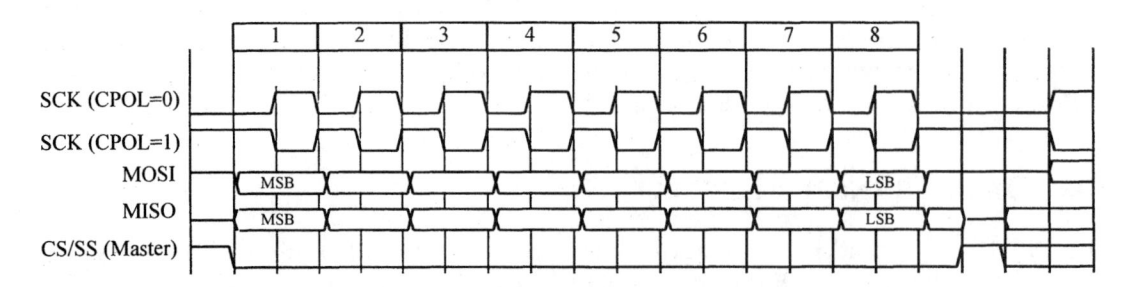

Figure 10.5: SPI Transfer for `CPHA = 0`, `LSBF = 0`, `SSOE = 1`

Because the master and slave's most significant data bit are placed on the MOSI and MISO pins prior to the first clock edge on the SCK pin, the first clock edge causes the data to be latched into the master and slave's shift register simultaneously. The second clock edge of the cycle is utilized to shift the contents of the master and slave shift register by one bit, placing the next data bit on the MOSI and MISO pins. This pattern of *latch* and then *shift* is repeated for all eight clock cycles. Observe that after the final edge of the last clock cycle, the slave drives the MISO pin with data until its select line is negated. Typically, this data will be the most significant bit of the received byte, however, the value placed on the MISO pin will depend on the design of the connected peripheral device.

For M68HC12's that are configured as slaves, the transfer format selected when the CPHA control bit equals zero requires that the CS/SS line be negated and reasserted between each successive transfer. Failure to follow this procedure will prevent the slave from successfully writing a new value to the slave's SPI data register. Writes to the SPI data register when the CS/SS line is low are ignored and causes the Write Collision (WCOL) status bit in the SPI Status Register to be set.

Figure 10.6 presents the timing for the data transfer format when the CPHA control bit has a value of one. Again the transfer begins with the assertion of the CS/SS pin. However, instead of the slave placing the shift register's most significant bit on the MISO pin, the data appearing on the pin, though undefined, is typically the least significant bit of the previously transmitted byte. It is not until the first clock edge of the first SCK cycle that the most significant bit of the master and slave's shift registers are placed on the MOSI and MISO lines, respectively. The second edge of the clock cycle is used to simultaneously latch the data into the master and slave's shift register. This pattern of *shift* and then *latch*, which is is repeated for all eight clock cycles, is just the opposite of the transfer format shown in Figure 10.5. If the master automatically asserts the slave's select line, the CS/SS pin is asserted exactly one half SCK cycle before the first clock edge appears on the SCK line.

When the CPHA control bit has a value of one, M68HC12's configured as slaves are not required to have their slave select lines negated and reasserted between successive transfers. Although it will not improve the maximum data transfer rate, this format is sometimes preferred in systems having a single fixed master and a single slave microcontroller driving the MISO line.

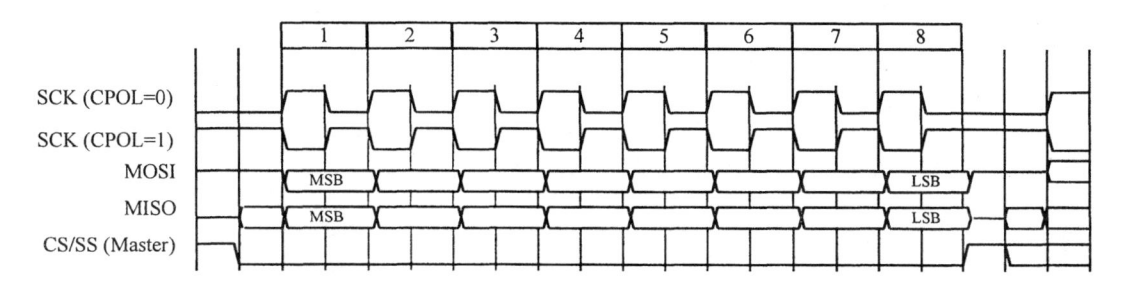

Figure 10.6: SPI Transfer for `CPHA = 1`, `LSBF = 0`, `SSOE = 1`

It is important to note for both transfer formats that there is a delay between sequential SPI transfers. When configured as a master, the delay is one half of an SCK cycle. This delay can be observed by the negation of the CS/SS pin when it is being used to automatically assert the slave's select line. If the CS/SS pin is not being used, the delay can be observed on the SCK pin where the clock line will remain in the idle state for a total of three, half clock periods. The SCK idle time includes not only the sequential delay transfer time, but also the half cycle clock idle time preceding the transfer and the half clock idle time after the last clock edge of the transfer. Because of this delay, the maximum sustained data transfer rate is somewhat less than the selected SCK frequency.

When configuring the SPI for various peripherals, it is important to carefully examine the peripheral's data sheet to determine the necessary transfer format and clock polarity. In some cases it may be necessary to change the SPI configuration between transfers to accommodate a mix of peripherals on the same SPI bus. In addition to the transfer format and clock polarity, each data sheet must be examined for the peripheral's timing requirements and chip select requirements. While the automatic assertion of the CS/SS pin by the SCI master reduces the requirements of a peripheral's software driver, it will probably not be useful with the vast majority of peripherals, especially those requiring data transfers longer than eight bits. In these cases, the peripheral's select line must be asserted by software at the beginning of a multi-byte transfer and negated by software at the completion of the transfer.

Because the M68HC12's SPI only supports transfers in multiples of eight bits, it may not accommodate some peripherals in a straightforward manner. In these cases it may be necessary to utilize a combination of SPI data transfers and software "bit banging" techniques to accommodate such peripherals. One such family of devices is Atmel's DataFlash memory devices. These serially accessed Flash devices require an additional clock pulse between the transmitted command phase and the reception of data from the memory device. Because all that is required is an additional clock pulse (the data supplied by the

Section 10.4: Bit Rate Selection

master during the clock pulse is ignored) the state of the CPOL bit can simply be toggled to produce the extra clock pulse. After the application of the additional clock pulse, the SPI can be used for normal data transfers.

Other devices requiring data transfers that are not an integer multiple of eight bits may require additional software for proper communication. In some cases, when peripherals require data transfers other than an even multiple of eight bits, it is sometimes possible to send more than the required number of bits. Many times, because these peripherals are made to be cascaded, they will ignore all but the most recent bits sent with the extra bits simply being ignored. In some cases, however, additional clock and/or data bits may alter the way in which the remaining bits are interpreted. In these cases, the SPI could be used to perform the data transfers up to the last full set of eight bits. But, the remaining bits would have to be transferred by disabling the SPI system and directly manipulating the associated port pins to generate the proper clock and data signals.

To summarize, the selection of the data transfer format and clock polarity depend upon the exact requirements of the attached peripheral. However, as a general guideline, slave peripherals placing their first data bit on the MISO line when the slave's select line is asserted are generally candidates for using the transfer format defined when the CPHA control bit is zero. On the other hand, peripherals requiring a clock edge before placing their first data bit on the MISO line will most likely require the transfer format defined when the CPHA control bit is one.

⚠ **M68HC12 Difference from the M68HC11**

10.4 BIT RATE SELECTION

The SPI clock rate selection is controlled by the lower three bits in the SPI Baud Rate Register (SP0BR). These three bits can select one of eight data rates ranging from the E-clock divided by two to the E-clock divided by 256. This provides four more transfer rate selections than the M68HC11 family's SPI module. The SP0BR may be read or written at any time and defaults to a value of zero selecting an SCK rate of one half the E-clock. While this allows the accommodation of peripherals with varying clock rate requirements, caution must be exercised when changing the baud rate between SPI transfers. From the timing diagrams in Figures 10.5 and 10.6 it can be seen that the SPI transfer does not actually end until one half SCK after the last SCK edge. Changing the bit rate before the transfer actually ends could cause timing problems that could result in unreliable data transfers. The table in Figure 10.7 shows the eight bit rates available for both a 4.0 MHz and 8.0 MHz E-clock operating frequency.

SPR2	SPR1	SPR0	E-Clock Divisor	SCK Frequency for E-Clock of 4.0 MHz	SCK Frequency for E-Clock of 8.0 MHz
0	0	0	÷ 2	2.0 MHz	4.0 MHz
0	0	1	÷ 4	1.0 MHz	2.0 MHz
0	1	0	÷ 8	500 KHz	1.0 MHz
0	1	1	÷ 16	250 KHz	500 KHz
1	0	0	÷ 32	125 KHz	250 KHz
1	0	1	÷ 64	62.5 KHz	125 KHz
1	1	0	÷ 128	31.3 KHz	62.5 KHz
1	1	1	÷ 256	15.6 KHz	31.3 KHz

Figure 10.7: SPI SCK Rate Selection

10.5 ACCESSING TRANSMITTED AND RECEIVED DATA

The SPI utilizes a single 8-bit register for both transmitted and received data much like the lower 8-bits of the SCI data register. Reads of this register are double buffered, allowing another transfer to start before the received data is read. Writes to the SPI data register, however, cause data to be latched directly to the shift register. Attempting to write to the SPI data register while a transfer is in progress causes the write to be ignored in order to avoid corruption of the transmitted or received data. This condition, known as a write collision, causes the WCOL bit in the SPI Status Register (SP0SR) to be set. The setting of the WCOL bit will not cause an SPI interrupt if interrupts are enabled, but the bit will remain set until the completion of the transmission in progress. It can then be read and appropriate action taken by the SPI driver software. The WCOL bit is cleared by reading the SP0SR register followed by a read or write access of the SPI data register. Although write collisions can occur when an M68HC12 is configured as a master or a slave, a write collision error is normally found in a slave because it has no control over when a master begins a transfer. Because a master initiates all SPI transfers, the software should always know when a transfer is in progress. Generally the only reason a write collision error would occur on a master is faulty software design.

Bit 7	6	5	4	3	2	1	Bit 0
SPIF	WCOL	0	MODF	0	0	0	0

Figure 10.8: SPI Status Register (SP0SR)

Section 10.5: Accessing Transmitted and Received Data

The completion of an SPI transfer is indicated when the SPIF bit in the `SP0SR` register is set. Because the SPI receiver is double buffered, the master may initiate a new transfer as soon as the SPIF bit becomes set. After initiating the new transfer, both the master and slave can read the previously received data. When performing successive transfers using high SCK rates, care must be taken to ensure that the slave microcontroller has enough time to write a new value into its data register before the next transfer begins.

When configured as a master, the SPIF flag is always set at the end of the eighth clock cycle. However, when the SPI is configured as a slave, the slave's SPIF bit is set by the last clock edge of the eighth clock cycle. When the CPHA bit is equal to one, the last clock edge of the transfer occurs in the middle of the eighth clock cycle, as shown in Figure 10.6. This causes the slave's SPIF flag to be set approximately one half SCK cycle earlier than the master's SPIF flag, giving the slave some additional time to load the next byte into the SPI data register. Even if the master initiates another transfer as soon as its SPIF flag is set, the one half SCK cycle delay inserted between transfers provides time for the slave to perform its required tasks. At lower SCK transfer rates, this additional time should provide adequate opportunity for the slave to preload its shift register with a new value before the master initiates a new transfer.

When the CPHA bit is equal to zero, the end of the of the eighth clock cycle coincides with the last clock edge, as shown in Figure 10.5. In this case, the SPIF flag for the master and slave microcontroller are set at virtually the same time leaving only the half clock transfer delay for the slave to load a new value into its SPI shift register. However, there is another potential problem that is sometimes overlooked but can easily be solved by proper software design. Remember that even though the slave's SPIF status bit is set at the end of the eighth clock cycle, the slave's select line must be negated and reasserted before a new value can be written to the SPI data register. If the master is using its CS/SS line to automatically assert and negate the slave's select line, the select line will be negated at the same time its SPIF bit is set. If, however, the master is controlling the slave's select line with software it is possible that the slave's select line will remain asserted longer than expected if the master is busy performing some other task. In this case, the slave should check the value of port pin PS7 to ensure that its slave select line has been negated before writing a new value to its SPI data register.

It is important to note that the SPIF bit is used to indicate the completion of an SPI transfer and does not necessarily indicate the SPI's readiness to initiate a transfer. This characteristic is important to understand when writing software drivers for SPI peripherals. For instance, after power-up or reset the SPIF flag has a value of zero. While this is consistent with the functional definition for the SPIF flag, this is the same value the flag has when a transfer is in process. Even after data transfers have taken place, the SPIF flag is cleared when an read of the `SP0SR` register is followed by an access of the SPI data register. Clearly, for this reason, SPI data transfers should be performed on a block or message basis rather than a byte at a time.

10.6 SPI Interrupts

Even though two conditions can potentially generate an SPI interrupt, the SPI utilizes only one of the 64 interrupt vectors available on the M68HC12 family. Resolution of the interrupt condition must be determined by the interrupt service routine. Both SPI interrupts are enabled by setting the SPIE bit in the `SP0CR1` control register. An interrupt is generated when either the SPIF or the MODF bit in the `SP0SR` register are set. Interrupts are cleared reading the `SP0SR` register followed by a read or write to the SPI data register.

10.7 SPI Software Driver Strategy

The exact strategy to use when writing software drivers for SPI peripherals depends on the data transfer format, maximum allowable clock rate, and number of connected peripherals. If only a single peripheral is attached to the SPI bus, the only necessary choice is whether the SPI software will be written to operate in an interrupt driven mode or in a polled mode. When operating at the maximum data transfer rate of the E-clock divided by 2, it makes little sense to operate the SPI in an interrupt driven manner because of the overhead involved in entering and exiting the interrupt service routine. Transmitting a single byte at an SCK rate of 4.0 MHz requires nine SCK clock cycles as shown in Figure 10.5 and 10.6, requiring 2.25 µS. Simply responding to and returning from an SPI interrupt requires 17 E-clock cycles or 2.125 µS. This cycle count includes nine cycles to respond to the interrupt, eight for the RTI instruction, and does not include any interrupt service routine overhead involved transmitting the next byte of data. For maximum SPI throughput at the highest SCK rate it is best to operate the SPI in polled mode.

When multiple peripherals with varying data transfer format requirements are connected to the SPI bus, each transfer must begin by configuring the SPI according to the data transfer criteria of the selected peripheral. At the end of each transfer, the SPI may remain enabled, or if desired, may be disabled by clearing the SPIE bit in the SP0CR1 control register. Remember that when the SPI is disabled, any pins that are defined as inputs when the SPI is enabled, will revert to the general purpose I/O function defined by the value in the Port S data direction register, DDRS. Utilizing the SPI in an interrupt driven manner with multiple peripherals attached to the bus will most likely require additional software in the interrupt service routine to determine the peripheral to which data is being transferred.

10.8 SPI Parallel Output Port Example

SPI peripherals range from complex functions such as LCD and LED display drivers to simple I/O functions utilizing general CMOS logic circuits. This example illustrates the use of a 74HC595 to add eight output port pins utilizing the SPI. The 74HC595 consists of an eight bit shift register and an eight bit D-type latch with three state parallel outputs. The D-

Section 10.8: SPI Parallel Output Port Example

type parallel output latches allow the outputs to remain constant as new data to be shifted into the shift register. The shift register accepts serial data on the rising edge of the shift clock and also provides a serial output. The serial output allows multiple 74HC595s to be connected together in series to provide multiple eight bit output ports with a single connection to the SPI port. A block diagram of the 74HC595 is shown in Figure 10.9.

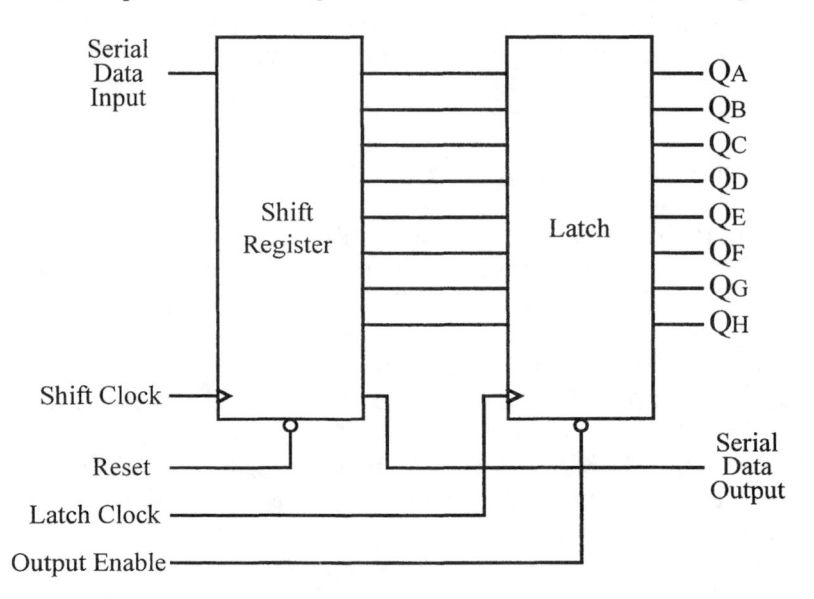

Figure 10.9: 74HC595 Block Diagram

Connecting the 74HC595 to the M68HC12's SPI is relatively straightforward. The Serial Data Input and Shift Clock input of the 74HC595 are connected to the SPI's MOSI and SCK outputs respectively. The Latch Clock input, which is used to transfer the contents of the shift register to the output data latches on a rising clock edge, can be connected directly to the SPI's CS/SS output pin. In most applications, the Output Enable pin can be permanently connected to Vss keeping the outputs of the 74HC595 active at all times. Applications requiring one or more outputs to assume a known value while the M68HC12 is in reset or before valid data is transferred into the data latches will require MCU control of this pin. If this is the case, the 74HC595's Output Enable pin should be connected one of the M68HC12's I/O pins and a pull-up resistor. In addition, each of the outputs requiring a known initial value must have either a pull-up or pull-down connected to the pin. These resistors will provide the proper voltage levels to the devices connected to the output pins during the time that the Output Enable pin is negated. As soon as the M68HC12 has initialized the 74HC595 with the first SPI transfer, the Output Enable may be permanently asserted by writing a zero to the data register of its associated I/O pin.

The active low Reset input resets the shift register portion of the device only. The values contained in the output data latch are unaffected. This pin may be connected directly to the M68HC12's reset pin, however, there is little to be gained from initializing the shift register contents to zero unless the initial value shifted out the Serial Data Output pin is important.

Finally, when cascading multiple 74HC595 devices, the Serial Data Output pin of one device is connected to the Serial Data Input pin of the next device in the chain. For all cascaded devices, the SPI signals connected to the Shift Clock, Latch Clock, Output Enable, and Reset may all be connected in parallel. However, when cascading multiple 74HC595's, the CS/SS output used to drive the Latch Clock must be asserted during the entire transfer. This means that for cascaded operation, the automatic assertion and negation capabilities of the CS/SS output may not be used. Instead, the SPI driver software must assert and negate the Latch Clock signal.

The timing requirements of the 74HC595 are flexible enough to allow the SPI to utilize either of its two data transfer formats. However, because the data on the Serial Data Input must be present at least 30 nS prior to the rising edge of the Shift Clock pin, a different clock polarity must be used for each of the data transfer formats. When the `CPHA` control bit is zero, the `CPOL` bit must also be zero. As shown in the timing diagram in Figure 10.5, the SPI transfer begins by placing the data on the MOSI pin one half clock cycle before the first clock edge on SCK. This time period is more than enough to meet the 30 nS data setup time specification of the 74HC595 even with a 4.0 MHz SCK frequency. Therefore the first rising edge must be used to shift the data into the 74HC595. When the `CPHA` control bit is one, the `CPOL` bit must also be one. Examining the timing diagram of Figure 10.6 shows that because the first clock edge is used to place the data on the MOSI pin, the second clock edge must be used to shift the data into the 74HC595.

The `LSBF` control bit may be programmed to either a zero or a one. If `LSBF` has a value of zero the most significant bit will be shifted out first and will appear on the 74HC595's Q_H output pin and the least significant bit will appear on the Q_A output. If the `LSBF` has a value of one the opposite will be true. Because the maximum Shift Clock rate of the 74HC595 is specified as 20 MHz, the maximum SCK rate of 4.0 MHz may safely be used.

Section 10.8: SPI Parallel Output Port Example

```
;
InitSPI595: ldab    #SPE+MSTR+SSOE ; enable SPI as master, auto assert SS/CS.
            stab    SP0CR1
            ldab    #0             ; use SCK rate of 4 MHz.
            stab    SP0BR
            ldab    DDRS           ; get current value of DDRS.
            andb    #$0f           ; don't disturbe lower 4 bits
            addb    #$e0           ; make SS/CS, SCK & MOSI outputs.
            stab    DDRS           ; update DDR.
            rts                    ; return
;
Out595:     stab    SP0DR          ; send data to HC595.
            brclr   SP0SR,#SPIF,*  ; wait till transfer is complete.
            rts                    ; return.
;
```

Figure 10.10: 74HC595 SPI Output Subroutine, Single Peripheral

The listing in Figure 10.10 contains the necessary software for initialization and data transfer to a single 74HC595 connected to the SPI port. It is interesting to see that the software required to initialize the SPI requires three times the number of instructions as the software required to transmit data to the 74HC595. The initialization code begins by enabling the SPI, configuring it as a master and setting the SSOE bit. Setting the SSOE bit enables the automatic assertion of the SS/CS line each time a transfer is performed. The CPHA and CPOL bits are both cleared and the SCK rate is set at 4.0 MHz. The remainder of the initialization code is used to configure the SPI pins used as outputs by setting the associated bits in the Port S Data Direction Register. Because the lower four bits of the Port S DDR are associated with the SCI and the Port S general purpose I/O pins the initialization software takes care not to modify the lower four bits of the DDR.

The data transfer subroutine, Out595, is written assuming that the 74HC595 is the only device attached to the SPI bus. If the the 74HC595 shared the SPI bus with other peripherals or SPI bus masters, the Out595 subroutine may have to call the InitSPI595 subroutine to configure the SPI properly. In addition, both subroutines would need to be modified so the 74HC595's Latch Clock was not automatically asserted by the SPI.

A modified version of these routines utilizing PS7 as a general purpose I/O pin to drive the 74HC595's Latch Clock appears in Figure 10.11. Notice that the Port S pin initialization portion of the InitSPI595 subroutine has been moved to the beginning of the subroutine. This change is necessary to ensure that the SS/CS pin (PS7) is initialized as an output *before* the SPI is enabled as a master. If the SS/CS pin is allowed to remain an input when the SPI is enabled, there is a danger that the pin will float to a logic low level and cause an SPI mode fault unless the pin is pulled up to VDD through an external pullup resistor.

```
;
InitSPI595: bset    PORTS,#$80      ; Init PS7 (595 Latch Clock) to 1.
            ldab    DDRS            ; get current value of DDRS.
            andb    #$0f            ; don't disturbe lower 4 bits
            addb    #$e0            ; make SCK, MOSI & PS7 outputs.
            stab    DDRS            ; update DDR.
            ldab    #SPE+MSTR       ; enable SPI as a master.
            stab    SP0CR1
            ldab    #0              ; use SCK rate of 4 MHz
            stab    SP0BR
            rts                     ; return
;
Out595:     pshb
            bsr     InitSPI595      ; init the SPI for 595 transfer.
            pulb
            stab    SP0DR           ; send data to HC595.
            brclr   SP0SR,#SPIF,*   ; wait till transfer is complete.
            bclr    PORTS,#$80      ; transfer data to latches.
            bset    PORTS,#$80
            rts                     ; return.
;
```

Figure 10.11: 74HC595 SPI Output Subroutine, Multiple Peripherals

The changes made to the Out595 subroutine include calling the InitSPI595 subroutine before each transfer and the addition of software necessary to assert the 74HC595's Latch Clock. Notice that the two instruction sequences used to transfer data from the shift register to the output latches appear one after the other at the end of the subroutine. Unlike the previous example where the SPI automatically asserted the Latch Clock during the entire transfer, this will only produce a narrow pulse after the completion of the data transfer. This arrangement is possible because the 74HC595's Latch Clock only requires a rising edge to transfer the shift register contents to the output latches.

The alert reader will notice that because the 74HC595 does not include an enable input, new data will be clocked into the shift register when data transfers are made to other peripherals attached to the SPI bus. As long as the 74HC595's Latch Clock remains inactive, the Output Latch contents will not change. The only side effect of the additional clocking of the 74HC595's shift register on each SPI data transfer would be a slight increase in the system's overall current consumption.

Section 10.9: SPI Parallel Input Port Example

10.9 SPI Parallel Input Port Example

This example provides the capabilities opposite those of the last example. It uses a 74HC597 Parallel-Input/Serial-Output shift register to provide 8-bits of parallel input utilizing the SPI. The 74HC597 consists of an 8-bit storage latch feeding parallel data from eight data inputs to an 8-bit shift register. The 8-bit input latch loads the parallel data present on the A - H inputs on the rising edge of the Latch Clock input. Once the input latch has been loaded with data, a low level must be applied to the Serial Shift/Parallel Load pin to transfer the data to the shift register. Before the data in the shift register can be transferred out the Q$_H$ output, the Serial Shift/Parallel Load pin must be returned to a logic one. A rising edge on the Shift Clock input causes data to be shifted into the Serial Data Input A and the data at the Q$_H$ output is shifted out, being replaced by the data previously stored in stage G. Because of the availability of the serial input to the shift register, multiple 74HC597's can be cascaded providing additional inputs. A block diagram of the 74HC597 is shown in Figure 10.12.

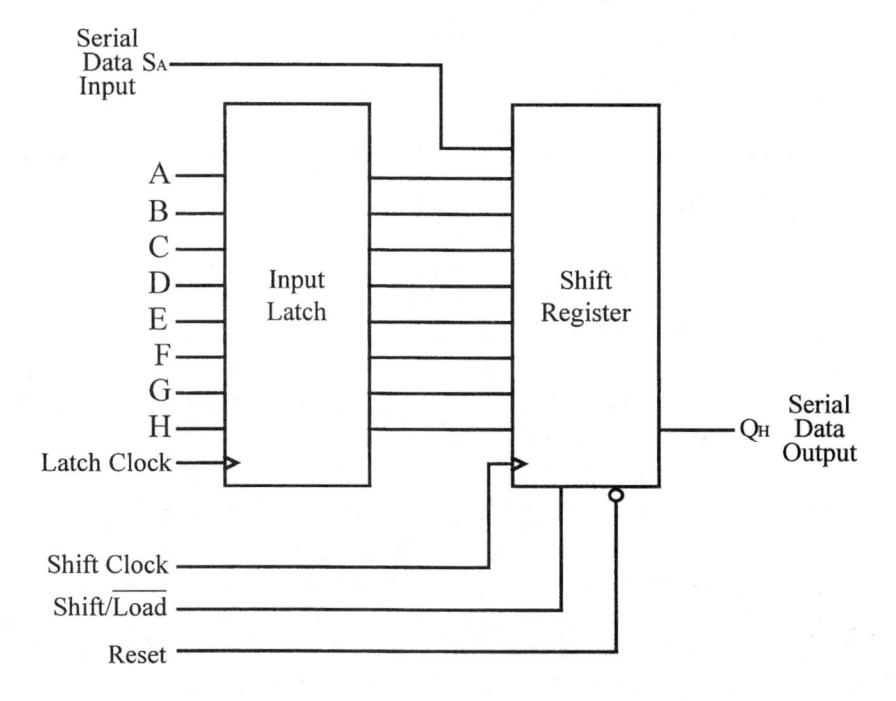

Figure 10.12: 74HC597 Block Diagram

Connecting the 74HC597 to the M68HC12's SPI pins is straightforward, although it requires one more connection than the 74HC595. The Serial Data Output and Shift Clock input of the 74HC597 are connected to the SPI's MISO and SCK outputs respectively.

Because of the timing requirements of the Latch Clock and Shift/Load clocks, each one must be connected to a separate general purpose I/O pin that is individually controlled. In the software example shown in Figure 10.14, PS7 is used to control the Latch Clock and PS3 controls the Serial Shift/Parallel Load input. Finally, the Reset input pin can be connected to the M68HC12's reset pin or connected directly to VDD.

Multiple 74HC597's may be cascaded to provide additional parallel inputs for the M68HC12. When cascading multiple 74HC597's, the Serial Data Output QH of each device in the chain, with the exception of the last device, is connected to the Serial Data Input A of the next device in the chain. For all cascaded devices, the SPI signals connected to the Shift Clock, Latch Clock, the Shift/Load Clock and Reset may be connected in parallel.

The timing requirements of the 74HC597 requires the use of the data transfer format defined by the `CPHA` control bit equal to zero and the `CPOL` bit equal to one. Examining the timing diagram in Figure 10.13, shows that for this configuration, the first clock edge of a transfer is a falling edge. It is this clock edge that is used to transfer the data present on the 74HC597's QH Serial Data Output pin into the SPI's shift register. At the time of the falling edge, the data on the 74HC597's QH Serial Data Output has been present for more than one half an SCK clock cycle, which is more than enough to meet the input setup time of the SPI. If a `CPOL` value of zero was used, the first SCK edge would be a rising edge. This would cause the data on the QH output of the 74HC597 to change at the same time, minus a propagation delay, that the data was being clocked into the SPI's shift register. Even though the M68HC12's SPI does not require any data hold time on the MISO pin when configured as a master, this configuration could result in corrupt data transfers if timing delays are present in the system.

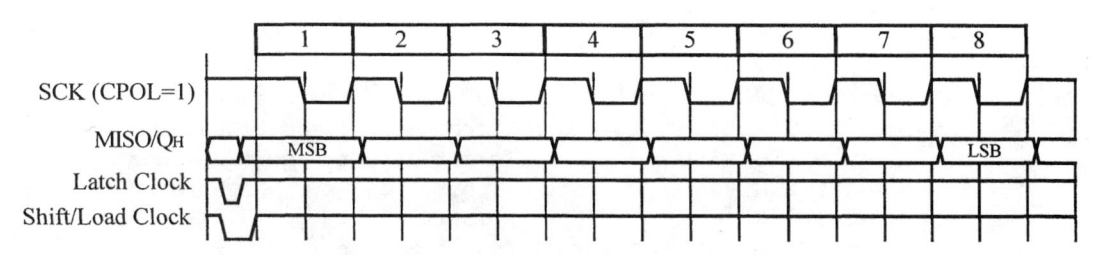

Figure 10.13: 74HC597/SPI Transfer Timing Diagram

The software required to read eight data bits from a single 74HC597 is presented in Figure 10.14. The `InitSPI597` subroutine is nearly identical to the `InitSPI595` subroutine with the exception of the values used to initialize the Port S data direction register. Notice once again that the Port S pins used as general purpose I/O are initialized before the SPI is enabled. If the port pin PS7 is allowed to remain an input when the SPI is enabled, there is a danger that the pin will float to a logic low level and cause an SPI mode fault unless the pin has been pulled up to VDD through an external pullup resistor.

Section 10.9: SPI Parallel Input Port Example

The `In597` subroutine begins the transfer by driving both the Latch Clock and Shift/Load signals low. Driving the Shift/Load signal low simultaneously with the Latch Clock allows data at the input pins to be transferred to the shift register on the rising edge of the Latch Clock. Immediately after the Latch clock is driven high, the Shift/Load signal is driven high allowing the transfer of the shift register contents the SPI data register. Finally, the contents of the B accumulator is written to the SPI data register to begin the data transfer. Because there is no connection to the MOSI pin in this example, the value written to the SPI data register is not important. When the transfer is complete, the data is read into the B accumulator and the subroutine returns.

Examining the block diagram of the 74HC597 in Figure 10.12, the perceptive reader may have noticed that the output of the shift register, QH, does not have the ability to be placed in a Tri-state condition so other SPI peripherals can share the bus. This is a limitation can be easily overcome by substituting a 74HC589 for the 74HC597 and making a slight modification to the `In597` subroutine.

```
;
InitSPI597:bset   PORTS,#$88       ; Init PS7 &PS3 to 1.
           ldab   DDRS             ; get current value of DDRS.
           andb   #$07             ; don't disturb lower 3 bits
           addb   #$e8             ; make SCK, MOSI, PS7 & PS3 outputs.
           stab   DDRS             ; update DDR.
           ldab   #SPE+MSTR+CPOL   ; enable SPI as master, CPOL = 1.
           stab   SP0CR1
           ldab   #0               ; use SCK rate of 4 MHz
           stab   SP0BR
           rts                     ; return
;
In597:     bsr    InitSPI597       ; init the SPI for 597 transfer.
           bclr   PORTS,#$88       ; make latch clock & shift/load low.
           bset   PORTS,#$80       ; transferfer data to input latches
           bset   PORTS,#$08       ; and to shift reg.
           stab   SP0DR            ; begin transfer from HC597.
           brclr  SP0SR,#SPIF,*    ; wait till transfer is complete.
           ldab   SP0DR            ; get received data.
           rts                     ; return.
;
```

Figure 10.14: 74HC597 SPI Input Subroutine

The pin out and block diagram of the 74HC589 is identical to the 74HC597 except that a Serial Data Output enable pin is substituted for the shift register reset. It would seem having to control the output enable would require an additional general purpose I/O pin.

Chapter 10: Serial Peripheral Interface

However, with some creative software, the output enable can simply be tied to the same I/O pin used to drive the Latch Clock pin. Figure 10.15 presents a modified version of the `In597` subroutine, `In589`. The `InitSPI589` subroutine referred to in the listing is identical to the `InitSPI597` subroutine and is therefore not included.

```
;
In589:      bsr     InitSPI589          ; init the SPI for 589 transfer.
            bclr    PORTS,#$88          ; transfer data to input latches.
            bset    PORTS,#$80
            bset    PORTS,#$08          ; and to shift reg.
            bclr    PORTS,#$80          ; drive latch clk & OE low.
            stab    SP0DR               ; begin transfer from HC589.
            brclr   SP0SR,#SPIF,*       ; wait till transfer is complete.
            bset    PORTS,#$80          ; put Shift reg. in Hi-Z.
            ldab    SP0DR               ; get received data.
            rts                         ; return.
;
```

Figure 10.15: 74HC589 SPI Input Subroutine

The only real difference between the In589 and In597 subroutines is the addition of a BCLR instruction just before the the beginning of the SPI data transfer and the addition of a BSET instruction immediately after the transfer is complete. The timing diagram in Figure 10.16 shows the waveforms for the data transfer utilizing the software in Figure 10.15. Observe that the transfer begins much the same as for the 74HC597 with the Latch Clock and Shift/Load Clocks transferring data to the input latches and then the shift register. Notice also that because the Output Enable is connected to the same I/O pin as the Latch Clock signal, the QH pin goes to a tri-state condition when the I/O pin is high. Before the data transfer can begin, the Latch Clock/OE signal must be driven low to enable the QH output. At the end of the transfer, the Latch Clock/OE signal must be driven high to place the QH output back to a tri-state condition so other peripherals may use the bus. Obviously, the rising edge on the Latch Clock/OE signal at the end of the transfer will load the input latches with the values present on the input pins. However, this additional load is simply ignored, as the latches are reloaded at the beginning of the next transfer.

Section 10.10: SPI Display Driver Example

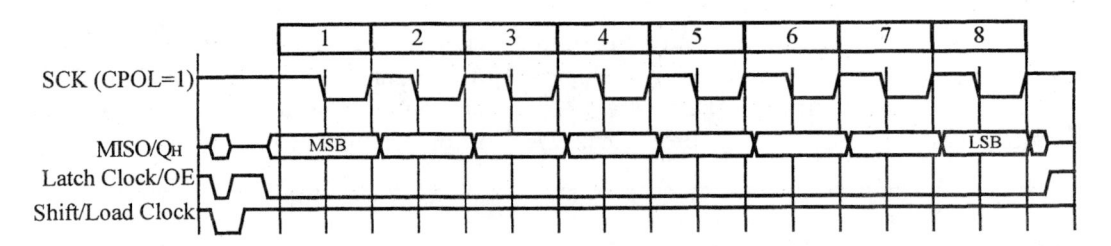

Figure 10.16: 74HC589/SPI Transfer Timing Diagram

One of the obvious questions to ask is why use a 74HC597 when the 74HC589 requires no additional general purpose I/O pins for control and only requires two additional instructions. The reason is cost. As this is being written, Motorola's price for an MC74HC589AN was listed at $1.17 in single unit quantities, while the single unit price of the MC74HC597AN was only $0.47. Clearly there is a substantial cost savings using a 74HC597 if the design allows it.

10.10 SPI DISPLAY DRIVER EXAMPLE

The final SPI peripheral example utilizes the MC14489 Multi-Character Display Driver. The MC14489 is designed to directly drive individual lamps, 7-segment displays, or various combinations of both. The LEDs must be wired in a common cathode arrangement and are driven in a multiplexed by five arrangement. In this example, it will be used to drive a four digit seven segment display with decimal points and four individual LED indicators. From a hardware standpoint, the MC14489 connects directly to the display elements without requiring any current limiting resistors or external high-current drivers. The only external components required are a single resistor connected to the Rx pin to set the peak segment drive current and a bypass capacitor. A block diagram of the MC14489 is shown in Figure 10.17. SPI connection to the MC14489 is straightforward with its Data In pin connected to the MOSI pin, its Clock pin connected to the SCK pin, and its Enable pin is connected to PS7. Because the MC14489 requires its Enable pin to be low during the entire transfer to its 24-bit Display Register, PS7 must be configured as a general purpose I/O pin and controlled by software.

Chapter 10: Serial Peripheral Interface

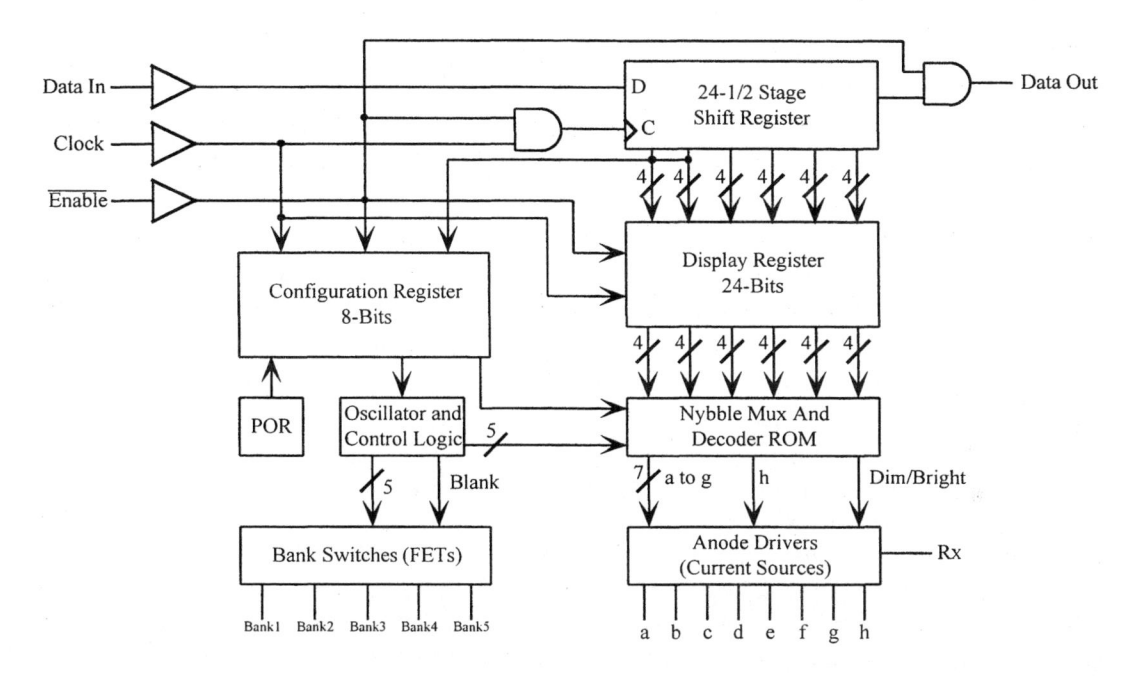

Figure 10.17: MC14489 Block Diagram

From a software viewpoint, the MC14489 consists of an 8-bit configuration register and a 24-bit display register. Because of the MC14489's register design, no address or steering bits are required to access either register. A 24-bit data transfer simply updates the Display Register while an 8-bit transfer changes the Configuration Register. The 8-bit Configuration Register is connected to the Nibble Mux and Decoder ROM block and is used to determine how the data in the display register is interpreted when driving the connected display. In addition, the least significant bit, C0, is used to place the MC14489 in a low power mode and at the same time blanks the entire display. The Configuration Register bits C1 through C5 control the decoding of each associated 4-bit nybble in the display register. When any of these bits is low, their default value, the associated nybble in the display register is decoded and displayed as a hexadecimal digit, $0 through $F. If any of the bits C1 through C3 contain a value of one, the associated nybble in the display register is either decoded as a special symbol, if C6 has a value of one, or is used to directly drive the segments a through d if C6 has a value of zero. If either C4 or C5 contain a value of one, the associated nybble in the display register is decoded as a special symbol, if C7 has a value of one, or is used to directly drive the segments a through d if C7 has a value of zero.

When the no decoding is selected, which is used in this example to drive the four individual LEDs, the least significant bit of each nybble is used to drive segment a, the next most significant bit is used to drive segment b and so forth. Segments e, f, and g are unused in this mode and are forced to an inactive low level. The h segment output, which is

Section 10.10: SPI Display Driver Example

normally used to drive the decimal point of a numeric display, is unaffected by any decode selections and is controlled solely by bits D20 through D22 in the Display register.

Because this example does not utilize the letters or symbols selected by the special decode mode they are not presented here but can be found in the MC14489 data sheet. These symbols can be used in conjunction with the letters $A through $F provided by the hexadecimal decoding to provide a limited vocabulary of text messages.

In addition to utilizing an external current setting resistor to determine the peak LED segment drive current and therefore LED brightness, the most significant bit of the Display Register, D23, can be used to control display brightness. When D23 has a value of one, the peak current through each display segment is approximately 10 times the current flowing through the Rx pin. When D23 has a value of zero, the peak segment current is reduced by approximately 50% dimming the display by about half.

The default value of all bits in the configuration register is zero placing the MC14489 in the low power mode, blanking the display, and selecting hexadecimal decode mode for all five digits. However, the reverse is true of the Display Register where the default state of all bits is one. Enabling the MC14489 by writing a $01 to the control register without first writing a value to the the Display Register will cause hexadecimal $F to be displayed in each digit position and the illumination of all decimal points at maximum brightness.

Display Register

D23	D22	D21	D20	D19	D18	D17	D16	D15	D14	D13	D12	D11	D10	D9	D8	D7	D6	D5	D4	D3	D2	D1	D0
Segment h Control			Bank5					Bank4					Bank3				Bank2				Bank1		

Display Brightness Control

| C7 | C6 | C5 | C4 | C3 | C2 | C1 | C0 |

— Low Power/Normal Mode Contro

Configuration Register

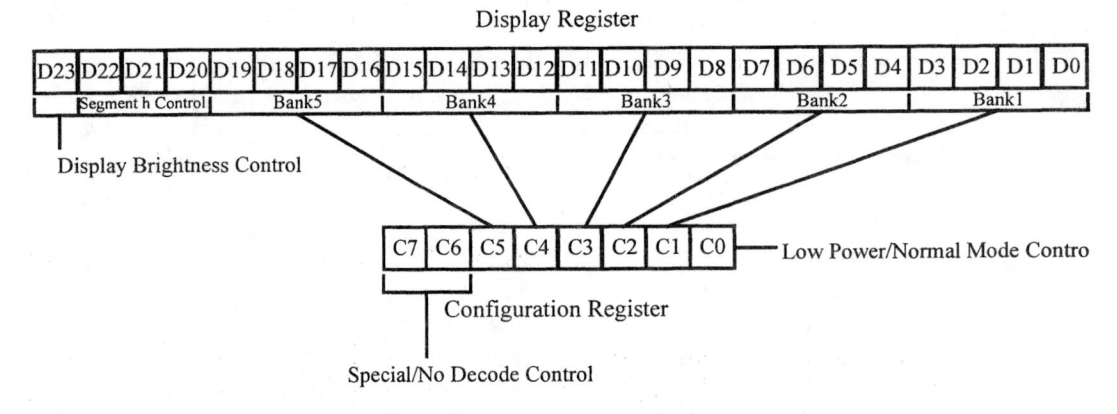

Special/No Decode Control

Figure 10.18: Configuration and Display Register Format

Figure 10.19 presents a basic block diagram of the MC14489 configuration used for this example. The four digit common cathode display can be obtained from a number of different vendors. For this example a Lumex LDQ-N516RI display is used. The four individual LED indicators can be of a size and color suitable to the application.

Chapter 10: Serial Peripheral Interface

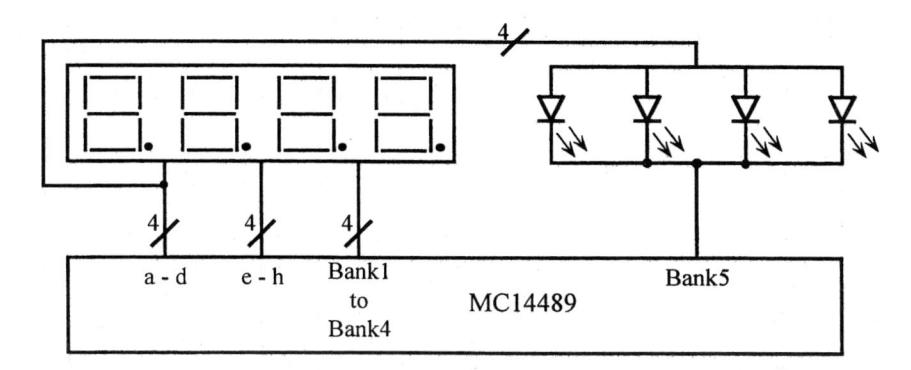

Figure 10.19: Four Digit Display with Decimals and Four LED indicators

The basic driver software necessary to communicate with the MC14489 Display Driver is shown in Figure 10.20. The listing begins with the declaration of two variables, `DispBuff` and `CfgRegVal`. The `DispBuff` variable consists of three bytes and contains the data sent to the MC14489's Display Register by the `SndDispReg` subroutine. The `CfgRegVal` variable holds an image of the value that is sent to the Configuration Register. Initially this variable may seem unnecessary; however, it is required for some of the utility routines presented later in the chapter.

Section 10.10: SPI Display Driver Example

```
;
DispBuff:    ds.b   3              ; holds value to be sent to Display Reg.
CfgRegVal:   ds.b   1              ; holds value to be sent to Config. Reg.
;
DispInit:    bset   PORTS,#$80     ; Init PS7 (14489 enable) to 1.
             ldab   DDRS           ; get current value of DDRS.
             andb   #$0f           ; don't disturbe lower 4 bits
             addb   #$e0           ; make SCK, MOSI & PS7 outputs.
             stab   DDRS           ; update DDR.
             bsr    ConfigDSPI     ; (re)initialize the SPI for the 14489.
             clrb                  ; send $00 to config reg for reset.
             jsr    SndCfgReg      ; write the control register.
             ldab   #$21           ; put $21 to config reg for normal.
             stab   CfgRegVal
             clr    DispBuff       ; display dim, no DP, no lamps.
             rts                   ; return.
;
ConfigDSPI:  ldab   #SPE+MSTR      ; enable SPI as master.
             stab   SP0CR1
             ldab   #0             ; use SCK rate of 4 MHz
             stab   SP0BR
             rts                   ; return
;
SndCfgReg:   bclr   PORTS,#$80     ; drive 14489 enable low.
             stab   SP0DR          ; begin transfer.
             brclr  SP0SR,#SPIF,*  ; wait till transfer is complete.
             bset   PORTS,#$80     ; drive 14489 enable high.
             rts                   ; return.
;
SndDispReg:  ldaa   #3             ; byte count.
             ldx    #DispBuff      ; point to display buffer.
             bclr   PORTS,#$80     ; drive 14489 enable low.
NextByte:    ldab   1,x+           ; get byte, advance pointer
             stab   SP0DR          ; begin transfer.
             brclr  SP0SR,#SPIF,*  ; wait till transfer is complete.
             dbne   a,NextByte     ; loop till all 3 bytes transfered.
             bset   PORTS,#$80     ; drive 14489 enable high.
             rts                   ; return.
;
```

Figure 10.20: MC14489 Driver Software

The `DispInit` subroutine begins by initializing the Port S I/O pins used as SPI outputs including PS7 used to drive the MC14489's Enable line. Next, the `ConfigSPI` subroutine is called to enable and configure the SPI as a master with a clock polarity and clock phase of zero and a data rate of 4.0 MHz. This small piece of code is included as a subroutine rather than in line code in the `DispInit` subroutine so the SPI can be reinitialized by the display utility subroutines presented in the remainder of the chapter. If

Chapter 10: Serial Peripheral Interface

the MC14489 is used as the sole SPI peripheral in a system, this code could be incorporated into the `DispInit` subroutine and references to it removed from the utility subroutines.

The final action of the `DispInit` subroutine writes a value of zero to the Configuration Register. This action may seem unnecessary given the fact that the default value of the Configuration Register is zero; however, this action is included because of a power-up restriction imposed by the MC14489. For the MC14489's internal Power On Reset (POR) to operate properly, its Clock line must not be floated or toggled during power-up. The Clock pin must be stable until VDD reaches at least 3.0 volts. Because the SPI's SCK pin is initially configured as an input during the M68HC12 power-up/reset sequence, the MC14489's Clock pin is allowed to float. Writing a zero to bit C0 of the Configuration Register and then writing it to a one performs a proper reset of the MC14489. Finally, the `CfgRegVal` variable is initialized with the value of $21, but is not written to the Configuration Register since the Display Register has not been initialized. When this value is written to the Configuration Register it configures the MC14489 to drive a four digit display and four individual LED lamps.

The remaining two subroutines in Figure 10.20, `SndCfgReg` and `SndDispReg` are used to write values to the Configuration and Display Register respectively. The value sent to the Configuration Register is passed to the `SndCfgReg` in the B accumulator. Again this may seem strange since the `CfgRegVal` variable contains the value to be written; however, it is required for other utility routines. The value written to the 24-bit Display register is read directly from the `DispBuff` variable and sent, most significant byte first, to the MC14489. While these two subroutines provide the basic capability for writing values to the MC14489's two registers, they do not provide any display formatting or high level control for the display's decimal points or the four LED lamps connected to bank 5 of the display driver.

It may seem unnecessary to have a separate subroutine to send numeric data to the display driver; however, there is a desirable feature of numeric displays not supported in hardware by the MC14489: leading zero suppression. Leading zero suppression makes a number in a multi-digit display more readable by blanking all digits containing zeros, beginning at the left most digit in the display, prior to the first non-zero digit. If the number zero is presented for display, a single zero is displayed in the right-most digit of the display.

Figure 10.21 presents the source code for the `DispNum` subroutine. It furnishes the capability to display a four digit packed BCD or hexadecimal number with leading zero suppression. Blanking the leading zeros in the display is accomplished by examining each digit of the number, beginning with the most significant digit, and building a value for the Configuration Register that will blank a digit with a nybble value of zero. Writing a value of one to the a bank's associated bank decode control bits, C1 through C5, will cause the nybble decoding to be determined by the Configuration Register bits C6 and C7. If these two bits contain a value of zero, no decoding is performed by the Nybble Mux and Decoder ROM. Instead, the display segments a through d are driven directly by the value in and

345

Section 10.10: SPI Display Driver Example

associated bank nybble and the segments e through g are turned off. This results in all segments being extinguished when a value of zero is written to the associated bank nybble.

The `DispNum` subroutine listing begins with the declaration of two variables required for its operation. The value in `ZSLoopCnt` controls the maximum number of leading zeros that will be blanked in the display. For a four digit display, this variable is initialized with a value of three so that a value of $0000 written to the lower 16-bits of the display register will display a single zero in the least significant digit of the display. The value in the `ZSCtrlBit` variable, initialized with a value of $10, is used to write a one to the associated bank decode control bit in the `CfgRegVal` variable. In each pass through the subroutine's loop where a leading zero is found, the value of `ZSCtrlBit` is added to the value in `CfgRegVal` and then the value of `ZSCtrlBit` shifted right one bit. The shift operation places the '1' in the next lower bit position ready to be added into the `CfgRegVal` if the next digit examined has a value of zero. Note that the initial value of the `CfgRegVal` variable is set to $21. This value places the MC14489 in the normal display mode and configures Bank 5, used to drive the discrete LEDs, for no decoding.

Chapter 10: Serial Peripheral Interface

```
;
                offset  0
ZSLoopCnt:      ds      1
ZSCtrlBit:      ds      1
;
DispNum:        std     DispBuff+1      ; save the number in the display buffer.
                jsr     ConfigDSPI      ; (re)initialize the SPI for the 14489.
                ldab    #$10            ; init the zero supress control bit.
                pshb
                ldab    #3              ; supress a max of 3 leading 0s.
                pshb
                ldab    #$21            ; init base value of the config reg.
                stab    CfgRegVal
                ldd     DispBuff+1      ; get value to display from buffer.
ZSLoop:         ldy     #16             ; shift it left 4 bits.
                emul
                exg     d,y             ; put MS digit in b. save remaining.
                tstb                    ; MS digit zero?
                bne     NoZS            ; no. we're done.
                ldab    CfgRegVal       ; yes. get the config register value.
                addb    ZSCtrlBit,sp    ; add in the zero supress control bit.
                stab    CfgRegVal       ; save the new config register value.
                lsr     ZSCtrlBit,sp    ; shift the ZS bit to the next digit.
                exg     d,y             ; restore remaining digits.
                dec     ZSLoopCnt,sp    ; checked for max leading zeros?
                bne     ZSLoop          ; no. check for more.
NoZS:           ldab    CfgRegVal       ; yes. get the config reg value built.
                bsr     SndCfgReg       ; send it to the 14489.
                bsr     SndDispReg      ; send number to display.
                leas    LocalSize,sp    ; remove the stack storage.
                rts                     ; return.
;
```

Figure 10.21: DispNum Subroutine

Each digit of the number to be displayed, passed to the subroutine in the D accumulator, is examined by shifting the four most significant bits of the D accumulator into the lower four bits of the Y index register. This shift operation is accomplished by multiplying the contents of the D accumulator by 16. To examine the four bits shifted into the Y index register and save the remaining portion of the D accumulator, the contents of the two registers are exchanged. The four bits examined end up in the B accumulator where a TSTB instruction performs the check for zero. When a non-zero digit is found or when three digits have been examined, the value in CfgRegVal is sent to the MC14489 followed by the 24-bits of data in DispBuff. Finally, the two local variables are removed from the stack and the subroutine returns.

Section 10.10: SPI Display Driver Example

Note that the zero suppression algorithm used in this subroutine only works for integer numbers or numbers displayed with one digit to the right of the decimal point. If the display shows fractional numbers where the decimal point is fixed at two or three digits to the right of the decimal point, the simple solution would be to reduce the maximum number of suppressed leading zeros to two or one respectively. If the decimal point moves depending on the quantity or type of data displayed, a leading zero suppression algorithm that examines the position of the decimal point would have to be used.

```
;
DispOff:    bsr     ConfigDSPI      ; (re)initialize the SPI for the 14489.
            clrb                    ; send $00 to config reg for reset.
            bsr     SndCfgReg       ; write the control register.
            rts
;
DispOn:     bsr     ConfigDSPI      ; (re)initialize the SPI for the 14489.
            ldab    CfgRegVal       ; config normal mode, no decode on bank 5.
            bsr     SndCfgReg       ; write the control register.
            rts
;
DispBright: bsr     ConfigDSPI      ; (re)initialize the SPI for the 14489.
            bset    DispBuff,#$80   ; MSB of display buff = 1 is bright LEDs.
            bsr     SndDispReg      ; send the display buffer.
            rts                     ; return.
;
DispDim:    bsr     ConfigDSPI      ; (re)initialize the SPI for the 14489.
            bclr    DispBuff,#$80   ; MSB of display buff = 0 sets dim LEDs.
            bsr     SndDispReg      ; send the display buffer.
            rts                     ; return.
;
DispSetDP:  pshb                    ; save the DP position.
            bsr     ConfigDSPI      ; (re)initialize the SPI for the 14489.
            pulb                    ; restore the DP position.
            cmpb    #$04            ; greater than 4 DP?
            bhi     BadDP           ; yes. just ignore.
            ldaa    #16             ; shift left 4 bits by multiply.
            mul
            ldaa    DispBuff        ; get MS Byte of display buffer.
            anda    #$8f            ; mask off DP bits.
            aba                     ; add desired DP to other bits.
            staa    DispBuff        ; update the display buffer.
            bsr     SndDispReg      ; update the display register.
BadDP:      rts                     ; return.
;
```

Figure 10.22: MC14489 Utility Subroutines

Chapter 10: Serial Peripheral Interface

In addition to the basic routines presented so far, Figure 10.22 contains several utility subroutines allowing easy use of some of the additional features of the MC14489. The first two subroutines, `DispOff` and `DispOn`, can be used to blank and enable the display respectively. The display is blanked simply by writing a value of $00 to the Configuration Register placing the MC14489 in low power mode. To re-enable the display, the `DispOn` subroutine writes the value contained in `CfgRegVal` to the Configuration Register. These two routines are the reason that the `CfgRegVal` variable must maintain a copy of the value in the Configuration Register. Using these two routines along with a time delay routine allows an application to blink the display, possibly indicating an error or other unusual condition.

The next two subroutines, `DispBright` and `DispDim`, allow the brightness of the display to be set to normal or half brightness respectively. Because the display brightness control bit is contained in the most significant bit of the display register, the entire contents of the Display Register must be written to the MC14489 after the most significant bit of the `DispBuff` variable is manipulated.

The final subroutine in Figure 10.22, `DispSetDP`, is used to illuminate or extinguish the decimal points of the display. While the MC14489 provides the ability to illuminate all of the decimal points simultaneously, the `DispSetDP` subroutine does not support this option. The bank number of the decimal point to be illuminated is passed to the subroutine in the B accumulator. A value of one will illuminate the decimal point associated with Bank 1, a value of two illuminates the decimal point associated with Bank 2 and so fourth. Passing a value of greater than four will cause the subroutine to return without modifying the displayed decimal point. Passing a value of zero causes all of the decimal points to be extinguished. As shown in Figure 10.18, the control bits for the decimal points, or segment h, are contained in bits D20 through D22 of the Display Register and are decoded according to the table in Figure 10.23. Because these bits are part of the 24-bit Display Register, the entire Display Register must be written when changing these control bits.

D22	D21	D20	Segment h Active
0	0	0	All Off
0	0	1	Bank 1
0	1	0	Bank 2
0	1	1	Bank 3
1	0	0	Bank 4
1	0	1	Bank 5
1	1	0	Bank 1 & Bank 2
1	1	1	All Banks On

Figure 10.23: Segment h Control Bits Decoding

Section 10.10: SPI Display Driver Example

The last two utility subroutines listed in Figure 10.24, `DispLampOn` and `DispLampOff`, provide the ability to illuminate or extinguish the four individual LEDs associated with Bank 5. Each LED can be turned on or off individually by passing an LED number, one through four, to the subroutines in the B accumulator. LED number one is associated with display segment a, LED two is associated with display segment b and so fourth. Passing a value of zero to the `DispLampOn` subroutine will illuminate all four LEDs at once while passing a value of zero to the `DispLampOff` subroutine will extinguish all four LEDs at once. If a value greater than four is passed to either routine, the lamps' state will remain unchanged.

After performing a range check on the input value, both subroutines generate a bit mask used to set or clear one of the lower four bits in the byte at `DispBuff`. The bit mask generation in the `DispLampOn` subroutine begins by clearing the A accumulator and setting the carry. The accumulator is then rotated left by the count contained in the B accumulator. This operation places a one in the bit position corresponding to the LED's control bit and zeros in all remaining bits in the A accumulator. Performing a logical OR of the mask value and the value in the byte at `DispBuff` causes the corresponding LED control bit to be set to a one. The `DispLampOff` subroutine works in a very similar manner. In this case the LED's corresponding control bit in the upper byte of the display buffer must be cleared. An initial value $FF is loaded into the A accumulator and the carry is cleared. Rotating the A accumulator to the left by the count in accumulator B causes a zero to end up in the position of the corresponding LED control bit. When a logical AND is performed with the resulting bit mask and the value in the byte at `DispBuff`, the LED control bit is cleared while all remaining bits in the byte remain unchanged.

Before returning, both subroutines call the SndDispReg subroutine to update the MC14489's display register.

```
;
DispLampOn:     tstb                    ; turn all 4 LEDs on?
                bne     LOnChkMax       ; no. just one.
                ldaa    #$0f            ; yes. bit mask for all 4 LED
                bra     LOnDone         ; go turn all the lamps on.
LOnChkMax:      cmpb    #$04            ; valid LED number?
                bhi     BadLOn          ; no. just return.
                clra                    ; initial bit mask.
                sec                     ; rotate a 1 in to turn the LED on.
LOnLoop:        rola                    ; shift the '1' to the left.
                dbne    b,LOnLoop       ; 1 in the proper location? no.
LOnDone:        oraa    DispBuff        ; yes. set bit of LED to be turned on.
                staa    DispBuff        ; update the value in DispBuff.
                jsr     SndDispReg      ; send the display data to the 14489.
BadLOn:         rts                     ; done.
;
DispLampOff:    tstb                    ; turn all 4 lamps off?
                bne     LOffChkMax      ; no. just one.
                ldaa    #$f0            ; yes. bit mask for all 4 lamps.
                bra     LOffDone        ; go turn all the lamps off.
LOffChkMax:     cmpb    #$04            ; valid lamp number?
                bhi     BadLOff         ; no. just return.
                ldaa    #$ff            ; yes. initial bit mask.
                clc                     ; must rotate a 0 in to clear a bit.
LOffLoop:       rola                    ; rotate the 0 in the mask.
                dbne    b,LOffLoop      ; rotate till 0 in proper bit loc.
LOffDone:       anda    DispBuff        ; yes. clear the proper bit in DispBuff
                staa    DispBuff        ; update the value in DispBuff.
                jsr     SndDispReg      ; send the display data to the 14489.
BadLOff:        rts                     ; done.
;
```

Figure 10.24: DispLampOn and DispLampOff Subroutines

Questions/Exercises

10.1   How many pins are associated with the SPI? What are the pin names?

10.2   What effect do the Port S data direction register bits have on the pins associated with the SPI when it is enabled? How does this compare with the SCI?

10.3   How is the function of the Slave Select pin (SS/CS) different on the M68HC12 than on the M68HC11 family?

Section 10.10: SPI Display Driver Example

10.4 Under what circumstances is the additional functionality of the Slave Select pin of limited use?

10.5 What new operating mode is present on the M68HC12's SPI?

10.6 What is the main difference between the two transfer modes supported by the SPI?

10.7 What limits the maximum sustained data transfer rate of the SPI?

10.8 What are the minimum and maximum bit rates available to the SPI?

10.9 What techniques can be used to communicate with peripherals that require a combination of clock and/or data pulses that is not an even multiple of eight bits?

10.10 How does the configuration of the SPI data register affect when SPI data can be read or written? How is this different from the SCI?

10.11 What potential data transfer problem exists for M68HC12's when configured as slaves? How can this problem be avoided?

10.12 How is the function of the SPIF status bit different from the TDRE and RDRF status bits of the SPI? How does this affect the method used to transfer data to or from peripherals?

10.13 When operating the SPI at its maximum bit rate, is it better to write the software drivers to operate in a polled or interrupt driven mode? Why?

10.14 What software considerations must be addressed when multiple peripherals with varying data transfer formats are connected to the SPI bus?

10.15 Rewrite the software in Figure 10.10 to allow the contents of a data buffer of arbitrary length to be transferred to a like number of 74HC595s.

10.16 Rewrite the software in Figure 10.14 to allow the data from an arbitrary number of 74HC597s to be read and placed in a data buffer.

10.17 What is the reason to use a 74HC589 instead of a 74HC597 for an SPI input port?

10.18 What components might be used when a 16-bit SPI input port is required to share the SPI bus with other peripherals?

10.19   Why does the DispInit subroutine write a zero to the MC14489's Configuration register?

10.20   What is 'leading zero suppression'? Why is this feature desirable?

10.21   The DispNum subroutine is capable of displaying a four digit packed BCD or hexadecimal number. Write a subroutine to convert a 16-bit binary number to a four digit packed BCD number.

10.22   Rewrite the DispNum subroutine to perform correct leading zero suppression when fractional numbers are displayed. Hint: Examine the decimal point control bit to determine how many leading zeros to suppress.

10.23   The MC14489 has a Data Out pin that allows multiple devices to be cascaded. Rewrite the MC14489 driver routines to support a 10 digit display utilizing two MC14489s.

Chapter 11 STANDARD TIMER MODULE

This chapter covers the Standard Timer Module present on the MC68HC912B32 and other M68HC12 family members. The Standard Timer Module is designed to be functionally upward compatible with timer systems on the M68HC11 family while providing additional features and functionality. The timer system is based on a 16-bit free-running counter driven by a three stage prescaler. To allow the timing of events longer than periods directly supported by the 16-bit counter and prescaler, a counter overflow function is provided allowing software to extend the timer's range beyond 16-bits. Timing functions are performed utilizing eight independent timing channels. Unlike many of the M68HC11 family members, each of the eight channels may be individually programmed to act as an input capture or output compare. An input capture function allows the value of the free running counter to be captured when a selected edge occurs on the associated timer channel's input pin. An output compare function allows an output signal to be generated when the value in the timer channel's compare register matches the value of the free running counter.

In addition to the input capture and output compare functions, a 16-bit pulse accumulator is also part of the Standard Timer Module. The pulse accumulator is based on a simple 16-bit up counter that can be configured for simple event counting or gated time accumulation. Unlike the counter associated with the input capture and output compare functions, the pulse accumulator may be preset to any desired value. This feature allows a preset number of input pulses to be accumulated before the counter overflows and sets a bit in the pulse accumulator's status register. Two of the timer module's 11 interrupt vectors are associated with the pulse accumulator allowing each accumulated event or a pulse accumulator overflow to generate a separately vectored interrupt.

Section 11.1: Input Capture Concepts

The Standard Timer Module occupies a block of 48 bytes in the I/O register space - more than any other single peripheral module on the MC68HC912B32. In addition to numerous control and status registers, each timer channel has an associated 16-bit register used for the input capture or output compare function. Although hardware logic is included to automate some of the timer's functions, the timer architecture is basically software oriented. Even though this type of timer architecture is not as efficient as dedicated hardware in some specific applications, its software programmability makes it easily adaptable to a wide variety of applications.

Though the basic timer architecture of the M68HC12 family is very similar to the timer architecture used in the M68HC11 microcontrollers, there are significant differences and enhancements. For those not familiar with the basic timer architecture supported by the M68HC11, M68HC12 and other Motorola microcontroller families, a brief discussion of the timer's two basic timing functions is provided.

11.1 INPUT CAPTURE CONCEPTS

For the M68HC12, time is represented by the value of a 16-bit free running counter clocked by the timer prescaler. The input capture function of the M68HC12 timer provides the ability to record the value of the counter when an external event occurs. When a selected edge is detected at an input capture pin, the value of the 16-bit free running counter is latched into the timer channel's capture/compare register. The latched value is held there until it can be read by software. Note that if a second edge is detected on the input capture pin before the first value is read, the first value will be overwritten with the new counter value.

By recording the counter values for successive edges of an incoming signal, software can determine the period or pulse width of the signal with simple arithmetic. In general, when measuring signal periods, the value of the counter is captured using two successive edges of the same polarity. The signal period, in timer clock ticks, is calculated by simply subtracting the first captured value from the second. Measuring the pulse width of a signal involves a similar process except that two alternate polarity edges are used to capture the value of the counter. Each time a selected edge is detected at an input capture pin, a flag bit is set and can optionally cause an interrupt. Obviously when the period or pulse width of a signal or event is less than the time represented by 65,535 timer counts, a simple subtraction is all that is necessary to calculate the signal's time value. By selecting an appropriate prescale value, the time period represented by a full count of the 16-bit counter should be adequate for all timing functions in an application. If, however, the range of timing measurements exceeds the capabilities of the 16-bit counter, the timer counter overflow function can be used to extend the length of the timer to any arbitrary size using software.

In addition to using the input capture function to measure the amount of time between two edges of an external event, it can be used in conjunction with the output compare to provide a precision delayed output that is related to the input capture event. For example, if an application requires the activation of an output a fixed time period after the occurrence of an input event, a count representing the delay period can simply be added to the value latched into the input capture register and written to an output compare register. Because both input capture and output compare registers use the same 16-bit counter, the delay can be very precisely controlled without regard to the software latency times involved in reading the registers and performing the required calculations.

11.2 OUTPUT COMPARE CONCEPTS

Like the input capture, the output compare forms one of the basic timing functions of the M68HC12 timer system. The output compare function of the M68HC12 timer provides the ability to cause an event to occur at a specific time relative to the value of the 16-bit free running counter. When a timer channel is configured as an output compare, a dedicated 16-bit comparator is used to compare the value in the free running counter to the compare register during every CPU12 bus cycle. When the compare register value matches the free running counter, a compare status flag is set, optionally causing a timer channel interrupt. In addition, the output pin control logic may be programmed to cause the associated timer channel pin to be driven high, low or toggled.

Because many embedded control systems require that tasks be performed on a regular basis, one of the most common uses of the output compare function is for generating an interrupt at a fixed time interval. Because the value of the compare register does not change after the output compare occurs, the interrupt service routine simply adds a 16-bit constant to the value in the compare register and writes the result back to the compare register. This action configures the output compare register for the next compare which will occur when the value of the counter "catches up" with the value in the compare register. Because the free running counter operates in a modulo 65,536 manner, any overflows from the addition of the 16-bit constant can be ignored. If the range of time delays or pulse generation required by a system's firmware exceeds the range of the 16-bit counter, the time delays can be extended through the use of additional software.

The second most common use of the output compare function is for the generation of output waveforms. Waveform generation can range from a simple fixed frequency square wave, to a fixed frequency Pulse Width Modulated (PWM) waveform, to output waveforms of arbitrary complexity. Because of the software oriented nature of the timer, the more complex an output waveform becomes, the greater the software overhead becomes. The amount of software overhead and interrupt response time required to produce high frequency, complex waveforms, can require a significant portion of the CPU12's available bandwidth. Careful analysis of a system's timing requirements must be performed to ensure that the time required for waveform generation, timing measurements, and other tasks does not exceed the available bandwidth of the M68HC12 at a particular operating frequency.

Section 11.3: Timer Structure and Physical Interface

⚠ **M68HC12 Difference from the M68HC11**

11.3 TIMER STRUCTURE AND PHYSICAL INTERFACE

As shown in the simplified block diagram of Figure 11.1, all eight timer channels share the single 16-bit counter for timing measurements and pulse train generation. In addition to the Input Capture/Output Compare functions, a 16-bit pulse accumulator is provided to enable event counting or gated pulse accumulation. This function is an expansion of the 8-bit pulse accumulator provided in the M68HC11 standard timer module and allows a much greater number of events to be counted without requiring CPU intervention. As shown, the pulse accumulator shares its input with the same pin, PT7, as the channel seven timer function. This, however, does not imply that a choice must be made to use one function or the other. On the contrary, these two functions can be used in combination to perform some unusual or complex timing functions by allowing the output compare function of timer channel seven to control the input to the pulse accumulator. Using this arrangement, timer channel seven can be used to create the events counted by the pulse accumulator or it could be used as the gating signal in the pulse accumulator's gated time accumulation operating mode.

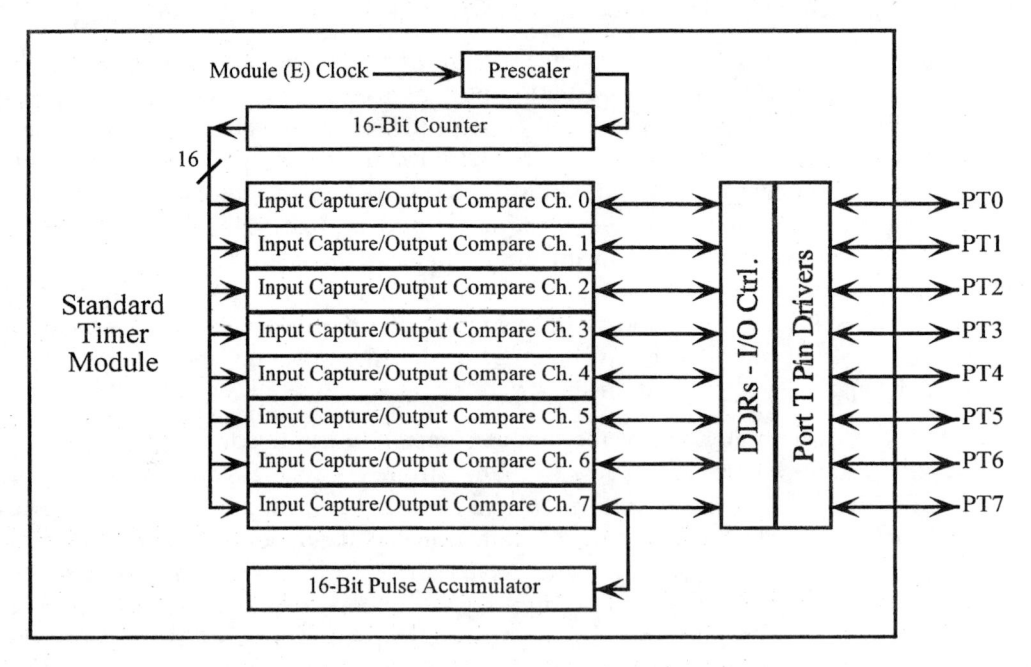

Figure 11.1: Standard Timer Block Diagram

Figure 11.2 presents a more detailed block diagram of a single timer capture/compare channel. Each channel consists of a 16-bit capture latch, a 16-bit comparator and pin control logic. In addition, control and status bits for each timer channel are distributed among the timer module's control and status bits. The block labeled TCx in the block diagram is a 16-bit register allowing access to the capture and compare register. When a channel is configured as an input capture, the value of the associated capture latch may be read at any time, however writes are ignored. When configured as an output compare, the value of the 16-bit comparator may be read or written at any time.

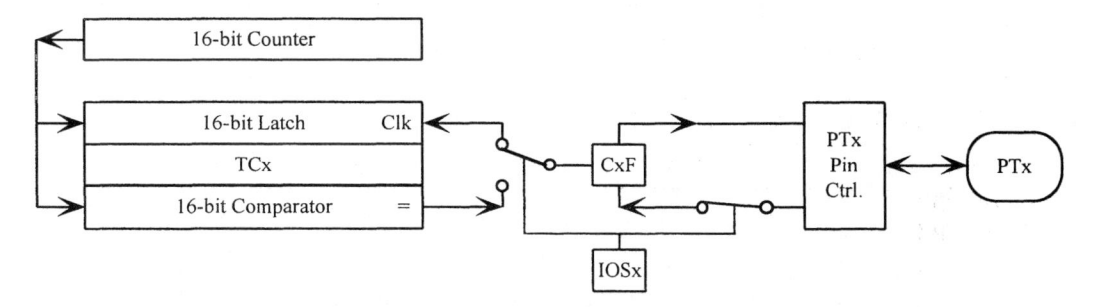

Figure 11.2: Timer Channel Block Diagram

The IOSx block represents one of eight configuration bits residing in the Timer Input Capture/Output Compare Select (`TIOS`) register allowing the configuration of each timer channel as an input capture or output compare. Each timer channel is configured as an input capture after reset, but may be reconfigured at any time. The CxF block represents one of eight flag bits residing in the Timer Input Capture/Output Compare Flag 1 (TFLG1) register. When an event occurs on a particular timer channel, a flag bit is set. When a timer channel is configured as an output compare, its associated flag bit is set when the contents of the 16-bit free running counter matches the value previously written to the 16-bit comparator. When configured as an input capture, each channel's related flag bit is set when an edge is detected on the corresponding I/O pin. The Timer Interrupt Mask 1 (TMSK1) register contains eight control bits corresponding one-for-one with the bits in the TFLG1 register. Setting any of the bits in the TMSK1 register causes a timer channel interrupt when the corresponding bit in the TFLG1 register is set.

The circuitry associated with the PTx Pin Control block of Figure 11.2 contains the necessary logic to allow each timer pin to be configured for one of three functions. When the associated timer channel is configured as an output compare, the timer logic forces the I/O pin to become an output regardless of the state of the associated Port T data direction register bit. In this case, the state of the data direction register bit is not changed but has no affect on the direction of the pin. If the associated port pin is later configured as a general purpose I/O, the Port T DDR bit controls the configuration of the I/O pin. As shown in

Section 11.3: Timer Structure and Physical Interface

Figure 11.3, each timer channel, when configured as an output compare, has two associated control bits that determine the action performed when an output compare occurs.

TCTL1	Bit 7	6	5	4	3	2	1	Bit 0
	OM7	OL7	OM6	OL6	OM5	OL5	OM4	OL4

TCTL2	Bit 7	6	5	4	3	2	1	Bit 0
	OM3	OL3	OM2	OL2	OM1	OL1	OM0	OL0

OMx	OLx	Action
0	0	Timer disconnected from I/O pin logic
0	1	Toggle OCx timer pin
1	0	Clear OCx timer pin
1	1	Set OCx timer pin

Figure 11.3: Timer Output Compare Configuration

Especially note that no pin action is performed when OMx and OLx are both zero. This configuration is particularly useful when an output compare is simply used to produce a periodic timing reference. In this situation, the associated port pin can be utilized as a general purpose I/O pin without negating the use of the timer channel. The remaining three functions, toggle, set, or clear, allow complete flexibility when generating an arbitrary output waveform. The ability to toggle the output pin state is especially useful when generating simple periodic waveforms such as a square wave or a PWM signal.

When a timer channel is configured as an input capture, the Port T DDR bits retain configuration control of the Port T timer pins. Therefore, timer channels configured as input captures should have their related DDR bits cleared to connect the associated pin to the edge detection logic. Even though a timer channel is configured as an input capture, the associated DDR bit can be set, configuring the pin as an output. In this situation, writes to the related bit in the Port T data register will cause input captures to occur if the pin logic is configured to respond to input edges. Much like OMx and OLx bits controlling the action of the output compare function, each channel has a separate pair of control bits used to configure the response of the input capture function. As shown in Figure 11.4 the TCTL3 and TCTL4 registers contain eight pairs of EDGxB and EDGxA control bits. The default value of these control bits is zero after reset, disconnecting the input capture function from its associated port pin. The other combinations of the EDGxB and EDGxA control bits allow the value of the 16-bit counter to be captured on the rising, falling or both edges. These options, combined with appropriate software, allow pulse and/or period measurements to be performed.

	Bit 7	6	5	4	3	2	1	Bit 0
TCTL3	EDG7B	EDG7A	EDG6B	EDG6A	EDG5B	EDG5A	EDG4B	EDG4A

	Bit 7	6	5	4	3	2	1	Bit 0
TCTL4	EDG3B	EDG3A	EDG2B	EDG2A	EDG1B	EDG1A	EDG0B	EDG0A

EDGxB	EDGxA	Configuration
0	0	Capture function disabled
0	1	Capture on rising edges only
1	0	Capture on falling edges only
1	1	Capture on rising and falling edges

Figure 11.4: Input Capture Pin Configuration

When utilizing any of the timer port pins as a general purpose I/O, the pin's associated bit in the TIOS register and the associated EDGxB and EDGxA control bits must all contain zeros. As with other I/O pins related to on-chip peripherals, the Port T pins provide the option of active pull-ups and/or reduced drive capability. Like most of the other peripheral ports where the active pull-up and reduced drive options exist, these options must be enabled or disabled for all the pins on the port. These options are controlled by the PUPT and RDPT bits as shown in Figure 11.5.

	Bit 7	6	5	4	3	2	1	Bit 0
TMSK2	TOI	0	**PUPT**	**RDPT**	TCRE	PR2	PR1	PR0

Figure 11.5: Port T Reduced Drive and Pull-up Control Bits

11.4 TIMER PRESCALER AND COUNTER CLOCK SOURCE

Of the remaining bits in the TMSK2 register, only the most significant bit, the Timer Overflow Interrupt (TOI) enable bit, is actually an interrupt mask control bit. The three least significant bits of this register, PR2:PR0, comprise the timer prescaler select bits. These three

Section 11.4: Timer Prescaler and Counter Clock Source

bits specify the clock scale factor applied to the module or E-clock before a clock is applied to the 16-bit free running counter. Unlike the M68HC11 family that only allowed prescale factors of 1, 4, 8 and 16, the M68HC12 prescaler allows prescale factors of 1, 2, 4, 8, 16 and 32 as shown in Figure 11.6. Note that the last two prescale bit combinations are reserved and should not be used.

⚠ M68HC12 Difference from the M68HC11

Readers familiar with the M68HC11 will remember that the timer prescaler control bits are protected and can only be written once in the first 64 E-clock cycles. The M68HC12 timer module does not impose any protection mechanism on the prescaler control bits. The prescale factor may be changed at any time, however the newly selected prescale factor will not take effect until the next time where *all* prescale counter stages are equal to zero. While the ability to change the timer prescale factor provides an extra degree of flexibility, care must be exercised when manipulating the remaining bits in the TMSK2 register to avoid inadvertently changing the counter's prescale factor.

PR2	PR1	PR0	Prescale Factor
0	0	0	÷1
0	0	1	÷2
0	1	0	÷4
0	1	1	÷8
1	0	0	÷16
1	0	1	÷32

Figure 11.6: Timer Prescale Rate Selection

In addition to offering extra prescale factors, the M68HC12 standard timer module offers the selection of an alternate clock source for the 16-bit free running counter. By default, the counter is clocked by the output of the prescaler module. However, two control bits contained in the Pulse Accumulator Control (PACTL) register allow the pulse accumulator clock to be used as the input to the timer's 16-bit free running counter. Obviously, when this mode of operation is selected, the counter is no longer 'free running', but is dependent upon the clock source selected for the pulse accumulator. Used in this manner, the 16-bit counter could behave more like a second pulse accumulator depending on the clock input option selected.

Figure 11.7 presents the four counter clock source options available. The first option, as mentioned previously, uses the timer prescaler output to drive the 16-bit free running counter. The remaining three options route the scaled input of the pulse accumulator to the 16-bit free running counter. The input to the pulse accumulator depends on the pulse accumulator operating mode selected by the `PAMOD` bit in the `PACTL` register. When the pulse accumulator is configured as a simple event counter, a rising or falling edge (selectable) applied to the PT7 timer pin causes both the pulse accumulator and the free running counter to be incremented. When configured for the gated time accumulation mode, the module clock divided by 64 is applied to both counters when a gating pulse of the proper logic level is applied to timer pin PT7.

CLK1	CLK0	Selected Counter Clock Source
0	0	Prescaler used as counter clock source
0	1	Pulse Accumulator input ÷ 1 used as counter clock source
1	0	Pulse Accumulator input ÷ 256 used as counter clock source
1	1	Pulse Accumulator input ÷ 65536 used as counter clock source

Figure 11.7: Counter Clock Source Options

Using this particular option to clock the timer's free running counter may not seem to have much use for most applications. However, configuring the pulse accumulator as a simple event counter and applying a continuous frequency waveform to the PT7 input will allow the main timer system to be used in a normal manner, yet provides much greater flexibility in the range of clock frequencies used for the main timer system. Of course supplying the main timer clock in this manner would negate the use of the pulse accumulator for its intended purpose. It should be noted that using this method to clock the 16-bit counter requires the pulse accumulator to be enabled. When the pulse accumulator is disabled, the timer prescaler is used to clock the free running counter regardless of the state of the `CLK0` and `CLK1` control bits.

⚠ **M68HC12 Difference from the M68HC11**

11.5 TIMER COUNTER RESET

Bit three of the `TMSK2` register, the Timer Counter Reset Enable (`TCRE`) bit, provides an additional capability not available on M68HC11 timer systems. When `TCRE` has a value of zero, the timer system operates normally allowing the 16-bit counter to free run. When the `TCRE` bit is set, the 16-bit counter is reset to $0000 when a successful output compare occurs on timer channel seven. One application of this operating mode allows up to seven highly accurate PWM outputs using timer channels zero through six when configured as output compares. In such an application, a count representing the PWM period is loaded

Section 11.6: Timer Channel Flags and Interrupts

into the timer channel seven compare register, while a count representing the PWM duty cycle is written into each channel's output compare register. While this special operating mode would not negate the use of some of the timer channels as input captures for pulse or frequency measurement, additional arithmetic is required to obtain the proper results. If TC7 contains a value of $0000 when TCRE is set, the Timer Counter Register (TCNT) register will remain at $0000. If TC7 contains a value of $FFFF when TCRE is set, the timer will operate normally counting from $0000 through $FFFF except that the Timer Overflow Interrupt (TOI) flag will never be set.

11.6 Timer Channel Flags and Interrupts

As explained previously, each time a successful input capture or output compare occurs, a flag in the TFLG1 register is set. These flags can be polled by software to determine if a timer channel event has occurred. Alternately, if the corresponding bit in the TMSK1 register is set, a timer channel interrupt is generated if the I-bit in the CPU12's condition code register is clear. Whether utilizing the timer in a polled or interrupt driven manner, the timer channel flag must be cleared before another event on the same channel can be recognized by software. When operating the timer in an interrupt driven manner, it is imperative that a timer channel's flag is cleared before exiting the interrupt service routine. Failure to clear the flag will result in the generation of another interrupt by the same timer channel immediately after returning. This will cause the CPU12 to continually execute the interrupt service routine to the exclusion of all other software. The only way to terminate such a situation is through a CPU reset.

	Bit 7	6	5	4	3	2	1	Bit 0
TFLG1	C7F	C6F	C5F	C4F	C3F	C2F	C1F	C0F

	Bit 7	6	5	4	3	2	1	Bit 0
TMSK1	C7I	C6I	C5I	C4I	C3I	C2I	C1I	C0I

Figure 11.8: Timer Flag 1 and Timer Mask 1 Registers

Like the M68HC11 family, clearing the timer channel flags involves writing a value of one to the bit position corresponding to the set flag. Several different instruction sequences can be used to clear the flags. However, the most common method is to simply load the A or B accumulator with a value having a one in the bit position corresponding to the set bit and storing the value to the appropriate timer flag register. Note that the BSET instruction should *not* be used to clear bits in the timer flag registers because the instruction could unintentionally clear other bits in the register. For example, consider what might happen if bits C7F and C6F in TFLG1 are both set, and the `BSET TFLG1,#$80` instruction is executed in an attempt to clear C7F. Because the BSET is a read-modify-write instruction, it will read the value of $C0 from the TFLG1 register, perform a logical OR with the supplied mask value of $80 and then write the result back to TFLG1. The logical OR operation results in a value of $C0 being written to the TFLG1 register, clearing C7F *and* C6F.

A second method that can be used to clear the timer channel flags involves the use of the BCLR instruction. This at first may seem counter intuitive since the BSET cannot be used to clear the flags. However, close examination of the operations performed by the BCLR instruction reveal the reason why this instruction works properly. Like the BSET instruction, BCLR performs a read-modify-write operation on a referenced memory location. However, the BCLR instruction performs a logical AND operation with the *ones compliment* of the supplied mask value. By supplying a mask value that has a zero in the bit position of the flag to be cleared and ones in all the remaining bits, a one will be written only to the flag bit to be cleared. In the example presented in the previous paragraph, the ones compliment of $80 or $7F could be used with the BCLR instruction to clear the C7F timer channel flag. Note that the assembler's bit compliment operator can be used to calculate the proper bit mask making the assembler source more readable and less error prone. For example, rather than writing `BCLR TFLG1,#$7F` to clear the C7F flag the source line could be written `BCLR TFLG1,#~$80`.

⚠ M68HC12 Difference from the M68HC11

In addition to the standard method of clearing the timer flags, the M68HC12 standard timer module provides an additional feature that reduces the software overhead. This feature is controlled by the Timer Fast Flag Clear All (TFFCA) bit in the Timer System Control Register (TSCR). When the TFFCA has a value of zero, its default value, the timer flags are cleared as previously described. When TFFCA has a value of one, reads from an input capture or writes to an output compare will automatically clear the corresponding channel flag. In addition, a read of the TCNT register will cause the TOF bit in the TFLG2 register to be cleared. Likewise the two flags associated with the Pulse Accumulator, PAOVF and PAIF in the the Pulse Accumulator Flag (PAFLG) Register, are cleared with a read or write of the Pulse Accumulator Count (PACNT) register. While using this feature has the advantage of eliminating the small amount of software overhead in clearing the flags, extra care is required to avoid accidentally clearing a flag. This is especially true for applications requiring use of the timer overflow function since simply reading the value of the TCNT register when the TOF bit is set automatically clears the TOF bit. When selecting the Timer Fast Flag Clear All option, *none* of the timer flags can be cleared using the standard clearing mechanism. However, because the TFFCA is not write-once protected, it is possible, but not advisable, to change the timer flag clearing mechanism during program execution.

Section 11.7: Timer System Control

	Bit 7	6	5	4	3	2	1	Bit 0
TSCR	TEN	TSWAI	TSBCK	TFFCA	0	0	0	0

Figure 11.9: Timer System Control Register (TSCR)

⚠ **M68HC12 Difference from the M68HC11**

11.7 TIMER SYSTEM CONTROL

As shown in Figure 11.9, in addition to the TFFCA control bit, three additional control bits reside in the TSCR register. The Timer Enable (TEN) bit is used to enable or disable the entire timer system including the counter and prescaler. By default, the value of the TEN bit is zero placing the timer system in a disabled state. Even though the TEN bit must be set before normal timer operations can be performed, all of the timer registers may be read or written when the timer is disabled. Like the timer prescaler control bits, the TEN bit is not write-once protected and may be read and written at any time. While this provides a great deal of flexibility in using the timer system, most applications will set the TEN bit during system initialization and allow it to remain set during the remainder of program execution.

One example of a specialized application where the timer system is repeatedly enabled and disabled is the on-chip Flash memory bootloader presented in Chapter 8. In this example it was necessary to produce a short, accurate delay used to time the high-voltage programming pulse for the Flash memory. As shown in the listing in Figure 8.17, before each program cycle begins, the timer subsystem is disabled by clearing the TEN. When the timer is disabled, the contents of all timer registers, including the value of the TCNT, are maintained and may be read or written. This allows the software to read the value of the TCNT register, add a value that produces a 22 µS delay and write the result to the TC0 register. Using the timer in this manner allows a delay constant to be used without having to compensate for any intervening instruction execution time.

Bit six of the TSCR register, the Timer Stop in Wait (TSWAI) mode allows the timer system to be stopped when the timer enters the low power wait mode and then automatically be re-enabled when the M68HC12 exits the wait mode. While this feature can be useful in reducing power consumption especially in battery powered applications, none of the timer system functions can be used to exit the wait mode.

The Timer Stops while in Background mode (TSBCK) control bit is principally used by development tool software. When set, the timer system is automatically stopped when the CPU12 enters active background mode and then re-enabled when normal program execution resumes. It should be recognized that with the current implementation of the M68HC12 Single Wire Background Debug system, that even though the TCNT register always maintains an accurate count, the TCNT value may be advanced several counts when entering and exiting active background mode when this feature is enabled. The number of counts, if any, will depend on the setting of the timer prescaler and the value of the prescale counter when entering active background mode. For most applications, this slight difference in timer values between instruction traces should not cause a problem; however, it is something to keep in mind when debugging an application making extensive use of the timer system.

⚠ **M68HC12 Difference from the M68HC11**

11.8 Special Timer Features

Like the M68HC11 family, the timer system allows one of the output compare functions to simultaneously control the state of all pins configured as output compares. The M68HC11 family timer uses output compare one for this function; however, in the M68HC12 standard timer module this feature is assigned to timer channel seven.

Output compare seven uses the control bits in the Output Compare 7 Mask (OC7M) and Output Compare 7 Data (OC7D) registers to control the automatic timer output actions occurring as a result of a successful compare on timer channel seven. Each of the bits in these registers corresponds bit-for-bit with the Port T timer pins. For each of the Port T output compare pins to be affected by the output compare action on channel seven, the pin's corresponding bit in the OC7M register must be set. If a timer port pin is configured as an output compare pin, setting a bit in the OC7M register causes the corresponding Port T pin to be configured as an output regardless of the state of the corresponding data direction bit or the output compare action selected by the associated OMx and OLx control bits.

	Bit 7	6	5	4	3	2	1	Bit 0
OC7M	OC7M7	OC7M6	OC7M5	OC7M4	OC7M3	OC7M2	OC7M1	OC7M0

	Bit 7	6	5	4	3	2	1	Bit 0
OC7D	OC7D7	OC7D6	OC7D5	OC7D4	OC7D3	OC7D2	OC7D1	OC7D0

Figure 11.10: Output Compare 7 Mask (OC7M) and Output Compare 7 Data (OC7D) Registers

When an output compare occurs on channel seven, the value of the related data bit in the OC7D register is driven onto the Port T timer pin. In the event that an output compare occurs during the same cycle on channel seven and a timer channel whose associated OC7M bit is set, the timer channel's action will depend upon the value stored to the OC7D register.

Section 11.9: Timer Initialization

One other special feature of the standard timer module allows an output compare action to be forced without setting up an output compare event. The force compare feature is useful to establish an initial state of the output compare or to force an output compare event earlier than it was scheduled to occur. This feature is especially useful for a control system involving spark timing of an internal combustion engine. In this case the exact time to fire a cylinder's spark plug is based on a number of factors, but is primarily based upon the crank shaft position. For an engine running at steady state, the time at which to schedule an output compare event for spark firing is completely predictable and easily calculated. However, if factors, including engine speed, change between the time the spark event is scheduled and the time when it will actually occur, the force compare feature can be used to fire the spark plug earlier than scheduled. Without this feature, such an application would be required to read the value of the timer counter, add a constant to the timer value and update the output compare register so that the compare occurred on the timer clock cycle following the write to the output compare register. While using such a technique is not difficult, it can be error prone because the value of the constant depends on the setting of the timer prescaler and the number of clock cycles required to read the timer and update the output compare register.

The force compare mechanism is activated by writing ones to the bit positions in the Timer Force Compare (CFORC) register associated with the corresponding output compare channels. The next timer clock cycle following the write to the CFORC register causes the previously programmed output compare action to occur on the selected output compare channels. The only difference between a forced output compare action and one caused by a match between the TCNT and an output compare register is that a force compare does not set the timer channel event flag in the TFLG1 register.

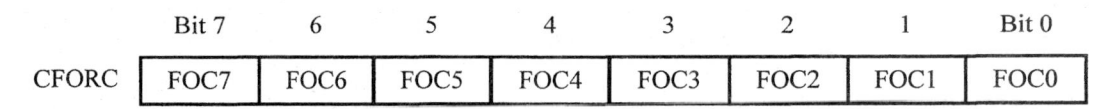

	Bit 7	6	5	4	3	2	1	Bit 0
CFORC	FOC7	FOC6	FOC5	FOC4	FOC3	FOC2	FOC1	FOC0

Figure 11.11: Timer Force Compare (CFORC) Register

11.9 TIMER INITIALIZATION

Because the timer module is disabled when the M68HC12 exits the reset state it must be enabled before any timer operations can be performed. However, as mentioned previously, even though the timer is disabled, all of the timer's registers are accessible and may be read or written as appropriate. All of the timer module's configuration registers may be initialized before or after the the timer is enabled. The exact order of initialization depends on each application and the timing functions used.

Basic initialization of the timer module involves writing the `TSCR` register with the appropriate to enable the timer system and select the other available options. If the required timer prescale factor is other than the default value, the `TMSK2` register can be written with the desired value either before or after enabling the timer system. Realize, however, that the new prescale factor does not take effect until the next time where all the prescale counter stages are equal to zero. This is the case even if the required prescale factor is written to the `TMSK2` register before the timer system is enabled.

After enabling the timer system, the `TIOS` register can be written to configure each timer channel as an input capture or output compare. Remember that for timer channels configured as input captures, the associated `EDGxA` and `EDGxB` bits in the `TCTL3` and `TCTL4` registers must also be configured to connect the input pin to the input edge detection circuitry. For channels configured as output compares, the associated `OMx` and `OLx` bits in the `TCTL1` and `TCTL2` registers need to be written only if a connection to the external pin is required.

Timer channels utilized in an interrupt driven manner must have their associated timer interrupt mask bits in the `TMSK1` register set before an interrupt can be generated. However, before enabling the interrupts, it is usually a good idea to reset all of the timer interrupt flags in the `TFLG1` register to avoid any spurious interrupts as a result of input captures or output compares that might have occurred during the timer initialization process.

11.10 Period Measurement

Measuring the period of a repetitive waveform involves capturing the value of the free running counter on successive edges of the same polarity and subtracting the two values. The result of the subtraction is the period of a single cycle of the waveform in timer clock cycles. Many applications are able to perform their required actions by utilizing the calculated period measurement directly or with a simple conversion through a look up table. Some applications may utilize complex calculations involving various scientific units of measurement or may use the time measurement to represent speed or angular position. In these cases there may be a need to convert the period measurement into the required units.

Section 11.10: Period Measurement

```
;
IC0Period:      ds.w    1               ; contains calculated period.
LastIC0:        ds.w    1               ; last input capture value.
ValidIC0:       ds.b    1               ; Flag for ISR to check for valid IC0.
;
IC0Setup:       clra
                clrb
                std     IC0Period       ; init period to zero.
                stab    ValidIC0        ; no valid ICs have occurred yet.
                ldab    #TEN+TFFCA      ; enable timer & select fast flag clear.
                stab    TSCR
                bset    TCTL4,#EDG0A    ; config Ch. 0 to capture on rising edges.
                ldd     TC0             ; clear possible spurious input capture.
                bset    TMSK1,#C0I      ; enable timer interrupts.
                cli                     ; enable cpu interrupts.
                bra     *               ; the ISR does all the work.
;
IC0ISR:         ldd     TC0             ; get IC value, clear IC0 flag.
                tfr     d,y             ; save a copy in y.
                tst     ValidIC0        ; LastIC0 contain a capture value?
                bne     CalcPeriod      ; yes. go calc the period.
                inc     ValidIC0        ; no. set the flag & go save the value.
                bra     NoPeriod
CalcPeriod:     subd    LastIC0         ; yes. sub current value from prev value.
                std     IC0Period       ; save the result as the period.
NoPeriod:       sty     LastIC0         ; update LastIC1 with current capture value
                rti                     ; return.
;
```

Figure 11.12: Period Measurement Using Input Capture With Interrupts

Figure 11.12 presents a code fragment that measures the period of a repetitive waveform applied to the PT0 timer port pin. In this example the timer is operated in an interrupt driven manner. The main portion of the code, beginning at the label `IC0Setup`, merely enables the timer module, configures timer channel zero to capture the timer value on every rising edge, and then enables the timer and CPU12 interrupts. At the end of the setup code, the M68HC12 executes a branch-to-self instruction allowing the timer interrupt service routine to perform all of the work. In an actual application, the branch-to-self instruction would be replaced with code that performs other tasks in the system. Because the interrupt service routine performs the task of period measurement, it will be discussed in detail.

The basic job of the TC0 interrupt service routine is to retrieve the captured value of the free running counter, subtract the value captured on a previous edge of the same polarity, and save the result in a global variable where it can be retrieved by other routines in the system. The timer channel zero interrupt service routine, beginning at label `IC0ISR`, starts by reading the value in the input capture register and saving a copy of the value in the Y index register. This copy is later used to update the value in the `LastIC0` variable which holds the previously captured counter value. Because the setup routine enabled the Timer Fast Flag Clear All option, this action also clears the timer interrupt flag associated with this channel.

The first time the interrupt service routine is executed, the value in the `LastIC0` variable will not contain a captured counter value. In fact, because it is not initialized by the setup routine, it will contain whatever value might have been left from a memory test routine or random power-up data. To avoid calculating an invalid period value, a flag variable, `ValidIC0`, is set to zero by the initialization routine. When the interrupt service routine is executed the first time, the value of the variable is checked before calculating a period value. If the value is zero, it is set to a non-zero value, the captured counter value is stored in the `LastIC0` variable and the interrupt service routine returns. All subsequent executions of the interrupt service routine will detect a non-zero value in `ValidIC0` and calculate a new period value updating the `LastIC0` and `IC0Period` variables. While this may seem to be a bit of overkill, it does ensure that the first non-zero value available in the `IC0Period` variable is valid. If an application can tolerate an invalid period value for one cycle of an incoming waveform, this portion of the interrupt service routine can be eliminated. This will help to reduce the total overhead of calculating a waveform's period.

There are a number of things to consider when using the timer input capture function to measure a waveform's period or frequency. Because there is a fixed amount of software overhead involved in servicing the timer interrupt and calculating the period, the highest measurable frequency will be limited by the amount of time required to execute the interrupt service routine. In addition, any time periods when interrupts are disabled, such as when other interrupt service routines are being executed, must be taken into account. Using the example presented in Figure 11.12, the total interrupt service routine overhead is equal to 27 E-clock cycles. Assuming that interrupts are never disabled and no other interrupt latencies exist, at a very minimum the execution time for longest instruction, `EMACS` which requires 13 clock cycles, must be added to this cycle count. This would bring the total cycle count to 40, which is equivalent to 5.0 µS utilizing an 8.0 MHz E-clock. This time period is equivalent to a single cycle of a waveform with a frequency of 200,000 Hz. While it is quite possible to perform period measurements on waveforms with frequencies in this range, the CPU12 would spend the majority of its time, more than 67% (27 ÷ 40), servicing this single timer input capture channel. Most applications do not require the measurement of waveforms with frequencies this high. In fact many applications involve period measurement of waveforms with frequencies from several hundred to several thousand hertz. However, this example does show the need for careful analysis of system requirements involving CPU time utilization in relationship to timer interrupt service routines.

An additional consideration is the range of frequencies that can be measured when performing period measurements. The previous paragraph discussed some of the considerations that limit the timer's ability to measure high frequency waveforms. However,

Section 11.10: Period Measurement

there are also some limitations in measuring the period of low frequency waveforms. While these limitations can be overcome utilizing the timer overflow interrupt and additional software, it is a good idea to avoid using these techniques if possible. Three things determine the lowest frequency that can be accurately measured: the module or E-clock frequency, the number of timer bits, and the timer prescaler setting. Obviously because the number of timer bits cannot be changed and because the microcontroller clock is usually chosen for system performance reasons, the only item that can easily be changed is the timer prescaler value. Figure 11.13 shows the lowest frequency that can be accurately measured for various prescale factors at module clock frequencies of 4.0 and 8.0 MHz.

Prescale Factor	Min Freq. w/ 4.0 MHz E-clock	Min Freq. w/ 8.0 MHz E-clock
÷ 1	61 Hz	122 Hz
÷ 2	30.5 Hz	61 Hz
÷ 4	15.25 Hz	30.5 Hz
÷ 8	7.63 Hz	15.25 Hz
÷ 16	3.8 Hz	7.63 Hz
÷ 32	1.9 Hz	3.8 Hz

Figure 11.13: Lowest Frequency Measurement vs Prescaler Setting

The prescale factor affects not only the lowest measurable frequency, it also influences the resolution of the measured period. The smaller the prescale factor, the greater the resolution of the period measurement. For many applications, especially those measuring the period of lower frequency signals, the resolution at even the highest prescaler factors is acceptable. However, for period measurements involving higher frequency waveforms, the prescale factor can make a significant difference in the smallest detectable variation of a measured signal. For example, if a periodic signal with a nominal frequency of 10,000 Hz is being measured and a prescale factor of ÷32 is chosen for an 8.0 MHz module clock, the measured period would result in a value of 25 timer counts. This number represents the period of one cycle of a 10,000 Hz signal *exactly*. Because because each timer count represents 4 µS, a measured period count of 24 would actually represent a frequency of 10,417 Hz and a count of 26 would represent a frequency of 9615 Hz. This measurement uncertainty represents an error of approximately 4% around the nominal frequency.

On the other hand, if a prescale factor of ÷1 is chosen for the same application, the measured period would result in a value of 800 timer counts for a 10,000 Hz signal. In this case, because each timer count represents .125 µS, a timer count of 799 would represent a frequency of 10,013 Hz and a count of 801 would represent a frequency of 9988 Hz. Here, the measurement uncertainty represents an error of a little more than 0.1% around the nominal frequency.

11.11 Pulse Width Measurement

Measuring the width of repetitive or non-repetitive pulses is similar to period measurement except the timer value is captured on edges of opposite polarity. For instance, if an application is required to measure the width of a negative going pulse, the value of the timer's counter is first captured on the falling edge and then on the rising edge. Subtracting the first value from the second value produces the width of the pulse in timer clock cycles.

Figure 11.14 presents a code fragment that performs pulse width measurement for negative going signals. The setup code beginning at label IC0Setup is very similar to that in Figure 11.13. However, in this case the timer prescaler is set to divide by four and input capture one is configured to capture the counter value on the first negative going edge applied to the PT0 pin. Like the period measurement example, most of the work is performed by the interrupt service routine.

The interrupt service routine, beginning at label IC0PWISR, starts by reading the value in the input capture register. Next, the interrupt service routine checks the state of the EDG0B control bit to determine if the capture resulted from a negative or positive edge on PT0. If the capture was the result of a negative edge, the counter value is saved in LastIC0 and the EDG0A and EDG0B control bits are reconfigured to perform the next capture on a rising edge. If a positive edge caused the capture, the value in LastIC0 is subtracted from the counter value and the result saved in IC0PW. The EDG0A and EDG0B control bits are reconfigured to perform the next capture on a falling edge. Finally, the code beginning at the label Finish is executed to prepare the input capture to respond to the next negative going edge. The method used to reconfigure the control bits involves inverting the bits using an exclusive-OR operation. This method has an advantage over using BSET and BCLR instructions and should be obvious by examining the interrupt service routine. Because both bits simply need to be inverted, the same instruction sequence can be used after a negative or positive edge has been detected resulting in a smaller interrupt service routine.

Section 11.11: Pulse Width Measurement

```
;
ICOPW:      ds.w    1               ; contains calculated pulse width.
LastIC0:    ds.w    1               ; last input capture value.
;
IC0Setup:   clra
            clrb
            std     ICOPW           ; init pulse width to zero.
            ldab    #2
            stab    TMSK2           ; set prescaler to /4.
            ldab    #TEN+TFFCA      ; enable timer & select fast flag clear.
            stab    TSCR
            bset    TCTL4,#EDG0B    ; config Ch. 0 to capture on falling edges.
            ldd     TC0             ; clear possible spurious input capture.
            bset    TMSK1,#C0I      ; enable timer interrupts.
            cli                     ; enable cpu interrupts.
            bra     *               ; the ISR does all the work.
;
ICOPWISR:   ldd     TC0             ; get IC value, clear IC0 flag.
            brclr   TCTL4,#EDG0B,CalcPW ; just captured a rising edge.
            std     LastIC0         ; captured a falling edge, save value.
Finish:     ldab    TCTL4           ; get EDG0B & EDG0A value.
            eorb    #EDG0B+EDG0A    ; invert them.
            stab    TCTL4           ; update the values.
            rti                     ; return.
CalcPW:     subd    LastIC0         ; subtract the value from the falling edge.
            std     ICOPW           ; save the pulse width.
            bra     Finish          ; go finish up.
;
```

Figure 11.14: Pulse Width Measurement Using Input Capture With Interrupts

Many of the same considerations and restrictions involved in period measurement also apply to pulse width measurement. Obviously, because of the overhead of the interrupt service routine and the need to reconfigure the edge detection logic, there is a minimum pulse width that can be measured for a given interrupt service routine, module clock frequency, and prescaler setting. What might not be quite as obvious is the fact that the restrictions regarding the minimum measurable pulse width also applies to the minimum allowable high time between the width of long, repetitive negative pulses. The minimum high time between negative going pulses, illustrated in Figure 11.15, is essentially equal to the minimum measurable negative going pulse.

Minimum Pulse Width

Minimum High Time Between Pulses

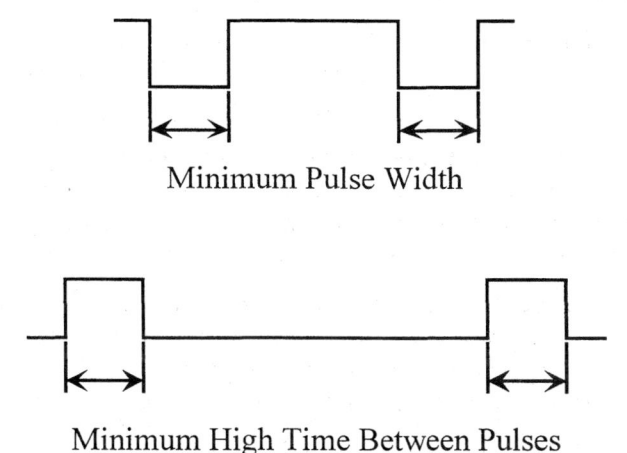

Figure 11.15: Pulse Width Measurement Restrictions

11.12 PULSE TRAIN PULSE MEASUREMENT

Some applications, such as a simple infrared (IR) or radio frequency (RF) communications data link, require the reception of data in the form of pulse width encoded signals. The input capture function can be used to measure both positive and negative going pulses of an incoming signal, storing the results in an array of variables for processing by other routines. This application combines the techniques for pulse width and period measurement presented in the two previous examples. Figure 11.16 presents the initialization code and interrupt service routine necessary to measure the high and low times of an incoming pulse train.

The listing begins with several declarations that allocate storage space for the required variables and sets the maximum number of pulses measured. Three variables are required in this example to measure the width of a variable number of pulses. The first variable, PWArray, is an array of 16-bit elements used to contain values representing the width of the measured pulses. In addition, each array element is used to save the captured value of the timer's counter at each edge so that the pulse width can be calculated at the next detected clock edge. The double use of each array element reduces the requirement for a separate variable to maintain the last captured counter value and also allows for an efficient implementation of the interrupt service routine. The second variable, PWArrayP, is a single 16-bit pointer used to access the various elements of PWArray. Finally, EdgeCount is a one byte variable containing a count of the *clock edges* to be detected for a given number of pulses. Because the number of clock edges is always one more than the number of pulses, this variable must be initialized with a count of one more than the number of pulses to be

Section 11.12: Pulse Train Pulse Measurement

measured. This restriction seems to limit the software to receiving a maximum of 254 pulses. However, if `EdgeCount` is initialized to zero, a total of 255 pulses may be measured.

The initialization code, beginning at `IC0Setup`, initializes the variables `EdgeCount`, `PWArrayP` and then initializes the timer using the same code appearing in Figure 11.12. As with the other two examples, after the initialization is complete, the CPU12 executes a branch-to-self instruction while the interrupt service routine performs the pulse measurement tasks.

The interrupt service routine begins by reading the value of timer channel zero's capture register, clearing the input capture flag. As when measuring the period of a fixed frequency signal, there is a need to check for the first detected edge so an erroneous pulse measurement is not performed. In the example of Figure 11.12, this function was performed by using a one byte flag variable set to a non zero value after the first edge was detected. In this example, rather than use an additional variable, we simply compare the value of the array pointer, `PWArrayP`, to the address of of `PWArray`. If the two values match, it indicates that the first edge has been detected. In this case, the captured value of the timer is saved in the first element of `PWArray`, `PWArrayP` is updated to point to the next array entry and the input capture edge detection logic is reconfigured to detect the next clock edge. Before returning, the value of `EdgeCount` is decremented. When its value reaches zero, indicating that the pulse train measurement is complete, channel zero interrupts are disabled preventing any additional interrupts until the data measurements can be processed.

```
MaxPulses:    equ     10
;
PWArray:      ds      2*MaxPulses    ; array for PW of incoming pulse train.
PWArrayP:     ds      2              ; pointer to the next PW array entry.
EdgeCount:    ds      1              ; number of edges remaining to be detected.
;
IC0Setup:     ldab    #MaxPulses+1   ; edges is # of pulses + 1.
              stab    EdgeCount
              ldx     #PWArray       ; init pointer to the PW storage array.
              stx     PWArrayP
              ldab    #TEN+TFFCA     ; enable timer & select fast flag clear.
              stab    TSCR
              bset    TCTL4,#EDG0A   ; config Ch. 0 to capture on rising edges.
              ldd     TC0            ; clear possible spurious input capture.
              bset    TMSK1,#C0I     ; enable timer interrupts.
              cli                    ; enable cpu interrupts.
              bra     *              ; the ISR does all the work.
;
IC0ISR:       ldd     TC0            ; get IC value, clear IC0 flag.
              tfr     d,y            ; save a copy in y.
              ldx     PWArrayP       ; get pointer to PW storage array.
              cpx     #PWArray       ; first edge?
              beq     NoPeriod       ; yes. go save captured value & return.
              subd    -2,x           ; no sub current value from prev value.
              std     -2,x           ; overwrite last captured value.
NoPeriod:     sty     2,x+           ; update LastIC1 with current capture value
              stx     PWArrayP       ; save updated pointer.
              ldab    TCTL4          ; get EDG0B & EDG0A value.
              eorb    #EDG0B+EDG0A   ; invert them.
              stab    TCTL4          ; update the values.
              dec     EdgeCount      ; done with all rcv'd pulses?
              bne     IC0ISRtn       ; no. just return.
              bclr    TMSK1,#C0I     ; yes. disable timer interrupts.
IC0ISRtn:     rti                    ; return.
;
```

Figure 11.16: Pulse Train Measurement Using Input Capture

For all subsequent executions of the interrupt service routine, the previously captured timer value is subtracted from the newly captured value with the result overwriting the previously saved capture value. Notice that because the value in PWArrayP is updated at the end of the interrupt service routine, the previously saved capture value is located at an offset of -2 from the value of the pointer. Finally, the instruction sequence beginning at the label FirstEdge is executed performing the same actions described for the first detected edge.

11.13 MEASURING VERY SHORT PULSES

As discussed in the previous section, because of the software overhead involved in servicing an input capture channel, there is a minimum pulse width that can be measured for a given interrupt service routine, module clock frequency, and prescaler setting using a single input capture channel. It is possible, however, to utilize two input capture channels connected to the same source signal to measure pulse widths as small as one timer count. To perform such a measurement, one input capture channel must be configured to capture the counter value on the leading edge of the pulse while the other channel is configured to capture the counter value on the trailing edge of the pulse. Determining the pulse width is simply a matter of subtracting the counter value captured on the leading edge of the pulse from the counter value captured on the trailing edge of the pulse.

11.14 ALTERNATE USES FOR INPUT CAPTURE CHANNELS

Because many applications do not require all eight timer channels, unused channels may be configured as input captures and used as edge sensitive interrupt inputs each with its own interrupt vector. Utilizing spare timer channels in this manner has two key advantages over the IRQ interrupt input of the M68HC12. First, because the input capture edge detection circuitry is configurable, each input may be configured to generate an interrupt on a rising edge, a falling edge, or both edges. This extra flexibility can be important for some specific applications and may simplify the interface of an external peripheral or signal. The second advantage is related to the status flags associated with each timer channel. Because these flags may be read by software, an application can determine if an interrupt is pending from one of these sources. This capability allows application software to clear a pending interrupt before enabling the source.

11.15 WAVEFORM GENERATION USING OUTPUT COMPARE

The output compare function, rather than being a dedicated function for generating output waveforms, is controlled by software, allowing a great variety of timing tasks to be performed. With the appropriate software, the output compare function can generate waveforms as simple as a square wave or pulse width modulated (PWM) signal, to complex pulse trains used to control fuel injection or ignition spark in automotive applications. Because of the software overhead involved in performing simple functions, the output compare function is not suitable for generating high frequency repetitive signals. While the PWM module, discussed in Chapter 12, is much better suited for such applications, the output compare function is more flexible and has a much wider range of applications than the PWM module.

Chapter 11: Standard Timer Module

Because each timer channel is configurable as an output compare, the MC68HC912B32 is capable of having up to eight output compare channels. Each channel has its own value compare register and a dedicated 16-bit comparator. Each timer clock cycle, the comparator compares the value of the counter to the value in the compare register. When the two match, the timer channel's interrupt flag is set, an interrupt is optionally generated and depending on the OMx and OLx settings in the `TCTL1` and `TCTL2` registers, the associated output pin is optionally changed. When configured as output compares, seven of the eight timer channels possess identical capabilities. Channel seven, however, can control any combination of the remaining timer channels configured as output compares.

From a CPU utilization viewpoint, even though it is more efficient to use the PWM module to generate a periodic signal of fixed frequency and duty cycle, there are still many situations that can benefit from using the output compare. One of the most common uses of the output compare function is to establish a reference time interval for the execution of periodic tasks. In many systems, for example, the application is structured in such a way that a main program loop is executed performing non-time critical tasks. An output compare is used to interrupt the main program at a fixed interval to execute one or more of the periodic tasks. Figure 11.17 shows a code fragment that initializes the timer system. Also included is an interrupt service routine that supports the output compare interrupt.

```
Period10mS: equ     SysClock/100/2
;
OC0Setup:   bset    TIOS,#IOS0      ; configure channel 0 as output compare.
            ldab    #1              ; set prescaler for ÷2.
            stab    TMSK2
            ldab    #TEN+TFFCA      ; enable timer & select fast flag clear.
            stab    TSCR
            ldd     #Period10mS     ; get value for 10mS period.
            addd    TCNT            ; add it to the current timer value
            std     TC0             ; setup OC0, clearing any pending IRQs.
            bset    TMSK1,#C0I      ; enable timer interrupts.
            cli                     ; enable cpu interrupts.
            bra     *               ; the ISR does all the work.
;
OC0ISR:     ldd     TC0             ; get IC value, clear IC0 flag.
            addd    #Period10mS     ; add value for 10mS period.
            std     TC0             ; setup OC0, clearing COF.
            rti                     ; return to main task.
;
```

Figure 11.17: Fixed Period Output Compare Example

Section 11.15: Waveform Generation Using Output Compare

It is obvious from the listing that the code required to setup the timer requires more than twice the number of instructions as the interrupt service routine. If this code were used as part of an application, the interrupt service routine would most likely be longer. However, if an application is only required to produce a fixed frequency, fixed duty cycle waveform, the setup code and interrupt service routine can be used with a couple of small modifications. In this example an interrupt period of 10 mS was arbitrarily chosen, producing interrupts at a rate of 100 per second. To generate an output waveform of 100 Hz, the constant, `Period10mS` would need to be half the 10 mS value. This would cause the output compare to keep the associated pin high for 5 mS and then low for the other half of the cycle. The other necessary change involves the initialization of timer channel zero's OL0 control bit allowing the output pin to be toggled automatically each time an output compare occurs.

Before proceeding to the next example, it is important to understand the calculation of the `Period10mS` constant. The value calculated for the `Period10mS` constant needs to represent the number of counter clocks required to produce a 10 mS period. Because a 10 mS period is equal to an interrupt frequency of 100 Hz, the input frequency to the timer counter must be divided by 100 to obtain the correct count. Initially, dividing the system clock of 8.0 MHz by 100 results in a count of 80,000 which is larger than can be represented by a 16-bit number. If the input frequency to the 16-bit counter is reduced to 4.0 MHz, a count value of 40,000 is required to produce a 10 mS period. Because a count of 40,000 is small enough to fit in the precision of a 16-bit number, the prescaler is initialized to divide the system clock by two. This is the reason for the additional division by two in the calculation of the `Period10mS` constant.

The listing in Figure 11.18 contains the necessary modifications to generate a 100 Hz square wave on pin PT0. Changes in the setup routine include the addition of an instruction to enable automatic output pin toggling and the removal of the instructions that set the prescaler to divide by two. In the previous example to allow a 10 mS interrupt period with an 8.0 MHz module clock the prescaler had to be set to divide by two. However, because the interrupt period is 5 mS for the 100 Hz signal, the prescaler can be left at its default setting.

When generating fixed or variable duty cycle waveforms utilizing the output compare function, several things must be taken into consideration. Like the timer input capture function, there is a fixed amount of software overhead involved in servicing an output compare interrupt. The interrupt execution time, plus the applications's interrupt latency, determines the highest frequency waveform that can practically be generated using the output compare. In the example given in Figure 11.18 the interrupt service routine requires 15 E-clock cycles. Assuming that interrupts are never disabled and no other interrupt latencies exist, the execution time for longest instruction, EMACS requiring 13 clock cycles, must be added to this cycle count. This brings the total cycle count to 28, which is equivalent to 3.5 µS utilizing an 8.0 MHz E-clock. This time period is approximately equivalent to a *half* cycle of a 143,000 Hz square wave. While it is possible to generate a square wave with a frequency this high, the CPU12 would have time to do little else. In fact, the CPU12 would spend the majority of its time, more than 53% (15 ÷ 28), servicing this single timer output compare channel. Most applications do not require the generation of signals with frequencies this high. In fact most applications involve waveform generation with frequencies from several hundred to several thousand hertz. However, this example does show the need for careful analysis of system requirements involving CPU time utilization with regards to timer interrupt service routines.

```
Hz100:      equ    SysClock/100/2
;
OC0Setup:   bset   TIOS,#IOS0        ; configure channel 0 as output compare.
            bset   TCTL2,#OL0        ; toggle PT0 at every output compare.
            ldab   #TEN+TFFCA        ; enable timer & select fast flag clear.
            stab   TSCR
            ldd    #Hz100            ; get value for 5mS interrupt period.
            addd   TCNT              ; add it to the current timer value
            std    TC0               ; setup OC0, clearing any pending IRQs.
            bset   TMSK1,#C0I        ; enable timer interrupts.
            cli                      ; enable cpu interrupts.
            bra    *                 ; the ISR does all the work.
;
OC0ISR:     ldd    TC0               ; get IC value, clear IC0 flag.
            addd   #Hz100            ; add value for 5mS half period.
            std    TC0               ; setup OC0, clearing C0F.
            rti                      ; return to main task.
;
```

Figure 11.18: Square Wave Generation Using Output Compare

An additional consideration when generating waveforms is the lowest frequency that can be produced. The previous paragraph discussed some of the considerations limiting the timer's ability to produce high frequency waveforms, however, there are also limitations when generating low frequency waveforms. While these limitations can be overcome utilizing the timer overflow interrupt and additional software, it is a good idea to avoid using these techniques if possible. Three things determine the lowest frequency that can be directly generated by an output compare: the module or E-clock frequency, the number of timer bits and the timer prescaler setting. Obviously because the number of timer bits cannot be changed and because the microcontroller clock is usually chosen for system performance reasons, the only factor that can be easily changed is the timer prescaler value. Figure 11.19 shows the lowest frequency square wave that can be generated for various prescale factors at module clock frequencies of 4.0 and 8.0 MHz.

Section 11.16: Pulse Width Modulated Waveform Generation

Prescale Factor	Min Freq. Waveform w/ 4.0 MHz E-clock	Min Freq. Waveform w/ 8.0 MHz E-clock
÷ 1	30.5 Hz	61 Hz
÷ 2	15.25 Hz	30.5 Hz
÷ 4	7.63 Hz	15.25 Hz
÷ 8	3.8 Hz	7.63 Hz
÷ 16	1.9 Hz	3.8 Hz
÷ 32	0.95 Hz	1.9 Hz

Figure 11.19: Lowest Frequency Waveform Generation vs Prescaler Setting

11.16 PULSE WIDTH MODULATED WAVEFORM GENERATION

As mentioned previously, the M68HC912B32 contains a dedicated PWM module that includes the necessary circuitry to generate PWM signals with no intervention from the CPU12. For applications that may require more than the four 8-bit or two 16-bit PWM channels provided by the PWM module, the output compare function can be used to perform this function. Examination of the listing in Figure 11.20 shows that the interrupt service routine is not much more involved than one required to generate a simple square wave. Even so, the additional length of the interrupt service routine, plus some additional factors discussed later, limit the maximum PWM frequency to less than that of a square wave.

The listing begins with the declaration of three constants and two variables required by the PWM routines. The first constant, PWMPeriod, represents the total number of timer clocks required for one cycle of the PWM waveform. In this case, because the prescaler is left at its default value, the system clock frequency simply needs to be divided by the desire PWM frequency to obtain the proper count. In this case, the value of SysClock is 8,000,000 resulting in a value of 8000 for PWMPeriod.

Because of the software overhead involved in the PWM interrupt service routine, it is not possible to achieve duty cycles of 0% or 100% using the interrupt service routine alone. The next two constants, PWMMinDty and PWMMaxDty, represent the minimum and maximum count values that can be used to generate the minimum and maximum allowable duty cycle respectively. The constant of 70 represents the number of clock cycles required by the interrupt service routine plus any interrupt latencies introduced by the rest of the system. In this case the interrupt service routine only requires 38 clock cycles including the eight clock cycles required to stack the CPU12 registers and fetch the interrupt vector. A value of

70 was chosen to allow for other possible interrupt latencies in the system. This value may actually be too small for a system where multiple interrupts may be pending simultaneously. Careful analysis of the entire system is required before choosing the proper value for this constant. Finally, the two variables, `OC0PWMHi` and `OC0PWMLo` represent the number of timer counts the PWM waveform remains high and low respectively. These 16-bit variables are initialized in the PWM initialization code to produce a waveform with the minimum duty cycle.

The PWM initialization code, beginning at label `OC0PWMSetup`, enables the timer system and configures timer channel zero as an output compare. The `OM0` and `OL0` bits for channel zero are both set configuring the output pin to be set at the first successful compare. Finally, timer and CPU interrupts are enabled, allowing the timer interrupt service routine to generate the PWM waveform. Notice that because the initial state of the PT0 pin out of reset is zero, the output compare register TC0 is initialized to start the PWM waveform in the low portion of the PWM period.

Section 11.16: Pulse Width Modulated Waveform Generation

```
;
PWMPeriod:    equ    SysClock/1000   ; counts (prescale ÷ 1) for 1000 Hz.
PWMMinDty:    equ    70              ; min timer counts for min duty cycle.
PWMMaxDty:    equ    PWMPeriod-70    ; max timer counts for max duty cycle.
;
OC0PWMHi:     ds.w   1               ; timer counts the PWM waveform is high.
OC0PWMLo:     ds.w   1               ; timer counts the PWM waveform is low.
;
OC0PWMSetup:  ldab   #TEN+TFFCA      ; enable timer & select fast flag clear.
              stab   TSCR
              bset   TIOS,#IOS0      ; config channel 0 as O.C.
              ldd    #PWMMinDty      ; default to minimum duty cycle.
              std    OC0PWMHi
              ldd    #PWMPeriod      ; get total PWM period count.
              subd   #PWMMinDty      ; subtract min high cnt to get low cnt.
              std    OC0PWMLo        ; init PWM low count.
              addd   TCNT            ; add to current counter value to
              std    TC0             ; start PWM in low portion of period.
              bset   TCTL2,#OL0+OL0  ; set pin at expiration of low period.
              bset   TMSK1,#C0I      ; enable timer interrupts.
              cli                    ; enable cpu interrupts.
              bra    *
;
OC0PWMISR:    ldd    OC0PWMHi        ; get PWM high count.
              brset  PORTT,#$01,DlyHi ; output was just set to 1.
              ldd    OC0PWMLo        ; output just went to 0. get low count.
DlyHi:        addd   TC0             ; add high or low count to O.C. 0.
              std    TC0             ; update O.C. 0, clearing C0F.
              ldab   #OL0            ; get OL0 bit.
              eorb   TCTL2           ; toggle with eor.
              stab   TCTL2           ; update OL0.
              rti
;
```

Figure 11.20: PWM Initialization and Interrupt Service Routine

The PWM interrupt service routine, beginning at label OC0PWMISR, begins by loading the D accumulator with the timer count for the high portion of the of the PWM period. It then checks the current state of the PWM waveform by examining bit zero of the PORTT data register. Even though the pin is configured as an output compare, a read of the data register will reflect the current state of the output latch which is shared by the output data register and the timer output compare function. If the output data latch contains a value of one, it indicates that the PWM low period has just expired and that the PWM high period has just begun. In this case, the OC0PWMHi value is added to the value in the TC0 register and TC0 is updated. If the output data latch contains a value of zero, the low portion of the PWM period has just begun. Because the BRSET instruction does not branch, the D accumulator is loaded with the count for the PWM low period. In both cases the value in the D accumulator is added to the value in the TC0 register and TC0 is updated. Finally, the OL0 bit is toggled to its opposite state by performing an exclusive OR operation with its current state. Using this method to toggle the output compare pin rather than initializing the OM0 and OL0 bits to automatically toggle the output at each compare operation is required for proper update of the OC0PWMLo and OC0PWMHi variables by the SetPWMDty subroutine described below.

While the PWM initialization code and the interrupt service routine are relatively simple, a mechanism is required to calculate new values for the OC0PWMHi and OC0PWMLo variables when establishing new PWM duty cycles. Figure 11.21 contains the listing for the SetPWMDuty subroutine that performs this function. The input to the subroutine is an integer duty cycle percentage between 1% and 99% passed in the B accumulator.

```
;
SetPWMDuty: tba                    ; move duty cycle into a for min/max .
            movw  #$0163,2,-sp     ; values for min(1) & max(99) on stack.
            maxa  1,sp+            ; bounds check against min. of 1%
            mina  1,sp+            ; bounds check against max. of 99%
            exg   a,d              ; a -> $00:b
            ldx   #100             ; calc ratio of d%/100%
            fdiv
            tfr   x,y              ; frac to y to mult by PWMPeriod in d.
            ldd   #PWMPeriod
            emul                   ; (d%/100%) * PWMPeriod
            pshy                   ; save high count for bounds check.
            ldd   #PWMMinDty       ; compare to min duty cycle count.
            emaxm 0,sp             ; low limit stored on stack.
            ldd   #PWMMaxDty       ; max duty cycle timer count.
            eminm 0,sp             ; high limit stored on stack.
            ldd   #PWMPeriod       ; calc. timer low count
            subd  0,sp             ; from PWMPeriod - OC0PWMHi.
            brset TCTL2,#OL0,*     ; if in low portion of cycle wait here.
            brclr TCTL2,#OL0,*     ; wait till O.C. transitions from 1 to 0.
            std   OC0PWMLo         ; update PWM low count
            puld
            std   OC0PWMHi         ; update PWM high count.
            rts                    ; return.
;
```

Figure 11.21: SetPWMDuty Subroutine

Section 11.16: Pulse Width Modulated Waveform Generation

As mentioned previously, because the interrupt service routine by itself does not support 0% or 100% duty cycle, the first action performed by the `SetPWMDuty` subroutine is a range check on the input value to ensure that it falls within the allowable range of 1% through 99%. Using the `MINA` and `MAXA` instructions not only allows the input range to be checked, but also forces the input value into the proper range. Because the minimum and maximum instructions may only utilize indexed addressing, the limit values are placed on the stack for comparison. The `MAXA` instruction compares the A accumulator to the minimum allowable duty cycle and places the larger of the two in the A accumulator. The `MINA` instruction compares the A accumulator to the maximum allowable duty cycle and places the smaller of the two in the A accumulator. Notice that in both cases the limit values placed on the stack are automatically removed from the stack using post increment indexed addressing.

After the limit check, the 8-bit duty cycle is zero extended into the D accumulator using the `EXG` instruction. This prepares the duty cycle percentage to be used in calculating a 16-bit binary weighted fraction, used to determine the number of timer counts representing the requested duty cycle percentage. After the high time count is calculated, the value must be limit checked against the `PWMMinDty` and `PWMMaxDty` constants to ensure that the requested duty cycle can actually be achieved at the desired PWM frequency. In this case where a 1,000 Hz PWM signal is generated, a 1% duty cycle equates to a timer count of 80 and a 99% duty cycle equates to a count of 7920. In both cases, these counts are within the range of the `PWMMinDty` and `PWMMaxDty` constants of 60 and 7940 respectively. Consider, however, that the 1% and 99% duty cycle counts for a 10,000 Hz signal are 8 and 792 respectively. These values are clearly outside the limits of 60 for `PWMMinDty` and 740 for `PWMMaxDty`. For a 10,000 Hz PWM signal the `PWMMinDty` count corresponds to a minimum achievable duty cycle of about 8% while the `PWMMaxDty` count corresponds to a maximum achievable duty cycle of about 92%. Notice that because a 16-bit value is involved, the EMIN and EMAX instructions are used. Also note that the forced limit value is left on the top of the stack rather than in the D accumulator.

After calculating the PWM low period count, two successive bit branch instructions are executed. These two instructions ensure that OC0PWMLo and OC0PWMHi are updated in a manner that guarantees no glitches or anomalies appear on the PWM output. This is achieved by updating the variables only during the low portion of the PWM waveform. When the PWM waveform is in the low portion of its cycle, the `OL0` bit will be set indicating that the next successful compare will cause the PWM output to transition from low to high. Because the software cannot be certain whether the low portion of the cycle just began or is about to finish, the `BRSET` instruction is continually executed until the PWM waveform transitions from low to high. Once the waveform transitions to the high state and the interrupt service routine has been executed, the `OL0` bit will be cleared indicating that the next successful compare will cause the PWM output to go low. At this point, the `BRSET` instruction will terminate and the `BRCLR` instruction will execute until the `OL0` bit transitions to a one indicating that the interrupt service routine executed and the PWM waveform has entered the beginning of its low period. Using this method to update

OC0PWMLo and OC0PWMHi can require close to one full PWM cycle for the update to occur, but guarantees that they are updated in a coherent manner.

11.17 General Purpose Waveform Generation

While generating single pulses, square waves and PWM signals are common uses of the output compare function, it can easily generate waveforms of arbitrary complexity. Figure 11.22 presents the initialization and interrupt service routine necessary to generate arbitrarily complex waveforms. The listing begins with the declaration of two variables. The first variable, WavTableP, is a pointer to a table of delay constants. Each table entry consists of a 16-bit constant representing the number of timer counts for each high and low portion of the output waveform. The variable is initialized to point to the beginning of a table and is incremented to point to the next table entry by the interrupt service routine. The second variable, EdgeCount, contains a count of the number of interrupt requests generated for the waveform described by the timer constant table. This value is initialized with a count of the number of entries in the timer constant table *plus one*. The additional count is required to generate an interrupt, and hence an output state change, after the delay specified by the last table entry. Examining the output waveform for this example in Figure 11.24 shows that 12 edges are required for a waveform consisting of 11 pulses.

Section 11.17: General Purpose Waveform Generation

```
;
WavTableP:      ds.w    1                   ; pointer to delay constant table.
EdgeCount:      ds.b    1                   ; number of table entries + 1.
;
OC0WavSetup:    ldab    #TEN+TFFCA          ; enable timer & select fast flag clear.
                stab    TSCR
                ldd     #WavTable           ; start of the waveform table.
                std     WavTableP
                ldab    #WavTblSize+1       ; size of the table + 1.
                stab    EdgeCount
                bclr    PORTT,#$01          ; make output latch 0
                bset    DDRT,#$01           ; make PT0 an output.
                bset    TIOS,#IOS0          ; config channel 0 as OC
                bset    TCTL2,#OL0          ; toggle OC at each compare.
                ldd     TCNT                ; get current value of the timer.
                addd    #10                 ; first OC in 10 clock cycles.
                std     TC0
                bset    TMSK1,#C0I          ; enable OC0 interrupts.
                cli                         ; enable CPU interrupts.
                bra     *                   ; allow ISR to do all the work.
;
OC0WavISR:      dec     EdgeCount           ; done with pulse transmission?
                bne     NotDone             ; no. setup OC for delay & gen next edge.
                bclr    TIOS,#IOS0          ; yes. reconfigure as GPIO.
                std     TC0                 ; clear the IC0 flag.
                rti                         ; return.
;
NotDone:        ldd     TC0                 ; get IC value.
                ldx     WavTableP           ; point to OC wave constant table.
                addd    2,x+                ; add to TC0 value, update pointer.
                std     TC0                 ; update TC0 & clear C0F.
                stx     WavTableP           ; update pointer.
                rti                         ; return.
;
```

Figure 11.22: Arbitrary Waveform Generation Using Output Compare

The timer and variable initialization code beginning at label `OC0WavSetup` are not much different than some of the other examples presented in this chapter. However, the code beginning at the BCLR instruction necessitates some explanation. The pulse train generated in this example begins and ends at a logic zero level as shown in Figure 11.24. Even though the reset state of all output data latches is zero, it is still a good idea to initialize them with the desired value. Though not explicitly stated or explained in the M68HC12 documentation, the output data latches for Port T are shared by the output compare and the general purpose I/O functions. Writing the desired initial value to the associated bits in the Port T data register *before* configuring the timer channel as an output compare will cause the timer channel pins to assume the value written to the Port data register. In addition to initializing the output data latch of PT0 with a value of zero the pin is also configured as a general purpose output. This ensures that PT0 will be driven with the value in the Port T data register when the pulse train is complete and the output compare function is disabled.

After enabling the output compare and configuring it to toggle the port pin at each compare, the waveform generation is begun by "forcing" an output compare to occur by adding a small value to the current value of the counter and writing to the output compare register. This method of forcing an output compare is required, rather than writing to bit zero of the CFORC, so that an output compare interrupt is produced, beginning the waveform generation process. Once this forced compare is set up, timer channel zero and CPU interrupts are enabled allowing the interrupt service routine to generate the output waveform.

The output compare interrupt service routine, starting at `OC0WavISR`, begins by decrementing the `EdgeCount` variable. If its value is not zero, execution continues at the label `NotDone` where a value is retrieved from the waveform table, added to the current value of the compare register and finally updating the compare register. In addition, the `WavTableP` variable is updated to point to the next table entry. When the value of `EdgeCount` reaches zero, the waveform generation is complete and the output compare function is disabled. This causes the Port P pin to revert back to a general purpose output pin driving the previously written value of zero onto the port pin. Also notice that even though channel zero has been configured as a general purpose output a write to the TC0 register is required to clear the C0F flag.

Section 11.18: Pulse Accumulator

```
;
WavTable:    dc.w SysClock/1000;  1 mS wide pulse.
             dc.w SysClock/500 ;  2 mS wide pulse.
             dc.w SysClock/500 ;  2 mS wide pulse.
             dc.w SysClock/1000;  1 mS wide pulse.
             dc.w SysClock/1000;  1 mS wide pulse.
             dc.w SysClock/1000;  1 mS wide pulse.
             dc.w SysClock/500 ;  2 mS wide pulse.
             dc.w SysClock/1000;  1 mS wide pulse.
             dc.w SysClock/500 ;  2 mS wide pulse.
             dc.w SysClock/1000;  1 mS wide pulse.
             dc.w SysClock/1000;  1 mS wide pulse.
;
WavTblSize:equ    (*-WavTable)/2
;
```

Figure 11.23: Arbitrary Waveform Generation Lookup Table

Figure 11.23 contains the table of constants used to generate the waveform in Figure 11.24. Even though the waveform is relatively simple and could be generated without the use of a table, the constants and/or the length of the table can easily be changed to accommodate a waveform of arbitrary complexity.

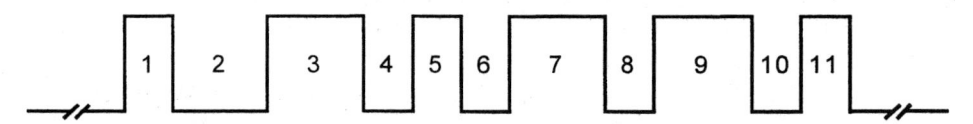

Figure 11.24: Output Waveform Generated By Lookup Table

⚠ **M68HC12 Difference from the M68HC11**

11.18 Pulse Accumulator

The M68HC12 pulse accumulator is comprised of a 16-bit up counter that can be operated as a simple event counter or in a gated time accumulation mode. As a simple event counter, the pulse accumulator is incremented at each active edge applied to the PT7 timer port pin. In the gated time accumulation mode, the PT7 timer port pin acts as an enable signal gating a free running clock signal into the pulse accumulator. The gated signal is tapped off of the main timer counter chain at a fixed frequency of the module clock ÷ 64. Unlike the timer's main counter, the pulse accumulator can be preloaded with a value at any time. Two maskable interrupts are associated with the pulse accumulator each having separate control bits and interrupt vectors.

As shown in the simple block diagram of Figure 11.25, the pulse accumulator utilizes timer port pin PT7 which it shares with timer channel seven. However, this does not imply that a choice must be made between using one function or the other. On the contrary, these two functions can be used in combination to perform some unusual or complex timing functions by allowing the output compare function of timer channel seven to control the input to the pulse accumulator. Using this arrangement, timer channel seven can be used to create the events counted by the pulse accumulator or it could be used as the gating signal in the pulse accumulator's gated time accumulation mode. When configured as an output compare, these two resources can also be used independently if the output compare remains disconnected from the port pin. Because the input capture function has its own input buffer and edge detection circuitry it can be used in conjunction with the pulse accumulator to "time stamp" each incoming clock edge.

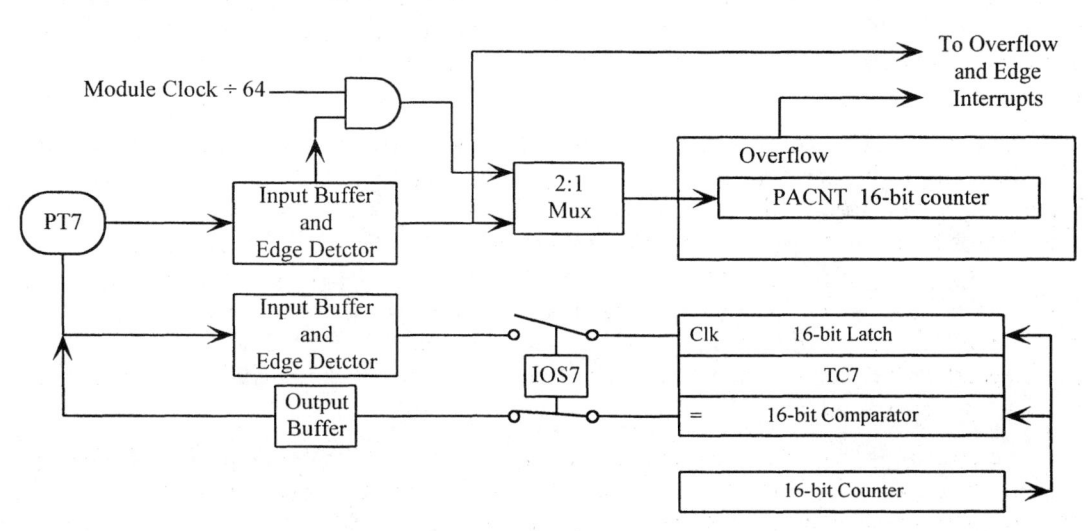

Figure 11.25: Simplified Pulse Accumulator Block Diagram

Although not shown in the simplified block diagram, the pulse accumulator input signals, edge selection, and interrupt control options are controlled by five bits in the PACTL register shown in Figure 11.26. The PAEN bit is used to enable or disable the entire pulse accumulator system. When this bit is clear, its default value, the pulse accumulator is disconnected from the input pin logic. However, like the main timer system, all of the pulse accumulator's associated registers can be read or written when the pulse accumulator is

Section 11.18: Pulse Accumulator

disabled. Also keep in mind that the pulse accumulator can be used in the event counting mode even when the main timer system is disabled.

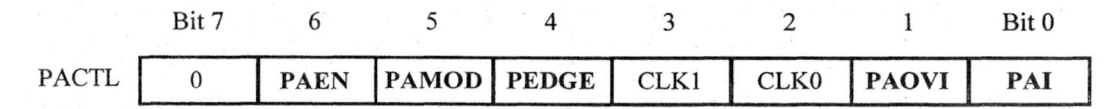

	Bit 7	6	5	4	3	2	1	Bit 0
PACTL	0	PAEN	PAMOD	PEDGE	CLK1	CLK0	PAOVI	PAI

Figure 11.26: Pulse Accumulator Control Register (PACTL)

Selection of the operating mode is controlled by the PAMOD bit. Its default value of zero selects the event counting mode and when equal to one selects the gated time accumulation mode. As mentioned in the preceding paragraph, only the event counting mode is valid when the main timer is disabled. The Pulse Accumulator Edge control bit (PEDGE) has two different functions depending on the operating mode of the pulse accumulator. When the event counting mode is selected, PEDGE chooses the clock edge that increments the 16-bit counter. When PEDGE is zero, falling edges on the pulse accumulator input pin cause the count to be incremented. When PEDGE has a value of one, a rising edge on the pulse accumulator input cause the count to be incremented. Notice that no option exists to allow the counter to be incremented on both rising and falling clock edges, however, this alternative could easily be performed by inverting the value of PEDGE in an interrupt service routine.

When the pulse accumulator is configured for the gated time accumulation mode, the PEDGE control bit selects the required signal polarity that applies the Module clock ÷ 64 to the pulse accumulator. In this case, when PEDGE has a value of zero, a logic high level on the pulse accumulator input pin applies the Module clock ÷ 64 to the 16-bit counter. When the enable signal transitions from a logic one to a zero, the Pulse Accumulator Input flag (PAIF) flag is set indicating the clock has been removed from the counter. When PEDGE has a value of one, a logic low level on the input pin applies the Module clock ÷ 64 to the pulse accumulator. In this instance the PAIF flag is set when the enable signal transitions from a logic zero to a one.

The remaining two bits in the PACTL register are utilized by the interrupt control logic in conjunction with the Pulse Accumulator Overflow Interrupt Flag (PAOVF) and the PAIF to control the two sources of pulse accumulator interrupts. When the pulse accumulator transitions from $FFFF to $0000 the PAOVF is set and if the Pulse Accumulator Overflow Interrupt enable bit (PAOVI) bit is set, a vectored interrupt will occur. Similarly, the PAIF bit is set for each selected transition on the pulse accumulator input pin causing a separately vectored interrupt if the Pulse Accumulator Interrupt enable (PAI) is set. Like the main timer system, an automatic flag clearing mechanism exists for the PAOVF or PAIF bits if the TFFCA bit in the Timer System Control Register is set. Reading or writing the PACNT register with either or both bits set causes the PAOVF and PAIF bit to be cleared. In addition, each of these bits can be cleared by writing a one to their respective bit positions in the PAFLG register when the TFFCA bit is clear.

	Bit 7	6	5	4	3	2	1	Bit 0
PAFLG	0	0	0	0	0	0	PAOVF	PAIF

Figure 11.27: Pulse Accumulator Flag Register (PAFLG)

11.18.1 Event Counting

Many applications require the ability to count events over a given time period or to count a fixed number of events before performing a specified action. For microcontrollers not possessing a pulse accumulator, the task must be performed in software utilizing an interrupt input or general purpose I/O pin. Employing one of these methods not only requires additional software, but also increases the CPU overhead required to perform the task. The pulse accumulator hardware helps to reduce the software and execution time associated with event counting.

For event counting, initialization of the pulse accumulator differs depending on how an application responds to counted events. Remember that the pulse accumulator does have the ability to interrupt the CPU12 at each counted event, however, many applications will find it more useful to have an interrupt generated only after a specific number of events have occurred. Because the pulse accumulator only has the ability to count up, the twos complement of the desired count must be written to the PACNT register rather than the desired count. This will cause the PAOVF flag to be set when the terminal count is reached. A pulse accumulator overflow interrupt will occur if the PAOVI bit in the pulse accumulator control register is set. Because the CPU12 does not contain an instruction to obtain the twos complement of the D accumulator, one of the instruction sequences shown in Figure 11.28 must be used.

```
;
        coma                ; 1's complement of upper 8-bits.
        comb                ; 1's complement of lower 8-bits.
        addd    #1          ; 16-bit twos complement.
;
        clra                ; clear d.
        clrb
        subd    PACount     ; 0 - PACount is twos complement of saved value.
;
```

Figure 11.28: Taking Twos Complement of D Accumulator

Section 11.18: Pulse Accumulator

The first three-instruction sequence is useful when the pulse accumulator contains the result of a calculation. In this case the twos complement is calculated in a straight forward manner by calculating the ones complement of the A and B accumulators and adding one to the result. The second instruction sequence is more efficient if the count value was previously calculated and saved in memory. In this case the twos complement is calculated by subtracting the saved value from zero.

Figure 11.29 presents a small code fragment that initializes the pulse accumulator and a pulse accumulator overflow interrupt handler that keeps a simple time of day clock. The portion of the interrupt handler that keeps time is nearly identical to the beginning of the time keeping interrupt service routine presented in Chapter 5. In that example, the IRQ input is used to interrupt the CPU12 at the line frequency rate to keep time. In this example, the pulse accumulator is used to count at the line frequency rate, interrupting the CPU12 at one second intervals when it overflows. Using the pulse accumulator in this type of application helps reduce the interrupt overhead associated with keeping a time of day clock in software.

The pulse accumulator setup software is simple and straightforward. The PACNT register is initialized with a value that is the two's complement of the line frequency, in this case 60 Hz. The pulse accumulator is then enabled, configured to count on rising edges, and overflow interrupts are enabled. Finally, the CPU interrupts are enabled allowing the pulse accumulator overflow interrupt service routine to execute, keeping the time of day. As mentioned, the interrupt service routine only keeps a simple time of day clock, keeping track of seconds, minutes and hours. If a more complete time keeping function is desired, the pulse accumulator interrupt service routine could be merged with the example presented in Chapter 5.

```
;
Seconds:        ds      1           ; seconds counter (0 - 59).
Minutes:        ds      1           ; minutes counter (0 - 59).
Hours:          ds      1           ; hour counter (0 - 23).
;
PACCSetup:      ldab    #TFFCA
                stab    TSCR        ; enable fast flag clear option for PACC.
                ldd     #-60        ; init PACNT with -60 for overflow after
                std     PACNT       ; 60 counts.
                ldab    #PAEN+PEDGE+PAOVI ; enable PACC, count on rising edge &
                stab    PACTL       ; enable PACC interrupts on overflow.
                cli                 ; enable CPU interrupts.
                bra     *           ; let ISR do all the work.
;
PACCISR:        ldd     #-60        ; init PACNT with -60 for overflow after
                std     PACNT       ; 60 counts.
                ldab    #60         ; compare count for seconds & minutes.
                inc     Seconds     ; Seconds = Seconds + 1.
                cmpb    Seconds     ; 60 seconds elapsed?
                bhi     Return      ; not yet. Just return.
                clr     Seconds     ; yes. set seconds counter to 0.
                inc     Minutes     ; add 1 to the minutes counter.
                cmpb    Minutes     ; 60 minutes elapsed?
                bhi     Return      ; not yet. Just return.
                clr     Minutes     ; yes. set minutes counter to 0.
                inc     Hours       ; add 1 to the hours counter.
                ldab    Hours       ; get the hours counter.
                cmpb    #24         ; did it roll over to the next day?
                blo     Return      ; no. return.
                clr     Hours       ; yes. 00:00 = 12:00 A.M.
Return:         rti                 ; return.
;
```

Figure 11.29: Using PACC Overflow Interrupt to Keep Time-of-Day

11.18.2 Gated Time Accumulation

In the gated time accumulation mode the function of the pulse accumulator effectively changes from a counter to a timer, similar in function to an input capture channel. However, because the module clock ÷ 64 can only be applied to the pulse accumulator when its input is high or low, the most useful task of the gated time accumulation mode is pulse width measurement. Because the counter does not start counting until its input is active, pulse

Section 11.18: Pulse Accumulator

width measurement is performed in a slightly different manner than with an input capture. Typically, before the pulse accumulator input becomes active the counter is set to zero. After the pulse is complete, the pulse width time can be read directly from the PACNT register. Unlike the input capture, this has the advantage of not having to capture a starting count, an ending count and subtracting the two values.

Even though the gated time accumulation mode is generally not used for measuring waveform periods, with some clever software it can easily be used to perform period measurement. In connection with the time of day clock example in Figure 11.29, it would be preferable if the initialization software could measure the line frequency so the software would work in countries having 60 Hz and 50 Hz line frequencies. The approach taken in the time of day clock example in Chapter 5 uses a simple software counting loop to determining the connected line frequency. In this case, because the line is connected to the pulse accumulator input, a measurement can be made that is independent of software and addressing modes.

```
;
PeriodCnt:  ds    2
;
PACCSetup:  ldab  #TEN+TFFCA      ; enable the timer so we can use the gated
            stab  TSCR            ; time accumulation mode.
            clra                  ; set the PACC to zero.
            clrb
            std   PACNT
            ldab  #PAEN+PAMOD+PAI ; PACC enable, time acc mode & edge ints.
            stab  PACTL           ; enable PACC interrupts on overflow.
            cli                   ; enable CPU interrupts.
            bra   *               ; let ISR do all the work.
;
PACCISR:    brclr PACTL,#PEDGE,DoLow ; if PEDGE=0, just measured high time.
            ldd   PACNT           ; PEDGE was = 1, just measured low time.
            std   PeriodCnt       ; save the count.
            clra
            clrb
            std   PACNT           ; set PACNT to 0 for next measurement.
            bclr  PACTL,#PEDGE    ; measure the high time first.
            rti                   ; return.
;
DoLow:      bset  PACTL,#PEDGE    ; continue with measurement of low time.
            ldd   PACNT           ; reset PAIF
            rti                   ; return.
;
```

Figure 11.30: Period Measurement Using Gated Time Accumulation Mode

Because the gated time accumulation mode only counts while the pulse accumulator is either high or low, the first approach might be to simply measure half the period of the incoming waveform. However, using this approach would make the time measurements dependent on the symmetry of the incoming waveform. For most applications, the circuitry used to isolate and condition the incoming line voltage would not produce a 50% duty cycle waveform, especially over time and temperature. The approach taken to solve this problem, presented in Figure 11.30, measures the full waveform period by changing the PEDGE bit in the interrupt service routine. This allows the module clock ÷ 64 to increment the counter while the pulse accumulator input is high and then while it is low. The setup code is similar to that for the clock example in Figure 11.29 except the counter is initialized to zero. Because the gated time accumulation mode is used, the main timer system must also be enabled.

As with the other timer examples, the interrupt service routine performs all of the work. The interrupt service routine begins by checking the state of the PEDGE bit. If the bit is clear, the pulse accumulator only contains a count representing the high portion of the incoming waveform. The PEDGE bit is set so that the pulse accumulator continues to accumulate counts during the signal's low time. Notice that before returning, the PACNT register is accessed to clear the PAIF flag. When the interrupt service routine is entered following the low portion of the waveform, the count contained in the PACNT register represents the waveform period in module clock ÷ 64 counts. For a nominal 60 Hz waveform the count would be approximately 2083. For a nominal 50 Hz line frequency the count would be 2500 assuming an 8.0 MHz module clock. Of course, because the short term stability of the AC line current varies, it is a good idea not to use these exact counts when determining the line frequency. The approach taken in the example in Chapter 5 used a count representing 55 Hz as a reference. If the count was above that reference value, a line frequency of 50 Hz was used. Any count below the 55 Hz reference assumed a line frequency of 60 Hz. Even this approach is not fool proof since the AC line is full of noise and the power companies regularly drop portions of cycles. The best approach is to average several readings and perform some bounds checking on the result to ensure that the proper line frequency is chosen.

When using the pulse accumulator to perform period measurements in this manner, there is a consideration regarding the accuracy of the measured period. Because the signal being measured runs asynchronously in relationship to the clock signal gated into the pulse accumulator, it is possible that the ÷ 64 counter will overflow just after the interrupt occurs but before the PEDGE control bit has been switched. This situation, which could happen at either or both interrupts, can cause the count to be two counts less than the actual period of the incoming waveform. For low frequency waveforms, such as the 50 Hz or 60 Hz line frequency used in this example, this slight discrepancy is not a problem. However, for higher frequency signals, the two counts can contribute a greater percentage of measurement error.

Section 11.18: Pulse Accumulator

A larger potential accuracy problem exists with system interrupt latencies. Even the time required for interrupt service routine execution can cause accuracy problems if it is not properly written. Because the `PEDGE` control bit must be switched in the interrupt service routine before the pulse accumulator can continue measurement of of the signal, any extended time period during which interrupts are masked will cause missed counts. Again, for low frequency signals, especially those not requiring extremely accurate measurement, this may not pose a problem. However, the magnitude of the problem will depend upon the length of time that interrupts remain masked. An additional source of potential measurement error can come from the length of time required by the interrupt service routine to save the measured count, clear the pulse accumulator, switch the `PEDGE` control bit and perform any additional functions. In the example presented, the total time required for the interrupt service routine until the `PEDGE` control bit is switched, including register stacking and vector fetch, is 27 cycles. As long as this total number is less than 64, no counts will be missed. If additional tasks must be performed in the interrupt service routine, they should be placed after the `BCLR` instruction that changes the `PEDGE` control bit. While this is a unique way to utilize the pulse accumulator in the gated time accumulation mode, careful examination of system latencies and period measurement accuracies is required.

Questions/Exercises

11.1 Explain the difference between the eight timer channels on the M68HC12 Standard Timer and the eight timer channels found on most M68HC11 family members. What advantage does the difference provide?

11.2 What is the major difference between the pulse accumulator of the M68HC12 and M68HC11 family?

11.3 Explain the main advantage and disadvantage of theM68HC12 timer architecture.

11.4 How is the input capture function used to measure waveform periods? Pulse widths?

11.5 How are waveform periods measured that exceed the 16-bit range of the M68HC12's timer system?

11.6 How is the output compare function used to generate waveforms?

11.7 What are the two main uses of the output compare function?

11.8 What two functions share timer pin PT7? Is there a potential problem with this arrangement? Explain.

Chapter 11: Standard Timer Module

11.9 How is each timer channel configured when the M68HC12 comes out of reset?

11.10 When a timer channel is configured as an output compare, what actions may be associated with each channel's related port pin? How are these actions configured?

11.11 Is it ever useful to utilize an output compare and have it remain disconnected from the port pin? Why?

11.12 How is the interaction between the Port T data direction control bits different when a timer channel is configured as an input capture and an output compare?

11.13 What port pin actions can cause an input capture event to occur? Must these actions be caused by an external signal? Explain.

11.14 How is the M68HC12 timer prescaler different from the M68HC11 family?

11.15 What mechanism is used to protect the M68HC12's prescaler from accidental modification by software?

11.16 Other than the prescaler, what other clock sources, if any, are available to be used as the main timer's clock source?

11.17 Explain the feature controlled by the Timer Counter Reset Enable (TCRE) bit. What is one application of this operating mode?

11.18 What condition will result from failure to clear a timer channel flag before exiting the channel's interrupt service routine?

11.19 What methods can be used to clear a timer channel flag? What new feature is available on the M68HC12 family?

11.20 What configuration must be performed before the timer system can be used?

11.21 Why is it useful to stop the timer system when the CPU12 enters the wait mode? What are the drawbacks?

11.22 What limitations are imposed when stopping the timer system after entering the background debug mode?

11.23 What other timer channels can be controlled by channel seven? What action will occur on these channels when a successful compare occurs on channel seven?

Section 11.18: Pulse Accumulator

11.24 What is the difference between a normal output compare event and a forced output compare event.

11.25 List the necessary steps involved in initializing the timer system.

11.26 What things must be considered when using the input capture function to perform period measurement?

11.27 Write a subroutine to convert a measured period value into a frequency value.

11.28 What are the main differences in performing period and pulse width measurement?

11.29 What are some alternate uses for input capture channels?

11.30 What techniques can be used to measure very short pulses using the input capture function?

11.31 Name some of the applications for the output compare function.

11.32 What changes might be necessary to an output compare interrupt service routine to produce an output waveform of 750 Hz rather than simply generating an interrupt at a 750 Hz rate?

11.33 List the things that must be considered when generating periodic waveforms using the output compare function.

11.34 What determines the lowest and highest PWM duty cycles that can be generated with the output compare? How is this affected by the frequency of the PWM signal?

11.35 What problems exist when updating the OC0PWMLo and OC0PWMHi variables in the PWM example of Figure 11.20? Why is it necessary to update them in a proper manner?

11.36 Modify the SetPWMDuty subroutine Figure 11.21 to support PWM duty cycles of 0% and 100%.

11.37 Construct a data table that will produce an output waveform with the following pulse widths using the exampe in Figure 11.22: 1 mS, 3 mS, 5 mS, 100 µS, 300 µS, 25 mS, 1 mS.

11.38 What are the two operating modes available with the timer's pulse accumulator?

Chapter 11: Standard Timer Module

11.39 How is the clock for the gated time accumulation mode derived?

11.40 What restrictions exist regarding the use of the pulse accumulator and the timer channel associated with port pin PT7?

11.41 What pulse accumulator events can cause interrupts to be generated? Are these events independently controllable? What are the names of the control bit(s) used for this purpose.

11.42 How is the pulse accumulator initialized to generate an interrupt after a specific number of counted events?

Chapter 12 PULSE WIDTH MODULATION MODULE

The MC68HC912B32 contains a four channel pulse width modulation (PWM) timer. Each of the channels can create independent continuous waveforms with software selectable duty cycles between 0% and 100%. Each of the four channels contains a resetable counter, a period register, and a duty cycle register. The frequency of each channel is determined by a match between the counter and the period register. The duty register contains a value that changes the state of the output during the period, determining the duty cycle of the waveform. An option exists allowing the counter, period, and duty registers for channels zero and one or channels two and three to be concatenated to form two 16-bit PWM timer channels. This option is independent for each channel pair allowing a configuration of a single 16-bit and two 8-bit PWM channels. The PWM outputs can also be programmed for either left aligned or center aligned output modes.

Both the period and duty cycle registers are double buffered so that writes to these registers while the channels are enabled will not take effect until the beginning of the next PWM period or until the channel is disabled. This double buffering ensures that the counters are updated in a coherent manner, preventing any glitches from appearing on the PWM output waveform. As discussed in Chapter 11, performing this operation using PWM signals generated with an output compare channel requires special software techniques. If a PWM channel is disabled, writes to period or duty cycle registers will go directly to the comparators as well as the buffer registers. This ensures that the output will always maintain a valid PWM waveform when the channel is enabled.

Section 12.1: Left Aligned Operation

The four PWM channel outputs share general purpose Port P pins PP0 through PP3. Enabling a PWM channel overrides the data direction register settings, automatically configuring the associated port pin as an output. When a PWM channel is not in use, the channel's port pin may be used for general purpose I/O. Port pins PP4 through PP7 are always available for use as general purpose I/O.

When referring to the PWM module's duty and period registers, the mnemonics PWPER and PWDTY are used to refer to any of the four channels registers. Using these mnemonics followed by a single digit (i.e., PWPER3) refers to a specific PWM timer channel's registers.

⚠ **M68HC12 Difference from the M68HC11**

Before beginning a detailed discussion of the PWM module, it must be noted that even though the programming model looks nearly identical to some M68HC11 PWM modules, the two are not software compatible. Changes to the Scaled Clock and Duty Cycle equations require driver code written for the M68HC11 PWM modules to be rewritten for the M68HC12 PWM module.

12.1 LEFT ALIGNED OPERATION

Figure 12.1 shows the major components of a single 8-bit PWM channel. As the diagram shows, the counter is actually a configurable up/down counter controlled by the Center aligned output mode (CENTR) control bit. When configured for left aligned operation, the counter operates in a count up mode. As each PWM cycle begins, the counter starts at zero and is incremented by the selected clock source. As the counter advances, the values of the PWDTY and PWPER registers are continuously compared to the value of the counter. When the counter value matches the value in the PWDTY register, the PWM output changes state on the *next* PWM clock by driving the set input of the attached flip-flop. As the counter continues to increment, it will eventually reach the value of the PWPER register. When this occurs, the flip-flop is reset on the *next* PWM input clock causing the output to change state, resetting the PWM counter at the same time.

The output of the flip-flop is applied to a multiplexer controlled by the channel's PWM Polarity (PPOL) control bit. This additional flexibility allows each cycle to begin with the output high or low. As shown in Figure 12.2, the output cycle begins and remains high for for the time defined by the channel's PWDTY register plus one when the PPOL bit is one. When the PPOL bit is zero, just the opposite is true, the output cycle begins and remains low for for the time defined by the channel's PWDTY register plus one.

Chapter 12: Pulse Width Modulation Module

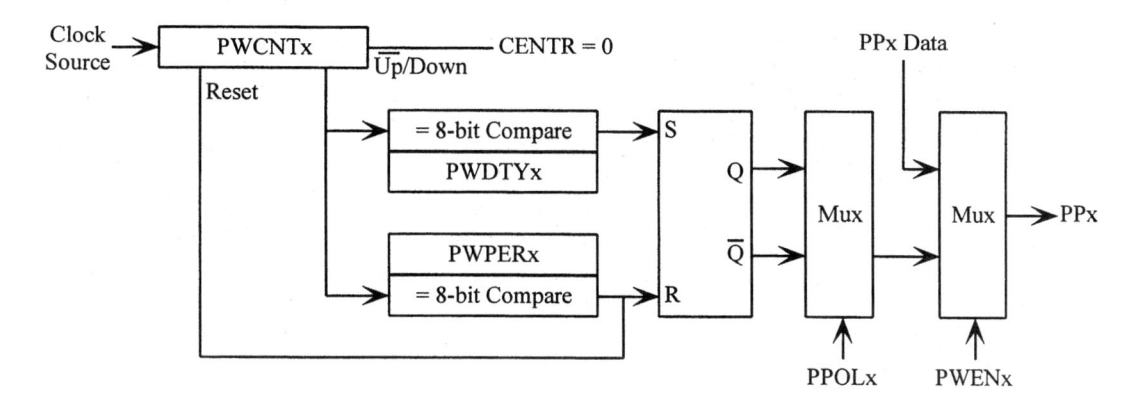

Figure 12.1: Left Aligned PWM Block Diagram

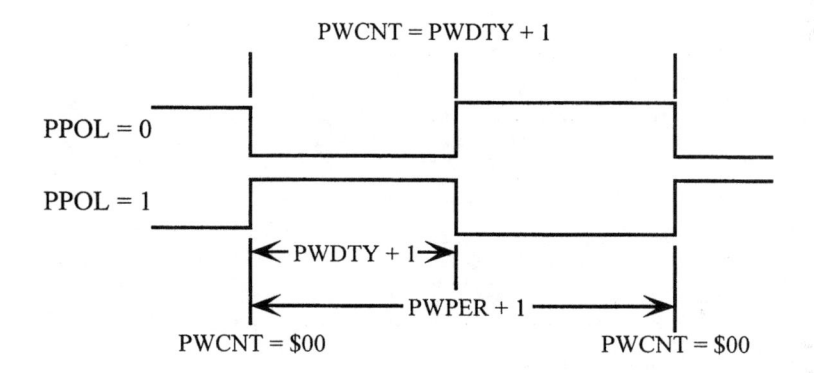

Figure 12.2: Output Waveform for Left Aligned PWM

12.2 CENTER ALIGNED OPERATION

When configured for center aligned operation, each of the PWM channels produce a waveform fundamentally the same as left aligned operation. However, because each channel's counter counts up during the first half of the cycle and counts down during the second half, the waveform is centered around the value in the PWPER register. Because the waveform is centered around the PWPER value, the frequency of the output waveform is one half that of left aligned operation for given values of PWDTY and PWPER. A single control bit, CENTR, in the PWCTL register configures all of the PWM timer channels for center aligned operation when set. As shown in Figure 12.3, the counter is configured for up and down counting with the counter direction being controlled by the output of the PWPER comparator. Also notice that the output of the PWDTY comparator is applied to the T (toggle) input of the flip-flop rather than the S (set) input.

Section 12.2: Center Aligned Operation

As each center aligned PWM cycle begins, a channel's counter starts at zero and is incremented by the selected clock source. As the channel's counter increments, the values of the `PWDTY` and `PWPER` registers are compared to the value of the counter. When the counter matches the value in the `PWDTY` register, the toggle input of the flip-flop is triggered, causing the PWM output to change state. As the counter continues to increment, it eventually reaches the value of the `PWPER` register. When the two values match, the `PWPER` comparator reconfigures the channel's counter to count down. As each each incoming clock pulse decrements the counter, the `PWDTY` value is again compared to the counter value. Once again, when the two values match, the toggle input of the flip-flop is triggered and the PWM output state changes. When the counter reaches zero, the `PWDTY` and `PWPER` registers are loaded with the contents of the the `PWDTY` and `PWPER` buffers, the counter is configured as an up counter and the next waveform cycle begins. Figure 12.4 provides visual detail of the center aligned PWM cycle showing the output waveform relative to PWM counter values and in relationship to `PWDTY` and `PWPER` at key points in the waveform.

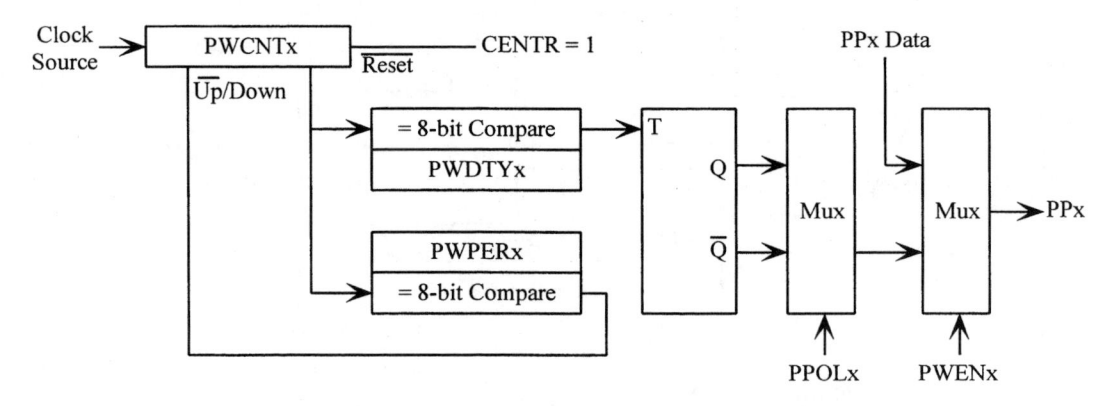

Figure 12.3: Center Aligned PWM Block Diagram

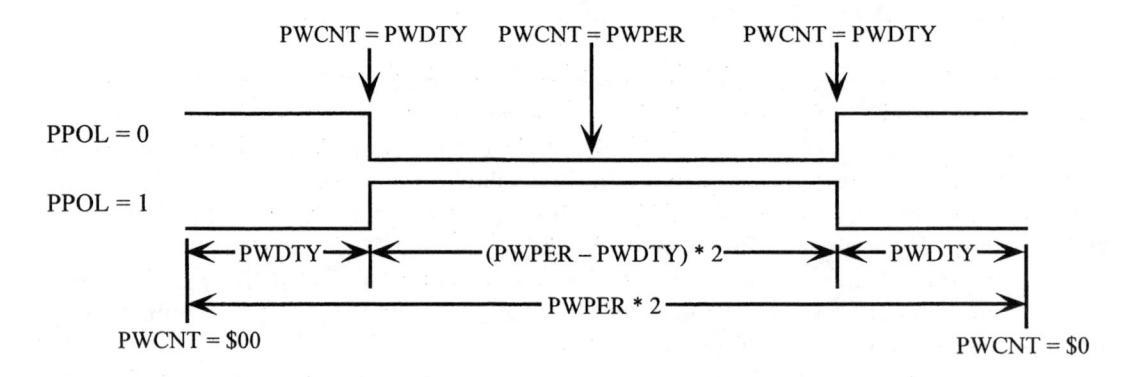

Figure 12.4: Output Waveform for Center Aligned PWM

12.3 PWM Clock Sources

The clock generator portion of the PWM module is shared by all four channels. However, several options allow a great deal of flexibility in the selection of the input clock for each PWM channel. As shown in Figure 12.5, the clock generator consists of two basic sections. The section on the left, the prescaler, consists of a simple 7-bit counter that successively divides the input clock by two. The input to the divider chain and the output of each divider stage is applied to two sets of multiplexers used to select a basic clock rate for each pair of PWM channels. Prescaled ClockA, controlled by PCKA0:2, can be applied directly to channel zero or channel one using the PCLK0 and PCLK1 control bits. In the same manner, prescaled ClockB controlled by PCKB0:2, can be applied directly to channel two or channel three using the PCLK2 and PCLK3 control bits. The prescale clock control bits are located in the PWM Clocks and Concatenate (PWCLK) control register shown in Figure 12.9. The PCLK0:3 control bit are located in the PWM Clock Select and Polarity register (PWPOL) along with the channel polarity select bits.

In addition to directly applying the prescaled clock to the PWM timer channels, a programmable scaling counter is provided for each channel pair. This feature provides additional flexibility by allowing the output from the prescaler section to be scaled by a number other than a power of two. As shown, each scale counter consists of an 8-bit down counter, 8-bit comparator, a scale register, and a divide by two counter. As each scaled clock count cycle begins, the 8-bit counter, PWSCNT, loads a user programmable value from the PWSCAL register and begins to count down. When the counter reaches zero, a pulse is applied to the divide by two counter and the counter is reloaded from the PWSCAL register. The actual scale factor produced by the counter is the value contained in the PWSCAL register *plus* one. With a divide by two circuit on the output of the comparator, a minimum scale factor of two is achievable for a PWSCAL value of $00. A maximum scale factor of 512 results from a PWSCAL value of $FF. Recognize that because of the divide by two circuit on the output of the comparator, only even scaling factors are achievable. The formula for the scaled clock period is: ClockxPeriod * (PWSCALx +1) * 2.

Section 12.4: Calculating Duty Cycle and Period

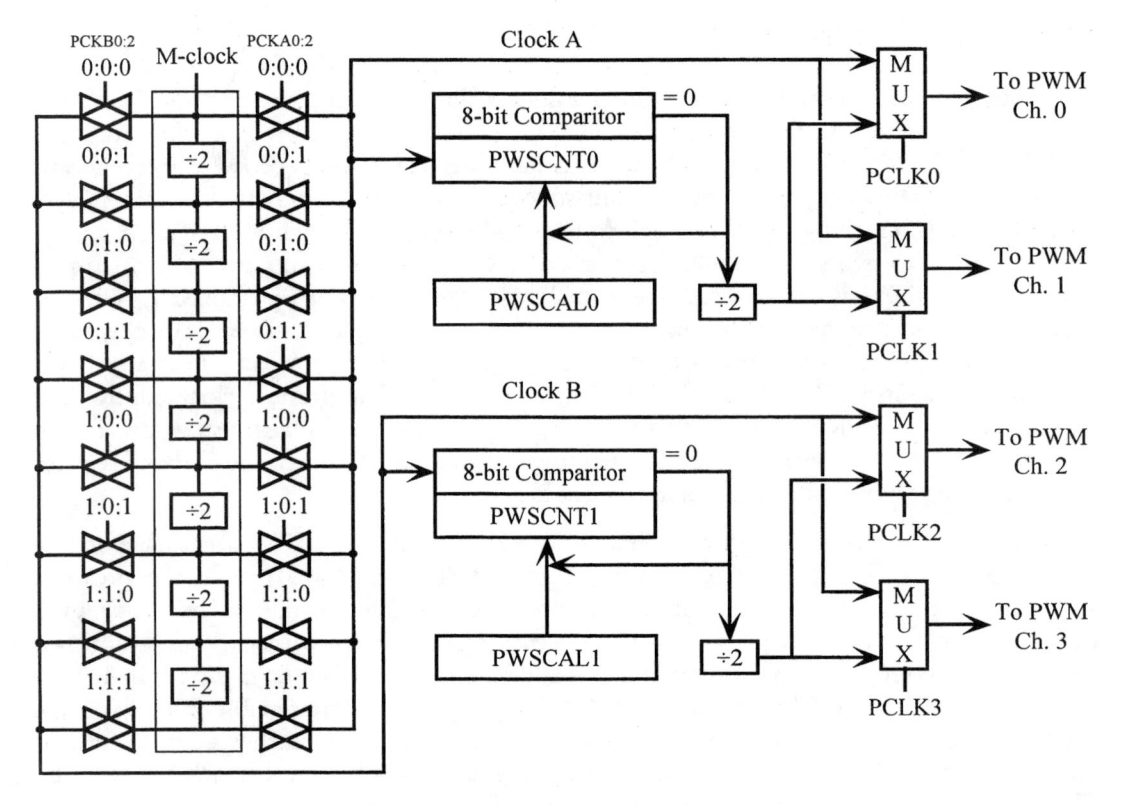

Figure 12.5: PWM Module Clock Sources

12.4 CALCULATING DUTY CYCLE AND PERIOD

Determining the period and duty cycle of a PWM waveform are relatively easy tasks based on a few simple formulas. However, determining the proper values for a channel's PWPER and PWDTY registers requires an analysis of the required waveform accuracy for a particular application.

Figure 12.6 presents the formulas used to determine period and duty cycle for various configurations of the PWM channels. As expected, the period of a PWM waveform is independent of its polarity, but as previously discussed it does depend on the state of the CENTR control bit. On the other hand, the duty cycle, which is defined as the percentage of time the waveform remains high, depends on the state of both the CENTR and PPOL bits. Examining the duty cycle formulas for left aligned mode reveals a characteristic about the PWM channels that is not immediately apparent. Notice that the denominator of both duty cycle formulas are the same. For the case when PPOL is zero, a duty cycle of 100% cannot be achieved by simply writing a value of zero to the PWDTY register since the formula becomes PWPER ÷ (PWPER + 1). Similarly, when the PPOL bit is one, a duty cycle of 0% cannot be achieved by simply writing a value of zero to the PWDTY register since the formula becomes 1 ÷ (PWPER + 1).

	Left Aligned (CENTR = 0)		Center Aligned (CENTR = 1)	
	PPOLx = 0	PPOLx = 1	PPOLx = 0	PPOLx = 1
Duty Cycle	$\frac{PWPERx - PWDTYx}{(PWPERx + 1)} * 100\%$	$\frac{PWDTYx + 1}{(PWPERx + 1)} * 100\%$	$\frac{PWPERx - PWDTYx}{PWPERx} * 100\%$	$\frac{PWDTYx}{PWPERx} * 100\%$
Period	Channel_Clock_Period * (PWPER + 1)		Channel_Clock_Period * PWPER * 2	

Figure 12.6: Period and Duty Cycle Formulas

Obtaining a duty cycle of exactly 0% or 100% for left aligned operation can be accomplished in several ways. The most straight forward manner is to configure the PWM channel's associated I/O as general purpose output by writing a one to the related data direction bit. When either 0% or 100% duty cycle is required, the appropriate value is written to the channel's Port P data bit and the PWM channel is disabled by clearing the channel's enable bit. This results in the port pin being driven to the value written to the channel's Port P data bit. While this method is straight forward and easy to understand, disabling the PWM channel in this manner will cause an immediate change in the output state rather than waiting until the end of the current cycle. This may result in a truncated PWM period and may lead to undesired operation of device being driven by the PWM signal.

To avoid any undesired operation when switching to 0% or 100% duty cycles for left aligned operation, special values involving boundary conditions for the PWDTY and PWPER registers may be utilized. These conditions, presented in Figure 12.7, show the state of a PWM output in relationship to the channel's PWDTY, PWPER and PPOL values. The selected combination of register and PPOL values used for 0% and 100% depends on the values employed for duty cycles other than 0% or 100%.

The first two boundary conditions listed in the table only apply to left aligned operation. In this case the PWM output will follow the *opposite* state of the PPOL bit whenever the PWDTY register contains a value of $FF. When a channel's PWPER register contains $FF, this boundary case makes it impossible for software to achieve 100% duty cycle simply by writing a value of $FF to the PWDTY register if PPOL equals one. Note, it is possible to achieve 100% duty cycle by manipulating a channel's PWDTY register and the PPOL bit. However, using such a method would cause a glitch to appear on the output between the time the PWDTY register is written to $FF and the state of the PPOL bit is changed. For left aligned operation where the PPOL bit equals one and the PWDTY register contains $FF, the best way to achieve 100% duty cycle is to utilize the fifth condition listed in the table. Obviously, the best way to realize 0% duty cycle is to write $FF to the PWDTY register when PPOL is one.

Section 12.4: Calculating Duty Cycle and Period

For left aligned operation, the last four boundary conditions only apply if the `PWDTY` register does not contain a value of $FF. Even though the last four conditions in the table apply to center aligned operation, the special boundary conditions are required to attain 0% or 100% duty cycle. When the `PPOL` bit has a value of one, writing zero to the `PWDTY` register will cause the output to remain low, while writing the `PWDTY` register with a value greater than or equal to the `PWPER` register will cause the output to stay high.

PWDTYx	PWPERx	PPOLx	Output
$FF	>$00	1	Low
$FF	>$00	0	High
PWPERx	–	1	High
PWPERx	–	0	Low
–	$00	1	High
–	$00	0	Low

Figure 12.7: PWDTY and PWPER Boundary Cases

Further examination of Figure 12.6 reveals that the 0% and 100% duty cycle restrictions for left aligned operation do not exist for center aligned operation. Zero percent duty cycle operation can be obtained by writing a value of zero to the `PWDTY` register. One hundred percent duty cycle can be accomplished by writing the `PWDTY` register with a value equal to or greater than the value in the `PWPER` register.

Determining the period of a waveform given the channel clock period and the value of the `PWPER` register is a simple matter of applying the proper formula from the table in Figure 12.6. Even though most system design specifications will usually provide a frequency at which the PWM is to operate, it is easy to obtain the formula for frequency by inverting the right hand side of the period equations. While the result is no more complex, the formula still contains two unknown values. The best approach to determine these values is to choose a value for the `PWPER` register that produces the required accuracy for the output waveform. If, for instance, an application requires duty cycle control to an accuracy of 1%, a `PWPER` value of 99 can be used for left aligned operation and 100 can be used for center aligned operation. Choosing this value provides a one-to-one correspondence between the duty cycle percentage and the value stored in the `PWDTY` register. As a result, no additional calculations are required when updating the PWM duty cycle. Obviously, increasing the value in the `PWPER` register will provide greater duty cycle accuracy. However, when operating a channel in 8-bit mode, the best accuracy that can be obtained is $1 \div 256$ for left aligned operation or $1 \div 255$ for center aligned operation. In both cases this produces an accuracy of approximately 0.4%. Applications requiring greater duty cycle accuracy will need to combine one of the 8-bit channel pairs to form a 16-bit PWM timer channel.

After determining the proper value for the `PWPER` register, the proper clock source value can easily be determined by solving a frequency equation for the channel clock period. For example, suppose an application requires a 25,000 Hz PWM waveform with a duty cycle accuracy of 0.5%. To satisfy the requirement of 0.5% duty cycle accuracy requires a `PWPER` register value of 199 for left aligned operation.

Rearranging and applying the period formula for left aligned operation as shown in Figure 12.8 results in a simple formula for determining the required prescale division factor based on the module clock frequency, the required PWM frequency and `PWPER` register value. Based on an M-clock frequency of 8.0 MHz, the required prescale division factor for the example is 1.6. Obviously, because the prescaler only supports integer division factors, a choice must be made to either round up to a prescale factor of two or truncate the value to a factor of one. Using a prescale factor of one will produce a waveform frequency of 40,000 Hz while utilizing a prescale factor of two will result in a PWM frequency of 20,000 Hz. If the specified frequency for an application is critical, it is possible to make an adjustment to the `PWPER` value to obtain an exact frequency, however, it may be at the expense of duty cycle accuracy or require the use of a second PWM channel.

If a prescale factor of two is chosen, a PWPER register value of 159 would produce a waveform frequency of exactly 25,000 Hz. However, this compromise would result in a duty cycle accuracy of 0.625% rather than the required 0.5%. This small difference may be acceptable for the application, but it would make the duty cycle calculations more complex. If the duty cycle accuracy variation were unacceptable, it is possible to achieve the required accuracy by configuring one of the PWM channel pairs for 16-bit operation. In this case the prescaler would be configured for one, using the M-clock directly, and the 16-bit `PWPER` register would be written with a value of 319. Again this would produce a waveform frequency of exactly 25,000 Hz and a duty cycle accuracy of 0.313%.

Section 12.5: PWM 16-bit Operation

$$F = \frac{1}{CCP * (PWPER + 1)} \Rightarrow CCP = \frac{1}{F * (PWPER + 1)}$$

$$CCP = \frac{1}{F * (PWPER + 1)} \Rightarrow CCF = F * (PWPER + 1)$$

$$PS = \frac{M\text{-clock}}{CCF} \Rightarrow PS = \frac{M\text{-clock}}{F * (PWPER + 1)}$$

Where: F is PWM frequency
CCP is Clock Channel Period
CCF is Clock Channel Frequency
PS is Prescaler divide factor
M-clock is the Module clock frequency

Figure 12.8: Prescale Factor Formulas for Left Aligned Mode

12.5 PWM 16-BIT OPERATION

The 16-bit PWM operation is governed by the CON23 and CON01 control bits in the PWM Clocks and Concatenate (PWCLK) register shown in Figure 12.9. These control bits permit the concatenation of each PWM channel pair allowing them to operate as a single 16-bit channel. When a channel pair is combined, the PWCNT, PWPER and PWDTY registers at the lower address becomes the high order byte of the 16-bit word. The next higher address becomes the low byte. Because no read or write hardware buffering exists, the resulting 16-bit registers must be read or written with a single 16-bit access to avoid data coherency problems. The clock source for the 16-bit channel is determined by the clock select control bit of the higher numbered 8-bit channel. While the resulting PWM waveform is output to the pin of the corresponding lower numbered 8-bit channel. Fortunately, the pin associated with the higher numbered 8-bit channel can be used for general purpose I/O. The 16-bit PWM channel may be configured for either left or center aligned mode, but remember that *all* the active PWM channels are affected by the mode selection.

	Bit 7	6	5	4	3	2	1	Bit 0
PWCLK	CON23	CON01	PCKA2	PCKA1	PCKA0	PCKB2	PCKB1	PCKB0

Figure 12.9: PWM Clocks and Concatenate (PWCLK) Register

Chapter 12: Pulse Width Modulation Module

12.6 CHANGING DUTY CYCLE AND PERIOD

As mentioned previously, the period and duty registers are double buffered so changes made to these registers will not take effect until the end of the current PWM cycle. This feature keeps the current PWM period from being truncated and thus from producing output waveform anomalies. When generating high frequency waveforms, the latency involved before a new period or duty cycle takes effect will be quite small. On the other hand, the latency period could be relatively long for low frequency waveforms. If an application requires the ability to make immediate changes to period or duty cycle, register changes can be forced into immediate effect by writing to the PWM channel counter after writing new period and/or duty register values. Writing to the counter register initiates a channel counter reset causing the new period and/or duty values to be latched.

An alternate method of forcing immediate changes to the period and/or duty registers involves disabling the associated PWM channel. Writes made to the period or duty register before or after a PWM channel is disabled causes the new period and duty values to be latched immediately. Like writing to the counter register this has the same effect of prematurely truncating the waveform period. Using either method, it is possible for software to read a channel's counter and duty cycle register to determine the current state of the waveform before forcing any changes. In addition, the current state of the PWM output pin may be determined by examining the state of the associated Port P data bit.

12.7 EIGHT BIT, LEFT ALIGNED PWM EXAMPLE

Initialization of each PWM channel is a relatively easy process. Before writing to the PWEN register to enable one or more channels, the prescaler, scale registers, clock select bits, output polarity, period and duty cycle registers should be initialized. The listing in Figure 12.10 presents the initialization code necessary to configure channel zero and one to produce an output waveform of 22,000 Hz and 2500 Hz with positive polarity, left aligned operation.

The two equate statements at the beginning of the listing define the PWPER values for channel zero and one. The value for channel zero, based on a prescale division factor of two, will produce a PWM waveform with a frequency just slightly less than 22 KHz with a module clock of 8.0 MHz. Remember, because this example uses the PWM channels in left aligned mode, the PWM period count is actually 182. To obtain a frequency of 2,500 Hz on channel one, the programmable clock scale counter must be used as the channel's clock source. Keep in mind that the input to the scaled clock divider is the output of the prescaler which is 4.0 MHz. For this example, a period count of 100 was arbitrarily choose. This value allows duty cycle adjustments as small as 1% which is adequate for many applications. To obtain a 2500 Hz waveform frequency with a period count of 100 requires an input frequency of 250 KHz. With an input frequency of 4.0 MHz, a scaled clock factor of 16 is required. Because the output of the scaled clock divider is divided by two, a scale factor of

Section 12.7: Eight Bit, Left Aligned PWM Example

eight is required. Due to the fact that the scaled clock divider divides its input by the value in the PWSCAL register minus one, a value of seven is written to the PWSCAL0 register.

After initializing the prescaler, scale registers, clock select bits, output polarity and period registers, the duty cycle registers of both channels are written with a value of $FF. This value, as shown in the table of Figure 12.7, utilizes one of the PWM's boundary conditions to ensure the output of both channels are at 0% duty cycle when the channels are enabled. For most applications this would be the desired state.

```
;
Ch0Period:  equ   181            ; PWPER value for 22 KHz waveform.
Ch1Period:  equ   99             ; PWPER value for 2500 Hz waveform.
;
PWM8Init:   ldab  #$08           ; set clock A prescaler to ÷ 2.
            stab  PWCLK
            ldab  #$23           ; Ch. 0 & 1 PPOL = 1 Ch.0 clk src = Clk A.
            stab  PWPOL          ; Ch. 1 clk src = scaled clk 0.
            ldab  #$07           ; scaled clk 0 = ÷ 16.
            stab  PWSCAL0
            ldab  #Ch0Period     ; init. channel 0 period
            stab  PWPER0
            ldab  #Ch1Period     ; init. channel 1 period
            stab  PWPER1
            ldab  #$ff           ; make output 0
            stab  PWDTY0         ; by setting PWDTY $ff for both channels.
            stab  PWDTY1
            ldab  #$3            ; enable both channels.
            stab  PWEN
;
```

Figure 12.10: Eight bit PWM Initialization

As stated previously, the PWM channel initialization is a straight forward process of writing the proper values to the control registers. Once the channels are enabled a mechanism is required to change each channel's duty cycle. For channel one, the process is fairly simple because a duty count of 100 was chosen. An application can simply write the desired duty cycle percentage minus one directly to the PWDTY1 register to achieve duty cycles from 0% through 100%. For 0% duty cycle the value written to the PWDTY1 register would be $FF ($00 - $01), utilizing the first boundary condition listed in the table of Figure 12.7 to output a continuous low. For 100% duty cycle, the value in the PWDTY register would be equal to the PWPER register. This corresponds to the third boundary condition listed in the table of Figure 12.7.

Unfortunately, the task of calculating and updating the PWDTY register for channel zero is not nearly as simple. The listing presented in Figure 12.11 is a general purpose duty cycle update subroutine that can be used to establish the duty cycle of any of the four PWM channels in 1% increments with a few restrictions. Because of the boundary conditions utilized for 0% and 100%, the subroutine may only be used with channels configured for left aligned operation, the PPOL bit set to one, and Period register values from from $01 through $FE. Even with these restrictions, the SetDty8LA subroutine is useful for many applications. The PWM channel number, zero through three, is passed in the A accumulator and the duty cycle percentage, zero through 100 is passed in the B accumulator. Note that no bounds checking is performed on the input values.

The subroutine begins by performing checks for 0% and 100% duty cycle. For 0% duty cycle, the boundary condition employed in the initialization code is used to establish a continuous low output. To establish 100% duty cycle, the channel's PWDTY register is set equal to the value in the PWPER register, producing a continuous high at the channel's output pin.

If a duty cycle other than 0% or 100% is requested, execution continues at OtherDty where the channel number is saved on the stack. To determine the duty register count necessary to represent the requested duty cycle percentage, a weighted binary fraction is calculated by dividing the requested duty cycle by 100. Even though the result of the FDIV instruction is a 16-bit weighted binary fraction, only the upper 8-bits are required to calculate an accurate value for the PWDTY register. After placing the fraction in the D accumulator, the lower 8-bits, in the B accumulator, are overwritten by the channel number. This in turn is used as an index to retrieve the value of the PWPER register for the associated PWM channel. Multiplying the 8-bit weighted binary fraction by the 8-bit integer value of the PWPER register produces a 16-bit number where the upper 8-bits represents the integer portion of the result and the lower 8-bits represents the fractional portion of the result. Rounding the result is accomplished by checking the state of the carry bit, which is set by the multiply instruction if the most significant bit of the lower eight bits of the result is set. In this case, the most significant bit of the lower byte of the result represents a value of 0.5. After the rounding operation, the channel number is removed from the stack, adjusted to point to the channel's PWDTY register and the PWDTY register is updated.

Even though this subroutine is written for a specific configuration of the PWM, the techniques can easily be adapted for other configurations. For example, when the module is configured for center aligned operation the only real change required to the subroutine is the elimination of the special case for 0%. Remember that for center aligned operation, writing zero to a channel's PWDTY register results in a continuous low output when the channel's PPOL bit is one. Adapting the routines for 16-bit operation requires more extensive modification because the arithmetic must be performed with 16-bit precision. However, the same basic calculation methods can be used.

Section 12.8: Sequenced Output Switching

```
;
SetDty8LA:  tstb                ; 0% duty cycle?
            bne     Chck100     ; no. go check for 100%.
            decb                ; yes. set PWDTYx to $ff to drive output
            ldx     #PWDTY0     ; to 0 (when PPOLx = 1).
            stab    a,x
            rts                 ; return.
;
Chck100:    cmpb    #100        ; 100% duty cycle?
            bne     OtherDty    ; no. go calc. PWDTYx val for requested %.
            ldx     #PWPER0     ; yes. point to base of PWPER registers
            ldab    a,x         ; get PWPER value for selected channel.
            adda    #4          ; offset to PWDTY registers.
            stab    a,x         ; PWDTY = PWPER makes out 1 (for PPOLx = 1).
            rts                 ; return.
;
OtherDty:   psha                ; save PWM channel number.
            clra                ; zero extend b into d.
            ldx     #100        ; divide requested % by 100%.
            fdiv                ; generate weighted binary fraction.
            exg     d,x         ; put fraction in d.
            ldx     #PWPER0     ; point to period registers.
            ldab    0,sp        ; overwrite lower half of fract w/ Ch. #.
            ldab    b,x         ; overwrite Ch. # with PWPERx value.
            mul                 ; mul 8-bit fraction by PWPERx value.
            bcc     NoRound     ; don't round if carry clear.
            inca                ; round result up.
NoRound:    ldab    1,sp+       ; get PWM channel #, remove from stack.
            addb    #4          ; offset to duty registers
            staa    b,x         ; update channel duty register.
            rts                 ; return.
;
```

Figure 12.11: Duty Cycle Update Subroutine For Left Aligned Mode

12.8 Sequenced Output Switching

One of the applications of PWM outputs is to vary the average power applied to external loads such as D.C. motors or incandescent lamps by controlling power devices such as transistors or MOSFETs. When utilizing multiple PWM outputs for controlling high current loads, it is desirable to minimize the switching transients caused by initial inrush currents at the beginning of each PWM cycle. Even though the PWM counters may not be written with a specific value, it is possible to offset the beginning of each channel's cycle relative to the other channels by enabling the channels in a time sequenced manner during the initialization process. For example, if all four PWM channels are used to drive loads at the same frequency, each channel can be successively enabled at a count interval representing one quarter of the PWM period so that none of the loads are switched on at the same time.

The software presented in Figure 12.12 performs the task of initializing the PWM module and successively enabling the each PWM channel. The code begins initializing each PWPER and PWDTY register with a value of $FF. This may seem redundant since $FF is the default value of theses registers, however, it's always a good idea to code defensively. The PPOL bits are all set to one so that each PWM output begins its cycle at a logic one. Finally, the A and B prescaler are both set to provide the module clock divided by eight to each PWM channel pair. This value was arbitrarily chosen for this example.

The channel sequencing begins by initializing four of the CPU12 registers then enabling channel zero before entering the channel enable loop at EnLoop. Before entering the loop at label OffsetLoop where the counter value is compared to the offset value in the B accumulator, a new channel enable bit mask is generated. Each time through the outer loop the value to be written to the PWEN register is shifted to the left and the least significant bit is set. This generates a mask value that enables the next higher channel in the sequence while keeping the currently enabled channels operating. When the value of the current PWM channel counter is greater than or equal to the offset value in accumulator B, the BHI instruction fails and the bit mask is written to the PWEN register enabling the channel. Finally the X index register is incremented to point to the next PWCNT register and the channel counter in the Y index register is decremented. When all four channels have been enabled, each channel's PWDTY register is set to produce a duty cycle of 50%. Examining the port pins PP0 through PP3 with an oscilloscope, using channel zero as the timing reference, triggering on the rising edge, should produce waveforms with the timing relationship shown in Figure 12.13. As expected, the rising edge of each channel lags the preceding channel by 90°.

While this technique can be used to skew the rising or falling edges of the PWM clocks of the same frequency, the technique has a couple of limitations. If channel zero and two are examined on an expanded horizontal sweep scale, it can be seen that the falling edge of channel two does not coincide *exactly* with the rising edge of channel zero. In fact the falling edge of channel two occurs one or two microseconds after the rising edge of channel zero. This time difference is caused by the overhead of the software and the fact that the prescaler counter chain runs asynchronously relative to the software.

Section 12.8: Sequenced Output Switching

```
PWMSeq:         ldab    #$ff            ; set period & duty values to $ff.
                ldaa    #8              ; number of registers to write.
                ldx     #PWPER0         ; point to period 0 register.
InitLoop:       stab    1,x+            ; init period or duty register.
                dbne    a,InitLoop      ; dec register count. loop till done.
                ldab    #$0f            ; start PWM cycle high.
                stab    PWPOL
                ldab    #$1b            ; set A & B prescaler to ÷ 8.
                stab    PWCLK
;
                ldy     #3              ; channel count - 1.
                ldx     #PWCNT0         ; pointer to PWM counter regs.
                ldaa    #$01            ; initial PWM enable bit mask.
                ldab    #63             ; PWCNT offset count between Ch. enable.
                staa    PWEN            ; enable PWM Ch. 0.
;
EnLoop:         lsla
                oraa    #$01            ; generate bit mask for next Ch. enable.
OffsetLoop:     cmpb    0,x             ; Ch. count < offset count?
                bhi     OffsetLoop      ; yes. compare until it is >=.
                staa    PWEN            ; no. enable the next PWM
                inx                     ; point to next PWCNT register.
                dbne    y,EnLoop        ; loop till all channels enabled.
;
                ldab    #$7f            ; set duty cycle to 50%.
                stab    PWDTY0          ; all channels.
                stab    PWDTY1
                stab    PWDTY2
                stab    PWDTY3
;
                bra     *               ; just hang.
;
```

Figure 12.12: Sequenced PWM Output Switching

Chapter 12: Pulse Width Modulation Module

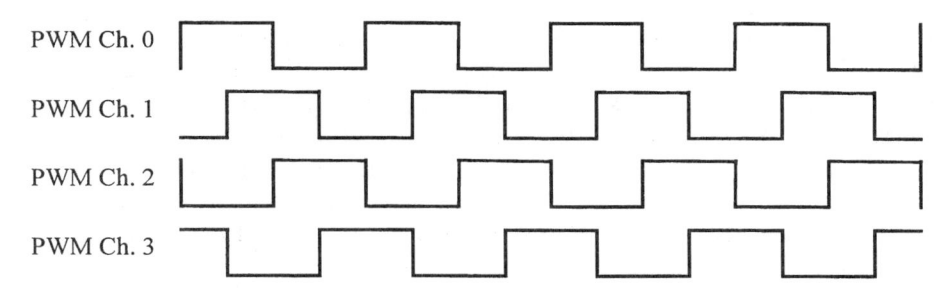

Figure 12.13: Skewed PWM Waveforms

For example, consider what happens if the channel counter becomes equal to the value in the B accumulator just after the `CMPB` instruction reads its value as shown in the cycle-by-cycle instruction activity of Figure 12.14. In this example, because the prescaler is set to divide by eight, the `PWCNT` register is incremented every eight module clock cycles. Remember that for the MC68HC912B32 the module and E-clock are the same. As the figure shows, the `CMPB` instruction performs the read of the register during the first clock of the instruction and `PWCNT` is incremented on the next rising edge. Because the value read is less than the value in the B accumulator, the `BHI` instruction executes three program fetch cycles to branch back to the `CMPB` instruction. This time, because `PWCNT` contains a value equal to the B accumulator, the second execution of the `CMPB` instruction sets the condition code register so that the `BHI` instruction will fail to branch. This causes the CPU12 to perform a single 16-bit aligned program fetch to replace the discarded branch instruction. Notice that when the `BHI` instruction executes the second time, the `PWCNT` register has been incremented again. By the time the `STAA` instruction enables the next PWM channel, the offset count between the channels is incorrect.

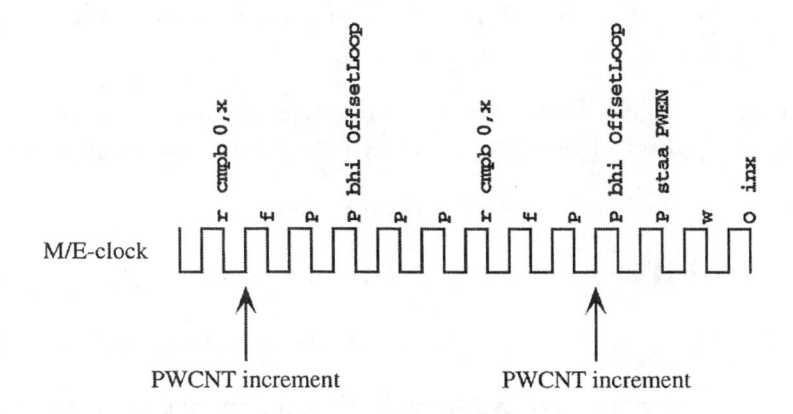

Figure 12.14: Skewed PWM Enable Cycle-by-Cycle Instruction Activity

Section 12.8: Sequenced Output Switching

If the prescale division factor is increased to a value above eight, the problem completely disappears as there is no possibility of the `PWCNT` register being incremented twice during the execution of the loop. On the other hand, using prescale division factors smaller than eight will exacerbate the problem because the `PWCNT` register is incremented multiple times during the execution of the update loop. Using additional software to compensate for the extra counts or adjusting the offset value can help to reduce the offset for prescale division factors of eight or less but the fact that the prescaler runs asynchronously relative to the software makes it difficult to eliminate the offset entirely.

Questions/Exercises

12.1 Why is double buffering of the period and duty cycle registers important? When, if ever, is the double buffering disabled?

12.2 Is the M68HC12 PWM module compatible with the M68HC11 PWM module? What differences, if any, exist between the two.

12.3 Explain the operation of a PWM channel configured for left aligned operation by describing a single PWM cycle.

12.4 What is the purpose of each channel's PPOL control bit?

12.5 Which of the PWM channels can be configured for center aligned operation?

12.6 What is different about the configuration of the counter for a PWM channel configured for Center Aligned operation?

12.7 Explain the operation of a PWM channel configured for center aligned operation by describing a single PWM cycle.

12.8 Given set of values for a channel's `PWPER` and `PWDTY` registers, what is the relationship between the waveforms for left and center aligned operation.

12.9 What is the clock source for the PWM's prescaler?

12.10 How many clock sources does each PWM channel have?

12.11 What is the clock source for the programmable scaling counter?

12.12 What is the maximum achievable division factor for the clock input to a PWM channel?

12.13 What operational limitations of left aligned operation can be deduced by examining the period and duty cycle formulas?

12.14 What techniques can be used to overcome these limitations? What are the advantages and disadvantages of using these techniques?

12.15 Do any of the limitations for left aligned operation also apply to center aligned operation? Why or why not?

12.16 What is the primary consideration when selecting a value for a channel's `PWPER` register?

12.17 What compromises and/or tradeoffs must be made when selecting a clock source division value for a given `PWPER` register value?

12.18 What restrictions are imposed for reading and writing a PWM channel configured for 16-bit operation? Why?

12.19 How is the clock source selected for a PWM channel configured for 16-bit operation?

12.20 On which port pin does the PWM waveform appear for a PWM channel configured for 16-bit operation?

12.21 What methods can be used to force new period or duty cycle register values to take effect immediately?

12.22 Write the software for an initialization sequence configuring channel zero for 33 KHz and channel one for 60 Hz operation. Both channels must have a duty cycle accuracy of at least 1% and be configured for left aligned operation. The generated waveform should begin each cycle high. At the end of initialization, set channel zero to 25% duty cycle and channel to 57% duty cycle.

12.23 Rewrite the `SetDty8LA` subroutine in Figure 12.11 so that the duty cycle will be properly set regardless of the state of a channel's PPOL control bit.

12.24 Write a subroutine similar to the one in Figure 12.11 for center aligned operation.

12.25 Write the software for an initialization sequence configuring one of the channel pairs for 16-bit operation. Set the waveform frequency to 100 Hz center aligned operation. The waveform must have a duty cycle accuracy of at least 0.1%.

Section 12.8: Sequenced Output Switching

12.26 Rewrite the initialization code in Figure 12.12 to sequence the switching of the output within the first 50% of the waveform.

Chapter 13 ANALOG-TO-DIGITAL MODULE

The analog-to-digital converter (ADC) module used in the M68HC12 family is a selectable 8-bit or 10-bit successive approximation converter that is nearly identical to the ADC module used in Motorola's M68HC16 modular microcontroller family. Even though the module utilizes an eight input multiplexer to select and convert one channel at a time, separate registers are used to hold the result of individual conversions. To allow additional flexibility for the conversion and processing of analog signals, the ADC module provides eight different conversion modes. These modes allow a single channel to be converted multiple times or multiple channels to be converted once each. Like the M68HC16 and M68HC11 family ADC modules, the M68HC12 ADC does not require an external sample and hold circuit because of the charge redistribution technique used in the conversion process. With a module clock of 8.0 MHz, the ADC can perform an 8-bit conversion in 9 µS and a 10-bit conversion in 10 µS.

13.1 THE ADC

As shown in the simplified block diagram of Figure 13.1, the ADC consists of an analog and digital section. The analog section consists of an input multiplexer, a sample amplifier, a digital-to-analog converter (DAC) and a comparator. The input multiplexer has a total of 16 inputs, allowing the selection of one of eight external or eight internal conversion sources. Three of the eight internal inputs are connected to the reference voltage inputs and an internally generated reference that is the difference of the reference voltages divided by two. Internal access to these three voltages simplifies testing of the ADC at the factory. However,

Section 13.1: The ADC

because these voltage sources are selectable by application software, they can be measured and used as part of a system's diagnostic routines.

The sample amplifier, connected to the output of the 16 channel multiplexer, is used to isolate a potentially high impedance analog source from the capacitance of the internal DAC array. As each channel conversion begins, a small capacitor connected to the input of the sample amplifier is charged for two module clock cycles. This initial sample time allows voltage on the capacitor to approach the value at the input pin without loading the source. At the end of the period, the source is disconnected from the input to the sample amplifier and the amplifier's output is connected to the DAC array. During the next four clock periods, the low impedance output of the sample amplifier charges the capacitance of the DAC array to a level that is close to that of the capacitor at its input. During the final input sampling period, the amplifier is effectively removed from the circuit and the input is connected directly to the DAC array. This allows the DAC array voltage to reach the voltage at the input pin while presenting very little capacitive load to the voltage source. Using this final sampling period provides an additional benefit of reducing or eliminating any errors introduced by the sample amplifier. In addition, because the final sampling period is programmable between two and sixteen clock periods, the ADC can easily be configured to work well with high impedance sources. The high voltage charge pump, connected to DAC array and the comparator, is used to generate a voltage several volts greater than the supply voltage. This higher voltage is used for transmission gate control and provides a higher operating voltage for the comparator thus allowing accurate measurements when the ADC input voltages approach the supply voltage.

The DAC array consists of parallel connected, binary-weighted capacitors and a resistor divisor chain. The DAC array is utilized for two functions during the conversion process. As described previously, the capacitive portion is utilized as a sample-and-hold circuit; maintaining the voltage applied to the input pin during the conversion process. Second, the binary-weighted capacitor array is used during the resolution process to determine a digital number proportionally equivalent to the applied voltage. The number is determined through a progressive switching sequence that compares the combined charge stored on the capacitors to a reference charge stored during the sampling period. The switching sequence begins with the largest capacitor and progresses toward the smallest in the array. The switching sequence, controlled by digital logic, is used in conjunction with the comparator to control the resolution process.

Notice that the negative input to the comparator is connected to a 'dummy' DAC array which is in turn connected to the ADC's V_{RH} input pin. During the channel sample and transfer period, the 'dummy' DAC array is used to obtain a sample of the voltage applied to the V_{RH} input pin. Sampling the V_{RH} voltage rather than applying it directly to the comparator during the resolution process helps prevent conversion errors due to high frequency noise that may be present on the V_{RH} input pin. As the digital control logic cycles through the resolution process, the output of the comparator is fed back into the control

Chapter 13: Analog-to-Digital Module

logic setting or clearing each bit in the successive approximation register. When the resolution process is complete, the contents of the successive approximation register is transferred to the appropriate result register where it can be read by application software.

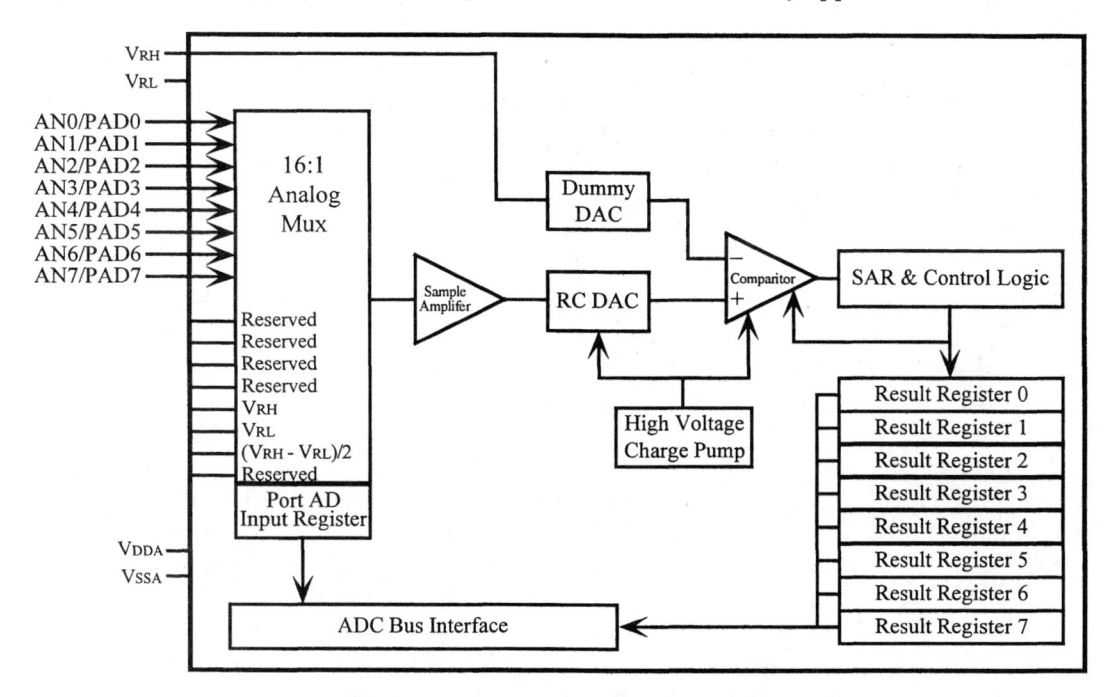

Figure 13.1: ADC Simplified Block Diagram

Like the M68HC11 family, the M68HC12 ADC has high (V_{RH}) and low (V_{RL}) analog reference voltage inputs. Having these independent reference inputs permits the system designer to achieve the greatest degree of conversion accuracy by connecting these pins to a well regulated, filtered supply not shared with the digital logic power supply. Unlike the M68HC11, separate V_{DDA} and V_{SSA} inputs are used to supply power to the analog circuitry associated with the sample amplifier and the DAC array. These dedicated power inputs help to isolate the sensitive analog circuitry from the switching noise present on the microcontroller's digital power supply.

13.2 ADC INITIALIZATION

As with all other M68HC12 peripherals, the ADC is disabled when the microcontroller exits the reset state. Before initiating an ADC measurement, the module must be enabled by setting the the `ADPU` control bit in the A-to-D Control Register 2 (`ATDCTL2`), shown in Figure 13.2. Unlike other peripherals, after enabling the ADC, an application program must

425

Section 13.3: Conversion Clock Prescaler and Final Channel Sample Time

wait a minimum of 10 µS before it can begin making measurements. This delay period is required for the charge pump to generate the proper voltage levels to obtain accurate measurements. Note that this delay period is also required when exiting the WAIT mode if the A-to-D Stop in WAIT mode (`ASWAI`) control bit is set or when exiting STOP mode. Stopping the ADC in wait mode disables the charge pump and removes bias voltages from the ADC's analog circuitry, reducing power consumption. Even when the ADC is disabled, all of its registers may be accessed, including the `PORTAD` input register.

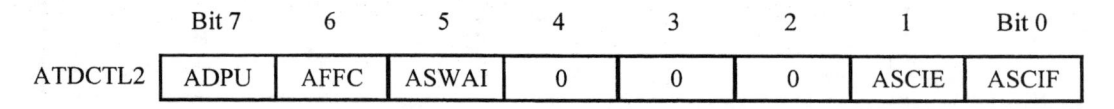

	Bit 7	6	5	4	3	2	1	Bit 0
ATDCTL2	ADPU	AFFC	ASWAI	0	0	0	ASCIE	ASCIF

Figure 13.2: A-to-D Control Register 2 (`ATDCTL2`)

In addition to the ADC power control bits, the `ATDCTL2` control register contains three control bits controlling the behavior of the ADC status flags and interrupts. The A-to-D Fast Flag Clear (`AFFC`) control bit is similar in function to the timer's `TFFCA` control bit. It allows any of the eight Conversion Complete Flags (`CCF`) to be cleared simply by reading the conversion result from a the channels's associated result register. Furthermore, the `SCF` bit is automatically cleared when one of the ADC's result registers involved in the conversion is read. If not using the fast flag clear option, the A-to-D Status Register (`ATDSTAT`) must be read before each read of a result register to clear the channel's associated `CCF` bit. When using the standard flag clearing mechanism, the `SCF` bit remains set after the first conversion sequence except when a conversion is in process. This behavior has several implications related to using the ADC in an interrupt driven mode and is discussed in one of the examples later in the chapter.

The least significant bit in this register, the A-to-D Sequence Complete Interrupt Flag (`ASCIF`), is set at the end of either four or eight channel conversion periods only if the A-to-D Sequence Complete Interrupt Enable (`ADSCIE`) control bit is set. In this case, if the I-bit in the CPU12 condition code register is clear, an interrupt is generated. Keep in mind that an interrupt cannot be generated at the completion of each channel conversion.

13.3 CONVERSION CLOCK PRESCALER AND FINAL CHANNEL SAMPLE TIME

Before enabling the ADC, the conversion clock prescaler and the final channel sample time should be set. Unlike other peripherals, the ADC has a minimum and maximum frequency at which it can operate. Because of the charge redistribution technique used in the conversion process, if the conversion is not performed quickly enough, the charge will eventually leak off of the DAC array resulting in conversion errors. Currently, the minimum operating frequency is specified at 500 KHz. Operating the ADC below this level may produce acceptable results, especially if the M68HC12 is operated at a temperature substantially below its maximum rating, however, the ADC's accuracy is not guaranteed below 500 KHz. Unlike the M68HC11, the ADC module does not contain an RC oscillator that can be used when the module clock falls below the specified minimum. Unfortunately, this renders the ADC unusable for systems that must operate at very low clock frequencies.

It may seem strange that there is a maximum operating frequency associated with the ADC. However, this restriction also has to do with the charge redistribution technique used in the conversion process. As with any electrical circuit, all of the signal paths used to transfer the sampled charge around during the conversion process have some amount of electrical resistance associated with them. The RC time constant resulting from the resistance and the DAC capacitance can introduce conversion errors if an attempt is made to move electrical charge through these connections too quickly. As stated in the current electrical specifications for the MC68HC912B32, the maximum conversion clock frequency for the ADC module is 2.0 MHz. This allows an 8-bit conversion in as little as 9 µS and a 10-bit conversion in in as little as 10 µS. The ADC conversion clock is controlled by the lower five bits in the ATDCTL4 register as shown in Figure 13.3.

The prescaler clock bits select a division factor for a 5-bit modulo counter used as the prescaler. The ADC module clock is divided by the value written to these bits plus one and is further divided by two to generate the ADC conversion clock. The additional divide by two stage assures symmetry of the conversion clock. The default value of the prescaler control bits is %00001 which selects a prescale factor of four. This value allows conversions to be performed at the maximum clock rate of 2.0 MHz with an 8.0 MHz module clock.

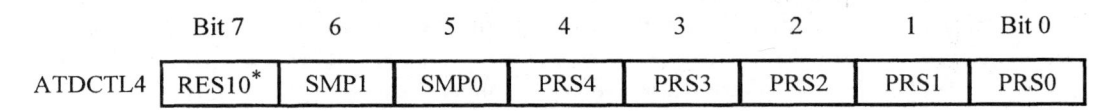

	Bit 7	6	5	4	3	2	1	Bit 0
ATDCTL4	RES10*	SMP1	SMP0	PRS4	PRS3	PRS2	PRS1	PRS0

Figure 13.3: ADC Control Register 4 (ATDCTL4)

Also contained in the ATDCTL4 control register are the Final Sample Time control bits, SMP0 and SMP1, allowing the selection of one of four final sampling times. As explained previously, this second sampling period occurs after the buffered sample and charge transfer period. This allows the the DAC array to be charged to its final value without excessively loading the measured source. Extending the final sample period permits accurate measurement of high impedance sources without requiring an external amplifier to buffer a sensor's output signal. The default value of both bits is zero selecting a final sample period of two ADC conversion clocks. Final sample periods of four, eight, and sixteen ADC conversion clocks are selectable as shown in Figure 13.4.

Section 13.3: Conversion Clock Prescaler and Final Channel Sample Time

SMP1	SMP0	Final Sample Time	8-Bit Conversion Time
0	0	2 ADC Clock Periods	18 ADC Clock Periods
0	1	4 ADC Clock Periods	20 ADC Clock Periods
1	0	8 ADC Clock Periods	24 ADC Clock Periods
1	1	16 ADC Clock Periods	32 ADC Clock Periods

Figure 13.4: Final Sample Time Selection

As expected, extending the final sample period lengthens the total conversion time of *all* ADC channels. For systems having a mixture of high and low impedance analog sources, tailoring the sample time for the high impedance sources will impose a conversion performance penalty for the low impedance sources without careful thought and planning. For such systems, for example, it may be possible to group all of the high impedance sources on the lower four channels while placing the low impedance sources on the upper four channels. With such an arrangement, the final sample time could be set to two clocks during the conversion of the low impedance sources, and lengthened as required when converting the high impedance sources. Of course, such a strategy makes the assumption that none of the analog sources needs to be converted continuously at the maximum rate.

While some applications may require the conversion of analog sensor signals at the maximum rate possible, there are many applications that can utilize lower conversion rates. Using a slower conversion clock rate will allow for additional settling time for node voltages in the analog portion of the ADC, however, it will not necessarily result in a more accurate reading. Because the total capacitance of the sample DAC is quite small, there is very little signal integration that takes place during the sampling and transfer period. The most critical period for ensuring an accurate reading is the exact moment when the final sample period ends. Because this event takes place on a clock edge, the sample period and conversion clock rate are less important as long as the sample has had time to settle. The most important consideration in obtaining an accurate conversion of the input signal is to reduce any high frequency noise that may be part of the signal.

Finally, the most significant bit in the ATDCTL4 register, RES10, is used to control the resolution of the ADC. When this bit is zero, its default value, the ADC operates in an 8-bit conversion mode, requiring a minimum of 18 ADC clocks to convert a single channel. When RES10 is one, the ADC operates in an 10-bit conversion mode requiring a minimum of 20 ADC clocks to convert each channel. Those familiar with the MC68HC912B32 will realize that the part's ADC is only specified for 8-bit resolution. In reality, the MC68HC912B32's ADC module is the same one used on the MC68HC912BC32, MC68HC912D60 and the MC68HC912DA/DG128 and is capable of 10-bit resolution. Even though the MC68HC912B32 documentation shows that the RES10 control bit contains a permanent value of zero, the bit may be written to a one and the ADC operated in 10-bit mode.

Recognize, however, that the accuracy of the MC68HC912B32's ADC module is only tested and guaranteed for 8-bit operation at this time.

13.4 OPERATING MODE SELECTION

The operating mode and conversion channel selection is made by the various control bits in the ATDCTL5 control register. As shown in Figure 13.5, the lower four bits CD through CA, are used to select the channel or group of channels to be converted during each sequence. The combination of the remaining three bits in the register are used to select one of eight operating modes.

	Bit 7	6	5	4	3	2	1	Bit 0
ATDCTL5	0	S8CM	SCAN	MULT	CD	CC	CB	CA

Figure 13.5: ADC Control Register 5 (ATDCTL5)

The Select Eight Channel Mode (S8CM) control bit chooses either a four or eight conversion sequence. Its default value of zero selects a four conversion sequence. Writing one to this bit selects an eight conversion sequence. When used in conjunction with the Multi Channel Conversion (MULT) control bit, the ADC sequencer will run four or eight conversions on either a single channel or on a multi-channel group. The Enable Continuous Channel Scan (SCAN) control bit selects either a single conversion sequence or sets the ADC to convert continuously without stopping. The table in Figure 13.6 summarizes the operating modes available utilizing the eight combinations of these three control bits.

S8CM	SCAN	MULT	ADC Action
0	0	0	Convert one channel four times & stop
0	0	1	Convert four channels one time & stop
0	1	0	Convert one channel four times continuously
0	1	1	Convert four channels continuously
1	0	0	Convert one channel eight times & stop
1	0	1	Convert eight channels one time & stop
1	1	0	Convert one channel eight times continuously
1	1	1	Convert eight channels continuously

Figure 13.6: ADC Conversion Mode Summary

Section 13.5: Result Registers

When converting a single channel, all four channel select bits are significant when selecting the channel to be converted. However, when converting either four or eight channels, the least significant two or three channel select bits are ignored. When converting only four channels, a restriction is imposed allowing the conversion of a single channel group consisting of inputs AN0 through AN3, AN4 through AN7 or one of the two internal channel groups in a single sequence. When the four channel group consisting of inputs AN4 through AN7 or the internal test channels are converted, the results are placed in result registers `ADR0` through `ADR3` rather than `ADR4` through `ADR7`.

13.5 Result Registers

To accommodate the conversion of all eight input channels in a single sequence, the ADC contains eight separate result registers. Each result register consists of two bytes to accommodate the 10-bit conversion mode. As shown in Figure 13.7, the positioning of the data within the 16-bit register is not necessarily what might be expected. For eight bit conversions, the result is placed in the high order byte of the 16-bit result register allowing the data to be accessed with a single 8-bit read access. When operating in 10-bit mode each conversion result is placed in a 16-bit result register left justified. Formatting the data in this manner, rather than right justifying it in the 16-bit register, allows the data to be treated as an unsigned binary fraction for calculation purposes. The data can easily be converted to right justified format after reading it into the D accumulator. Notice that bits zero through five of the `ADRxL` register always read zero.

	Bit 7	6	5	4	3	2	1	Bit 0
ADRxH	ADR9/7	ADR8/6	ADR7/5	ADR6/4	ADR5/3	ADR4/2	ADR3/1	ADR2/0
ADRxL	ADR1	ADR0	0	0	0	0	0	0

Figure 13.7: ADC Result Register

When a single channel is converted four or eight times, the results are placed in result registers ADR0 through ADR3 or ADR0 through ADR7 without regard to which channel was converted. When converting a group of four channels, either AD0 through AD3 or AD4 through AD7, the results are always placed in result registers ADR0 through ADR3. The contents of the result registers are undefined after a powerup reset and will retain the results of the last conversion after any other reset.

As each analog input channel is converted, the register's associated Conversion Complete Flag (`CCFx`) in the low byte of the `ATDSTAT` register is automatically set indicating that the related result register contains a valid conversion result. The CCF for each channel remains set until the affiliated result register is read. If the `AFFC` bit in the `ATDCTL2` register is clear, a read of the `ATDSTAT` register must be performed *before* reading a result register to clear the associated CCF bit. When the AFFC bit is set, a read of a result register is all that is required to clear a CCF flag.

The Sequence Complete Flag (SCF), found in the high byte of the ATDSTAT register, is set at the end of a four or eight conversion sequence when the ADC is configured for single conversion sequence mode. When the AFFC bit is zero, writing to the ATDCTL5 register to begin a new conversion sequence clears the SCF bit. Reading any of the result registers after the SCF bit becomes set, when AFFC is one, will automatically clear it. When the ADC is configured for continuous conversion mode, the SCF bit is set at the end of the first conversion sequence and then remains set.

	Bit 15	14	13	12	11	10	9	Bit 8
ADSTATH	SCF	0	0	0	0	CC2	CC1	CC0
ADSTATL	CCF7	CCF6	CCF5	CCF4	CCF3	CCF2	CCF1	CCF0
	Bit 7	6	5	4	3	2	1	Bit 0

Figure 13.8: ADC Status Register

13.6 SIMPLE ADC EXAMPLE

In many applications sensors are used to detect relatively slow changing analog signals. In such applications, the ADC may be configured to convert the desired channels in a continuous manner, leaving the results of each conversion in the channel's associated result register. Utilizing the ADC in this manner only requires setup during the application's initialization process. Thereafter, the application may read a sensor's value at any time by simply reading the channel's result register. The initialization of the ADC for such an application is shown in Figure 13.9.

While this simple code sequence requires little explanation, it can be noted that the writes to ATDCTL4 and ATDCTL5 could be combined into a single 16-bit write to the address of ATDCTL4 because the two 8-bit registers are adjacent to one another. For some applications, especially those that may need to change the final sample clock when converting different channels, a single write would be preferable since a write to either 8-bit register will initiate a new conversion sequence. Note also that a 10 µS delay is not included after writing to the ATDCTL2 register to enable the ADC. For most applications such a delay is unnecessary because of the elapsed time required for other system initialization.

Section 13.7: Timed Conversion Example

```
;
ADCInit: ldab   #80        ; power up the ADC.
         stab   ATDCTL2
         ldab   #$41       ; select a final sample time of 8 clocks
         std    ATDCTL4    ; and a /4 prescaler for 2 MHz conversion clock
                           ; @ 8 MHZ E-clock.
         ldab   #$30       ; convert Ch. 0 - 3 in a continuous manner.
         std    ATDCTL5
         rts               ; init finished.
;
```

Figure 13.9: ADC Initialization

13.7 TIMED CONVERSION EXAMPLE

While the previous example is adequate for some applications, there are numerous others requiring samples to be taken at regular intervals. Performing the conversions at regular intervals requires a time base to trigger a conversion sequence. The example presented in Figure 13.10 uses one of the timer channels as an output compare, initiating an ADC conversion every 10 mS or 100 times per second. Both the timer and the ADC are operated in an interrupt driven manner so other tasks may be performed between conversions and during the conversion process.

The initialization portion of the example begins by configuring timer channel zero as an output compare, setting up the TC0 register to produce an interrupt 10 mS after the timer is enabled. Notice that the Timer Fast Flag Clear All (TFFCA) option is enabled, allowing the clearing of the timer interrupt flag for channel zero by writing TC0 in the interrupt service routine. After the timer is initialized, the ADC is enabled by setting the ADPU bit in the ATDCTL2. In addition the ADC's Fast Flag Clear (AFFC) and ADC interrupts are enabled. Because all of the work is performed by the timer and ADC interrupt service routines, a branch-to-self is executed after the CPU12's interrupt mask is cleared.

Chapter 13: Analog-to-Digital Module

```
;
Ch4Rslt: ds      1                       ; averaged result.
;
CvtInit: ldab    #$01                    ; make Ch 0 an output compare.
         stab    TIOS
         ldab    #$03                    ; set prescaler to /8.
         stab    TMSK2
         ldd     #10000                  ; constant for 10 mS delay.
         std     TC0
         ldab    #$01                    ; enable interrupts for Ch 0.
         stab    TMSK1
         ldab    #TEN+TFFCA              ; enable timer & fast flag clear.
         stab    TSCR
         ldab    #ADPU+AFFC+ASCIE        ; powerup the ADC, use fast flag clear,
         stab    ATDCTL2                 ; enable ADC interrupts.
         cli
         bra     *
;
OC0ISR:  ldd     TC0                     ; get value of OC0 register.
         addd    #10000                  ; add in delay constant.
         std     TC0                     ; update OC0, clearing interrupt flag.
         ldab    #$04                    ; convert Ch 4 four times & stop
         stab    ATDCTL5                 ; initiate the conversion.
         rti                             ; return.
;
ADCISR:  clra                            ; initialize average accumulator.
         clrb
         pshd                            ; init temporary on the stack.
         ldx     #ADR0H                  ; point to the first ADC result register.
         ldy     #4                      ; number of conversions to average.
AvgLoop: movb    2,x+,1,sp               ; move ADC result into LSByte of temp.
         addd    0,sp                    ; add it to the accumulated result.
         dbne    y,AvgLoop               ; loop until all 4 Ch are added in.
         lsrd                            ; divide by 4 to get average.
         lsrd
         stab    Ch4Rslt                 ; save the result.
         puld                            ; remove temporary.
         rti                             ; return.
;
```

Figure 13.10: Periodic ADC Conversion

433

Section 13.7: Timed Conversion Example

The timer interrupt service routine, executed every 10 mS, performs two simple operations. First it reinitializes the output compare register for the next 10 ms period, initiates a sequence of four conversions on channel four and then returns. When the ADC finishes its conversion sequence, the SCF flag in the ATDSTAT register is set, generating an interrupt. Because the ADC conversion sequence involves four conversions of the same channel, the four results are averaged to help provide noise immunity for the measured signal. Notice that because the Fast Flag Clear option is enabled, no explicit action is needed to clear the SCF flag. Reading any of the result registers affected by the conversion automatically clears both the SCF and the ASCIF flags. When not using the Fast Flag Clear option, ADC interrupts must be enabled in the timer interrupt service routine *before* the ADC conversion sequence is initiated and then disabled within the ADC interrupt service routine before returning. If the interrupt is not enabled before initiating the conversion sequence, the conversion sequence will be aborted when writing the ATDCTL2 register. In addition, the AFFC and ASCIE bits must not be set in the initialization routine. The modified interrupt service routines are shown in Figure 13.11.

```
;
OC0ISR:     ldd     TC0                 ; get value of OC0 register.
            addd    #10000              ; add in delay constant.
            std     TC0                 ; update OC0, clearing interrupt flag.
            bset    ATDCTL2,#ASCIE      ; enable ADC interrupts.
            ldab    #$04                ; convert Ch 4 four times & stop
            stab    ATDCTL5             ; initiate the conversion.
            rti                         ; return.
;
ADCISR:     clra                        ; initialize average accumulator.
            clrb
            pshd                        ; init temporary on the stack.
            ldx     #ADR0H              ; point to the first ADC result register.
            ldy     #4                  ; number of conversions to average.
AvgLoop:    movb    2,x+,1,sp           ; move ADC result into LSByte of temp.
            addd    0,sp                ; add it to the accumulated result.
            dbne    y,AvgLoop           ; loop until all 4 Ch are added in.
            lsrd                        ; divide by 4 to get average.
            lsrd
            stab    Ch4Rslt             ; save the result.
            puld                        ; remove temporary.
            bclr    ATDCTL2,#ASCIE      ; disable ADC interrupts.
            rti                         ; return.
;
```

Figure 13.11: Using Standard ADC Interrupts

13.8 ADC PORT INPUT REGISTER

The ADC module has a single input port associated with the eight analog input pins of the ADC. This port was designed as an input–only port to provide the greatest ADC conversion accuracy possible. If the port pins were designed with bidirectional I/O drivers, the additional capacitance and leakage current added by the N-channel and P-channel output drivers could adversely affect readings. Reading the PORTAD input register will always return the digital level applied to the input pin. Any of the pins used as analog inputs will return an indeterminate value if the applied signal falls outside the M68HC12's electrical specifications for a logic high (VIH) or a logic low (VIL). Using some of the PORTAD pins for digital inputs does not preclude their use as analog inputs. Because the port is on an internally buffered register bus, reading the PORTAD register during an ADC conversion sequence will not affect the conversion accuracy.

Questions/Exercises

13.1   What is the resolution of the M68HC12 ADC module?

13.2   What is the purpose of the sample amplifier connected to the output of the channel multiplexer?

13.3   List the advantages of using the three different time periods utilized during the sampling portion of the channel conversion time.

13.4   What is the purpose of the high voltage charge pump in the ADC module?

13.5   Describe the two functions of the capacitive DAC array during the conversion process.

13.6   What is the function of the a 'dummy' DAC array?

13.7   What function do the VRH, VRL, VDDA, and VSSA inputs perform in the ADC module?

13.8   After enabling the ADC module, what restrictions must be observed?

13.9   Does the Fast Flag Clear option of the ADC have any advantages over the standard flag clearing mechanism? If so, what are they?

13.10 Give the reasons that the ADC module specifies both a minimum and maximum operating frequency.

Section 13.8: ADC Port Input Register

13.11 What is the purpose of providing a programmable final sample time?

13.12 How does the final sample time affect the total conversion time of the ADC? Is there a way to negate the time penalty imposed by mixing high and low impedance sources? Explain.

13.13 Is there any advantage using an ADC conversion clock slower than the specified maximum clock frequency? Explain.

13.14 Explain the purpose of each of the conversion mode select bits. How many conversion modes are available?

13.15 Explain the function of the channel select bits in the various conversion modes.

13.16 Where are the results of a conversion sequence involving channels AD4 through AD7 placed?

13.17 What is the functional difference between a Conversion Complete Flag (CCFx) and the Sequence Complete Flag (SCF).

13.18 Modify the example in Figure 13.10 to convert four channels at 10 mS intervals, averaging four readings for each channel.

13.19 What must be considered when interpreting the digital data read at PORTAD when both analog and digital signals are connected to port pins AD0 through AD7?

Chapter 14 HARDWARE BREAKPOINT MODULE

The hardware breakpoint module, included on most M68HC12 family members, provides software developers a powerful tool allowing code to be debugged directly from the on-chip Flash memory. The breakpoint module contains two sets of comparators capable of being configured to monitor the activity on the address and/or data bus. When the values appearing on the address and/or data bus' match those in the breakpoint module's address and/or data registers, the CPU12 can be forced to enter active background debug mode (BDM) or initiate a software interrupt sequence. In addition to its intended use as a debugging tool, the hardware breakpoint module can be used in a unique manner allowing the correction of software bugs in ROM code.

14.1 BREAKPOINT OPERATING MODES

The flexibility built into the breakpoint module allows it to be configured for operation in one of three basic modes. Two of these modes cause the CPU12 to enter the active background debug mode when the conditions specified for a breakpoint are met. The third mode causes the CPU12 to initiate a software interrupt sequence. The breakpoint operating mode is controlled by two bits, BKEN0 and BKEN1, contained in the Breakpoint Control Register 0 (BRKCT0). The three operating modes are summarized in the table of Figure 14.1.

Section 14.1: Breakpoint Operating Modes

BKEN1	BKEN0	Selected Mode	Address Register	Data Register	R/$\overline{\text{W}}$	Range
0	0	Breakpoints Off	—	—	—	—
0	1	SWI – Dual Address Mode	Address Match	Address Match	No	Yes
1	0	BDM – Full Breakpoint Mode	Address Match	Data Match	Yes	Yes
1	1	BDM – Dual Address Mode	Address Match	Address Match	Yes	Yes

Figure 14.1: Breakpoint Operating Mode Summary

As shown, two registers, 16-bits each, are provided allowing breakpoint triggering on address and/or data bus information. The address register, BRKAH:BRKAL, is used only for address information regardless of the operating mode. The data register, BRKDH:BRKDL, on the other hand, may be used to contain address or data information. In both the BDM and SWI dual address modes, the data register is only used for a second address breakpoint. In all modes a 256 byte range of addresses may be used as the breakpoint match criteria, but only in the BDM modes may the Read/write signal be used to qualify the breakpoint match.

In addition to the three main operating modes described above, the breakpoint module may be configured to initiate a breakpoint on either an opcode fetch or a data reference. When the breakpoint module is configured to generate a breakpoint on an opcode fetch, the CPU12's instruction tagging mechanism is used. The tagging mechanism allows prefetched instructions to be marked in the instruction prefetch queue, only causing a breakpoint if the instruction is actually executed by the CPU. While the SWI breakpoint mode is automatically forced to use the opcode tracking mechanism, the BDM dual address mode can use either opcode fetch or data reference to trigger a breakpoint. If configured for a breakpoint on an opcode fetch when the BDM full breakpoint mode is used, the data match specified by BRKDH:BRKDL and the control bits in the Breakpoint Control Register 1 (BRKCT1) are ignored.

The breakpoint range mode is controlled by the BK0ALE and BK1ALE control bits in the BRKCT0 register. These bits, when cleared, allow the contents of BRKAL and BRKDL respectively, to be ignored. When the breakpoint module is configured for full breakpoint mode, the state of the BK1ALE control bit is ignored. When utilizing the range mode together with instruction opcode tracking, a breakpoint is generated whenever an opcode is fetched from the 256 byte page specified by the upper eight bits of the address in BRKAH or BRKDH. When utilizing the range mode with the data access modes, a breakpoint is generated whenever the specified data reference occurs in the specified 256 byte page.

Figure 14.2 shows the Breakpoint Control Register 0 (BRKCT0) and the Breakpoint Control Register 1 (BRKCT1).

Bit 7	6	5	4	3	2	1	Bit 0	
BKEN1	BKEN0	BKPM	0	BK1ALE	BK0ALE	0	0	BRKCT0

Bit 7	6	5	4	3	2	1	Bit 0	
0	BKDBE	BKMPH	BKMPL	BK1RWE	BK1RW	BK0RWE	BK0RW	BRKCT1

Figure 14.2: Breakpoint Control Register 0 and 1

14.2 SWI Dual Address Mode

The SWI dual address mode utilizes the BRKAH:BRKAL and BRKDH:BRKDL registers to provide two program address-only breakpoints. Because the SWI breakpoint mode automatically utilizes the CPU12's instruction tagging mechanism, breakpoint addresses may *only* be set on instruction opcodes. With one exception, if either the breakpoint address or data register is set to an address not containing an instruction opcode, the breakpoint will effectively be ignored. If, however, the range option is selected, any opcode fetch from the selected 256 byte page will initiate an SWI breakpoint.

When an SWI breakpoint is recognized, the CPU12 performs the same actions as if it had executed an actual SWI instruction. The contents of the CPU registers are pushed onto the stack, the SWI vector is fetched, the CPU performs three program fetch cycles and executes the SWI interrupt service routine. There is one slight but important difference between the execution of an SWI instruction and the processing of the SWI breakpoint. When an SWI instruction is executed, as with all instructions, the program counter is advanced to point to the next instruction. Thus, the stacked value of the program counter will be the address of the SWI opcode plus one. However, when an SWI breakpoint is processed, the stacked value of the program counter will be the address of the opcode fetch invoking the breakpoint. This subtle difference is important to realize if returning from an SWI breakpoint using the RTI instruction. If the stacked value of the program counter is not adjusted before returning, another SWI breakpoint will be recognized and processed, placing the CPU12 in an endless loop.

As a debugging aid, the SWI breakpoint mode is useful in combination with ROM resident debug programs such as D-Bug12 that is resident on Motorola's MC68HC912B32 EVB. Utilizing the SWI breakpoints instead of the traditional software breakpoints provides the ability to perform instruction single stepping and setting breakpoints in nonvolatile memory. The second important use of the SWI breakpoint mode is illustrated in the ROM code patching example presented later in this chapter.

Section 14.3: BDM Full Breakpoint Mode

As shown in Figure 14.1, BKEN0 and BKEN1 must be initialized to one and zero respectively to enable the SWI breakpoint mode. The value of the BKPM bit is ignored in the SWI breakpoint mode and may be written to a one or zero. If not utilizing the address range feature of either breakpoint, BK0ALE and BK1ALE must both be written to one. To enable the second breakpoint, whose address is placed in the BRKDH:BRKDL register, a one must be written to the BKDBE bit in the BRKCT1 control register. The remaining bits in the BRKCT1 control register are ignored in the SWI breakpoint mode.

14.3 BDM Full Breakpoint Mode

BDM full breakpoint mode provides a single full featured breakpoint allowing a full combination of address and data bus information to trigger the breakpoint mechanism. Because this breakpoint mode places the M68HC12 into active background when the breakpoint criteria is met, this mode is not generally useful to an application program. This mode is most often supported by high level background debug tools that hide the configuration details from the developer. However, understanding the capabilities of this mode should help developers better understand the capabilities of the high level tools supporting the hardware breakpoint module.

In general, the BDM full breakpoint mode is used to detect a read or write of a specific data value to an 8-bit or 16-bit memory location. When configuring the BRKCT0 control register for full breakpoint mode, BKPM must be cleared to disable the instruction tagging mechanism, allowing data access compares. The BK0ALE bit may be used to specify an address range for the data access, however, the BK1ALE control bit has no meaning in full breakpoint mode. To enable data comparisons utilizing the value in the BRKDH and BRKDL registers requires that the BKDBE bit in the BRKCT1 control register be set. The state of other control bits in BRKCT1 will depend on the desired operation, though the BK1RWE and BK1RW bits have no meaning in full breakpoint mode.

Important Information

The Breakpoint Mask Byte High (BKMBH) and Breakpoint Mask Byte Low (BKMBL) bits control the comparison of the BRKDH and BRKDL registers respectively, to the M68HC12's data bus. Setting either of these bits causes the breakpoint module to ignore comparison of the data bus' corresponding byte. When configuring the module to detect data read from or written to an *aligned* word variable, both control bits should be cleared and the desired 16-bit data written to the BRKDH and BRKDL registers. To configure a data comparison for a *misaligned* internal word access to RAM, the contents written to the BRKDH and BRKDL registers must be *reversed* from the order the value is stored in memory. This byte reversal is related to the on-chip RAM's capability to allow 16-bit misaligned accesses in a single cycle. When a 16-bit misaligned word is read from the on-chip RAM, the data appears

Chapter 14: Hardware Breakpoint Module

on the bus in reverse byte order. However, an internal bus controller swaps the bytes before passing the data along to the CPU12. Conversely, when a misaligned word is written to the on-chip RAM, the internal bus controller swaps the bytes before placing the data on the internal bus. *Note that misaligned word data accesses to any other internal modules or external memory are not supported by the breakpoint module.*

When configuring the module to detect data read from or written to a byte variable, the BKMBH and BKMBL bits and the BRKDH and BRKDL registers must be properly configured to select comparison of the proper byte. As discussed in Chapter 1, data transactions involving bytes with even addresses utilize the upper eight bits (15:8) of the data bus while transactions involving bytes with odd addresses utilize the lower eight bits (7:0). When utilizing the full breakpoint mode for data comparison at an even address, the BKMBL bit must be set to ignore the lower 8-bit of the data bus and the BRKDH written with the desired 8-bit data. When comparing data at odd addresses, the BKMBH bit must be set and the BRKDL written with the desired 8-bit data.

Figure 14.3 summarizes the control and data register configuration required for utilizing the breakpoint module in full breakpoint mode. Remember the address range option is also available in this mode by clearing the BK0ALE bit in the BRKCT0 register. When utilizing the range option the value of BRKCT0 would become $80 instead of $84.

BRKCT0	BRKCT1	Data Bus Comparison	BRKDH	BRKDL
$84	$53	Even Byte Read	<data 7:0>	—
$84	$52	Even Byte Write	<data 7:0>	—
$84	$63	Odd Byte Read	—	<data 7:0>
$84	$62	Odd Byte Write	—	<data 7:0>
$84	$43	Aligned Word Read	<data 15:8>	<data 7:0>
$84	$42	Aligned Word Write	<data 15:8>	<data 7:0>
$84	$43	Misaligned Word Read*	<data 7:0>	<data 15:8>
$84	$42	Misaligned Word Write*	<data 7:0>	<data 15:8>

*Misaligned Access Supported Only In Internal RAM

Figure 14.3: BDM Full Breakpoint Mode Configuration Summary

14.4 BDM Dual Address Mode

The BDM dual address mode provides two address-only breakpoints placing the M68HC12 into active background mode when the breakpoint criteria is met. Like the BDM full breakpoint mode, this mode is not generally useful to an application program. Because the BRKDH and BRKDL registers are used to contain a second address, data bus comparisons are not supported. However, because BDM dual address mode allows the use of the BKPM bit to optionally use the CPU12's instruction tagging mechanism, the two breakpoints may be used as program breakpoints or data breakpoints.

Setting the BKPM bit in BDM dual address mode configures the breakpoint module to provide two program-only breakpoints. In this configuration, the breakpoint operates in a manner identical to the SWI dual breakpoint mode except that the CPU12 enters the active background mode when a breakpoint occurs. Because this mode utilizes the CPU12's instruction tagging mechanism, breakpoint addresses may *only* be set on instruction opcodes. If either the address or data register is set to an address not containing an instruction opcode, the breakpoint is effectively ignored. However, if the range option is selected, any opcode fetch from the 256 byte page will place the CPU12 in the active background mode.

When the BKPM bit is cleared, the breakpoint module provides two data-only breakpoints. In this mode, data accesses to the address in BRKAH:BRKAL or BRKDH:BRKDL will cause the CPU12 to enter the background mode. Even though the BRKDH:BRKDL is not available for comparison of specific values at either breakpoint address, the Read/write compare enable control bits (BKxRWE) in conjunction with the Read/write compare value control bits (BKxRW) may be used to qualify the access as a read or write cycle. Even though this operating mode does not provide the sophisticated data qualification of the full breakpoint mode, it does allow detection of an access to a specific address.

There is one limitation to this mode where a memory access is not detected by the breakpoint module. If one of the breakpoint registers is set to an odd address, and a word access is made to next lower even address, the breakpoint module will ignore the access to the odd address. This seemingly errant behavior is not caused by a design defect, but rather by the fact that when an aligned word access is performed, the address of the aligned word is all that ever appears on the address bus. All other cases of byte and misaligned word accesses are detected by the breakpoint module.

14.5 BDM Breakpoint Cautions

As mentioned earlier in the chapter, neither of the BDM breakpoint modes are normally utilized by application programs. However, application developers and development tool vendors must ensure that the BDM breakpoint modes are not enabled unless the Enable BDM (ENBDM) bit in the BDM Status Register (STATUS) has previously been set.

Unfortunately, there is no hardware locking mechanism preventing the recognition of hardware breakpoints if the ENBDM bit is not set. If the CPU12 enters the active background mode from a BDM breakpoint, the BDM firmware will check the state of the ENBDM bit and immediately return to the application program if it is not set. Because the program counter is not advanced as it is when a BGND instruction is executed, the CPU12 will return to the same address causing the hardware breakpoint. This will cause the breakpoint module to reassert the hardware breakpoint, placing the CPU12 into an endless loop entering and exiting the background mode.

It should be noted that the hardware breakpoints are disabled when the CPU12 is in the active background mode executing the BDM firmware. This ensures that hardware breakpoints may be set in the 256 byte memory area, $FF00 through $FFFF, that is occupied by the BDM firmware ROM without affecting the execution of the BDM firmware.

14.6 PROGRAM COUNTER AT DATA BREAKPOINTS

As discussed previously, when the breakpoint module is configured to break on a program address, the CPU12's instruction tagging mechanism is used to ensure that the breakpoint occurs only if an instruction is executed. This prevents a breakpoint from being asserted when the instruction is fetched and placed in the CPU12's prefetch queue and restricts the placement of program breakpoints to an opcode address. In addition, the tagging mechanism ensures that the breakpoint is recognized and processed *before* the instruction opcode at the breakpoint address is executed. The program counter will thus be pointing to the instruction opcode that caused the breakpoint.

Because data breakpoints cannot utilize the opcode tracking mechanism, a signal from the breakpoint module is asserted as soon as an instruction references a memory location specified in the breakpoint module. After the assertion of the breakpoint signal, the CPU12 will always complete execution of the current instruction, yet it requires 1.5 E-clock cycles to recognize and begin breakpoint processing. Depending on when the data access occurs in the instruction cycle, it is possible that an additional one or two instructions will be executed before the CPU12 enters the active background mode. At best, if the data access occurs early in the instruction execution, the program counter will end up pointing to the next instruction. At worst, if the data access takes place during the last cycle of the instruction, the program counter could end up pointing to an instruction that is not even close to the instruction causing the breakpoint.

For example, if a BSET or BCLR instruction (write occurs in the last cycle of the instruction for direct, extended and one byte indexed addressing modes) causing a breakpoint is followed by a JMP instruction, the program counter would point to the destination of the JMP instruction by time the CPU12 entered the active background mode. For this particular example, which is the worse case, in may be extremely difficult to determine the program instruction causing the assertion of the breakpoint. While this is a

Section 14.7: ROM Code Patching Example

recognized limitation of the breakpoint module when configured to break on data accesses, it does not completely negate its use for this purpose. For most other instruction combinations, it would be much easier to determine the instruction causing the breakpoint.

14.7 ROM CODE PATCHING EXAMPLE

Companies using large volumes of microcontrollers generally prefer to use parts containing masked ROM rather than One Time Programmable (OTP) EPROM or Flash EEPROM because of the cost savings associated with masked ROM parts. Although the masked ROM parts offer a lower piece price, there are significant risks associated with their use. In addition to the manufacturing lead time, inventory, and reduced development time associated with ROM parts, there is always a chance that a software bug will be found after the ROM parts have been fabricated and placed in service. If the discovered bug is severe enough to pose a safety or life threatening risk to the equipment's users, the entire module containing the microcontroller would have to be replaced. The example presented here illustrates how the M68HC12's breakpoint module can be used in conjunction with the on-chip EEPROM memory to correct up to two software bugs in ROM without having to replace the module or even the microcontroller. Because the on-chip EEPROM is used to contain the bug replacement code and a small address table, the complexity of the bug that can be fixed is limited by the amount of EEPROM not used by the application. In view of the fact that many applications only utilize a small amount of the on-chip EEPROM for data storage, most of the space would be available for the ROM code patch.

The use of this method places two requirements on the module. First, a small amount of additional code must be added to the application in ROM *before* the device is fabricated. The code contains fewer than 60 bytes and consists of an initialization subroutine and an SWI interrupt service routine. Second, a method must exist to allow the bug replacement code to be programmed into the on-chip EEPROM. If the code patch must be applied after the microcontroller has been soldered on to the circuit board, the EEPROM may easily be programmed through the BDM connector if available. In many cases, this operation could be performed as part of the module's final test. If a BDM connection is not available, some additional software development may be necessary to satisfy this requirement.

To perform the ROM code patching function, the breakpoint module must be configured to operate in the SWI dual address mode. The BRKAH:BRKAL and/or BRKDH:BRKDL registers are loaded with the opcode address(es) of the first instruction in the code sequence to be replaced. When an opcode fetch occurs at either of the breakpoint addresses, an SWI breakpoint is asserted. This causes the CPU12 to suspend instruction processing, fetching the SWI vector. The SWI interrupt service routine must then determine the breakpoint causing the SWI interrupt and execute the associated code patch.

Both the SWI interrupt service routine and the ROM patch setup routine require a small table of information to perform their functions. The table, located in EEPROM, is eight bytes long and is shown in Figure 14.4. The `ROMPatch1` and `ROMPatch2` variables are used to contain the address of the first instruction in the ROM code to be replaced. If a ROM patch is not required, both variables should contain the value of $FFFF, which is the erased state of the EEPROM memory. The `Patch1Code` and `Patch2Code` variables must contain the address of the first instruction of the replacement code. These instruction sequences would normally reside in the on-chip EEPROM.

```
;
ROMPatch1:  ds.w    1       ; ROM address #1 to patch.
Patch1Code: ds.w    1       ; Code patch #1 start address.
ROMPatch2:  ds.w    1       ; ROM address #2 to patch.
Patch2Code: ds.w    1       ; Code patch #2 start address.
;
```

Figure 14.4: ROM Code Patch Address Table

The `PatchSetup` subroutine, presented in Figure 14.5, is contained in ROM and should always be called as part of the application's initialization process, even if no ROM patches are required. If the EEPROM used for `ROMPatch1` and `ROMPatch2` remain in the erased state, the breakpoint module will remain disabled. If `ROMPatch1` contains a value other than $FFFF, the breakpoint module is configured for SWI dual address mode and the patch address is written to the `BRKAH:BRKAL` address register. Next, if the value of `ROMPatch2` contains a value other than $FFFF, the `BRKDH:BRKDL` register is written with the second address. Finally, the `BKDBE` bit in the `BRKCT1` register is set to enable address comparisons of the value in `BRKDH:BRKDL`. If `ROMPatch1` contains a value of $FFFF, the contents of `ROMPatch2` is not checked for a valid patch address. If only a single ROM patch is required, the patch address must be placed in the `ROMPatch1` variable for proper breakpoint module initialization.

The final piece of software required for patching the ROM code is the SWI interrupt service routine. This routine, also residing in ROM, is called through the SWI interrupt vector in response to the assertion of an SWI breakpoint. As shown in Figure 14.6, the stacked value of the program counter is retrieved from the stack and compared to the value stored in `ROMPatch1`. If the values do not match, the value is compared with the contents of `ROMPatch2`. If these values do not match, it is assumed that the SWI interrupt service routine was entered by the execution of an `SWI` instruction rather than the assertion of an SWI breakpoint. In this example, no SWI instruction handler is provided, instead, an `RTI` instruction is simply executed. If SWI instructions are not utilized by an application, the RTI instruction should be replaced with a code sequence that might attempt to recover from errant code execution.

Section 14.7: ROM Code Patching Example

```
;
PatchSetup: ldd    ROMPatch1          ; get ROM patch #1 address.
            cpd    #$ffff             ; valid patch address in ROMPatch1?
            bne    SetBrkPt1          ; yes. go setup breakpoint #1.
NoPatch2:   rts                       ; no. just return.
;
SetBrkPt1:  std    BRKAH              ; put ROM addr in breakpoint address reg.
            ldab   #$44               ; set to swi dual address mode,
                                      ; compare BRKAH & BRKAL to address bus.
            stab   BRKCT0
            ldd    ROMPatch2          ; get ROM patch #2 address.
            cpd    #$ffff             ; valid patch address in ROMPatch1?
            beq    NoPatch2           ; not valid address just return.
            std    BRKDH              ; put ROM addr in breakpoint 'data' reg.
            bset   BRKCT0,#BK1ALE     ; compare BRKDH & BRKDL to address bus.
            ldab   #BKDBE             ; enable compare of BRKDH:BRKDL.
            stab   BRKCT1
            rts                       ; patch setup done. return.
;
```

Figure 14.5: ROM Patch Setup Subroutine

If the stacked value of the program counter does match the value in ROMPatch1 or ROMPatch2, program execution continues at the location Patch1Code or Patch2Code respectively. The method used to begin execution of the code patch involves overwriting the stacked return address with the code patch address and executing an RTI instruction. Using this method, rather than just jumping to the instruction at Patch1Code or Patch2Code, completely restores the CPU12 register contents. This allows the patch code to utilize any values that may have been calculated or loaded into registers just prior to the assertion of the SWI breakpoint, thus, possibly reducing the amount of code required by the patch routine.

Other than possible size restrictions based on the amount of available EEPROM, there are no real limitations on the operations performed by the patch code itself. In fact, depending on the problem to be fixed, the patch code could utilize subroutines and functions in the ROM to help correct the software bug. When the patch code has completed execution, it must jump back into the ROM so that the application can continue its normal execution. When returning to ROM code execution from the patch, care must be exercised to ensure that the stack is in the state expected by the returning code. Failure to exercise careful attention to this detail could result in creating a worse problem that the original bug being fixed.

```
;
RtnPC:      equ     7               ; offset to return PC in ISR stack frame.
;
SWIIsr:     ldd     RtnPC,sp        ; get the return address from the stack.
            cpd     ROMPatch1       ; stacked pc the same as the ROM 1 patch addr?
            bne     ChkPatch2       ; no. go check the ROM 2 patch address.
            ldd     Patch1Code      ; yes. get the address of the patch code.
            std     RtnPC,sp        ; overwrite the return address.
            rti                     ; restore the regs & go to the patch routine.
;
ChkPatch2:  cpd     ROMPatch2       ; stacked pc the same as the ROM 2 patch addr?
            bne     DoSWI           ; no. we got here by an actual swi instruction.
            ldd     Patch2Code      ; yes. get the address of the patch code.
            std     RtnPC,sp        ; overwrite the return address.
            rti                     ; restore the regs & go to the patch routine.
;
DoSWI:      rti                     ; put swi instruction handler here if desired.
;
```

Figure 14.6: ROM Patch SWI Interrupt Service Routine

14.8 PROTECTING THE EEPROM TABLE AND CODE PATCH

Placing this 'back door' into an application may seem to pose more of a potential for problems than the possible benefit it might provide on the chance a software bug will be discovered after device fabrication. While no technique such as this can be guaranteed to be 100% free from possible problems, there are additional steps than can be taken to help ensure that the ROM patching procedure presented here operates reliably.

The greatest potential for problems exists with the unintentional modification of the on-chip EEPROM memory. It is strongly suggested that both the code patch address table *and* the patch code itself be placed in areas of the EEPROM memory that are separate from the areas used by the application for data storage. This separation would allow the EEPROM used for ROM code patching to be protected from being accidentally altered by using the EEPROM block protect mechanism.

While the SWI interrupt service routine does check the stacked return address to make sure that it corresponds to either the ROMPatch1 or ROMPatch2 address, some additional range checking or reinitialization of the breakpoint module could be performed if neither of the addresses match. The PatchSetup subroutine could also perform some additional checks to ensure that the addresses in ROMPatch1 and ROMPatch2 correspond to actual ROM addresses before initializing the breakpoint module.

Section 14.8: Protecting the EEPROM Table and Code Patch

Questions/Exercises

14.1 How many major operating modes are provided by the breakpoint module? Name them.

14.2 What restrictions are placed on the use of the SWI dual address mode?

14.3 Why are the BDM full breakpoint mode and the BDM dual address mode not useful to an application program?

14.4 How must the BRKDH and BRKDL registers be configured to recognize a misaligned data access to an internal memory location?

14.5 When configured for BDM full breakpoint mode, what register must contain the match data for a byte with an even address? What register must contain the match data for a byte with an odd address?

14.6 What flexability does the BDM dual address mode have that the BDM full breakpoint mode does not provide?

14.7 What limitation does the BDM dual address mode have when utilized for data access breakpoints?

14.8 What actions occur if a BDM breakpoint occurs and the BDM mode has not been enabled?

14.9 What limitations does the breakpoint module have in stopping the CPU12 when a data access breakpoint is asserted?

14.10 How must an application be altered to utilize the ROM code patching example presented in this chapter?

Chapter 15 BACKGROUND DEBUG - A SOFTWARE PERSPECTIVE

An abundance of documentation exists covering the M68HC12's Background Debug Module (BDM), but little has been written about the firmware that exists in the BDM or how the firmware interacts with debugging tools that communicate with a target M68HC12 using the BKGD pin. This chapter presents the complete BDM firmware code, and a set of routines that can be used in an external M68HC12-based pod to communicate with a target MCU through the BDM system.

The BDM firmware is a very unusual and interesting piece of assembly language code. The interactions between the code and the hardware logic implementing the BDM module are so closely coupled that the cycle-by-cycle bus activity of individual instructions is critical. In addition, this code makes use of temporary registers inside the CPU12 that are not normally available to programmers. Finally, the code employs Program Counter Relative (PCR) indexed addressing to transfer CPU12 execution from active background mode to the system's application code.

Furthermore, a unique set of M68HC12 assembly language routines are discussed that can be used to implement the lowest levels of communication between a development pod and the BDM interface of the M68HC12. The BDM pod firmware uses instructions with carefully selected addressing modes to control pulse timing on an I/O pin down to the cycle. Moreover, a technique is demonstrated for analyzing the cycle-by-cycle behavior of a routine which can be very helpful for code that is intimately tied to hardware.

Section 15.1: An Unusually Cozy Relationship Between Hardware and Software

Because higher level languages such as C do not provide enough subtle control of timing, instruction, and register usage, all of the presented code is written in assembly language. The extreme degree of control presented in this chapter is not required for most applications. However, when a situation is encountered where there is a need to squeeze a few extra bytes out of a program, or fine tune the speed of a driver routine, these techniques will come in handy. Studying code like this also provides insight into the subtle operation of instructions and the instruction set architecture of the CPU12.

15.1 An Unusually Cozy Relationship Between Hardware and Software

The BDM system in the M68HC12 is a mixture of hardware logic and a firmware program. The serial communication is handled by a section of hardware logic much like a timer or serial I/O peripheral module. Additionally, the BDM commands allowing target memory to be read and written are implemented with the same hardware logic. This feature is what provides the BDM the capability to access target memory without CPU12 intervention. The remainder of the BDM commands are implemented as a 240 byte firmware program. This program provides the capability to read and write the application's CPU registers, execute a single instruction and transfer CPU12 execution from the BDM firmware to the target system's application code.

For the BDM module to execute any of the firmware commands, the target M68HC12 device must be in *active background mode*; that is, the CPU12 must be executing the BDM firmware code instead of the target application. This is important to understand since the hardware portion of the BDM module is *always* active and allows reading and writing target memory regardless of the instructions being executed by the target application. The table in Figure 15.1 summarizes the various BDM firmware commands while Figure 15.2 summarizes the BDM hardware commands.

A few of the firmware commands fall in a gray area between hardware and firmware and will be examined in more detail in the remainder of the chapter. Even though the BACKGROUND command is classified as a hardware command, it causes the CPU12 to stop executing the target application code and begin executing the BDM firmware. In other words, it places the target M68HC12 device in active background mode. In addition to the BACKGROUND command three additional methods may be used to enter active background mode. Execution of the BDM firmware can be started by resetting the target M68HC12 in special single chip mode. In this case the BDM ROM is enabled when the target MCU exits reset and the reset vector is fetched out of the BDM firmware ROM rather than the target application memory. Although this is not a command, it is an important part of the interplay between the BDM hardware and firmware. In addition, if the application firmware executes the BGND instruction ($00), a transition to active background mode occurs if the ENABLE_FIRMWARE command has previously been issued. Alternately, if

Chapter 15: Background Debug - A Software Perspective

instruction tagging has been enabled, external debugging hardware can cause the CPU12 to enter the active background mode.

The GO, TRACE1, and TAG_GO firmware commands control the transfer of CPU12 execution from active BDM to target application code. These three firmware commands interact with the BDM hardware to trigger logic signals at very specific times during the transition process.

Command	Description
GO	Exit Active Background Mode; begin execution of target application
TRACE1	Execute a single target instruction and return to active background mode
TAGGO	Enable instruction tagging and begin execution of target application
WRITE_NEXT	X = X + 2; Write word at 0,X
WRITE_PC	Modify target application's Program Counter value
WRITE_D	Modify target application's D accumulator value
WRITE_X	Modify target application's X index register value
WRITE_Y	Modify target application's Y index register value
WRITE_SP	Modify target application's Stack Pointer value
READ_NEXT	X = X + 2; Read word at 0,X
READ_PC	Read target application's Program Counter value
READ_D	Read target application's D accumulator value
READ_X	Read target application's X index register value
READ_Y	Read target application's Y index register value
READ_SP	Read target application's Stack Pointer value

Figure 15.1: BDM Firmware Commands

Before discussing the process of transfers from active background mode to the execution of target application code, one additional concept must be understood. The BDM ROM and a small number of BDM registers occupy the address area from $FF00 through $FFFF in the M68HC12's 64K memory map. However, because the BDM hardware logic has control over access to this memory area on a cycle-by-cycle basis, these resources remain invisible to a target application. This means application code can never access these resources. Similarly, BDM firmware cannot access the user's memory at these locations. With a more complex logic design, the BDM could have provided a means for the BDM

Section 15.2: Separation of BDM vs User Applications

firmware to optionally access the application resources at these addresses, but present designs do not allow this.

Command	Description
BACKGROUND	Enter Active Background Mode if firmware has been enabled
READ_BD_BYTE	Read a byte from target memory with the BDM block in the memory map
STATUS	Read the BDM status register at $FF01 (special case of READ_BD_BYTE)
READ_BD_WORD	Read a word from target memory with the BDM block in the memory map
READ_BYTE	Read a byte from target memory with the BDM block out of the memory map
READ_WORD	Read a word from target memory with the BDM block out of the memory map
WRITE_BD_BYTE	Write a byte to target memory with the BDM block in the memory map
ENABLE_FIRMWARE	Write the BDM status register at $FF01 (special case of WRITE_BD_BYTE)
WRITE_BD_WORD	Write a word to target memory with the BDM block in the memory map
WRITE_BYTE	Write a byte to target memory with the BDM block out of the memory map
WRITE_WORD	Write a word to target memory with the BDM block out of the memory map

Figure 15.2: BDM Hardware Commands

Hardware commands can access either the BDM ROM and background register block or the application resources at these addresses because the BDM hardware logic has complete control over which resource is enabled on cycle-by-cycle basis. The READ_BYTE hardware command accesses the application memory space. The READ_BD_BYTE command enables the BDM ROM and background register block, placing them in the memory map for a single bus cycle while the BDM logic is reading or writing the location. This means a hardware BDM command can read the contents of the BDM ROM or a BDM register even while the target application program is running. Because the BDM hardware logic accesses the M68HC12's memory map during an instruction free cycle or halts the CPU12 for a single cycle if necessary, switching the BDM ROM into the memory map does not interfere with an executing application. This is true even if the application program is executing in the $FF00 - FFFF area and/or is accessing memory in this address range.

15.2 Separation of BDM vs User Applications

Some debug systems, such as ROM monitor programs, interfere with the target applications in ways that typically lead to problems during debugging. Most of these schemes require that additional software be present in the application code space and generally use some amount

Chapter 15: Background Debug - A Software Perspective

of application RAM for variables and/or stack space. In addition, these types of systems also utilize some of the I/O pins required by the target application. The M68HC11 bootstrap mode improved on this somewhat by having its firmware switch in and out of the memory map so it didn't interfere with the application program space and didn't need to be incorporated into the application program. However, it still shared the use of the SCI serial I/O pins. This meant that the bootstrap mode couldn't be used unless a system was specifically designed to avoid conflicts between an application's use and the bootstrap system's use of these pins.

The BDM system in the M68HC12 completes the separation of debug system and the application resources by having its own dedicated serial communication pin and by avoiding the use of any application memory. Like the M68HC11 bootstrap mode, the BDM system borrows the idea of switching its resources into and out of the memory map as needed; however, the M68HC12 takes this control a bit further by allowing the switch to work for a single bus cycle. In addition, by including BDM-related control and status registers in the resource block, no application resources are required by the BDM system.

While the CPU12 is executing the BDM firmware, the application's context (the values of the CPU12 registers at the time the switch to active background mode was made) must be saved so that the context can be restored when application program execution resumes. Even though entry into active background mode is performed by some of the same logic the CPU12 uses to respond to interrupts, the CPU registers are not automatically pushed onto the stack. Saving the application's registers on the stack would not usually be a problem; however, in some cases, this action could cause an application program to malfunction. Instead, a combination of techniques is used that do not require any application memory or registers. Two of the CPU12 registers, the program counter and D accumulator, are saved in two 16-bit CPU12 temporary registers, TMP2 and TMP3. The contents of the stack pointer, X, and Y index registers are saved by avoiding use of instructions that change them in BDM firmware. As discussed later, there are a few exceptions in the case of the X register, and are a result of executing the READ_NEXT and WRITE_NEXT commands. The condition code register is saved in an 8-bit register, CCRSAVE, which is part of the BDM ROM and background register block and is not accessible to application code. Making this technique work requires a combination of tricks in the use of the CPU logic, the BDM logic, and knowledge of subtle instruction behavior when writing the BDM firmware. From a firmware perspective, it would have been easier to simply include enough storage registers in the BDM logic to save all of the CPU register contents; however, that would have significantly increased the size and cost of the BDM logic block.

The main reason for saving the application's register values in this manner has more to do with protecting the integrity of the application's entire context. In most situations, placing the application's registers on the stack would do little more than increase the stack depth slightly. However, in cases where the depth of an application's stack is very close to its allowed limit, it would be possible to inadvertently overwrite other information, such as global variables, when the BDM became active. The most serious problem would involve situations where the stack pointer might not have been properly initialized or has an invalid value for some other reason. In this case, the register values may not be saved at all or might corrupt other data, making it more difficult to determine the exact source of a problem. Finally, there are certain situations where it would be difficult to properly trace instructions affecting the value of the stack pointer. While many attempts have been made in ROM debuggers to deal with these sorts of problems, the M68HC12's BDM system avoids these pitfalls completely by not making use of the application's stack at all.

15.3 ENTERING ACTIVE BACKGROUND MODE

As mentioned previously, there are four ways to enter the active background mode. In each case, the BDM ROM is enabled at the appropriate time so an interrupt or reset vector is fetched from the BDM ROM rather than the application's memory. When the M68HC12 is reset in the special single chip mode, the BDM ROM and background register block are simply enabled before the CPU12 performs the reset vector fetch. This results in the reset vector being fetched from the BDM ROM rather than application memory. This manner of entering active background mode is particularly useful for gaining control of an M68HC12 before anything is programmed into the application memory.

The other three methods of entering active background mode cause the SWI vector to be fetched from the BDM ROM. In these cases, the CPU detects what appears to be normal interrupt exception processing. However, additional control signals instruct the CPU to handle these exceptions in a slightly differently manner than a normal SWI interrupt. Execution of a BGND instruction invokes a CPU12 response very similar to an SWI instruction. However, instead of stacking the CPU registers when responding to these exceptions, the CPU stores the application's program counter in the TMP2 temporary register and fetches the SWI vector. At the appropriate time the BDM logic switches the BDM ROM into the map so the vector fetch and subsequent program fetches come from the BDM ROM instead of application memory.

On entry to active BDM mode, the first thing the BDM firmware needs to do is to save the value of the D accumulator and the condition code register. The D accumulator is saved in the CPU12 temporary register TMP3 and the condition code register is saved in the BDM's CCRSAVE register. This operation is a little tricky because the operation must be performed without disturbing the condition code register's value before it can be saved. The BDM firmware accomplishes this using the code sequence shown in Figure 15.3.

Notice that the first instruction in the listing is a general purpose exchange instruction involving one of the CPU12's internal temporary registers. Studying the postbyte encoding of the general purpose transfer and exchange instructions in Figure 2.35 of Chapter 2 shows why an EXG instruction is used rather than a TFR instruction. As shown, the temporary register TMP2 can only be used as the destination of a transfer or exchange while temporary register TMP3 can only be used as the source register of a transfer or exchange. Essentially, a `TFR D,TMP3` instruction does not exist, however, the exchange instruction performs the required action since the value placed in the D accumulator as a result of the exchange instruction is unimportant in this case.

```
;
; BDM ROM SWI vector points at START
;
START:     exg    tmp3,d        ; [P] save D without affecting CCR.
           tfr    ccr,a         ; [P] user CCR value to A.
           staa   CCRSAVE       ; [wOP] save user CCR value.
;
```

Figure 15.3: BDM SWI Entry Point

After saving the value of the D accumulator, the contents of the condition code register are transferred to the A accumulator and then saved in the BDM's CCRSAVE register. Remember that the transfer and exchange instructions do not affect any of the bits in the CPU12's condition code register.

The next task of the BDM firmware is to determine the mechanism causing the CPU12 to enter active background mode so the application's program counter can be adjusted if necessary. The need for the possible adjustment of the program counter is necessary to prevent the CPU12 from remaining in active background mode if the BDM has not been enabled by the reception of the ENABLE_FIRMWARE command. If the CPU12 enters active background mode as a result of executing a tagged instruction in the instruction queue or because a BDM BACKGROUND command was received, the application's program counter will point to the next instruction to be executed. If, however, active background mode is entered by executing a BGND instruction, the program counter remains pointing at the BGND opcode rather than the byte following the BGND opcode. Note that this behavior is different from an SWI instruction which advances the program counter to the address following the SWI opcode.

Consider the circumstance where a BGND instruction might be inadvertently executed as a result of program run-away in the target application and the ENBDM bit in the BDM's status register is clear. If the firmware were to simply execute an immediate return to the application without advancing the program counter to the next memory location, the CPU12 would re-execute the BGND instruction, causing the execution of an infinite loop.

As shown in figure 15.4, the firmware examines the opcode at the address of the program counter to determine if the program counter needs to be adjusted. This process is complicated slightly by the fact that the BDM firmware cannot read the contents of the application memory map in the area occupied by the BDM ROM and background register

Section 15.3: Entering Active Background Mode

block. To avoid the possibility of creating an infinite loop, the firmware automatically adds one to the saved value of the program counter if it falls within this range. Note that the development tool hosting the BDM connection is responsible for determining the validity of the program counter adjustment. This operation is easy for the debug system because it can use the BDM's hardware memory access commands to read the application memory space even when BDM is active.

One minor case surrounding the automatic increment of the application's program counter remains that cannot be resolved by a development tool. When the host debugging software reads a program counter value of $0000 it cannot determine if the program counter was $FFFF and incremented to $0000 by the BDM firmware or if it was $0000 on entry to active BDM mode. Fortunately, this is not a serious case because an application's program counter should never have a value of $FFFF since this value is the middle of the reset vector.

```
;
            exg    x,tmp2           ; [P] swap PC into X and save X for now.
            cpx    #$FF00           ; [OP] user PC in BDM space (ff00-ffff?).
            bhs    ROM_INC          ; [PPP/P] if so always increment.
            tst    0,x              ; [rOP] is opcode at user PC=0?
            bne    RES_X_T2         ; [PPP/P] if not, skip increment.
ROM_INC:    inx                     ; [O] adjust user PC=PC+1.
RES_X_T2:   exg    x,tmp2           ; [P] swap x and t2 back.
;
            brset  STATUS,#$80,INST_LOOP ; [rfPPP] go inst loop if ENBDM=1.
            clra                    ; [O] ENBDM,TRACE, & TAG bits = 0.
            bra    EXIT_SEQ         ; [PPP/P] exit to user code.
;
```

Figure 15.4: Testing for Application PC Adjustment

If a BDM BACKGROUND command is received just as the CPU12 is about to execute a BGND opcode, this increment mechanism can cause the BGND opcode to be skipped. Fortunately, this case is unimportant since the CPU12 is entering active background at the time anyway.

Notice that the X index register is used in this code sequence, however, its value is saved and then restored at the end of the sequence. Use of the X register was required because the saved value of the application's program counter cannot be modified while it is stored in the TMP2 register. It should be noted that the firmware designers were careful not to use instructions that modify the TMP2 or TMP3 registers. Even though there is nothing to prevent an application from using these internal CPU12 registers, it would be unwise to do so since no documentation exists explaining when and how the CPU12 uses these registers in other instructions.

After executing the code performing the optional adjustment to the value of the application's program counter, the BDM firmware checks the ENBDM bit in the BDM's STATUS register. If ENBDM is set, meaning active BDM mode has been enabled through the BDM serial interface, the BDM firmware continues execution at label INST_LOOP where it waits for firmware instructions to be received through the BDM serial interface. If the ENBDM is clear, the active BDM mode has not been enabled and execution continues at the label EXIT_SEQ where the firmware restores the application's CPU registers, switches the BDM ROM and registers out of the memory map, and resumes execution of the application. The firmware's exit sequence is the topic of the next section of this chapter.

Entering active background mode by resetting the target M68HC12 in special single chip mode is similar to the previously discussed methods with two exceptions. First, the address of the firmware entry point is fetched from the reset vector in the BDM ROM rather than the SWI vector. Second, rather than adding additional hardware logic to set the ENBDM bit before executing the BDM firmware at its entry point, a BSET instruction is used to set the ENBDM bit in the BDM STATUS register. Setting this bit causes the BRSET instruction in the listing of Figure 15.4 to continue execution at label INST_LOOP rather than attempting to exit the BDM firmware. Even though the BSET instruction will alter the initial value of the N-, Z-, and V-bits in the condition code register, the S-, X-, and I-bits remain set as they would after any CPU12 reset. Resetting a device in special single chip mode is the only practical way to get into active background mode without issuing a serial BDM command.

15.4 EXITING ACTIVE BACKGROUND MODE

Triggering the code sequence to exit active background mode and begin the execution of application code is initiated by the reception of one of three BDM firmware commands. However, the final trigger mechanism of this sequence, a write to the BDM STATUS register, involves the most intimate cooperation between software and hardware anywhere in the M68HC12. Before executing the exit sequence, presented in Figure 15.5, the A accumulator is loaded with a value that will be written to the BDM STATUS register. As shown in the listing, the write occurs just before the execution of the JMP instruction that transfers CPU12 execution to the application code. Before transferring CPU12 control to the target application program, the saved state of the CPU12 registers must first be restored. While this may not seem to be an overly complex task, care must be taken during the final steps of the process to ensure that the value restored to the CPU12's condition code register is not inadvertently modified.

Section 15.4: Exiting Active Background Mode

```
;
EXIT_SEQ:   clr     INSTR               ; [wOP] acknowledge any BDM command.
            ldab    CCRSAV              ; [rOP] re-entry value for user CCR.
            staa    CCRSAV              ; [wOP] temp save of STATUS value.
            exg     x,tmp2              ; [P] swap x->tmp2, user PC to x.
            stx     SHIFTER             ; [WOP] need user PC in memory.
            exg     x,tmp2              ; [P] to restore user X.
            tfr     b,ccr               ; [P] restore user CCR.
            exg     tmp3,d              ; [P] restore user D (A:B) from tmp3.
            movb    CCRSAVE,STATUS      ; [OrPwPO] write w/o CCR chg.
            jmp     [SHIFTER,pcr]       ; [fIPfPPP] exit to user PC.
;
```

Figure 15.5: Active BDM Exit Code

The first instruction in the exit sequence writes zero to the BDM's 8-bit instruction register. This action is required so the BDM firmware will not re-execute the command in the instruction register if active background mode is entered before another valid command is received through the BDM serial interface. The next two instructions may seem confusing, but the actions they perform are crucial to initiating the transition from active background mode without affecting the CPU12's restored register values. To accomplish this, the value passed to the exit sequence in the A accumulator must be placed in a memory location where it can later be copied into the BDM's STATUS register using a MOVB instruction. The only usable 8-bit location in the BDM's register block is the CCRSAV register. Because this register contains the value of the application's condition code register, a copy of its contents must be saved in the B accumulator.

In a situation similar to the STATUS register value, the application's program counter must be placed in a 16-bit memory location that can be accessed by the indirect jump instruction. The next three instructions place the application's program counter in the BDM's SHIFTER register. Even though the X index register is used in the process, its value is restored by the second EXG instruction. Before executing the two instruction exit sequence, the application's condition code register and D accumulator are restored.

As mentioned previously, the timing of the last two instructions in the exit sequence are the critical key to performing the switch from active background mode to the target application. A write to the BDM STATUS register with the BDACTV bit clear is the event that triggers the BDM hardware to switch the BDM ROM and register block out of the memory map. An understanding of how and when the switch occurs requires that the cycle-by-cycle instruction timing of the MOVB and the JMP instructions be studied. This information is provided between the square brackets at the beginning of the comment field. Examining the cycle-by-cycle timing of the MOVB instruction reveals that the write of the STATUS register occurs during the fourth clock of the instruction. Four clock cycles following the write, the BDM ROM and register block are removed from the M68HC12 memory map. By this time, the first two clock cycles of the indirect JMP instruction have been completed. The first cycle of the JMP instruction is a free cycle where the CPU12 is calculating the effective address of the BDM SHIFTER register. During the second cycle, an indirect address fetch cycle, the application's program counter is read from the SHIFTER register. At the end of this clock cycle, the map switch occurs. During the last three cycles of the JMP instruction, the CPU12's instruction queue is filled with three program words beginning at the location read from the BDM SHIFTER register.

Figure 15.6 presents the bit values written to the STATUS register for the various exit conditions. The value for the first exit condition listed in the table, $00, is used when the CPU12 has entered active background mode when the ENBDM bit is cleared. As the code in Figure 15.4 shows, the A accumulator is cleared and the BDM firmware branches to the beginning of the exit sequence. The values written to the STATUS register for the remaining exit conditions result from the reception of one of the three BDM firmware commands listed in the table. If the TRACE bit is set when the status register is written, the BDM hardware asserts an internal signal during the final P cycle of the JMP instruction allowing a a single instruction of the application code to execute before returning to active background mode.

Exit Condition	Status Register							
	bit-7	6	5	4	3	2	1	bit-0
	ENBDM	BDACTV	TAG	VALID	TRACE	*	reserved	reserved
ENBDM=0	0	0	0	0	0	0	0	0
GO	1	0	0	0	0	0	0	0
TRACE1	1	0	0	0	1	0	0	0
TAG_GO	1	0	1	0	0	0	0	0

Figure 15.6: Active BDM Status Register Exit Values

When the TAG bit is written to a one, the basic exit sequence is the same as the others except that it triggers a sequence switching the LSTRB/TAGLO and BKGD/TAGHI pins from their LSTRB and BKGD functions to their tagging input functions. The BDM logic considers the command complete at the sample point in the last logic zero bit time (12 target E cycles into the last bit time). As soon as the BDM firmware can interpret this command and exit, the BKGD pin switches from the BDM serial communication input to the tagging input function. By this time, the debugging system must have stopped driving the pin low, or an active tag input signal will be erroneously detected. Care must be taken not to continue driving the BKGD pin low for too long after the last bit of the TAG_GO command. Examining the complete listing of the BDM firmware reveals a cycle count of about 33 target CPU cycles from the sample point of the last command bit time until the pin function switch between the I and PPP cycles of the final jmp in the exit sequence.

15.5 TIMING CONSIDERATIONS BETWEEN DEBUGGER HARDWARE AND BDM FIRMWARE

Timing requirements for firmware commands depend on the interaction of the host debugger hardware, the BDM logic, and the BDM firmware. The BDM hardware logic receiving the serial commands considers the last bit of an instruction to be complete at the 12th target BDM clock after the start of the bit was recognized. Note, however, that because of synchronization uncertainty, there could be up to one additional target cycle after the actual start edge from the debugger hardware until the BDM logic recognizes it. This is slightly earlier than the end of the bit time which is equal to 16 target BDM clocks. Also keep in mind that the BDM firmware is essentially asynchronous to the arrival of any new command from a debug pod.

When the target M68HC12 is in active background mode, the BDM firmware waits in the two-instruction loop as shown in Figure 15.7. When the BDM hardware logic receives a complete command, the command byte is stored into the BDM's INSTR register. The LDAA instruction retrieves the value and modifies the condition code register so that the BLE branch instruction can test for the reception of hardware commands and null commands simultaneously. Because all hardware commands have their most significant bit set, the loop will continue to execute allowing the hardware logic to perform the memory read or write.

```
;
INST_LOOP:   ldaa    INSTR       ; [rOP] wait for non-zero non-hdw command.
             ble     INST_LOOP   ; [PPP/P] $00 is null command
;
```

Figure 15.7: BDM Command loop

This two-instruction loop requires six bus cycles as long as no firmware commands are received. Examining the cycle-by-cycle operation of these two instructions reveals a subtle but important detail if a hardware command arrives when the target MCU is in active background mode. When a hardware command is received requesting access to a target memory location, the BDM logic monitors the bus for a CPU free cycle when the CPU12 does not require the bus. If a free cycle is not located within 128 bus cycles, the CPU12 is halted so the BDM can steal a single bus cycle for the requested BDM memory access. As the listing shows, neither of the two instructions contains a free cycle as part of its bus activity. However, if the load instruction is aligned to an even byte boundary, the O (optional) cycle is treated as a free cycle. Care was taken when writing the BDM firmware to assure that this instruction is located on an even byte boundary. This ensures that the BDM hardware does not have to wait for 128 cycles to perform a memory read or write when the target is in active background mode. In fact, this arrangement ensures that a BDM memory

Chapter 15: Background Debug - A Software Perspective

access can take place within six bus cycles without having to steal a bus cycle. Host debugger hardware can take advantage of this detail to maximize the data transfer rate between the target and host computer when the target is in active background mode by avoiding the 128 cycle delay.

Like the hardware commands, the BDM firmware commands have timing restrictions due to the overhead of the BDM firmware. Once the firmware detects the presence of the received command, it must determine the requested action and then perform the command. This overhead places restrictions on the minimum amount of time that must elapse between the issuance of a command and when data may be read or written. In addition, because the shifter register is needed during the exit sequence, commands such as GO, TRACE1, and TAG_GO may not be issued until the overhead period has expired. To determine this time period, the source code for the BDM firmware must be examined in detail.

When a firmware command arrives, the BLE instruction fails, causing the CPU12 to exit the two-instruction loop. However, because the BDM firmware timing is asynchronous with respect to the BDM hardware logic, it could require a maximum of 10 target CPU clock cycles before decoding of the received command can begin. Consider the case where the received command is placed in the BDM's INSTR register just after the point where it can be recognized by the read cycle of the LDAA instruction. This means that the complete loop, requiring six cycles, would need to be executed before the firmware command was loaded into the A accumulator. This would have to be added to the four cycles after the read cycle for the branch not-taken case of the loop, resulting in a total of 10 cycles.

As shown in Figure 15.8, all firmware commands are initially checked to determine if they are one of the three possible execution commands. If the received command is a GO, TRACE1, or TAG_GO command, the A accumulator is loaded with the appropriate value and branches to the EXIT_SEQ code discussed earlier. The first two instructions of the listing are in the decode path for all firmware instructions, requiring four bus cycles when the BEQ instruction is taken. Adding this to the worst-case time of 10 cycles from the arrival of a command to the point of the NOT_EXE label is a total of 14 cycles.

For the case where one of the three execution commands is received, the cycles from the command detection until the value in the BDM SHIFTER register is no longer needed in the exit sequence must be added. From command detection to the completion of the BEQ instruction when the branch is not taken is a total of 12 cycles. From EXIT_SEQ until after the I cycle in the final indirect jump in EXIT_SEQ, is 24 cycles. The total firmware delay for TRACE is 12 + 8 + 24 or 44 cycles. For GO the firmware delay is 12 + 9 + 24 or 45 clocks, and for TAG_GO the delay is 12 + 7 + 24 or 43 cycles. As mentioned previously, the reception of the last bit of a command actually occurs at the twelfth BDM bit time. If the bit times of the debugging hardware are significantly longer than the minimum 16 target BDM clocks, some overlap of the firmware instruction decoding and next instruction can be assumed.

461

Section 15.5: Timing Considerations Between Debugger Hardware and BDM Firmware

```
;
          bita    #$18        ; [P] TAGGO,TRACE, or GO commands?
          beq     NOT_EXE     ; [PPP/P] branch if not execution command.
          cmpa    #$10        ; [P] %xxx10xxx ?
          beq     TRACE       ; [PPP/P] branch if TRACE command.
          bmi     GO          ; [PPP/P] %xxx01xxx ?
;
; if not TRACE or GO, must be TAG_GO %xxx11xxx (fall through).
;
          ldaa    #$A0        ; [P] enBDM + TAG bits in STATUS.
          bra     EXIT_SEQ    ; [PPP] Controlled exit (3 of 4).
TRACE:    ldaa    #$88        ; [P] enBDM + TRACE bits in STATUS.
          bra     EXIT_SEQ    ; [PPP] Controlled exit (2 of 4).
GO:       ldaa    #$80        ; [P] enBDM bit only in STATUS.
          bra     EXIT_SEQ    ; [PPP] Controlled exit (1 of 4).
;
```

Figure 15.8: Initial Firmware Command Decoding

When the BDM firmware arrives at the NOT_EXE label, only four of the bits in the command byte are significant for the remaining decode process. Bit five of the command byte is used to indicate if the command involves a read or a write operation. When bit five is one, a read operation is performed and when zero, a write is performed. The lower three bits of the command byte are used to encode the CPU12 register or action involved in the firmware command as shown in the table of Figure 15.10. The first two bit combinations in the table are currently ignored by the BDM firmware, although the second table entry is reserved for future use. The third bit combination is used for the READ_NEXT and WRITE_NEXT commands and the remainder of the bit combinations designate an action on one of the application's CPU registers. Examining the table it is evident that a firmware command does not exist to access the value of the condition code register. Because the application's condition code register is saved in the BDM's CCRSAV register ($FF06) hardware read and write commands may be used to access or modify its value.

The code segment beginning at label NOT_EXE, presented in Figure 15.9, is used to perform an initial decode on the register read/write commands. After making a copy of the command byte in the B accumulator and masking off all but the lower three bits of the command, two is subtracted from the value remaining in the A accumulator. This subtraction actually performs a dual purpose. If the value remaining in the A accumulator is either zero or one, the subtraction will produce a negative result, allowing the Illegal and Reserved bit pattern to be detected with a single branch instruction. In addition, by performing the subtraction rather than a compare, the A accumulator will contain a value of zero through five, corresponding to register codes two through seven. This value is used for computed GOTO operations.

```
;
NOT_EXE:  tfr    a,b            ; [P] extra copy of command.
          anda   #$07           ; [P] save only lower 3 bits.
          suba   #2             ; [P] 0-orient codes 2-7.
          bmi    INST_DONE      ; [PPP/P] reject codes 0 and 1.
          bitb   #$20           ; [P] check R/W bit.
          bne    COMP_GOTO      ; [PPP/P] branch if read command.
;
```

Figure 15.9: Initial Firmware Read/Write Decode

Assuming a valid command is received, the execution of the initial decode segment in Figure 15.9 requires eight cycles if it is a read operation and six cycles if it is a write operation. When a firmware write command is received, the BNE instruction at the end of the listing fails resulting in the execution of the code segment in Figure 15.11. Because firmware write commands involve the reception of 16-bits of data, the firmware overhead is inconsequential compared to the 256 BDM clocks (16-bits at 16 BDM clocks per bit) required to receive the data.

I2	I1	I0	Register/Usage
0	0	0	Illegal
0	0	1	Reserved
0	1	0	Read/Write Next
0	1	1	Program Counter
1	0	0	D Accumulator (A:B)
1	0	1	X Index Register
1	1	0	Y Index Register
1	1	1	Stack Pointer

Figure 15.10: Firmware Register Decode Bit Patterns

The three instructions beginning at the label WAIT_DATA in Figure 15.11 wait for the BDM serial I/O hardware to receive the data portion of the write command to complete. While waiting for the data to be received, the first two instructions in this loop check the value of the BDM INSTRUCTION register to insure that the command has not been aborted before receiving the 16-bits of data. To prevent the BDM firmware or the hardware state machine from becoming stuck in an indeterminate state if a command is terminated,

Section 15.5: Timing Considerations Between Debugger Hardware and BDM Firmware

the hardware clears the INSTRUCTION register if 512 BDM clock cycles occur between falling edges on the BKGD pin. If the command has not been terminated, the BRCLR instruction checks the state of the SDV (Shifter Data Valid) bit in the BDM STATUS register to determine when all 16 bits have been received. Once the data has been received, the last three instructions of this sequence perform a computed GOTO operation.

Utilizing a computed GOTO operation to perform the the final command decoding has the advantage of requiring only five bytes to decode all six of the write commands. Using a compare and branch approach to the decoding process would have required additional object code and time to perform the operation. A typical compare and branch implementation would require four bytes for five of the six cases, for a total of 20 bytes. Even a decrement and branch approach would require three bytes for five of the six cases resulting in a total of 15 bytes. Although it may seem unusual to go to this extreme to save a few bytes of memory, if the size of the BDM ROM needed to be increased because of the additional bytes, it would raise the cost of the BDM system for every M68HC12 device.

```
;
WAIT_DATA:  tst    INSTR                    ; [rOP] check for aborted command.
            beq    INST_LOOP                ; [PPP/P] branch if aborted.
            brclr  STATUS,$10,WAIT_DATA;    [rfPPP] wait for data done.
;
            ldab   #7                       ; [P] 7-bytes per command.
            mul                             ; [ffO] 7*(register_code-2).
            jmp    b,pc                     ; [PPP] computed GOTO.
;
```

Figure 15.11: Firmware Write Command Decode Completion

To understand why the value in the A accumulator is multiplied by seven requires an analysis of the code sequences implementing the write commands. Examining the listing in Figure 15.12 reveals that the first three commands each require three instructions, with each of the three commands occupying seven bytes. As the listing shows, the remaining commands actually require fewer than seven bytes, however, for the computed GOTO to work properly, each command must be the same length. For this reason, the WRITE_X and WRITE_Y commands have had two NOP instructions added to them. However, notice that the WRITE_SP command does not require the byte padding because it is the last command in the table.

Before examining the firmware write instructions in more detail, one additional item regarding the computed GOTO must be pointed out. Notice that the JMP instruction does not use the assembler notation for program counter relative indexed addressing, but instead uses the notation for program counter indexed addressing. In this case the B accumulator contains an offset that is added to the value of the program counter. The value of the

Chapter 15: Background Debug - A Software Perspective

program counter used in the calculation of the effective address is the address of the instruction following the JMP instruction. For the computed GOTO to work properly, the code for the firmware write routines must immediately follow the JMP instruction.

The first write command appearing in Figure 15.12 is one of the exceptions in the BDM firmware where one of the application's registers is modified and not restored to its original value. This command preincrements the value in the X index register and stores the received 16-bit value into memory. Because the command only requires the transmission of an 8-bit command and the 16-bit data, it is more efficient than the WRITE_WORD hardware command, especially when writing numerous data words to successive memory locations. Obviously, before using this firmware command, the value of the X index register should be saved by the debugger and restored after the block of data is written.

Due to the fact that the application's program counter and D accumulator values are saved in the CPU12's temporary registers TMP2 and TMP3 respectively, an exchange instruction must be used to modify their values. Because the values of the application's remaining registers stay in their respective register while the CPU12 is in active background mode, the value in the SHIFTER register is loaded directly into the register.

Now that the code for the firmware write commands has been presented, the worst-case execution time can be determined. Remember that the reason this time must be determined is so that the debugger will not issue a new command until the current command is complete. To avoid corruption of the data in the SHIFTER register, the first bit of a new command must not reach its data sense point before SHIFTER is read by the firmware write command. Because all six write commands read SHIFTER during the first cycle after the indexed jump in the computed GOTO, only one cycle needs to be added to the previously computed cycle counts. Adding the 14 cycles for the WAIT_DATA loop and the seven cycles required for the computed GOTO brings the worse-case cycle count to 22 cycles. In reality this number could be reduced somewhat because the last data bit received in the SHIFTER register overlaps this delay by at least 3 or 4 BDM clock cycles. Because the first bit of a new command isn't placed into SHIFTER until the data sense point, which is BDM clock cycle 12 after the falling edge of the first bit, the total could be reduced even further.

Section 15.5: Timing Considerations Between Debugger Hardware and BDM Firmware

```
;
W_NXT_WRD:      ldd     SHIFTER         ; [ROP] get data for write.
                std     2,+x            ; [P] pre-inc X by 2 & store word.
INST_DONE1:     bra     INST_DONE       ; [PPP] to main instruction loop.
;
WRITE_PC:       ldd     SHIFTER         ; [ROP] modify application PC.
                exg     d,tmp2          ; [P] user PC in temp 2 reg.
                bra     INST_DONE       ; [PPP] to main instruction loop.
;
WRITE_D:        ldd     SHIFTER         ; [ROP] get data for write.
                exg     tmp3,d          ; [P] modify application D accumulator.
                bra     INST_DONE       ; [PPP] to main instruction loop.
;
WRITE_X:        ldx     SHIFTER         ; [ROP] modify application X index register.
                bra     INST_DONE       ; [PPP] to main instruction loop.
                nop                     ; [O] fill to make seq 7 bytes.
                nop                     ; [O]
;
WRITE_Y:        ldy     SHIFTER         ; [ROP] modify application Y index register.
                bra     INST_DONE       ; [PPP] to main instruction loop.
                nop                     ; [O] fill to make seq 7 bytes.
                nop                     ; [O]
;
WRITE_SP:       lds     SHIFTER         ; [ROP] modify application's SP.
                bra     INST_DONE       ; [PPP] to main instruction loop.
;
```

Figure 15.12: Firmware Write Commands

Like the firmware write commands, the read commands also utilize a computed GOTO for final command decoding. But unlike the write commands, four of the six read commands only require four bytes for their implementation. For this reason the computed GOTO, shown at the beginning of the listing in Figure 15.13, utilizes two ASLA instructions to perform a multiply by four. Because the READ_PC command requires more than four bytes, a branch to the actual implementation is used as the first instruction with the remaining two bytes filled with NOP instructions. Notice that all of the firmware read commands branch to a common section of code beginning at the label R_COMMON. This code segment places the data in the BDM's SHIFTER register and waits in a loop until the host debugger has shifted out all 16 bits of data. Like the related code for the firmware write instructions, a test is placed within the loop to detect the possible termination of the read command.

Analyzing the timing of the computed GOTO and read commands reveals the worst-case timing path is for the READ_NEXT command. This path includes five cycles for the computed GOTO and seven cycles until the memory data is written into the SHIFTER register. These 12 cycles are added to the 14 cycles in INST_LOOP code and the eight

Chapter 15: Background Debug - A Software Perspective

cycles required to decode a read command for a total of 34 BDM clock cycles. As with the write commands, this number can be reduced because the last data bit of the command overlaps this delay by three BDM clock cycles. Also, because the first bit of data isn't shifted out of the BDM's SHIFTER register until the data sense point, the total can be reduced even further. This analysis suggests that Motorola's specification of 32 cycles of delay between the transmission of a read command and reading the data and the 32 cycle delay at the end of a write command for firmware commands is somewhat conservative. However, because of possible timing mismatches between the BDM clock and the debugging hardware, it is probably a good idea to use the minimum specified time.

```
;
COMP_GOTO: asla                    ; [O] multiply by 2.
           asla                    ; [O] A=4*(register_code-2).
           jmp       a,pc          ; [PPP] computed GOTO.
;
R_NXT_WRD: ldd       2,+x          ; [RfP] pre-inc X by 2 & read word.
           bra       R_COMMON      ; [PPP] D->SHIFTER, wait done, go INST_DONE.
;
READ_PC:   bra       READ_PC1      ; [PPP] can't fit in 4 bytes.
           nop                     ; [O] fill to exactly 4 bytes.
           nop                     ; [O]
;
READ_D:    tfr       tmp3,d        ; [P] user D was in temp 3.
           bra       R_COMMON      ; [PPP] D->SHIFTER, wait done, go INST_DONE.
;
READ_X:    tfr       x,d           ; [P] move user X to D.
           bra       R_COMMON      ; [PPP] D->SHIFTER, wait done, go INST_DONE.
;
READ_Y:    tfr       y,d           ; [P] move user Y to D.
           bra       R_COMMON      ; [PPP] D->SHIFTER, wait done, go INST_DONE.
;
READ_SP:   tfr       sp,d          ; [P] move user SP to D.
R_COMMON:  std       SHIFTER       ; [WOP] make data available for serial xfer.
WAIT:      tst       INSTR         ; [rOP] check for aborted command.
           lbeq      INST_LOOP     ; [OPPP/OPO] branch if aborted.
           brclr     STATUS,#$10,WAIT ; [rfPPP] wait for data done.
           bra       INST_DONE1    ; [PPP] clr INSTR and go loop top.
;
READ_PC1:  exg       d,tmp2        ; [P] user PC to D, junk to temp 2.
           std       SHIFTER       ; [WOP] user PC to SHIFTER.
           exg       d,tmp2        ; [P] user PC to temp 2, junk to D.
           bra       WAIT          ; [PPP] wait for done, go INST_DONE.
;
```

Figure 15.13: Computed GOTO and Firmware Read Commands

Section 15.6: Implementing a BDM Debugger Interface

Before ending the discussion of the BDM firmware, it is useful to point out a simple byte saving technique that is used at the end of the wait loop sequence in Figure 15.13. After the completion of the data phase of the read command, the firmware needs to return to the code at the label INST_DONE. However, the instruction at this label is too far away to be reached by a short branch instruction. A LBRA or JMP instruction could have been used here, but would have required an additional one or two bytes of object code. Instead, a label, INST_DONE1, was created at an existing branch instruction that is within the range of a short branch to the label INST_DONE. While the technique of using a branch to a branch instruction can be valuable in saving a byte or two, it does result in a slightly longer execution time.

15.6 Implementing a BDM Debugger Interface

To utilize the M68HC12's BDM system requires an interface device that can convert a standard communications protocol from a host computer to the custom serial communications protocol utilized by the BDM system. There are numerous ways that such debugger 'pods' can be built, however, the most common method is to use a microcontroller to convert serial or parallel data from a host computer into BDM commands. At least one low cost BDM pod has been constructed using a small high-speed microcontroller to receive simple ASCII commands from a host computer and convert them into equivalent BDM serial commands. Using this approach allowed for a very simple pod design, but placed the burden of supplying a high-level debug system on the host computer. The Motorola Serial Debug Interface (SDI) utilizes an M68HC11 family microcontroller to implement their M68HC12 family BDM interface pod. The M68HC11 utilizes a Motorola-defined serial command protocol to communicate with a host computer and converts generalized data requests into one or more BDM commands to obtain the requested data. This generalized approach has made it possible for numerous third-party development tool vendors to design complex software debug tools including such advanced features as C source-level debug.

A third approach, utilized by the M68EVB912B32 evaluation board, includes a complete command line based debugger program and the BDM serial communications primitives in the evaluation board's MC68HC912B32. This approach has the advantage of allowing the debugger to be used with any host computer capable of supporting a simple ASCII terminal emulator. In addition, the MC68HC912B32 EVB can also act as a stand-alone evaluation system utilizing the built in debugger as a ROM monitor much like the M68HC11EVBU with its BUFFALO program. A jumper on the EVB selects the ROM monitor or POD operating mode. When operating the EVB in POD mode, the debugger commands access an M68HC12 target, connected through a 6-pin BDM cable.

This section presents example CPU12 assembly language routines implementing the lowest level single-wire BDM communications protocol. These communications primitives are then used to build higher level routines implementing the entire BDM command set. These routines are essentially what was used in the original MC68HC912B32 evaluation board. Although Motorola has since enhanced the low-level communication routines to allow the MC68HC912B32 evaluation board to communicate with target M68HC12 devices operating at any speed, the routines presented in this chapter assume that the EVB POD and target are operating at approximately the same frequency. In addition to the BDM primitives, a few additional commands are provided to check the BDM status, enable the BDM firmware, and read or write the application's condition code register. As can be determined by examining the source code, these additional commands are special cases of the BDM hardware commands.

All of the routines were written such that they can be loaded into the EEPROM of an MC68HC912B32 evaluation board for experimentation and study. Because these routines rely on cycle-by-cycle timing of instructions to generate timed waveforms, interrupts should not be enabled while these routines are executing. The routines themselves do not mask interrupts because the debugger in the EVB does not enable interrupts when it is operating in POD mode. To allow these routines to operate in a more flexible environment, the I-bit in the condition code register should be set before calling any of the BDM routines. If using these routines in another environment, such as the MC68HC812A4 EVB, the routines can be reassembled to locate them in the MC68HC812A4's EEPROM. However, because the routines depend on the cycle-by-cycle instruction timing, the routines should not be run from external memory where the instruction timing could be different depending on the speed of the memory devices being used.

15.7 BDM COMMUNICATION PRIMITIVES

The BDM communication primitives, `WSerial_16`, `WSerial_8`, and `RSerial_16` are unusual because they rely on the cycle-by-cycle instruction timing of the implementation to execute the BDM serial protocol. To show the unique relationship of each instruction to the generated waveform, portions of the code for these three routines is presented in a unique manner. By modifying a standard program listing to add additional lines, (one for each cycle in each instruction), and writing down the cycle codes from the CPU12 Reference Manual, the relationship between the software routine and signal timing on the BKGD pin can easily be documented. The listings are rotated sideways so the timing pattern can be drawn like an oscilloscope trace below this listing. The listings are not quite like assembly listings because they show instructions in execution order as opposed to source listing order. For example, in the case when a branch instruction is taken, these listings show the next instruction that executes rather than the instruction at the address following the branch. Furthermore, one instruction from the assembly listing can appear several times in these execution order listings. In addition to demonstrating the critical timing involved in writing the BDM primitives, the routines also demonstrate techniques allowing a single pin to be

Section 15.7: BDM Communication Primitives

utilized as both an input and an output. All three subroutines use the timer port pin PT7 for communication with the target system.

Figure 15.14 presents the timing for the `WSerial_16` subroutine entry overhead and the timing involved in the transmission of a logic zero and a logic one bit-time. Before calling the routine, the Port T bit-7 pin is configured as a high-impedance input. At reference point [1], the pin changes to an actively driven logic one. The falling edge at reference point [2] starts the first bit-time of the 16-bit word transmission. However, because the two microcontrollers run asynchronously in relationship to one another, the target can require up to one BDM clock cycle to notice the falling edge at reference point [3]. For this reason, there is actually one clock cycle of uncertainty regarding the point where the target senses the bit level at reference point [4]. Note that Figure 15.14 is presented from the POD's viewpoint while the timing reference diagrams in Motorola's data sheets are drawn from the target's viewpoint. Obviously, from the POD's reference point there is no uncertainty about when the BKGD pin is driven low, however because of the edge synchronization required by the target there is one clock of uncertainty regarding when the target samples the data on the BKGD pin. Even though the target samples the BKGD pin at a fixed number of clocks after the falling edge of the start of a bit time, the end of a bit time, represented by a rising edge on the BKGD pin, can vary from 10 to more than 500 target BDM clock times. Although as shown in Figure 15.14 the minimum time between falling edges is 16 BDM clock periods.

If the target microcontroller operates at a lower frequency than the POD, the bit sample points would appear to move to the right. If the target operates significantly slower than the POD and the target requires a whole BDM clock cycle to detect the falling edge at the start because of synchronization, the sample point could move far enough to the right that it would move past the next rising edge on BKGD. Obviously, this would cause the bit level to be sensed incorrectly. When the target operates at a higher frequency than the POD, the sample point would appear to move to the left and into the start pulse of a logic one bit time.

The best way to incorporate speed tolerance into the BDM write routines is make the low period for the logic zero bit-time as long as possible while making the low period for the logic one bit-time as short as possible. Effectively, this allows the sample periods to slide in time, to either the left or right, the maximum amount without the target incorrectly detecting a transmitted bit. Of course there are practical limits to the minimum width of the high time at the end of a logic zero bit-time and the minimum width of the low time at the beginning of a logic one bit-time. For the target to correctly synchronize to the falling edge of the start-bit, both of the pulse widths must be slightly longer than one target BDM clock cycle. Clearly if the Start pulse of a logic one becomes too narrow, there is a risk that the pulse will be too narrow for the BDM state machine logic to recognize. Other areas exist where a faster or slower target could cause the communications to fail. On a practical level the overall tolerance is approximately ± 20% which is a much wider band of tolerance than an RS-232 asynchronous serial interface.

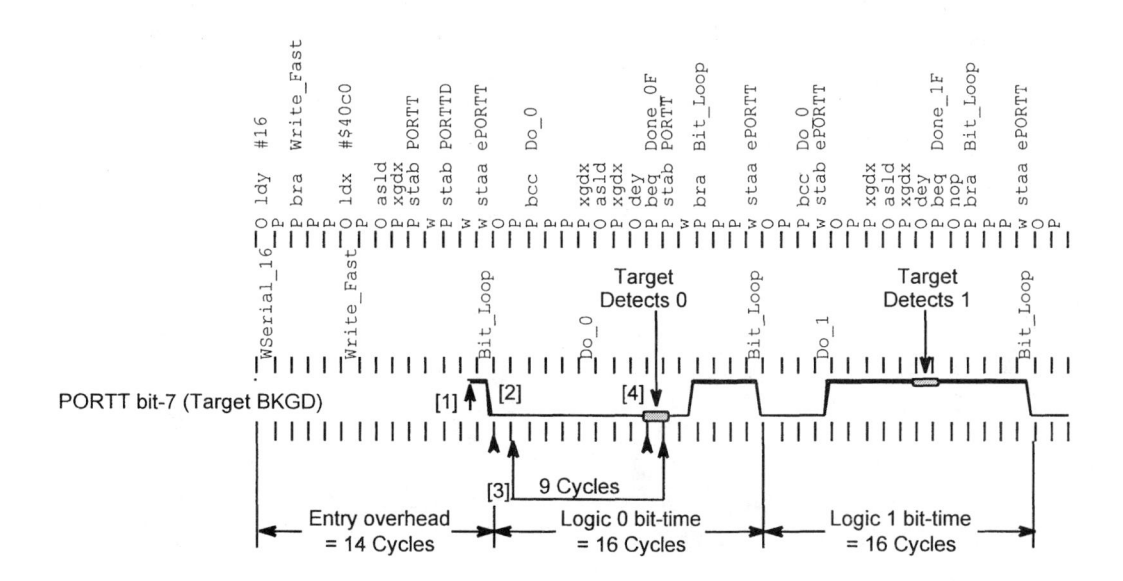

Figure 15.14: WSerial_16 Subroutine Entry and 0 and 1 Bit Time Transitions

The instructions in the `WSerial_16` primitive subroutine were carefully selected, the order of operations was carefully arranged, and delay padding was added in strategic places to cause all paths through the routine to match, so each bit time would be exactly 16 cycles long. This was accomplished through a combination of trial and error as well as using cycle-by-cycle timing diagrams like the one in Figure 15.14. Fortunately, most assembly language programming does not require such extraordinary measures. With a little more effort, the entry and exit sequences could have been fine tuned to match as well, but that was not important in this case. The additional effort expended fine tuning the data bit timing portion of the routines made the operation of the communication routines independent of the transmitted data which simplified the testing of the finished routines. Note that the `WSerial_8` primitive subroutine is simply an alternate entry into `WSerial_16` where a value of eight, the number of transmitted bits, is loaded into the Y index register instead of 16. The source code for the `WSerial_16` and `WSerial_8` primitive subroutine is presented in figure 15.15

Figure 15.16 presents the timing for the `RSerial_16` subroutine entry overhead and the timing involved in the POD's reception of a logic one and a logic zero. Because the POD must initiate all data transfers between itself and the target, the I/O pin used by the read routine must be configured as an output to generate a falling edge on the BKGD pin,

471

Section 15.7: BDM Communication Primitives

then reconfigured as an input so the POD can read the value placed on the BKGD pin by the target. Examining the first four instructions in the timing diagram shows how the edge is generated. When the subroutine is entered, the BCLR instruction clears bit seven of the Port T data direction register to ensure that pin PT7 is a high impedance input. The second BCLR instruction writes a zero to bit seven of the Port T data register, preloading the output data latch with the value driven onto pin PT7 when it is configured as an output.

```
;
WSerial_16: ldy   #16          ; [2]   bit count = 16.
            bra   Write_Fast   ; [3]   Rest is same as Write8.
;
WSerial_8:  ldy   #8           ; [2]   bit count = 8.
;
Write_Fast: ldx   #$40c0       ; [2]   Patterns for BKGD low:hi.
            asld               ; [1]   MSB of data to C-bit.
            xgdx               ; [1]   data to X, $40c0 to D.
            stab  PORTT        ; [2]   Pw Write BKGD output to 1.
            stab  PORTTD       ; [2]   Pw BKGD to active high.
Bit_Loop:   staa  ePORTT       ; [3]   wOP BKGD output to 0.
            bcc   Do_0         ; [1/3] Branch if bit is a 0.
Do_1:       stab  ePORTT       ; [3]   wOP force BKGD back high.
            xgdx               ; [1]   data to D, $40c0 to X.
            asld               ; [1]   next data bit to C-bit.
            xgdx               ; [1]   data to X, $40c0 to D.
            dey                ; [1]   Update bit counter.
            beq   Done_1F      ; [1/3] If last data bit sent.
            nop                ; [1]   delay.
            bra   Bit_Loop     ; [3]   Loop for next bit.
Do_0:       xgdx               ; [1]   data to D, $40c0 to X.
            asld               ; [1]   next data bit to C-bit.
            xgdx               ; [1]   data to X, $40c0 to D.
            dey                ; [1]   Update bit counter.
            beq   Done_0F      ; [1/3] If last data bit sent.
            stab  PORTT        ; [2]   Pw BKGD output to 1.
            bra   Bit_Loop     ; [3]   Loop for next bit.
Done_0F:    stab  ePORTT       ; [3]   wOP force BKGD high.
Done_1F:    clr   ePORTTD      ; [3]   wOP force BKGD to hi-z.
            rts                ; [5]   ** return **.
;
```

Figure 15.15: WSerial_16 and WSerial_8 Subroutine

The next two instructions, the `BSET` and `BCLR`, configure PT7 as an output driving the pin to a logic zero and then immediately reconfiguring the pin as an input. As shown in the timing diagram, because the `BSET` and `BCLR` instructions each require four clock cycles, the pin is driven low for exactly four clocks. When the pin is reconfigured as an input by the `BCLR` instruction, the pin level begins to rise to a logic one as a result of a pullup resistor and stray capacitance on the pin. During this time, the D accumulator is initialized and a `BRA` instruction is executed, transferring execution into the data receive loop. During the execution of the `BRA` instruction, the target drives the BKGD pin to a logic one for one target BDM clock cycle. This speedup pulse ensures that the BKGD pin reaches the proper level of a logic one before the POD reads the state of the BKGD pin.

The `LDX` instruction reads the Port T data and data direction register, placing the state of the BKGD pin in the most significant bit of the X index register. The data read from the data direction register is not necessary to the subroutine; however, it was necessary to use the X index register because of the value preloaded into the D accumulator. The first `XGDX` instruction places the data read by the `LDX` instruction in the D accumulator where the most significant bit is shifted into the carry by the `ASLD` instruction. The second `XGDX` instruction restores the previous value of the D accumulator, leaving the state of the BKGD pin in the carry. A `BSET/BCLR` instruction pair is executed initiating the next bit time before the carry is rotated into the least significant bit of the D accumulator. The `BCC` instruction at the end of the loop checks to see if a one was rotated out of the most significant bit of D into the carry. If not, execution continues at the top of the loop where the state of the BKGD pin is read by the `LDX` instruction. As the timing diagram shows, during the second bit time where the target transmits a logic zero to the POD, the target keeps the BKGD pin held low until the start of the 14th target BDM clock. Again, the target drives the BKGD pin to a logic one for one target BDM clock cycle to ensure that the BKGD pin assumes a logic one level and is ready to begin the next bit transmission.

The complete source listing for the `RSerial_16` Subroutine appears in Figure 15.17. Like the `WSerial_16` primitive subroutine, the instructions were carefully selected, the order of operations carefully arranged, and delay padding added in strategic places to cause all paths through the routine to match. Although the the reception of each bit requires more than the 16 BDM clock minimum, the time required to receive a logic one or zero is the same, thus simplifying the testing of the finished routines.

Examining the complete source listing reveals the reason for loading the D accumulator with a value of three before entering the loop at label `Read_1F`. As explained previously, the receive loop terminates when a one is rotated into the carry as the recently received data bit is rotated into the least significant bit of the D accumulator. It may seem that initializing the D accumulator with a one in the second least significant bit of D would cause the loop to terminate after receiving only 15 bits. This is, in fact, the case. The last bit is read and shifted into the D accumulator by the code beginning at label `Read_Done`.

Section 15.8: Implementing BDM Commands

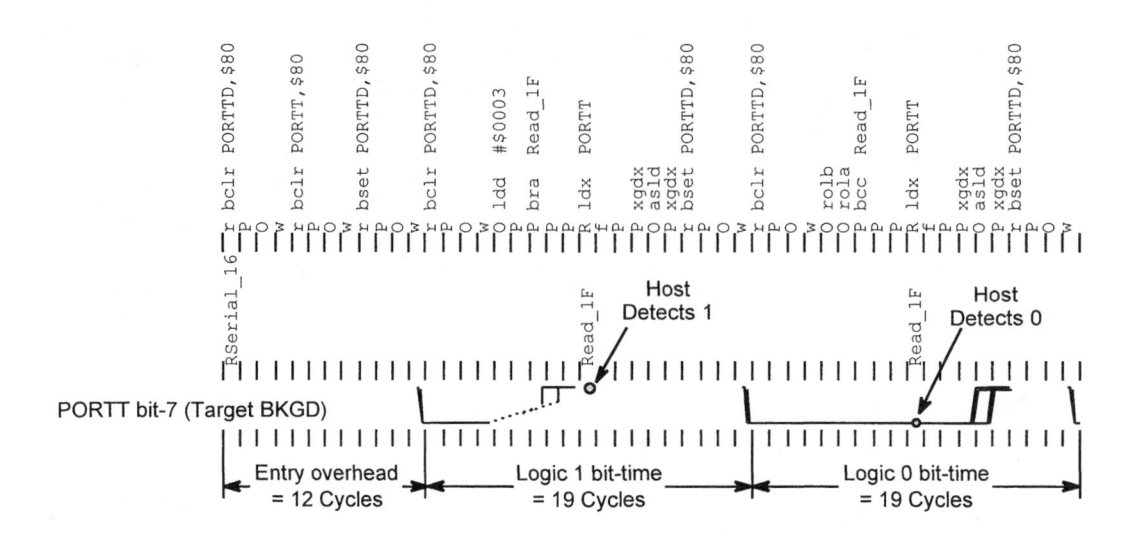

Figure 15.16: `RSerial_16` Subroutine Entry and 1 and 0 Bit Time Transitions

15.8 IMPLEMENTING BDM COMMANDS

The BDM primitives presented in the previous section provide the bare minimum firmware necessary to begin building a set of BDM routines required to communicate with a target M68HC12. With these routines plus some delay subroutines, subroutines for all of the BDM commands listed in Figures 15.1 and 15.2 can be implemented. Because the source code for the BDM primitives is well-commented and is included on a disk with the book, each of the primitives are not discussed. Also see Appendix C for a complete commented source listing. of the BDM primitives. To help the reader understand the routines in the listing, several of the primitives are discussed in the remainder of this chapter.

Figure 15.18 presents the source code implementing the WRITE_WORD BDM command plus two support subroutines. The format of the WRITE_WORD command consists of an 8-bit command followed by a 16-bit address and the 16-bits of data. The address is passed to the subroutine in the D accumulator and the data is passed in the X index register. Because the BDM hardware commands only support reading or writing 16-bit quantities to aligned word addresses, the Test4odd subroutine checks for an odd address. If the address is even, the WRITE_WORD subroutine continues by saving the address and data on the stack. Studying the source for the Test4odd subroutine shows a common technique used by assembly language programmers known as a 'double return'. If the address is odd, the carry bit is set indicating the error. Then the return address, placed on the stack when the Test4odd subroutine was called, is removed from the stack by the LEAS instruction. When the RTS is executed, a return is made to the routine that called the WRITE_WORD subroutine. This technique helps to minimize the amount of stack and program space required by the BDM routines, however, unless it is applied carefully and well documented it can easily cause program run away.

```
;
RSerial_16:bclr  PORTTD,$80 ; [4] rPOw be sure BKGD is hi-z.
           bclr  PORTT,$80  ; [4] rPOw write BKGD output to 0.
;
; BKGD will go to 0 when a 1 is written to PORT T DDR bit-7.
;
           bset  PORTTD,$80 ; [4] rPOw BKGD low to start bit time.
           bclr  PORTTD,$80 ; [4] rPOw return BKGD to hi-z.
           ldd   #$0003     ; [2] end when 1 shifts out MSB of D.
           bra   Read_1F    ; [3] delay to match timing.
Read_1F:   ldx   PORTT      ; [3] RfP read next data bit to MSB.
           xgdx             ; [1] new bit to MSB of A, data to X.
           asla             ; [1] shift new data bit into Carry.
           xgdx             ; [1] data to D, C not changed.
           bset  PORTTD,$80 ; [4] rPOw BKGD low to start bit time.
           bclr  PORTTD,$80 ; [4] rPOw return BKGD to hi-z.
           rolb             ; [1] shift new bit to LSB from right.
           rola             ; [1] 16-bit rotate.
           bcc   Read_1F    ; [1/3] bra=more bits, else done.
Read_done: xgdx             ; [1] data to X.
           nop              ; [1] delay.
           ldaa  PORTT      ; [3] rfP read last data bit to MSB.
           asla             ; [1] shift last data bit to carry.
           xgdx             ; [1] data to D, C not affected.
           rolb             ; [1] shift new bit to LSB from right.
           rola             ; [1] 16-bit rotate.
           rts              ; [5] ** return **.
;
```

Figure 15.17: RSerial_16 subroutine

Section 15.8: Implementing BDM Commands

```
;
WRITE_WORD: jsr    Test4odd      ; [4+10] proceed only if addr even.
                                 ; NOTE: double returns if address was bad.
            pshx                 ; [2] save data.
            pshd                 ; [2] save address.
            ldaa   #$c8          ; [1] WRITE_WORD command code.
WTw_com:    jsr    WSerial_8     ; [4+146] send command.
            puld                 ; [3] recover address and deallocate.
            jsr    WSerial_16    ; [4+277] send address.
            puld                 ; [3] recover data and deallocate.
            jsr    WSerial_16    ; [4+277] send data.
            jsr    Dly_175       ; [4+173] wait for free cycle.
            clc                  ; [1] indicate no error.
            rts                  ; [5] ** return **.
;
Test4odd:   bitb   #$01          ; [1] check for odd (illegal).
            beq    notodd        ; [1/3] bra if addr was even.
            sec                  ; [1] indicate error.
            leas   2,sp          ; [2] addr was odd so double return.
notodd:     rts                  ; [5] ** return or double return **.
;
Dly_175:    ldx    #42           ; [2] initialize loop count.
dlydecx:    dex                  ; [1] update loop count=count-1.
            bne    dlydecx       ; [1/3] loop till X=0.
            rts                  ; [5] ** return **.
;
```

Figure 15.18: WRITE_WORD BDM Subroutine

After saving the data and address on the stack, the value $C8, representing the WRITE_WORD command, is loaded into the A accumulator and sent to the target by calling the WSerial_8 primitive. Upon return, the address and data are recovered from the stack and sent to the target using the WSerial_16 primitive. Because all hardware commands require a minimum delay of 150 BDM clock cycles as they search for a target CPU free cycle to complete the requested write operation, the Dly_175 subroutine is called to wait for 175 target BDM clock cycles before returning. Finally, the condition code register carry bit is cleared before returning, indicating that no errors occurred. The label WTw_com is used as an entry point by the WRITE_BD_WORD subroutine.

Figure 15.19 contains the source code implementing the WRITE_BYTE BDM command. Even though the command only writes a byte to target memory, its format consists of an 8-bit command followed by a 16-bit address and 16-bits of data. If the target memory address is odd, the 8-bits of data must be transmitted in the low order byte of the data field. If the address is even, the data must be transmitted in the high order byte of the data field. Because the 8-bits of data is passed to the subroutine in the low byte of the X

Chapter 15: Background Debug - A Software Perspective

index register, the WRITE_BYTE routine tests the address and rearranges the data byte as necessary.

As with the WRITE_WORD subroutine, the Dly_175 subroutine is called to wait for a hardware command to complete before returning. Because of the absence of error conditions within the WRITE_BYTE subroutine, it does not return an error indicator like the WRITE_WORD subroutine. The label WTb_com is used as an entry point by the WRITE_BD_BYTE subroutine.

```
;
WRITE_BYTE: pshx              ; [2] save data.
            pshd              ; [2] save address.
            ldaa  #$c0        ; [1] WRITE_BYTE command code.
WTb_com:    jsr   WSerial_8   ; [4+146] send command.
            ldd   0,sp        ; [3] address of byte to write.
            jsr   WSerial_16  ; [4+277] send address.
            puld              ; [3] recover address and deallocate.
            bitb  #$01        ; [1] test for odd/even address.
            puld              ; [3] recover data and deallocate.
            bne   arn_swp0    ; [1/3] bra if addr odd (data in B).
            exg   b,a         ; [1] even addr so swap data to A.
arn_swp0:   jsr   WSerial_16  ; [4+277] send 16-bits of data.
            jmp   Dly_175     ; [3+173] wait for free cycle.
                              ; double return after Dly_175.
;
```

Figure 15.19: WRITE_BYTE BDM Subroutine

The source code for the READ_WORD and READ_BYTE subroutines is presented in Figure 15.20 and 15.21. Examining the routines reveals that both are similar to the WRITE_WORD and WRITE_BYTE subroutines, however, the command sent to the target consists only of an 8-bit command and a 16-bit address. The 16-bit data is read from the target device after calling the Dly_175 subroutine to allow the target to detect a CPU free cycle for accessing the memory data.

Like the WRITE_BYTE routine, even though READ_BYTE involves reading a byte from target memory, 16-bits of data must be transferred from the target BDM system. The eight bits of data transferred from the target system are returned in the lower byte for odd addresses and in the upper byte of the 16-bit data stream for even addresses. For either case, the READ_BYTE routine clears the A accumulator and returns the 8-bit data in the B accumulator.

Section 15.8: Implementing BDM Commands

```
;
READ_WORD: bsr   Test4odd     ; [4+10] cont. only if addr even.
                              ; NOTE: double returns if address was bad.
           pshd               ; [2] save address.
           ldaa  #$e8         ; [1] command code for READ_WORD.
RDw_com:   jsr   WSerial_8    ; [4+146] send command.
           puld               ; [3] recover address and deallocate.
           jsr   WSerial_16   ; [4+277] send address.
           bsr   Dly_175      ; [4+173] wait for free cycle.
           jsr   RSerial_16   ; [4+317] get 16-bits of data.
           clc                ; [1] indicate no error.
           rts                ; [5] ** return **.
;
```

Figure 15.20: READ_WORD BDM Subroutine

```
;
READ_BYTE: pshd               ; [2] save address.
           ldaa  #$e0         ; [1] command code for READ_BYTE.
RDb_com:   jsr   WSerial_8    ; [4+146] send command.
           ldd   0,sp         ; [3] address of byte to read.
           jsr   WSerial_16   ; [4+277] send address.
           bsr   Dly_175      ; [4+173] wait for free cycle.
           jsr   RSerial_16   ; [4+317] get 16-bits of data.
           pulx               ; [3] recover address and deallocate.
           xgdx               ; [1] swap address to D for tests.
           bitb  #$01         ; [1] test for odd/even address.
           xgdx               ; [1] swap address and data back.
           bne   arn_tfr0     ; [1/3] bra if addr odd (data in B).
           tfr   a,b          ; [1] even addr so move data to B.
arn_tfr0:  clra               ; [1] clear upper byte of returned D.
           rts                ; [5] ** return **.
;
```

Figure 15.21: READ_Byte BDM Subroutine

Questions/Exercises

15.1   Why is the M68HC12's BDM system capable of reading and writing target memory without intervention from the CPU12?

15.2   What does the term *active background* infer?

Chapter 15: Background Debug - A Software Perspective

15.3 How many different ways can the CPU12 be placed into the active background mode? Briefly describe each method.

15.4 What area of memory does the BDM ROM and control register block occupy? In what way does it interfere with the target application? Why?

15.5 What restrictions does the BDM firmware have regarding access to the application memory map? Does this restriction apply to the BDM hardware logic?

15.6 Explain the advantages of the M68HC12 BDM debug system over conventional strategies used in the past.

15.7 Where or how is an application's context saved when the CPU12 enters active background? What are the advantages or disadvantages of using this method?

15.8 When entering active background mode, where is the application's program counter saved?

15.9 What CPU12 mechanism is used to enter active background?

15.10 What is the first thing the BDM firmware is required to do after entering active background? What is critical about this operation?

15.11 Where is the value of the application's D accumulator saved? What mechanism is used to save its contents?

15.12 Where is the application's condition code register saved?

15.13 When does the application's program counter require adjustment after entering active background? Why?

15.14 What condition must be true for the CPU12 to remain in active background mode?

15.15 What is the critical code sequence that initiates the switch from active BDM to the execution of application code? What condition must be true when this event occurs?

15.16 What occurs during the exit sequence that causes the CPU12 to execute a single application instruction and then return to active background mode?

15.17 Explain the importance of the location of two instruction code sequence executed by the CPU12 while it waits for the reception of a BDM firmware command?

Section 15.8: Implementing BDM Commands

15.18   Why is a computed GOTO operation used to perform the final decoding of received firmware commands?

15.19   Explain what precautions are necessary when using the READ_NEXT and WRITE_NEXT firmware commands.

15.20   What timing restrictions exist for a debugger POD when sending firmware commands to a target M68HC12 device?

15.21   What restrictions regarding execution speed are placed on the POD primitive routines presented in this chapter?

15.22   Why is a high level language such as C not suitable for writing software like the BDM POD primitives?

Appendix A: Instruction Set Summary

The author and publisher thank Motorola, Inc. for the permission to reprint the following information from the CPU 12 Reference Guide.

Motorola Semiconductor Technical Data

Order this document
by CPU12RG/D Rev. 1

CPU12 Reference Guide

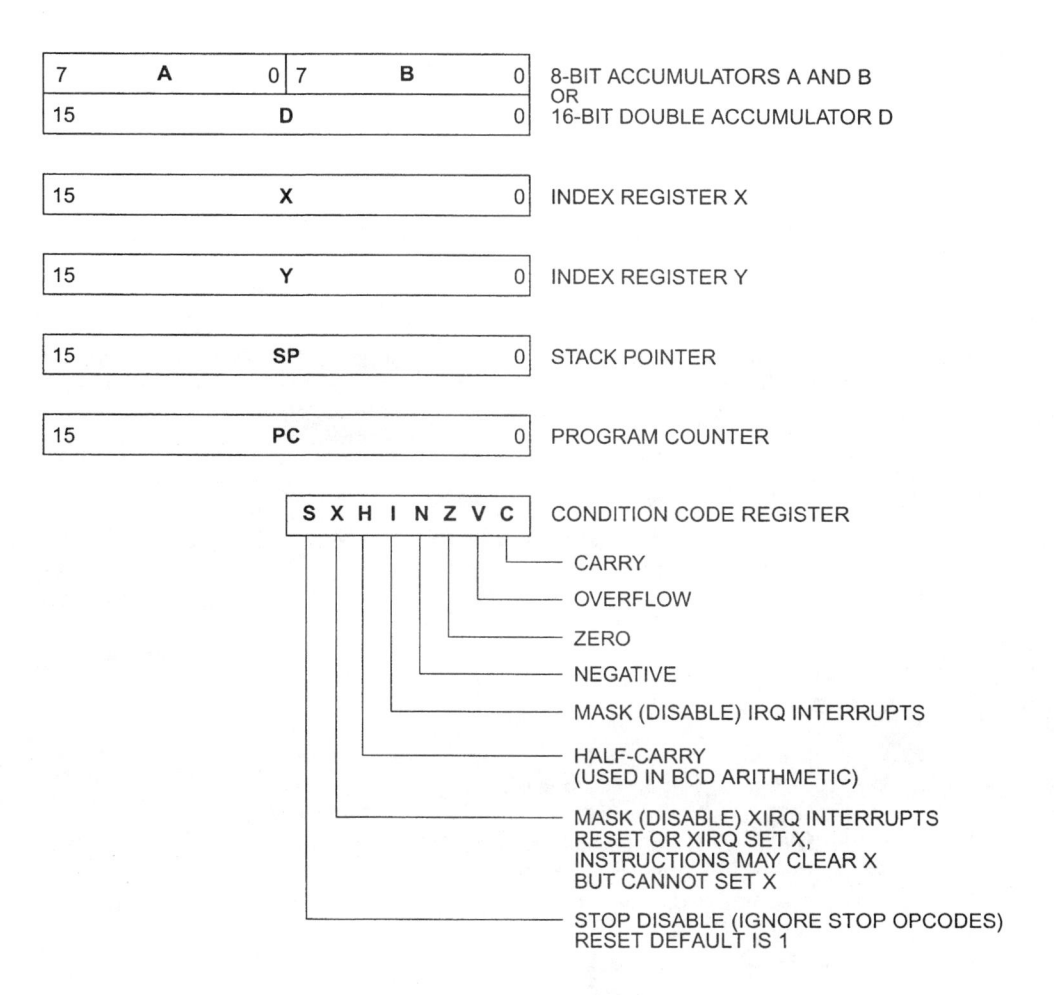

```
 7     A     0 7     B     0    8-BIT ACCUMULATORS A AND B
                                 OR
15           D             0    16-BIT DOUBLE ACCUMULATOR D

15           X             0    INDEX REGISTER X

15           Y             0    INDEX REGISTER Y

15           SP            0    STACK POINTER

15           PC            0    PROGRAM COUNTER

             S X H I N Z V C    CONDITION CODE REGISTER
                         └──── CARRY
                       └────── OVERFLOW
                     └──────── ZERO
                   └────────── NEGATIVE
                 └──────────── MASK (DISABLE) IRQ INTERRUPTS
               └────────────── HALF-CARRY
                               (USED IN BCD ARITHMETIC)
             └──────────────── MASK (DISABLE) XIRQ INTERRUPTS
                               RESET OR XIRQ SET X,
                               INSTRUCTIONS MAY CLEAR X
                               BUT CANNOT SET X
           └────────────────── STOP DISABLE (IGNORE STOP OPCODES)
                               RESET DEFAULT IS 1
```

Figure 1. Programming Model

CPU12 Reference Guide

Stack and Memory Layout

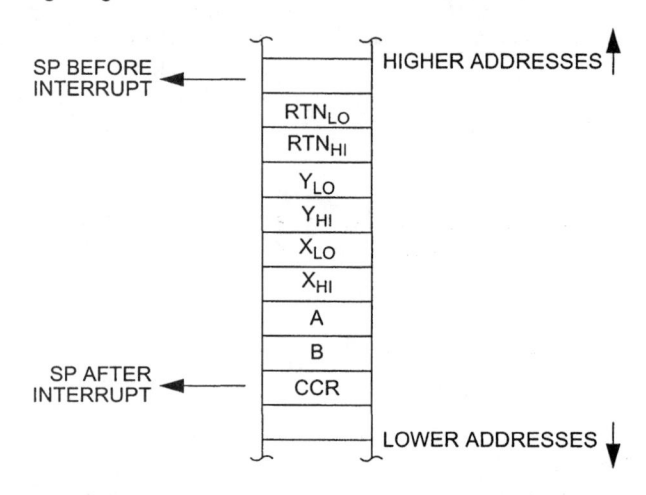

SP BEFORE INTERRUPT →	RTN$_{LO}$ ← HIGHER ADDRESSES
	RTN$_{HI}$
	Y$_{LO}$
	Y$_{HI}$
	X$_{LO}$
	X$_{HI}$
	A
	B
SP AFTER INTERRUPT →	CCR
	← LOWER ADDRESSES

STACK UPON ENTRY TO SERVICE ROUTINE IF SP WAS ODD BEFORE INTERRUPT

SP +8	RTN$_{LO}$		SP +9
SP +6	Y$_{LO}$	RTN$_{HI}$	SP +7
SP +4	X$_{LO}$	Y$_{HI}$	SP +5
SP +2	A	X$_{HI}$	SP +3
SP	CCR	B	SP +1
SP –2			SP –1

STACK UPON ENTRY TO SERVICE ROUTINE IF SP WAS EVEN BEFORE INTERRUPT

SP +9			SP +10
SP +7	RTN$_{HI}$	RTN$_{LO}$	SP +8
SP +5	Y$_{HI}$	Y$_{LO}$	SP +6
SP +4	X$_{HI}$	X$_{LO}$	SP +4
SP +1	B	A	SP +2
SP –1		CCR	SP

Interrupt Vector Locations

$FFFE, $FFFF	Power-On (POR) or External Reset
$FFFC, $FFFD	Clock Monitor Reset
$FFFA, $FFFB	Computer Operating Properly (COP Watchdog Reset
$FFF8, $FFF9	Unimplemented Opcode Trap
$FFF6, $FFF7	Software Interrupt Instruction (SWI)
$FFF4, $FFF5	XIRQ
$FFF2, $FFF3	IRQ
$FFC0–$FFF1	Device-Specific Interrupt Sources

Notation Used in Instruction Set Summary

Explanation of Italic Expressions in Source Form Column

- *abc* — A or B or CCR
- *abcdxys* — A or B or CCR or D or X or Y or SP. Some assemblers also allow T2 or T3.
- *abd* — A or B or D
- *abdxys* — A or B or D or X or Y or SP
- *dxys* — D or X or Y or SP
- *msk8* — 8-bit mask, some assemblers require # symbol before value
- *opr8i* — 8-bit immediate value
- *opr16i* — 16-bit immediate value
- *opr8a* — 8-bit address used with direct address mode
- *opr16a* — 16-bit address value
- *oprx0_xysp* — Indexed addressing postbyte code:
  - *oprx3,–xys*   Predecrement X or Y or SP by 1 . . . 8
  - *oprx3,+xys*   Preincrement X or Y or SP by 1 . . . 8
  - *oprx3,xys–*   Postdecrement X or Y or SP by 1 . . . 8
  - *oprx3,xys+*   Postincrement X or Y or SP by 1 . . . 8
  - *oprx5,xysp*   5-bit constant offset from X or Y or SP or PC
  - *abd,xysp*   Accumulator A or B or D offset from X or Y or SP or PC
- *oprx3* — Any positive integer 1 . . . 8 for pre/post increment/decrement
- *oprx5* — Any value in the range –16 . . . +15
- *oprx9* — Any value in the range –256 . . . +255
- *oprx16* — Any value in the range –32,768 . . . 65,535
- *page* — 8-bit value for PPAGE, some assemblers require # symbol before this value
- *rel8* — Label of branch destination within –256 to +255 locations
- *rel9* — Label of branch destination within –512 to +511 locations
- *rel16* — Any label within 64K memory space
- *trapnum* — Any 8-bit value in the range $30-$39 or $40-$FF
- *xys* — X or Y or SP
- *xysp* — X or Y or SP or PC

CPU12 Reference Guide

Address Modes

IMM	— Immediate
IDX	— Indexed (no extension bytes) includes: 5-bit constant offset Pre/post increment/decrement by 1 . . . 8 Accumulator A, B, or D offset
IDX1	— 9-bit signed offset (1 extension byte)
IDX2	— 16-bit signed offset (2 extension bytes)
[D, IDX]	— Indexed indirect (accumulator D offset)
[IDX2]	— Indexed indirect (16-bit offset)
INH	— Inherent (no operands in object code)
REL	— 2's complement relative offset (branches)

Machine Coding

`dd` — 8-bit direct address $0000 to $00FF. (High byte assumed to be $00).

`ee` — High-order byte of a 16-bit constant offset for indexed addressing.

`eb` — Exchange/Transfer post-byte. See **Table 3** on page 23.

`ff` — Low-order eight bits of a 9-bit signed constant offset for indexed addressing, or low-order byte of a 16-bit constant offset for indexed addressing.

`hh` — High-order byte of a 16-bit extended address.

`ii` — 8-bit immediate data value.

`jj` — High-order byte of a 16-bit immediate data value.

`kk` — Low-order byte of a 16-bit immediate data value.

`lb` — Loop primitive (DBNE) post-byte. See **Table 4** on page 24.

`ll` — Low-order byte of a 16-bit extended address.

`mm` — 8-bit immediate mask value for bit manipulation instructions. Set bits indicate bits to be affected.

`pg` — Program page (bank) number used in CALL instruction.

`qq` — High-order byte of a 16-bit relative offset for long branches.

`tn` — Trap number $30–$39 or $40–$FF.

`rr` — Signed relative offset $80 (–128) to $7F (+127). Offset relative to the byte following the relative offset byte, or low-order byte of a 16-bit relative offset for long branches.

`xb` — Indexed addressing post-byte. See **Table 1** on page 21 and **Table 2** on page 22.

Access Detail

Each code letter equals one CPU cycle. Uppercase = 16-bit operation and lowercase = 8-bit operation. For complex sequences see the *CPU12 Reference Manual* (CPU12RM/AD).

- f — Free cycle, CPU doesn't use bus
- g — Read PPAGE internally
- I — Read indirect pointer (indexed indirect)
- i — Read indirect PPAGE value (call indirect)
- n — Write PPAGE internally
- O — Optional program word fetch (P) if instruction is misaligned and has an odd number of bytes of object code — otherwise, appears as a free cycle (f)
- P — Program word fetch (always an aligned word read)
- r — 8-bit data read
- R — 16-bit data read
- s — 8-bit stack write
- S — 16-bit stack write
- w — 8-bit data write
- W — 16-bit data write
- u — 8-bit stack read
- U — 16-bit stack read
- V — 16-bit vector fetch
- t — 8-bit conditional read (or free cycle)
- T — 16-bit conditional read (or free cycle)
- x — 8-bit conditional write

Special Cases

- PPP/P — Short branch, PPP if branch taken, P if not
- OPPP/OPO — Long branch, OPPP if branch taken, OPO if not

Condition Codes Columns

- – — Status bit not affected by operation.
- 0 — Status bit cleared by operation.
- 1 — Status bit set by operation.
- ∆ — Status bit affected by operation.
- ⇓ — Status bit may be cleared or remain set, but is not set by operation.
- ⇑ — Status bit may be set or remain cleared, but is not cleared by operation.
- ? — Status bit may be changed by operation but the final state is not defined.
- ! — Status bit used for a special purpose.

CPU12 Reference Guide

Instruction Set Summary

Source Form	Operation	Addr. Mode	Machine Coding (hex)	Access Detail	S	X	H	I	N	Z	V	C
ABA	(A) + (B) ⇒ A Add Accumulators A and B	INH	18 06	OO	–	–	Δ	–	Δ	Δ	Δ	Δ
ABX	(B) + (X) ⇒ X Translates to LEAX B,X	IDX	1A E5	PP[1]	–	–	–	–	–	–	–	–
ABY	(B) + (Y) ⇒ Y Translates to LEAY B,Y	IDX	19 ED	PP[1]	–	–	–	–	–	–	–	–
ADCA #opr8i ADCA opr8a ADCA opr16a ADCA oprx0_xysp ADCA oprx9,xysp ADCA oprx16,xysp ADCA [D,xysp] ADCA [oprx16,xysp]	(A) + (M) + C ⇒ A Add with Carry to A	IMM DIR EXT IDX IDX1 IDX2 [D,IDX] [IDX2]	89 ii 99 dd B9 hh ll A9 xb A9 xb ff A9 xb ee ff A9 xb A9 xb ee ff	P rfP rOP rfP rPO frPP fIfrfP fIPrfP	–	–	Δ	–	Δ	Δ	Δ	Δ
ADCB #opr8i ADCB opr8a ADCB opr16a ADCB oprx0_xysp ADCB oprx9,xysp ADCB oprx16,xysp ADCB [D,xysp] ADCB [oprx16,xysp]	(B) + (M) + C ⇒ B Add with Carry to B	IMM DIR EXT IDX IDX1 IDX2 [D,IDX] [IDX2]	C9 ii D9 dd F9 hh ll E9 xb E9 xb ff E9 xb ee ff E9 xb E9 xb ee ff	P rfP rOP rfP rPO frPP fIfrfP fIPrfP	–	–	Δ	–	Δ	Δ	Δ	Δ
ADDA #opr8i ADDA opr8a ADDA opr16a ADDA oprx0_xysp ADDA oprx9,xysp ADDA oprx16,xysp ADDA [D,xysp] ADDA [oprx16,xysp]	(A) + (M) ⇒ A Add without Carry to A	IMM DIR EXT IDX IDX1 IDX2 [D,IDX] [IDX2]	8B ii 9B dd BB hh ll AB xb AB xb ff AB xb ee ff AB xb AB xb ee ff	P rfP rOP rfP rPO frPP fIfrfP fIPrfP	–	–	Δ	–	Δ	Δ	Δ	Δ
ADDB #opr8i ADDB opr8a ADDB opr16a ADDB oprx0_xysp ADDB oprx9,xysp ADDB oprx16,xysp ADDB [D,xysp] ADDB [oprx16,xysp]	(B) + (M) ⇒ B Add without Carry to B	IMM DIR EXT IDX IDX1 IDX2 [D,IDX] [IDX2]	CB ii DB dd FB hh ll EB xb EB xb ff EB xb ee ff EB xb EB xb ee ff	P rfP rOP rfP rPO frPP fIfrfP fIPrfP	–	–	Δ	–	Δ	Δ	Δ	Δ
ADDD #opr16i ADDD opr8a ADDD opr16a ADDD oprx0_xysp ADDD oprx9,xysp ADDD oprx16,xysp ADDD [D,xysp] ADDD [oprx16,xysp]	(A:B) + (M:M+1) ⇒ A:B Add 16-Bit to D (A:B)	IMM DIR EXT IDX IDX1 IDX2 [D,IDX] [IDX2]	C3 jj kk D3 dd F3 hh ll E3 xb E3 xb ff E3 xb ee ff E3 xb E3 xb ee ff	OP RfP ROP RfP RPO fRPP fIfRfP fIPRfP	–	–	–	–	Δ	Δ	Δ	Δ
ANDA #opr8i ANDA opr8a ANDA opr16a ANDA oprx0_xysp ANDA oprx9,xysp ANDA oprx16,xysp ANDA [D,xysp] ANDA [oprx16,xysp]	(A) • (M) ⇒ A Logical And A with Memory	IMM DIR EXT IDX IDX1 IDX2 [D,IDX] [IDX2]	84 ii 94 dd B4 hh ll A4 xb A4 xb ff A4 xb ee ff A4 xb A4 xb ee ff	P rfP rOP rfP rPO frPP fIfrfP fIPrfP	–	–	–	–	Δ	Δ	0	–
ANDB #opr8i ANDB opr8a ANDB opr16a ANDB oprx0_xysp ANDB oprx9,xysp ANDB oprx16,xysp ANDB [D,xysp] ANDB [oprx16,xysp]	(B) • (M) ⇒ B Logical And B with Memory	IMM DIR EXT IDX IDX1 IDX2 [D,IDX] [IDX2]	C4 ii D4 dd F4 hh ll E4 xb E4 xb ff E4 xb ee ff E4 xb E4 xb ee ff	P rfP rOP rfP rPO frPP fIfrfP fIPrfP	–	–	–	–	Δ	Δ	0	–

Note 1. Due to internal CPU requirements, the program word fetch is performed twice to the same address during this instruction.

Instruction Set Summary (Continued)

Source Form	Operation	Addr. Mode	Machine Coding (hex)	Access Detail	S	X	H	I	N	Z	V	C
ANDCC #opr8i	(CCR) • (M) ⇒ CCR Logical And CCR with Memory	IMM	10 ii	P	⇓	⇓	⇓	⇓	⇓	⇓	⇓	⇓
ASL opr16a ASL oprx0_xysp ASL oprx9,xysp ASL oprx16,xysp ASL [D,xysp] ASL [oprx16,xysp] ASLA ASLB	Arithmetic Shift Left Arithmetic Shift Left Accumulator A Arithmetic Shift Left Accumulator B	EXT IDX IDX1 IDX2 [D,IDX] [IDX2] INH INH	78 hh ll 68 xb 68 xb ff 68 xb ee ff 68 xb 68 xb ee ff 48 58	rOPw rPw rPOw frPPw fIfrPw fIPrPw O O	–	–	–	–	Δ	Δ	Δ	Δ
ASLD	Arithmetic Shift Left Double	INH	59	O	–	–	–	–	Δ	Δ	Δ	Δ
ASR opr16a ASR oprx0_xysp ASR oprx9,xysp ASR oprx16,xysp ASR [D,xysp] ASR [oprx16,xysp] ASRA ASRB	Arithmetic Shift Right Arithmetic Shift Right Accumulator A Arithmetic Shift Right Accumulator B	EXT IDX IDX1 IDX2 [D,IDX] [IDX2] INH INH	77 hh ll 67 xb 67 xb ff 67 xb ee ff 67 xb 67 xb ee ff 47 57	rOPw rPw rPOw frPPw fIfrPw fIPrPw O O	–	–	–	–	Δ	Δ	Δ	Δ
BCC rel8	Branch if Carry Clear (if C = 0)	REL	24 rr	PPP/P[1]	–	–	–	–	–	–	–	–
BCLR opr8a, msk8 BCLR opr16a, msk8 BCLR oprx0_xysp, msk8 BCLR oprx9,xysp, msk8 BCLR oprx16,xysp, msk8	(M) • (mm) ⇒ M Clear Bit(s) in Memory	DIR EXT IDX IDX1 IDX2	4D dd mm 1D hh ll mm 0D xb mm 0D xb ff mm 0D xb ee ff mm	rPOw rPPw rPOw rPwP frPwOP	–	–	–	–	Δ	Δ	0	–
BCS rel8	Branch if Carry Set (if C = 1)	REL	25 rr	PPP/P[1]	–	–	–	–	–	–	–	–
BEQ rel8	Branch if Equal (if Z = 1)	REL	27 rr	PPP/P[1]	–	–	–	–	–	–	–	–
BGE rel8	Branch if Greater Than or Equal (if N ⊕ V = 0) (signed)	REL	2C rr	PPP/P[1]	–	–	–	–	–	–	–	–
BGND	Place CPU in Background Mode see CPU12 Reference Manual	INH	00	VfPPP	–	–	–	–	–	–	–	–
BGT rel8	Branch if Greater Than (if Z + (N ⊕ V) = 0) (signed)	REL	2E rr	PPP/P[1]	–	–	–	–	–	–	–	–
BHI rel8	Branch if Higher (if C + Z = 0) (unsigned)	REL	22 rr	PPP/P[1]	–	–	–	–	–	–	–	–
BHS rel8	Branch if Higher or Same (if C = 0) (unsigned) same function as BCC	REL	24 rr	PPP/P[1]	–	–	–	–	–	–	–	–
BITA #opr8i BITA opr8a BITA opr16a BITA oprx0_xysp BITA oprx9,xysp BITA oprx16,xysp BITA [D,xysp] BITA [oprx16,xysp]	(A) • (M) Logical And A with Memory	IMM DIR EXT IDX IDX1 IDX2 [D,IDX] [IDX2]	85 ii 95 dd B5 hh ll A5 xb A5 xb ff A5 xb ee ff A5 xb A5 xb ee ff	P rfP rOP rfP rPO frPP fIfrfP fIPrfP	–	–	–	–	Δ	Δ	0	–
BITB #opr8i BITB opr8a BITB opr16a BITB oprx0_xysp BITB oprx9,xysp BITB oprx16,xysp BITB [D,xysp] BITB [oprx16,xysp]	(B) • (M) Logical And B with Memory	IMM DIR EXT IDX IDX1 IDX2 [D,IDX] [IDX2]	C5 ii D5 dd F5 hh ll E5 xb E5 xb ff E5 xb ee ff E5 xb E5 xb ee ff	P rfP rOP rfP rPO frPP fIfrfP fIPrfP	–	–	–	–	Δ	Δ	0	–

Notes: 1. PPP/P indicates this instruction takes three cycles to refill the instruction queue if the branch is taken and one program fetch cycle if the branch is not taken.

CPU12 Reference Guide

Instruction Set Summary (Continued)

Source Form	Operation	Addr. Mode	Machine Coding (hex)	Access Detail	S	X	H	I	N	Z	V	C
BLE rel8	Branch if Less Than or Equal (if Z + (N ⊕ V) = 1) (signed)	REL	2F rr	PPP/P[1]	–	–	–	–	–	–	–	–
BLO rel8	Branch if Lower (if C = 1) (unsigned) same function as BCS	REL	25 rr	PPP/P[1]	–	–	–	–	–	–	–	–
BLS rel8	Branch if Lower or Same (if C + Z = 1) (unsigned)	REL	23 rr	PPP/P[1]	–	–	–	–	–	–	–	–
BLT rel8	Branch if Less Than (if N ⊕ V = 1) (signed)	REL	2D rr	PPP/P[1]	–	–	–	–	–	–	–	–
BMI rel8	Branch if Minus (if N = 1)	REL	2B rr	PPP/P[1]	–	–	–	–	–	–	–	–
BNE rel8	Branch if Not Equal (if Z = 0)	REL	26 rr	PPP/P[1]	–	–	–	–	–	–	–	–
BPL rel8	Branch if Plus (if N = 0)	REL	2A rr	PPP/P[1]	–	–	–	–	–	–	–	–
BRA rel8	Branch Always (if 1 = 1)	REL	20 rr	PPP	–	–	–	–	–	–	–	–
BRCLR opr8a, msk8, rel8 BRCLR opr16a, msk8, rel8 BRCLR oprx0_xysp, msk8, rel8 BRCLR oprx9,xysp, msk8, rel8 BRCLR oprx16,xysp, msk8, rel8	Branch if (M) • (mm) = 0 (if All Selected Bit(s) Clear)	DIR EXT IDX IDX1 IDX2	4F dd mm rr 1F hh ll mm rr 0F xb mm rr 0F xb ff mm rr 0F xb ee ff mm rr	rPPP rfPPP rPPP rffPPP frPffPPP	–	–	–	–	–	–	–	–
BRN rel8	Branch Never (if 1 = 0)	REL	21 rr	P	–	–	–	–	–	–	–	–
BRSET opr8, msk8, rel8 BRSET opr16a, msk8, rel8 BRSET oprx0_xysp, msk8, rel8 BRSET oprx9,xysp, msk8, rel8 BRSET oprx16,xysp, msk8, rel8	Branch if (M̄) • (mm) = 0 (if All Selected Bit(s) Set)	DIR EXT IDX IDX1 IDX2	4E dd mm rr 1E hh ll mm rr 0E xb mm rr 0E xb ff mm rr 0E xb ee ff mm rr	rPPP rfPPP rPPP rffPPP frPffPPP	–	–	–	–	–	–	–	–
BSET opr8, msk8 BSET opr16a, msk8 BSET oprx0_xysp, msk8 BSET oprx9,xysp, msk8 BSET oprx16,xysp, msk8	(M) + (mm) ⇒ M Set Bit(s) in Memory	DIR EXT IDX IDX1 IDX2	4C dd mm 1C hh ll mm 0C xb mm 0C xb ff mm 0C xb ee ff mm	rPOw rPPw rPOw rPwP frPwOP	–	–	–	–	Δ	Δ	0	–
BSR rel8	(SP) – 2 ⇒ SP; RTN$_H$:RTN$_L$ ⇒ M$_{(SP)}$:M$_{(SP+1)}$ Subroutine address ⇒ PC Branch to Subroutine	REL	07 rr	PPPS	–	–	–	–	–	–	–	–
BVC rel8	Branch if Overflow Bit Clear (if V = 0)	REL	28 rr	PPP/P[1]	–	–	–	–	–	–	–	–
BVS rel8	Branch if Overflow Bit Set (if V = 1)	REL	29 rr	PPP/P[1]	–	–	–	–	–	–	–	–
CALL opr16a, page CALL oprx0_xysp, page CALL oprx9,xysp, page CALL oprx16,xysp, page CALL [D,xysp] CALL [oprx16, xysp]	(SP) – 2 ⇒ SP; RTN$_H$:RTN$_L$ ⇒ M$_{(SP)}$:M$_{(SP+1)}$ (SP) – 1 ⇒ SP; (PPG) ⇒ M$_{(SP)}$; pg ⇒ PPAGE register; Program address ⇒ PC Call subroutine in extended memory (Program may be located on another expansion memory page.) Indirect modes get program address and new pg value based on pointer.	EXT IDX IDX1 IDX2 [D,IDX] [IDX2]	4A hh ll pg 4B xb pg 4B xb ff pg 4B xb ee ff pg 4B xb 4B xb ee ff	gnfSsPPP gnfSsPPP gnfSsPPP fgnfSsPPP fIignSsPPP fIignSsPPP	–	–	–	–	–	–	–	–
CBA	(A) – (B) Compare 8-Bit Accumulators	INH	18 17	OO	–	–	–	–	Δ	Δ	Δ	Δ
CLC	0 ⇒ C Translates to ANDCC #$FE	IMM	10 FE	P	–	–	–	–	–	–	–	0
CLI	0 ⇒ I Translates to ANDCC #$EF (enables I-bit interrupts)	IMM	10 EF	P	–	–	–	0	–	–	–	–

Notes
1. PPP/P indicates this instruction takes three cycles to refill the instruction queue if the branch is taken and one program fetch cycle if the branch is not taken.

Instruction Set Summary (Continued)

Source Form	Operation	Addr. Mode	Machine Coding (hex)	Access Detail	S	X	H	I	N	Z	V	C
CLR opr16a CLR oprx0_xysp CLR oprx9,xysp CLR oprx16,xysp CLR [D,xysp] CLR [oprx16,xysp]	0 ⇒ M Clear Memory Location	EXT IDX IDX1 IDX2 [D,IDX] [IDX2]	79 hh ll 69 xb 69 xb ff 69 xb ee ff 69 xb 69 xb ee ff	wOP Pw PwO PwP PIfPw PIPPw	–	–	–	–	0	1	0	0
CLRA CLRB	0 ⇒ A Clear Accumulator A 0 ⇒ B Clear Accumulator B	INH INH	87 C7	O O								
CLV	0 ⇒ V *Translates to* ANDCC #$FD	IMM	10 FD	P	–	–	–	–	–	–	0	–
CMPA #opr8i CMPA opr8a CMPA opr16a CMPA oprx0_xysp CMPA oprx9,xysp CMPA oprx16,xysp CMPA [D,xysp] CMPA [oprx16,xysp]	(A) – (M) Compare Accumulator A with Memory	IMM DIR EXT IDX IDX1 IDX2 [D,IDX] [IDX2]	81 ii 91 dd B1 hh ll A1 xb A1 xb ff A1 xb ee ff A1 xb A1 xb ee ff	P rfP rOP rfP rPO frPP fIfrfP fIPrfP	–	–	–	–	Δ	Δ	Δ	Δ
CMPB #opr8i CMPB opr8a CMPB opr16a CMPB oprx0_xysp CMPB oprx9,xysp CMPB oprx16,xysp CMPB [D,xysp] CMPB [oprx16,xysp]	(B) – (M) Compare Accumulator B with Memory	IMM DIR EXT IDX IDX1 IDX2 [D,IDX] [IDX2]	C1 ii D1 dd F1 hh ll E1 xb E1 xb ff E1 xb ee ff E1 xb E1 xb ee ff	P rfP rOP rfP rPO frPP fIfrfP fIPrfP	–	–	–	–	Δ	Δ	Δ	Δ
COM opr16a COM oprx0_xysp COM oprx9,xysp COM oprx16,xysp COM [D,xysp] COM [oprx16,xysp]	(M̄) ⇒ M *equivalent to* $FF – (M) ⇒ M 1's Complement Memory Location	EXT IDX IDX1 IDX2 [D,IDX] [IDX2]	71 hh ll 61 xb 61 xb ff 61 xb ee ff 61 xb 61 xb ee ff	rOPw rPw rPOw frPPw fIfrPw fIPrPw	–	–	–	–	Δ	Δ	0	1
COMA COMB	(Ā) ⇒ A Complement Accumulator A (B̄) ⇒ B Complement Accumulator B	INH INH	41 51	O O								
CPD #opr16i CPD opr8a CPD opr16a CPD oprx0_xysp CPD oprx9,xysp CPD oprx16,xysp CPD [D,xysp] CPD [oprx16,xysp]	(A:B) – (M:M+1) Compare D to Memory (16-Bit)	IMM DIR EXT IDX IDX1 IDX2 [D,IDX] [IDX2]	8C jj kk 9C dd BC hh ll AC xb AC xb ff AC xb ee ff AC xb AC xb ee ff	OP RfP ROP RfP RPO fRPP fIfRfP fIPRfP	–	–	–	–	Δ	Δ	Δ	Δ
CPS #opr16i CPS opr8a CPS opr16a CPS oprx0_xysp CPS oprx9,xysp CPS oprx16,xysp CPS [D,xysp] CPS [oprx16,xysp]	(SP) – (M:M+1) Compare SP to Memory (16-Bit)	IMM DIR EXT IDX IDX1 IDX2 [D,IDX] [IDX2]	8F jj kk 9F dd BF hh ll AF xb AF xb ff AF xb ee ff AF xb AF xb ee ff	OP RfP ROP RfP RPO fRPP fIfRfP fIPRfP	–	–	–	–	Δ	Δ	Δ	Δ
CPX #opr16i CPX opr8a CPX opr16a CPX oprx0_xysp CPX oprx9,xysp CPX oprx16,xysp CPX [D,xysp] CPX [oprx16,xysp]	(X) – (M:M+1) Compare X to Memory (16-Bit)	IMM DIR EXT IDX IDX1 IDX2 [D,IDX] [IDX2]	8E jj kk 9E dd BE hh ll AE xb AE xb ff AE xb ee ff AE xb AE xb ee ff	OP RfP ROP RfP RPO fRPP fIfRfP fIPRfP	–	–	–	–	Δ	Δ	Δ	Δ
CPY #opr16i CPY opr8a CPY opr16a CPY oprx0_xysp CPY oprx9,xysp CPY oprx16,xysp CPY [D,xysp] CPY [oprx16,xysp]	(Y) – (M:M+1) Compare Y to Memory (16-Bit)	IMM DIR EXT IDX IDX1 IDX2 [D,IDX] [IDX2]	8D jj kk 9D dd BD hh ll AD xb AD xb ff AD xb ee ff AD xb AD xb ee ff	OP RfP ROP RfP RPO fRPP fIfRfP fIPRfP	–	–	–	–	Δ	Δ	Δ	Δ

CPU12 Reference Guide

Instruction Set Summary (Continued)

Source Form	Operation	Addr. Mode	Machine Coding (hex)	Access Detail	S	X	H	I	N	Z	V	C
DAA	Adjust Sum to BCD Decimal Adjust Accumulator A	INH	18 07	OfO	–	–	–	–	Δ	Δ	?	Δ
DBEQ *abdxys, rel9*	(cntr) – 1 ⇒ cntr if (cntr) = 0, then Branch else Continue to next instruction Decrement Counter and Branch if = 0 (cntr = A, B, D, X, Y, or SP)	REL (9-bit)	04 lb rr	PPP	–	–	–	–	–	–	–	–
DBNE *abdxys, rel9*	(cntr) – 1 ⇒ cntr If (cntr) not = 0, then Branch; else Continue to next instruction Decrement Counter and Branch if ≠ 0 (cntr = A, B, D, X, Y, or SP)	REL (9-bit)	04 lb rr	PPP	–	–	–	–	–	–	–	–
DEC *opr16a* DEC *oprx0_xysp* DEC *oprx9,xysp* DEC *oprx16,xysp* DEC [D,*xysp*] DEC [*oprx16,xysp*] DECA DECB	(M) – $01 ⇒ M Decrement Memory Location (A) – $01 ⇒ A Decrement A (B) – $01 ⇒ B Decrement B	EXT IDX IDX1 IDX2 [D,IDX] [IDX2] INH INH	73 hh 11 63 xb 63 xb ff 63 xb ee ff 63 xb 63 xb ee ff 43 53	rOPw rPw rPOw frPPw fIfrPw fIPrPw O O	–	–	–	–	Δ	Δ	Δ	–
DES	(SP) – $0001 ⇒ SP *Translates to* LEAS –1,SP	IDX	1B 9F	PP[1]	–	–	–	–	–	–	–	–
DEX	(X) – $0001 ⇒ X Decrement Index Register X	INH	09	O	–	–	–	–	–	Δ	–	–
DEY	(Y) – $0001 ⇒ Y Decrement Index Register Y	INH	03	O	–	–	–	–	–	Δ	–	–
EDIV	(Y:D) ÷ (X) ⇒ Y Remainder ⇒ D 32 × 16 Bit ⇒ 16 Bit Divide (unsigned)	INH	11	ffffffffffO	–	–	–	–	Δ	Δ	Δ	Δ
EDIVS	(Y:D) ÷ (X) ⇒ Y Remainder ⇒ D 32 × 16 Bit ⇒ 16 Bit Divide (signed)	INH	18 14	OfffffffffO	–	–	–	–	Δ	Δ	Δ	Δ
EMACS *opr16a* [2]	$(M_{(X)}:M_{(X+1)}) \times (M_{(Y)}:M_{(Y+1)}) + (M\sim M+3) \Rightarrow M\sim M+3$ 16 × 16 Bit ⇒ 32 Bit Multiply and Accumulate (signed)	Special	18 12 hh 11	ORROffRRfWWP	–	–	–	–	Δ	Δ	Δ	Δ
EMAXD *oprx0_xysp* EMAXD *oprx9,xysp* EMAXD *oprx16,xysp* EMAXD [D,*xysp*] EMAXD [*oprx16,xysp*]	MAX((D), (M:M+1)) ⇒ D MAX of 2 Unsigned 16-Bit Values N, Z, V and C status bits reflect result of internal compare ((D) – (M:M+1))	IDX IDX1 IDX2 [D,IDX] [IDX2]	18 1A xb 18 1A xb ff 18 1A xb ee ff 18 1A xb 18 1A xb ee ff	ORfP ORPO OfRPP OfIfRfP OfIPRfP	–	–	–	–	Δ	Δ	Δ	Δ
EMAXM *oprx0_xysp* EMAXM *oprx9,xysp* EMAXM *oprx16,xysp* EMAXM [D,*xysp*] EMAXM [*oprx16,xysp*]	MAX((D), (M:M+1)) ⇒ M:M+1 MAX of 2 Unsigned 16-Bit Values N, Z, V and C status bits reflect result of internal compare ((D) – (M:M+1))	IDX IDX1 IDX2 [D,IDX] [IDX2]	18 1E xb 18 1E xb ff 18 1E xb ee ff 18 1E xb 18 1E xb ee ff	ORPW ORPWO OfRPWP OfIfRPW OfIPRPW	–	–	–	–	Δ	Δ	Δ	Δ
EMIND *oprx0_xysp* EMIND *oprx9,xysp* EMIND *oprx16,xysp* EMIND [D,*xysp*] EMIND [*oprx16,xysp*]	MIN((D), (M:M+1)) ⇒ D MIN of 2 Unsigned 16-Bit Values N, Z, V and C status bits reflect result of internal compare ((D) – (M:M+1))	IDX IDX1 IDX2 [D,IDX] [IDX2]	18 1B xb 18 1B xb ff 18 1B xb ee ff 18 1B xb 18 1B xb ee ff	ORfP ORPO OfRPP OfIfRfP OfIPRfP	–	–	–	–	Δ	Δ	Δ	Δ
EMINM *oprx0_xysp* EMINM *oprx9,xysp* EMINM *oprx16,xysp* EMINM [D,*xysp*] EMINM [*oprx16,xysp*]	MIN((D), (M:M+1)) ⇒ M:M+1 MIN of 2 Unsigned 16-Bit Values N, Z, V and C status bits reflect result of internal compare ((D) – (M:M+1))	IDX IDX1 IDX2 [D,IDX] [IDX2]	18 1F xb 18 1F xb ff 18 1F xb ee ff 18 1F xb 18 1F xb ee ff	ORPW ORPWO OfRPWP OfIfRPW OfIPRPW	–	–	–	–	Δ	Δ	Δ	Δ
EMUL	(D) × (Y) ⇒ Y:D 16 × 16 Bit Multiply (unsigned)	INH	13	ffO	–	–	–	–	Δ	Δ	–	Δ

Notes
1. Due to internal CPU requirements, the program word fetch is performed twice to the same address during this instruction.
2. *opr16a* is an extended address specification. Both X and Y point to source operands.

Instruction Set Summary (Continued)

Source Form	Operation	Addr. Mode	Machine Coding (hex)	Access Detail	S	X	H	I	N	Z	V	C
EMULS	(D) × (Y) ⇒ Y:D 16 × 16 Bit Multiply (signed)	INH	18 13	OfO	–	–	–	–	Δ	Δ	–	Δ
EORA #*opr8i* EORA *opr8a* EORA *opr16a* EORA *oprx0_xysp* EORA *oprx9,xysp* EORA *oprx16,xysp* EORA [D,*xysp*] EORA [*oprx16,xysp*]	(A) ⊕ (M) ⇒ A Exclusive-OR A with Memory	IMM DIR EXT IDX IDX1 IDX2 [D,IDX] [IDX2]	88 ii 98 dd B8 hh ll A8 xb A8 xb ff A8 xb ee ff A8 xb A8 xb ee ff	P rfP rOP rfP rPO frPP fIfrfP fIPrfP	–	–	–	–	Δ	Δ	0	–
EORB #*opr8i* EORB *opr8a* EORB *opr16a* EORB *oprx0_xysp* EORB *oprx9,xysp* EORB *oprx16,xysp* EORB [D,*xysp*] EORB [*oprx16,xysp*]	(B) ⊕ (M) ⇒ B Exclusive-OR B with Memory	IMM DIR EXT IDX IDX1 IDX2 [D,IDX] [IDX2]	C8 ii D8 dd F8 hh ll E8 xb E8 xb ff E8 xb ee ff E8 xb E8 xb ee ff	P rfP rOP rfP rPO frPP fIfrfP fIPrfP	–	–	–	–	Δ	Δ	0	–
ETBL *oprx0_xysp*	(M:M+1)+ [(B)×((M+2:M+3) − (M:M+1))] ⇒ D 16-Bit Table Lookup and Interpolate Initialize B, and index before ETBL. <ea> points at first table entry (M:M+1) and B is fractional part of lookup value (no indirect addr. modes or extensions allowed)	IDX	18 3F xb	ORRfffffP	–	–	–	–	Δ	Δ	–	?
EXG *abcdxys,abcdxys*	(r1) ⇔ (r2) (if r1 and r2 same size) *or* $00:(r1) ⇒ r2 (if r1=8-bit; r2=16-bit) *or* (r1$_{low}$) ⇔ (r2) (if r1=16-bit; r2=8-bit) r1 and r2 may be A, B, CCR, D, X, Y, or SP	INH	B7 eb	P	–	–	–	–	–	–	–	–
FDIV	(D) ÷ (X) ⇒ X; Remainder ⇒ D 16 × 16 Bit Fractional Divide	INH	18 11	OfffffffffO	–	–	–	–	–	Δ	Δ	Δ
IBEQ *abdxys, rel9*	(cntr) + 1 ⇒ cntr If (cntr) = 0, then Branch else Continue to next instruction Increment Counter and Branch if = 0 (cntr = A, B, D, X, Y, or SP)	REL (9-bit)	04 lb rr	PPP	–	–	–	–	–	–	–	–
IBNE *abdxys, rel9*	(cntr) + 1 ⇒ cntr if (cntr) not = 0, then Branch; else Continue to next instruction Increment Counter and Branch if ≠ 0 (cntr = A, B, D, X, Y, or SP)	REL (9-bit)	04 lb rr	PPP	–	–	–	–	–	–	–	–
IDIV	(D) ÷ (X) ⇒ X; Remainder ⇒ D 16 × 16 Bit Integer Divide (unsigned)	INH	18 10	OfffffffffO	–	–	–	–	–	Δ	0	Δ
IDIVS	(D) ÷ (X) ⇒ X; Remainder ⇒ D 16 × 16 Bit Integer Divide (signed)	INH	18 15	OfffffffffO	–	–	–	–	Δ	Δ	Δ	Δ
INC *opr16a* INC *oprx0_xysp* INC *oprx9,xysp* INC *oprx16,xysp* INC [D,*xysp*] INC [*oprx16,xysp*] INCA INCB	(M) + $01 ⇒ M Increment Memory Byte (A) + $01 ⇒ A Increment Acc. A (B) + $01 ⇒ B Increment Acc. B	EXT IDX IDX1 IDX2 [D,IDX] [IDX2] INH INH	72 hh ll 62 xb 62 xb ff 62 xb ee ff 62 xb 62 xb ee ff 42 52	rOPw rPw rPOw frPPw fIfrPw fIPrPw O O	–	–	–	–	Δ	Δ	Δ	–
INS	(SP) + $0001 ⇒ SP *Translates to* LEAS 1,SP	IDX	1B 81	PP[1]	–	–	–	–	–	–	–	–
INX	(X) + $0001 ⇒ X Increment Index Register X	INH	08	O	–	–	–	–	–	Δ	–	–
INY	(Y) + $0001 ⇒ Y Increment Index Register Y	INH	02	O	–	–	–	–	–	Δ	–	–

Note 1. Due to internal CPU requirements, the program word fetch is performed twice to the same address during this instruction.

CPU12 Reference Guide

Instruction Set Summary (Continued)

Source Form	Operation	Addr. Mode	Machine Coding (hex)	Access Detail	S	X	H	I	N	Z	V	C
JMP opr16a	Subroutine address ⇒ PC	EXT	06 hh ll	PPP	–	–	–	–	–	–	–	–
JMP oprx0_xysp		IDX	05 xb	PPP								
JMP oprx9,xysp	Jump	IDX1	05 xb ff	PPP								
JMP oprx16,xysp		IDX2	05 xb ee ff	fPPP								
JMP [D,xysp]		[D,IDX]	05 xb	fIfPPP								
JMP [oprx16,xysp]		[IDX2]	05 xb ee ff	fIfPPP								
JSR opr8a	(SP) – 2 ⇒ SP;	DIR	17 dd	PPPS	–	–	–	–	–	–	–	–
JSR opr16a	RTN$_H$:RTN$_L$ ⇒ M$_{(SP)}$:M$_{(SP+1)}$;	EXT	16 hh ll	PPPS								
JSR oprx0_xysp	Subroutine address ⇒ PC	IDX	15 xb	PPPS								
JSR oprx9,xysp		IDX1	15 xb ff	PPPS								
JSR oprx16,xysp	Jump to Subroutine	IDX2	15 xb ee ff	fPPPS								
JSR [D,xysp]		[D,IDX]	15 xb	fIfPPPS								
JSR [oprx16,xysp]		[IDX2]	15 xb ee ff	fIfPPPS								
LBCC rel16	Long Branch if Carry Clear (if C = 0)	REL	18 24 qq rr	OPPP/OPO[1]	–	–	–	–	–	–	–	–
LBCS rel16	Long Branch if Carry Set (if C = 1)	REL	18 25 qq rr	OPPP/OPO[1]	–	–	–	–	–	–	–	–
LBEQ rel16	Long Branch if Equal (if Z = 1)	REL	18 27 qq rr	OPPP/OPO[1]	–	–	–	–	–	–	–	–
LBGE rel16	Long Branch Greater Than or Equal (if N ⊕ V = 0) (signed)	REL	18 2C qq rr	OPPP/OPO[1]	–	–	–	–	–	–	–	–
LBGT rel16	Long Branch if Greater Than (if Z + (N ⊕ V) = 0) (signed)	REL	18 2E qq rr	OPPP/OPO[1]	–	–	–	–	–	–	–	–
LBHI rel16	Long Branch if Higher (if C + Z = 0) (unsigned)	REL	18 22 qq rr	OPPP/OPO[1]	–	–	–	–	–	–	–	–
LBHS rel16	Long Branch if Higher or Same (if C = 0) (unsigned) same function as LBCC	REL	18 24 qq rr	OPPP/OPO[1]	–	–	–	–	–	–	–	–
LBLE rel16	Long Branch if Less Than or Equal (if Z + (N ⊕ V) = 1) (signed)	REL	18 2F qq rr	OPPP/OPO[1]	–	–	–	–	–	–	–	–
LBLO rel16	Long Branch if Lower (if C = 1) (unsigned) same function as LBCS	REL	18 25 qq rr	OPPP/OPO[1]	–	–	–	–	–	–	–	–
LBLS rel16	Long Branch if Lower or Same (if C + Z = 1) (unsigned)	REL	18 23 qq rr	OPPP/OPO[1]	–	–	–	–	–	–	–	–
LBLT rel16	Long Branch if Less Than (if N ⊕ V = 1) (signed)	REL	18 2D qq rr	OPPP/OPO[1]	–	–	–	–	–	–	–	–
LBMI rel16	Long Branch if Minus (if N = 1)	REL	18 2B qq rr	OPPP/OPO[1]	–	–	–	–	–	–	–	–
LBNE rel16	Long Branch if Not Equal (if Z = 0)	REL	18 26 qq rr	OPPP/OPO[1]	–	–	–	–	–	–	–	–
LBPL rel16	Long Branch if Plus (if N = 0)	REL	18 2A qq rr	OPPP/OPO[1]	–	–	–	–	–	–	–	–
LBRA rel16	Long Branch Always (if 1=1)	REL	18 20 qq rr	OPPP	–	–	–	–	–	–	–	–
LBRN rel16	Long Branch Never (if 1 = 0)	REL	18 21 qq rr	OPO	–	–	–	–	–	–	–	–
LBVC rel16	Long Branch if Overflow Bit Clear (if V=0)	REL	18 28 qq rr	OPPP/OPO[1]	–	–	–	–	–	–	–	–
LBVS rel16	Long Branch if Overflow Bit Set (if V = 1)	REL	18 29 qq rr	OPPP/OPO[1]	–	–	–	–	–	–	–	–
LDAA #opr8i	(M) ⇒ A	IMM	86 ii	P	–	–	–	–	Δ	Δ	0	–
LDAA opr8a	Load Accumulator A	DIR	96 dd	rfP								
LDAA opr16a		EXT	B6 hh ll	rOP								
LDAA oprx0_xysp		IDX	A6 xb	rfP								
LDAA oprx9,xysp		IDX1	A6 xb ff	rPO								
LDAA oprx16,xysp		IDX2	A6 xb ee ff	frPP								
LDAA [D,xysp]		[D,IDX]	A6 xb	fIfrfP								
LDAA [oprx16,xysp]		[IDX2]	A6 xb ee ff	fIPrfP								
LDAB #opr8i	(M) ⇒ B	IMM	C6 ii	P	–	–	–	–	Δ	Δ	0	–
LDAB opr8a	Load Accumulator B	DIR	D6 dd	rfP								
LDAB opr16a		EXT	F6 hh ll	rOP								
LDAB oprx0_xysp		IDX	E6 xb	rfP								
LDAB oprx9,xysp		IDX1	E6 xb ff	rPO								
LDAB oprx16,xysp		IDX2	E6 xb ee ff	frPP								
LDAB [D,xysp]		[D,IDX]	E6 xb	fIfrfP								
LDAB [oprx16,xysp]		[IDX2]	E6 xb ee ff	fIPrfP								

Note 1. OPPP/OPO indicates this instruction takes four cycles to refill the instruction queue if the branch is taken and three cycles if the branch is not taken.

Instruction Set Summary (Continued)

Source Form	Operation	Addr. Mode	Machine Coding (hex)	Access Detail	S	X	H	I	N	Z	V	C
LDD #opr16i	(M:M+1) ⇒ A:B	IMM	CC jj kk	OP	-	-	-	-	Δ	Δ	0	-
LDD opr8a	Load Double Accumulator D (A:B)	DIR	DC dd	RfP								
LDD opr16a		EXT	FC hh ll	ROP								
LDD oprx0_xysp		IDX	EC xb	RfP								
LDD oprx9,xysp		IDX1	EC xb ff	RPO								
LDD oprx16,xysp		IDX2	EC xb ee ff	fRPP								
LDD [D,xysp]		[D,IDX]	EC xb	fIfRfP								
LDD [oprx16,xysp]		[IDX2]	EC xb ee ff	fIPRfP								
LDS #opr16i	(M:M+1) ⇒ SP	IMM	CF jj kk	OP	-	-	-	-	Δ	Δ	0	-
LDS opr8a	Load Stack Pointer	DIR	DF dd	RfP								
LDS opr16a		EXT	FF hh ll	ROP								
LDS oprx0_xysp		IDX	EF xb	RfP								
LDS oprx9,xysp		IDX1	EF xb ff	RPO								
LDS oprx16,xysp		IDX2	EF xb ee ff	fRPP								
LDS [D,xysp]		[D,IDX]	EF xb	fIfRfP								
LDS [oprx16,xysp]		[IDX2]	EF xb ee ff	fIPRfP								
LDX #opr16i	(M:M+1) ⇒ X	IMM	CE jj kk	OP	-	-	-	-	Δ	Δ	0	-
LDX opr8a	Load Index Register X	DIR	DE dd	RfP								
LDX opr16a		EXT	FE hh ll	ROP								
LDX oprx0_xysp		IDX	EE xb	RfP								
LDX oprx9,xysp		IDX1	EE xb ff	RPO								
LDX oprx16,xysp		IDX2	EE xb ee ff	fRPP								
LDX [D,xysp]		[D,IDX]	EE xb	fIfRfP								
LDX [oprx16,xysp]		[IDX2]	EE xb ee ff	fIPRfP								
LDY #opr16i	(M:M+1) ⇒ Y	IMM	CD jj kk	OP	-	-	-	-	Δ	Δ	0	-
LDY opr8a	Load Index Register Y	DIR	DD dd	RfP								
LDY opr16a		EXT	FD hh ll	ROP								
LDY oprx0_xysp		IDX	ED xb	RfP								
LDY oprx9,xysp		IDX1	ED xb ff	RPO								
LDY oprx16,xysp		IDX2	ED xb ee ff	fRPP								
LDY [D,xysp]		[D,IDX]	ED xb	fIfRfP								
LDY [oprx16,xysp]		[IDX2]	ED xb ee ff	fIPRfP								
LEAS oprx0_xysp	Effective Address ⇒ SP	IDX	1B xb	PP[1]	-	-	-	-	-	-	-	-
LEAS oprx9,xysp	Load Effective Address into SP	IDX1	1B xb ff	PO								
LEAS oprx16,xysp		IDX2	1B xb ee ff	PP								
LEAX oprx0_xysp	Effective Address ⇒ X	IDX	1A xb	PP[1]	-	-	-	-	-	-	-	-
LEAX oprx9,xysp	Load Effective Address into X	IDX1	1A xb ff	PO								
LEAX oprx16,xysp		IDX2	1A xb ee ff	PP								
LEAY oprx0_xysp	Effective Address ⇒ Y	IDX	19 xb	PP[1]	-	-	-	-	-	-	-	-
LEAY oprx9,xysp	Load Effective Address into Y	IDX1	19 xb ff	PO								
LEAY oprx16,xysp		IDX2	19 xb ee ff	PP								
LSL opr16a		EXT	78 hh ll	rOPw	-	-	-	-	Δ	Δ	Δ	Δ
LSL oprx0_xysp		IDX	68 xb	rPw								
LSL oprx9,xysp		IDX1	68 xb ff	rPOw								
LSL oprx16,xysp	Logical Shift Left	IDX2	68 xb ee ff	frPPw								
LSL [D,xysp]	same function as ASL	[D,IDX]	68 xb	fIfrPw								
LSL [oprx16,xysp]		[IDX2]	68 xb ee ff	fIPrPw								
LSLA	Logical Shift Accumulator A to Left	INH	48	O								
LSLB	Logical Shift Accumulator B to Left	INH	58	O								
LSLD	Logical Shift Left D Accumulator same function as ASLD	INH	59	O	-	-	-	-	Δ	Δ	Δ	Δ
LSR opr16a		EXT	74 hh ll	rOPw	-	-	-	-	0	Δ	Δ	Δ
LSR oprx0_xysp		IDX	64 xb	rPw								
LSR oprx9,xysp		IDX1	64 xb ff	rPOw								
LSR oprx16,xysp	Logical Shift Right	IDX2	64 xb ee ff	frPPw								
LSR [D,xysp]		[D,IDX]	64 xb	fIfrPw								
LSR [oprx16,xysp]		[IDX2]	64 xb ee ff	fIPrPw								
LSRA	Logical Shift Accumulator A to Right	INH	44	O								
LSRB	Logical Shift Accumulator B to Right	INH	54	O								

Note 1. Due to internal CPU requirements, the program word fetch is performed twice to the same address during this instruction.

CPU12 Reference Guide

Instruction Set Summary (Continued)

Source Form	Operation	Addr. Mode	Machine Coding (hex)	Access Detail	S	X	H	I	N	Z	V	C
LSRD	$0 \to$ [b7 A b0] [b7 B b0] $\to$ C Logical Shift Right D Accumulator	INH	49	O	–	–	–	–	0	Δ	Δ	Δ
MAXA oprx0_xysp MAXA oprx9,xysp MAXA oprx16,xysp MAXA [D,xysp] MAXA [oprx16,xysp]	MAX((A), (M)) $\Rightarrow$ A MAX of 2 Unsigned 8-Bit Values N, Z, V and C status bits reflect result of internal compare ((A) – (M)).	IDX IDX1 IDX2 [D,IDX] [IDX2]	18 18 xb 18 18 xb ff 18 18 xb ee ff 18 18 xb 18 18 xb ee ff	OrfP OrPO OfrPP OfIfrfP OfIPrfP	–	–	–	–	Δ	Δ	Δ	Δ
MAXM oprx0_xysp MAXM oprx9,xysp MAXM oprx16,xysp MAXM [D,xysp] MAXM [oprx16,xysp]	MAX((A), (M)) $\Rightarrow$ M MAX of 2 Unsigned 8-Bit Values N, Z, V and C status bits reflect result of internal compare ((A) – (M)).	IDX IDX1 IDX2 [D,IDX] [IDX2]	18 1C xb 18 1C xb ff 18 1C xb ee ff 18 1C xb 18 1C xb ee ff	OrPw OrPwO OfrPwP OfIfrPw OfIPrPw	–	–	–	–	Δ	Δ	Δ	Δ
MEM	μ (grade) $\Rightarrow M_{(Y)}$; (X) + 4 $\Rightarrow$ X; (Y) + 1 $\Rightarrow$ Y; A unchanged if (A) < P1 or (A) > P2 then μ = 0, else μ = MIN[((A) – P1)×S1, (P2 – (A))×S2, $FF] where: A = current crisp input value; X points at 4-byte data structure that describes a trapezoidal membership function (P1, P2, S1, S2); Y points at fuzzy input (RAM location). See CPU12 Reference Manual for special cases.	Special	01	RRfOw	–	–	?	–	?	?	?	?
MINA oprx0_xysp MINA oprx9,xysp MINA oprx16,xysp MINA [D,xysp] MINA [oprx16,xysp]	MIN((A), (M)) $\Rightarrow$ A MIN of 2 Unsigned 8-Bit Values N, Z, V and C status bits reflect result of internal compare ((A) – (M)).	IDX IDX1 IDX2 [D,IDX] [IDX2]	18 19 xb 18 19 xb ff 18 19 xb ee ff 18 19 xb 18 19 xb ee ff	OrfP OrPO OfrPP OfIfrfP OfIPrfP	–	–	–	–	Δ	Δ	Δ	Δ
MINM oprx0_xysp MINM oprx9,xysp MINM oprx16,xysp MINM [D,xysp] MINM [oprx16,xysp]	MIN((A), (M)) $\Rightarrow$ M MIN of 2 Unsigned 8-Bit Values N, Z, V and C status bits reflect result of internal compare ((A) – (M)).	IDX IDX1 IDX2 [D,IDX] [IDX2]	18 1D xb 18 1D xb ff 18 1D xb ee ff 18 1D xb 18 1D xb ee ff	OrPw OrPwO OfrPwP OfIfrPw OfIPrPw	–	–	–	–	Δ	Δ	Δ	Δ
MOVB #opr8, opr16a[1] MOVB #opr8i, oprx0_xysp[1] MOVB opr16a, opr16a[1] MOVB opr16a, oprx0_xysp[1] MOVB oprx0_xysp, opr16a[1] MOVB oprx0_xysp, oprx0_xysp[1]	$(M_1) \Rightarrow M_2$ Memory to Memory Byte-Move (8-Bit)	IMM-EXT IMM-IDX EXT-EXT EXT-IDX IDX-EXT IDX-IDX	18 0B ii hh ll 18 08 xb ii 18 0C hh ll hh ll 18 09 xb hh ll 18 0D xb hh ll 18 0A xb xb	OPwP OPwO OrPwPO OrPwP OrPwP OrPwO	–	–	–	–	–	–	–	–
MOVW #oprx16, opr16a[1] MOVW #opr16i, oprx0_xysp[1] MOVW opr16a, opr16a[1] MOVW opr16a, oprx0_xysp[1] MOVW oprx0_xysp, opr16a[1] MOVW oprx0_xysp, oprx0_xysp[1]	$(M:M+1_1) \Rightarrow M:M+1_2$ Memory to Memory Word-Move (16-Bit)	IMM-EXT IMM-IDX EXT-EXT EXT-IDX IDX-EXT IDX-IDX	18 03 jj kk hh ll 18 00 xb jj kk 18 04 hh ll hh ll 18 01 xb hh ll 18 05 xb hh ll 18 02 xb xb	OPWPO OPPW ORPWPO OPRPW ORPWP ORPWO	–	–	–	–	–	–	–	–
MUL	(A) × (B) $\Rightarrow$ A:B 8 × 8 Unsigned Multiply	INH	12	ffo	–	–	–	–	–	–	–	Δ
NEG opr16a NEG oprx0_xysp NEG oprx9,xysp NEG oprx16,xysp NEG [D,xysp] NEG [oprx16,xysp] NEGA NEGB	0 – (M) $\Rightarrow$ M or $(\overline{M})$ + 1 $\Rightarrow$ M Two's Complement Negate 0 – (A) $\Rightarrow$ A equivalent to $(\overline{A})$ + 1 $\Rightarrow$ A Negate Accumulator A 0 – (B) $\Rightarrow$ B equivalent to $(\overline{B})$ + 1 $\Rightarrow$ B Negate Accumulator B	EXT IDX IDX1 IDX2 [D,IDX] [IDX2] INH INH	70 hh ll 60 xb 60 xb ff 60 xb ee ff 60 xb 60 xb ee ff 40 50	rOPw rPw rPOw frPPw fIfrPw fIPrPw O O	–	–	–	–	Δ	Δ	Δ	Δ
NOP	No Operation	INH	A7	O	–	–	–	–	–	–	–	–

Note 1. The first operand in the source code statement specifies the source for the move.

Instruction Set Summary (Continued)

Source Form	Operation	Addr. Mode	Machine Coding (hex)	Access Detail	S	X	H	I	N	Z	V	C
ORAA #opr8i ORAA opr8a ORAA opr16a ORAA oprx0_xysp ORAA oprx9,xysp ORAA oprx16,xysp ORAA [D,xysp] ORAA [oprx16,xysp]	(A) + (M) ⇒ A Logical OR A with Memory	IMM DIR EXT IDX IDX1 IDX2 [D,IDX] [IDX2]	8A ii 9A dd BA hh ll AA xb AA xb ff AA xb ee ff AA xb AA xb ee ff	P rfP rOP rfP rPO frPP fIfrfP fIPrfP	–	–	–	–	Δ	Δ	0	–
ORAB #opr8i ORAB opr8a ORAB opr16a ORAB oprx0_xysp ORAB oprx9,xysp ORAB oprx16,xysp ORAB [D,xysp] ORAB [oprx16,xysp]	(B) + (M) ⇒ B Logical OR B with Memory	IMM DIR EXT IDX IDX1 IDX2 [D,IDX] [IDX2]	CA ii DA dd FA hh ll EA xb EA xb ff EA xb ee ff EA xb EA xb ee ff	P rfP rOP rfP rPO frPP fIfrfP fIPrfP	–	–	–	–	Δ	Δ	0	–
ORCC #opr8i	(CCR) + M ⇒ CCR Logical OR CCR with Memory	IMM	14 ii	P	⇑	–	⇑	⇑	⇑	⇑	⇑	⇑
PSHA	(SP) – 1 ⇒ SP; (A) ⇒ M$_{(SP)}$ Push Accumulator A onto Stack	INH	36	Os	–	–	–	–	–	–	–	–
PSHB	(SP) – 1 ⇒ SP; (B) ⇒ M$_{(SP)}$ Push Accumulator B onto Stack	INH	37	Os	–	–	–	–	–	–	–	–
PSHC	(SP) – 1 ⇒ SP; (CCR) ⇒ M$_{(SP)}$ Push CCR onto Stack	INH	39	Os	–	–	–	–	–	–	–	–
PSHD	(SP) – 2 ⇒ SP; (A:B) ⇒ M$_{(SP)}$:M$_{(SP+1)}$ Push D Accumulator onto Stack	INH	3B	OS	–	–	–	–	–	–	–	–
PSHX	(SP) – 2 ⇒ SP; (X$_H$:X$_L$) ⇒ M$_{(SP)}$:M$_{(SP+1)}$ Push Index Register X onto Stack	INH	34	OS	–	–	–	–	–	–	–	–
PSHY	(SP) – 2 ⇒ SP; (Y$_H$:Y$_L$) ⇒ M$_{(SP)}$:M$_{(SP+1)}$ Push Index Register Y onto Stack	INH	35	OS	–	–	–	–	–	–	–	–
PULA	(M$_{(SP)}$) ⇒ A; (SP) + 1 ⇒ SP Pull Accumulator A from Stack	INH	32	ufO	–	–	–	–	–	–	–	–
PULB	(M$_{(SP)}$) ⇒ B; (SP) + 1 ⇒ SP Pull Accumulator B from Stack	INH	33	ufO	–	–	–	–	–	–	–	–
PULC	(M$_{(SP)}$) ⇒ CCR; (SP) + 1 ⇒ SP Pull CCR from Stack	INH	38	ufO	Δ	⇓	Δ	Δ	Δ	Δ	Δ	Δ
PULD	(M$_{(SP)}$:M$_{(SP+1)}$) ⇒ A:B; (SP) + 2 ⇒ SP Pull D from Stack	INH	3A	UfO	–	–	–	–	–	–	–	–
PULX	(M$_{(SP)}$:M$_{(SP+1)}$) ⇒ X$_H$:X$_L$; (SP) + 2 ⇒ SP Pull Index Register X from Stack	INH	30	UfO	–	–	–	–	–	–	–	–
PULY	(M$_{(SP)}$:M$_{(SP+1)}$) ⇒ Y$_H$:Y$_L$; (SP) + 2 ⇒ SP Pull Index Register Y from Stack	INH	31	UfO	–	–	–	–	–	–	–	–

CPU12 Reference Guide

Instruction Set Summary (Continued)

Source Form	Operation	Addr. Mode	Machine Coding (hex)	Access Detail	S	X	H	I	N	Z	V	C
REV (add if interrupted)	MIN-MAX rule evaluation Find smallest rule input (MIN). Store to rule outputs unless fuzzy output is already larger (MAX). For rule weights see REVW. Each rule input is an 8-bit offset from the base address in Y. Each rule output is an 8-bit offset from the base address in Y. $FE separates rule inputs from rule outputs. $FF terminates the rule list. REV may be interrupted.	Special	18 3A	ORf(ttx)O[1] ff + Orf	–	–	?	–	?	?	Δ	?
REVW (add 2 at end of ins if wts) (add if interrupted)	MIN-MAX rule evaluation Find smallest rule input (MIN), Store to rule outputs unless fuzzy output is already larger (MAX). Rule weights supported, optional. Each rule input is the 16-bit address of a fuzzy input. Each rule output is the 16-bit address of a fuzzy output. The value $FFFE separates rule inputs from rule outputs. $FFFF terminates the rule list. REVW may be interrupted.	Special	18 3B	ORf(tTx)O[2] (rffRf)[2] fff + ORft	–	–	?	–	?	?	Δ	!
ROL opr16a ROL oprx0_xysp ROL oprx9,xysp ROL oprx16,xysp ROL [D,xysp] ROL [oprx16,xysp] ROLA ROLB	Rotate Memory Left through Carry Rotate A Left through Carry Rotate B Left through Carry	EXT IDX IDX1 IDX2 [D,IDX] [IDX2] INH INH	75 hh ll 65 xb 65 xb ff 65 xb ee ff 65 xb 65 xb ee ff 45 55	rOPw rPw rPOw frPPw fIfrPw fIPrPw O O	–	–	–	–	Δ	Δ	Δ	Δ
ROR opr16a ROR oprx0_xysp ROR oprx9,xysp ROR oprx16,xysp ROR [D,xysp] ROR [oprx16,xysp] RORA RORB	Rotate Memory Right through Carry Rotate A Right through Carry Rotate B Right through Carry	EXT IDX IDX1 IDX2 [D,IDX] [IDX2] INH INH	76 hh ll 66 xb 66 xb ff 66 xb ee ff 66 xb 66 xb ee ff 46 56	rOPw rPw rPOw frPPw fIfrPw fIPrPw O O	–	–	–	–	Δ	Δ	Δ	Δ
RTC	$(M_{(SP)}) \Rightarrow PPAGE; (SP) + 1 \Rightarrow SP;$ $(M_{(SP)}):M_{(SP+1)} \Rightarrow PC_H:PC_L;$ $(SP) + 2 \Rightarrow SP$ Return from Call	INH	0A	uUnPPP	–	–	–	–	–	–	–	–
RTI (if interrupt pending)	$(M_{(SP)}) \Rightarrow CCR; (SP) + 1 \Rightarrow SP$ $(M_{(SP)}):M_{(SP+1)} \Rightarrow B:A; (SP) + 2 \Rightarrow SP$ $(M_{(SP)}):M_{(SP+1)} \Rightarrow X_H:X_L; (SP) + 4 \Rightarrow SP$ $(M_{(SP)}):M_{(SP+1)} \Rightarrow PC_H:PC_L; (SP) - 2 \Rightarrow SP$ $(M_{(SP)}):M_{(SP+1)} \Rightarrow Y_H:Y_L;$ $(SP) + 4 \Rightarrow SP$ Return from Interrupt	INH	0B	uUUUUPPP uUUUUVfPPP	Δ	⇓	Δ	Δ	Δ	Δ	Δ	Δ
RTS	$(M_{(SP)}):M_{(SP+1)} \Rightarrow PC_H:PC_L;$ $(SP) + 2 \Rightarrow SP$ Return from Subroutine	INH	3D	UfPPP	–	–	–	–	–	–	–	–
SBA	$(A) - (B) \Rightarrow A$ Subtract B from A	INH	18 16	OO	–	–	–	–	Δ	Δ	Δ	Δ

Notes:
1. The 3-cycle loop in parentheses is executed once for each element in the rule list. When an interrupt occurs, there is a 2-cycle exit sequence, a 4-cycle re-entry sequence, then execution resumes with a prefetch of the last antecedent or consequent being processed at the time of the interrupt.
2. The 3-cycle loop in parentheses expands to 5 cycles for separators when weighting is enabled. The loop is executed once for each element in the rule list. When an interrupt occurs, there is a 2-cycle exit sequence, a 4-cycle re-entry sequence, then execution resumes with a prefetch of the last antecedent or consequent being processed at the time of the interrupt.

Instruction Set Summary (Continued)

Source Form	Operation	Addr. Mode	Machine Coding (hex)	Access Detail	S	X	H	I	N	Z	V	C
SBCA #opr8i SBCA opr8a SBCA opr16a SBCA oprx0_xysp SBCA oprx9,xysp SBCA oprx16,xysp SBCA [D,xysp] SBCA [oprx16,xysp]	(A) – (M) – C ⇒ A Subtract with Borrow from A	IMM DIR EXT IDX IDX1 IDX2 [D,IDX] [IDX2]	82 ii 92 dd B2 hh 11 A2 xb A2 xb ff A2 xb ee ff A2 xb A2 xb ee ff	P rfP rOP rfP rPO frPP fIfrfP fIPrfP	–	–	–	–	Δ	Δ	Δ	Δ
SBCB #opr8i SBCB opr8a SBCB opr16a SBCB oprx0_xysp SBCB oprx9,xysp SBCB oprx16,xysp SBCB [D,xysp] SBCB [oprx16,xysp]	(B) – (M) – C ⇒ B Subtract with Borrow from B	IMM DIR EXT IDX IDX1 IDX2 [D,IDX] [IDX2]	C2 ii D2 dd F2 hh 11 E2 xb E2 xb ff E2 xb ee ff E2 xb E2 xb ee ff	P rfP rOP rfP rPO frPP fIfrfP fIPrfP	–	–	–	–	Δ	Δ	Δ	Δ
SEC	1 ⇒ C Translates to ORCC #$01	IMM	14 01	P	–	–	–	–	–	–	–	1
SEI	1 ⇒ I; (inhibit I interrupts) Translates to ORCC #$10	IMM	14 10	P	–	–	–	1	–	–	–	–
SEV	1 ⇒ V Translates to ORCC #$02	IMM	14 02	P	–	–	–	–	–	–	1	–
SEX abc,dxys	$00:(r1) ⇒ r2 if r1, bit 7 is 0 or $FF:(r1) ⇒ r2 if r1, bit 7 is 1 Sign Extend 8-bit r1 to 16-bit r2 r1 may be A, B, or CCR r2 may be D, X, Y, or SP Alternate mnemonic for TFR r1, r2	INH	B7 eb	P	–	–	–	–	–	–	–	–
STAA opr8a STAA opr16a STAA oprx0_xysp STAA oprx9,xysp STAA oprx16,xysp STAA [D,xysp] STAA [oprx16,xysp]	(A) ⇒ M Store Accumulator A to Memory	DIR EXT IDX IDX1 IDX2 [D,IDX] [IDX2]	5A dd 7A hh 11 6A xb 6A xb ff 6A xb ee ff 6A xb 6A xb ee ff	Pw wOP Pw PwO PwP PIfPw PIPPw	–	–	–	–	Δ	Δ	0	–
STAB opr8a STAB opr16a STAB oprx0_xysp STAB oprx9,xysp STAB oprx16,xysp STAB [D,xysp] STAB [oprx16,xysp]	(B) ⇒ M Store Accumulator B to Memory	DIR EXT IDX IDX1 IDX2 [D,IDX] [IDX2]	5B dd 7B hh 11 6B xb 6B xb ff 6B xb ee ff 6B xb 6B xb ee ff	Pw wOP Pw PwO PwP PIfPw PIPPw	–	–	–	–	Δ	Δ	0	–
STD opr8a STD opr16a STD oprx0_xysp STD oprx9,xysp STD oprx16,xysp STD [D,xysp] STD [oprx16,xysp]	(A) ⇒ M, (B) ⇒ M+1 Store Double Accumulator	DIR EXT IDX IDX1 IDX2 [D,IDX] [IDX2]	5C dd 7C hh 11 6C xb 6C xb ff 6C xb ee ff 6C xb 6C xb ee ff	PW WOP PW PWO PWP PIfPW PIPPW	–	–	–	–	Δ	Δ	0	–
STOP (entering STOP) (exiting STOP) (continue) (if STOP disabled)	(SP) – 2 ⇒ SP; RTN$_H$:RTN$_L$ ⇒ M$_{(SP)}$:M$_{(SP+1)}$; (SP) – 2 ⇒ SP; (Y$_H$:Y$_L$) ⇒ M$_{(SP)}$:M$_{(SP+1)}$; (SP) – 2 ⇒ SP; (X$_H$:X$_L$) ⇒ M$_{(SP)}$:M$_{(SP+1)}$; (SP) – 2 ⇒ SP; (B:A) ⇒ M$_{(SP)}$:M$_{(SP+1)}$; (SP) – 1 ⇒ SP; (CCR) ⇒ M$_{(SP)}$ STOP All Clocks If S control bit = 1, the STOP instruction is disabled and acts like a two-cycle NOP. Registers stacked to allow quicker recovery by interrupt.	INH	18 3E	OOSSSfSs fVfPPP fO OO	–	–	–	–	–	–	–	–

Instruction Set Summary (Continued)

Source Form	Operation	Addr. Mode	Machine Coding (hex)	Access Detail	S	X	H	I	N	Z	V	C
STS opr8a STS opr16a STS oprx0_xysp STS oprx9,xysp STS oprx16,xysp STS [D,xysp] STS [oprx16,xysp]	$(SP_H:SP_L) \Rightarrow M:M+1$ Store Stack Pointer	DIR EXT IDX IDX1 IDX2 [D,IDX] [IDX2]	5F dd 7F hh ll 6F xb 6F xb ff 6F xb ee ff 6F xb 6F xb ee ff	PW WOP PW PWO PWP PIfPW PIPPW	–	–	–	–	Δ	Δ	0	–
STX opr8a STX opr16a STX oprx0_xysp STX oprx9,xysp STX oprx16,xysp STX [D,xysp] STX [oprx16,xysp]	$(X_H:X_L) \Rightarrow M:M+1$ Store Index Register X	DIR EXT IDX IDX1 IDX2 [D,IDX] [IDX2]	5E dd 7E hh ll 6E xb 6E xb ff 6E xb ee ff 6E xb 6E xb ee ff	PW WOP PW PWO PWP PIfPW PIPPW	–	–	–	–	Δ	Δ	0	–
STY opr8a STY opr16a STY oprx0_xysp STY oprx9,xysp STY oprx16,xysp STY [D,xysp] STY [oprx16,xysp]	$(Y_H:Y_L) \Rightarrow M:M+1$ Store Index Register Y	DIR EXT IDX IDX1 IDX2 [D,IDX] [IDX2]	5D dd 7D hh ll 6D xb 6D xb ff 6D xb ee ff 6D xb 6D xb ee ff	PW WOP PW PWO PWP PIfPW PIPPW	–	–	–	–	Δ	Δ	0	–
SUBA #opr8i SUBA opr8a SUBA opr16a SUBA oprx0_xysp SUBA oprx9,xysp SUBA oprx16,xysp SUBA [D,xysp] SUBA [oprx16,xysp]	$(A) - (M) \Rightarrow A$ Subtract Memory from Accumulator A	IMM DIR EXT IDX IDX1 IDX2 [D,IDX] [IDX2]	80 ii 90 dd B0 hh ll A0 xb A0 xb ff A0 xb ee ff A0 xb A0 xb ee ff	P rfP rOP rfP rPO frPP fIfrfP fIPrfP	–	–	–	–	Δ	Δ	Δ	Δ
SUBB #opr8i SUBB opr8a SUBB opr16a SUBB oprx0_xysp SUBB oprx9,xysp SUBB oprx16,xysp SUBB [D,xysp] SUBB [oprx16,xysp]	$(B) - (M) \Rightarrow B$ Subtract Memory from Accumulator B	IMM DIR EXT IDX IDX1 IDX2 [D,IDX] [IDX2]	C0 ii D0 dd F0 hh ll E0 xb E0 xb ff E0 xb ee ff E0 xb E0 xb ee ff	P rfP rOP rfP rPO frPP fIfrfP fIPrfP	–	–	–	–	Δ	Δ	Δ	Δ
SUBD #opr16i SUBD opr8a SUBD opr16a SUBD oprx0_xysp SUBD oprx9,xysp SUBD oprx16,xysp SUBD [D,xysp] SUBD [oprx16,xysp]	$(D) - (M:M+1) \Rightarrow D$ Subtract Memory from D (A:B)	IMM DIR EXT IDX IDX1 IDX2 [D,IDX] [IDX2]	83 jj kk 93 dd B3 hh ll A3 xb A3 xb ff A3 xb ee ff A3 xb A3 xb ee ff	OP RfP ROP RfP RPO fRPP fIfRfP fIPRfP	–	–	–	–	Δ	Δ	Δ	Δ
SWI	$(SP) - 2 \Rightarrow SP$; $RTN_H:RTN_L \Rightarrow M_{(SP)}:M_{(SP+1)}$; $(SP) - 2 \Rightarrow SP; (Y_H:Y_L) \Rightarrow M_{(SP)}:M_{(SP+1)}$; $(SP) - 2 \Rightarrow SP; (X_H:X_L) \Rightarrow M_{(SP)}:M_{(SP+1)}$; $(SP) - 2 \Rightarrow SP; (B:A) \Rightarrow M_{(SP)}:M_{(SP+1)}$; $(SP) - 1 \Rightarrow SP; (CCR) \Rightarrow M_{(SP)}$ $1 \Rightarrow I; (SWI\ Vector) \Rightarrow PC$ Software Interrupt	INH	3F	VSPSSPSsP[1]	–	–	–	1	–	–	–	–
TAB	$(A) \Rightarrow B$ Transfer A to B	INH	18 0E	OO	–	–	–	–	Δ	Δ	0	–
TAP	$(A) \Rightarrow CCR$ Translates to TFR A , CCR	INH	B7 02	P	Δ	$\Downarrow$	Δ	Δ	Δ	Δ	Δ	Δ
TBA	$(B) \Rightarrow A$ Transfer B to A	INH	18 0F	OO	–	–	–	–	Δ	Δ	0	–

Note 1. The CPU also uses the SWI processing sequence for hardware interrupts and unimplemented opcode traps. A variation of the sequence (VfPPP) is used for resets.

Instruction Set Summary (Continued)

Source Form	Operation	Addr. Mode	Machine Coding (hex)	Access Detail	S	X	H	I	N	Z	V	C
TBEQ abdxys,rel9	If (cntr) = 0, then Branch; else Continue to next instruction Test Counter and Branch if Zero (cntr = A, B, D, X,Y, or SP)	REL (9-bit)	04 lb rr	PPP	–	–	–	–	–	–	–	–
TBL oprx0_xysp	$(M) + [(B) \times ((M+1) - (M))] \Rightarrow A$ 8-Bit Table Lookup and Interpolate Initialize B, and index before TBL. <ea> points at first 8-bit table entry (M) and B is fractional part of lookup value. (no indirect addressing modes or extensions allowed)	IDX	18 3D xb	OrrffffP	–	–	–	–	Δ	Δ	–	?
TBNE abdxys,rel9	If (cntr) not = 0, then Branch; else Continue to next instruction Test Counter and Branch if Not Zero (cntr = A, B, D, X,Y, or SP)	REL (9-bit)	04 lb rr	PPP	–	–	–	–	–	–	–	–
TFR abcdxys,abcdxys	$(r1) \Rightarrow r2$ or $\$00:(r1) \Rightarrow r2$ or $(r1[7:0]) \Rightarrow r2$ Transfer Register to Register r1 and r2 may be A, B, CCR, D, X, Y, or SP	INH	B7 eb	P or Δ	– or Δ	⇓	– or Δ	– or Δ	– or Δ	– or Δ	– or Δ	– or Δ
TPA	$(CCR) \Rightarrow A$ Translates to TFR CCR,A	INH	B7 20	P	–	–	–	–	–	–	–	–
TRAP trapnum	$(SP) - 2 \Rightarrow SP$; $RTN_H:RTN_L \Rightarrow M_{(SP)}:M_{(SP+1)}$; $(SP) - 2 \Rightarrow SP$; $(Y_H:Y_L) \Rightarrow M_{(SP)}:M_{(SP+1)}$; $(SP) - 2 \Rightarrow SP$; $(X_H:X_L) \Rightarrow M_{(SP)}:M_{(SP+1)}$; $(SP) - 2 \Rightarrow SP$; $(B:A) \Rightarrow M_{(SP)}:M_{(SP+1)}$; $(SP) - 1 \Rightarrow SP$; $(CCR) \Rightarrow M_{(SP)}$ $1 \Rightarrow I$; (TRAP Vector) $\Rightarrow PC$ Unimplemented opcode trap	INH	18 tn tn = $30-$39 or $40-$FF	OfVSPSSPSsP	–	–	–	1	–	–	–	–
TST opr16a TST oprx0_xysp TST oprx9,xysp TST oprx16,xysp TST [D,xysp] TST [oprx16,xysp] TSTA TSTB	$(M) - 0$ Test Memory for Zero or Minus $(A) - 0$ Test A for Zero or Minus $(B) - 0$ Test B for Zero or Minus	EXT IDX IDX1 IDX2 [D,IDX] [IDX2] INH INH	F7 hh 11 E7 xb E7 xb ff E7 xb ee ff E7 xb E7 xb ee ff 97 D7	rOP rfP rPO frPP fIfrfP fIPrfP O O	–	–	–	–	Δ	Δ	0	0
TSX	$(SP) \Rightarrow X$ Translates to TFR SP,X	INH	B7 75	P	–	–	–	–	–	–	–	–
TSY	$(SP) \Rightarrow Y$ Translates to TFR SP,Y	INH	B7 76	P	–	–	–	–	–	–	–	–
TXS	$(X) \Rightarrow SP$ Translates to TFR X,SP	INH	B7 57	P	–	–	–	–	–	–	–	–
TYS	$(Y) \Rightarrow SP$ Translates to TFR Y,SP	INH	B7 67	P	–	–	–	–	–	–	–	–
WAI (before interrupt) (when interrupt comes)	$(SP) - 2 \Rightarrow SP$; $RTN_H:RTN_L \Rightarrow M_{(SP)}:M_{(SP+1)}$; $(SP) - 2 \Rightarrow SP$; $(Y_H:Y_L) \Rightarrow M_{(SP)}:M_{(SP+1)}$; $(SP) - 2 \Rightarrow SP$; $(X_H:X_L) \Rightarrow M_{(SP)}:M_{(SP+1)}$; $(SP) - 2 \Rightarrow SP$; $(B:A) \Rightarrow M_{(SP)}:M_{(SP+1)}$; $(SP) - 1 \Rightarrow SP$; $(CCR) \Rightarrow M_{(SP)}$ WAIT for interrupt	INH	3E	OSSSfSsf VfPPP or –	– or –	– or 1	–	– or 1	1	–	–	–

Instruction Set Summary (Continued)

Source Form	Operation	Addr. Mode	Machine Coding (hex)	Access Detail	S	X	H	I	N	Z	V	C
WAV (add if interrupt)	$\sum_{i=1}^{B} S_i F_i \Rightarrow Y:D$ $\sum_{i=1}^{B} F_i \Rightarrow X$ Calculate Sum of Products and Sum of Weights for Weighted Average Calculation. Initialize B, X, and Y before WAV. B specifies number of elements. X points at first element in S_i list. Y points at first element in F_i list. All S_i and F_i elements are 8-bits. If interrupted, six extra bytes of stack used for intermediate values	Special	18 3C	Off(frrfffff)O SSS + UUUrr	–	–	?	–	?	Δ	?	?
wavr pseudo-instruction	see WAV Resume executing an interrupted WAV instruction (recover intermediate results from stack rather than initializing them to zero)	Special	3C		–	–	?	–	?	Δ	?	?
XGDX	(D) ⇔ (X) Translates to EXG D, X	INH	B7 C5	P	–	–	–	–	–	–	–	–
XGDY	(D) ⇔ (Y) Translates to EXG D, Y	INH	B7 C6	P	–	–	–	–	–	–	–	–

Table 1. Indexed Addressing Mode Postbyte Encoding (xb)

00 0,X 5b const	10 −16,X 5b const	20 1,+X pre-inc	30 1,X+ post-inc	40 0,Y 5b const	50 −16,Y 5b const	60 1,+Y pre-inc	70 1,Y+ post-inc	80 0,SP 5b const	90 −16,SP 5b const	A0 1,+SP pre-inc	B0 1,SP+ post-inc	C0 0,PC 5b const	D0 −16,PC 5b const	E0 n,X 9b const	F0 n,SP 9b const
01 1,X 5b const	11 −15,X 5b const	21 2,+X pre-inc	31 2,X+ post-inc	41 1,Y 5b const	51 −15,Y 5b const	61 2,+Y pre-inc	71 2,Y+ post-inc	81 1,SP 5b const	91 −15,SP 5b const	A1 2,+SP pre-inc	B1 2,SP+ post-inc	C1 1,PC 5b const	D1 −15,PC 5b const	E1 −n,X 9b const	F1 −n,SP 9b const
02 2,X 5b const	12 −14,X 5b const	22 3,+X pre-inc	32 3,X+ post-inc	42 2,Y 5b const	52 −14,Y 5b const	62 3,+Y pre-inc	72 3,Y+ post-inc	82 2,SP 5b const	92 −14,SP 5b const	A2 3,+SP pre-inc	B2 3,SP+ post-inc	C2 2,PC 5b const	D2 −14,PC 5b const	E2 n,X 16b const	F2 n,SP 16b const
03 3,X 5b const	13 −13,X 5b const	23 4,+X pre-inc	33 4,X+ post-inc	43 3,Y 5b const	53 −13,Y 5b const	63 4,+Y pre-inc	73 4,Y+ post-inc	83 3,SP 5b const	93 −13,SP 5b const	A3 4,+SP pre-inc	B3 4,SP+ post-inc	C3 3,PC 5b const	D3 −13,PC 5b const	E3 [n,X] 16b indr	F3 [n,SP] 16b indr
04 4,X 5b const	14 −12,X 5b const	24 5,+X pre-inc	34 5,X+ post-inc	44 4,Y 5b const	54 −12,Y 5b const	64 5,+Y pre-inc	74 5,Y+ post-inc	84 4,SP 5b const	94 −12,SP 5b const	A4 5,+SP pre-inc	B4 5,SP+ post-inc	C4 4,PC 5b const	D4 −12,PC 5b const	E4 A,X A offset	F4 A,SP A offset
05 5,X 5b const	15 −11,X 5b const	25 6,+X pre-inc	35 6,X+ post-inc	45 5,Y 5b const	55 −11,Y 5b const	65 6,+Y pre-inc	75 6,Y+ post-inc	85 5,SP 5b const	95 −11,SP 5b const	A5 6,+SP pre-inc	B5 6,SP+ post-inc	C5 5,PC 5b const	D5 −11,PC 5b const	E5 B,X B offset	F5 B,SP B offset
06 6,X 5b const	16 −10,X 5b const	26 7,+X pre-inc	36 7,X+ post-inc	46 6,Y 5b const	56 −10,Y 5b const	66 7,+Y pre-inc	76 7,Y+ post-inc	86 6,SP 5b const	96 −10,SP 5b const	A6 7,+SP pre-inc	B6 7,SP+ post-inc	C6 6,PC 5b const	D6 −10,PC 5b const	E6 D,X D offset	F6 D,SP D offset
07 7,X 5b const	17 −9,X 5b const	27 8,+X pre-inc	37 8,X+ post-inc	47 7,Y 5b const	57 −9,Y 5b const	67 8,+Y pre-inc	77 8,Y+ post-inc	87 7,SP 5b const	97 −9,SP 5b const	A7 8,+SP pre-inc	B7 8,SP+ post-inc	C7 7,PC 5b const	D7 −9,PC 5b const	E7 [D,X] D indirect	F7 [D,SP] D indirect
08 8,X 5b const	18 −8,X 5b const	28 8,−X pre-dec	38 8,X− post-dec	48 8,Y 5b const	58 −8,Y 5b const	68 8,−Y pre-dec	78 8,Y− post-dec	88 8,SP 5b const	98 −8,SP 5b const	A8 8,−SP pre-dec	B8 8,SP− post-dec	C8 8,PC 5b const	D8 −8,PC 5b const	E8 n,Y 9b const	F8 n,PC 9b const
09 9,X 5b const	19 −7,X 5b const	29 7,−X pre-dec	39 7,X− post-dec	49 9,Y 5b const	59 −7,Y 5b const	69 7,−Y pre-dec	79 7,Y− post-dec	89 9,SP 5b const	99 −7,SP 5b const	A9 7,−SP pre-dec	B9 7,SP− post-dec	C9 9,PC 5b const	D9 −7,PC 5b const	E9 −n,Y 9b const	F9 −n,PC 9b const
0A 10,X 5b const	1A −6,X 5b const	2A 6,−X pre-dec	3A 6,X− post-dec	4A 10,Y 5b const	5A −6,Y 5b const	6A 6,−Y pre-dec	7A 6,Y− post-dec	8A 10,SP 5b const	9A −6,SP 5b const	AA 6,−SP pre-dec	BA 6,SP− post-dec	CA 10,PC 5b const	DA −6,PC 5b const	EA n,Y 16b const	FA n,PC 16b const
0B 11,X 5b const	1B −5,X 5b const	2B 5,−X pre-dec	3B 5,X− post-dec	4B 11,Y 5b const	5B −5,Y 5b const	6B 5,−Y pre-dec	7B 5,Y− post-dec	8B 11,SP 5b const	9B −5,SP 5b const	AB 5,−SP pre-dec	BB 5,SP− post-dec	CB 11,PC 5b const	DB −5,PC 5b const	EB [n,Y] 16b indr	FB [n,PC] 16b indr
0C 12,X 5b const	1C −4,X 5b const	2C 4,−X pre-dec	3C 4,X− post-dec	4C 12,Y 5b const	5C −4,Y 5b const	6C 4,−Y pre-dec	7C 4,Y− post-dec	8C 12,SP 5b const	9C −4,SP 5b const	AC 4,−SP pre-dec	BC 4,SP− post-dec	CC 12,PC 5b const	DC −4,PC 5b const	EC A,Y A offset	FC A,PC A offset
0D 13,X 5b const	1D −3,X 5b const	2D 3,−X pre-dec	3D 3,X− post-dec	4D 13,Y 5b const	5D −3,Y 5b const	6D 3,−Y pre-dec	7D 3,Y− post-dec	8D 13,SP 5b const	9D −3,SP 5b const	AD 3,−SP pre-dec	BD 3,SP− post-dec	CD 13,PC 5b const	DD −3,PC 5b const	ED B,Y B offset	FD B,PC B offset
0E 14,X 5b const	1E −2,X 5b const	2E 2,−X pre-dec	3E 2,X− post-dec	4E 14,Y 5b const	5E −2,Y 5b const	6E 2,−Y pre-dec	7E 2,Y− post-dec	8E 14,SP 5b const	9E −2,SP 5b const	AE 2,−SP pre-dec	BE 2,SP− post-dec	CE 14,PC 5b const	DE −2,PC 5b const	EE D,Y D offset	FE D,PC D offset
0F 15,X 5b const	1F −1,X 5b const	2F 1,−X pre-dec	3F 1,X− post-dec	4F 15,Y 5b const	5F −1,Y 5b const	6F 1,−Y pre-dec	7F 1,Y− post-dec	8F 15,SP 5b const	9F −1,SP 5b const	AF 1,−SP pre-dec	BF 1,SP− post-dec	CF 15,PC 5b const	DF −1,PC 5b const	EF [D,Y] D indirect	FF [D,PC] D indirect

Key to Table 1

- postbyte (hex)
- B0 #,REG type — source code syntax
- type offset used

CPU12 Reference Guide

Table 2. Indexed Addressing Mode Summary

Postbyte Code (xb)	Operand Syntax	Comments
rr0nnnnn	,r n,r –n,r	**5-bit constant offset** n = –16 to +15 rr can specify X, Y, SP, or PC
111rr0zs	n,r –n,r	**Constant offset** (9- or 16-bit signed) z- 0 = 9-bit with sign in LSB of postbyte (s) 1 = 16-bit if z = s = 1, 16-bit offset indexed-indirect (see below) rr can specify X, Y, SP, or PC
rr1pnnnn	n,–r n,+r n,r– n,r+	**Auto pre-decrement /increment or Auto post-decrement/increment;** p = pre-(0) or post-(1), n = –8 to –1, +1 to +8 rr can specify X, Y, or SP (PC not a valid choice)

111rr1aa	A,r
	B,r
	D,r
		Accumulator offset (unsigned 8-bit or 16-bit)
		aa - 00 = A
		      01 = B
		      10 = D (16-bit)
		      11 = see accumulator D offset indexed-indirect
		rr can specify X, Y, SP, or PC

111rr011	[n,r]	**16-bit offset indexed-indirect** rr can specify X, Y, SP, or PC
111rr111	[D,r]	**Accumulator D offset indexed-indirect** rr can specify X, Y, SP, or PC

Table 3. Transfer and Exchange Postbyte Encoding

TRANSFERS

⇓LS \ MS⇒	0	1	2	3	4	5	6	7
0	A ⇒ A	B ⇒ A	CCR ⇒ A	TMP3$_L$ ⇒ A	B ⇒ A	X$_L$ ⇒ A	Y$_L$ ⇒ A	SP$_L$ ⇒ A
1	A ⇒ B	B ⇒ B	CCR ⇒ B	TMP3$_L$ ⇒ B	B ⇒ B	X$_L$ ⇒ B	Y$_L$ ⇒ B	SP$_L$ ⇒ B
2	A ⇒ CCR	B ⇒ CCR	CCR ⇒ CCR	TMP3$_L$ ⇒ CCR	B ⇒ CCR	X$_L$ ⇒ CCR	Y$_L$ ⇒ CCR	SP$_L$ ⇒ CCR
3	sex:A ⇒ TMP2	sex:B ⇒ TMP2	sex:CCR ⇒ TMP2	TMP3 ⇒ TMP2	D ⇒ TMP2	X ⇒ TMP2	Y ⇒ TMP2	SP ⇒ TMP2
4	sex:A ⇒ D SEX A,D	sex:B ⇒ D SEX B,D	sex:CCR ⇒ D SEX CCR,D	TMP3 ⇒ D	D ⇒ D	X ⇒ D	Y ⇒ D	SP ⇒ D
5	sex:A ⇒ X SEX A,X	sex:B ⇒ X SEX B,X	sex:CCR ⇒ X SEX CCR,X	TMP3 ⇒ X	D ⇒ X	X ⇒ X	Y ⇒ X	SP ⇒ X
6	sex:A ⇒ Y SEX A,Y	sex:B ⇒ Y SEX B,Y	sex:CCR ⇒ Y SEX CCR,Y	TMP3 ⇒ Y	D ⇒ Y	X ⇒ Y	Y ⇒ Y	SP ⇒ Y
7	sex:A ⇒ SP SEX A,SP	sex:B ⇒ SP SEX B,SP	sex:CCR ⇒ SP SEX CCR,SP	TMP3 ⇒ SP	D ⇒ SP	X ⇒ SP	Y ⇒ SP	SP ⇒ SP

EXCHANGES

⇓LS \ MS⇒	8	9	A	B	C	D	E	F
0	A ⇔ A	B ⇔ A	CCR ⇔ A	TMP3$_L$ ⇒ A $00:A ⇒ TMP3	B ⇒ A A ⇒ B	X$_L$ ⇒ A $00:A ⇒ X	Y$_L$ ⇒ A $00:A ⇒ Y	SP$_L$ ⇒ A $00:A ⇒ SP
1	A ⇔ B	B ⇔ B	CCR ⇔ B	TMP3$_L$ ⇒ B $FF:B ⇒ TMP3	B ⇒ B $FF ⇒ A	X$_L$ ⇒ B $FF:B ⇒ X	Y$_L$ ⇒ B $FF:B ⇒ Y	SP$_L$ ⇒ B $FF:B ⇒ SP
2	A ⇔ CCR	B ⇔ CCR	CCR ⇔ CCR	TMP3$_L$ ⇒ CCR $FF:CCR ⇒ TMP3	B ⇒ CCR $FF:CCR ⇒ D	X$_L$ ⇒ CCR $FF:CCR ⇒ X	Y$_L$ ⇒ CCR $FF:CCR ⇒ Y	SP$_L$ ⇒ CCR $FF:CCR ⇒ SP
3	$00:A ⇒ TMP2 TMP2$_L$ ⇒ A	$00:B ⇒ TMP2 TMP2$_L$ ⇒ B	$00:CCR ⇒ TMP2 TMP2$_L$ ⇒ CCR	TMP3 ⇒ TMP2	D ⇔ TMP2	X ⇔ TMP2	Y ⇔ TMP2	SP ⇔ TMP2
4	$00:A ⇒ D B ⇒ CCR	$00:B ⇒ D	$00:CCR ⇒ D B ⇒ CCR	TMP3 ⇔ D	D ⇔ D	X ⇔ D	Y ⇔ D	SP ⇔ D
5	$00:A ⇒ X X$_L$ ⇒ A	$00:B ⇒ X X$_L$ ⇒ B	$00:CCR ⇒ X X$_L$ ⇒ CCR	TMP3 ⇔ X	D ⇔ X	X ⇔ X	Y ⇔ X	SP ⇔ X
6	$00:A ⇒ Y Y$_L$ ⇒ A	$00:B ⇒ Y Y$_L$ ⇒ B	$00:CCR ⇒ Y Y$_L$ ⇒ CCR	TMP3 ⇔ Y	D ⇔ Y	X ⇔ Y	Y ⇔ Y	SP ⇔ Y
7	$00:A ⇒ SP SP$_L$ ⇒ A	$00:B ⇒ SP SP$_L$ ⇒ B	$00:CCR ⇒ SP SP$_L$ ⇒ CCR	TMP3 ⇔ SP	D ⇔ SP	X ⇔ SP	Y ⇔ SP	SP ⇔ SP

TMP2 and TMP3 registers are for factory use only.

Table 4. Loop Primitive Postbyte Encoding (lb)

00 A DBEQ (+)	10 A DBEQ (−)	20 A DBNE (+)	30 A DBNE (−)	40 A TBEQ (+)	50 A TBEQ (−)	60 A TBNE (+)	70 A TBNE (−)	80 A IBEQ (+)	90 A IBEQ (−)	A0 A IBNE (+)	B0 A IBNE (−)
01 B DBEQ (+)	11 B DBEQ (−)	21 B DBNE (+)	31 B DBNE (−)	41 B TBEQ (+)	51 B TBEQ (−)	61 B TBNE (+)	71 B TBNE (−)	81 B IBEQ (+)	91 B IBEQ (−)	A1 B IBNE (+)	B1 B IBNE (−)
02 —	12 —	22 —	32 —	42 —	52 —	62 —	72 —	82 —	92 —	A2 —	B2 —
03 —	13 —	23 —	33 —	43 —	53 —	63 —	73 —	83 —	93 —	A3 —	B3 —
04 D DBEQ (+)	14 D DBEQ (−)	24 D DBNE (+)	34 D DBNE (−)	44 D TBEQ (+)	54 D TBEQ (−)	64 D TBNE (+)	74 D TBNE (−)	84 D IBEQ (+)	94 D IBEQ (−)	A4 D IBNE (+)	B4 D IBNE (−)
05 X DBEQ (+)	15 X DBEQ (−)	25 X DBNE (+)	35 X DBNE (−)	45 X TBEQ (+)	55 X TBEQ (−)	65 X TBNE (+)	75 X TBNE (−)	85 X IBEQ (+)	95 X IBEQ (−)	A5 X IBNE (+)	B5 X IBNE (−)
06 Y DBEQ (+)	16 Y DBEQ (−)	26 Y DBNE (+)	36 Y DBNE (−)	46 Y TBEQ (+)	56 Y TBEQ (−)	66 Y TBNE (+)	76 Y TBNE (−)	86 Y IBEQ (+)	96 Y IBEQ (−)	A6 Y IBNE (+)	B6 Y IBNE (−)
07 SP DBEQ (+)	17 SP DBEQ (−)	27 SP DBNE (+)	37 SP DBNE (−)	47 SP TBEQ (+)	57 SP TBEQ (−)	67 SP TBNE (+)	77 SP TBNE (−)	87 SP IBEQ (+)	97 SP IBEQ (−)	A7 SP IBNE (+)	B7 SP IBNE (−)

Key to Table 4

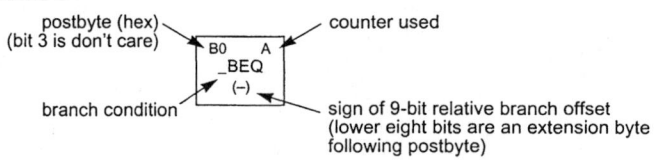

postbyte (hex) (bit 3 is don't care) — B0 A _BEQ (−) — counter used

branch condition — sign of 9-bit relative branch offset (lower eight bits are an extension byte following postbyte)

Table 5. Branch/Complementary Branch

Branch				Complementary Branch			
Test	Mnemonic	Opcode	Boolean	Test	Mnemonic	Opcode	Comment
r>m	BGT	2E	Z + (N ⊕ V) = 0	r≤m	BLE	2F	Signed
r≥m	BGE	2C	N ⊕ V = 0	r<m	BLT	2D	Signed
r=m	BEQ	27	Z = 1	r≠m	BNE	26	Signed
r≤m	BLE	2F	Z + (N ⊕ V) = 1	r>m	BGT	2E	Signed
r<m	BLT	2D	N ⊕ V = 1	r≥m	BGE	2C	Signed
r>m	BHI	22	C + Z = 0	r≤m	BLS	23	Unsigned
r≥m	BHS/BCC	24	C = 0	r<m	BLO/BCS	25	Unsigned
r=m	BEQ	27	Z = 1	r≠m	BNE	26	Unsigned
r≤m	BLS	23	C + Z = 1	r>m	BHI	22	Unsigned
r<m	BLO/BCS	25	C = 1	r≥m	BHS/BCC	24	Unsigned
Carry	BCS	25	C = 1	No Carry	BCC	24	Simple
Negative	BMI	2B	N = 1	Plus	BPL	2A	Simple
Overflow	BVS	29	V = 1	No Overflow	BVC	28	Simple
r=0	BEQ	27	Z = 1	r≠0	BNE	26	Simple
Always	BRA	20	—	Never	BRN	21	Unconditional

For 16-bit offset long branches preceed opcode with a $18 page prebyte.

Memory Expansion

Some M68HC12 derivatives support >4 megabytes of program memory.

Memory precedence
— Highest —
On-chip registers (usually $0000 or $1000)
BDM ROM (only when BDM active)
On-chip RAM
On-chip EEPROM
On-chip program memory (FLASH or ROM)
Expansion windows (on MCUs with expanded memory)
Other external memory
— Lowest —

CPU sees 64 Kbytes of address space (CPU_ADDR [15:0])
PPAGE 8-bit register to select 1 of 256 —16 Kbyte program pages
DPAGE 8-bit register to select 1 of 256 — 4 Kbyte data pages
EPAGE 8-bit register to select 1 of 256 — 1 Kbyte extra pages

Extended address is 22 bits (EXT_ADDR [21:0])
Program expansion window works with CALL and RTC instructions to simplify program access to extended memory space. Data and extra expansion windows (when present) use traditional banked expansion memory techniques.

Program window
    If   CPU_ADDR [15:0] = $8000–BFFF and PWEN = 1
    Then   EXT_ADDR [21:0] = PPAGE [7:0]:CPU_ADDR [13:0]
Program window works with CALL/RTC to automate bank switching. 256 pages (banks) of 16 Kbytes each = 4 M.

Data window
    If   CPU_ADDR [15:0] = $7000–7FFF and DWEN = 1
    Then   EXT_ADDR [21:0] = 1:1:DPAGE [7:0]:CPU_ADDR [11:0]
User program controls DPAGE value

Extra window
- If   CPU_ADDR [15:0] = $0000–03FF and EWDIR = 1 and EWEN = 1
- or   CPU_ADDR [15:0] = $0400–07FF and EWDIR = 0 and EWEN = 1
- Then   EXT_ADDR [21:0] = 1:1:1:1:EPAGE [7:0]:CPU_ADDR [9:0]

User program controls EPAGE value

CPU address not in any enabled window

EXT_ADDR [21:0] = 1:1:1:1:1:1:CPU_ADDR [15:0]

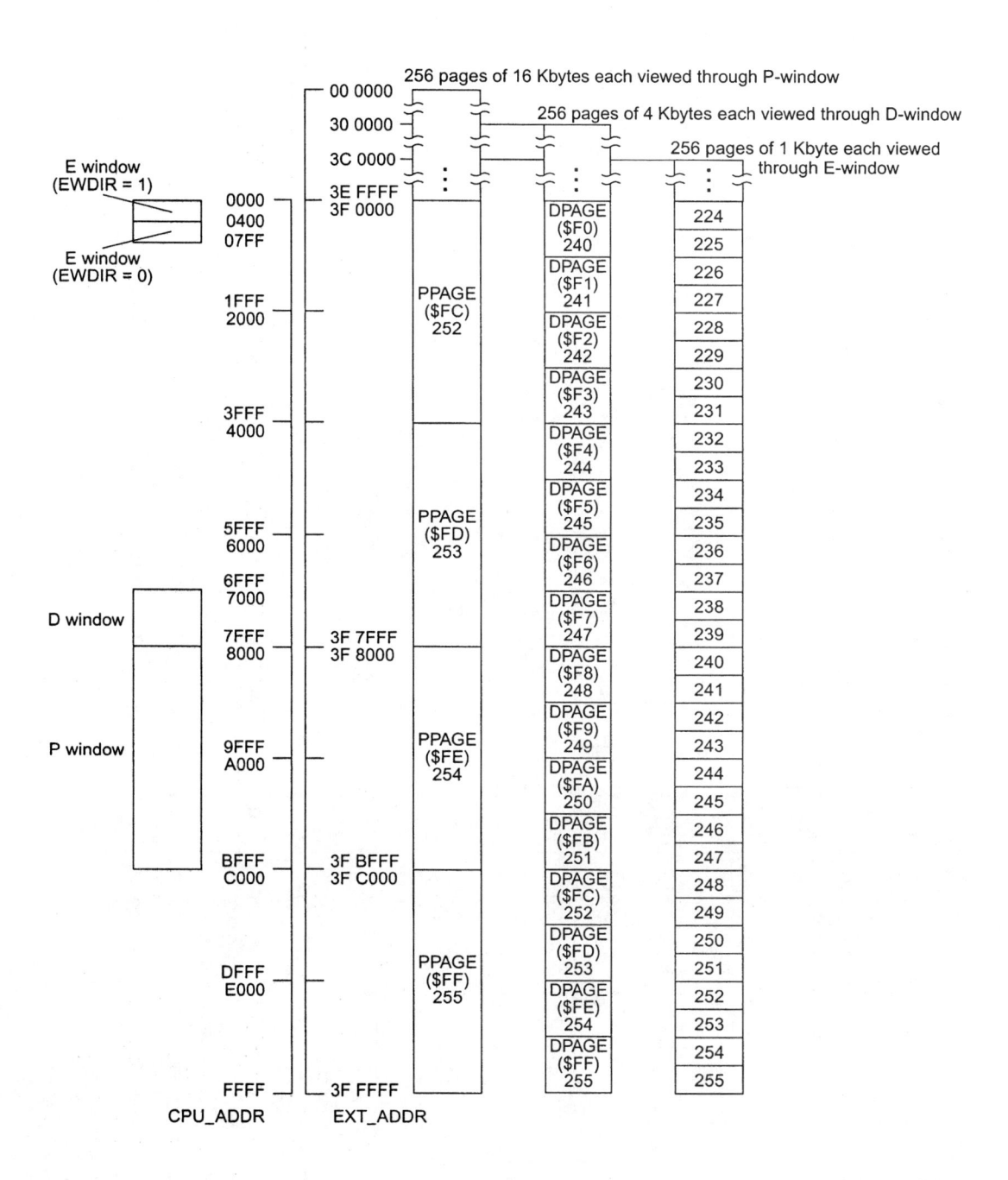

CPU12 Reference Guide

256 pages of 16 Kbytes each viewed through P-window

256 pages of 4 Kbytes each viewed through D-window

256 pages of 1 Kbyte each viewed through E-window

CPU_ADDR	EXT_ADDR	PPAGE	DPAGE	E-window
0000–07FF (E window EWDIR=1 / EWDIR=0)	00 0000			
	30 0000			
	3C 0000			
	3E FFFF			
0000 / 0400 / 07FF	3F 0000		DPAGE ($F0) 240	224 / 225
		PPAGE ($FC) 252	DPAGE ($F1) 241	226 / 227
1FFF / 2000			DPAGE ($F2) 242	228 / 229
			DPAGE ($F3) 243	230 / 231
3FFF / 4000			DPAGE ($F4) 244	232 / 233
			DPAGE ($F5) 245	234 / 235
5FFF / 6000		PPAGE ($FD) 253	DPAGE ($F6) 246	236 / 237
6FFF / 7000 (D window)			DPAGE ($F7) 247	238 / 239
7FFF / 8000	3F 7FFF / 3F 8000		DPAGE ($F8) 248	240 / 241
			DPAGE ($F9) 249	242 / 243
9FFF / A000 (P window)		PPAGE ($FE) 254	DPAGE ($FA) 250	244 / 245
			DPAGE ($FB) 251	246 / 247
BFFF / C000	3F BFFF / 3F C000		DPAGE ($FC) 252	248 / 249
			DPAGE ($FD) 253	250 / 251
DFFF / E000		PPAGE ($FF) 255	DPAGE ($FE) 254	252 / 253
			DPAGE ($FF) 255	254 / 255
FFFF	3F FFFF			

CPU12 Reference Guide

Table 6. CPU12 Opcode Map (Sheet 1 of 2)

Table 6. CPU12 Opcode Map (Sheet 2 of 2)

	00	10	20	30	40	50	60	70	80	90	A0	B0	C0	D0	E0	F0
0	MOVW 4/IM-ID 5	IDIV 12/IH 2	LBRA 4/RL 3	TRAP 10/IH 2	TRAP 10/IH 2	TRAP 10/IH 2	TRAP 10/IH 2	TRAP 10/IH 2	TRAP 10/IH 2	TRAP 10/IH 2	TRAP 10/IH 2	TRAP 10/IH 2	TRAP 10/IH 2	TRAP 10/IH 2	TRAP 10/IH 2	TRAP 10/IH 2
1	MOVW 5/EX-ID 5	FDIV 12/IH 2	LBRN 3/RL 3	TRAP 10/IH 2	TRAP 10/IH 2	TRAP 10/IH 2	TRAP 10/IH 2	TRAP 10/IH 2	TRAP 10/IH 2	TRAP 10/IH 2	TRAP 10/IH 2	TRAP 10/IH 2	TRAP 10/IH 2	TRAP 10/IH 2	TRAP 10/IH 2	TRAP 10/IH 2
2	MOVW 5/ID-ID 4	EMACS 13/SP 4	LBHI 4/3 RL 4	TRAP 10/IH 2	TRAP 10/IH 2	TRAP 10/IH 2	TRAP 10/IH 2	TRAP 10/IH 2	TRAP 10/IH 2	TRAP 10/IH 2	TRAP 10/IH 2	TRAP 10/IH 2	TRAP 10/IH 2	TRAP 10/IH 2	TRAP 10/IH 2	TRAP 10/IH 2
3	MOVW 5/IM-EX 6	EMULS 3/IH 2	LBLS 4/3 RL 4	TRAP 10/IH 2	TRAP 10/IH 2	TRAP 10/IH 2	TRAP 10/IH 2	TRAP 10/IH 2	TRAP 10/IH 2	TRAP 10/IH 2	TRAP 10/IH 2	TRAP 10/IH 2	TRAP 10/IH 2	TRAP 10/IH 2	TRAP 10/IH 2	TRAP 10/IH 2
4	MOVW 6/EX-EX 6	EDIVS 12/IH 2	LBCC 4/3 RL 4	TRAP 10/IH 2	TRAP 10/IH 2	TRAP 10/IH 2	TRAP 10/IH 2	TRAP 10/IH 2	TRAP 10/IH 2	TRAP 10/IH 2	TRAP 10/IH 2	TRAP 10/IH 2	TRAP 10/IH 2	TRAP 10/IH 2	TRAP 10/IH 2	TRAP 10/IH 2
5	MOVW 5/ID-EX 5	IDIVS 12/IH 2	LBCS 4/3 RL 4	TRAP 10/IH 2	TRAP 10/IH 2	TRAP 10/IH 2	TRAP 10/IH 2	TRAP 10/IH 2	TRAP 10/IH 2	TRAP 10/IH 2	TRAP 10/IH 2	TRAP 10/IH 2	TRAP 10/IH 2	TRAP 10/IH 2	TRAP 10/IH 2	TRAP 10/IH 2
6	ABA 2/IH 2	SBA 2/IH 2	LBNE 4/3 RL 4	TRAP 10/IH 2	TRAP 10/IH 2	TRAP 10/IH 2	TRAP 10/IH 2	TRAP 10/IH 2	TRAP 10/IH 2	TRAP 10/IH 2	TRAP 10/IH 2	TRAP 10/IH 2	TRAP 10/IH 2	TRAP 10/IH 2	TRAP 10/IH 2	TRAP 10/IH 2
7	DAA 3/IH 2	CBA 2/IH 2	LBEQ 4/3 RL 4	TRAP 10/IH 2	TRAP 10/IH 2	TRAP 10/IH 2	TRAP 10/IH 2	TRAP 10/IH 2	TRAP 10/IH 2	TRAP 10/IH 2	TRAP 10/IH 2	TRAP 10/IH 2	TRAP 10/IH 2	TRAP 10/IH 2	TRAP 10/IH 2	TRAP 10/IH 2
8	MOVB 4/IM-ID 4	MAXA 4-7/ID 3-5	LBVC 4/3 RL 4	REV *3n/SP 2	TRAP 10/IH 2	TRAP 10/IH 2	TRAP 10/IH 2	TRAP 10/IH 2	TRAP 10/IH 2	TRAP 10/IH 2	TRAP 10/IH 2	TRAP 10/IH 2	TRAP 10/IH 2	TRAP 10/IH 2	TRAP 10/IH 2	TRAP 10/IH 2
9	MOVB 5/EX-ID 5	MINA 4-7/ID 3-5	LBVS 4/3 RL 4	REVW *3n/SP 2	TRAP 10/IH 2	TRAP 10/IH 2	TRAP 10/IH 2	TRAP 10/IH 2	TRAP 10/IH 2	TRAP 10/IH 2	TRAP 10/IH 2	TRAP 10/IH 2	TRAP 10/IH 2	TRAP 10/IH 2	TRAP 10/IH 2	TRAP 10/IH 2
A	MOVB 5/ID-ID 4	EMAXD 4-7/ID 3-5	LBPL 4/3 RL 4	WAV *8B/IH 2	TRAP 10/IH 2	TRAP 10/IH 2	TRAP 10/IH 2	TRAP 10/IH 2	TRAP 10/IH 2	TRAP 10/IH 2	TRAP 10/IH 2	TRAP 10/IH 2	TRAP 10/IH 2	TRAP 10/IH 2	TRAP 10/IH 2	TRAP 10/IH 2
B	MOVB 5/IM-EX 5	EMIND 4-7/ID 3-5	LBMI 4/3 RL 4	TBL 8/ID 3	TRAP 10/IH 2	TRAP 10/IH 2	TRAP 10/IH 2	TRAP 10/IH 2	TRAP 10/IH 2	TRAP 10/IH 2	TRAP 10/IH 2	TRAP 10/IH 2	TRAP 10/IH 2	TRAP 10/IH 2	TRAP 10/IH 2	TRAP 10/IH 2
C	MOVB 6/EX-EX 6	MAXM 4-7/ID 3-5	LBGE 4/3 RL 4	LBLT 4/3 RL 4	TRAP 10/IH 2	TRAP 10/IH 2	TRAP 10/IH 2	TRAP 10/IH 2	TRAP 10/IH 2	TRAP 10/IH 2	TRAP 10/IH 2	TRAP 10/IH 2	TRAP 10/IH 2	TRAP 10/IH 2	TRAP 10/IH 2	TRAP 10/IH 2
D	MOVB 5/ID-EX 5	MINM 4-7/ID 3-5	LBLT 4/3 RL 4	STOP *9+5/IH 2	TRAP 10/IH 2	TRAP 10/IH 2	TRAP 10/IH 2	TRAP 10/IH 2	TRAP 10/IH 2	TRAP 10/IH 2	TRAP 10/IH 2	TRAP 10/IH 2	TRAP 10/IH 2	TRAP 10/IH 2	TRAP 10/IH 2	TRAP 10/IH 2
E	TAB 2/IH 2	EMAXM 4-7/ID 3-5	LBGT 4/3 RL 4	ETBL 10/ID 3	TRAP 10/IH 2	TRAP 10/IH 2	TRAP 10/IH 2	TRAP 10/IH 2	TRAP 10/IH 2	TRAP 10/IH 2	TRAP 10/IH 2	TRAP 10/IH 2	TRAP 10/IH 2	TRAP 10/IH 2	TRAP 10/IH 2	TRAP 10/IH 2
F	TBA 2/IH 2	EMINM 4-7/ID 3-5	LBLE 4/3 RL 4	TRAP 10/IH 2	TRAP 10/IH 2	TRAP 10/IH 2	TRAP 10/IH 2	TRAP 10/IH 2	TRAP 10/IH 2	TRAP 10/IH 2	TRAP 10/IH 2	TRAP 10/IH 2	TRAP 10/IH 2	TRAP 10/IH 2	TRAP 10/IH 2	TRAP 10/IH 2

* Refer to instruction summary for more information.
‡ The opcode $04 corresponds to one of the loop primitive instructions DBEQ, DBNE, IBEQ, IBNE, TBEQ, or TBNE.

511

Table 7. Hexadecimal to ASCII Conversion

Hex	ASCII	Hex	ASCII	Hex	ASCII	Hex	ASCII
$00	NUL	$20	SP *space*	$40	@	$60	` *grave*
$01	SOH	$21	!	$41	A	$61	a
$02	STX	$22	" *quote*	$42	B	$62	b
$03	ETX	$23	#	$43	C	$63	c
$04	EOT	$24	$	$44	D	$64	d
$05	ENQ	$25	%	$45	E	$65	e
$06	ACK	$26	&	$46	F	$66	f
$07	BEL *beep*	$27	' *apost.*	$47	G	$67	g
$08	BS *back sp*	$28	(	$48	H	$68	h
$09	HT *tab*	$29	)	$49	I	$69	i
$0A	LF *linefeed*	$2A	*	$4A	J	$6A	j
$0B	VT	$2B	+	$4B	K	$6B	k
$0C	FF	$2C	, *comma*	$4C	L	$6C	l
$0D	CR *return*	$2D	- *dash*	$4D	M	$6D	m
$0E	SO	$2E	. *period*	$4E	N	$6E	n
$0F	SI	$2F	/	$4F	O	$6F	o
$10	DLE	$30	0	$50	P	$70	p
$11	DC1	$31	1	$51	Q	$71	q
$12	DC2	$32	2	$52	R	$72	r
$13	DC3	$33	3	$53	S	$73	s
$14	DC4	$34	4	$54	T	$74	t
$15	NAK	$35	5	$55	U	$75	u
$16	SYN	$36	6	$56	V	$76	v
$17	ETB	$37	7	$57	W	$77	w
$18	CAN	$38	8	$58	X	$78	x
$19	EM	$39	9	$59	Y	$79	y
$1A	SUB	$3A	:	$5A	Z	$7A	z
$1B	ESCAPE	$3B	;	$5B	[	$7B	{
$1C	FS	$3C	<	$5C	\	$7C		
$1D	GS	$3D	=	$5D	]	$7D	}
$1E	RS	$3E	>	$5E	^	$7E	~
$1F	US	$3F	?	$5F	_ *under*	$7F	DEL *delete*

Hexadecimal to Decimal Conversion

To convert a hexadecimal number (up to four hexadecimal digits) to decimal, look up the decimal equivalent of each hexadecimal digit in **Table 8**. The decimal equivalent of the original hexadecimal number is the sum of the weights found in the table for all hexadecimal digits.

Table 8. Hexadecimal to/from Decimal Conversion

15	Bit		8	7	Bit		0
15		12	11	8	7	4	3	0
4th Hex Digit		3rd Hex Digit		2nd Hex Digit		1st Hex Digit	
Hex	Decimal	Hex	Decimal	Hex	Decimal	Hex	Decimal
0	0	0	0	0	0	0	0
1	4,096	1	256	1	16	1	1
2	8,192	2	512	2	32	2	2
3	12,288	3	768	3	48	3	3
4	16,384	4	1,024	4	64	4	4
5	20,480	5	1,280	5	80	5	5
6	24,576	6	1,536	6	96	6	6
7	28,672	7	1,792	7	112	7	7
8	32,768	8	2,048	8	128	8	8
9	36,864	9	2,304	9	144	9	9
A	40,960	A	2,560	A	160	A	10
B	45,056	B	2,816	B	176	B	11
C	49,152	C	3,072	C	192	C	12
D	53,248	D	3,328	D	208	D	13
E	57,344	E	3,484	E	224	E	14
F	61,440	F	3,840	F	240	F	15

Decimal to Hexadecimal Conversion

To convert a decimal number (up to $65,535_{10}$) to hexadecimal, find the largest decimal number in **Table 8** that is less than or equal to the number you are converting. The corresponding hexadecimal digit is the most significant hexadecimal digit of the result. Subtract the decimal number found from the original decimal number to get the *remaining decimal value*. Repeat the procedure using the remaining decimal value for each subsequent hexadecimal digit.

CPU12 Reference Guide

Motorola reserves the right to make changes without further notice to any products herein. Motorola makes no warranty, representation or guarantee regarding the suitability of its products for any particular purpose, nor does Motorola assume any liability arising out of the application or use of any product or circuit, and specifically disclaims any and all liability, including without limitation consequential or incidental damages. "Typical" parameters which may be provided in Motorola data sheets and/or specifications can and do vary in different applications and actual performance may vary over time. All operating parameters, including "Typicals" must be validated for each customer application by customer's technical experts. Motorola does not convey any license under its patent rights nor the rights of others. Motorola products are not designed, intended, or authorized for use as components in systems intended for surgical implant into the body, or other applications intended to support or sustain life, or for any other application in which the failure of the Motorola product could create a situation where personal injury or death may occur. Should Buyer purchase or use Motorola products for any such unintended or unauthorized application, Buyer shall indemnify and hold Motorola and its officers, employees, subsidiaries, affiliates, and distributors harmless against all claims, costs, damages, and expenses, and reasonable attorney fees arising out of, directly or indirectly, any claim of personal injury or death associated with such unintended or unauthorized use, even if such claim alleges that Motorola was negligent regarding the design or manufacture of the part. Motorola and (M) are registered trademarks of Motorola, Inc. Motorola, Inc. is an Equal Opportunity/Affirmative Action Employer.

How to reach us:
  USA/EUROPE/Locations Not Listed: Motorola Literature Distribution, P.O. Box 5405, Denver, Colorado 80217, 1-800-441-2447 or
    1-303-675-2140. Customer Focus Center, 1-800-521-6274
  JAPAN: Nippon Motorola Ltd.: SPD, Strategic Planning Office, 141, 4-32-1 Nishi-Gotanda, Shinigawa-Ku, Tokyo, Japan. 03-5487-8488
  ASIA/PACIFIC: Motorola Semiconductors H.K. Ltd., 8B Tai Ping Industrial Park, 51 Ting Kok Road, Tai Po, N.T., Hong Kong. 852-26629298
  Mfax™, Motorola Fax Back System: RMFAX0@email.sps.mot.com; http://sps.motorola.com/mfax/;
    TOUCHTONE, 1-602-244-6609; US and Canada ONLY, 1-800-774-1848
  HOME PAGE: http://motorola.com/sps/

Mfax is a trademark of Motorola, Inc.

© Motorola, Inc., 1998

CPU12RG/D

APPENDIX B: CONFIGURATION CODE

```
;
;               Configuration values for MC68HC912B32
;
OprMode:        equ     $90             ; run in normal single-chip mode.
;
Regbase:        equ     $0000           ; base address of I/O register block.
INITRGDF:       equ     $0011           ; default (out of reset) of INITRG.
SysClock:       equ     8000000         ; system clock frequency.
RAMBase:        equ     $0800           ; base address of on chip RAM.
RAMSize:        equ     1024            ; number of bytes of on-chip RAM
EEBase:         equ     $0d00           ; base address of on-chip EEPROM.
EESize:         equ     768             ; number of bytes of on-chip EEPROM.
FEEBase:        equ     $8000           ; base address of on-chip Flash EEPROM.
FEESize:        equ     32768           ; number of bytes of on-chip Flash EEPROM.
;
COPOff:         equ     0
COPRate1:       equ     1
COPRate2:       equ     2
COPRate3:       equ     3
COPRate4:       equ     4
COPRate5:       equ     5
COPRate6:       equ     6
COPRate7:       equ     7
```

Appendix B: Configuration Code

```
;
;               A-to-D Module Register and bit definitions
;
ATDCTL0:        equ     RegBase+$0060 ; Reserved.
ATDCTL1:        equ     RegBase+$0061 ; Reserved.
ATDCTL2:        equ     RegBase+$0062 ; A-to-D Control register 2.
ATDCTL3:        equ     RegBase+$0063 ; A-to-D Control register 3.
ATDCTL4:        equ     RegBase+$0064 ; A-to-D Control register 4.
ATDCTL5:        equ     RegBase+$0065 ; A-to-D Control register 5.
ATDSTATH:       equ     RegBase+$0066 ; A-to-D status register high byte.
ATDSTATL:       equ     RegBase+$0067 ; A-to-D status register low byte.
ATDTSTH:        equ     RegBase+$0068 ; A-to-D test register high byte.
ATDTSTL:        equ     RegBase+$0069 ; A-to-D test register low byte.
PORTAD:         equ     RegBase+$006f ; Port AD Input Register.
ADR0:           equ     RegBase+$0070 ; A-to-D Result register 0.
ADR1:           equ     RegBase+$0072 ; A-to-D Result register 1.
ADR2:           equ     RegBase+$0074 ; A-to-D Result register 2.
ADR3:           equ     RegBase+$0076 ; A-to-D Result register 3.
ADR4:           equ     RegBase+$0078 ; A-to-D Result register 4.
ADR5:           equ     RegBase+$007a ; A-to-D Result register 5.
ADR6:           equ     RegBase+$007c ; A-to-D Result register 6.
ADR7:           equ     RegBase+$007e ; A-to-D Result register 7.
ADR0H:          equ     RegBase+$0070 ; A-to-D Result register 0.
ADR1H:          equ     RegBase+$0072 ; A-to-D Result register 1.
ADR2H:          equ     RegBase+$0074 ; A-to-D Result register 2.
ADR3H:          equ     RegBase+$0076 ; A-to-D Result register 3.
ADR4H:          equ     RegBase+$0078 ; A-to-D Result register 4.
ADR5H:          equ     RegBase+$007a ; A-to-D Result register 5.
ADR6H:          equ     RegBase+$007c ; A-to-D Result register 6.
ADR7H:          equ     RegBase+$007e ; A-to-D Result register 7.
;
;
;               Bit definitions for the ATDCTL2 register
;
ADPU:           equ     $80             ; enable/disable A-to-D module.
AFFC:           equ     $40             ; A-to-D Fast Flag Clear All Control bit.
ASWAI:          equ     $20             ; Stop A-to-D module in Wait mode.
ASCIE:          equ     $02             ; A-to-D Sequence complete Interrupt Enable.
ASCIF:          equ     $01             ; A-to-D Sequence complete Interrupt Flag.
;
;               Bit definitions for the ATDCTL3 register
;
```

Appendix B: Configuration Code

```
FRZ1:       equ     $02             ; A-to-D module mode in Background.
FRZ0:       equ     $01             ; A-to-D module mode in Background.
;
;                   Bit definitions for the ATDCTL4 register
;
RES10:      equ     $80             ; A-to-D resolution select bit.
SMP1:       equ     $40             ; A-to-D sample time select.
SMP0:       equ     $20             ; A-to-D sample time select.
;
;                   Bit definitions for the ATDCTL5 register
;
S8CM:       equ     $40             ; Select number of channels to convert.
SCAN:       equ     $20             ; Enable continuous channel scan.
MULT:       equ     $10             ; Enable multi-channel conversion.
;
;                   Bit definitions for the ATDSTATH register
;
SCF:        equ     $80             ; Sequence complete flag.
;
;                   Bit definitions for the ATDSTATL register
;
CCF7:       equ     $80             ; Channel 7 conversion complete flag.
CCF6:       equ     $40             ; Channel 6 conversion complete flag.
CCF5:       equ     $20             ; Channel 5 conversion complete flag.
CCF4:       equ     $10             ; Channel 4 conversion complete flag.
CCF3:       equ     $08             ; Channel 3 conversion complete flag.
CCF2:       equ     $04             ; Channel 2 conversion complete flag.
CCF1:       equ     $02             ; Channel 1 conversion complete flag.
CCF0:       equ     $01             ; Channel 0 conversion complete flag.
;
;                   Bit definitions for the ATDTESTL register
;
RST:        equ     $20             ; Module reset control bit.
TSTOUT:     equ     $10             ; Mux. output of TST[3:0].


;
;                   BDLC Module Register and bit definitions
;
BCR1:       equ     RegBase+$00f8;  BDLC Control Register 1.
BSVR:       equ     RegBase+$00f9;  BDLC State Vector Register.
BCR2:       equ     RegBase+$00fa;  BDLC Control Register 2.
BDR:        equ     RegBase+$00fb;  BDLC Data Register.
```

Appendix B: Configuration Code

```
BARD:       equ     RegBase+$00fc;  BDLC Analog Roundtrip Delay Register.
DLCSCR:     equ     RegBase+$00fd;  Port DLC Control Register.
PORTDLC:    equ     RegBase+$00fe;  Port DLC Data Register.
DDRDLC:     equ     RegBase+$00ff;  Port DLC Data Direction Register.
;
;                   Bit definitions for the BCR1 register
;
IMSG:       equ     $80             ; Ignore incomming message control bit.
CLCKS:      equ     $40             ; Integer/binary clovk source select.
R1:         equ     $20             ; BDLC clock rate select bit 1.
R0:         equ     $10             ; BDLC clock rate select bit 0.
IE:         equ     $02             ; BDLC Interrupt enable.
WCM:        equ     $01             ; Stop BDLC in CPU WAIT mode.
;
;                   Bit definitions for the BCR2 register
;
ALOOP:      equ     $80             ; Put BDLC in analog loopback mode.
DLOOP:      equ     $40             ; Put BDLC in digital loopback mode.
RX4XE:      equ     $20             ; Enable 4x receive mode.
NBFS:       equ     $10             ; Normalization Bit Format select.
TEOD:       equ     $08             ; Xmit End Of Data (8-bit CRC).
TSIFR:      equ     $04             ; Xmit In-frame response.
TMIFR1:     equ     $02             ; Xmit multi-byte In-frame response w/ CRC.
TMIFR0:     equ     $01             ; Xmit multi-byte In-frame response w/o CRC.
;
;                   Bit definitions for the BARD register
;
ATE:        equ     $80             ; On-chip analog transceiver enable.
RXPOL:      equ     $40             ; Receive pin polarity.
;
;                   Bit definitions for the BDLSCR register
;
BDLCEN:     equ     $04             ; BDLC Enable.
PUPDLC:     equ     $02             ; Port DLC active pull-up enable.
RDPDLC:     equ     $01             ; Port DLC reduced enable.


;
;                   Breakpoint Module Register and bit definitions
;
BRKCT0:     equ     RegBase+$20     ; Breakpoint Control Register 0.
BRKCT1:     equ     RegBase+$21     ; Breakpoint Control Register 1.
BRKAH:      equ     RegBase+$22     ; Breakpoint Address Register, High Byte.
```

Appendix B: Configuration Code

```
BRKAL:      equ     RegBase+$23     ; Breakpoint Address Register, Low Byte.
BRKDH:      equ     RegBase+$24     ; Breakpoint Data Register, High Byte.
BRKDL:      equ     RegBase+$25     ; Breakpoint Data Register, Low Byte.
;
;                   Bit definitions for the BRKCT0 register
;
BKEN1:      equ     $80             ; Breakpoint mode enable 1.
BKEN0:      equ     $40             ; Breakpoint mode enable 0.
BKPM:       equ     $20             ; Break on program address.
BK1ALE:     equ     $08             ; Breakpoint 1 range control.
BK0ALE:     equ     $04             ; Breakpoint 0 range control.
;
;                   Bit definitions for the BRKCT1 register
;
BKDBE:      equ     $40             ; Enable data bus.
BKMBH:      equ     $20             ; Breakpoint Mask High.
BKMBL:      equ     $10             ; Breakpoint Mask Low.
BK1RWE:     equ     $08             ; Breakpoint 1 R/w Compare Enable.
BK1RW:      equ     $04             ; Breakpoint 1 R/w Compare Value.
BK0RWE:     equ     $02             ; Breakpoint 0 R/w Compare Enable.
BK0RW:      equ     $01             ; Breakpoint 0 R/w Compare Value.
;


;
;                   Clock Synthesizer Module Register and bit definitions
;
SYNR:       equ     RegBase+$0038   ; Synthesizer loop count register.
REFDV:      equ     RegBase+$0039   ; Synthesizer reference divider register.
CGTFLG:     equ     RegBase+$003a   ; Clock generator test register.
PLLFLG:     equ     RegBase+$003b   ; PLL Flag register.
PLLCR:      equ     RegBase+$003c   ; PLL control register.
CLKSEL:     equ     RegBase+$003d   ; Clock generator Clock select register.
SLOW:       equ     RegBase+$003e   ; Slow mode divider register.
CGTCTL:     equ     RegBase+$003f   ; Clock generator test control register.
;
;                   Bit definitions for the PLLFLG register
;
LOCKIF:     equ     $80             ; PLL lock interrupt flag.
LOCK:       equ     $40             ; PLL locked flag.
LHIF:       equ     $02             ; Limp-Home interrupt flag.
LHOME:      equ     $01             ; Limp-Home mode status.
;
```

Appendix B: Configuration Code

```
;               Bit definitions for the PLLCR register
;
LOCKIE:     equ     $80         ; PLL lock interrupt enable.
PLLON:      equ     $40         ; PLL on/off control bit.
AUTO:       equ     $20         ; PLL automatic bandwidth control.
ACQ:        equ     $10         ; PLL not in acquisition.
PSTP:       equ     $04         ; Pseudo-STOP Enable control bit.
LHIE:       equ     $02         ; Limp-Home Interrupt Enable.
NOLHM:      equ     $01         ; Limp-Home mode disable/enable.
;
;               Bit definitions for the CLKSEL register
;
BCSP:       equ     $40         ; SYSCLK (bus) source select.
BCSS:       equ     $20         ; SYSCLK (bus) slow mode clock select.
MCS:        equ     $04         ; Module clock source select.
;
;               Bit definitions for the CGTCTL register
;
OPNLE:      equ     $80         ;
TRK:        equ     $40         ;
TSTCLKE:    equ     $20         ;


;
;               EEPROM Register definitions
;
EEMCR:      equ     Regbase+$f0 ; EEPROM Module Configuration Register.
EEPROT:     equ     Regbase+$f1 ; EEPROM Block Protect Register.
EETST:      equ     Regbase+$f2 ; EEPROM Test Register.
EEPROG:     equ     Regbase+$f3 ; EEPROM Control Register.
;
;
;               Bit definitions for the EEMCR register
;
EESWAI:     equ     $04         ; enable (0)/disable (1) EE in wait mode.
PROTLCK:    equ     $02         ; lock (1)/unlock (0) block protect bits.
EERC:       equ     $01         ; Use sys (0)/RC (1) clock for charge pump.
;
;               Bit definitions for the EEPROT register
;
BPROT4:     equ     $10         ; protect 256 bytes xd00 - xdff.
BPROT3:     equ     $08         ; protect 256 bytes xe00 - xeff.
BPROT2:     equ     $04         ; protect 128 bytes xf00 - xf7f.
```

Appendix B: Configuration Code

```
BPROT1:     equ     $02             ; protect 64 bytes xf80 - xfbf.
BPROT0:     equ     $01             ; protect 64 bytes xfbf - xfff.
;
;                   Bit definitions for the EETST register
;
EEODD:      equ     $80             ; enable (1)/disable(0) odd row programming.
EEVEN:      equ     $40             ; enable (1)/disable(0) even row programming.
MARG:       equ     $20             ; enable (1)/disable(0) voltage margin test.
EECPD:      equ     $10             ; enable (0)/disable(1) EE charge pump.
EECPRD:     equ     $08             ; enable (0)/disable(1) EE charge pump ramp.
EECPM:      equ     $02             ; (1) rut EE charge pump on IRQ/Vpp pin.
;
;                   Bit definitions for the EEPROG register
;
BULKP:      equ     $80             ; enable (0)/disable (1) EE bulk erase.
BYTE:       equ     $10             ; (0) bulk or row, (1) byte or word erase.
ROW:        equ     $08             ; (0) erase EEP array; (1) erase 32-byte row.
ERASE:      equ     $04             ; (0) program or read EE; (1) erase EE.
EELAT:      equ     $02             ; enable (1)/disable(0) pgm/erase latches.
EEPGM:      equ     $01             ; apply (1)/remove (0) Vpp from EE array.
;


;
;                   Flash EEPROM Register definitions
;
FEELCK:     equ     Regbase+$00f4 ; Flash Lock Control Registers.
FEEMCR:     equ     Regbase+$00f5 ; Flash Module Configuration Register.
FEETST:     equ     Regbase+$00f6 ; Flash Module Test Register.
FEECTL:     equ     Regbase+$00f7 ; Flash Control Register.
;
;
;                   Bit definitions for the FEELCK register
;
LOCK:       equ     $01             ; enable/disable writes to FEEMCR register.
;
;                   Bit definitions for the FEEMCR register
;
BOOTP:      equ     $01             ; enable/disable erase & program bootblock.
;
;                   Bit definitions for the FEETST register
;
FSTE:       equ     $80             ; enable/disable gate/drain stress circuitry.
```

Appendix B: Configuration Code

```
GADR:       equ     $40             ; Select drain or gate stress circuitry.
HVT:        equ     $20             ; High voltage present/not during stress test
FENLV:      equ     $10             ; Select low V xsistor in I ref. circuit.
FDISVFP:    equ     $08             ; Select automatic lock if Vfp is low.
VTCK:       equ     $04             ; Select Vt test.
STRE:       equ     $02             ; Select spare row test.
MWPR:       equ     $01             ; Select multiple word programming.
;
;                   Bit definitions for the FEECTL register
;
FEESWAI:    equ     $10             ; enable (0) Flash when in wait mode.
SVFP:       equ     $08             ; Vfp present (1)/not present (0).
ERAS:       equ     $04             ; configure for programming (0) or erase (1).
LAT:        equ     $02             ; enable (1) programming/erase latches.
ENPE:       equ     $01             ; apply (1) Vfp to Flash EEPROM array.
;


;
;                   LIM Module Register and bit definitions
;
PORTA:      equ     RegBase+$0000   ; Port A data register.
PORTB:      equ     RegBase+$0001   ; Port B data register.
DDRA:       equ     RegBase+$0002   ; Port A data direction register.
DDRB:       equ     RegBase+$0003   ; Port B data direction register.
PORTE:      equ     Regbase+$0008   ; Port E data register.
DDRE:       equ     RegBase+$0009   ; Port E data direction register.
PEAR:       equ     RegBase+$000a   ; Port E pin asignment register.
MODE:       equ     RegBase+$000b   ; CPU operating mode select register.
PUCR:       equ     RegBase+$000c   ; Port A, B & E pullup control register.
RDRIV:      equ     RegBase+$000d   ; Port A, B & E drive reduction control
                                    ; register.
INITRM:     equ     RegBase+$0010   ; RAM base address register.
INITRG:     equ     Regbase+$0011   ; I/O Register base address.
INITEE:     equ     RegBase+$0012   ; EEPROM Base address.
MISC:       equ     RegBase+$0013   ; miscellaneous control bit register.
RTICTL:     equ     RegBase+$0014   ; Real Time Interrupt Control register.
RTIFLG:     equ     RegBase+$0015   ; Real Time Interrupt Flag register.
COPCTL:     equ     RegBase+$0016   ; Watchdog timer control register.
COPRST:     equ     RegBase+$0017   ; Watchdog timer reset register.
ITST0:      equ     RegBase+$0018   ; Interrupt test register #0
ITST1:      equ     RegBase+$0019   ; Interrupt test register #1
ITST2:      equ     RegBase+$001a   ; Interrupt test register #2
```

Appendix B: Configuration Code

```
ITST3:      equ     RegBase+$001b;  Interrupt test register #3
INTCR:      equ     RegBase+$001e;  IRQ Interrupt Control Register.
HPRIO:      equ     RegBase+$001f;  Highest priority interrupt source.
;
;           Bit definitions for the PEAR register
;
NDBE:       equ     $80             ; enable/disable the DBE signal on PE7.
PIPOE:      equ     $20             ; enable/disable pipe sigs on PE5 & PE6.
NECLK:      equ     $10             ; enable/disable the E-clock on PE4.
LSTRE:      equ     $08             ; enable/disable the low strobe sig pin PE3.
RDWE:       equ     $04             ; enable/disable the R/w signal on pin PE2.
;
;
;           Bit definitions for the MODE register
;
SMODN:      equ     $80             ; Special mode select bit.
MODB:       equ     $40             ; Mode control 'B' bit.
MODA:       equ     $20             ; Mode control 'A' bit.
ESTR:       equ     $10             ; E-clock stretch enable bit.
IVIS:       equ     $08             ; Internal visibility enable bit.
EBSWAI:     equ     $04             ; External bus stop control bit in WAIT mode.
EME:        equ     $01             ; Emulate port E control bit.
;
;
;           Bit definitions for the PUCR register
;
PUPK:       equ     $80             ; Port K pullup enable control bit.
PUPJ:       equ     $40             ; Port J pullup enable control bit.
PUPH:       equ     $20             ; Port H pullup enable control bit.
PUPE:       equ     $10             ; Port E pullup enable control bit.
PUPB:       equ     $02             ; Port B pullup enable control bit.
PUPA:       equ     $01             ; Port A pullup enable control bit.
;
;
;           Bit definitions for the RDRIV register
;
RDPK:       equ     $80             ; Port K reduced drive control bit.
RDPJ:       equ     $40             ; Port J reduced drive control bit.
RDPH:       equ     $20             ; Port H reduced drive control bit.
RDPE:       equ     $10             ; Port E reduced drive control bit.
RDPB:       equ     $02             ; Port B reduced drive control bit.
RDPA:       equ     $01             ; Port A reduced drive control bit.
;
```

Appendix B: Configuration Code

```
;
;               Bit definitions for the INITRG register
;
MMSWAI:         equ     $01
;
;
;               Bit definitions for the INITEE register
;
EEON:           equ     $01             ; EEPROM enable control bit.
;
;
;               Bit definitions for the MISC control register
;
NDRF:           equ     $40             ; Narrow Data Bus for Register-Following Map.
RFSTR1:         equ     $20             ; Register-Following Stretch bit #1.
RFSTR0:         equ     $10             ; Register-Following Stretch bit #0.
EXSTR1:         equ     $08             ; External Access stretch bit #1.
EXSTR0:         equ     $04             ; External Access stretch bit #0.
MAPROM:         equ     $02             ; memory map location of on-chip Flash
                                        ; EEPROM.
ROMON:          equ     $01             ; Flash EEPROM enable bit.
;
;
;               Bit definitions for the RTICTL control register
;
RTIE:           equ     $80             ; real time interrupt enable control bit.
RSWAI:          equ     $40             ; disable COP & RTI when in WAIT mode.
RSBCK:          equ     $20             ; disable COP & RTI when in background mode.
RTBPY:          equ     $08             ; RTI prescaler bypass.
;
;
;               Bit definitions for the RTIFLG control register
;
RTIF:           equ     $80             ; Real Time Interrupt Flag bit.
;
;
;               Bit definitions for the COPCTL control register
;
CME:            equ     $80             ; Clock monitor control bit.
FCME:           equ     $40             ; Force clock monitor control bit.
FCM:            equ     $20             ; Force clock monitor reset.
FCOP:           equ     $10             ; Force a watchdog timer reset.
DISR:           equ     $08             ; Disable resets from COP & clock monitor.
```

Appendix B: Configuration Code

```
;
;
;               Bit definitions for the INTCR control register
;
IRQE:           equ     $80             ; IRQ edge sensitive only select.
IRQEN:          equ     $40             ; External IRQ enable.
DLY:            equ     $40             ; Enable osc start-up dly on exit from STOP.
;


;
;               MSI Module Register and bit definitions
;
SC0BD:          equ     RegBase+$c0     ; SCI 0 baud rate register word.
SC0BDH:         equ     RegBase+$c0     ; SCI 0 baud rate register high byte.
SC0BDL:         equ     RegBase+$c1     ; SCI 0 baud rate register low byte.
SC0CR1:         equ     RegBase+$c2     ; SCI 0 control register 1.
SC0CR2:         equ     RegBase+$c3     ; SCI 0 control register 2.
SC0SR1:         equ     RegBase+$c4     ; SCI 0 status register 1.
SC0SR2:         equ     RegBase+$c5     ; SCI 0 status register 2.
SC0DRH:         equ     RegBase+$c6     ; SCI 0 data register high byte.
SC0DRL:         equ     RegBase+$c7     ; SCI 0 data register low byte.
SP0CR1:         equ     RegBase+$d0     ; SPI 0 control register 1.
SP0CR2:         equ     RegBase+$d1     ; SPI 0 control register 2.
SP0BR:          equ     RegBase+$d2     ; SPI 0 baud rate register.
SP0SR:          equ     RegBase+$d3     ; SPI 0 status register.
SP0DR:          equ     RegBase+$d5     ; SPI 0 data register.
PORTS:          equ     RegBase+$d6     ; Port S data register.
DDRS:           equ     RegBase+$d7     ; Port S data direction register.
PURDS:          equ     RegBase+$db     ; Port S Pull-up and Reduced Drive Control
                                        ; Register.
;
;               Bit definitions for the SC0BDH register
;
BTST:           equ     $80             ; reserved for factory test.
BSPL:           equ     $40             ; reserved for factory test.
BRDL:           equ     $20             ; reserved for factory test.
;
;               Bit definitions for the SC0CR1 register
;
LOOPS:          equ     $80             ; Loop/Single wire mode select.
WOMS:           equ     $40             ; Tx/Rx pin Open drain enable.
RSRC:           equ     $20             ; Select receiver source.
```

Appendix B: Configuration Code

```
M:          equ     $10             ; Data length select control bit.
WAKE:       equ     $08             ; Address Mark/Idle Line wake-up mode select.
ILT:        equ     $04             ; short/long idle line wake-up mode select.
PE:         equ     $02             ; parity enable/disable control bit.
PT:         equ     $01             ; odd/even parity select control bit.
;
;                   Bit definitions for the SC0CR2 register
;
TIE:        equ     $80             ; Transmit interrupt enable.
TCIE:       equ     $40             ; Transmit complete interrupt enable.
RIE:        equ     $20             ; Receive interrupt enable.
ILIE:       equ     $10             ; Idle line interrupt enable.
TE:         equ     $08             ; Transmitter enable.
RE:         equ     $04             ; Receiver enable.
RWU:        equ     $02             ; Receiver wake-up mode enable.
SBK:        equ     $01             ; Send break control bit.
;
;                   Bit definitions for the SC0SR1 register
;
TDRE:       equ     $80             ; Transmit data register empty status bit.
TC:         equ     $40             ; Transmit data complete flag.
RDRF:       equ     $20             ; Receive data register full flag.
IDLE:       equ     $10             ; Receiver idle line detect flag.
OR:         equ     $08             ; Receiver data overrun flag.
NF:         equ     $04             ; Noise detect flag.
FE:         equ     $02             ; Framing error flag.
PF:         equ     $01             ; Parity error flag.
;
;                   Bit definitions for the SC0SR2 register
;
RAF:        equ     $01             ; receiver active flag.
;
;                   Bit definitions for the SC0DRH register
;
R8:         equ     $80             ; Received Ninth data bit.
T8:         equ     $40             ; Transmitted Ninth data bit.
;
;                   Bit definitions for the SP0CR1 register
;
SPIE:       equ     $80             ; SPI interrupt enable.
SPE:        equ     $40             ; SPI system enable.
SWOM:       equ     $20             ; enable open drain outputs on pins PS7:PS4.
MSTR:       equ     $10             ; Master/Slave mode select.
```

Appendix B: Configuration Code

```
CPOL:       equ     $08             ; Clock polarity select.
CPHA:       equ     $04             ; Clock phase select.
SSOE:       equ     $02             ; Slave select output enable.
LSBF:       equ     $01             ; LSB first enable.
;
;                   Bit definitions for the SP0CR2 register
;
PUPS:       equ     $08             ; Port S pullup enable.
RDPS:       equ     $04             ; Port S reduced drive enable.
SSWAI:      equ     $02             ; Disable SPI system in WAIT mode.
SPC0:       equ     $01             ; SPI pin control.
;
;                   Bit definitions for the SP0SR register
;
SPIF:       equ     $80             ; SPI interrupt flag.
WCOL:       equ     $40             ; Write collision Flag.
MODF:       equ     $01             ; SPI mode fault interrupt flag.


;
;                   PWM Register definitions
;
PWCLK:      equ     Regbase+$0040;  PWM Clocks and Concatenate Register.
PWPOL:      equ     Regbase+$0041;  PWM Clock & Polarity Select Register.
PWEN:       equ     Regbase+$0042;  PWM Channel Enable Register.
PWPRES:     equ     Regbase+$0043;  PWM Prescaler Counter Register.
PWSCAL0:    equ     Regbase+$0044;  PWM Scale Register #0.
PWSCNT0:    equ     Regbase+$0045;  PWM Scale Counter Value #0.
PWSCAL1:    equ     Regbase+$0046;  PWM Scale Register #1.
PWSCNT1:    equ     Regbase+$0047;  PWM Scale Counter Value #1.
PWCNT0:     equ     Regbase+$0048;  PWM Channel #0 Counter Register.
PWCNT1:     equ     Regbase+$0049;  PWM Channel #1 Counter Register.
PWCNT2:     equ     Regbase+$004a;  PWM Channel #2 Counter Register.
PWCNT3:     equ     Regbase+$004b;  PWM Channel #3 Counter Register.
PWPER0:     equ     Regbase+$004c;  PWM Channel #0 Period Register.
PWPER1:     equ     Regbase+$004d;  PWM Channel #1 Period Register.
PWPER2:     equ     Regbase+$004e;  PWM Channel #2 Period Register.
PWPER3:     equ     Regbase+$004f;  PWM Channel #3 Period Register.
PWDTY0:     equ     Regbase+$0050;  PWM Channel #0 Duty Cycle Register.
PWDTY1:     equ     Regbase+$0051;  PWM Channel #1 Duty Cycle Register.
PWDTY2:     equ     Regbase+$0052;  PWM Channel #2 Duty Cycle Register.
PWDTY3:     equ     Regbase+$0053;  PWM Channel #3 Duty Cycle Register.
PWCTL:      equ     Regbase+$0054;  PWM Control Register.
```

Appendix B: Configuration Code

```
PWTST:      equ     Regbase+$0055;  PWM test register.
PORTP:      equ     Regbase+$0056;  Port P data register.
DDRP:       equ     Regbase+$0057;  Port data direction register.
;
;                   Bit definitions for the PWCLK register
;
CON23:      equ     $80             ; enable concatenation of channels 2 & 3.
CON01:      equ     $40             ; enable concatenation of channels 0 & 1.
PCKA2:      equ     $20             ; Prescaler bit 2 for clock A source.
PCKA1:      equ     $10             ; Prescaler bit 1 for clock A source.
PCKA0:      equ     $08             ; Prescaler bit 0 for clock A source.
PCKB2:      equ     $04             ; Prescaler bit 2 for clock B source.
PCKB1:      equ     $02             ; Prescaler bit 1 for clock B source.
PCKB0:      equ     $01             ; Prescaler bit 0 for clock B source.
;
;                   Bit definitions for the PWPOL register
;
PCLK3:      equ     $80             ; PWM Channel 3 clock select.
PCLK2:      equ     $40             ; PWM Channel 2 clock select.
PCLK1:      equ     $20             ; PWM Channel 1 clock select.
PCLK0:      equ     $10             ; PWM Channel 0 clock select.
PPOL3:      equ     $08             ; PWM Channel 3 polarity select.
PPOL2:      equ     $04             ; PWM Channel 2 polarity select.
PPOL1:      equ     $02             ; PWM Channel 1 polarity select.
PPOL0:      equ     $01             ; PWM Channel 0 polarity select.
;
;                   Bit definitions for the PWEN register
;
PWEN3:      equ     $08             ; PWM Channel 3 enable.
PWEN2:      equ     $04             ; PWM Channel 2 enable.
PWEN1:      equ     $02             ; PWM Channel 1 enable.
PWEN0:      equ     $01             ; PWM Channel 0 enable.
;
;                   Bit definitions for the PWCTL register
;
PSWAI:      equ     $10             ; Stop PWM Channels in Wait mode.
CENTR:      equ     $08             ; Center-aligned output mode.
RDPP:       equ     $04             ; enable/disable reduced drive on Port P.
PUPP:       equ     $02             ; enable/disable pull-ups on Port P.
PSBCK:      equ     $01             ; Stop PWM Channels in Background mode.
;
;                   Bit definitions for the PWTST register
;
```

Appendix B: Configuration Code

```
DISCR:    equ    $80          ; Disable rst of ch. ctr on write to ch ctr.
DISCP:    equ    $40          ; Disable compare count period.
DISCAL:   equ    $20          ; Disable load of scale-ctrs on write
                              ; to associated scale-registers.

;
;              Standard Timer Module Register and bit definitions
;
TIOS:     equ    RegBase+$0080 ; Timer Input Capture/Output Compare Select.
CFORC:    equ    RegBase+$0081 ; Timer Compare Force Register.
OC7M:     equ    RegBase+$0082 ; Output Compare 7 Mask Register.
OC7D:     equ    RegBase+$0083 ; Output Compare 7 Data Register.
TCNT:     equ    RegBase+$0084 ; Timer Count Register.
TSCR:     equ    RegBase+$0086 ; Timer System Control Register.
TQCR:     equ    RegBase+$0087 ; Reserved for future use.
TCTL1:    equ    RegBase+$0088 ; Timer Control Register #1.
TCTL2:    equ    RegBase+$0089 ; Timer Control Register #2.
TCTL3:    equ    RegBase+$008a ; Timer Control Register #3.
TCTL4:    equ    RegBase+$008b ; Timer Control Register #4.
TMSK1:    equ    RegBase+$008c ; Timer Interrupt Mask #1.
TMSK2:    equ    RegBase+$008d ; Timer Interrupt Mask #2.
TFLG1:    equ    RegBase+$008e ; Timer Interrupt Flag #1.
TFLG2:    equ    RegBase+$008f ; Timer Interrupt Flag #2.
TC0:      equ    RegBase+$0090 ; Input Capture/Output Compare Channel 0.
TC1:      equ    RegBase+$0092 ; Input Capture/Output Compare Channel 1.
TC2:      equ    RegBase+$0094 ; Input Capture/Output Compare Channel 2.
TC3:      equ    RegBase+$0096 ; Input Capture/Output Compare Channel 3.
TC4:      equ    RegBase+$0098 ; Input Capture/Output Compare Channel 4.
TC5:      equ    RegBase+$009a ; Input Capture/Output Compare Channel 5.
TC6:      equ    RegBase+$009c ; Input Capture/Output Compare Channel 6.
TC7:      equ    RegBase+$009e ; Input Capture/Output Compare Channel 7.
PACTL:    equ    RegBase+$00a0 ; Pulse accumulator control register.
PAFLG:    equ    RegBase+$00a1 ; Pulse accumulator flag register.
PACNT:    equ    RegBase+$00a2 ; 16-bit pulse accumulator count register.
TIMTST:   equ    RegBase+$00ad ; Timer test register.
PORTT:    equ    RegBase+$00ae ; Timer port data register.
PORTTD:   equ    RegBase+$00af ; Timer port data direction register.
DDRT:     equ    RegBase+$00af ; Timer port data direction register.
;
;              Bit definitions for the TIOS register
;
IOS7:     equ    $80          ; Input Capture/Output Compare Select Ch 7.
```

Appendix B: Configuration Code

```
IOS6:       equ     $40             ; Input Capture/Output Compare Select Ch 6.
IOS5:       equ     $20             ; Input Capture/Output Compare Select Ch 5.
IOS4:       equ     $10             ; Input Capture/Output Compare Select Ch 4.
IOS3:       equ     $08             ; Input Capture/Output Compare Select Ch 3.
IOS2:       equ     $04             ; Input Capture/Output Compare Select Ch 2.
IOS1:       equ     $02             ; Input Capture/Output Compare Select Ch 1.
IOS0:       equ     $01             ; Input Capture/Output Compare Select Ch 0.
;
;                   Bit definitions for the CFORC register
;
FOC7:       equ     $80             ; Force Compare Select On Channel 7.
FOC6:       equ     $40             ; Force Compare Select On Channel 6.
FOC5:       equ     $20             ; Force Compare Select On Channel 5.
FOC4:       equ     $10             ; Force Compare Select On Channel 4.
FOC3:       equ     $08             ; Force Compare Select On Channel 3.
FOC2:       equ     $04             ; Force Compare Select On Channel 2.
FOC1:       equ     $02             ; Force Compare Select On Channel 1.
FOC0:       equ     $01             ; Force Compare Select On Channel 0.
;
;                   Bit definitions for the OC7M register
;
OC7M7:      equ     $80             ; Force Compare Mask For Channel 7.
OC7M6:      equ     $40             ; Force Compare Mask For Channel 6.
OC7M5:      equ     $20             ; Force Compare Mask For Channel 5.
OC7M4:      equ     $10             ; Force Compare Mask For Channel 4.
OC7M3:      equ     $08             ; Force Compare Mask For Channel 3.
OC7M2:      equ     $04             ; Force Compare Mask For Channel 2.
OC7M1:      equ     $02             ; Force Compare Mask For Channel 1.
OC7M0:      equ     $01             ; Force Compare Mask For Channel 0.
;
;                   Bit definitions for the OC7D register
;
OC7D7:      equ     $80             ; Force Compare Data For Channel 7.
OC7D6:      equ     $40             ; Force Compare Data For Channel 6.
OC7D5:      equ     $20             ; Force Compare Data For Channel 5.
OC7D4:      equ     $10             ; Force Compare Data For Channel 4.
OC7D3:      equ     $08             ; Force Compare Data For Channel 3.
OC7D2:      equ     $04             ; Force Compare Data For Channel 2.
OC7D1:      equ     $02             ; Force Compare Data For Channel 1.
OC7D0:      equ     $01             ; Force Compare Data For Channel 0.
;
;                   Bit definitions for the TSCR register
;
```

Appendix B: Configuration Code

```
TEN:        equ     $80             ; Timer Enable.
TSWAI:      equ     $40             ; Stop Timer in Wait Mode.
TSBCK:      equ     $20             ; Stop Timer in Background Mode.
TFFCA:      equ     $10             ; Timer Fast Flag Clear Mode.
;
;                   Bit definitions for the TCTL1 register
;
OM7:        equ     $80             ; Output Mode For Channel 7.
OL7:        equ     $40             ; Output Level For Channel 7.
OM6:        equ     $20             ; Output Mode For Channel 6.
OL6:        equ     $10             ; Output Level For Channel 6.
OM5:        equ     $08             ; Output Mode For Channel 5.
OL5:        equ     $04             ; Output Level For Channel 5.
OM4:        equ     $02             ; Output Mode For Channel 4.
OL4:        equ     $01             ; Output Level For Channel 4.
;
;                   Bit definitions for the TCTL2 register
;
OM3:        equ     $80             ; Output Mode For Channel 3.
OL3:        equ     $40             ; Output Level For Channel 3.
OM2:        equ     $20             ; Output Mode For Channel 2.
OL2:        equ     $10             ; Output Level For Channel 2.
OM1:        equ     $08             ; Output Mode For Channel 1.
OL1:        equ     $04             ; Output Level For Channel 1.
OM0:        equ     $02             ; Output Mode For Channel 0.
OL0:        equ     $01             ; Output Level For Channel 0.
;
;                   Bit definitions for the TCTL3 register
;
EDG7B:      equ     $80             ; Input Capture Edge Control For Channel 7.
EDG7A:      equ     $40             ; Input Capture Edge Control For Channel 7.
EDG6B:      equ     $20             ; Input Capture Edge Control For Channel 6.
EDG6A:      equ     $10             ; Input Capture Edge Control For Channel 6.
EDG5B:      equ     $08             ; Input Capture Edge Control For Channel 5.
EDG5A:      equ     $04             ; Input Capture Edge Control For Channel 5.
EDG4B:      equ     $02             ; Input Capture Edge Control For Channel 4.
EDG4A:      equ     $01             ; Input Capture Edge Control For Channel 4.
;
;                   Bit definitions for the TCTL4 register
;
EDG3B:      equ     $80             ; Input Capture Edge Control For Channel 3.
EDG3A:      equ     $40             ; Input Capture Edge Control For Channel 3.
EDG2B:      equ     $20             ; Input Capture Edge Control For Channel 2.
```

Appendix B: Configuration Code

```
EDG2A:      equ     $10             ; Input Capture Edge Control For Channel 2.
EDG1B:      equ     $08             ; Input Capture Edge Control For Channel 1.
EDG1A:      equ     $04             ; Input Capture Edge Control For Channel 1.
EDG0B:      equ     $02             ; Input Capture Edge Control For Channel 0.
EDG0A:      equ     $01             ; Input Capture Edge Control For Channel 0.
;
;                   Bit definitions for the TMSK1 register
;
C7I:        equ     $80             ; Channel 7 Interrupt Enable.
C6I:        equ     $40             ; Channel 6 Interrupt Enable.
C5I:        equ     $20             ; Channel 5 Interrupt Enable.
C4I:        equ     $10             ; Channel 4 Interrupt Enable.
C3I:        equ     $08             ; Channel 3 Interrupt Enable.
C2I:        equ     $04             ; Channel 2 Interrupt Enable.
C1I:        equ     $02             ; Channel 1 Interrupt Enable.
C0I:        equ     $01             ; Channel 0 Interrupt Enable.
;
;                   Bit definitions for the TMSK2 register
;
TOI:        equ     $80             ; Timer Overflow Interrupt Enable.
PUPT:       equ     $20             ; Port T Pull-up Resistor Enable.
RDPT:       equ     $10             ; Port T Reduced Drive Enable.
TCRE:       equ     $08             ; Timer Counter Reset Enable.
PR2:        equ     $04             ; Timer Prescaler Select Bit 2.
PR1:        equ     $02             ; Timer Prescaler Select Bit 1.
PR0:        equ     $01             ; Timer Prescaler Select Bit 0.
;
;                   Bit definitions for the TFLG1 register
;
C7F:        equ     $80             ; Channel 7 Interrupt Flag.
C6F:        equ     $40             ; Channel 6 Interrupt Flag.
C5F:        equ     $20             ; Channel 5 Interrupt Flag.
C4F:        equ     $10             ; Channel 4 Interrupt Flag.
C3F:        equ     $08             ; Channel 3 Interrupt Flag.
C2F:        equ     $04             ; Channel 2 Interrupt Flag.
C1F:        equ     $02             ; Channel 1 Interrupt Flag.
C0F:        equ     $01             ; Channel 0 Interrupt Flag.
;
;                   Bit definitions for the TFLG2 register
;
TOF:        equ     $80             ; Timer Overflow Interrupt Flag.
;
;                   Bit definitions for the PACTL register
```

Appendix B: Configuration Code

```
;
PAEN:       equ     $40             ; Pulse Accumulator System Enable.
PAMOD:      equ     $20             ; Pulse Accumulator Mode Select.
PEDGE:      equ     $10             ; Pulse Accumulator Edge Select.
CLK1:       equ     $08             ; Pulse Accumulator Clock Select.
CLK0:       equ     $04             ; Pulse Accumulator Clock Select.
PAOVI:      equ     $02             ; Pulse Accumulator Overflow Interrupt
Enable.
PAI:        equ     $01             ; Pulse Accumulator Input Interrupt Enable.
;
;           Bit definitions for the PAFLG register
;
PAOVF:      equ     $02             ; Pulse Accumulator Overflow Interrupt Flag.
PAIF:       equ     $01             ; Pulse Accumulator Input Interrupt Flag.
;
;           Bit definitions for the TIMTST register
;
TCBYP:      equ     $02             ; Timer Divider Chain Bypass.
PCBYP:      equ     $01             ; Pulse Accumulator Divider Chain Bypass.
;
```

APPENDIX C: BDM PRIMITIVES LISTINGS

```
PORTT:          EQU     $00AE       ;Timer port data
PORTTD:         EQU     $00AF       ;Timer port ddr

                ORG     $0E00       ;B32 EEPROM past Dbug12 pod use.
;
;************************************************************
; Serial BDM data writes. Alternate entry pionts for
; 8-bit and 16-bit values.
;
; WSerial_8 - Enter with data in A, D value lost.
; WSerial_16 - Enter with data in D, D value lost.
;   X, Y, and D used in sub but not restored
;
; Port T bit-7 is tied to target BKGD for serial comm
; Port T bit-6 is tied to target RESET (=1 in this sub)
; This routine writes zero to bits 5-0 if GP output
;
; 16 clocks per bit time. Entry overhead to first
; falling edge is 11 cyc (8-bit) or 14 cyc (16-bit)
; Exit overhead from end of last bit time is 5 cyc if
; last bit=1, 7 cyc if last bit=0
; Total (+0/-2 cyc): 146 (8-bit)  277 (16-bit) cycles
;
;*** CAUTION: CRITICALLY TIMED ROUTINE *****************
;   assumes internal execution or no stretches
```

Appendix C: BDM Command Listings

```
;***********************************************************
;
WSerial_16:     ldy     #16             ; [2] bit count = 16
                bra     Write_Fast      ; [3] Rest is same as Write8
WSerial_8:      ldy     #8              ; [2] bit count = 8
Write_Fast:     ldx     #$40c0          ; [2] Patterns for BKGD low:hi
                asld                    ; [1] MSB of data to C-bit
                xgdx                    ; [1] data to X, $40c0 to D
                stab    PORTT           ; [2] Pw Write BKGD output to 1
                stab    PORTTD          ; [2] Pw BKGD to active high
Bit_Loop:       staa    ePORTT          ; [3] wOP BKGD output to 0
                bcc     Do_0            ; [1/3] Branch if bit is a 0
Do_1:           stab    ePORTT          ; [3] wOP force BKGD back high
                xgdx                    ; [1] data to D, $40c0 to X
                asld                    ; [1] next data bit to C-bit
                xgdx                    ; [1] data to X, $40c0 to D
                dey                     ; [1] Update bit counter
                beq     Done_1F         ; [1/3] If last data bit sent
                nop                     ; [1] delay
                bra     Bit_Loop        ; [3] Loop for next bit
Do_0:           xgdx                    ; [1] data to D, $40c0 to X
                asld                    ; [1] next data bit to C-bit
                xgdx                    ; [1] data to X, $40c0 to D
                dey                     ; [1] Update bit counter
                beq     Done_0F         ; [1/3] If last data bit sent
                stab    PORTT           ; [2] Pw BKGD output to 1
                bra     Bit_Loop        ; [3] Loop for next bit
Done_0F:        stab    ePORTT          ; [3] wOP force BKGD high
Done_1F:        clr     ePORTTD         ; [3] wOP force BKGD to hi-z
                rts                     ; [5] ** return **
;
;***********************************************************
; Serial BDM data read. All background read operations
; involve 16-bit data even if only a byte is being read.
; Byte operations return data from odd addresses in B
; and data from even addresses in A. This routine always
; returns 16-bits of data in D (A:B).
;
; RSerial_16 - Returns data in D.
;   X used in subroutine but not restored
;
; Port T bit-7 is tied to target BKGD for serial comm
; Port T bit-6 is tied to target RESET (=1 in this sub)
```

Appendix C: BDM Command Listings

```
; This routine writes $C0 to DDRT
;
; 19 clocks per bit time. Entry overhead to first
; BKGD edge is 12 cycles. Exit overhead is 1 cycle.
; Total 317 cycles
;
;*** CAUTION: CRITICALLY TIMED ROUTINE *****************
;** assumes internal execution or no stretches
;********************************************************

RSerial_16:     bclr    PORTTD,$80  ; [4] rPOw be sure BKGD is hi-z
                bclr    PORTT,$80   ; [4] rPOw write BKGD output to 0
;
; BKGD will go to driven 0 when 1 written to PORTTD bit-7
;
                bset    PORTTD,$80  ; [4] rPOw BKGD low to start bit tim
                bclr    PORTTD,$80  ; [4] rPOw return BKGD to hi-z
                ldd     #$0003      ; [2] end when 1 shifts out MSB of D
                bra     Read_1F     ; [3] delay to match timing
Read_1F:        ldx     PORTT       ; [3] RfP read next data bit to MSB
                xgdx                ; [1] new bit to MSB of A, data to X
                asla                ; [1] shift new data bit into Carry
                xgdx                ; [1] data to D, C not changed
                bset    PORTTD,$80  ; [4] rPOw BKGD low to start bit tim
                bclr    PORTTD,$80  ; [4] rPOw return BKGD to hi-z
                rolb                ; [1] shift new bit to LSB from rt
                rola                ; [1] 16-bit rotate
                bcc     Read_1F     ; [1/3] bra=more bits, else done
Read_done:      xgdx                ; [1] data to X
                nop                 ; [1] delay
                ldaa    PORTT       ; [3] rfP read last data bit to MSB
                asla                ; [1] shift last data bit to carry
                xgdx                ; [1] data to D, C not affected
                rolb                ; [1] shift new bit to LSB from rt
                rola                ; [1] 16-bit rotate
                rts                 ; [5] ** return **
;
; PORT and ddr defined earlier, these EQUs force the
; assembler to use extended addressing rather than direct

ePORTT:         EQU     $00AE       ; Extended mode Timer port data
ePORTTD:        EQU     $00AF       ; Extended mode Timer port ddr
```

Appendix C: BDM Command Listings

```
;******************************************************
; Some BDM command subroutines end in a jmp to
; a primitive subroutine. The rts at the end of that
; routine returns to the program that called the
; command subroutine (double return).
;
; These routines require interrupts to be masked.
; If needed, mask interrupts before calling.
;******************************************************
; There are two groups of BDM commands. The first group
; consists of hardware commands which do not require
; the MCU to be in active BDM mode. The second group of
; commands are firmware commands which require that
; BDM is active.
;
; The hardware commands are...
;
;   BACKGROUND - Go to active background mode
;   WRITE_BYTE - Write a byte with BDM not in map
;   WRITE_BD_BYTE - Write a byte with BDM in map
;   WRITE_WORD - Write a word with BDM not in map
;   WRITE_BD_WORD - Write a word with BDM in map
;   READ_BYTE - Read a byte with BDM not in map
;   READ_BD_BYTE - Read a byte with BDM in map
;   READ_WORD - Read a word with BDM not in map
;   READ_BD_WORD - Read a word with BDM in map
;
; Next four cammands are not basic BDM commands,
; they are built from basic BDM hardware commands.
;
;   ENABLE_FIRM - Set ENBDM bit in BDM status reg
;                 Enables firmware command group
;                 and BGND instruction (opcode)
;   BDM_STATUS - Read BDM status register
;   WRITE_CCR - Write user CCR
;   READ_CCR - Read user CCR
;******************************************************
;
;******************************************************
; BACKGROUND - $90 - Enter background mode
;
; skip if ENBDM bit not set - it would just return
; to user code anyway
```

538

Appendix C: BDM Command Listings

```
;*****************************************************
;
BACKGROUND:     jsr     BDM_STATUS  ; [4+958] read current status
                tstb                ; [1] see if firmware enabled
                bpl     Exit_BGND   ; [1/3] exit if not enabled
                ldaa    #$90        ; [1] BACKGROUND command code
                jsr     WSerial_8   ; [4+146]
                jmp     Dly_40      ; [3+45] delay then double return
Exit_BGND:      rts                 ; [5] return
;
;*****************************************************
; WRITE_BYTE - $C0 aaaa oooo
;    Write byte - BDM out of map
;
; On entry D=addr to write,
; data byte (dd) to write in low half of X (??:dd)
;*****************************************************
;
WRITE_BYTE:     pshx                ; [2] save data
                pshd                ; [2] save address
                ldaa    #$c0        ; [1] WRITE_BYTE command code
WTb_com:        jsr     WSerial_8   ; [4+146] send command
                ldd     0,sp        ; [3] address of byte to write
                jsr     WSerial_16  ; [4+277] send address
                puld                ; [3] recover address and deallocate
                bitb    #$01        ; [1] test for odd/even address
                puld                ; [3] recover data and deallocate
                bne     arn_swp0    ; [1/3] bra if addr odd (data in B)
                exg     b,a         ; [1] even addr so swap data to A
arn_swp0:       jsr     WSerial_16  ; [4+277] send 16-bits of data
                jmp     Dly_175     ; [3+173] wait for free cycle
                                    ; NOTE: double return after Dly_175
;
;*****************************************************
; WRITE_BD_BYTE - $C4 aaaa oooo
;    Write a byte with BDM in map
;
; On entry D=addr to write,
; data byte (dd) to write in low half of X (??:dd)
;*****************************************************
;
WRITE_BD_BYTE:  pshx                ; [2] save data
                pshd                ; [2] save address
```

539

Appendix C: BDM Command Listings

```
                        ldaa    #$c4        ; [1] WRITE_BD_BYTE command code
                        bra     WTb_com     ; [3] rest is same as WRITE_BYTE
;
;*****************************************************
; WRITE_WORD - $C8 aaaa oooo
;   Write word - BDM out of map
;
; On entry D=addr to write, data word to write in X
; Carry set on return if address was illegal (odd)
;*****************************************************
;
WRITE_WORD:     jsr     Test4odd    ; [4+10] proceed only if addr even
                                    ; NOTE: double returns if address was bad
                pshx                ; [2] save data
                pshd                ; [2] save address
                ldaa    #$c8        ; [1] WRITE_WORD command code

WTw_com:        jsr     WSerial_8   ; [4+146] send command
                puld                ; [3] recover address and deallocate
                jsr     WSerial_16  ; [4+277] send address
                puld                ; [3] recover data and deallocate
                jsr     WSerial_16  ; [4+277] send data
                jsr     Dly_175     ; [4+173] wait for free cycle
                clc                 ; [1] indicate no error
                rts                 ; [5] ** return **
;
;*****************************************************
; WRITE_BD_WORD - $CC aaaa oooo
;   Write a word with BDM in map
;* NOTE: there are no writable words in BD space
;*       (so this command is not useful)
;
; On entry D=addr to write, data word to write in X
; Carry set on return if address was illegal (odd)
;*****************************************************
;
WRITE_BD_WORD:  bsr     Test4odd    ; [4+10] proceed only if addr even
                                    ; NOTE: double returns if address was bad
                pshx                ; [2] save data
                pshd                ; [2] save address
                ldaa    #$cc        ; [1] WRITE_BD_WORD command code
                bra     WTw_com     ; [3] rest is same as WRITE_WORD
;
```

Appendix C: BDM Command Listings

```
;****************************************************
; READ_BYTE - $E0 aaaa iiii
;    Read byte - BDM out of map
;
; On entry D=address to read,
; return data byte in D (00:B)
;****************************************************
;
READ_BYTE:      pshd                    ; [2] save address
                ldaa        #$e0        ; [1] command code for READ_BYTE
RDb_com:        jsr         WSerial_8   ; [4+146] send command
                ldd         0,sp        ; [3] address of byte to read
                jsr         WSerial_16  ; [4+277] send address
                bsr         Dly_175     ; [4+173] wait for free cycle
                jsr         RSerial_16  ; [4+317] get 16-bits of data
                pulx                    ; [3] recover address and deallocate
                xgdx                    ; [1] swap address to D for tests
                bitb        #$01        ; [1] test for odd/even address
                xgdx                    ; [1] swap address and data back
                bne         arn_tfr0    ; [1/3] bra if addr odd (data in B)
                tfr         a,b         ; [1] even addr so move data to B
arn_tfr0:       clra                    ; [1] clear upper byte of returned D
                rts                     ; [5] ** return **
;
;****************************************************
; READ_BD_BYTE - $E4 aaaa iiii
;    Read a byte with BDM in map
;
; On entry D=address to read,
; return data byte in D (00:B)
;****************************************************
;
READ_BD_BYTE:   pshd                    ; [2] save address
                ldaa        #$e4        ; [1] command code for READ_BD_BYTE
                bra         RDb_com     ; [3] rest is same as READ_BYTE
;
;****************************************************
; READ_WORD - $E8 aaaa iiii
;    Read word - BDM out of map
;
; On entry D=address to read,
; return data word in D (A:B)
; Carry set on return if address was illegal (odd)
```

541

Appendix C: BDM Command Listings

```
;****************************************************
;
READ_WORD:        bsr     Test4odd    ; [4+10] cont. only if addr even
                                      ; NOTE: double returns if address was bad
                  pshd                ; [2] save address
                  ldaa    #$e8        ; [1] command code for READ_WORD
RDw_com:          jsr     WSerial_8   ; [4+146] send command
                  puld                ; [3] recover address and deallocate
                  jsr     WSerial_16  ; [4+277] send address
                  bsr     Dly_175     ; [4+173] wait for free cycle
                  jsr     RSerial_16  ; [4+317] get 16-bits of data
                  clc                 ; [1] indicate no error
                  rts                 ; [5] ** return **
;
;****************************************************
; READ_BD_WORD - $Ec aaaa iiii
;    Read a word with BDM in map
;
; On entry D=address to read,
; return data word in D (A:B)
; Carry set on return if address was illegal (odd)
;****************************************************
;
READ_BD_WORD:     bsr     Test4odd    ; [4+10] cont. only if addr even
                                      ; NOTE: double returns if address was bad
                  pshd                ; [2] save address
                  ldaa    #$ec        ; [1] command code for READ_BD_WORD
                  bra     RDw_com     ; [3] rest is same as READ_WORD
;
;****************************************************
; ENABLE_FIRM - $C4 $FF01 %1x000000
;
; This command optionally writes $80 or $C0 to
; BDM address $FF01 depending upon the current
; value in BDM Status register $FF01.
;****************************************************
;
ENABLE_FIRM:      bsr     BDM_STATUS  ; [4+958] first read current status
                  tstb                ; [1] See if ENBDM already enabled
                  bmi     Exit_EF     ; [1/3] exit if already enabled
                  andb    #$40        ; [1] keep current BDMACT status
                  orab    #$80        ; [1] set FIRMware enable bit
                  clra                ; [1] clear other half of D
```

Appendix C: BDM Command Listings

```
                tfr     d,x             ; [1] move data to X
                ldd     #$ff01          ; [2] address of BDM status register
                bsr     WRITE_BD_BYTE   ; [4+909] update STATUS register
Exit_EF:        rts                     ; [5] ** return **
;
;*****************************************************
; BDM_STATUS - $E4 FF01 iiii
;   Read BDM status register
;*****************************************************
;
BDM_STATUS:     ldd     #$ff01          ; [2] addr of BDM status register
                bra     READ_BD_BYTE    ; [3+953] execute and double return
;
;*****************************************************
; WRITE_CCR - $c4 FF06 oooo
;   Write user CCR register, enter with data in A
;*****************************************************
;
WRITE_CCR:      tfr     d,x             ; [1] move data to X
                ldd     #$ff06          ; [2] addr of CCRSAV register
                jmp     WRITE_BD_BYTE   ; [3+909] write & double return
;
;*****************************************************
; READ_CCR - $E4 FF06 iiii
;   Read user CCR register, data returned in A
;*****************************************************
;
READ_CCR:       ldd     #$ff06          ; [2] addr of CCRSAV register
                bra     READ_BD_BYTE    ; [3+953] read and double return
;
;** Local subroutine to delay about 175 target E cycles
;** to allow wait for dead cycle to complete access
;** overhead here is 9 cycles, n is 42, loop is 4(n-1)
;** total delay is 9+164=173 cycles (plus ext overhead)
;
Dly_175:        ldx     #42             ; [2] initialize loop count
dlydecx:        dex                     ; [1] update loop count=count-1
                bne     dlydecx         ; [1/3] loop till X=0
                rts                     ; [5] ** return **
;
;** Local subroutine to check for illegal odd address
;** returns to calling routine or sets carry
;** (to indicate error) and double returns
```

Appendix C: BDM Command Listings

```
;** to program that called calling routine
;
Test4odd:      bitb      #$01       ; [1] check for odd (illegal)
               beq       notodd     ; [1/3] bra if addr was even
               sec                  ; [1] indicate error
               leas      2,sp       ; [2] addr was odd so double return
notodd:        rts                  ; [5] ** return or double return **
;
;** Local subroutine to delay about 40 target E cycles
;** to allow time for BDM to complete command or
;** to allow time for firmware to complete access
;** overhead here is 9 cycles, n is 10, loop is 4(n-1)
;** total delay is 9+36=45 cycles (plus ext overhead)
;
Dly_40:        ldx       #10        ; [2] initialize loop count
dly40decx:     dex                  ; [1] update loop count=count-1
               bne       dly40decx  ; [1/3] loop till X=0
               rts                  ; [5] ** return **
;
;*****************************************************
; Firmware commands can only be executed while the
; background mode is active. If BDM is not active,
; these commands should not be issued.
; To find out if BDM is active, you can execute a
; BDM_STATUS command and check bit-6 of returned
; value in A (0=not active).
;
; The firmware commands are...
;
;   WRITE_NEXT - Pre-inc X by 2 and write word
;   WRITE_PC - Write user PC
;   WRITE_D - Write user D accumulator
;   WRITE_X - Write index register X
;   WRITE_Y - Write index register Y
;   WRITE_SP - Write stack pointer
;   READ_NEXT - Pre-inc X by 2 and read word
;   READ_PC - Read user PC
;   READ_D - Read user D accumulator
;   READ_X - Read index register X
;   READ_Y - Read index register Y
;   READ_SP - Read stack pointer
;   BDM_GO - Resume user program from active BDM
;   BDM_TRACE - Do 1 user inst. and return to BDM
```

Appendix C: BDM Command Listings

```
;   TAG_GO - Enable tagging and go to user program
;****************************************************
;
;****************************************************
; WRITE_NEXT - $42 - Pre-inc X by 2 and write word
;****************************************************
;
WRITE_NEXT:     pshd                    ; [2] save data
                ldaa    #$42            ; [1] WRITE_NEXT command code
;
;** Local common routine
;
Write_Firm:     jsr     WSerial_8       ; [4+146] send command
                puld                    ; [3] recover data
                jsr     WSerial_16      ; [4+277] send data
                bra     Dly_40          ; [3+45] allow time to do write
                                        ; double returns from end of delay routine
;
;****************************************************
; WRITE_PC - $43 - Write user PC
;****************************************************
;
WRITE_PC:       pshd                    ; [2] save data
                ldaa    #$43            ; [1] WRITE_PC command code
                bra     Write_Firm      ; [3+482] double return
;
;****************************************************
; WRITE_D - $44 - Write user D accumulator
;****************************************************
;
WRITE_D:        pshd                    ; [2] save data
                ldaa    #$44            ; [1] WRITE_D command code
                bra     Write_Firm      ; [3+482] double return
;
;****************************************************
; WRITE_X - $45 - Write index register X
;****************************************************
;
WRITE_X:        pshd                    ; [2] save data
                ldaa    #$45            ; [1] WRITE_X command code
                bra     Write_Firm      ; [3+482] double return
;
;****************************************************
```

Appendix C: BDM Command Listings

```
; WRITE_Y - $46 - Write index register Y
;****************************************************
;
WRITE_Y:        pshd                ; [2] save data
                ldaa    #$46        ; [1] WRITE_Y command code
                bra     Write_Firm ; [3+482] double return
;
;****************************************************
; WRITE_SP - $47 - Write stack pointer
;****************************************************
;
WRITE_SP:       pshd                ; [2] save data
                ldaa    #$47        ; [1] WRITE_SP command code
                bra     Write_Firm ; [3+482] double return
;
;****************************************************
; READ_NEXT - $62 - Pre-inc X by 2 and read word
;****************************************************
;
READ_NEXT:      ldaa    #$62        ; [1] READ_NEXT command code
;
;** Local common routine
;
Read_Firm:      jsr     WSerial_8  ; [4+146] send command
                bsr     Dly_40     ; [4+45] allow firmware to do access
                jmp     RSerial_16 ; [3+317] read data & double return
;
;****************************************************
; READ_PC - $63 - Read user PC
;****************************************************
;
READ_PC:        ldaa    #$63        ; [1] READ_PC command code
                bra     Read_Firm  ; [3+519] double return
;
;****************************************************
; READ_D - $64 - Read user D accumulator
;****************************************************
;
READ_D:         ldaa    #$64        ; [1] READ_D command code
                bra     Read_Firm  ; [3+519] double return
;
;****************************************************
; READ_X - $65 - Read index register X
```

```
;***************************************************
;
READ_X:            ldaa      #$65        ; [1] READ_X command code
                   bra       Read_Firm   ; [3+519] double return
;
;***************************************************
; READ_Y - $66 - Read index register Y
;***************************************************
;
READ_Y:            ldaa      #$66        ; [1] READ_Y command code
                   bra       Read_Firm   ; [3+519] double return
;
;***************************************************
; READ_SP - $67 - Read stack pointer
;***************************************************
;
READ_SP:           ldaa      #$67        ; [1] READ_SP command code
                   bra       Read_Firm   ; [3+519] double return
;
;***************************************************
; BDM_GO - $08
;    Resume user program from active BDM
;***************************************************
;
BDM_GO:            ldaa      #$08        ; [1] BDM_GO command code
Go_8:              jsr       WSerial_8   ; [4+146] send command
                   bra       Dly_40      ; [3+45] double return
;
;***************************************************
; BDM_TRACE - $10
;    Do 1 user instruction and return to BDM
;***************************************************
;
BDM_TRACE:         ldaa      #$10        ; [1] BDM_TRACE command code
                   bra       Go_8        ; [3+198] send, dly & dbl return
;
;***************************************************
; TAG_GO - $18
;    Enable tagging and go to user program
;***************************************************
;
TAG_GO:            ldaa      #$18        ; [1] TAG_GO command code
                   bra       Go_8        ; [3+198] send, dly & dbl return
;
```

Due to a production error, the page numbers listed in the index are incorrect. The subjects can be found four pages after the page number indicated. We apologize for the inconvenience.

Index

16-bit offset · 45
5-bit signed offset · 43
74HC589 · 334
74HC595 · 329
74HC597 · 332
9-bit offset · 44

A

absolute addressing · 128
accessing data · 325
accumulator · 21, 22
accumulator offset indexed addressing · 47, 63
active background mode · 110, 175, 362, 446
active background mode exit · 453
active background mode, entering · 450
actuator · 222
ADC example · 427
ADC initialization · 421
ADC input port · 431
ADC interrupt · 430
ADC min, max frequency · 422
ADC module · 419
ADC operating mode selection · 425
ADC resolution · 424
ADC result register · 426
addition and subtraction instructions · 69
addition, BCD · 70
address arithmetic · 71
address calculation · 71
addressing mode · 35, 55, 83, 99
addressing mode summary table · 53
algorithm, Flash erase · 260
aligned access · 192
alignment · 21
allocation of stack space · 120
alpha-numeric display · 226
analog reference voltage input · 421
analog-to-digital converter (ADC) module · 419

application/debug separation · 449
arithmetic instruction · 54
arithmetic shift instructions · 80
arithmetic, address · 71
arithmetic, mixed 8 and 16 bit · 68
array · 48
ASCII character format · 139
ASCII character output · 232
ASCII colon character · 34
ASCII data, display · 226
ASCII pound sign · 37
ASCII to binary conversion · 142
ASCII to binary hex conversion · 277
assembler section · 124
assembly language · xiv, 73, 446
assembly language syntax · 33
assertion and negation, automatic · 329
ATDCTL2 control register · 422
Atmel · 323
auto increment/decrement indexed addressing · 134
auto post increment indexed addressing example · 59
autoincrement and autodecrement · 42
automatic increment or decrement operation · 48
automatic register stacking · 191

B

back door · 443
BACKGROUND command · 446
Background Debug mode · 171
Background Debug Mode (BDM) firmware · 68
Background Debug Module (BDM) · 110, 445
background mode · 362, 439
bank switching · 90
base address · 22, 43
base index register · 127

549

Index

basic architecture · 21
baud rate · 296
Baud Rate Control Register · 300
baud rate generator · 299
baud rate mismatch · 295
BCD (binary coded decimal) · 19, 139
BCD data arithmetic · 70
BCLR · 361
BDLC · 256, 265
BDM (Background Debug Module) firmware · 69
BDM (Background Debug Module) · 445
BDM breakpoint cautions · 438
BDM command inplementation · 470
BDM Command loop · 456
BDM communication primitives · 465
BDM communications protocol, single-wire example · 464
BDM dual address mode · 438
BDM firmware timing · 456
BDM full breakpoint mode · 436
BDM system implementation · 464
BGND · 109
bidirectional communication · 298
bidirectional I/O pin · 207
bidirectional mode · 320
big endian · 18
binary coded decimal (BCD) · 19
binary number · 35
binary point · 20
binary to ASCII conversion · 139
bit data · 19
bit manipulation instruction · 86, 206
bit mask · 218
bit position encoding · 242
bit rate selection · 324
bit synchronization · 294
bit-test-and-branch · 39, 40
blank and enable display · 345
block diagram, timer · 355
block move · 134
block move routine · 49
block protect · 239
block protect bit · 250
block protect mechanism · 239, 443
boolean logic instructions · 82

boot block · 256
boot loader · 265
boot loader example · 271
boot loader startup code · 269
BOOTP bit · 257
bootstrap mode · 449
borrow · 30
bounce, switch · 211
branch · 92
branch always, relative · 88
branch instruction · 39, 59
branch instruction example · 62
branch instruction, signed · 65
branch instruction, simple · 60
branch instruction, unconditional · 59
branch instruction, unsigned · 63
branching range · 40
branching, program · 28
break · 294
breakpoint · 110, 436, 438
breakpoint module · 433
breakpoint, program counter · 439
brightness, display · 345
Bruce, Bill · xi
BSET instruction · 453
buffer · 18, 294, 296
buffer pointer · 95
buffer, elastic · 306
bug correction, ROM · 440
bug replacement code · 440
built-in active pull-up device · 210
bulk erase · 250, 255
Bulk Erase Protection (BULKP) · 241
bulk erasure · 240
BULKP (Bulk Erase Protection control bit) · 241
bus control signal configuration · 163
bus frequency · 53
bus timing · 161, 162
busy flag polling · 227
byte count value · 244
byte erasable EEPROM · 258
byte ordering · 18
byte reversal · 436
byte size variable · 123
byte, defined · 18

Index

C

C · 73, 446
C bit · 61
C compiler · xiv
C programming language · 49
ca6812 assembler · 124
calculating offset · 121
CAN · 256, 265
capacitive load to the microcontroller · 163
capacitor, variable · 169
carry · 30
carry bit · 70
carry/borrow status bit · 27
cascaded device · 329
cascading 74HC597 inputs · 333
C-bit · 30
CCR (Condition Code Register) · 21, 27
CCRSAV register · 454
center aligned operation · 401
CFORC register · 364
changing period and duty cycle · 409
channel sequencing · 413
charge pump · 237, 238, 246, 422
charge redistribution technique · 422
checksum · 145, 277
chip power · 239
Chip Select/Slave Select · 318
clearing global variable storage · 130
clearing interrupt status flag · 188
clearing sequence · 166
CLI instruction · 188
CLI instruction sequence · 190
clock disabling · 239
clock generator, PWM · 403
Clock Monitor · 167, 176, 182
clock polarity · 323
clock rate selection · 324
clock signal · 227
clock stretching · 162
clock, time of day · 390
clocks, disabling · 97
code patch · 440
colon character · 34
comment field · 35
commercial at character (@) · 35

communication primitives, BCM · 465
communication, high speed · 317
communications primitives · 464
comparator · 419
compare · 99, 134
compare instructions · 82
compare status flag · 353
comparing unsigned data · 63
compiler package · xiv
computed GOTO · 462
Computer Operating Properly (COP) · 164
condition code register (CCR) ·21, 27, 55, 184, 186, 188, 450
condition code register instructions · 91
condition code register interrupt mask bit · 189
condition code register, save and restore contents · 85
configuring the SPI · 323
constant data · 91, 129
constant definitions area · 269
constant offset indexed addressing · 43, 51
context saving time · 191
control algorithm · 101
control program · 169
control register · 54, 155, 160
conversion clock prescaler · 422
conversion modes, ADC · 419
conversion sequence, ADC · 425
conversion, binary to ASCII · 139
COP (Computer Operating Properly) · 164
COP Control register · 166
COP watchdog · 182
COP watchdog timer · 176
Cosmic Software · xiv
Cosmic Software assembler · 124
count value · 244
counter · 299
counter chain · 165
counter clock source · 358
counter overflow · 351
counter, programmable · 403
counting events · 389
CPHA bit · 326
CPS instruction · 84
CPU context · 24

Index

CPU12 · 17
CPU12 difference · 23, 24, 57, 59, 66, 70, 74, 84, 86, 88, 91, 96, 99, 104, 155, 164, 194, 238, 239, 245, 318, 319, 324, 354, 358, 359, 361, 362, 363, 400
CPU12 instruction set · 33
CPU12 Reference Manual · 54
CRC (cyclic redundancy check) · 145
critical event · 30
cross assembler · xiv
crystal oscillator, disabling · 109
CS/SS pin · 321
current consumption · 209
current drive capability · 222
current limiting resistor · 222
current setting resistor · 338
cursor · 232
custom instructions · 96
cyclic redundancy check (CRC) · 145

D

D accumulator · 47
D.C. motor · 412
DAA (Decimal Adjust accumulator A) · 29
damage to output devices · 209
damage, EEPROM · 252
data access · 325
data alignment · 238
data bit, serial communication · 293
data direction · 318
data direction register · 206, 327
data latch · 328
data organization in memory · 20
data register · 207, 297
data retention life · 238
data sampling · 294
data size · 18
data table · 129, 256
data transfer · 324
data transfer format, SPI · 321
data transfer rate · 323
data transfer subroutine · 330
data transfer, full duplex synchronous · 320
data type · 19

DataFlash · 323
DayOfWeek variable · 195
Days per Month Lookup Table · 201
D-Bug12 · xv, 95
DDR bit · 356
debounce · 211, 214
debounce delay · 213
debug · 207, 433, 435, 448
debug module · 110
debug timing requirements · 456
debug tool · 436, 445
debug/application separation · 449
debugger pod · 464
debugging · 109, 118
Decimal Adjust accumulator A (DAA) · 29
decimal number · 35
decimal point · 344
decimal point display · 224
decimal to binary conversion · 142
decrement · 92
decrement instruction · 64
Define Storage (DS) directive · 123
defuzzification · 105, 107
delay loop · 227
delay subroutine · 470
delay time, programmed · 109
design fault, peripheral · 188
destination index register · 72
diagnostic routine · 420
diagnostics · 299
Digital Equipment · 17
digital-to-analog converter (DAC) · 419
direct addressing · 38, 78
disabling XIRQ interrupts · 29
dispatch routine example · 96
display · 222
display brightness · 338, 345
display driver · 336
display module · 226
display module initialization · 228
divide instruction · 74
DLY (oscillator startup delay) · 184
DLY bit · 185
dollar sign ($) · 35
DOS · 34
double buffering · 294

Index

double return · 470
drive capability · 163, 222
driver, software · 327
DS (Define Storage) directive · 123
dual address mode · 438
duty cycle calculation · 404
duty cycle register · 399

E

E-clock · 299
E-clock stretching · 192, 193
edge detect IRQ · 185
edge sensitive interrupt input · 374
EEMCR (EEPROM Module Configuration Register) · 238
EEPGM bit · 248
EEPROG register · 245
EEPROM · 440
EEPROM characteristics · 241
EEPROM damage · 252
EEPROM data loss · 252
EEPROM memory modification · 252
EEPROM memory, protecting · 443
EEPROM Module Configuration Register (EEMCR) · 238
EEPROM programming and erasure · 241, 244
EEPROM structure · 237
EEPROM, on-chip · 237
EERC bit · 239
EESWAI bit · 239
elastic buffer · 306
electrical noise · 206, 209, 295
EMACS · 191
EMACS instruction · 192
emulator · 161
ENABLE_FIRMWARE command · 446
ENBDM bit · 453
endless loop · 164, 176, 439
engine controller · xiii
EPROM, UV-erasable · 237
erase and write cycles, minimum · 241
erase command, boot loader · 284
ERASE control bit · 246

erase operation · 246
erase protected boot block · 256, 265
erase pulse · 260
erase time delay · 269
erase, byte and word · 248
erase, row · 249
erased state, EEPROM · 241
erasing display line · 233
erasure · 257
erasure of EEPROM · 239
erasure of Flash EEPROM · 260
errata, mask set · xv
evaluation board · xv, 464
event counting · 351, 389
examples, programming · 117
exception · 450
exception types · 182
exception, processing · 181
exchange instruction · 66
execution speed, multiply and divide · 76
EXG instruction · 450
exit active background mode · 453
expanded memory · 89, 181
Expanded mode · 161
expansion address mapping logic · 162
extended addressing · 37, 95
extended addressing mode · 87, 206
extension byte · 42
external access · 162
external buffer · 222
external bus · 161
external load · 412
external memory · 192
external memory and peripherals · 161
external memory, width and speed · 193

F

factory test · 300
FEESWAI bit · 257
final channel sample time · 422
firmware · 255
firmware read command · 462
firmware timing requirements · 456
firmware write instruction · 460

Index

firmware, BDM · 445
First-In-First-Out (FIFO) buffer · 274
Flash device · 323
Flash EEPROM · 237
Flash EEPROM memory · 255
Flash erase algorithm · 284
Flash memory · 161, 128, 362
Flash module · 256
Flash paging mechanism · 259
Flash program/erase life · 259
Flash programming algorithm · 259
Flash programming control loop · 274
Flash serial boot loader · 265
floating gate · 241
floating point hardware · 101
force compare · 364
forced idle period · 297
FProg subroutine · 274
fractional divide instruction · 75
fractional number display · 344
framing error · 295
free cycle · 456
free-running counter chain · 165
frequency measurement · 365
frequency variation, AC power · 198
fuel injection · 374
full breakpoint mode · 436
full duplex synchronous data transfer · 320
fuzzification · 99
fuzzy logic · 104
fuzzy logic instruction · 188, 191

G

gated time accumulation · 351
gated time accumulation mode · 388, 391
general purpose I/O examples · 210
general purpose I/O port · 205
generating polynomial · 145
getchar subroutine · 276, 310
global data access · 129
global variable · 118, 121, 287
global variable storage · 130
GOTO, computed · 462
Gregorian calendar · 200

H

half carry · 29
half carry status bit · 27
half carry bit · 70
handshaking · 274
handshaking signal · 292
hardware breakpoint · 439
hardware breakpoint module · 433
hardware command · 448
hardware divide · 74
hardware handshaking · 274
hardware interface · 185
hardware interlock · 256
hardware interrupt · 95, 169
hardware priority encoder · 182
hardware/firmware, BDM · 446
H-bit · 29
HD44780 LCD controller · 230
hexadecimal number · 35
high speed communication · 317
Highest Priority Maskable Interrupt (HPRIO) register · 186
high-voltage breakdown · 252
Hours variable · 195
HPRIO (Interrupt Priority Conrol Register) · 194
HPRIO control register · 186

I

I Mask bit · 29
I/O · 291
I/O and control registers · 54
I/O pin configuration · 205
I/O pin, unused · 208
I/O port initialization · 208
I/O port, general purpose · 205
I/O register access · 129
I/O register block · 156
I/O registers · 87
I-bit · 29, 184, 186, 190, 194
ICMAX · 193
idle frame · 298
ignition spark · 374

Index

illegal opcodes · 96
immediate addressing · 36
inadvertent switching · 209
incandescent lamp · 412
increment · 92
index register · 22, 127
indexed addressing · 41, 51, 78
indexed addressing enhancements · 42
indexed addressing mode · 33
indexed indirect addressing · 50
indirect addressing · 50
infrared communications · 371
inherent addressing · 34, 36
inhibited interrupts · 190
initialization code example · 172
initialization process · 441
initialization sequence · 155
INITRG Register · 158
input capture · 352, 374
input latch · 332
input multiplexer · 419
input port, ADC · 431
inrush current · 412
instruction mnemonic field · 34
instruction pipe · 58
Instruction Pointer (IP) · 27
instruction queue · 18, 27
instruction set overview · 53
instruction stream · 36
instruction tagging · 447
INTCR (Interrupt Control Register) · 184
integer data · 19
interpolation · 76, 101
interrupt · 24, 28, 29, 109, 169, 181, 353, 389
interrupt and reset vectors · 266
Interrupt Control Register (INTCR) · 184
interrupt dispatch routine · 308
interrupt driven mode · 327
interrupt driven SCI example · 306
interrupt driven system · 252
interrupt exception processing · 450
interrupt input · 374
interrupt latency · 266, 394
interrupt latency calculation · 192
interrupt latency period · 191
interrupt masking bit · 27

interrupt nesting · 189
interrupt pending · 194
Interrupt Priority Control Register (HPRIO) · 194
interrupt response · 97
interrupt response time · 193
interrupt service routine · 54, 95, 166, 187, 207, 441
interrupt service routine speed · 189
interrupt status flag · 187
interrupt vector · 327, 351
interrupt vector fetch delay · 110
interrupt vector fetch time · 192
interrupt vector map · 186
interrupt, ADC · 430
interrupt, SCI · 303
interrupt, timer channel · 360
interrupts inhibited · 190
interrupts, disabled · 85
IP (Instruction Pointer) · 27
IRQ bit · 29
IRQ edge select (IRQE) · 184
IRQ interrupt · 202
IRQ Interrupt Example · 194
IRQ interrupt pin · 184
IRQE bit · 185
IVIS bit · 160, 161

J

jump · 88
jump table · 266
junction temperature · 222

K

key rollover capability · 218
key scanning · 220
knowledge base · 105

L

label field · 34
lamp driver · 336

555

Index

last used stack · 67
last used style stack · 23
latch · 258
latch, address and data · 246
LCD · 226
LCD controller · 230
LEA (Load Effective Address) · 71
leading zero suppression · 140, 341
leap year · 199
leap year defined · 200
LeapYear variable · 195
LED · 222
LED brightness · 338
LED indicator · 336
left aligned operation · 400
limit check example · 99
line frequency · 392
line wrapping · 232
linear equation · 101
linear interpolation · 101
LineFreq subroutine (50/60 Hz) · 195
linker · 124
Lite Module Bus (LMB) · 17
LMB (Lite Module Bus) · 17
load and store instructions · 54
Load Effective Address (LEA) · 71
local area network · 299
local data storage · 117
local variable access · 121
local variable allocation · 120
local variable, removing · 125
local variables · 119
location counter · 122, 124
LOCK bit · 257
lock up · 53
logic analyzer · 161
logic instruction · 54
logical shift · 79
long branch instruction · 39
long word variable · 123
long word, defined · 18
longest uninterruptable instruction · 191
lookup table · 91, 101
loop · 39, 41, 60, 109
loop counter · 138
loop primitive instruction · 92, 130

loop, endless · 164, 176
loop, infinite · 451
loop, timing · 196
loopback test mode · 298
LOOPS bit · 298
low power standby state · 109
low power state · 28, 97
low power wait mode · 362
Lumex LDQ-N516RI display · 338

M

M clock · 300
M6801 · xiii
M68HC11 · xiii
M68HC12 · xiv
M68HC12 family · 17
M68HC12B32EVB · xv
Macintosh · 34
mapping register · 157
mask bit, interrupt · 184
mask, bit · 91
maskable exception (interrupt) · 184
maskable interrupt priority · 186
masked ROM · 440
master · 321
master and slave microcontroller · 326
master mode · 318
mathematical expression · 34
mathematical operation · 74
maximum data transfer rate · 327
maximum instruction · 131
maximum instructions · 99
maximum interrupt latency · 192
MC14489 · 336
mechanical switch · 211
membership function · 105
memory mapped I/O · 205
memory modification, EEPROM · 252
memory word organization · 19
memory, expanded · 89
memory, external · 161
memory-mapped I/O · 54
memory-to-memory move instruction · 49, 54
memory-to-memory move instructions · 57

Index

microcontroller, uses · xiii
microprocessor · xiii
minimum and maximum instructions · 99, 131
MinMax routine · 132
misaligned read · 192
MISC register · 161
MODE register · 159
modular programming · 118
Module clock · 299
modulus counter · 299
MOSFET · 412
motor speed control example · 211
move · 134
move instructions · 57
multiple digit display · 225
multiple precision arithmetic example · 62
multiple precision computation · 69
multiple pushbutton switches · 218
multiplex display driver · 226
multiplexed address, data, and bus control signals · 163
multiplexer, input · 419
multiplexing · 226
multiply instruction · 74
multi-precision operations · 81

N

N bit · 30, 61
narrow mode · 192
Narrow operating mode · 193
NECLK bit initialization · 177
negative status bit · 27
nesting interrupts · 189
networking applications · 291
next available style stack · 23
NMI (Non-Maskable Interrupt) · 28
non-maskable exception · 182
Non-Maskable Interrupt (NMI) · 28
nonvolatile data storage · 245
NOP · 109
NRZ data format · 291, 293
null terminated string · 49
number base · 35
numeric constant · 121

numeric display · 138, 222

O

O (optional) cycle · 456
object code · 46
object code compatibility · 17, 42
octal number · 35
odd byte count · 18
offset · 43, 51, 127
offset indexed addressing · 46
offset range · 43, 44
offset section · 124
offset size · 46
offset, signed and unsigned · 39
on-chip memory system · 156
on-chip peripheral · 54
on-chip peripheral systems · 184
on-chip volatile memory, clearing · 130
opcode tracking mechanism · 439
open drain · 319
operand alignment · 21
operand field · 34
operand location · 193
operating mode · 159
operating mode selection, ADC · 425
operating mode switching · 175
operating mode, SPI · 320
operating modes, wide and narrow · 193
operating system service request · 96
Optrex DMC-16249 · 226
oscillator startup delay (DLY) · 184
output compare · 353, 359, 363
output compare waveform generation · 374
output compare, timer · 356
output indicator · 222
output waveform generation · 353
overflow · 30
overflow status bit · 27
overrun error · 295, 309

P

packed BCD data · 29

557

Index

PACNT register · 361
PACTL register · 358
PAFLG Register · 361
PAOVI · 388
parallel input port example · 332
parallel output port example · 327
parameter passing · 118, 123
parameter, removing · 125
parameters · 119
parity · 293
parity generation and checking · 291
passing parameters · 118
PC (Program Counter) · 21, 27
PCR (Program Counter Relative) Indexed Addressing · 52
PCU12 difference · 109
PDP-8 · 17
PEDGE · 388
pending interrupt · 191
percent character (%) · 35
period calculation · 404
period measurement · 365, 392
period register · 399
peripheral access · 205
peripheral connection · 185
peripheral module design fault · 188
peripheral, external · 161
physical interface, SCI · 292
pipe · 18
polled mode · 327
polled SCI example · 305
polynomial, generating · 145
Port D · 298
Port S · 292
Port T · 356
Ports A, B, and E drive levels · 163
position independent code · 128, 266
post auto-increment indexed addressing · 130
post increment indexed addressing · 95
postbyte · 42, 48
postbyte encoding, transfer/exchange · 68
pound sign · 37
power consumption · 97, 163, 168, 239
power failure · 252
power line frequency reference · 170
power line timing reference · 194
power state · 28
preamble word · 297
prebyte · 42
prefetch queue · 256
prescaler · 165, 351, 358, 422
priority encoder · 182
priority, maskable interrupt · 186
processing exception · 181
program breakpoint · 439
Program Counter (PC) · 21, 27
program counter as an index register · 43
program counter as base index register · 129
program counter as base index register, special considerations · 58
Program Counter Relative (PCR) indexed addressing · 445
program counter relative notation · 52
program loop · 109
program relative addressing · 39
program verification delay · 270
program/erase life, Flash · 259
programming and erase time delays · 269
programming and erasing on-chip Flash memory · 265
programming and erasure, EEPROM · 244
programming EEPROM · 241
programming examples · 117
programming Flash block · 279
programming operation, Flash · 259
programming the Flash array · 262
programming voltage · 251
programming/erase voltage, Flash · 260
protected register · 156, 176
protection mechanism · 156, 252
PROTLCK bit · 239
pull · 84
pull-down resistor · 208
pull-up · 292, 319
pull-up / pull-down · 328
pull-up control bit · 210
pull-up or pull-down resistor · 208
pull-up resistor · 298
pulse accumulator · 351, 386, 391
pulse train generation · 354
pulse train measurement · 371
pulse width · 352

Index

pulse width encoded signal · 371
pulse width measurement · 369, 392
pulse width modulation (PWM) module · 399
PURDS (Pull-up and Reduced Drive) control register · 292
push · 84, 119, 121
push and pull instructions · 127
pushbutton switches, multiple · 218
putchar subroutine · 312
PWM 16-bit operation · 408
PWM clock · 403
PWM clock skew · 413
PWM module · 378, 399
PWM output · 359
PWM signal · 374
PWM waveform · 353

Q

quartz crystal accuracy · 169
queue · 49
queue index value · 308
queue management · 306
queue size · 307

R

race condition · 186
Radio Frequency Interference (RFI) · 163
radix · 20
range option · 435
range, branching · 40
RC oscillator · 238
read command, firmware · 462
read/modify/write instructions · 77
Real Time Interrupt (RTI) · 169, 186
Real Time Interrupt (RTI) timer · 216
Real Time Operating System (RTOS) · 169
receive interrupt service routine · 309
receiver · 294
receiver interrupt · 308
Receiver Source (RSRC) control bit · 298
recursive subroutine · 117
reduced drive capability · 163, 319
reduced drive option · 292
reentrant · 190
reentrant routine · 117
reference input · 421
register pre-stacking · 98
register protection mechanism · 175
register specification · 34
register stacking sequence · 191
register transfer/exchange instruction · 66
relative addressing · 39, 266
relative branch instruction · 129
relocatable code · 128
remapping · 238
removing local variables and parameters · 125
reprogramming · 240
reset · 159, 163, 164, 167, 171, 176, 181, 182, 186, 205, 206, 240, 252, 355, 421, 446, 450
reset exception · 182
reset vector · 267
resolution, ADC · 424
resource mapping · 156
response speed · 191
result register, ADC · 426
return address · 22, 119
ReTurn from Interrupt (RTI) · 29
return result · 50
RF communications · 371
RFI (Radio Frequency Interference) · 163
ROM code patch · 440
ROM monitor · 448
ROM patching procedure · 443
rotate · 30
rotating multi-precision values · 81
row erase · 241, 249
RS-232 translator chip · 266
RTI (Real Time Interrupt) · 169
RTI (ReTurn from Interrupt) · 29
RTI instruction · 194, 435
RTOS (Real Time Operating System) · 169
rule base · 106
rule evaluation · 105, 106
run away · 96, 183

Index

S

S control bit · 28
sample amplifier · 419
sample time · 422
sample-and-hold · 420
sampling time · 423
scanned switch matrix · 220
SCI (Serial Communications Interface) · 56, 94, 266, 291
SCI character receive routine · 274
SCI interrupt · 303
SCI physical interface · 292
SCI receiver · 294
SCI transmitter · 296
SCK · 324
SDI (Serial Debug Interface) · 464
section, assembler · 124
SEI instruction · 188
selective-write · 242
semicolon · 35
sequential SPI transfers · 323
serial communication, BDM · 449
Serial Communications Interface (SCI) · 56, 94, 291, 317
Serial Debug Interface (SDI) · 464
Serial Interface module · 317
Serial Peripheral Interface (SPI) · 317
service request · 182
service request, urgent · 183
services, operating system · 96
setting the time and date variables · 202
seven segment display · 223
Shadow and Test Row Protection control bit (STPROT) · 241
shift · 30
shift and rotate instructions · 79
shifting multi-precision values · 81
short branch instruction · 39
short pulse measurement · 374
Sibigtroth, Jim · xii
signal period · 352
signed branch example · 65
signed branch instruction · 65
signed data · 65
signed multiply · 75
signed offsets · 43
signed subtraction · 66
simple branch instruction · 60
single byte instruction · 18
single chip mode · 161, 446, 453
single wire bus · 299
single wire operating mode · 298
slave · 321
Slave Select · 318
slave select line · 326
SMODN bit · 160
software breakpoint · 110
software counter · 216
software debugging · 175
software driver · 327
software driver for SPI peripheral · 326
software handshaking · 274
software interrupt · 95
Software Interrupt vector (SWI) · 188
software recovery · 164
software timing loop · 54
source code compatibility · 42
source line layout · 33
source loading, DAC · 420
SP (Stack Pointer) · 21
spark timing · 364
special decode mode · 338
Special mode · 160, 164
special single chip mode · 453
speed tolerance, BDM · 466
speedup pulse · 469
SPI (Serial Peripheral Interface) · 317
SPI configuration · 323
SPI data transfer format · 321
SPI initialization · 330
SPI interrupt · 325, 327
SPI operating modes · 320
SPI physical interface · 318
SPI transfer · 324
SPIF flag · 326
square wave · 374
S-Record · 276
stack · 49
stack data · 43
stack frame · 119
stack location · 191

Index

stack pointer · 22, 67, 194
Stack Pointer (SP) · 21
stack pointer alignment · 26
stack pointer as a base index register · 121, 127
stack pointer as a counter register · 93
stack pointer initialization · 24
stack pointer relative addressing · 24
stack space · 74
stack type · 23
stack usage · 117
stacking order · 25, 98
stack-related instructions · 84
Standard Timer Module · 351
standby state · 109
start bit · 295
Start Of Record (SOR) · 276
state diagram, switch detection · 214
status bit · 27
stealing a bus cycle · 457
STOP · 28, 109
stop bit · 295
stop bit detection · 294
stop disable bit · 168
STOP instruction control bit · 27
STOP mode · 422
store instructions · 54
STPROT (Shadow and Test Row Protection control bit) · 241
stray capacitance · 163
stretch bit · 162
string copy example · 56
structure · 137
subroutine · 89, 181, 187
subroutine parameter access · 121
subroutine sharing · 190
subtraction instruction · 69
subtraction, BCD · 70
subtraction, signed and unsigned · 66
support routines · 287
SWI (Software Interrupt vector) · 188, 450
SWI breakpoint endless loop · 435
SWI dual address mode · 435
SWI instruction exception · 182
SWI interrupt service routine · 441
switch closure detection example · 213

switch connection · 212
switch detection state diagram · 214
switch matrix · 220
switch pressed status · 211
switch, mechanical · 211
switches, multiple pushbutton · 218
switching transient · 412
switching, inadvertent · 209
switching, sequenced · 412
symbolic name · 121
synchronization uncertainty · 456
synchronization, POD · 466
syntax, assembly language · 33
system clock · 97
system failure · 28, 183, 190
system firmware · 255
system reset · 252

T

table · 256
table lookup · 76
target memory access · 446
target system development · 175
TCRE (Timer Counter Reset Enable) · 359
temporary data storage · 117
terminating null character · 57
test · 92
test register · 160
text display · 231
TFFCA (Timer Fast Flag Clear All) · 361
TFLG1 register · 355
TFR instruction · 450
Ticks variable · 195
time · 352
time and date keeping functions · 198
time and date, accessing · 202
time delay creation · 281
time delay, programming and erase · 269
time keeping software · 195
time of day · 169
time of day and date · 194
time of day clock · 390
time stamp · 202
timed ADC conversion example · 428

Index

timeout mechanism · 156
timeout period · 164
timer · 216, 285, 351, 391
timer channel · 354
timer channel flag/interrupt · 360
timer channel interrupt · 353
timer channel seven · 363, 387
timer channels · 88
Timer Counter Reset Enable (TCRE) · 359
Timer Enable (TEN) bit · 362
Timer Fast Flag Clear All (TFFCA) · 361
timer initialization · 364
timer module · 217, 269
Timer Overflow Interrupt (TOI) · 357
timer port · 466
timer prescaler · 357
timer prescaler value · 368
timer system control · 362
timing · 462
timing diagram · 321
timing loop · 196
timing loop compatibility · 53
timing measurement · 354
timing reference · 194
timing requirements, firmware · 456
timing, data input · 333
TIOS register · 355
TMP register · 449, 452, 461
TMSK1 register · 355
TOI (Timer Overflow Interrupt) · 357
transfer and exchange instructions · 66
transfer format · 323
transfer functions · 101
Transfer/Exchange postbyte encoding · 68
transistor controlling · 412
transmit interrupt service routine · 311
transmitter interrupt · 308
transmitter, SCI · 296
trap · 182
TRAP · 96
trapezoidal membership function · 105
TSCR · 361
TSWAI mode · 362
two's compliment arithmetic overflow · 30

U

UART · 274
unconditional branch instruction · 59
unconnected pins · 209
unimplemented opcode trap · 182
unimplemented opcodes · 96
unintended system reset · 252
uninterruptable instruction · 191
UNIX · 34
unreliable data · 252
unsigned branch instruction · 63
unsigned subtraction · 65
unused I/O pin · 208
UV erasable EPROM · 237

V

V bit · 30, 62
valid addressing mode · 52
variable · 123
variable capacitor · 169
variable name · 121
vector fetch · 194
vector map, exception · 183
vector table · 181, 266
very short pulse measurement · 374
volatile memory, on-chip · 130

W

WAI (Wait for Interrupt) · 190
wait mode · 171, 239, 362, 422
watchdog · 182
watchdog reset · 176
watchdog timer · 164
watchdog timer reset · 165
waveform generation · 374
waveform generation, general purpose · 383
WCOL bit · 325
weighted binary fraction · 20
Wide and Narrow operating modes · 193
Window COP Mode · 165
Windows · 34

Index

Wired-Or · 319
Wired-Or mode · 298
word alignment · 18, 21, 436
word organization · 19
word variable · 123
word, defined · 18
worst-case execution time, firmware write · 461
worst-case timing, firmware write · 462
write collision · 325
Write Collision (WCOL) status bit · 322
write command, firmware · 459
write once mechanism · 156, 239
write-once mechanism · 185
write-once register protection mechanism · 175

X

X index register · 42

X/Y/ZModem protocol · 145
X-bit · 28, 183
XIRQ bit · 28
XIRQ interrupt · 252
XIRQ interrupt, disabling · 29
Xon/Xoff · 274

Y

Y index register · 42
year, determining type · 200

Z

Z bit · 61, 73
Z-bit · 30
zero extending 8 bit value · 68
zero-page addressing · 38

Notes

Notes

Notes

Notes

Notes

Notes

Notes

Notes

Notes

Notes

Notes

Notes

The author and publisher appreciate your comments and suggestions.
You may contact us at info@annabooks.com

For information regarding books, classes, workshops, and conferences regarding computer design topics, please see http://www.annabooks.com.

For those interested in learning about fuzzy logic, we recommend

Fuzzy Logic for Real World Design
by Ted Heske and Jill Neporent Heske
Including a fuzzy engine for the Motorola M68HC11 on CD-ROM

order from www.annabooks.com

Annabooks
12860 Danielson Court
Poway, California, USA 92064
858-391-5600